INVESTIGATING BEHAVIOR
Principles of Psychology

Harper & Row, Publishers
New York, Hagerstown, San Francisco, London

Otello Desiderato
Connecticut College

Diane Black Howieson
Connecticut College

Joseph H. Jackson

INVESTIGATING BEHAVIOR
Principles of Psychology

To Dorothy, John, Jane, and our parents

Sponsoring Editor: George A. Middendorf
Project Editor: David Nickol
Designer: Emily Harste
Production Supervisor: Will C. Jomarrón
Compositor: Progressive Typographers, Inc.
Printer and binder: Rand McNally & Company
Art Studio: Lou Bonamarte, John Martin, and J&R Technical Services Inc.

INVESTIGATING BEHAVIOR
Principles of Psychology

Library of Congress Cataloging in Publication Data

Desiderato, Otello.
    Investigating behavior.

    Bibliography: p.
    Includes indexes.
    1. Psychology. 2. Psychological research.
I. Howieson, Diane Black, joint author.
II. Jackson, Joseph Hollister, joint author.
III. Title.
BF121.D45   150'.1'8   76-18293
ISBN 0-06-041614-9

Contents

6

States of Consciousness
157

7

Conditioning
185

8 Behavioral Technology and Self-Control 215

9 Human Learning 243

10 Memory 271

11

Mediation, Problem Solving, and Creativity
295

12

Motivation and Emotion
327

13

Anxiety, Frustration, and Conflict
359

14

Personality
391

15

Behavior Disorders
423

16

Psychotherapy
451

17

Social Behavior
485

Appendix Statistics
517

Preface

This book is for those who wish to understand more about people. All of us, students and teachers of psychology alike, yearn for greater knowledge of the overt behavior and the inner life of human beings—male and female, young and old, hesitant and determined, calm and excited, frustrated and satisfied, parent and child, achiever and failure, friend and foe alike.

The keynote of significant and responsible investigation sounds throughout this book, as its title implies. From its opening on the principal divisions and methods of the science of psychology to its closing with an appendix on practical statistics and their applications, the book is empirically based and research oriented. Attention is given throughout to everyday applications of the research discussed, as well as to many topics of current interest to both students and instructors.

The book first examines the foundations of behavior in the physical organism and its heritage, its nervous system, and its behavioral development from infancy onward. Then it delves into the sources of behavior in sensory processes and in perception. It moves on to varied human experiences in states of consciousness including alert awareness, sleep and dreams, hypnotic and drugged conditions, and meditation. Modifications in behavior are then discussed, along with classical and instrumental conditioning, conceptual processes of learning, memory, and symbolic mediation, problem solving, and creativity. The treatment of behavioral technology describes practical methods of self-control, relating basic principles to real-life problems. The springs of behavior in motives and emotions are sought, leading into a thorough analysis of anxiety, frustration, and conflict. The sources of individuality in patterns of personality are explored, with side trips into type theory and even astrology. Then the breakdown of these patterns in maladaptive behavior disorders is delineated, and current attempts to treat such disorders in terms of psychodynamic, behavioral, and drug therapies are compared and evaluated. The discussion of the interplay of people in social encounters covers such topics as personal space, conformity and independence, and friendship and love, with a look at recent attempts to measure interpersonal attraction by means of Kirlian auras.

The emphasis on discovery, exploration, and investigation is highlighted throughout the book by dozens of brief investigative activities that will immerse students in experiences with the topics discussed and facilitate a quick recognition and grasp of the factors involved in these topics. These activities reveal the immediacy and richness of the subject matter and provide common experiences that lead to productive class discussions. Thus the individual student data from the activities involving TV violence in Chapter 1, "afterglow" sensations in Chapter 4, or the tracing of an opened paperclip in Chapter 9, can be combined for class discussions. The activities are not full-fledged, controlled experiments, but they provide a springboard for discussion in the recitation or laboratory sessions that often accompany introductory courses. In addition, many recent, significant research studies are presented in some detail separate from the text to highlight current advances for special attention.

Students will find that the brief summary at the end of each chapter helps them to organize and remember the main points covered. The exercises following the summaries are designed to reinforce and integrate the knowledge of the contents by encouraging students to act as "experts" in applying concepts or using procedures discussed in each chapter. In addition, the glossary at the back of the book provides thorough definitions of all the key terms in the text. It also relates these terms by means of a system of cross-references, so that families of terms can be located quickly, involving strategies of "clustering" and "hierachies" as aids to retrieval, as discussed in Chapter 10 on memory. The references can lead interested students into the original source material. Appropriate general books for further reading are recommended in the *Workbook and Study Guide,* which also provides many review and self-testing questions and additional work on chapter contents.

Whether students are looking for a sound introduction to the discipline, new perspectives on the human condition, or a framework within which to organize their own life experiences, the straightforward presentation, the many activities, applications, and exercises—in fact every page and chapter in this book—have been designed to stimulate and involve them. Furthermore, the book presents a broad variety of the most fundamental issues, methods, and theories in contemporary psychology for the free-ranging selection of the instructor. It does not bypass significant concepts merely because they might be deemed too complicated or difficult; rather, it attempts to present these concepts in simple and clear fashion.

The book is concise enough to serve for a short but intensive course. A plentiful supply of cross-references between chapters ensures that related materials and relevant background in other chapters can be found, so chapters can be skipped or taken out of order without raising difficulties. However, the book's comprehensive yet compact treatment of the basic psychological principles, concepts, and techniques also makes it suitable for a longer, more thorough course.

An old hand at the textbook game warned us early on that we would "never be the same after producing a psychology text"—and we never will! From its conception onward, every chapter in the book expresses something of what has happened to us: Altered states of consciousness, conditioning, behavioral self-control and learning, problem solving, and creativity—to say nothing of anxiety, frustration, and conflict—have all been our lot as we carried on the project. And surely our needs for affiliation and achievement have been stimulated, with a host of other motives and emotions, some even of the peak variety, including the flowering of cooperation, trust, and friendship as the work progressed.

But the book would not be what it is without the knowledge and skills countless others have contributed. Many reviewers and readers, notably Herbert A. Alpern, University of Colorado at Boulder; Charles N. Cofer, The Pennsylvania State University; Thomas Fitzpatrick, Rockland Community College; Richard A. Kasschau, University of Houston; Gregory A. Kimble, University of Colorado at Boulder; R. A. Kinchla, Princeton University; W. Daniel Phillips, Trenton State College; and Richard L. Solomon, University of Pennsylvania, have vitally improved the text with their suggestions. We greatly appreciate those who have lent their perceptive editorial skills, including George Middendorf, David Nickol, Emily Harste, Charles Woodford, Genia Graves, and Barbara Salazar. The illustrations owe a great deal to the art of Lou Bonamarte and John Martin and the photographs of Philip Biscuti, Dorothy Desiderato, and Victor Miano. Claire Gadaree, Deborah Spiegel, Lorrie

Siedlecki, Nancy MacLeod, Betty Morrison, Patricia Minucci, Ann Gregory, and Jane Carnaghan have labored intelligently and exhaustively to move the manuscript along from one stage to the next. At Connecticut College we are also indebted to Helen Aitner and James MacDonald for library assistance, to Margaret Thompson of the News Office, to Mollie Brooks of the Counseling Staff and to James Crabtree of the Theater Department; and at the Norwich (Connecticut) Hospital to Joseph Marone and his staff. Many students have also lent helping minds and hands to work that varied from questions and discussions to proposing or testing activities, shaping up exercises and test items, serving as subjects for photographs, and typing or proofing manuscript at various stages. And our debts to many others who graciously shared their professional knowledge are cordially recognized in the acknowledgments and references.

As the activity on acoustic confusion (Chapter 4) clearly demonstrates, errors in reading or writing are all too easy to make. But for whatever errors may still remain in this book, we take the sole responsibility.

Otello Desiderato
Diane Black Howieson
Joseph H. Jackson

Acknowledgments

FIGURES

Chapter 1

1-1 Deer and bison (sorcerers): Marshack, A. *The roots of civilization: The cognitive beginnings of man's first art, symbol and notation.* New York: McGraw-Hill Book Co., 1972. Copyright © Alexander Marshack, 1972. Bison with arrows: Bandi, H.-G., Breuil, H., Berger-Kirchner, L., Lhote, H., Holm, E., & Lomell, A. *The art of the Stone Age: Forty thousand years of rock art.* New York: Crown Publishers, 1961. **1-2** Bandi, et al., *op. cit.* **1-3** Marshack, *op. cit.* **1-4, 1-5** Philip A. Biscuti. **1-6** Victor Miano. **1-7** Dorothy Desiderato. **1-8** Philip A. Biscuti. **1-9** *New London Day.* **1-10** Dorothy Desiderato. **1-11** Bandi, et al., *op. cit.* **1-12** Philip A. Biscuti. **Box page 17** Adapted from drawing on p. 24 of *TV Guide*, June 14, 1975 (Triangle Publications, Inc.); excerpts in box on *Violence on TV* taken from *TV Guide* advertisement, *N. Y. Times*, p. 72M, June 10, 1975. **1-17** Courtesy Hilltop Lab Animals. **1-18** Frank Kiernan.

Chapter 2

Photos page 34 Dorothy Desiderato. **2-1** Tinbergen, N. *The study of instinct.* Oxford: The Clarendon Press, 1969. **2-2** Eibl-Eibesfeldt, I., *Ethology: The biology of behavior.* New York: Holt, Rinehart and Winston, 1970. **2-3** Drawings by Hermann Kacher. **2-4** Hailman, J. P., The pecking response in chicks of the laughing gull (*larus articilla L.*) and related species. *Behaviour Supplement,* XV, 1967. Copyright © 1967 by E. J. Brill Publishers. **2-5, 2-6, 2-7** Tinbergen, N., *The study of instinct.* Oxford: The Clarendon Press, 1969. **2-8** Thorpe, W. H., *Bird-song.* New York: Cambridge University Press, 1961. **2-9** Steiner, J. E., Innate discriminative human facial expressions to taste and smell stimulation. *Annals of the New York Academy of Sciences,* 1974, *237,* 229–233. **2-10** Adapted from Karl von Frisch. *Bees: Their vision, chemical senses, and language.* Copyright © 1950 by Cornell University. Used by permission of Cornell University Press. **2-11** Adapted from V. G. Dethier & E. Stellar. *Animal behavior* (3rd ed.). Englewood Cliffs, N. J.: Prentice-Hall, 1970. **2-15** Victor Miano. **2-16** Victor Miano. **2-17** Adapted from R. C. Tryon. Genetic differences in maze-learning ability in rats. *39th Yearbook of the National Society for the Study of Education,* Part I, 1940, 111–119. **2-18** Adapted from R. Ashman. The inheritance of simple musical memory. Reprinted with permission from *The Journal of Heredity,* 43: 51–52, 1952. Copyright © 1952 by the American Genetic Association. **2-23** Vesalius, Andreas, *Icones anatomicae,* 1934. Permission granted by the New York Academy of Medicine Library.

Chapter 3

Photo page 70 Degrés des Ages. Courtesy of Bernard I. Murstein. **3-1** Patten, W., *Evolution.* Hanover, N. H.: Dartmouth College Press, 1922. **3-2** Fantz, R. L., Pattern vision in newborn infants. *Science,* 1963, *140,* 296–297. Copyright © 1963 by the American Association for the Advancement of Science. **3-3** Fantz, R. L., Visual perception from birth as shown by pattern selectivity. *Annals of the New York Academy of Sciences,* 1965, *118,* 793–814. **3-4, 3-5** Kagan, J., The determinants of attention in the infant. *American Scientist,* 1970, *58,* 298–305. Reprinted by permission, *American Scientist,* journal of Sigma Xi, The Scientific Research Society of North America. **3-7** Walk, R. D., & Gibson, E. J., A comparative and analytical study of visual depth perception. *Psychological Monographs,* 1961, *75,* Whole No. 512. Copyright © 1961 by the American Psychological Association. Reprinted by permission. **3-8** Frankenburg,

W. K., Dodds, J. B., and Fandal, A. W., Denver Developmental Screening Test Manual (Revised). Copyright © 1970. **3-12** Philip A. Biscuti. Test Materials of 1960 Stanford-Binet kit. Printed with permission of Houghton Mifflin Company. **3-13** Copyright © 1949, 1960, Institute for Personality and Ability Testing, Champaign, Illinois. Reproduced by permission. **3-16** Victor Miano. **3-17** Bandura, A., Ross, D., & Ross, S. A., Imitation of film-mediated aggressive models. *Journal of Abnormal and Social Psychology*, 1963, *66*, 3-11. Copyright © 1963 by the American Psychological Association. Reprinted by permission.

Chapter 4

4-1, 4-2 Philip A. Biscuti. **4-5** Tanner, W. P., Jr., & Swets, J. A., A decision-making theory of visual detection. *Psychological Review,* 1954, *61*, 401–409. Copyright © 1954 by the American Psychological Association. Reprinted by permission. **4-12** Emily Harste. **4-14** Pritchard, R. M., Stabilized images in the retina. *Scientific American*, 1961, *204* (June), 72–78. Copyright © 1961 by Scientific American, Inc. All rights reserved. **4-16** Brown, P. K., & Wald, G., Visual pigments in single rods and cones of the human retina. *Science*, 1964, *144*, 45–52. Copyright © 1964 by the American Association for the Advancement of Science. **4-17** Philip A. Biscuti. **4-22** von Békésy, G., The variation of phase along the basilar membrane with sinusoidal vibrations. *Journal of the Acoustical Society of America*, 1947, *19*, 452–460. **4-25** Zotterman, Y., Special senses: thermal receptors. In V. E. Hall (Ed.) *Annual Review of Physiology*. Stanford, Calif.: Annual Reviews, 1953, pp. 357–372. **4-27** Krieg, W. J. S., *Functional Neuroanatomy*. New York: McGraw-Hill, 1953. **4-28** Heron, W., The pathology of boredom. *Scientific American*, 1957, *196* (January), 52–56. Copyright © 1957 by Scientific American, Inc. All rights reserved.

Chapter 5

5-4 Philip A. Biscuti. **5-6** Escher Foundation — Haags Gemeentemuseum — The Hague. **5-7** Davenport, R. K., & Rogers, C. M., Intermodal equivalence of stimuli in apes. *Science*, 1970, *168*, 279–280. Copyright © 1970 by the American Association for the Advancement of Science. **5-8** Bryant, P. E., Jones, P., Clayton, V., & Perkins, G. M., Recognition of shapes across modalities by infants. *Nature*, 1972, *240*, 303–304. **5-9** Robinson, J. O., & Wilson, J. A., The impos-

sible colonnade and other variations of a well-known figure. *British Journal of Psychology*, 1973, *64*, 363–365. **5-10** Philip A. Biscuti. **5-11b and c.** Victor Miano. **5-12** Philip A. Biscuti. **5-13** Coren, S., Subjective contours and apparent depth. *Psychological Review*, 1972, *79*, 359–367. Copyright © 1972 by the American Psychological Association. Reprinted by permission. **5-14** Petry, H., Paper presented at the meeting of the Eastern Psychological Association, New York, April, 1975. **5-15** (bottom) Kanizsa, G., Marzini quasi-percettivi in campi con stimolazione omogenea. *Rivista di Psicologia*, 1955, *49*, 7–30. **5-16** Cormack, R. M., Haptic illusion: Apparent elongation of a disk rotated between the fingers. *Science*, 1973, *179*, 590–592. Copyright © 1973 by the American Association for the Advancement of Science. **5-17** Adapted from Brunswik, E., *Perception and the representative design of perceptual experiments*. Berkeley: University of California Press, 1956. Copyright © 1956 by the Regents of the University of California; reprinted by permission of the University of California Press. Originally appearing in Brunswik, E., & Reiter, L., Eindrucks-charactere schematisierter Gesichter. *Zeitschrift fur Psychologie*, 1938, *142*, 67–134. **5-18** Victor Miano. **5-19** Boring, E. G., Apparatus notes: a new ambiguous figure. *American Journal of Psychology*, 1930, *42*, 444–445. **5-21** Targ, R., & Puthoff, H., Information transmission under conditions of sensory shielding. *Nature*, 1974, *251*, 602–607.

Chapter 6

Photo page 158 David Desiderato. **6-2** Kleitman, N., Patterns of dreaming. *Scientific American*, 1960, *203* (November), 82–88. Copyright © by Scientific American, Inc. All rights reserved. **6-3** Roffwarg, H. P., Muzio, J. N., & Dement, W. C., Ontogenetic development of the human sleep-dream cycle. *Science*, 1966, *152*, 604–619. Copyright © 1966 by the American Association for the Advancement of Science. Revised since publication in *Science* by Dr. Roffwarg. **6-5** Wallace, R. K., & Benson, H., The physiology of meditation. *Scientific American*, 1972, *226* (February), 85–90. Copyright © 1972 by Scientific American, Inc. All rights reserved. **6-6** Vesalius, Andreas, *Icones anatomicae*, 1934. Permission granted by the New York Academy of Medicine Library. **6-7, 6-8, 6-9** Gazzaniga, M., The split brain in man. *Scientific American*, 1967, *217* (August), 24–29. Copyright © 1967 by Scientific American, Inc. All rights reserved.

Chapter 7

7-3 Pavlov, I., *Lectures on conditioned reflexes.* Vol. 1. New York: International Publishers, 1928, p. 271. **7-13a** Adapted from Fig. 5 in J. W. Moore, Stimulus control: Studies of auditory generalization in rabbits, in Abraham H. Black, William F. Prokasy, *Classical Conditioning II: Current Theory and Research.* Copyright © 1972. Reprinted by permission of Prentice-Hall, Inc., Englewood Cliffs, N. J. **7-13b** Jenkins, H. M., & Harrison, R. H., The effect of discrimination training on auditory generalization. *Journal of Experimental Psychology,* 1960, *59,* 246–253. Copyright © 1960 by the American Psychological Association. Reprinted by permission. **7-14** Yerkes Primate Research Center of Emory University. **7-15** Adapted from Fig. 1 in Hoffman, H. S., Fleshler, M., & Jensen, P., Stimulus aspects of aversive controls: The retention of conditioned suppression. *Journal of the Experimental Analysis of Behavior,* 1963, *6,* 575–583. Copyright © 1963 by the Society for the Experimental Analysis of Behavior, Inc. **Photo on page 212** Philip A. Biscuti.

Chapter 8

Photo page 216 Philip A. Biscuti. **8-1** Adapted from a chart in *Psychology Today* Magazine, March 1974. Copyright © 1974, Ziff-Davis Publishing Company. All rights reserved. **8-2** "Dennis the Menace" Copyright © 1975 by Field Newspaper Syndicate, T.M.R. **8-5** Shapiro, D., Schwartz, G. E., & Tursky, B., Control of diastolic blood pressure in man by feedback and reinforcement. *Psychophysiology,* 1972, *9,* 296–304. Copyright © 1972 by the Society for Psychophysiological Research. Reprinted by permission. **8-6** Courtesy Biofeedback Systems, Inc., 2736 47th Street, Boulder, Colo. 80301. **8-7** Budzynski, T. H., Stoyva, J. M., & Adler, C. S., Feedback-induced muscle relaxation: Application to tension headache. *Behavior Therapy and Experimental Psychiatry,* 1970, *1,* 205–211. Reprinted with permission from author and Pergamon Press. **8-10** Nolan, J. D., Self-control procedures in the modification of smoking behavior. *Journal of Consulting and Clinical Psychology,* 1968, *32,* 92–93. Copyright © 1968 by the American Psychological Association. Reprinted by permission.

Chapter 9

Photo page 244 Philip A. Biscuti. **9-2** Ostwald, P., The sounds of infancy. *Developmental Medicine & Child Neurology,* 1972, *14,* 350–361. Reprinted by permission of the author and the Editors of Spastics International Medical Publications. **9-3** Lovaas, O. I., et al., Acquisition of imitative speech by schizophrenic children. *Science,* 1966, *151,* 705–707. Copyright © 1966 by the American Association for the Advancement of Science. **9-4** Cohen, B. D., et al., Experimental manipulation of verbal behavior. *Journal of Experimental Psychology,* 1954, *47,* 106–110. Copyright © 1954 by the American Psychological Association. Reprinted by permission. **9-5** Spielberger, C. D., The role of awareness in verbal conditioning. In C. W. Eriksen (Ed.), *Behavior and awareness.* Copyright © 1962, Duke University Press. **9-6** Spielberger, C. D., et al., The effects of awareness and attitude toward the reinforcement on the operant conditioning of verbal behavior. *Journal of Personality,* 1962, *30,* 106–121. Copyright © by Duke University Press, Durham, N. C. **9-7** DeNike, L. D., The temporal relationship between awareness and performance in verbal conditioning. *Journal of Experimental Psychology,* 1964, *68,* 521–529. Copyright © 1964 by the American Psychological Association. Reprinted by permission. **9-9, 9-10** Courtesy Lafayette Instrument Co. **9-12** Courtesy Aetna Life & Casualty. **9-19** Woodworth, R. S., & Schlosberg, H., *Experimental psychology* (Revised). Copyright © Henry Holt & Company. **9-20** Harry F. Harlow, University of Wisconsin Primate Laboratory. **9-21** Harlow, H. F., The formation of learning sets. *Psychological Review,* 1949, *56,* 51–65. Copyright © 1949 by the American Psychological Association. Reprinted by permission.

Chapter 10

Photo page 272 Philip A. Biscuti. **10-1** Krueger, W. C. F., The effect of overlearning on retention. *Journal of Experimental Psychology,* 1929, *12,* 71–78. Copyright © 1929 by the American Psychological Association. **10-2** Gates, A. I., Recitation as a factor in memorizing. *Archives of Psychology,* 1917, *6* (40). **10-6** Underwood, B. J., Interference and forgetting. *Psychological Review,* 1957, *64,* 49–60. Copyright © 1957 by the American Psychological Association. Reprinted by permission. **10-8** Peterson, L. R., & Peterson, M. J., Short-term retention of individual verbal items. *Journal of Experimental Psychology,* 1959, *58,* 193–198. Copyright © 1959 by the American Psychological Association. Reprinted by permission. **10-9** Bower, G. H., Organizational factors in memory. *Cognitive Psychology,* 1970, *1,*

18–46. Reprinted by permission of the author and Academic Press, Inc. **10-10** Penfield, W., *The excitable cortex in conscious man.* Liverpool: Liverpool University Press, 1958. **10-11** Bennett, A., Diamond, E. L., Krech, D., & Rosenzweig, M. R., Chemical and anatomical plasticity of brain. *Science*, 1964, *146*, 610–619. Copyright © 1964 by the American Association for the Advancement of Science. Reprinted by permission.

Chapter 11

Photo page 296 Philip A. Biscuti. **Cartoon page 301** Field Newspaper Syndicate. **11-6** Osgood, C. E., The nature and measurement of meaning. *Psychological Bulletin*, 1952, *49*, 197–237. Copyright © 1952 by the American Psychological Association. Reprinted by permission. **11-12** Munn, N. L., The evolution of mind. *Scientific American*, 1957, *196* (6), 140–150. **11-13** Thorndike, E. L., *Animal intelligence — Psychological Monographs*, 1898, *2* (Whole No. 8). Copyright © 1898 by the American Psychological Association.

Chapter 12

12-1 Philip A. Biscuti. **12-2** Brown, J. S., *The motivation of behavior.* Copyright © 1964, The McGraw-Hill Book Co. **12-9, 12-10** Philip A. Biscuti. **12-11** Solomon, R. L., & Corbit, J. D., An opponent process theory of motivation: I. Temporal dynamics of affect. *Psychological Review*, 1974, *81*, 119–145. Copyright © 1974 by the American Psychological Association. Reprinted by permission. **12-12** Adapted from Fig. 1, NEUROPHYSIOLOGY AND EMOTION. Proceedings of a conference under the auspices of Russell Sage Foundation and the Rockefeller University, David C. Glass, editor. Copyright © 1967 by the Rockefeller University Press and Russell Sage Foundation. **12-16, 12-17, 12-18** Cabanac, M., Physiological role of pleasure. *Science*, 1971, *173*, 1103–1107. Copyright © 1971 by the American Association for the Advancement of Science. **12-19** Bridges, K. M. B., Emotional development in early infancy. *Child Development*, 1932, *3*, 324–341. Copyright © 1932 by the Society for Research in Child Development, Inc. **12-20** Schlosberg, H., The description of facial expression in terms of two dimensions. *Journal of Experimental Psychology*, 1952, *44*, 229–237. Copyright © 1952 by the American Psychological Association. Reprinted by permission. Photos Philip A. Biscuti.

Chapter 13

13-2 Taylor, J. A., A personality scale of manifest anxiety. *Journal of Abnormal and Social Psychology*, 1953, *48*, 285–290. Copyright © 1953 by the American Psychological Association. Reprinted by permission. **13-3** Taylor, J. A., The relationship of anxiety to the conditioned eyelid response. *Journal of Experimental Psychology*, 1951, *41*, 81–92. Copyright © 1951 by the American Psychological Association. Reprinted by permission. **13-4** Spielberger, C. D., The effects of manifest anxiety on the academic achievement of college students. *Mental Hygiene*, 1962, *46*, 420–426. Reprinted by permission of the National Association for Mental Health, Inc. **13-8** Masserman, J. H., *Principles of dynamic psychiatry.* W. B. Saunders, 1946. By permission of author and publisher. **13-14** Thomas Höpker, Woodfin Camp. **13-16** Epstein, S., & Fenz, W. O., Steepness of approach and avoidance gradients in humans as a function of experience: Theory and experiment. *Journal of Experimental Psychology*, 1965, *70*, 1–12. Copyright © 1965 by the American Psychological Association. Reprinted by permission. **13-17** *Sacrifice of Abraham.* Rembrandt von Rijn, Netherlands, 1606–1669. Etching. Harvey D. Parker Collection, H. 283. Courtesy Museum of Fine Arts, Boston.

Chapter 14

Photo page 392 Philip A. Biscuti. **14-3** Allport, G. W., Vernon, P. E., & Lindzey, G., *Manual: Study of values.* Houghton Mifflin Co., 1970. **14-4** Reprinted with permission of the publisher from the *Profile for the Strong-Campbell Interest Inventory, Form T325* of the STRONG VOCATIONAL INTEREST BLANKS. Copyright © 1974 by the Board of Trustees of the Leland Stanford Junior University. **14-6** Dorothy Desiderato. **14-8** Philip A. Biscuti. **14-10** Reprinted by permission from TIME, The Weekly Newsmagazine; copyright © Time, Inc.

Chapter 15

Drawing page 424 from Roubíček, J., Anxiety and higher nervous functions. In Studies of anxiety, *British Journal of Psychiatry*, Special Publication, No. 3, 1969. **15-1** Agras, W., Sylvester, D., & Oliveau, D., The epidemiology of common fears and phobias. *Comprehensive Psychiatry*, 1969, *10*, 151–156. Reprinted by permission of Greene & Stratton, Inc. **15-3** From Roubíček, J., Anxiety and higher nervous functions. In Studies of anxiety, *British Journal of Psychiatry*, Special Publication No. 3, 1969. **15-4** Leff, M., Roatch, J. F., & Bunney, W. E., Jr., Environmental factors preceding the onset of severe depressions. *Psychiatry*, 1970, *33*, 293–311.

Chapter 16

Photo page 452 Dorothy Desiderato. **16-2, 16-4** The Bettmann Archive. **16-3** Courtesy of the Trustees of Sir John Soane's Museum. **16-5** Rogers, C. R., *On becoming a person*. Copyright © 1961 by Houghton Mifflin Company. Reprinted by permission of the publisher. **16-6** Deke Simon. **16-7** Moreno Institute Inc., Beacon, N. Y., George Zimbel. **16-8** Courtesy Louis A. Gottschalk; ch. B. 8 in H. I. Kaplan & B. J. Sadock (Eds.) *Comprehensive Group Psychotherapy*. Copyright © 1971 by the Williams & Wilkins Company. Reprinted by permission of the author and publisher. **16-11** King, G. F., Armitage, S. G., & Tilton, J. R., A therapeutic approach to schizophrenics of extreme pathology. *Journal of Abnormal and Social Psychology*, 1960, *61*, 276–286. Copyright © 1960 by the American Psychological Association. Reprinted by permission. **16-12** Dorothy Desiderato. **16-13** Ayllon, T., & Azrin, N. H., The measurement and reinforcement of behavior of psychotics. *Journal of the Experimental Analysis of Behavior*, 1965, *8*, 357–383. Copyright © 1965 by the Society for the Experimental Analysis of Behavior, Inc. **16-14** Fairweather, G. W., et al., *Community life for the mentally ill*. Copyright © 1969, Aldine Publishing Company. **16-15** Scoville, W. B., Recent trends in lobotomy. *Acta Neurologica Latinoamericana*, 1955, *1*, 353. By permission of the author and editor.

Chapter 17

Photo page 486 Dorothy Desiderato. **17-1** Dorothy Desiderato. **17-2** through **17-6** Philip A. Biscuti.

TABLES

Chapter 2

Table 2-1 Adapted from E. J. Gardner. *Principles of genetics* (4th ed.). New York: Wiley, 1972. **Table 2-2** Cooper, R. M., & Zubek, J. P., Effects of enriched and restricted early environments on the learning ability of bright and dull rats. *Canadian Journal of Psychology*, 1958, *12*, 159–164. **Table 2-3** Arthur R. Jensen, How much do we boost IQ and scholastic achievement? *Harvard Educational Review* 39, Winter 1969, 1–123. Copyright © 1969 by President and Fellows of Harvard College. **Table 2-4** Adapted from G. S. Claridge, S. Carter, & W. I. Hume. *Personality differences and biological variations: A study of twins*. Oxford: Pergamon, 1973.

Chapter 3

Table 3-1 Reprinted by permission of New York University Press from *Behavioral Individuality in Early Childhood* by Alexander Thomas and others. Copyright © 1963 by New York University. **Table 3-2** Pinneau, S. R., *Changes in Intelligence Quotient: Infancy to Maturity*, Boston: Houghton Mifflin, 1961. Copyright © 1961 by the Houghton Mifflin Company. **Table 3-4** Braine, M. D. S., The ontogeny of English phrase structure: the first phase. *Language*, 1963, *39*, 1–13.

Chapter 6

Table 6-1 Weitzenhoffer, A. M., & Hilgard, E. R., *Stanford Hypnotic Susceptibility Scale, Forms A and B*. Stanford, Calif.: Stanford University Press, 1959.

Chapter 10

Table 10-1 Glucksberg, S., & King, L. J., Motivated forgetting mediated by implicit verbal chaining: A laboratory analog of repression. *Science*, 1967, *158*, 517–518. Copyright © 1967 by the American Association for the Advancement of Science.

Chapter 11

Table 11-1 Razran, G., The observable unconscious and the inferable conscious in current Soviet Psychophysiology. *Psychological Review*, 1961, *68*, 81–147. Copyright © 1961 by the American Psychological Association. Reprinted by permission.

Chapter 15

Table 15-2 Cochrane, R., & Robertson, A., The life events inventory. *Journal of Psychosomatic Research*, 1973, *17*, 135–139. Reprinted by permission, copyright © 1973, Pergamon Press. **Table 15-3** Greden, J. F., Anxiety of caffeinism: A diagnostic dilemma. *American Journal of Psychiatry*, 1974, *131*, 1089–1092. Copyright © 1974, the American Psychiatric Association. **Table 15-4** Beck, A. T., *Depression: Causes and Treatment*. Philadelphia: University of Pennsylvania Press, 1972. **Table 15-5** de Lint, J., & Schmidt, W., The epidemiology of alcoholism. In Y. Israel & J. Mardones (Eds.) *Biological basis of alcoholism.* Copyright © 1971, John Wiley & Sons, Inc.

Chapter 16
Table 16-2 Wolpe, J., *The practice of behavior therapy* (2nd ed.). Copyright © 1973, Pergamon Press. Reprinted by permission.

Chapter 17
Tables 17-1, 17-2, 17-3 Karlins, M., Coffman, T. L., & Walters, G., On the fading of stereotypes: Studies in three generations of college students. *Journal of Personality and Social Psychology*, 1969, *13*, 1–16. Copyright © 1969 by the American Psychological Association. Reprinted by permission.

INVESTIGATING BEHAVIOR
Principles of Psychology

1

Psychological Approach

Figure 1-1 Typical figures engraved and painted on the walls of caves in France by pre-literate people tens of thousands of years ago. The bison (center) pierced with arrows and the humans dressed in masks of deer (left) and bison (right) may represent season dances or ceremonies in which sorcerers, or shamans, practiced their magic arts for the benefit of the tribe.

Of the countless questions that have puzzled human beings since time immemorial, none have been so fascinating and persistent, so perplexing and consuming, as questions about themselves and their place in the whole scheme of things. So far as anyone knows, *Homo sapiens* is the only species that studies itself.

PERSISTENT QUESTIONS

It's impossible to determine when this examination of the nature of human nature began. It must have started long before human experiences were first recorded in writing. Early men and women must have had many of the experiences and emotions that each of us has today, and they must have been just as puzzled about many of them. Evidence has accumulated that prehistoric peoples wondered about the human spirit or soul. Burial sites of those long-past eras indicate the practice of funeral rites.

The dead were equipped with tools, weapons, provisions, and ornaments, indicating a belief in life after death. Furthermore, ancient cave paintings show that prehistoric people held magical ceremonies, perhaps to give them success in the hunt (see Figure 1-1). People as well as other animals are pictured in many of these cave and rock paintings, drawn with great artistry (see Figure 1-2). Although the exact beliefs that led to such rituals and artistic representations cannot be reconstructed, their remains do imply that human beings were even then a puzzle for themselves and were subjects for human observation and explanation.

Long before there was any thought of written language, people were counting the days in the lunar month from new moon to new moon and recording their observations in tallies scratched on bones or stones, many of which have been unearthed from caves they inhabited (see Figure 1-3). Studies of these first ''calendars'' have proved that their obser-

Figure 1-2 These highly abstract representations of warriors dancing or attacking (left), archers fighting (center), and dancing women (right) from primitive Spanish cave paintings convey a sense of movement demonstrating the great artistry of early humans.

vations were most accurate, and demonstrate the observational and cognitive capacities that enabled human beings gradually to develop science as we know it today (Marshack, 1972).

Mind and Body

Prehistoric people must have wondered how, while their bodies stilled and slept, they could experience in dreams another strange and varied existence in which they could love and hate, play and fight, laugh and cry, among both friends and strangers. Preliterate Australian aborigines believed in the reality of a dream world, peopled with their ancestors and interwoven with their daily existence. This part of a human individual, which could reach far-off places in an instant and revisit both the living and the dead, was under one severe constraint, however: It had to return to the

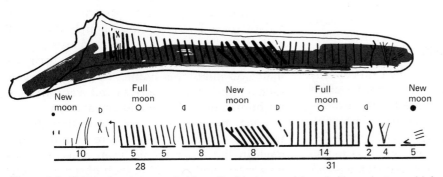

Figure 1-3 This broken bone, probably a ritual baton used by primitive priests or chiefs, was found in a French cave. The marks engraved on it are shown in the drawing to correspond to the 59 days of two full lunar cycles, each actually passing in 29.5 days from new moon to full moon and back to new moon. Many such "calendars" have been found with which early peoples demonstrated their ability to keep track of the seasons through the year.

sleeping form before the body resumed its customary waking activities. And early humans had other striking experiences, like sudden encounters with their own images when they looked down into a pool of still water, and the return of a cry—at once muted and haunting—echoing from the hill across the valley. Undoubtedly such experiences compelled people to adopt a **dualistic conception** of their nature. Two worlds exist, the early human must have concluded: the world of the body, the material, physical world, and the world of the spirit, mysterious, powerful, but immaterial. The forces of the world of the spirit underlie and govern the material world that we see, hear, and touch, and control the activities of our own bodies as well, according to this view. The word "animism" (from the Latin *anima*, meaning soul) expresses the idea that events in the universe, including our own behavior, are governed by spiritual forces.

Such dualistic interpretations have persisted into and through recorded history, with the emphasis sometimes on one side (spirit) and sometimes on the other (matter). In Eastern civilizations, with their mystical concepts of the spiritual quest for Nirvana, ultimate reality is to be found in the depths of the soul, penetrated with difficulty by various methods of meditation. In Western civilizations, the similar view that the spiritual component of the human being is somehow more real, pure, perfect, or good than the material body runs through the writings of the Greek philosopher Plato, the early Christians, and the church philosophers of the Middle Ages. Opposed to this view, and expressed perhaps first by the Greek Democritus, was the idea that human beings, like everything else in the universe, were composed of mere bits of matter that were indestructible in themselves, creating all things and events as they combined and recombined. These conflicting Western views of the physical and spiritual nature of humankind were integrated in the seventeenth century in the philosophical system of René Descartes, who conceived of mind and body as two distinct yet interacting entities.

Most psychologists today do not think of mind and body as separate and distinct. Mental phenomena are distinguished primarily by their relative inaccessibility and privacy, not by any supposed supernatural quality. Thoughts, perceptions, memories, emotions, dreams, and self-awareness may be studied, but only indirectly, through verbal reports or other measurable behaviors. To be sure, verbal reports of inner thoughts and feelings are extremely useful sources of information about the nature of mental events. But these verbal reports will probably never provide a full resolution of the mind-body distinction.

TRY IT YOURSELF

■ After you read this paragraph, sit down in a comfortable chair, relax, and close your eyes. Then concentrate on your body. Feel your fingers and toes, your legs, arms, stomach, chest, and head. Notice your breathing, any other movements that you make, and the placement or posture of your body, legs, and arms. Keep your eyes closed as you explore your bodily experiences for a few minutes.

Now that you have observed your body, how do you interpret the experiences involved in these observations? For example, are you directly aware of your fingers and toes? Do you have to wiggle them in order to feel them, or are you immediately aware of them at any time your attention shifts in that direction? Is it the activities or behaviors of parts of your body that give you your experiences of them? What are your fingers and toes beyond the feelings or sensations you have from them? Are you aware of your fingers and toes, or any other parts of your body, or are you only aware of certain feelings and sensations? What is the difference, if any, between your sensations and the things that you infer you are sensing? Close your eyes again and see if you can find answers to these questions.

Are all of us enclosed in private worlds of our own minds, including our feelings, sensations, memories, images, and thoughts, or do we all make real contact in our experiences with the world of our bodies and other objects around us? Does reality consist solely of mental events, solely of physical events, or of some vital blending of the two? Can you see why such questions have mystified humankind, from prehistoric hunters and gatherers to sophisticated religious thinkers, philosophers, and psychologists, and still puzzle all of us today?

The Quest for Self-Knowledge

Dualistic conceptions are still influential in every human being's quest for self-knowledge. What are dreams and what do they mean? What compels us to behave as we do? Is there a spiritual mind guiding our behavior? Can we always control our behavior voluntarily? Why is our behavior so often erratic and occasionally even bizarre? What is the mind and how does it work? How can the ways we behave, think, and feel be changed? Why does our resolve so often come to be, like Hamlet's, "sicklied o'er with the pale cast of thought"? Why does our courage melt into timidity, our skill deteriorate into fumbling ineptitude?

Many of the questions that have puzzled humanity since prehistoric times thus arise in each developing individual. Every growing child must struggle to make some sense out of the same mass of experiences that the human nervous system and the physical world conspire to produce in each of us. In a sense, every child is compelled to rediscover the questions of the past and formulate his or her own set of answers. The educational process in every culture serves to transmit to all of its members their own culture's interpretations of experience. More important, cultures provide conventional strategies whereby individuals construct still more adequate views of themselves and the world they live in and discover how to behave more adequately and competently.

Among these cultural interpretations and strategies are those that psychology can provide. We do not claim that the psychological approach is the best or the only way to understand human nature. Attempts at such understanding take many and vastly differing forms — religious, historical, literary, and artistic, as well as scientific. And to be truly free to choose from among the many methods and viewpoints, one must understand all of them. We provide here an account of what psychology has to offer in its approach to human nature and the way psychologists go about the task of studying human and animal behavior.

THE SCIENCE OF PSYCHOLOGY

Psychology can be broadly defined as the investigation of human and animal behavior, and of the mental and physiological processes associated with this behavior. Thus the province of psychology ranges all the way from studies of the growth of affectionate behavior between mothers and infants to studies of heart and respiration rates in relation to meditation and the modification of behavior by changing the pattern of rewards and punishments that result from the behavior. This brief definition of psychology can be given substance by a look at what various kinds of psychologists actually do.

There are over 50,000 psychologists in the United States today. About 35,000 of them are members of the American Psychological Association (APA), the national organization of psychologists. The number of psychologists has been increasing at an enormous rate; APA membership alone has multiplied by eight times in the last 25 years, prompting one psychologist to predict that by the year 2000 one out of every two Americans will work in psychology. About a quarter of the psychologists are women. Eight out of 10 have the Ph.D. degree and most others a master's degree. About 25,000 psychology majors receive bachelor's degrees each year. Most psychologists are fairly young; the largest number are between 30 and 34 years of age. The majority work in schools and colleges, where they are engaged in teaching, research, or more usually both. Some of these psychologists do some clinical or counseling work as well, and many act as consultants to public or private institutions and organizations. The practice of applied psychology engages close to 4 out of 10 psychologists. Most of these professional psychologists work in hospitals and clinics; others work in industry and private practice (Boneau & Cuca, 1974). As you can see, psychology includes people whose work ranges from pure research to purely applied work. To get a better idea of what psychologists do, let's briefly examine some of the major fields of psychology.

Experimental Psychology

The oldest division of the discipline, **experimental psychology,** usually involves basic, or theoretical, research aimed more toward the discovery of laws of behavior than toward devising practical applications of known laws (see Figure 1-4). The research experiments are designed to reveal what conditions influence human and animal perception, learning, memory, and motivation, and to enable the researcher to state the principles or laws of the relationships between these processes and behavior. **Laws** are general statements of uniform, invariant relationships between events. Eventually a **theory** may be formulated, pulling together principles or laws into a logically coherent structure and explaining a number of related events. For example, learning researchers vary training conditions such as amount of practice and rewards for good performance in order to study the effects of these conditions on rate of learning. Then they integrate well-established cause–effect principles into a learning theory. A good theory not only summarizes such laws, but also suggests additional relations between conditions and behavior that the psychologist can check in further experiments.

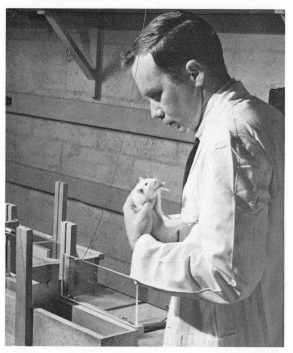

Figure 1-4 The experimental psychologist conducts research often designed to reveal basic principles of human and animal behavior.

Physiological Psychology

Although similar in its aims and methods to experimental psychology, **physiological psychology** concentrates on the biological rather than the environmental determinants of behavior (see Figure 1-5). For example, while the experimental psychologist studies the effects of reward on rate of learning, the physiological psychologist might conduct experiments aimed at ascertaining which portions of the brain are involved with rewarding mechanisms and what chemical transformations take place in the brain at work. Or if the experimental psychologist discovers that newborn animals that are handled grow into less emotional adults than others that are not handled, the physiological psychologist might study how changes in endocrine gland functioning

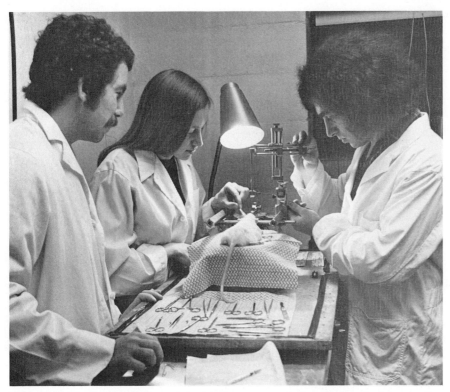

Figure 1-5 The physiological psychologist often uses surgical procedures to determine the effects of neural and endocrine processes on behavior.

produced by the early handling may account for the reduced emotionality of adult animals.

Developmental Psychology

Concerned with the changing patterns of behavior from conception to old age, **developmental psychology** concentrates on relating these behavioral changes to genetic, organic, and environmental influences (see Figure 1-6). For example, some developmental psychologists study infant-mother interaction, others language development, still others emotional development. During the last decade the psychologies of both adolescence and old age have made rapid strides. Much of this research requires careful observation in natural settings, as in studies of infant orangutans in the jungles of Burma and the exploratory behavior of human infants as they begin to crawl and walk.

Clinical, Counseling, and School Psychology

Clinical, counseling, and school psychology are grouped together because all of them provide professional services for people who need help in understanding and changing their own behavior and in dealing with their emotional conflicts. They account for over half of all American psychologists. The doctoral training of all three types of psychologists requires an internship in a hospital, clinic, or school setting. **Clinical psychology** is concerned with people who suffer emotional or adjustment

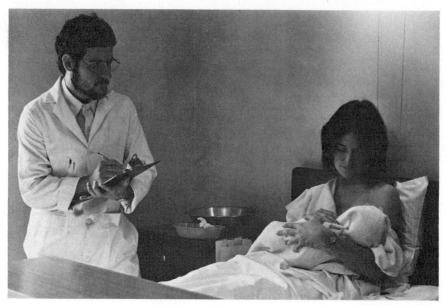

Figure 1-6 The growth and development of sensory and motor functions is one type of behavior change studied by the developmental psychologist.

Figure 1-7 The clinical psychologist helps individuals understand and resolve emotional problems.

Figure 1-8 Most counseling psychologists work in educational settings, helping students define and solve academic and interpersonal problems.

problems, and the clinical psychologist may work in a hospital or clinic or in private practice (see Figure 1-7). Unlike practitioners of **psychiatry,** who have medical degrees, clinical psychologists or clinicians do not prescribe drugs. Some clinicians are trained to practice **psychoanalysis,** a special form of psychotherapy developed by Sigmund Freud and his followers. Psychoanalysts must have undergone psychoanalysis themselves. While most psychoanalysts have medical degrees and have had further training in psychiatry, psychologists, social workers, and even people in

entirely different professions may train to become lay psychoanalysts.

Counseling psychology gives much more emphasis to techniques and theories of personal advising and guidance than clinical psychology does, though its practitioners receive much the same training. Counseling psychologists are likely to work in educational settings and in upper levels of business management, dealing with less severe problems than those encountered by clinicians in mental hospitals (see Figure 1-8). The counseling psychologist should not be confused with the high school

Figure 1-9 A school psychologist administers a school readiness test to a preschooler. Such tests help kindergarten teachers individualize their instruction according to each child's strengths and weaknesses.

guidance counselor, who is primarily responsible for assisting the academic and vocational planning of students.

Practitioners of **school psychology** deal with the emotional and developmental problems of children in elementary and secondary schools (see Figure 1-9). School psychologists are really clinicians in a school setting and must be well trained in diagnostic testing and counseling as well as in methods and theories of learning and instruction. In most states they must also have teaching certificates.

FINDING A GOOD PSYCHOLOGIST

Suppose you needed to find a psychologist, either for yourself, for someone in your family, or for a friend. How would you go about it? At one time just about anyone could claim to be a psychologist, hang out a shingle, and start "practicing." Many of these people had little or no formal training in psychology, and their competence was not examined by either responsible psychologists or any state or municipal agency. As you can imagine, people who sought help from these self-proclaimed psychologists usually did not get it, despite frequently exorbitant fees. Some patients were actually harmed, either by the "treatment" itself or because they failed to receive the help they needed.

Today almost every state has its own licensing or certification laws, which make it illegal for an unqualified person to provide professional psychological services to the public. Eligibility for licensing in most states requires the Ph.D. degree, some postdoctoral experience, and often a passing grade on an examination constructed and administered for the state by a board of psychologists. People who are not licensed may use the title of "psychologist" if they are employed in an academic, governmental, or hospital setting, but not in private practice.

It is now possible to locate a licensed psychol-

Figure 1-10 Educational psychologists conduct research designed to develop and evaluate innovative methods of instruction.

ogist just by turning to the Yellow Pages of the phone book. In the past, "Psychic Mediums" were sometimes not separated from "Psychologists" in the listings, but today they are. The psychologists' listings sometimes also give areas of specialization, such as clinical psychology or child–parent guidance. Some listings also include the notation "Diplomate in Clinical Psychology, ABPP," indicating that the person has also "passed his boards"—that is, has met the rigorous standards of the American Board of Professional Psychologists, a group selected by the APA to evaluate the credentials of professional psychologists. Psychologists in private practice, like physicians, are ethically restrained from advertising their services

While current laws and the Yellow Pages help you avoid the unqualified, you might also seek the advice of a university psychology department or counseling office for the names of psychologists specially trained to deal with your problem. Finally, if there is time, you could also seek infor-

mation from the secretary of the psychological association of your state whose address can be found in the *Directory of the American Psychological Association,* available in most college and public libraries.

All these efforts will not necessarily guarantee that the psychologist you locate will turn out to be satisfactory, just as not every physician well qualified by training and experience turns out to be the one for you. What this information does provide is a way of finding psychologists who have met definite standards of training and competence.

Educational Psychology

Don't confuse the school psychologist with the educational psychologist; they don't perform the same functions. **Educational psychology** is concerned with the study of normal learning processes, usually in the classroom (see Figure 1-10). For example, educational psychologists

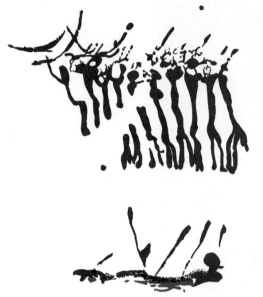

Figure 1-11 This primitive Spanish rock painting has been interpreted as an execution of a victim (below) by the armed men of the tribe (above).

may study the effects of alternate methods of instruction on the efficiency and permanence of learning; they may devise new objective measures of teacher performance or new methods of teacher training; or they may investigate the influence of teachers' expectations on their pupils' achievement (Rosenthal & Jacobson, 1968).

Social Psychology

Social psychology investigates the way the behavior of individuals is influenced by that of other individuals and of groups. We human beings are not islands unto ourselves. What we feel and do is largely the result of what others feel about us and do with or to us. So it will not surprise you to learn that social psychologists study such things as obedience, altruism, conformity, attitudes, prejudice, and interpersonal attraction, and aggression (see Figure 1-11). The relatively new field of **environmental psychology** is concerned with the effects of such factors as population density,

housing design, and urban noise on social behavior. Most social psychologists are researchers, but only in some instances does their research take the form of experiments. Surveys, case studies, and observations in natural settings are more often employed by social psychologists than by physiological or experimental psychologists.

Industrial Psychology

Industrial psychology is generally concerned with the efficiency of human performance in an organizational setting (see Figure 1-12). As human engineers, industrial psychologists try to design complex equipment with the sensory and motor capacities of the human being in mind. They aim for the best "fit" of the capabilities of the machine and those of the person who must operate it.

Personnel psychology is concerned with devising selection procedures that maximize the probability of assigning employees to tasks commensurate with their temperaments, interests, and abilities. Personnel psychologists frequently design and administer aptitude and personality tests. They may be responsible for devising more efficient training methods and for measuring employee morale and improving working conditions, all leading to greater job satisfaction and increased productivity.

Management psychology is a specialized area of personnel psychology. Management psychologists study patterns of intense stress under which executives must sometimes function, recommend organizational changes, improve executive evaluation techniques, and provide psychological counseling to help executives resolve business or personal problems that may be impairing their corporate functioning.

The Crossroad Discipline

These highlights of the principal divisions of the science of psychology reveal it to be a broad and diversified collection of fields, some

Figure 1-12 The design of complex human-machine systems requires the engineering psychologist to understand fully the sensory and motor capabilities of the human organism.

of which appeal to the scientifically oriented person, while others, like clinical psychology, attract those with a strong desire to help troubled individuals. Both the scholarly person who enjoys teaching and the concerned citizen who wants to work for social change can find niches in psychology that correspond with their interests.

Cradled by philosophy and nurtured by physics and physiology, psychology has always been a crossroad discipline. To this day, certain fields within psychology maintain firm ties to a number of outside fields, making it most attractive, and possible, for those with interests or training in other fields to find places in psychology. Such interconnections with a host of other, often very different fields are one reason that the number of people studying and working in psychology has increased so rapidly in the last decade. Another

reason is the growing evidence that psychological techniques can produce desirable personal and social changes.

BECOMING A PSYCHOLOGIST

Although most psychologists hold the Ph.D. degree, recent developments, especially in professional psychology, have shown that people with master's and bachelor's degrees may contribute effectively in the mental health field. Thus, college graduates who majored in psychology are finding places as child-care workers in residential treatment centers, as mental health technicians in community agencies, as counselors in independent schools, and as instructors in rehabilitation centers. The conception of the psychologist's role is being intensively examined and vigorously debated, and the tendency is to conclude that intelligent, sensitive, well-adjusted, and caring individuals armed only with the B.A. degree can be rapidly trained to assume many of the roles traditionally reserved for the Ph.D. in psychology. Accordingly, professional opportunities and responsibilities given the M.A.-level psychologist are also expanding to meet society's increasing need for psychological services. It should be noted, however, that the higher the degree, the wider the range of functions and responsibilities the psychologist may enjoy. Students who aspire to a decision-making, policy-setting role in a clinical setting, for example, are strongly advised to continue their training for the three or four postgraduate years required for the Ph.D. degree. This advice is consistent with a position recently taken by the American Psychological Association restricting professional status (in the form of full APA membership) to holders of the Ph.D. degree. Thus while opportunities are increasing for the B.A. or M.A. degree holder who seeks to provide some professional services to the public, full-fledged professional status requires training at the Ph.D. level.

PSYCHOLOGICAL METHODS

Psychologists use a great variety of methods in acquiring their knowledge about human and animal behavior. Some of their methods are more complicated than others, but all come down to various forms of **observation,** the act of attending to, recognizing, and recording facts or events, and often of measuring them in one way or another.

Figure 1-13 Scenes of violence saturate the airways. Does exposure to such scenes affect our behavior?

SAMPLE OBSERVATIONS

■ The roots of the science of psychology lie deep within each person in mental activities of which the individual alone is aware, but they flower in overt behavior, which everyone can observe. You can get some sense of one type of observation, **self-observation,** by carefully examining your internal and external reactions to a fairly complex situation. Then you can observe the reactions of others to the same kind of situation and see what you can make out of all this behav-

ior. Psychologists have made many investigations of people's reactions to a particular kind of situation: to take just one example, the viewing of violent TV dramas. Figure 1-13 illustrates a few violent scenes from TV dramas.

A. Pick out a TV drama you are sure will involve a good deal of violence and watch it alone. Try to see what goes on within you and in your overt behavior as you watch the drama. For example, what kinds of feelings, images, memories, thoughts, and attitudes do you have? How do you behave throughout the program? Do you find yourself staring at the screen? Do you fidget nervously or shudder at some scenes? When the show is concluded, write down your observations. A compact paragraph or two will do.

B. Then arrange to watch another violent TV drama with someone else, without telling the other person why you are doing so. This time, observe as much about the other person's behavior during the show as you can. When the program is over, explain that you are examining reactions to TV shows and ask your companion the following questions:

1. Did you pay attention to the TV show throughout, or did your mind wander?
2. Did you become involved in the drama?
3. With what character(s) did you tend to identify most?
4. What feelings and emotions did you have as you watched the show?
5. What were your reactions to the scenes of violence in the show?
6. What effects do you think the regular watching of such shows would have on you? On children?
7. Do you think watching TV violence would tend to make children more aggressive?
8. Would you approve or disapprove of your watching such shows regularly? Of children watching such shows regularly?

C. Think over the data you now have from your observations of yourself and another person, and recall your own past reactions to viewing violent TV shows. Then write down whatever conclusions you can draw about the effects violent TV shows have on viewers, both adults and children, again in a paragraph or two. Of course, any conclusions you draw will necessarily be speculative since they will not be based on *objective* evidence.

As you will see in reading further, you have been using a variety of observational methods in this activity.

Naturalistic Observation

One way to study behavior is to go where it's happening and make observations right then and there. **Naturalistic observation** is the study of behavior as it is occurring in "real life." You can observe your own behavior and that of another person in an immediate way in the TV activity. Similarly, social psychologists interested in what turns a crowd into a mob could try to observe the dynamics of mob formation on the spot. They could attempt to identify the background issues, the motives of the participants, the roles played by leaders, the ways in which plans and intentions are communicated, the reasons for failure of normal inhibiting mechanisms, and so on. They might also interview participants both during and after the event. Many such naturalistic observations were made, for example, during the Los Angeles riots that shocked the country in 1965 (Cohen, 1970).

If psychologists know ahead of time that a certain behavioral event is going to take place, they can plan their observations systematically. Such an opportunity enabled Festinger, Riecken, and Schachter (1956), for example, to study the intensely religious members of a small sect who had been told by spiritual messengers that a deluge would soon destroy the world, engulfing their city at a precise time on a given date, but that they would be saved by flying saucers. The naturalistic observers described in detail the intricate preparations made by these people: selling their homes, resigning from their jobs, selling or giving away all their possessions before the world ended. Knowing the precise time of the expected cataclysm, the observers were on the spot, watching and interviewing. When the appointed hour came and went without a trace of either floods or saucers, what then? The observers were interested in learning what people do when such a personally significant prophecy fails. How do they reconcile their beliefs with the facts? The observers reported that the believers became puzzled and confused, but finally, constructed an explanation that satisfied them: Because of their own faith, the gods had decided to spare the world.

As you can imagine, the naturalistic observer must exercise great care and skill to avoid disturbing and distorting the very behavior being studied. The act of observing people, as you may have noted while observing another person watching a TV show, or even the mere presence of another person, will often change the behavior under observation. Suppose you wanted to study pilfering behavior in a bookshop. Stationing yourself at a convenient vantage point, pencil and pad at the ready, would actually guarantee your failure to observe anyone stealing anything. A naive observer might conclude that little or no stealing ever takes place. In the study of socially proscribed behavior, it is especially important that naturalistic observation be carried out unobtrusively.

Unobtrusive measures are observations of behavior of which the subject is totally unaware. Psychologists use such measures to keep the behavior under observation from becoming distorted by the effects of the measurement process (Webb, Campbell, Schwartz, & Sechrest, 1966). The use of unobtrusive measures need not constitute an objectionable invasion of privacy. Periodic drops in municipal water pressure tend to occur between TV programs (when viewers stampede to the bathroom before the next program begins), and hence can be used as one measure of TV viewing. The number of empty liquor bottles found in trash cans has been used as an index of alcohol consumption in a "dry" town. Racial attitudes among students have been inferred from the degree to which black and white students cluster together in dining halls and classrooms. The ethical standards of psychology require that the rights of individuals should not be violated (APA *Ethical Principles*, 1973), and unobtrusive measures help psychologists to avoid potentially damaging activities.

Another serious problem that limits the usefulness of naturalistic observation is that the observations themselves can be interpreted in a variety of ways, and it is not easy to distinguish correct from incorrect conclusions. Take the question you asked your companion in the TV activity: Do you think watching TV violence would tend to make children more ag-

gressive? What could you conclude from the answer of the other person and of yourself to this question? Nothing, really, for such conclusions are full of inferences. But suppose you went further and observed that a group of four young boys always begins to fight after watching a half-hour TV program filled with violent scenes. How can you be sure that the violent scenes they witnessed caused the boys' aggressive behavior? It could have resulted from sitting still for 30 minutes. It might be correlated with the time of day—say, just before dinnertime. Without some controls like these, over other possible causes of aggressiveness, the conclusion that the TV violence the boys watched caused their aggressive behavior is suspect. The method of naturalistic observation does not normally provide such controls.

VIOLENCE ON TV—DOES IT AFFECT OUR SOCIETY?

The following quotations are excerpts from articles on "Violence on TV" that appeared in an issue of *TV Guide* (June 14, 1975) entirely devoted to this controversy or in an advertisement for this issue:

". . . in 1969 we called upon the Surgeon General to marshal the best minds in America and determine whether there is a connection between violence on television and antisocial behavior. In 1972—when the Surgeon General appeared before our committee—he substantiated these fears and declared in no uncertain terms that there is a causal relationship between violence on television and the behavior of children. Subsequent research has further confirmed the validity of this conclusion."
    J. O. Pastore, Chairman
    Senate Communications Subcommittee

"America is a troubled nation, and violence is undoubtedly part of what's troubling it. Yet violence is part of life, and it has always been part of fiction and drama. No one sensibly suggests its banishment from storytelling. The real concern is how we *deal* with violence."
    Robert T. Howard, President
    NBC-TV Network

"I was interested by a recent interview in the New York

in this regard will satisfy everyone. But we believe that the direction of our intent will be clear even to the most critical."
   Robert D. Wood, President
   CBS-TV Network

". . . if we continue to amuse ourselves with violence just because that worked for thousands of years, then the enemies that can't be conquered by violence (overpopulation, famine, pollution, scarcity) will conquer us, and it will all be over."
   Isaac Asimov

"If, indeed, the 'cumulative' watching of evil is turning us all, gradually, into depraved beings, then the 'cumulative' watching of good must be turning us all, gradually, into saints!"
   Edith Efron
   TV Guide Contributing Editor

Times with members of a New York street gang in which they rated the new program *S.W.A.T.* (ABC) as their favorite because 'lots of cops get hurt.' Actually, one of the gang members made a very perceptive point about the effect of televised violence when she said: 'Kids are curious and if you tell 'em "Don't watch" then that's the show they're gonna watch first chance they get.'"
   Torbert H. MacDonald, Chairman
   House Subcommittee on Communications

"If television is to focus on meaningful themes and mirror the reality of our times, television must continue to deal with mature and sensitive subjects. Our concern for any effect this might have will continue. And we will evidence this concern by how we refine our treatment of these themes."
   Frederick S. Pierce, President
   ABC Television

". . . the specter of censorship wafts into view like an unwelcome visitor. It's a solution nobody claims to want, but it may become less unthinkable in the current atmosphere of dismay over televised violence and the industry's stewardship of the public's airwaves."
   Neil Hickey
   TV Guide New York Bureau Chief

"In short, our goal is to be responsive to potential problems without at the same time destroying the creative freedom that has made television the country's most popular source of entertainment. Not all our efforts

Retrospective Methods

Since it is often not possible or feasible to observe natural behavior on the spot, psychologists are frequently restricted to learning about behavior that has already happened. **Retrospective methods** rely on accounts of prior behavior recalled by participants in events. Thus information about the ways people react under extreme stress can be obtained by reading the narratives they later compose. The manner in which survivors of a plane crash high in the Andes coped with cold, injuries, and starvation is recounted in the book *Alive* (Read, 1974), for example. Interviews with the survivors of sinking ocean liners, skyscraper fires, the air bombings of London and Dresden in World War II, and concentration camps all provide valuable information about human behavior. But these accounts are subject to considerable error because of the stressful conditions under which the observations were made, because of normal forgetting, and because of errors of reconstruction due to the emotional significance of the original events for the reporters.

   Questionnaires, often used by psychologists, consist of a group of systematically arranged and often pretested questions about respondents' past or usual behavior, opinions, or feelings. You used a brief questionnaire in the *B* part of your TV activity, for example, in interviewing your subject. Some questionnaires are used as personality tests; these are called **self-report inventories.** Others are used in attitude and opinion surveys. Questionnaires are usually easy to administer to groups of lay people and often provide useful descriptions of behaviors and attitudes. As you might suspect, the manner in which people respond to questionnaires is strongly dependent on the interviewer's approach, the respondents' memories, their ability to observe their own behavior, and their willingness to cooperate with the interviewer. Moreover, although such procedures at their best provide a description of typical feelings or attitudes, they seldom identify the factors that *caused* these reactions. For example, while survey data have repeatedly shown that the average American child spends more time in front of the television set (about 1200 hours a year) than in school, they provide little understanding of the causes of this "addiction." Along the same line, although 95 per cent of the TV cartoons viewed by children contain violent episodes (Surgeon General, 1971), this fact alone does not establish television viewing as a cause of aggressive behavior in children.

The **case history technique** is a special kind of retrospective method in which psychologists attempt to reconstruct significant events in their subjects' pasts on the basis of the subjects' own reports, reports of family members and others, and school, work, or other records. This technique is used primarily by clinical and counseling psychologists and by psychiatrists, in order to identify specific experiences that patients may have had that would help explain their current problems. Sometimes the traumatic effects of past experiences are so anxiety-provoking that patients find themselves unable to recall and face them. Special techniques, such as hypnosis, dream analysis, and free association, are sometimes used to help such patients remember.

One famous and detailed case history is that of Anna O., a seriously neurotic women studied by Breuer and Freud (1936). Fräulein O. suffered from a number of hysterical symptoms (see Chapter 15), including blurred vision, gagging, inability to swallow, and paralysis. While in a hypnotic trance, Anna was able to recall several episodes in her life that seemed to be related to her current problems. For example, her inability to swallow seemed related to the revulsion she had experienced as a child as she watched a large dog that belonged to her governess, a woman she disliked, drink from a drinking glass. Anna also remembered that as her father lay dying, he asked her for the time, but her eyes were so filled with tears that she had trouble seeing the hands on her watch. Her blurred vision seemed to date from that terribly upsetting episode.

How could the case history technique be used in studying the effects of TV violence on children's behavior? Imagine a young child afflicted with recurrent nightmares, afraid to go to sleep at night, and shrieking with terror at the slightest display of aggressiveness among family members or playmates. In addition to observations of the child's behavior at play and otherwise, and face-to-face talks, the case history approach would include questioning of the parents about events occurring around the time the child's symptoms began. The parents might recall that the symptoms seemed to coincide with the development of a habit of TV watching, perhaps initiated by a series of particularly violent adult dramas. Finding no evidence of a poor child–parent relationship and encountering no other history of trauma, the clinician might well conclude that the TV violence was the cause of the child's problems and that the remedy should include revised viewing habits.

Such a conclusion might be quite correct, but the case history technique can only *suggest* that TV was the culprit; it cannot provide proof. If frequent exposure to TV violence is identified as a common condition in the case histories of a number of disturbed children, one might conclude that such viewing was a cause of some children's disturbances. But again, this would be very little proof that TV violence necessarily caused the children's emotional upsets, nor would it identify the exact conditions under which it might have such effects. The case history technique is eminently suited for the clinical analysis of the individual case, but not for the establishment of **generalizations,** statements applicable to all members of a group, such as all children or all people who are left-handed.

Correlational Methods

When things or events tend to accompany each other in a consistent way, it is said that they are correlated, or that a **correlation** exists between them. **Correlational methods** are techniques designed to reveal events that are related positively or negatively to each other. These events may also have a **causal relationship,** as cause and effect, although not all correlated events are causally related. Things or events that are related may be measured over a wide range of values. For example, you know that when you hear a sudden loud noise, you tend to jump, in a general bodily reaction psychologists call a **startle response.** The noise represents one point on a wide continuum of intensities ranging from soft to loud. The startle response, too, varies in magnitude; it may be barely noticeable or it may actually lift you from your chair. These measures show a **positive correlation;** you will find that the louder the noise, the greater your startle response. The size of the iris opening of the eye, on the other hand, shows a **negative correlation** with the intensity of light, since the stronger the intensity of light, the smaller the iris opening becomes, decreasing as the light intensity increases.

To return to TV violence, the belief that watching violent TV shows causes aggressiveness in children would be weakened indeed if groups of children who watched dif-ferent amounts of television (one set of measures) did not differ in the aggressiveness they displayed (the second set of measures). But suppose you found a series of children who differed in the amounts of television they watched—4, 8, 12, and so on up to 20 hours a week. And suppose that you observed greater and greater amounts of aggressiveness as you passed from group to group watching television for greater lengths of time. You'd have to agree from this positive correlation that there's some connection, a positive correlation, between TV watching and aggressive behavior. But does this correlation *prove* that TV viewing causes the aggressiveness? Not at all. Think of some other possibilities: The more aggressive the child is, the more pleasure he obtains from watching television (here aggressiveness seems to be the "cause" of TV viewing). Or the more aggressive the child is, the more likely his parents are to use television as a pacifier (here also aggressiveness leads to TV viewing). Similarly, if a social psychologist found a high correlation between the number of churches in towns and the rate of alcoholism in those towns, he could not conclude that religious activities cause alcoholism. High correlations do not prove the relationship is causal, for there is always the possibility that some underlying condition is causally related to both of the correlated measures. In this instance, the underlying dimension of population density in the towns may give rise to both the varying number of churches and the varying rates of alcoholism. Some people try to cope by going to church, others by drinking.

Despite this weakness, correlational methods are very useful and powerful tools that many psychologists employ whenever they wish to determine in a general way whether some behavior is related to (*a*) external environmental factors, (*b*) internal biological factors, or (*c*) some other aspect of behavior. The correlation of TV viewing *with* aggressiveness exemplifies *a*; the correlation of concentrations of hormones like epinephrine (adrenaline) in the blood with aggressiveness illustrates *b*; and the correlation of the amount of aggressive behavior displayed at home with the amount displayed at school exemplifies *c*. Very precise ways of expressing the degree of the relationship in numerical terms have been worked out by statisticians (see Appendix: Statistics). Think how valuable it would be, for example, to find a very high correlation between aggressiveness at home and at school. The advantage is **predictability,** or the capacity to tell beforehand that an event will probably occur, given a certain condition or conditions. In this case, if you knew a boy's level of aggressiveness at home, you could predict how aggressive he'd probably be when he entered school. Knowledge of a strong correlation doesn't immediately tell you how behavior can be controlled, for it may not tell you the cause, but it does help you to predict behavior with some degree of probability, although never with certainty.

Now you can also see why so many psychologists devote much time and energy trying to improve the correlations between measures of performance on clinical diagnostic tests, such as a test for neurotic tendencies, and behavior in real life. The higher the correlation, the better clinicians can predict from the tests how the individual is likely to function when confronted with everyday stresses and conflicts. Similarly, the higher the correlation between personnel selection test results and job performance, the better the individual's performance and adjustment on the job can be predicted. And the higher the correlation between school aptitude tests and academic performance, the better a school psychologist can identify students who may need special instruction if they are to succeed in school. Correlations don't establish causes, only probable relationships. But these can be very valuable.

Experimental Methods

Experimental methods provide the most reliable knowledge about the causes of behavior because they do the best job of isolating the relevant factor or factors responsible for it. These methods assume that all behavior has causes; that is, every behavior is the result of some antecedent condition or conditions. If we grant that behavior has causes, but we don't know what they are in the case of some specific behavior that we are interested in understanding, one experimental method, the **method of difference,** is to present the individual with one possible causal situation and see if the behavior occurs. On another occasion the suspected cause is eliminated, and the psychologist observes whether the behavior occurs or not. If the behavior occurs only when the suspected causal factor is present, never when it is absent, we are confident of having identified one of the causes of the behavior in question.

Let's apply the method of difference to the question of whether viewing TV violence causes aggressive behavior in children. If it should be found that large numbers of children display aggressive behavior only after watching TV violence, but do not display this behavior after watching TV programs free of violent scenes, then the viewing of TV violence has been identified as at least one of the causes of aggressive behavior in children.

In experimental methods like the method of difference, the change or event that occurs first in a causal relationship is called the **independent variable,** while the change or event that follows it is called the **dependent variable.** Thus in causal relationships the cause is the independent variable and the effect the dependent variable, since it depends on the cause. In our example, an attempt was made to see whether children's aggressiveness (the dependent variable) depended on watching violent TV shows (the independent variable). In experiments, one or more independent variables are manipulated; other conditions are kept the same; and the consequences of such variations on the dependent variable, the behavior, are carefully noted.

Another powerful experimental method for identifying causes is called the **method of con-**

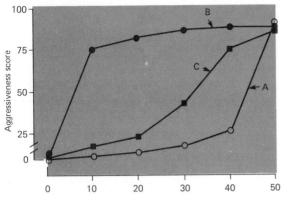

Figure 1-14 Several hypothetical functional relationships between number of violent TV scenes viewed in an average week (independent variable) and aggressive behavior (dependent variable).

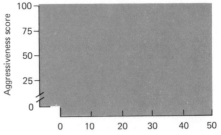

Figure 1-15 Copy this graph and draw a separate curve for each of the groups identified in the text expressing the functional relationship you would expect to find between number of violent scenes viewed and aggressiveness score.

comitant variations, or variations that occur together. This method identifies causes by the observation of functional relationships between variables. A **functional relationship** describes the way a dependent variable changes as some property of the independent variable changes. If precise variation in the dependent variable occurs as the independent variable is systematically changed, the independent variable is then known to be the cause of the dependent variable, the effect. The relationship between viewing violent TV shows and aggressive behavior of children would be called a functional relationship if, for example, it were found that increases in the independent variable (viewing violent TV scenes) were followed by precise increases in the dependent variable (the aggressiveness of the children). Figure 1-14 illustrates three hypothetical functional relationships that might hold between these two variables. Relationship A indicates that watching TV violence has little effect on aggressive behavior until the amount of exposure to the shows is extreme. Relationship B suggests that even a few viewings will increase aggressiveness. Is this the way you think it is? Or do you think relationship C accurately reflects the real nature of

the causal relationship? Perhaps the true relationship is a horizontal line, high across the graph if you think children are generally pretty aggressive regardless of the amount of TV exposure, and low if you think they're not.

PREDICTED FUNCTIONAL RELATIONSHIPS

■ Copy the graph in Figure 1-15 on graph or unlined paper and draw on it the functional relationships you think you would find if you carried out an experiment in which six groups of children were exposed to 50 different scenes of televised violence and their aggressive behavior was measured throughout the experiment. Draw separate curves representing the relationships you'd expect to find for groups of (a) randomly selected boys, (b) randomly selected girls, (c) male juvenile delinquents, (d) female juvenile delinquents, (e) shy, withdrawn boys, and (f) shy, withdrawn girls.

When you have finished drawing the curves, label them a, b, c, and so on, and examine them to see how you thought sex and delinquency conditions affected these functional relationships. Now examine the bases for your predictions. Are they based on any observations you've made? On observations made by others? On some logical deductions?

If the magnitude of an independent variable is systematically changed and corresponding orderly changes are observed in the measures of the behavioral dependent variable, not only has a determinant of behavior been identified, but also one learns how much the independent variable needs to be changed in order to obtain a given behavioral effect. Since specific environmental conditions are often manipulated in experiments, the independent variable, which affects the individual subjects, is often called the **stimulus condition.** Since the effects of variations in stimulus conditions on some specific kind of behavior are often observed, the dependent variable is known as the **response** of the individual subjects. Thus the psychological experiment can be interpreted as a way of studying **stimulus–response (S–R) relationships.**

Some of the stimulus and response variables are relatively simple to observe and measure, like the stimulus of number of hours of TV viewing and the response of number of temper tantrums. Others are more difficult, like the stimulus intensity of televised scenes of violence and the response of improvement during psychotherapy. So all investigators must define their stimulus and response terms as objectively as possible so that others can know precisely what the terms mean in the context of the experiments. Psychologists try to use **operational definitions,** defining their variables in terms of the observational or measurement procedures used in their experiments. An operational definition of aggressiveness, for example, might consist of a list of behaviors like hitting, pushing, shoving, and kicking, with a child's aggressiveness score based on the number of times within a specified period the child displayed such responses. Without such precise operational definitions of the variables used in an experiment, the investigator's report may not be understood and cannot be exactly repeated by others who wish to see if they will obtain the same results. Experimental replication is a crucial requirement in the establishment of a reliable body of knowledge about ourselves and the world around us.

A Typical Experiment

Let's now examine an actual experiment designed to determine the effect of viewing violent television programs on aggressive behavior (Feshbach & Singer, 1971). The investigators wanted to be sure the subjects would be watching either an aggressive or a nonaggressive series of TV programs during the six weeks of the experiment. Fortunately, what and how much the subjects watched could be precisely controlled, for the subjects were all boys in residential private schools and homes for the underprivileged. All subjects watched a minimum of six hours of television a week. Boys assigned to **experimental groups** (those exposed to the independent variable by the experimenters) had to select their programs from a list of particularly aggression-rich programs, in which fighting, shooting, and other types of mayhem figured prominently. Other boys were assigned to **control groups** (those not exposed to the independent variable), and selected their TV fare from a list of nonaggressive programs.

What was the dependent variable? There were several, for the investigators wanted to see the effects of television on several different types of behavior. Personality tests and attitude scales were administered to the subjects at the beginning and end of the experiment to measure changes in such traits as suppressed hostility and impulsiveness. One form of the **Thematic Apperception Test** (*TAT*) was used to measure aggressive fantasies. This test required the boys to make up stories about people shown on slides in somewhat ambiguous situations (see Chapter 14). Presumably the boys' own feelings were projected onto the characters in their stories. To measure the dependent variable of aggressiveness further, each boy was rated by his house parent, teacher, or supervisor for the frequency of well-defined aggressive acts—mild, moderate, or strong—whether the acts were provoked or unprovoked.

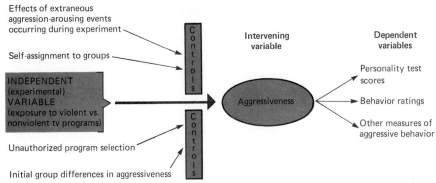

Effects of extraneous
aggression-arousing events
occurring during experiment

Self-assignment to groups

INDEPENDENT
(experimental)
VARIABLE
(exposure to violent vs.
nonviolent tv programs)

Unauthorized program selection

Initial group differences in aggressiveness

Controls

Controls

Intervening
variable

Aggressiveness

Dependent
variables

Personality test
scores

Behavior ratings

Other measures of
aggressive behavior

Figure 1-16 A well-controlled experiment prevents extraneous, or nonexperimental, variables from affecting the dependent variable(s). Thus observed differences in behavior can
be more confidently attributed to the experimental variable: exposure (experimental group)
vs. no exposure (control group) to programs depicting violence. Aggressiveness is an intervening variable, since it is a trait or state aroused by certain conditions (one of which *may* be
exposure to TV violence) and expressed in a variety of behaviors. Intervening variables summarize relationships between independent and dependent variables.

Now imagine that the experimental groups
showed more aggressive behavior at the end of
the experiment. Could this be explained by
saying that they happened to be more aggressive to begin with? Hardly, for measures of
aggressiveness were taken before the experiment started, and the investigators could observe how much change in aggressiveness occurred during the six weeks. Couldn't more
aggressive boys tend to select the more aggressive programs? Not in this case, for self-selection of programs was ruled out. The experimenter decided who was exposed to which
programs. Every experiment must be designed
to control for, or minimize, the effects of extraneous factors on the dependent variable.

The main components of this experiment
are diagrammed in Figure 1-16. Note the addition of a new term, **intervening variable** (in
this case, aggressiveness), which summarizes
relationships between the independent variable and the various dependent variable measures. As you can see, if watching TV violence
produces all or even a part of the behavioral
consequences listed, it is possible to summarize these relationships under the character-

istic (or trait) of aggressiveness, expressed in
many kinds of responses. Thus an intervening
variable is a concept for a hypothetical process
that stands for or expresses a number of relationships between independent and dependent variables.

What were the results of the Feshbach and
Singer experiment? In general, exposure to
violent TV programs over the six-week period
did not produce an increase in aggressive
behavior. In fact, the indications were that,
among residents of boys' homes, *less* behavioral aggression toward other boys and supervisors was displayed by the boys who watched
violent shows. This effect was especially
marked in boys with typically strong aggressive tendencies. The investigators tentatively
concluded that exposure to violent scenes on
television may help highly aggressive boys to
control their behavior. It is only fair to note,
however, that this conclusion is not final. It
has not been accepted by other investigators
(Eron, Huesmann, Lefkowitz, & Walder, 1972;
Liebert, Sobol, & Davidson, 1972), and some
have reported increases in aggression following the viewing of violent TV programs

(Steuer, Applefield, & Smith, 1971). The issue has not yet been settled, but the only way to do it is with carefully designed and controlled experiments.

STAGES IN INVESTIGATION

We all start with commonsense notions about the world and about ourselves. Many of these beliefs, like the idea that genius and madness are somehow related, are based on anecdotal and hearsay evidence. Many are traditions or myths that attempt to explain the puzzles in and between human beings by appealing to intrinsic properties of "human nature," thereby begging the question. For example, racial and ethnic prejudice was "explained" at one time by postulating an instinctive "dislike for the unlike" (Sumner, 1906).

Scientific psychology attempts to go beyond common sense, myth, and presumably self-evident beliefs by subjecting its statements about behavior to the test of verification. Just as the "obvious" conclusion that the world was flat was, through observations, tested and refuted (although a Flat Earth Society still exists), so too, many "obvious" conclusions about behavior are not accepted by psychologists in the absence of objective evidence or in the presence of evidence to the contrary. Although there is evidence in the history of psychology of reluctance to abandon cherished beliefs despite evidence to the contrary (Kamin, 1974), the commitment to keep the path to inquiry open and to put statements about behavior to empirical test runs strong. How does this scientific approach to investigating behavior work?

Problem Formulation

Statements about behavior may be guesses about relationships between behavior and environmental events (for example, neurotic behavior may be a result of inconsistently applied punishment), or between different cat-egories of behavior (people of low self-esteem tend to be very critical of others). They may also arise from casual observations, be formally deduced from a body of general principles or theory, or emerge out of ongoing research. Whatever the source, the requirements are the same. Statements about behavior must be expressed clearly enough to be put to an empirical, or observational, test. To achieve effective results, psychologists must work with statements about behavior that are both verifiable and communicable.

See how easy it is for research problems to develop: Some years ago it was discovered that infant rats handled by people prior to weaning grew to become generally less emotional adults than their nonhandled litter mates (Levine, Chevalier, & Korchin, 1956; see Figure 1-17). Note how the next set of questions arises almost immediately: (1) What is it about the handling that produces this result? Is it removal from the mother or from siblings? Changes in temperature, in tactual sensations, or in the mother's behavior when the infant

Figure 1-17 Rat pups removed from the nest for a few minutes a day prior to weaning develop into less emotional adult rats than those that have not been exposed to human handling.

pup is returned to the nest after handling? (2) What physiological changes are produced by the handling? Are these changes merely hormonal, or do they involve changes in neural structures as well? How do such physiological changes, if found, account for the reduction in emotionality in adulthood? (3) Will the adult rat that receives early handling respond less emotionally to all forms of adult stimulation? Isn't it more adaptive to respond emotionally under some conditions and calmly in nonthreatening circumstances? (4) What are the implications for humans of the effects of early handling on rats? Are babies who are exposed to a rich and varied stimulus environment likely to show lowered emotionality when they become adults? Does infant stimulation influence the intellectual development of the child, as well as the emotional or social development (Denenberg, 1975)? Clearly one question planted in a fertile medium begets many others, the answers to which might be most significant.

Review of Current Knowledge

Once a problem has been formulated, it becomes important to find out what is already known about the issue. To conduct a research project on a question that has long since been answered adequately would certainly be a waste of time and money. Both new and experienced investigators are wise to consult specialized guides to the research literature, and this is also a good way to learn what research is currently being done on any subject in which you may be interested. For psychologists, the *Psychological Abstracts*, published monthly, provide brief summaries of articles in print, with both subject and author indexes to enable you to locate articles and books relevant to the subject in which you are interested. If the problem also includes physiological elements, reference to *Biological Abstracts* is also worthwhile. Many journals and books also carry occasional reviews of the work that has

been done recently on a topic, summarizing the current state of knowledge on that topic and providing extensive bibliographies. A good example is the *Annual Review of Psychology*. Students interested in the effects of early handling on subsequent emotionality would certainly be amply rewarded with a rich crop of research references on this topic if they conducted a systematic survey of the literature. The review of current knowledge often enables investigators to restate their questions more effectively and exposes areas of the subject in which little or no research has been done, which may then be worth pursuing.

Research Design

In the next stage, the actual research procedures to be carried out to answer the question are planned. Investigators must decide whether to use naturalistic, retrospective, correlational, experimental, or other methods. They also have to decide what kind of subjects to use and how many, what control groups will be necessary if an experimental approach is to be used, what observations and equipment will be needed, and how these will relate to the problem posed. If the observations can be expressed **quantitatively,** in numbers, some decision about the statistical analyses to be applied to the numerical data will also need to be made (see Appendix: Statistics).

If an experimental approach is to be used, the investigation must be designed very carefully to control all the variables that may be involved. Suppose you had found a good reason, based on previous research, for predicting what would happen to the emotional development of infant rabbits if, during the very frequent and prolonged periods when the mother is customarily absent from the nest, half the infants were handled (experimental group) and half were not handled (control group). You'd then be able to set up a **predictive hypothesis,** indicating the results you would expect to observe if your idea were correct. Such a hypothesis takes the form "I bet this would happen if . . ." or, more formally, "If conditions *a* are applied, effect *b* should be observed." In our example, a predictive hypothesis might take this form: "Handling will produce less emotional adult rabbits if the handled infants are always returned to the nest while the mother is present, but not if they are returned while she is absent." This hypothesis implies that something about the mother's behavior toward handled and returned infants is critical. Rabbits would be an especially good species to work with since, unlike rat mothers, who rarely leave the nest, rabbit mothers naturally stay away from the nest, returning several times daily for periods of three to ten minutes to feed their bunnies.

You might choose a **descriptive hypothesis,** however, if you were unsure about the probable outcome of the experiment. A descriptive hypothesis seems to say, "I wonder what would happen if . . ." or, more formally, "To determine the effects of conditions *a* on events *b* . . ." using the experiment to answer a question without predicting just what the results will be. In our example, a descriptive hypothesis might begin this way: "To determine the effect of early handling on the subsequent emotional development of rabbits, if the handled infants are returned to the nest while the mother is present or absent from it . . ."

EXPERIMENT WITH INFANT RABBITS

■ Do you think the hypothesis about the treatment of infant rabbits could best be answered by the experimental approach? If so, how would you design an appropriate experiment? Remember that it's first necessary to show that the lawful relationship between handling and lower emotionality in adulthood found in rats is also true for rabbits. You could start by treating litters of rabbits like the litters in the rat experiments. Half the litter mates in a particular rabbit hutch would be removed for daily handling and then returned to the mother and litter mates, the other half being left undisturbed. Later, tests for emotionality would be administered to all litter mates.

Suppose the handled infant rabbits, like handled rat pups, grow up to be less emotional. Is this because the doe (mother) gives the handled bunnies some special treatment when they are returned to the hutch? Now you're ready to do the experiment to determine the role played by the mother's presence or absence from the hutch when the bunnies are returned after being handled. Give daily handling to all bunnies in the litter of another rabbit mother, but after each handling, be careful to return only half the bunnies to the hutch when the mother is absent, the other half being returned to the hutch when the mother is present. Usually, of course, many more than two litters would be used in order to obtain reliable statistical results.

What variables do you think need to be controlled in this research design? What is the dependent variable (or variables)? What do you think the outcome of such an experiment would be? Would it be valuable to compare the way the mother rabbit behaves toward the handled bunnies when they are returned to the hutch when she's in it, as opposed to the way she behaves toward them when she returns to the hutch and finds them there?

Assessment of Results

Once the observations have been made and the data collected, the investigator interprets them and determines how they bear on the initial hypothesis. Were clear-cut differences obtained between the experimental groups? Was the predicted hypothesis confirmed or refuted? What other implications do the results carry? If a descriptive hypothesis was involved, what possible explanations for the results can be offered? How confidently can the findings be generalized to other groups?

These are some of the questions to be considered in the final stages of a research project, even when nonexperimental methods are employed. In our example of the bunny study, suppose handled infant rabbits grew up to be less emotional than their nonhandled litter mates, regardless of the presence or absence of the mother when they were returned to the nest. This result would tend to rule out maternal behavior toward handled infants returned to the hutch as an explanation of the effects of handling. It would imply that something about the handling itself was the causal factor. What could this factor or factors be? Here is where theory comes into play. One theory offered to explain the effect of early handling of rat pups is that this experience causes an excessive adrenal response, one product being the hormone corticosterone. This hormone, the theory asserts, acts on the developing brain structures to bring about a neural organization that renders the animal permanently less emotional (Denenberg & Zarrow, 1971). A theory of this kind is said to be **reductionistic,** for it employs concepts from a lower or simpler level of explanation, in terms of hormones and brain structures, than those found at the level of behavior being explained. By contrast, some theories are **abstract,** in that they use mathematical or purely imaginary concepts to summarize and explain relationships. An intervening variable such as aggressiveness used earlier, is an example of such abstract concepts.

MISCONCEPTIONS OF PSYCHOLOGY

Before we start to investigate specific fields of psychology, it may be worthwhile to discuss a number of questions that people beginning the study of psychology often raise. People are often skeptical of the feasibility of a science of psychology, impatient with the frequency with which animal subjects are used, or fearful of the possibility that techniques of behavior control will harm the individual or fall into the hands of the unscrupulous.

Is a Science of Human Behavior Feasible?

Skepticism sometimes arises because it is difficult to see how the objective methods of science can be applied to subjective processes like mental events. But the events psychologists study, both objective and subjective, are every bit as much a part of the natural world as are genes, hormones, and muscular contractions. What psychologists study is what they can observe, directly or by means of instruments, of the overt, internal, or verbal behavior of subjects. Though a subjective event, such as one verbally expressed as "I feel delighted!" is ultimately experienced by only one organism, it can be indirectly indicated by the objectively observable behavior of that organism. It is understood, of course, that the relationship between a subjective state (feeling of delight) and the verbal or behavioral expression of it ("I feel delighted!" or a broad smile) cannot be taken for granted. A fearful state, for example, is a process *inferred* on the basis of the individual's verbal, physiological, gestural, and postural behavior. However, the inference is subject to error, particularly when the state is hidden or reported incorrectly by the individual. But the error inherent in inferences about processes that are not directly observable is not a problem unique to psychology. It appears in all the sciences, as in the concepts of protons and electrons in physics.

"But every person is unique," runs another criticism, "and science deals only with general principles." This statement fails to appreciate the way that general principles assist the understanding of uniqueness. Thus the science of genetics explains under what circumstances an albino is born to parents who are not themselves albinos. Similarly, in psychology, the principle of reinforcement (see Chapter 7) applies to all persons, but may also explain how it is that some individuals throw tantrums when they can't get their way while others turn on the charm. The two groups may have learned to *reduce their frustration* (a reinforcing effect) by means of very different behavioral strategies. Thus the same reinforcement principle is manifested in different behaviors. True, every individual is unique as an unrepeated combination of numerous personality traits and ways of behaving, but the relationships between these many variable factors in the individual may be explained by general principles that apply uniformly to all individuals.

"But behavior is too complex. You can't predict everything a rat will do, much less a person." True again, and nobody really wants to. Psychologists are more interested in understanding and predicting rather large and abstract classes of behavior, like "persistence in the face of obstacles" or "development of a favorable self-concept," for example. The psychologist's goal is more often the development of an appropriate degree of self-esteem in an individual than the determination of very specific attributes of the self-concept. Isn't it more important to understand and possibly assist the growth of appropriate levels of self-assertiveness in shy persons than to determine the precise words one shy person will use when he or she is treated unfairly?

"But people are perverse: Announce a behavioral law and you can be sure they'll try to break it!" But unlike laws enacted and enforced by human agencies, behavioral laws do not prescribe what a person ought to do or will do; they merely describe what a person in fact usually tends to do in a given set of circumstances, as you have seen. Because behavioral laws merely describe regularities in the manner in which subjects have been observed to react, they cannot be broken. Since they are descriptive rather than prescriptive, they are not coercive. It makes as much sense to try to break a behavioral law as it does to defy the law of gravity.

Isn't Animal Behavior Overemphasized?

"The true study of the human race is human beings. Why bother studying the behavior of animals?" Most psychologists who use animal subjects in their research are profoundly interested in applying to people the knowledge they gain from animals. One investigator, who is largely responsible for the application of principles acquired in the animal laboratory to the fields of psychotherapy and education, has this to say:

We study the behavior of animals because it is simpler. Basic processes are revealed more easily and can be recorded over longer periods of time. Our observations are not complicated by the social relations between subject and experimenter. Conditions may be better controlled. We may arrange genetic histories to control certain variables and special life histories to control others — for example, if we are interested in how an organism learns to see, we can raise an animal in darkness until the experiment is begun. . . . It would be rash to assert at this point that there is no essential difference between human behavior and the behavior of lower species; but until an attempt has been made to deal with both in the same terms, it would be equally rash to assert that there is [Skinner, 1953, pp. 38–39].

In addition, psychologists often study animal behavior when an experimental treatment might have undesirable consequences for the subjects. Just as a medical researcher would never use human subjects in the study of viruses that might cause cancer, a psychologist would not expose human subjects to painful or severe conditions in the study of the effects of stress on infant behavior.

Even language, the clearest boundary that has traditionally separated the human from other species, is proving to be a less and less reliable criterion for preserving humanity's claim to special status. By giving a chimpanzee, Lana, the use of a computer panel that she can operate to "speak" with her human attendants, psychologists have succeeded in teaching her a vocabulary of 80 symbols (Rumbaugh, Gill, & von Glasersfeld, 1973). (See Figure 1-18.) Some symbols allow her to ask, "What's this?" and even "What name this?" Lana's efforts in learning her language may help psychologists develop ways of teaching language to retarded or emotionally disturbed children who have failed to learn language for themselves.

Who Will Control Behavioral Control?

"If psychology succeeds in discovering principles of behavior, isn't it possible that this knowledge might be used to develop a tech-

Figure 1-18 Having communicated her wants by pressing a number of computer keys in the proper grammatical sequence, finishing with a period at the end of the sentence, Lana reaches for her reward.

nology of behavior controlled by a few to the disadvantage of the many?" This is not a trivial question. A behavioral technology is rapidly developing (see Chapter 8) that has already made it possible to effect desirable changes in a number of areas of human functioning, such as child rearing, the rechanneling of abnormal behavior, and education. But as knowledge of the determinants of behavior increases, could not techniques of behavior control fall into the hands of the unscrupulous, the privileged, the powerful? There is always the possibility that new knowledge will be put to evil ends. We already have the example of a nuclear technology that can create a world-destroying holocaust as well as produce energy for peaceful purposes and radiation to kill marauding cancer cells.

The question "Who controls?" has no easy answer. Most psychologists would hold that prohibition of further progress in their science is neither an effective nor a possible answer. The human being's exploration of human nature is an inherent part of that nature. The need to know oneself and others can never be drowned in a sea of official prohibitions. Nor can a virtue be made of ignorance. As Socrates observed 2500 years ago, "The unexamined life is not worth living." Probably the safest course is to keep the path to inquiry open, to continue learning as much as we can about ourselves. The knowledge that can be provided by a science of behavior should be disseminated as widely as possible, without restrictions as to color or class, to parents and teachers, to children and students, to people of stations high and low, to all who can be reached. If none is ignorant of the principles that govern behavior, those who yearn for power over others will have to rely on other, coercive measures, as they always have. Widespread knowledge of behavioral laws may be the best answer to such coercive measures and the only defense against any threat of behavior control.

SUMMARY

Human beings have always been interested in examining their own behavior. The earliest conceptions about behavior, some of which persist to this day, were dualistic in that they attributed both physical and spiritual properties to the individual. Dualistic interpretations in Western philosophy have centered largely around the mind–body relationship, as exemplified by the system of Descartes. Although earlier systems of psychology concentrated only on mental events, or only on physical or bodily events, modern psychology studies human and animal behavior and associated mental and physiological processes.

Contemporary psychology can be divided into a number of fields. In experimental psychology, basic theoretical research seeks to discover fundamental laws of behavior. Theories are formulated in order to integrate laws into a logical and coherent system. Physiological psychology concentrates on biological rather than environmental determinants of behavior. Developmental psychology studies the interaction of genetic, organic, and environmental determinants of behavior change from conception to old age. Clinical, counseling, and school psychology provide professional services for people with emotional problems in hospitals, in private practice, and in educational settings. Educational psychology studies normal learning processes in the classroom. Social psychology investigates both the effect of other people's behavior on one or more individuals and interactions within groups. Personnel and management psychologists are generally grouped within industrial psychology, the field concerned with effective performance in organizational settings.

All psychological methods of study are based on observation. Naturalistic observation is used to study behavioral phenomena in real life settings. Unobtrusive measures are useful in minimizing the tendency of people to behave differently when they know they are being observed. Retrospective methods, such as historical accounts, self-report inventories, and case histories, attempt to account for behavior that has already occurred. Correlational methods are used to establish the degree to which different measures of behavior are related. They provide information about covariation, not causality. Experimental methods provide the most reliable information about the causes of behavior. They involve the careful observation of a measure of behavior (dependent variable) to determine how it changes as another measure (independent variable) is systematically manipulated. Since the independent variable is often an environmental or stimulus condition, the psychological experiment is a way of studying stimulus–response, or S–R, relationships. Operational definitions, which describe the observational or measurement procedures used in the experiment, help to give definitional clarity to the terms and concepts employed.

Scientific psychology goes beyond common sense, myth, and "self-evident" beliefs about human and animal behavior by subjecting statements about behavior to empirical test. Stages in the investigation of propositions about behavior include clear formulation of the problem, review of existing knowledge, construction of an appropriate research design to facilitate collection of data relevant to the hypotheses posed, and careful assessment of the results obtained.

The view that the objective methods of science cannot be applied to subjective processes like mental events neglects the fact that in every science, unobservable processes are inferred on the basis of objective data. The assertion that the general principles sought by scientific psychology cannot apply to the unique qualities of each individual's behavior fails to appreciate the fact that the same general principles may account for quite different behaviors. Psychology attempts to understand, predict, and control large and important classes of behavior, not every trivial response. Behavioral laws cannot be broken, since they describe rather than prescribe the determinants of behavior.

The threat of behavior control is an important one in society. While the question "Who controls?" has no easy answer, the safest course may be to disseminate as widely as possible the rapidly accumulating knowledge of behavioral laws.

TRY BEHAVING LIKE A PSYCHOLOGIST

1. Think of a striking and unusual event that happened to you at some time in the past, recollect as much as you can about it, and write a brief narrative report of your own reactions and behavior in the situation, as well as of the behavior of any others involved in it. When you have finished the report, go back over it and pick out items that you are not sure about and places where it is incomplete. Does your report stand up

fairly well under your careful analysis, or does it show some of the weaknesses of the retrospective method?

2. Suppose you suspect from casual observations of various students that those who have great ability in mathematics will also have great ability in logic. To try out your hypothesis, you have administered mathematical and logical aptitude tests to 10 students, on which they have obtained the following scores:

| Student | Scores on | |
	Mathematics Test	Logic Test
1	75	74
2	89	90
3	100	98
4	92	94
5	57	53
6	87	85
7	60	63
8	71	67
9	82	80
10	67	66

Examine the scores of these students. Would you say that they show a low, moderate, or high degree of correlation between mathematical and logical aptitudes? Copy the graph shown in Figure 1–19 on a sheet of graph paper or unlined paper and plot the place of each student on it. Does this **scatter diagram** seem to indicate a low, moderate, or high degree of correlation? What kind of relationship does it show? If you are interested in carrying your analysis further, turn to "Appendix: Statistics" and use the product-moment method of correlation described there to determine the degree of correlation more precisely. What is the coefficient of correlation (r)? Would these prelimi-

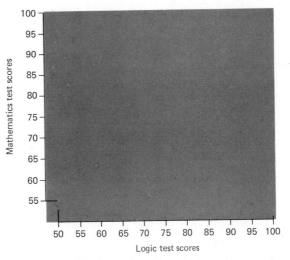

Figure 1-19 The form of graph used to make a scatter diagram showing the relationship between mathematical and logical aptitude test scores.

nary data support your hypothesis enough so that it would be worthwhile to test it out on a much larger number of students?

3. Do you agree or disagree with the proposed answers to the questions under "Misconceptions of Psychology"? Take each question in turn, either by yourself or with other students in the course. If you agree with the answer, try taking the other side and presenting arguments against the answer. If you disagree with the answer, see if you can add to the arguments for the answer given. When you (and any others) have done this for all the questions, look back over them and see if this role playing that you (and they) have done, defending the positions you reject, has tended to change your attitudes on any of these questions. (Also, when you have finished this course, you might check back on these questions and see whether and how much your position on any of your answers has changed.)

2

The Organism

Who you are and why you behave the way you do can be understood only by considering many factors. Our physical structures and psychological capacities are influenced by our biological inheritance and our experiences. The term **heredity** refers to the biological transmission of potentialities from parents to offspring. For thousands, perhaps millions, of years, people have observed that individuals resemble their ancestors. Many physical features are influenced by hereditary factors: eye color, skin color, curliness of hair, shape of the ears, size of the hands, body build, to name only a few. You probably have features similar to those of your parents. (Notice the strong family resemblance in the photographs at the beginning of the chapter.) If you are unusually tall, chances are your mother and (or) father are also very tall. If not, perhaps you have a grandparent who is unusually tall. Somewhere in the family the hereditary potential for tallness can probably be located. But hereditary factors alone do not determine an individual's physical characteristics. Heredity provides the biological instructions for development, but the environment influences the way in which these instructions are carried out. For example, an individual who suffers from malnutrition during childhood will probably not develop the normal body structure indicated by heredity. If an individual is to reach his full heredi-

tary potential with respect to a characteristic (in this case, height), the environmental conditions (nutrition) must be adequate. We often wrongly use the terms "inherited characteristics" or "innate characteristics" when we refer to those characteristics strongly influenced by hereditary factors. Actually, characteristics are not inherited. Biological instructions for characteristics are inherited—*potentialities* are inherited.

The biological inheritance of organisms has a profound effect on behavior. In a general way, heredity influences *all* behavior by providing instruction for the development of physical structures that mediate behavior. As an example, humans, in contrast to most other animals, have unique hand skills made possible because the thumb is opposable to the fingers. The degree to which humans develop these hand skills, however, depends upon practice or experience. Similarly, heredity plays a role in behavior by determining an organism's sensory capabilities. Organisms react only to stimuli that they detect. Some stimuli are more readily detected by certain species of animals than others. The common laboratory rat, for instance, possesses a highly sensitive olfactory system, allowing it to detect smell stimuli better than most other animals. Birds, on the other hand, have a remarkably sensitive visual system. Heredity also influences behavior by setting broad limits on more complex functions of the organism. Some species of animals are more intelligent or more successful in adapting to their environments than others.

In some organisms heredity strongly influences specific behaviors by specifying a tendency to respond to certain stimuli in the environment with behavior of a precise or fixed form. **Instincts,** or instinctive behaviors, are highly specific behaviors that are common to a species of animals and are strongly influenced by hereditary factors. Historically, the term "instinct" has been used to describe both specific behaviors primarily governed by hereditary factors, like nest-building behavior, and inherited motivational tendencies, like "maternal instinct," that direct behavior of a more general form. In this chapter the use of the term "instinct" will be restricted to the former meaning. Inherited motivational tendencies, sometimes referred to as instincts, will be discussed in Chapter 12 along with other biological drives like hunger and thirst.

SPECIES-CHARACTERISTIC BEHAVIORS

The term "instinct" became unpopular in psychology several decades ago, when the word was used loosely by many people to explain a variety of puzzling behaviors. For instance, a man who searched for and finally found a child lost in the woods might have said then that his "instincts" had led him to the right location. Actually, there is no reason to conclude that the successful rescue was based on specific innate human behavior. Currently the popular terms for innate behavior characteristic of a species are **species-characteristic behavior** or **species-specific behavior.** Species-characteristic behaviors have a number of features in common: (1) The behaviors occur frequently in all or nearly all members of a species in their natural environment. (2) They have a fixed form or pattern that is fairly stable under varying environmental conditions.

(3) Prior experience or learning is unnecessary for their development. At their first occurrence, the behaviors usually appear in a fully organized form. (4) They represent adaptive ways of interacting with the environment; that is, they have a beneficial value to the species.

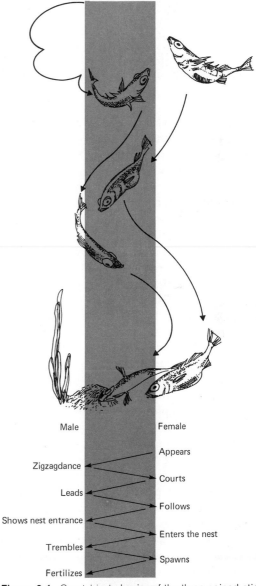

Male   Female

                        Appears

Zigzagdance ←   → Courts

Leads ←   → Follows

Shows nest entrance ← → Enters the nest

Trembles ←   → Spawns

Fertilizes ←

Figure 2-1 Courtship behavior of the three-spined stickleback fish. (Adapted from Tinbergen, 1969)

Courtship, mating, feeding, parental care, and aggressive behaviors of many animals fall into this category. The male three-spined stickleback fish, for example, builds a nest during breeding season, leads egg-carrying females to the nest with a zigzag dance, and, after the female has deposited her eggs there, fertilizes them (see Figure 2-1). This courtship behavior takes the same form for all or nearly all mating stickleback fish.

WHO SHOWED YOU HOW TO FLIRT?

When someone of the opposite sex is flirting with you or responding to your own flirting, you are quite well aware of it. But did you know that this is probably an inherited behavior pattern? The flirting pattern has been discovered by means of motion pictures taken while people were unaware that they were being photographed and then projected in slow motion. It appears in both old and young people, male and female. A flirting girl, for example, first smiles at the person who has attracted her attention. Then she lifts her eyebrows far up with a swift, jerky movement that takes about a sixth of a second, briefly opening the eyes wider (see Figure 2-2). She follows this by looking away with head lowered and eyelids dropped, then raises her head again for full contact with the eyes. Often the girl may cover her face with a hand and smile with some embarrassment, while still looking out of the corner of her eye. The same flirting behavior has been filmed, with agreement in the finest details, in Samoa, Papua, France, Japan, Africa, and South America (Eibl-Eibesfeldt, 1970).

The raising of the eyebrows is probably a universal response of friendly greeting, accompanying smiling and often nodding of the head. The next time someone is flirting with you or greeting you warmly, notice whether or not the eyebrows are raised swiftly in this manner. The behavior has to be spontaneous. It won't work to ask someone to flirt with you, for then the person

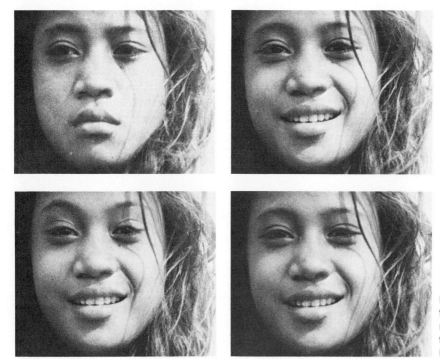

Figure 2-2 A Samoan girl first smiles, then swiftly raises her eyebrows in the typical flirting pattern. (Eibl-Eibesfeldt, 1970)

simply begins to play a role, like an actor or actress, and key elements of the pattern may be lost. If the flirting pattern proves to be universally present in all peoples, it may be an inherited behavior.

Several closely related species may have similar species-characteristic behaviors. Many species of surface-feeding ducks have similar courtship ritualizations. As may be seen in Figure 2-3, the behavior consists of bill shaking, head flicking, tail shaking, grunt-whistling, head bobbing, head turning, and so forth. Usually minute variations in forms of species-characteristic behaviors occur even in closely related species. Because behavioral as well as physical characteristics are important features of each species' heritage, they are used to describe the similarities and differences between species.

Since species-characteristic behaviors are inborn, experience is unnecessary for their development. In most natural circumstances, it is difficult to tell from observation whether a behavior is innate or learned on the basis of prior experience. One exception is the study of the nest-building behavior of insects. Since many insects undergo a period of development as larvae in a nest without any contact with parents, the elaborate nest-building behavior that isolated females later perform must be innate, rather than learned from the previous generation.

One good way of studying the innateness of behavior is to combine observation in nature with laboratory experimentation. A behavior that has been observed to occur frequently in all members of a species may be studied under the controlled conditions of a laboratory, where opportunities for learning are eliminated. Animals have been shown to demonstrate completely organized species-characteristic behaviors when they have had no experience with other members of their species. One investigator hatched and reared laughing gull

chicks in a laboratory in order to determine whether their feeding behavior was learned or inborn (Hailman, 1967). Feeding in this species starts with the young chick pecking the bill of the parent. After repeated pecks, the parent regurgitates partly digested food, which the chick then eats. When laboratory-reared chicks are presented with cardboard models of the parent's head, the chicks readily peck at the model. By comparing features of the model that do and do not elicit pecking, it has been shown that the red bill is the stimulus to which newly hatched chicks respond most strongly. Other features of the model have little influence on the pecking. Older chicks that have had experience feeding from the parents, however, develop a strong preference for an accurate model of the parent's head (see Figure 2-4).

Such highly specific cues in the environment that serve to elicit species-characteristic behaviors are called **sign stimuli.** Like the behaviors they evoke, these stimuli are species-characteristic. That is, the stimulus that is effective in triggering the behavior in one individual is effective for others of the same species. Nikolaas Tinbergen (1969), in a study of the sign stimulus of aggression in male stickleback fish, observed that in the breeding season the male lures females into his established territory but attacks any other male that tries to enter the territory. Tinbergen showed that the sign stimulus for aggression directed only at males is the presence of a red belly, which the males develop during breeding season. Models of sticklebacks with varying characteristics were presented to a number of male sticklebacks (see Figure 2-5). The fish reacted to all models that had red bellies, even though some of these models were very crude imitations of the fish. They did not react to otherwise accurate models lacking red bellies.

The sign stimulus for most species-characteristic behaviors is an external stimulus found in the organism's natural environment. In

Figure 2-3 Motor patterns of the courtship display of the mallard (A) and European teal (B). The basic movements of the ritualization consist of (1) bill shake, (2) head flick, (3) tail shake, (4) grunt whistle, (5) head-up-tail-up movement, (6) turning head toward female, (7) nod-swimming, (8) turning back of head toward female, (9) down-up movement, (10) bridling (This movement occurs in the mallard exclusively in after-copulation display: in the European teal it occurs as an independent courtship movement). In the diagram the thin line connotes pre-display attitude; the thick line indicates motor patterns of courtship proper. The dots between the thick lines indicate a non-obligatory coupling of motor patterns. In the teal, at high courtship intensity the motor patterns 4, 3, 2, 5, 6 and 8 are run through in one sequence of constant speed. At low intensity 4, 3 and 2 can be performed separately while 5, 6 and 8 are one inseparable unit. (Courtesy of Konrad Lorenz)

Pecks/30 sec

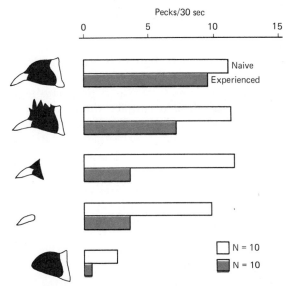

Figure 2-4 Models of a laughing gull head used to test pecking preferences in young chicks. Newly hatched chicks peck at all models that have a bill (hollow bars). Week-old chicks that had experience in feeding from the parent show a preference for models that accurately represent all of the features of the parent's head (solid bars). Lengths of bars indicate mean pecking rates. (Hailman, 1967)

some instances, however, the sign stimulus is a specific internal stimulus, arising from within the organism. Internal stimuli for species-characteristic behaviors are usually hormonal. The female pigeon will begin building a nest for her eggs when certain reproductive hormones signal the presence of fertilized eggs within her body. Fortunately she does not have to await the arrival of the eggs before building a nest which secures their safety.

It is more difficult to identify internal sign stimuli than external stimuli because they are not readily observable. It is tempting to assume that a particular species-characteristic behavior is triggered by an internal stimulus when no external stimulus is obvious. To be fully understood, however, the sign stimulus, whether internal or external, must be identified and experimentally tested.

Fixed-Action Patterns

Species-characteristic behaviors are often described in terms of fixed-action patterns. A **fixed-action pattern** is a relatively complex, repetitious set of responses of unchanging form; once initiated by a single sign stimulus, the pattern continues independently of further environmental control. Let's look at an example. The greylag goose retrieves an egg that has rolled out of her nest by rolling the egg

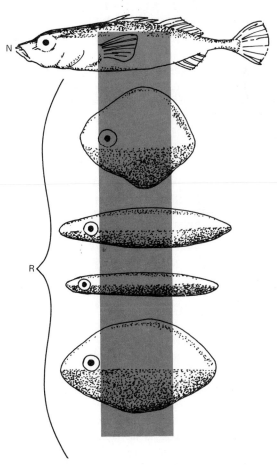

Figure 2-5 Models of male sticklebacks used to elicit aggression. The first model (N) is an accurate representation of a stickleback without a red belly. Each of the remaining models (Rs) has a red belly, but does not accurately represent the shape of a stickleback. (Tinbergen, 1969)

Figure 2-6   Greylag goose retrieving an egg. (Tinbergen, 1969)

back to the nest with her beak (see Figure 2-6). Once the goose has begun her repetitious egg-rolling movements, triggered by the sight of the egg out of the nest, the form of the response during the retrieval is no longer controlled by the presence of the egg. If the egg the goose is rolling slips sideways away from its beak, the unperturbed goose will continue her egg-rolling motions until she reaches the nest, but, alas, with no egg.

A species-characteristic behavior is usually composed of more than one fixed-action pattern. The whole behavior can be split into successive fixed-action patterns that often occur in the same order, but that depend on different eliciting stimuli. Many social behaviors depend on stimuli arising from reciprocal responses of two individuals of the same species. The zigzag dance of the stickleback fish is composed of a series of responses triggered by successive stimuli from the male and female (see Figure 2-1). The presence of the female triggers the male's zigzag dance, which in turn signals the female to court, and so forth. The courtship ritualization of ducks also involves a series of fixed-action patterns, each set off by a specific gesture of the partner. The reciprocal responses are important for coordinating the courtship duet.

The presence of a sign stimulus does not necessarily mean that the organism will manifest the appropriate fixed-action pattern. Behavior is much too complex to be that easily predicted. As is true of all behavior, situational and motivational factors will influence the

appearance or absence of the fixed-action pattern. The young laughing gull chick that is hungry is more likely to peck the parent's beak to obtain food than one that has just eaten.

On occasion a fixed-action pattern may occur in the absence of the appropriate sign stimulus. Animals in conflict situations often display fixed-action patterns that are inappropriate to the situation; these are called **displacement activities.** One common displacement activity in herring gulls consists of nesting movements in threat situations, when the bird seems to be in conflict between fighting and escaping (see Figure 2-7). Displacement activities are usually recognizable by their jerky, irregular, or incomplete expression of natural fixed-action patterns. No one really knows why displacement activities have established their place in the behavior repertoires of animals. One researcher has suggested that the conflict situation produces two competing response tendencies that block each other's expression, thereby allowing a seemingly irrelevant response to occur (Andrew, 1956). The irrelevant response, or displacement activity, is one the animal tends to engage in frequently in its normal life situation.

But an animal will sometimes perform an irrelevant fixed-action pattern when it is in no apparent conflict. In these cases, it is hypothesized that the animal is so highly motivated to engage in a given activity (for instance, feeding) that the behavior, called **vacuum**

Figure 2-7   Nesting movements in herring gulls as a displacement activity. (Tinbergen, 1969)

behavior, occurs even in the absence of the stimulus.

As you can see from these examples, fixed-action patterns are relatively complex responses involving many parts of the body. Their complexity distinguishes them from the simpler innate responses called reflexes. If someone taps your knee in the right spot, your reflexive response will be a knee jerk. A **reflex** is an automatic, inborn response to a specific stimulus. Unlike fixed-action patterns, reflex responses terminate as soon as the eliciting stimulus is withdrawn and occur independently of motivational factors.

Experience and Species-Characteristic Behaviors

Although species-characteristic behaviors are not learned, experience nevertheless plays an essential role in the precise development of certain of these behaviors. One particularly interesting example is the development of bird vocalizations. Each bird species has species-specific vocalizations. Although most birds reared in isolation from other members of the species exhibit normal vocalizations at maturity, the chaffinch's song is influenced by experience with other members of the species. As may be seen in Figure 2-8, chaffinches reared in isolation from adult chaffinches develop only a very simple type of song. The basic characteristics are appropriate for the species and the song is of about the right length and number of notes, but it lacks the complexity and terminal flourish of the adult's normal song. The opportunity to imitate the song of adults is necessary for the development of the full song. The influence of experience in the development of bird song is also demonstrated by the different dialects that occur in the songs of bird species in different regions of the country.

The importance of experience in the development of species-characteristic behaviors also is seen in **imprinting,** the tendency to follow a

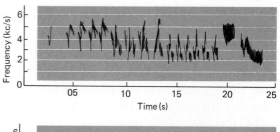
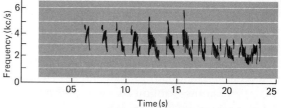
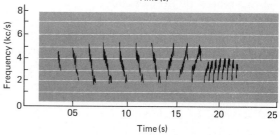

Figure 2-8 Sound spectrograph of the chaffinch song. Pitch of the notes is indicated on the vertical axis as frequency; amplitude is represented by the depth of shading. Top record, characteristic normal song; Middle record, song of an individual hand-reared in auditory isolation; Bottom record, song of a hand-reared bird after tutoring during one season with a tree pipit song. Although the chaffinch song was influenced by the song of the other species, the following season the chaffinch dropped its tree pipit song and reverted to a modified version of its innate song. (Thorpe, 1961)

moving object during early development and to form a lasting attachment to that object. Many animals capable of a high degree of independent activity from birth, like ducklings, will tend to follow any moving object that they encounter during a limited period early in their lives. As adults these animals show a preference for the object followed during their early development. The tendency to follow a moving object is innate. The exact object that is followed, however, depends on the experience of the animal. Normally, that object is the mother.

One of the first investigators to examine imprinting was Konrad Lorenz (1935). He divided greylag goose eggs into two groups. One group was hatched by the mother and one was hatched in an incubator. The goslings hatched in the incubator were cared for by Lorenz during the early posthatch days, while the others stayed with their mother. Then Lorenz placed the two groups together (after marking each distinctively) and observed their social preferences. The goslings hatched and reared by their mother followed her, while the goslings reared by Lorenz chose to follow him.

A wide range of stimuli, including inanimate objects, may be imprinted (Hess, 1964). The time during which the social attachment is established is confined to a **critical period** early in the life of the organism; after that time has passed, imprinting does not occur. For most species of birds that show imprinting, this period is 11 to 19 hours after hatching, when the animal is most likely to follow a moving object.

The established attachment to the imprinted object lasts throughout the life of the animal. Lorenz has suggested that imprinting may be important in determining preferences in sexual pairing later in life. The greylag gander includes among its courtship rituals the fetching of food and feeding it to his beloved. One of Lorenz's goslings, upon reaching maturity, persisted in trying to deposit succulent morsels in Lorenz's ear. Normally, of course, the young bird imprints to its mother, and at maturity shows a mating preference for another goose of the same species.

When imprinting occurs in an unnatural setting, it may not be as effective as when it occurs in a natural environment. Thus birds imprinted to humans in laboratories, but reared in adolescence with other members of their species, often develop a sexual preference for a mate of their own species (Guiton, 1962).

Human Species-Characteristic Behaviors

Species-characteristic behaviors are not a predominant part of adult human behavior. Newborns do show fairly simple behaviors that appear to be innate, although it is open to question whether these behaviors should be classed as reflexes or as species-characteristic behaviors. Newborns cry, a response that may have the evolutionary function of attracting the attention of their parents, who provide comfort and protection. When their lips are touched, newborns turn their heads back and forth in what appears to be a search for the breast. This "rooting response" is also observed in the young of many other species of mammals. Suckling is also a characteristic behavior, although it changes after the first few days and is affected by experience.

Newborns respond to loud noises with crying and to loss of support with a sort of protective huddling reaction that is called the Moro reflex. And even during the first weeks of life, infants begin to smile. Since the smiling is observed in infants born blind, or deaf and blind, in the same form as it occurs in normal newborns it has been c assified as a species-characteristic behavior (Freedman, 1964). Infant smiles are very rewarding for parents and tend to increase parental attachment, particularly when they become a social response to the parents' own smiles.

INNATE EXPRESSIONS OF EMOTION

An Israeli physiologist has tested the facial expressions of 15 newborns of both sexes, both black and white, in reaction to smelly substances placed near their noses prior to their first feeding (Steiner, 1974). The odorants used were an artificial butter to give a milky odor, vanilla and banana extracts for a fruity odor, and artificial shrimp and "rotten egg" extracts for rotten odors. The newborns all reacted to the milky and fruity odors with facial relaxation, pulling back of the mouth into a smiling expression, and sucking-licking movements of the lips (see Figure 2-9). These facial expressions are similar to those produced in infants by sweet tastes. The fishy, rotten odors, however, produced facial reactions that are normally elicited by bitter tastes, with pulling down of the mouth angles and raising of the center part of the upper lip in an archlike mouth opening, accompanied by salivation and spitting. Good fresh foods, with milky or fruity odors, thus elicit facial expressions of acceptance and satisfaction, while odors typical of rotten foods elicit expressions of aversion and rejection.

J. E. Steiner suggests that these facial expressions in reaction to both odors and tastes are innate response patterns of infants. He concludes that "food-related odors are properly evaluated by the human neonate in the very first hours of its extrauterine life according to their hedonic value [pleasantness]. Furthermore, this evaluation can lead to the elicitation of facial expressions seemingly serving communication purposes" (p. 232).

C.   BA./VA.   FI.   BU.   R.E.

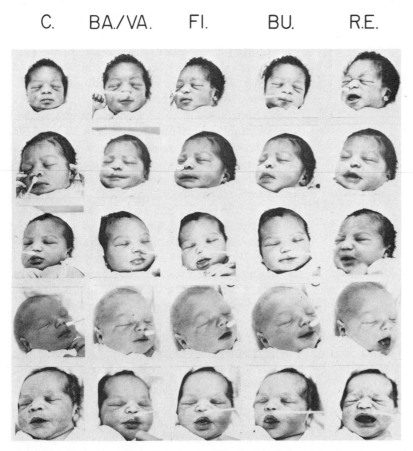

Figure 2-9 Facial reactions of newborn babies, before their first feeding, to odor stimulants of rotten eggs (RE), butter (BU), "fishy" shrimp (FI), and banana or vanilla extract (BA/VA), and under control conditions (C). Can you see acceptance and pleasure on their faces at the banana, vanilla, and butter odors, as opposed to aversion to the fishy and rotten-egg odors? (Steiner, 1974)

From these basic innate facial expressions showing liking and disliking, approval and disapproval, people develop many facial expressions in reaction to all kinds of stimuli in their environments.

The ability to recognize the meanings of facial expressions accompanying many emotions may be an innate ability of humans (Ekman, Sorenson, & Friesen, 1969). In one worldwide study, 30 photographs of male and female Caucasians, adults and children, depicting basic expressions of happiness, surprise, fear, anger, disgust-contempt, and sadness, were shown to people in many countries, including both literate and preliterate cultures. The subjects were given a set of names in their own languages of a variety of emotions and asked to identify the photographs expressing the emotions named. The subjects from literate cultures had greater success in recognizing the emotions named than those from preliterate cultures, possibly because the investigators were less fluent in the languages of the preliterate people. Additional studies, in which photos of preliterate people were judged by preliterate subjects, yielded similar results. These studies indicate that facial expressions of primary emotions may be inborn and universal to the human species but that they may be affected later by cultural customs that reinforce the display of emotions.

Is Language Species Characteristic? Like all animals, humans are biologically endowed with certain potentialities for behavior that are characteristic of the species. Perhaps the most important of these is the tremendous human capacity for language. Although many other animals are capable of communicating certain limited kinds of information through physical actions and vocalizations, these simple languages lack the variety and flexibility of human language. Recent long-term experiments in teaching apes nonoral languages, however, suggest that they are far more capable of learning language than was previously thought (see Chapter 3).

Sound films of adults talking to infants have shown that infants respond to adult speech with varied movements of the head, eyes, shoulders, elbows, hips, and feet (Condon & Smith, 1974). The infant responses are synchronized with human speech sounds, whether English or Chinese, within fractions of a second, but not synchronized with tapping or simple vowel sounds. Neonates thus move in organized rhythms in interaction with the language they hear from birth. They seem to be stimulated by human language long before they understand it. Such speech-synchronized rhythmic behavior may well be species characteristic and may facilitate the innate tendency to learn to use language.

Evolution and Behavior

Why do some animals show a lot of species-characteristic behaviors and others not? Why doesn't man have more such behaviors? Charles Darwin's theory of natural selection has contributed greatly to our understanding of phylogenetic differences in behavior. A **phylum** is a primary division of the animal kingdom, and **phylogenetic** refers to the natural evolutionary relationships among phyla.

According to evolutionary theory, animal species survive by adapting to their environments. Well-adapted species survive more successfully and outbreed less well-adapted animals. Through this natural selection process, behaviors have evolved that permit various species of animals to adjust to their particular environments. Species developing early in the history of animal life were selected that adapt to their environments through many innate behaviors. Thus behaviors that promote the survival of a species, such as those that result in efficient food seeking and mating, are transmitted across generations of surviving organisms. If you take a moment to think about the particular species-characteristic behaviors described in this chapter, you will see that each provides a survival advantage for the species.

One dramatic example of a highly complex species-characteristic behavior that assists the survival of a species is the food-seeking behavior of honeybees. Karl von Frisch (1950) has observed that "scout" honeybees search for food and, back at the hive, communicate the location of the food source to worker bees through an elaborate "dance," rather than leading the worker bees to the food. Characteristics of the dance indicate such precise information about the distance, direction, and quality of the nectar that the dance has been called a bee "language." Von Frisch studied the rela-

tionship of food location and richness to characteristics of the dance by systematically varying one aspect of the food source at a time and observing the effect on the dance of the scouts. He found that when food was as far away as 200 yards from the hive, the worker bees made a "beeline" to the location the scout had found. The scout bee's dance consisted of a series of wagging runs and 360° turns (see

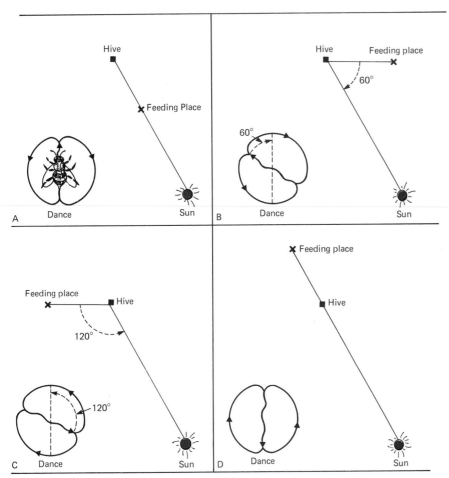

Figure 2-10 Round dance of the honeybee. The orientation of the middle tail-wagging runs on the vertical comb varies with the angle of the relationship between the feeding place, the hive, and the sun. A, the feeding place is in the direct line of the sun and hive, and the dance is oriented vertically up the hive; B–C, the feeding place is located at an angle from the sun, and the dance is appropriately angled from the vertical axis of the hive; D, the feeding place is in a straight line behind the sun and hive, and the dance is oriented vertically down the hive. (Von Frisch, 1950)

Figure 2-10). The distance of the food source to the hive was indicated by the speed of the scout's 360° turn. The farther the distance, the faster the turn. The direction of the food source was relayed by the angle of the straight runs with respect to the sun. The angle of the straight runs from the vertical axis of the hive corresponded to the angle of the food from an imaginary line connecting the sun with the hive. The richness of the food was correlated with the vigor of the tail-wagging dance.

The explicitness of the bee's food-location dance has obvious survival advantages. A study of food-seeking behaviors in more primitive species of bees has shown how the honeybee's dance gradually evolved (Esch, 1967). At the most primitive levels, the bee scout directly leads the group to the food. In one primitive species of stingless bees, the scout leaves a scented trail from a food source to the hive by stopping every two or three yards to mark a bush or stone with an odorous secretion. At the hive the scout collects a group of hivemates and leads them along the scented trail to the food.

A more advanced species of stingless bees uses a combination of guided tour and simple language to indicate a food source. The scout uses a sound code to indicate the distance to the food source. A series of sounds of short duration indicates that the food is nearby; sounds of longer duration say that the food is farther away. To show the direction of the food source, the scout leads the others from the hive in the direction of the food. After leading for a short distance, the scout takes off to the food and leaves the others behind. The hivemates return to the hive and wait for the scout to come back and lead them again. After several partial guidances, some members of the group get the message and make their own way to the food source.

Esch found that if he eliminated necessary hive conditions for the honeybee dance (by blocking light from the sun and tipping the hive horizontally), the honeybees reverted to the more primitive sound-coded language of the stingless bee.

It seems that bee food-seeking behavior evolved slowly from a stage in which no symbolic communication existed between scout and worker bees to one in which a sophisticated dance is used to relay precise information about the food source. Successive species of bees have developed a communication system that provides more explicit detail about a food source, and these species are therefore better adapted to their environment.

Animals that evolved late in phylogeny have developed more flexible forms of adaptation to their environment. Instead of predominantly fixed behavior patterns triggered by specific environmental cues, humans and other mammals have developed a considerable capacity for flexible responses to an ever changing environment. They have developed the capacity to modify all aspects of their behavior through experience in the environment —a process called **learning** (see Figure 2-11).

The 1973 Nobel Prize for Medicine and Physiology went to Nikolaas Tinbergen,

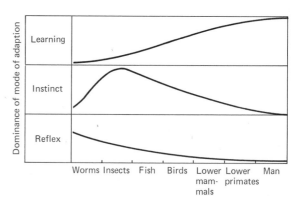

Animals from phylogenetic scale

Figure 2-11 The relative amounts of reflex, instinct, and learning in the phylogenetic series. The relative amount of each behavior is shown by the height of each curve within its own block. For instance, human beings have few reflexes and instincts, and learning is important for adaptation to the environment. (Adapted from Dethier & Stellar, 1970)

Konrad Lorenz, and Karl von Frisch for their work with instincts, discussed in this chapter, in recognition of the significant contribution their studies have made to an understanding of the biological features of behavior.

GENETICS

How are species-characteristic behaviors and general behavioral potentialities transmitted from generation to generation? They are transmitted from parents to offspring genetically in the same way in which potentials for developing physical traits such as eye color, height, and body build are transmitted. Heredity influences behavior by influencing the physical structure of the nervous system, muscles, and glands that mediate behavior. Underlying species-characteristic behaviors are structural features of the organism's nervous system that to a large degree have built into them a sensitivity to certain stimuli (sign stimuli) and a tendency for appropriate fixed-action patterns to occur in response to those stimuli.

Coded Genetic Messages

Although the genetic material of all cells was identified nearly a hundred years ago, it was not known until recently how this material carries coded messages that govern inherited traits. **Chromosomes** in the nuclei of all living cells are threadlike materials composed of genes. The **gene** is the smallest amount of chromosome material that can influence an inherited trait. Several thousand genes may be located in one chromosome. Specific genetic messages are written in a "four-letter alphabet" of the DNA (deoxyribonucleic acid) molecule that makes up the genes (Crick, 1962). Each of the four letters (A, C, G, and T, standing for their chemical names) represents a different type of molecular fragment of the DNA molecule. The order of occurrence of the different molecular fragments determines the genetic message (see Figure 2-12). It has

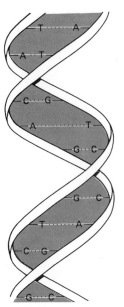

Figure 2-12 Structure of the DNA molecule.

been estimated that several hundred to several thousand occurrences of these letters form one genetic message. For the sake of time and space, let's consider an abbreviated example. The message for a simple genetic trait like brown eyes might read ACTTAGCCGATATC-GGCTAA. Since the possible number of arrangements of four letters in a message length of several thousand letters is very large, many genetic messages are possible.

The genetic message coded in the DNA molecule specifies the proteins that that cell is to manufacture. Proteins govern all activities of a cell by regulating the structural characteristics and chemical processes of the cell. All of the various proteins in the body are synthesized by DNA control of specific combinations of the 20 essential amino acids obtained from the diet. The genetic code for each amino acid has been deciphered (see Table 2-1). Therefore, the code for each protein found in cells may be constructed by arranging the message for particular amino acids in the order appropriate for that protein. Many scientists believe that the

Table 2-1 Genetic Codes for Amino Acids*

Amino Acid	DNA Code
1. Alanine	CGA CGG CGT CGC
2. Arginine	GCA GCT GCC TCT GCG TCC
3. Asparagine	TTA TTG
4. Aspartic acid	CTA CTG
5. Cysteine	ACA ACG
6. Glutamine	GTT GTC
7. Glutamic acid	CTT CTC
8. Glycine	CCA CCG CCT CCC
9. Histidine	GTA GTG
10. Isoleucine	TAA TAG TAT
11. Leucine	AAT AAC GAA GAG GAT GAC
12. Lysine	TTT TTC
13. Methionine	TAC
14. Phenylalanine	AAA AAG
15. Proline	GGA GGG GGT GGC
16. Serine	AGA AGG AGT AGC TCA TCG
17. Threonine	TGA TGG TGT TGC
18. Tryptophan	ACC
19. Tyrosine	ATA ATG
20. Valine	CAA CAG CAT CAC
Terminating triplets	ATT ATC ACT

Adapted from Gardner, 1972.

* In most cases, several combinations of letters code the same amino acid. The occurrence of the sequence CGA, CGG, CGT, or CGC on a DNA strand indicates instructions for the amino acid alanine at that location in the protein sequence. The terminating triplets ATT, ATC, and ACT are punctuation marks that indicate the beginning and end of the message. Following the code indicating the beginning of a message, the code is read in terms of three letters for each amino acid without punctuations between amino acids.

breaking of the genetic code is the greatest discovery of this century (Watson, 1968).

Hereditary Transmission

Each species of animals has a fixed number of chromosomes per cell. Each human cell (except the gametes, discussed later) contains 46 chromosomes arranged in 23 pairs. Two genes work together in determining a trait—genes from identical locations on each member of the chromosome pair. When two genes of a pair are identical, carrying the same instructions for a trait, the person is said to be **homozygous** (*homo* means same) for the gene. When the two genes carry different instructions, the person is **heterozygous** (*hetero* means different) for that gene. In heterozygous cases, the expressed trait is usually determined by one gene of the pair, called the **dominant gene.** The dominant gene has the ability to express itself wholly to the exclusion of the other member of the pair. The unexpressed, masked gene is called the **recessive gene.** Recessive genes, such as those for red hair and for blue eyes, are expressed

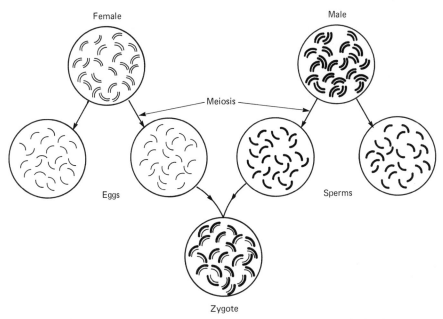

Female

Male

Meiosis

Eggs

Sperms

Zygote

Figure 2-13 During meiosis, gametes (eggs and sperms) that have 23 single chromosomes are produced. At fertilization the 23 chromosomes of an egg and sperm unite, giving the zygote 23 pairs of chromosomes.

only when the individual is homozygous for the recessive gene.

Each individual inherits one chromosome of each pair from one parent and the second from the other parent. The combination of chromosomes from the two parents produces a new combination of genetic material and results in a new individual. Offspring resemble parents because they possess many of the same genes, roughly 50 per cent. On the other hand, offspring are also different in many features because of the unique ways in which genetic material from both parents are combined.

In order for a parent to donate one chromosome of each pair to an offspring, the parent's genetic material must be reduced from 23 *pairs* of chromosomes to 23 *single* chromosomes. Although the process is more complex than can be indicated here, **meiosis** essentially consists of the formation of two reproductive cells, called **gametes,** from one cell of parental reproductive tissue; each gamete has one member of

each of the original 23 chromosome pairs. A cell in the reproductive tissue in the male testis, for example, produces two male **sperms,** each with one-half of the number of chromosomes from the parental cell. Similarly, the female ovary produces two female **eggs,** each with one-half of the number of chromosomes from the parental cell. At fertilization, the 23 chromosomes of the sperm and egg unite in a single cell, the **zygote,** so that the new individual has 23 pairs of chromosomes (see Figure 2-13). Chromosomes with genes for the same traits pair during this process. Different genetic instructions may be transmitted to different gametes from one parent. For instance, if the female possesses a dominant gene for brown eyes and a recessive gene for blue eyes, one-half of her reproductive cells would contain genes for brown eyes and one-half would contain genes for blue eyes. The chance that an offspring would inherit the dominant gene would be 50–50.

The process of segregation of chromosomes to gametes is similar to that of randomly dealing a deck of cards into two piles, with the restriction in this case that each pile (gamete) must contain one member of each chromosome pair. If you repeatedly dealt a deck of 46 cards into two piles, shuffling between deals, what are the chances that you would deal exactly the same two piles twice? Very remote. In the same way, several offspring from the same parents have very little chance of inheriting exactly the same set of chromosomes from each parent. It has been estimated that the probability of two sibling's inheriting exactly the same genetic instructions is one in 281 trillion. The exception to the rule that each individual has a unique genetic constitution is the case of **identical twins.** Identical twins develop from the splitting of a single fertilized egg, and therefore have exactly the same genetic material. **Fraternal twins,** on the other hand, result from the simultaneous fertilization and development of two eggs and are genetically no more alike than any other siblings.

Traits possessed by all members of a species are governed by genes that are common to all members of that species. These traits are very stable because they are continuously passed on from one generation to the next by common gene pools. Of course, each individual within a species is somewhat unique, since it results from a new combination of genetic material. Variation within a species also can occur through mutation. A **mutation** is a sudden change in the genetic material of a cell. Mutations may occur in any cell, and those that occur in gametes, or in tissue giving rise to gametes, will be passed on to the next generation, since mutations are as stable and reproducible as the original genetic information.

Evolution favors the strongest members of a species. These organisms reach sexual maturity, reproduce, and pass their genes on to their offspring. The weak die early, seldom having produced offspring. If a mutated gene happens to make an organism more likely to survive, the mutation may be genetically transmitted for many generations and become a part of the genetic inheritance of many members of a species. **Sickle-cell anemia** is a trait resulting from a mutation that is prevalent in the population of large parts of Africa, Sicily, southern Italy, Greece, the Near East, and certain parts of India. Evolutionary factors *favored* the selection of people carrying this trait. Although severe anemia results when an individual is homozygous for the recessive gene, the heterozygous carriers of the gene are better able to withstand malaria than are those who are homozygous for the dominant, normal gene. Since the regions of the world where this mutation is prevalent have a high incidence of malaria, carriers from these regions have had a survival advantage. In other parts of the world where malaria is almost unknown, selection *against* the gene has occurred because persons homozygous for the gene usually die of sickle-cell anemia before they can reproduce.

The traits of eye color, hair color, and sickle-cell anemia are determined by one gene pair and are called **monogenetic traits.** Every person has one or another specific expression of the trait. Most traits, however, are determined by more than one gene pair. Height is an example of such a **polygenetic trait.** The expression of polygenetic traits shows continuous variation because a number of genes make contributions to the expressed trait. Suppose the genetic trait of height is determined by the joint action of four gene pairs. Furthermore, suppose that the gene may exist in either a dominant (tall) or recessive (short) form at each gene pair. For any gene pair, the genetic trait of tallness would be indicated if one or both genes were of the dominant form. Ultimately a person's tallness would be influenced by the number of gene pairs indicating "tall" that were inherited. The offspring might receive three talls and one short, two talls and two shorts, or any of the other possible combinations.

Genetic Counseling

Our understanding of the way genetic material is passed on from parents to offspring is a useful tool in predicting whether an individual is likely to inherit a particular genetic trait. This becomes especially important when the trait involved is undesirable. **Genetic counseling** consists of tracing the incidence of a particular genetic trait in a family for the purpose of predicting the presence of an undesirable trait in an individual or in future offspring.

The prediction of monogenetic traits is straightforward. If both parents are homozygous for one gene form, whether it be a dominant or recessive form, the offspring will also be homozygous for that gene form. Therefore, if both parents have red hair (recessive), their progeny will have red hair. If one parent is homozygous for a dominant gene and the other parent is homozygous for the recessive, all offspring will be heterozygous for that trait and show the dominant gene expression.

Three other gene combinations are possible, and in each of these cases it is not possible to say with certainty what **genotype** (gene make-up) the individual will inherit (see Figure 2-14). However, it is possible to predict the individual's **phenotype** (expressed or observable trait) in one of these cases. If one parent is heterozygous for this trait and the other is homozygous for the dominant form of the trait, will their offspring display the dominant trait? The answer is yes. The potential for the trait will be inherited either from a heterozygous gene pair or a homozygous dominant gene pair (see Figure 2-14). The dominant gene is expressed in both cases. If one parent is homozygous for the recessive gene and the other is heterozygous, their offspring will have a 50–50 chance of inheriting the potential for the dominant trait.

In many cases it is not possible to know with certainty the parents' genotype. If a mother, say, expresses a dominant trait, she may be homozygous for the dominant gene or she may be heterozygous. Sometimes it's possible to find out which by tracing the expression of the trait in her parents. If this information is not available, prediction of the occurrence of the trait in the offspring is uncertain.

A disorder known as **phenylketonuria (PKU)** is a good example of the usefulness of genetic counseling in predicting monogenetic traits. A child with this disorder suffers from a metabolic deficiency that produces, among other symptoms, mental retardation. If the child is put on a special diet from birth, the metabolic deficiency can be controlled and the mental retardation prevented. The desirability of anticipating the occurrence of the disorder is obviously great.

PKU is inherited from a recessive gene. Both members of a couple may be normal and yet be carriers of the recessive gene. If so, there is one chance in four that an offspring will be homozygous for the recessive gene and will therefore inherit the unfortunate trait. Using the knowledge available to a genetic counselor, let's see how this probability was determined. If both parents are heterozygous for the gene (Pp), then the following combinations of gene forms are possible: PP, Pp, pP, pp (refer back to Figure 2-14). Since any one possible gene combination is as likely to occur as any of the others, there is a 25 per cent chance that any offspring from this couple may inherit the PKU phenotype.

Couples who have reason to believe there may be PKU in their family histories should seek genetic counseling when planning a family. A blood test is now available that can identify carriers of the trait. (Many states now require that all newborn babies be tested for PKU.) Similarly, couples with family histories of sickle-cell anemia, hemophilia, cystic fibrosis, and numerous other genetic disorders should seek genetic counseling when planning families. On the basis of family histories and the severity of the disorder, a couple can make

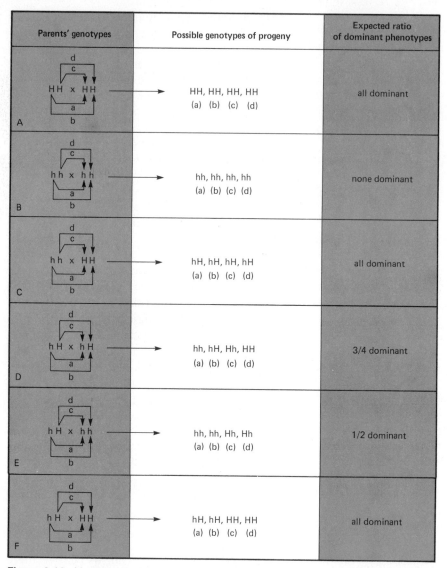

Parents' genotypes	Possible genotypes of progeny	Expected ratio of dominant phenotypes
A d / c / H H x H H / a / b	HH, HH, HH, HH (a) (b) (c) (d)	all dominant
B d / c / h h x h h / a / b	hh, hh, hh, hh (a) (b) (c) (d)	none dominant
C d / c / h h x H H / a / b	hH, hH, hH, hH (a) (b) (c) (d)	all dominant
D d / c / h H x h H / a / b	hh, hH, Hh, HH (a) (b) (c) (d)	3/4 dominant
E d / c / h H x h h / a / b	hh, hh, Hh, Hh (a) (b) (c) (d)	1/2 dominant
F d / c / h H x H H / a / b	hH, hH, HH, HH (a) (b) (c) (d)	all dominant

Figure 2-14 Monogenetic inheritance. For each possible combination of parental geno-types, possible genotypes and phenotypes of the progeny are indicated. Standard genetic notation is used, with a capital letter indicating a dominant gene and a small letter indicating a recessive gene. The letter *H* was arbitrarily chosen to stand for *hereditary trait*. For in-stance, if the mother's and father's genotypes are homozygous for the dominant gene (A), all offspring will be homozygous for the dominant gene and will have the dominant phenotype.

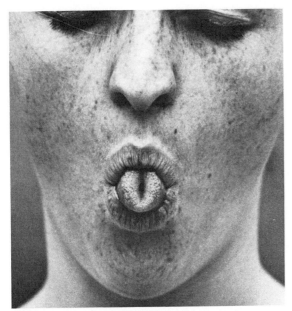

Figure 2-15 Tongue rolling. The ability to roll the tongue is a monogenetic dominant trait.

an informed judgment concerning the risk of conceiving a child with the trait. If all couples who are carriers or possible carriers of undesirable genetic defects would refrain from having children, in one generation these disorders would be eliminated from the world population. (Mutation, however, might reintroduce them at a later time.) Ethical, political, and moral considerations prevent mandatory enforcement of such a regulation.

GENETIC STUDIES OF BEHAVIOR

So far we have discussed relatively simple genetic traits. Inherited behavioral traits are often difficult to study because they may be strongly influenced by environmental factors and are usually polygenetic in nature. Therefore, there is much variability in the expression of behavioral traits within the species. Although species-characteristic behaviors are influenced by environmental factors, they show less variability than other polygenetic inherited behavior traits because they are

governed by genes that are common to all members of that species.

CAN YOU ROLL YOUR TONGUE?

■ Very few human behavioral traits are monogenetic. One such trait, controlled by a dominant gene, is the ability to stick the tongue out between the lips and roll it tightly, as shown in Figure 2-15 (Reedy, Szczes, & Downs, 1971). Another dominant gene also controls the ability to fold back the tip of the tongue toward its base, but this trait is not as common as rolling the tongue.

Can you roll your tongue this way? When you have the opportunity, see how many of your relatives and friends can roll their tongues. Are some of them incapable of rolling their tongues although both their parents can? You should be able to figure out the genetic makeup, as far as this trait is concerned, of such individuals and both of their parents. If you have trouble, refer back to Figure 2-14.

When you clasp your hands together as shown in Figure 2-16, do you put your right or left thumb on top? Try clasping your hands so that the other

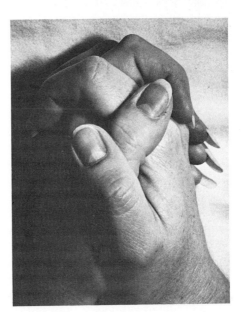

Figure 2-16 Clasping of hands. The tendency to put either the right or left thumb on top when clasping the hands seems to be inherited.

thumb is on top. Does it feel awkward? Some genetic studies indicate that the position of the thumb in this human mannerism is influenced by hereditary factors, although the exact hereditary mechanism has not been established (Winchester, 1972). You might be interested in tracing the expression of this trait in your family.

Heritability of Behavioral Traits

The term **heritability** refers to the degree to which a trait is controlled by genetic factors as opposed to environmental factors. In animals, one way to study the heritability of a trait is through **selective breeding.** Let's say you are interested in knowing whether a complex trait like the intelligence of rats is influenced by genetic factors. This question has been studied in many experiments, the results of one of which are illustrated in Figure 2-17. In this experiment, maze-learning performance was used as an index of intelligence in a group of rats. In a complex maze with many choice points, correct responses led along a path to food at the end, while incorrect responses led into blind alleys. Animals that were poor learners were inbred together and those that learned rapidly also were inbred. The inbreeding of poor learners with poor learners and of good learners with good learners continued for eight generations. Two distinct populations of offspring with respect to intelligence would be expected to emerge if maze learning is a heritable trait. This indeed happened, as you can see. The number of animals showing few errors in each generation of "bright" animals increased with successive generations, while the number showing many errors increased with successive generations of "dull" animals.

This experiment suggests that genetic factors can influence the maze-learning ability of rats. No attempt was made to assess the possible influence of environmental factors. A subsequent experiment compared both factors (Cooper & Zubek, 1958). As in the previous experiment, genetically derived bright and dull

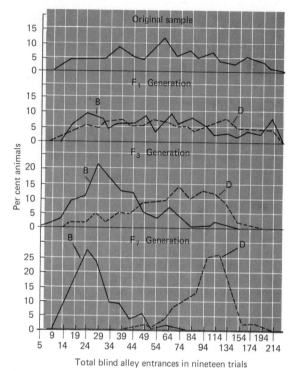

Figure 2-17 Maze-learning performance of different generations of rats selectively bred for maze brightness (B) or dullness (D). The performance of the original sample and the first, third, and seventh generations (F_1, F_3, and F_7) are shown. (Adapted from Tryon, 1940)

rats were trained to solve a maze. Half of the bright and dull rats had been raised in a restricted environment. Their laboratory cages were painted gray and contained only a food box and a water pan. The other half of the animals in both groups had been raised in enriched environments, their cages painted black and white and furnished with ramps, mirrors, swings, polished balls, marbles, barriers, slides, tunnels, bells, teeter-totters, and springboards, in addition to food and water containers. Bright and dull animals from a previous experiment that had been raised in a "normal" laboratory environment served as controls. The normal laboratory environment provided stimulation and opportunity for experience intermediate between the enriched and restricted environments.

Table 2-2 Mean Error Scores for Bright and Dull Animals Reared in Enriched, Normal, and Restricted Environments

Type of Animal	Error Scores		
	Enriched Environment	Normal Environment	Restricted Environment
Bright	111.2	117.0	169.7
Dull	119.7	164.0	169.5

Adapted from Cooper & Zubek, 1958.

As shown in Table 2-2, the genetically derived bright animals had fewer errors than the dull animals, in agreement with the previous experiment. However, environmental factors contributed significantly to the maze-learning ability of the animals. When both bright and dull rats were raised in enriched environments, the performance of the dull animals was nearly as good as that of the bright animals. When reared in restricted environments, the bright rats performed as poorly as did the dull rats. Thus environmental factors interacted with genetic factors in determining the learning capacity of the animals. Other behavioral traits such as general activity level, emotionality (fear), and aggressiveness have shown some heritability in animals.

Studying Human Behavioral Traits

Do human beings have many inherited behavioral traits? Since selective breeding experiments are obviously out of the question, human genetics must be studied by observing naturally occurring families. The occurrence of certain traits in blood relatives (such as parents, siblings, and grandparents) is compared with their incidence in the population at large. This technique is called **pedigree analysis.** Since blood relatives have more genes in common than nonrelated people, it would be expected that traits influenced by genetic factors would be more similar within a family than among a group of people selected at random. A pedigree analysis chart for the ability to recall simple musical tunes in three family lines is presented in Figure 2-18. This behavioral trait occurs more frequently in one family than in the others. Before we conclude that musical memory is influenced by genetic factors, differences in the frequency of occurrence of the trait in a large number of families should be found.

An even better experimental design, from a genetic viewpoint, is the comparison of behavioral trait similarities and differences in identical twins. If twins have the same phenotype, there is reason to believe that the trait may be genetically influenced. However, trait similarity may be due to the fact that both twins were raised in the same or similar environments. Some twins are treated so similarly that they are even dressed alike. In order to assess the importance of environmental influences on a trait, a comparison may be made of identical twins living together and those living apart. Twins living together should be more similar with respect to the behavioral trait than twins living apart, if the trait is one that is influenced by environmental factors. Since the number of cases of twins separated at an early age is small, data from this type of comparison are not easily obtained.

Another way of trying to reach the goal of assessing genetic as opposed to environmental influences on a behavioral trait is to compare similarities among identical twins and among same-sex fraternal twins. Both kinds of twins presumably have similar environmental experiences, but only identical twins have the same genetic makeup. Any difference in degree of similarity between the two twin types should be due to genetic factors.

A number of human behavioral traits seem to have some degree of heritability. One such trait is intelligence. Pedigree analyses and twin studies have shown that scores on intelligence tests have a significant genetic component (see Table 2-3). In general, as the degree of genetic similarity increases, similarity among in-

Generation

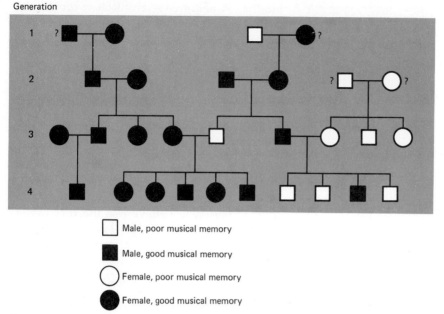

◻ Male, poor musical memory

◼ Male, good musical memory

◯ Female, poor musical memory

⬤ Female, good musical memory

Figure 2-18 Pedigree chart for the ability to recall musical melodies traced through four generations. In cases where an individual's trait was uncertain, a question mark occurs by that individual's symbol. In the family in which both parents have good musical memories (left), the progeny do too. Many offspring from parents who have poor musical memories also lack the ability to recall tunes (right). (Ashman, 1952)

telligence test scores increases. These correlations have recently come under question (Kamin, 1974), however. The number of studies showing the correlations is small, and the way in which intelligence was measured in some of the studies is not clear. Also, the similarity of age of the individuals being compared may have contributed to the high correlations in certain critical comparisons. Individuals of the same age would be expected to have more similar intelligence test scores than individuals of widely divergent ages. Therefore, the high correlations of twins and siblings of similar ages as compared to unrelated persons of varied ages may be due to an age factor rather than to a genetic factor. These and other arguments have made dubious the claim that genetic factors are stronger than environmental factors in the development of intelligence. Since intelligence is a complex behavioral trait

comprising many different types of aptitude, it is probably influenced by many genes.

AN ISSUE OF INTELLIGENCE

A controversy has been raging for several decades as to whether or not some races are more intelligent than others. In the United States this controversy has come down specifically to the issue of whether whites are on the average more inherently intelligent than blacks. What are the pros and cons on this issue and where can you find more information that may assist you in making up your own mind on it?

Intelligence is usually defined in a broad way as the capacity to solve all kinds of problems effectively, drawing on a variety of verbal and numerical abilities. Intelligence quotient (IQ) is measured by means of a variety of individual and group tests that have been developed since the turn of the century. IQ tests are used in schools, in

Table 2-3 Correlations for Intellectual Ability: Obtained and Theoretical Values

Correlations Between	Number of Studies	Obtained Median	Theoretical Value*
Unrelated persons			
Children reared apart	4	−.01	.00
Foster parent and child	3	+.20	.00
Children reared together	5	+.24	.00
Collaterals			
Second cousins	1	+.16	+.14
First cousins	3	+.26	+.18
Uncle (or aunt) and nephew (or niece)	1	+.34	+.31
Siblings reared apart	3	+.47	+.52
Siblings reared together	36	+.55	+.52
Fraternal twins, different sex	9	+.49	+.50
Fraternal twins, same sex	11	+.56	+.54
Identical twins reared apart	4	+.75	+1.00
Identical twins reared together	14	+.87	+1.00
Direct Line			
Grandparent and grandchild	3	+.27	+.31
Parent (as adult) and child	13	+.50	+.49
Parent (as child) and child	1	+.56	+.49

Adapted from Jensen, 1969.
* Expected value if genetic factors alone were operating.

business and industry, and in clinical and counseling psychology to help fit people into appropriate positions and to help give them proper treatment (see Chapter 3). Theories of intelligence range from the view that it is one general mental capacity to the view that it is composed of about 120 special abilities, and definitions of intelligence vary accordingly. Most psychologists agree, however, that intelligence is a complex polygenetic trait. They also agree that the average IQ scores of blacks on current intelligence tests run from 10 to 15 points below those of whites. Until the 1930s, the IQ scores of girls between the ages of 7 and 14 were higher on the average than the IQ scores of boys of the same age. Then the questions in IQ tests on which the girls scored higher were taken out on the ground that the girls' experiences, not their intelligence, enabled them to answer these questions better. However, few of the tests have been similarly adjusted for the cultural or environmental experiences that might enable whites to score generally higher than blacks.

Proponents of the view that whites are on the average inherently superior to blacks in intelligence hold that IQ tests do not discriminate against blacks in this manner. They also present such evidence as the high correlations in IQ scores of identical and fraternal twins, and low correlations of other siblings and relations, which they claim supports this view (Jensen, 1973).

Opponents of the view that the IQ difference reflects a genetic difference argue that a variety of environmental factors, such as family and schooling, have a predominant effect on intelligence, at least as measured by current IQ tests. Furthermore, opponents hold that the heritability of such a complex and undoubtedly polygenetic trait as intelligence (if it is a trait at all) has not been proved and probably is only a minor determinant of observed intelligence (Dobzhansky, 1973). In addition, recent evidence has indicated that black African infants of Nairobi, Kenya, are precocious in both neuromuscular and mental development during their first year of life. The evidence suggests that motor and mental test scores in black infants as well as Arab infants in Lebanon are superior to scores from white and black infants in the United States, and infants (white) in England (Leiderman, Babu, Kagla, Kraemer, & Leiderman, 1973; McLaren & Yaktin, 1973).

Other scientists, who maintain that there is not sufficient evidence to settle this question now, argue that polygenetic inheritance involves incredibly complex interactions among genes, as well as gene interactions with environmental factors. None of these can yet be specified in regard to intelligence or other complex human traits in the present state of the science of genetics. Such scientists maintain a cautious attitude toward this issue, holding that we do not, or cannot, know the answer (Layzer, 1974). Intelligence and tests for it are discussed in more detail in Chapter 3.

Personality traits seem to have much lower heritability than intelligence. The results of one representative study of personality traits of identical and fraternal twins are presented in Table 2-4. Since identical twins are not identical in any of the traits listed in the table, genetic factors alone cannot be governing these traits. Thus environmental differences experienced by members of the twin pairs must account for the variability.

Good evidence exists for a genetic component in several types of behavior disorders. The best documented example is the heritability of schizophrenia (see Chapter 15). **Schizophrenia** is a serious disorder characterized by disturbances in thinking, inappropriate emotional responses, social withdrawal, and sometimes hallucinations (sensory experiences that lack an external cause) and delusions (bizarre ideas that usually involve feelings of persecution or of grandeur). Studies of the incidence of schizophrenia in identical twins have indicated that if one member of a twin pair developed schizophrenia, in 42 per cent of the cases the other one developed the disorder also (Gottesman & Shields, 1966). The incidence in the second member of the twin pairs is over four times greater than the incidence in both members of fraternal twin pairs and is much greater than would be expected for any two people selected at random, since only about 0.8 per cent of the population develops schizophrenia. In one study that is particularly impressive because of its large sample size, the incidence of schizophrenia was compared in the biological and adoptive families of all children who were given up for adoption in Denmark over a 23-year period and who later developed schizophrenia (Kety, Rosenthal, Wender, & Schulsinger, 1968). About 5500 children were adopted during this period, and of those, 33 developed schizophrenia. If genetic factors are stronger than environmental factors in producing schizophrenia, then the biological families of these

Table 2-4 Correlations for Personality Traits

Trait	Identical Twins	Number of Pairs	Fraternal Twins	Number of Pairs
Neuroticism	.36*	39	.06	44
Anxiety	.56*	39	.33*	44
Extroversion	.43*	39	.08	44
Sociability (females)	.62*	31	.08	31
Sociability (males)	.79*	9	.61*	14
Impulsivity (females)	.28*	31	−.08	31
Impulsivity (males)	.16	9	.09	14

Adapted from Claridge, Carter, & Hume, 1973.
* Significant correlation.

33 schizophrenic children should have had a higher incidence of schizophrenia than the adoptive families. Exactly this was found. The incidence of schizophrenia in the biological families of schizophrenic adoptives was much higher than the incidence in the adoptive families. Other behavior disorders that show some degree of heritability are certain forms of depression. The environment undoubtedly plays a significant role in the development of these disorders, but the tendency to be susceptible to them seems to have a genetic base.

GENETIC INTERVENTION

With our rapidly expanding understanding of the way in which genes influence traits, a time is fast approaching when we might be able to manipulate genes for the purpose of changing traits. But should we? If we could prevent the occurrence of a hereditary disorder by changing genes, should we try? Although most geneticists believe that genetic intervention could be of immense potential benefit to the human race, the general public is resistant to the idea. Genetic intervention raises the problem of changing the course of nature and possibly, through our ignorance of the delicate balance of life forces, producing an unstable environment on earth. It also raises possibilities of the misuse of genetic technology for political purposes. Think what a powerful force governments would have if they could tamper with our inner nature.

The State of Genetic Technology

Spectacular accomplishments have already been achieved in **genetic technology,** the alteration and direction of the gene action of a cell. The composition of several genes has been worked out, and in 1970, H. Gobkind Khorana and coworkers synthesized in a test tube a potentially functioning gene (Agarival et al., 1970). A method for inserting and incorporating a gene into living cells has been es-

tablished (Aaronson & Todaro, 1969). Perhaps in the near future it will be possible to replace a defective gene in a gamete and thus avert a hereditary disorder in a future offspring. It may even be possible to replace defective genes in cells of individuals already born with a hereditary disorder.

It is now possible to determine certain genetic characteristics of embryos, unborn organisms in the early stages of development. The procedure, called **amniocentesis**, consists of inserting a needle through a pregnant woman's abdominal wall and uterus into the amniotic fluid surrounding the embryo and collecting a sample of the fluid. Examination of the cells sloughed off into the fluid by the embryo can indicate the embryo's sex and the presence of certain chromosomal abnormalities. It is therefore possible to abort an embryo that has a defective characteristic.

Genetic Alteration of Behavioral Traits?

Despite the amazing successes in the field of genetic technology, the possibility of altering significant inherited behavioral traits seems highly unlikely. One researcher in the field states:

In contrast to the cure of specific monogenic diseases, improvement of the highly polygenetic behavioral traits . . . will remain indefinitely in the realm of science fiction, like the currently popular extrapolation from the transplantation of a kidney or a heart, with a few tubular connections, to that of a brain with hundreds of thousands of specific neural connections [Davis, 1970, p. 1280].

Since behavioral traits are largely polygenetic in nature, the task of identifying genes that contribute to a trait and selectively altering them in a desired manner seems prohibitively difficult. Even if it should turn out that a few genes play critical roles in determining various intellectual or emotional characteristics, Davis believes that the possibility of manipulating the genes for the purpose of altering these traits seems unlikely.

What seems more likely is the possible use of a process called **cloning,** which consists of replicating the entire genetic makeup of an individual in a new organism, thereby producing an exact genetic copy. Cloning has been accomplished with frogs (Briggs & King, 1959). When the genetic material of a frog's egg cell is replaced with genetic material from the cell of another frog, an exact genetic replica of the donor is produced. Although the technique has not yet been worked out with cells from human beings or other mammals, at some time in the future it may be possible for a single parent to reproduce himself or herself genetically or for a society to produce multiple copies of an individual with desirable qualities. Can you picture a society with hundreds of Einsteins? Or even two? The current science fiction book *Joshua Son of None*, by Nancy Freedman, is the story of a human cloning experiment.

The *realistic* dangers from genetic intervention do not seem to outweigh the immense potential benefits. It is unlikely that genetic tools will ever be used to regulate behavior, and although human cloning may someday become a possibility, would society really want to produce multiple copies of any individual?

CONTROL SYSTEMS

Evolution has been kind to so-called higher animals. It has given them two sophisticated systems for the control of body functions and behavior. The **endocrine system** of glands of internal secretion is specialized for the control of ongoing, principally metabolic body functions. The **nervous system,** on the other hand, intervening between sense organs and muscles, is well designed to provide more rapid control of discrete functions such as activation of a specific set of muscles. Furthermore, the nervous system somehow controls consciousness, sensory experience, learning, memory, emotions, and other mental activities.

The Endocrine System

The endocrine glands regulate metabolism, growth, and behavior by discharging complex chemical substances called **hormones** into the bloodstream. The hormones affect specific target tissues by altering the rate of chemical processes in the tissues. The seven types of endocrine glands that regulate our internal environment are presented in Figure 2-19.

Two endocrine glands have special relevance for behavior. The **adrenal glands** secrete a hormone, **epinephrine** (or adrenaline) that is instrumental in the production of the peripheral activation or excitement accompanying many emotions. Epinephrine causes an increase in muscle tone, an increase in blood pressure and heart rate, dilation of the pupils, and an increase in blood sugar, providing quick energy. This peripheral excitement contributes to many emotional experiences: anxiety (butterflies in the stomach), fright (pounding of the heart), and exuberance (abounding energy), to name only a few.

The adrenal glands also secrete **adrenocortical hormones,** which are essential for life through their regulation of metabolic functions of the body. In addition, these hormones play a critical role in the body's adaptive adjustment to physical stress (such as bodily injury or exposure to extreme temperatures) and to psychological stress (such as loss of a job or loss of a loved one).

The **gonads** affect behavior through the release of the sex hormones, **androgens** (higher concentration in males) and **estrogens** (higher concentration in females). The sex hormones are responsible for the development of male and female secondary sex characteristics, such as a beard and a deep voice for the male, curved hips and developed breasts for the female. The sex hormones are also probably crucial at some stage for the development of normal adult sexual motivation, although the extent of their influence on sexual motivation in humans is not known. The effects of epinephrine and sex hormones on behavior will be discussed more fully in Chapter 12.

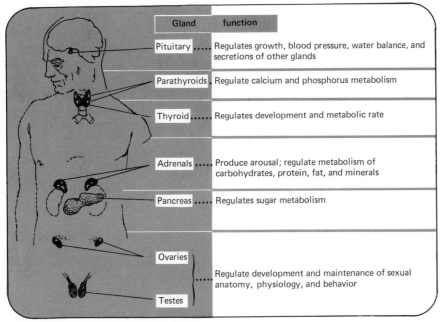

Gland	function
Pituitary	Regulates growth, blood pressure, water balance, and secretions of other glands
Parathyroids .	Regulate calcium and phosphorus metabolism
Thyroid	Regulates development and metabolic rate
Adrenals	Produce arousal; regulate metabolism of carbohydrates, protein, fat, and minerals
Pancreas	Regulates sugar metabolism
Ovaries	Regulate development and maintenance of sexual anatomy, physiology, and behavior
Testes	

Figure 2-19 The endocrine glands, showing their locations within the body and their general functions.

The Nervous System

The nervous system consists of two major divisions, the peripheral and central nervous systems. The **peripheral nervous system** consists of all nerves and **ganglia** (clusters of nerve cells) lying outside the skull and spine. The **central nervous system,** composed of the brain and spinal cord, lies within the bony skull and spine.

The cells of the nervous system are of two types: **neurons** and **glia.** Only neurons have the specialized ability to transmit nerve messages. Neurons may be divided into three classes, depending on their function: sensory neurons are activated by environmental stimuli and carry messages about the environment to the brain or spinal cord; motor neurons control the activity of the body's muscles and glands; and interneurons are links between sensory and motor neurons (activated by other neurons, they send their information to other interneurons or to motor neurons). Although the function of glial cells is unclear, they are

thought to provide nourishment to neurons and to give structural support to the nervous system.

A typical neuron is illustrated in Figure 2-20. The basic parts of a neuron are the cell body, the dendrites, and the axon. The cell body and the branched **dendrites** receive information (either from the environment or

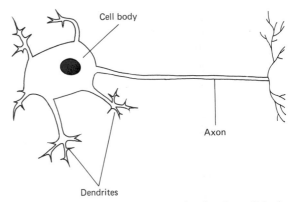

Figure 2-20 Drawing of a neuron showing the cell body, axon, and dendrites.

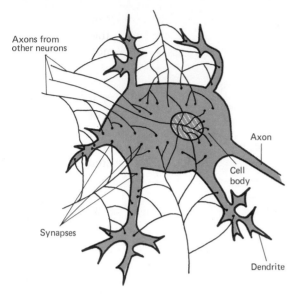

Figure 2-21 Many synapses on a single neuron. Synapses occur primarily on the dendritic branches and cell body of the neuron.

from other cells) and the **axon** transmits information away from the cell to other neurons, or to muscles or glands. Although some neurons have a large receiving end with many dendrites, only one axon leads away from the cell body.

Messages are transmitted in the nervous system in the form of nerve impulses. A **nerve impulse** is a brief bioelectrical change in a neuron that travels from the initial segment of the axon near the cell body to the terminal ends of the axon. Although the characteristic amplitude (voltage) and duration of nerve impulses are constant for all neurons, any given neuron may send different messages by varying the frequency and pattern of nerve impulse discharge in a coded fashion. (Refer to Chapter 4 for a fuller discussion of information coding in the nervous system.)

Most neurons fire nerve impulses at a spontaneous, low rate. When stimulated, they change their rate of firing from the baseline rate. Sensory neurons are stimulated by an environmental source; for example, pressure on the arm stimulates sensory "touch" neu-

rons there. Motor neurons and interneurons are stimulated by other neurons.

Each neuron, is physically isolated from others by extremely small gaps, called **synapses.** Neurons have hundreds of synapses with other neurons where stimulation may take place (see Figure 2-21).

Neurons stimulate one another chemically. When a nerve impulse reaches the terminal end of an axon, the axon releases a chemical, a **synaptic transmitter,** that diffuses across the synapse to the next neuron in the communication chain (see Figure 2-22). A number of chemicals serve as synaptic transmitters; **acetylcholine** is one known example. **Excitation** occurs when the synaptic transmitter causes a neuron to increase its rate of firing. Synaptic transmitters also can inhibit the activity of a neuron. **Inhibition** occurs when the transmitter causes a neuron to decrease its rate of firing. Since a neuron receives stimulation at many synapses simultaneously, it must sum up the excitatory and inhibitory inputs occurring at the same time in calculating the net amount of stimulation.

The nervous system processes information and executes its control over the body by increasing the rate of firing of some cells (exci-

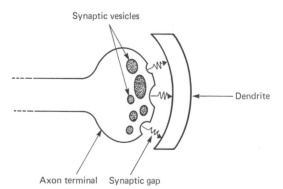

Figure 2-22 Chemical communication at the synapse. When a nerve impulse reaches the axon terminal, it stimulates the release of a chemical transmitter stored in synaptic vesicles. When the transmitter reaches the dendrite or cell body of the receiving neuron, it causes electrical changes in the neuron that may excite or inhibit the receiving cell.

peripheral nerve carries two-way messages —sensory information from the body to the central nervous system and motor commands from the central nervous system to the body's muscles and organs. Of the many axons making up a nerve, some carry information in one direction and some in the other. Any one axon, however, always transmits nerve impulses in one direction—away from its cell body.

The **autonomic nervous system** controls the activity of glands and organs; it also relays sensory information from the glands and organs to the central nervous system. It consists of a system of ganglia and associated nerves (see Figure 2-24). Two divisions of

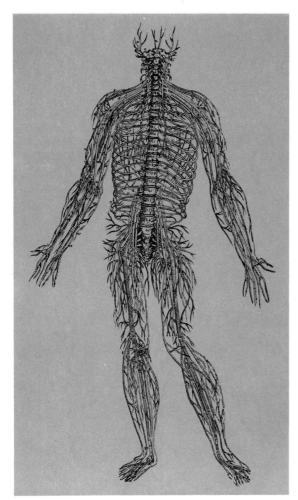

Figure 2-23 The distribution of somatic nerves in the body.

tation) and decreasing the rate of firing of others (inhibition).

The Peripheral Nervous System. The peripheral nervous system has two divisions, the somatic and the autonomic. The **somatic nervous system** consists of (1) all sensory neurons and their associated nerve fibers (axons) connecting the sense organs with the central nervous system, and (2) all nerve fibers leading from the central nervous system to the body's muscles (see Figure 2-23). A **nerve** is a bundle of fibers from many neurons covered by a protective sheath. With few exceptions a

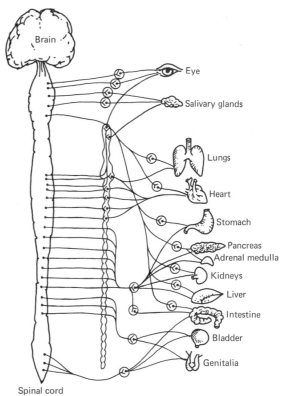

Figure 2-24 The autonomic nervous system. Nerves from the sympathetic division originate from the middle region of the spinal cord. They connect with ganglia lying just outside the cord. The parasympathetic division consists of nerves originating from higher and lower sections of the spinal cord. Their ganglia are near the organs stimulated. Most organs are innervated by nerves from both divisions, which usually have antagonistic functions.

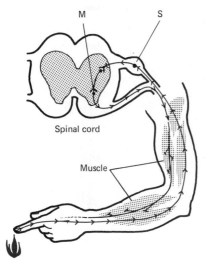

Figure 2-25 Neural circuitry of the withdrawal reflex. A painful stimulus from the hand stimulates sensory fibers originating in the hand. Sensory information is carried to the sensory neurons (S) lying outside the spinal cord, and to the motor neurons (M) inside the cord that govern the movement of the hand.

the autonomic nervous system work antagonistically to prepare the body either for activity by increasing heart rate and blood sugar levels **(sympathetic division)** or to promote the body's maintenance processes such as digestion **(parasympathetic division)**.

The Central Nervous System. The spinal cord and brain comprise the central nervous system. The **spinal cord** has two functions. It transmits messages to and from the brain by means of interneurons that travel up and down the cord, and it also controls many spinal reflexes. A **spinal reflex** occurs when sensory information originating in the body enters the cord and causes automatic activation of motor neurons. The relationship between the stimulus and response is invariant because it is "wired" into the organism much as an electrical circuit is wired, so that every time you flick a switch a particular light comes on. One

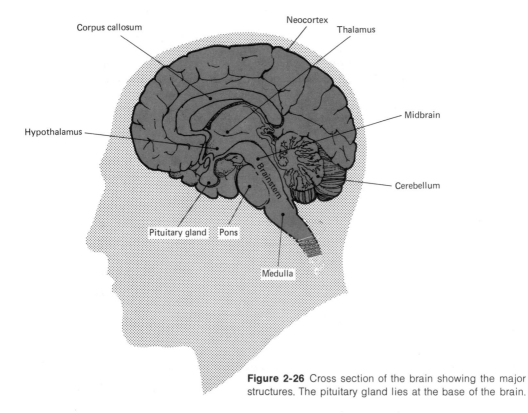

Figure 2-26 Cross section of the brain showing the major structures. The pituitary gland lies at the base of the brain.

important protective reflex is the withdrawal reflex. Any painful stimulus will cause automatic withdrawal of the part of the body being stimulated (see Figure 2-25).

Many reflexes can occur in the absence of the brain. For example, a cat can be made to stand after removal of its brain. The standing is controlled by spinal reflexes initiated in the pads of the feet. Penile erection in response to tactile stimulation can also occur even if the brain is absent. (However, erection as the result of sexual excitement by any other form of stimulation, such as visual stimulation, requires control from higher brain centers.) Normally the brain regulates all but a few simple reflexes.

The **brain stem** connects the spinal cord with higher brain regions (see Figure 2-26). It consists of the medulla, pons, and midbrain. These structures regulate the body's many automatic vegetative functions such as respiration, blood pressure, and heart rate. Close to the brain stem is the **cerebellum,** an important control center for movement, muscle coordination, and balance.

Several major structures are located between the brain stem and the highest brain centers. Together with the **limbic system,** a group of closely interconnected structures illustrated in Figure 12-5, the **hypothalamus** controls emotions and basic motivations such as hunger, sex, and temperature (see Chapter 12 for a full discussion).

The major relay station for the transmission of sensory messages to the cortex is the **thalamus.** Processing of incoming sensory information begins here in the brain.

The **cerebral hemispheres,** finally, represent the largest part of the brain. The thin surface layer is called the **neocortex,** or more commonly, the **cortex.** The human cortex is divided into lobes—frontal, parietal, occipital, and temporal—as shown in Figure 2-27. Most complex behaviors involving conscious experience are controlled by the cortex. The regions of the cortex devoted to sensory and motor functions are shown in the figure. The remaining

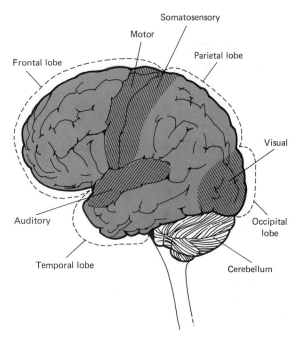

Figure 2-27 The four lobes of the left cerebral cortex, showing localization of sensory and motor functions. Note that most of the cortex is neither purely sensory nor purely motor, but rather associative in function.

regions are involved in complex cognitive functions like thinking and reasoning.

SUMMARY

An individual's characteristics are determined by biological inheritance and experience. The biological transmission of potentialities from parents to offspring is called heredity.

Instinctive or species-characteristic behaviors are behaviors primarily governed by hereditary rather than environmental influences. These behaviors (1) occur frequently in all or nearly all members of a species, (2) have a fixed form, (3) develop independently of experience or learning (although they may be modified by experience), and (4) represent adaptive ways of interacting with the environment. Stimuli that elicit species-characteristic behavior are called sign stimuli.

Most species-characteristic behaviors are

composed of a number of fixed-action patterns. A fixed-action pattern is a repetitious response of a fixed form that, once initiated, persists in the absence of the eliciting stimulus. Displacement activities and vacuum behavior are fixed-action patterns that occur in the absence of appropriate stimuli.

Imprinting is a good example of a species-characteristic behavior that is modified by the experience of the animal. Newly hatched goslings or ducklings will follow almost any moving object during a limited period of their development, and will form a lasting attachment or preference for that object. Another example is the song of some species of birds. The young chaffinch's song is improved by experience with other members of the species.

Species-characteristic behaviors are not a prominent part of adult human behavior. Basic human facial expressions, however, may be species characteristic. Language is a behavioral potentiality made possible by human species heritage.

Through evolution, higher animals have developed behavior that represents flexibility in adapting to the environment. Hereditary behavioral potentialities and species-characteristic behaviors are transmitted from generation to generation genetically. Heredity influences behavior by influencing the physical structure that mediates behavior.

Chromosomes, the hereditary material of all cells, are composed of genes. Genes from maternal and paternal gametes combine at conception, establishing the genetic makeup (genotype) of the new offspring. Monogenetic traits are influenced by a single gene pair, one member of the pair from each parent. Polygenetic traits are determined by many gene pairs. An observable trait (phenotype) in an individual can be predicted from a knowledge of that individual's genotype.

The heritability of behavioral traits in animals is studied through selective breeding experiments. In humans, useful information concerning heritability of traits may be obtained by comparing pedigree analyses of naturally occurring families. If genetic factors influence a trait, members within a family would be expected to resemble one another more than do randomly selected individuals, since members of a family share many of the same genes. Particularly useful in such studies is a comparison of trait similarities in identical twins, who have the same genotypes. Among the behavioral traits that may have some degree of heritability are schizophrenia and, possibly, intelligence.

Human biological inheritance has provided us with sophisticated endocrine and nervous systems to control bodily functions and behavior. Two endocrine glands that have a direct relevance for the study of behavior are the adrenal glands and the gonads. Hormones from these glands affect arousal, mood, and motivation.

The nervous system is composed of cells called neurons, which have the special ability to transmit nerve messages or impulses. Communication between cells in the nervous system is chemical. Information is somehow processed in the nervous system through changes in the rate of firing of certain cells. The peripheral nervous system consists of all somatic nerves and autonomic ganglia with associated nerves. The central nervous system consists of the brain and spinal cord. The main structures of the brain are the brain stem, cerebellum, limbic system, hypothalamus, thalamus, and cortex.

TRY IT YOURSELF

1. What features do species-characteristic behaviors of all animals have in common? Think of examples of differences in species-characteristic behaviors that exist among various species of animals.
2. Describe human beings in terms of (1) species-characteristic behaviors, (2) genetic makeup, and (3) endocrine and nervous systems.

3. In what ways can people use the knowledge obtained from the study of genetics to benefit humanity?

4. Imagine, for the moment, that ways have been found to carry out the cloning of human beings entirely successfully. How would you propose that individuals be selected for cloning? What kinds of individuals would you yourself select? What effects would this have on human cultures? What advantages and disadvantages would such cloning have, and which set outweighs the other? Would cloning be morally right or morally wrong, in your view?

3

Development

DEGRÉS DES AGES.

A CLOSED BOOK?

■ What do you know about your own infancy and childhood? Search your memory and then sit down and write a biography entitled "My First Six Years." What do you recall, or what have you heard, about your first few years? When did you sit up and when did you walk? When did you learn to talk? When were you toilet-trained, and how? Did you have any serious physical illnesses? Do you recall any psychological problems or conflicts? What do you recall of your mother and father in your first six years? Who were your first companions? When did you first go to school? Was school a happy or unhappy experience? How were you encouraged and disciplined? What impressive events happened to you during your first six years?

Your biography is probably very short. We usually have few actual memories of our first six years, psychologists have found. Often supposed memories are simply what our parents or others have told us, or are scenes that we have seen in photographs and assume that we recall. The first years of life must be observed, described, and explained by others, for we can't depend on our own memories alone.

The first six years of life, often called the formative years, have long been regarded as critical in the psychological development of the individual. The old adage "As the twig is bent the tree will grow" expresses this belief. Freud's psychoanalytic theory of personality takes the position that adult maladaptive behavior, injurious to the individual and to others, can always be traced to problems beginning in early childhood (see Chapter 14).

Development psychology is the field of psychology concerned with the combined physical and psychological growth of the individual from conception to maturity and on to old age. In this chapter we shall concentrate mainly on the childhood years. Early development occurs through an interaction of **maturation** (changes in behavior that occur as a result of physiological growth) and experience. For example, during early adolescence the body undergoes many changes, primarily hormonal, that prepare the individual for adult sexual behavior. This maturational process is genetically programmed to occur at about this time of life in all individuals regardless of environmental circumstances. The form that adult sexual behavior takes, however, is dependent also on experience in one's environment. Thus prison inmates, lacking the opportunity for normal heterosexual activity, sometimes engage in homosexual activity.

INFANCY

Prenatal Growth

Once the male sperm fertilizes the egg of the female, the process of development begins. During the 38-week gestation period, development proceeds in an orderly fashion through various stages. Most of the information about prenatal development (before birth) has been obtained by studying immature organisms ex-

pelled from the uterus by miscarriage or abortion. The unborn organism is called an **embryo** during the first eight weeks of gestation, and thereafter a **fetus.**

During early development, the human embryo resembles those of other vertebrates (see Figure 3-1). By the end of the second month of gestation the embryo is unquestionably human in form. During the third month, the sex organs develop sufficiently for the sex to be distinguishable. The first movements of the fetus occur during the third month; by the fourth month the mother can feel the movements. An infant born seven months after conception has a chance of survival even though the finishing touches of prenatal development are not complete.

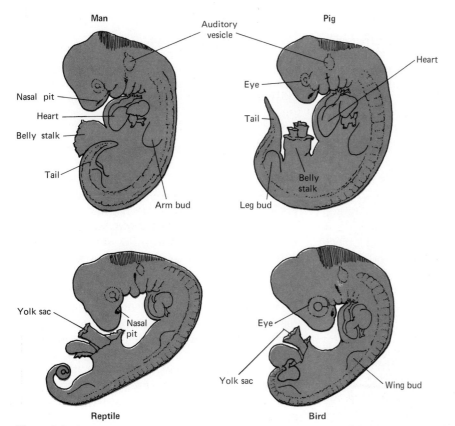

Figure 3-1   Structure of the young embryos of a human, pig, reptile, and bird. (Patten, 1922)

Newborn Equipment

Psychologists long believed that a newborn child is a completely helpless creature incapable of making any sense out of its new environment. This belief was largely fostered by casual observations of the newborn, whose behavioral repertoire is very limited. A newborn child spends approximately 17 hours each day sleeping and about 4 hours eating. At other times, casual observation would suggest that the infant isn't doing much of anything. By careful observation and clever experimentation, however, psychologists have learned that the newborn possesses a remarkable variety of behavioral skills.

To begin with, the newborn has many inborn reflexes such as sucking, rooting (orienting the mouth in the direction of a tactile stimulus, normally a nipple), sneezing, and blinking. The arms and legs will jerk away from a source of pain. One of the most amazing reflexes possessed by the newborn is the grasping reflex. The infant's fingers and toes will tighten around an object with remarkable strength. The grasp is so firm that an infant clutching a bar can be lifted into the air with no support but the grip of the fingers on the bar. The newborn also possesses perceptual abilities that until recently were attributed only to older infants. It was long believed that the newborn could not see or hear very well. Researchers have demonstrated, however, that only a few minutes after birth a baby's eyes can track a slowly moving object and move in the direction of a sound (Wertheimer, 1961; Wolff, 1966). Both of these skills require sophisticated nervous system control. Newborn infants also can smell perfectly adequately.

NEWBORN RESPONSES TO ALCOHOLS

Newborn capacities, even smelling, have been greatly underestimated. Psychologists used to believe that infants could smell a bit, perhaps, although only at a rudimentary level. But research has shown that "the human newborn has a much keener olfactory apparatus capable of making finer discriminations than previously thought" (Rovee, 1969, p. 253). The limited olfactory experience of infants makes them useful subjects for olfactory investigations.

Newborn discrimination of smells has been observed by noting changes in infants' respiration and movement in cribs when odors are introduced. The procedure simply calls for giving them a whiff of some odorous substance on cotton-swathed ends of glass rods held about a quarter-inch below their noses. In recent experiments, newborns averaging 60 hours old discriminated among five alcohols, ranging from short-chain propanol to long-chain decanol. The infants reacted most vigorously to the short-chain, low-carbon alcohols and less and less vigorously as the alcohols progressed to long-chain, high-carbon alcohols. Their smelling capacities seemed to be as efficient as those of adults. Furthermore, newborns showed differential responses to various odors, accepting some and rejecting others. Newborns have not been exposed to a great variety of odors and have had little opportunity to learn reactions to them. Their reactions to odors must therefore be based on innate preferences.

Young infants have preferences for certain visual stimuli. In an apparatus like that shown in Figure 3-2, infants in one experiment were placed face-up in a crib. Stimuli were then exposed about nine inches above the infant. The baby's attention to the stimulus was determined by recording the length of time the eyes remained fixed on it. Preferences for certain stimuli were determined by presenting various combinations of pairs of stimuli and observing to which member of the pair the infant attended most. In general, newborn infants prefer rather complex visual stimuli, such as bull's-eye designs and drawings of faces, to plainer solid-color figures and simple designs (see Figure 3-3). Certain features of complex designs attract more attention than others. Given an equal number of squares or other elements in the design, newborns prefer a de-

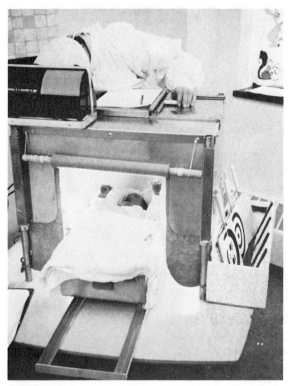

Figure 3-2 Apparatus used to test visual preferences in young infants. (Fantz, 1963)

sign with a larger pattern. Holding size of elements constant, newborns prefer a design with more elements. For example, newborns fixate longer on a white card with four large black squares than one with four smaller squares; and they fixate longer on a card with four squares than one with two of the same size. When size and number of variations vary in opposing directions, size preference tends to dominate. As infants get older, a shift occurs from size to number as the more dominant variable for attention (Fantz & Fagan, 1975). Newborns also prefer to look at curved rather than straight contours (Fantz & Miranda, 1975).

One- or two-week-old infants look equally long at photographs or drawings of regular human faces and photographs or drawings of faces in which the features are scrambled (see Figure 3-4). Thus there seems to be no innate

preference specifically for viewing a human face. Interestingly, by the time children are 27 months old they begin to fixate longer to the *irregular* face. Apparently these children have a concept of what the human face should look like and attend longer to the extremely irregular face because it diverges from their expectations (see Figure 3-5).

As seen in Figure 3-6, an infant as young as two weeks old will show a defense response to an approaching object (Ball & Tronick, 1971; Bower, 1971). The defense response implies that the infant perceives the oncoming object to be solid. This recent observation contradicts most traditional theories of perception, which have held that the association of visual cues and tactile qualities is learned. According to this older view, the infant must repeatedly see and touch solid objects in order to recognize solidity visually. But it is unlikely that infants less than two weeks old have learned to fear approaching objects and to expect them to have solidity. The expectation of solidity has been shown in somewhat older infants by stereoscopically presenting the illusion of a solid object on a screen in front of the infants and noting their surprise when they try to

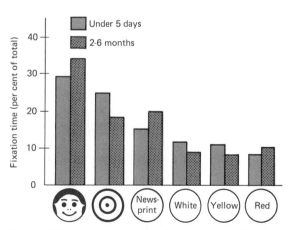

Figure 3-3 Visual preferences of young infants. The bars show the per cent of time infants under five days of age and infants from two to six months old spent looking at each stimulus. (Fantz, 1965)

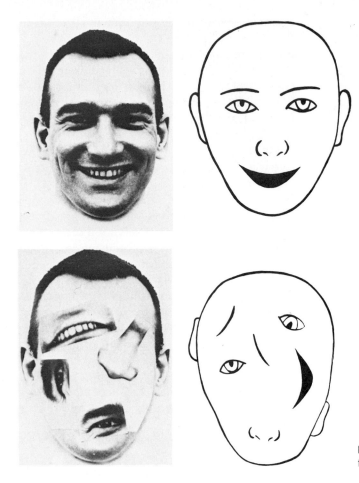

Figure 3-4 Photographs and drawings of human faces shown to young infants. (Kagan, 1970)

grasp the image (Bower, 1971). When they touched the real object in front of them, none of the infants showed surprise by crying, change in facial expressions, or other appropriate behaviors. Yet all appeared to be surprised when they grasped thin air in reaching for the visually projected three-dimensional image.

Young infants also perceive depth and avoid sharp drops, although they probably have not learned to do so through any direct experience. In one experiment, infants six to seven months old were placed on a wide board several inches above a clear glass support (see Figure 3-7). On one side of the board a checkerboard pattern on the floor, three or four

feet below, could be seen through the glass, giving the impression of a steep drop-off or "visual cliff." On the other side the same checkerboard pattern was attached to the undersurface of the glass, only a few inches below the infant. For each infant tested, the mother randomly walked either to the "shallow" or the "deep" side. Infants crawled to their mothers on the shallow side but not on the deep side. Therefore the perception of depth is probably innate and does not require learning.

The human infant is not, then, entirely helpless at birth, but rather displays a rich variety of perceptual skills that contribute to survival.

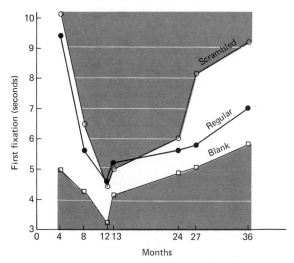

Figure 3-5 Fixation times of infants of various ages to regular and scrambled masks of a human face similar to those shown in Figure 3-4 or to a blank mask. (Kagan, 1970)

Figure 3-6 Defense reaction of a two-week-old infant to an approaching object. The reaction consists of raising the hand, pulling back the head, and blinking the eyes.

Early Personality

Great individual differences are observed in children from the moment of birth. The shaping of personality occurs through the interaction of their innate temperaments and their experiences. **Temperament** can be broadly defined as a person's characteristic inclination, emotional response, or frame of mind, tendencies to be contented or discontented, to accept or reject, to adjust to new conditions or struggle against them. Some infants are born cuddlers and some aren't (Schaffer & Emerson, 1964).

One long-term observation of 141 children from birth to 14 years showed that distinct individual differences in the children evident in the first week of life persisted through adolescence (Thomas, Chess, & Birch, 1970). On the basis of their temperaments, the children were described as "easy children" (about 40 per cent), "difficult children" (about 10 per cent), and "slow-to-warm-up children" (about 15 per cent). The remaining 35 per cent of the children did not fall into any one category, but showed mixed characteristics. The easy chil-

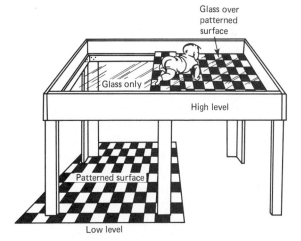

Figure 3-7 The visual cliff, consisting of two checkerboard surfaces. One is directly under the glass on which the infant is crawling; the other is several feet below the glass, giving the appearance of a drop-off. The infant refuses to cross to the "deep" side, thereby showing an ability to perceive depth. (Walk & Gibson, 1961)

Table 3-1 Stability of Temperament Traits over the First Two Years of Life

Trait	Per Cent of Individuals with Interperiod Stability
Activity	27.5%
Rhythmicity	65.0
Adaptability	83.8
Approach	81.2
Threshold	41.2
Intensity	87.5
Mood	92.5
Distractibility	36.2
Persistence	65.0

Source: Thomas, Chess, Birch, Hertzig, & Korn, 1964.

dren were generally content, slept well, had regular bodily functions, and adapted well to novel situations. The difficult children were just the opposite. They cried a great deal, did not eat or sleep well, and showed intense negative reactions to new situations. The slow-to-warm-up children tended to withdraw on their first exposure to new situations and were somewhat negative in mood. The individual temperament of each infant was a relatively stable characteristic that persisted over time. Table 3-1 shows the per cent of cases of the first 80 children studied that exhibited stability of a temperament trait over the first two years of life.

A later follow-up of these children showed that about 70 per cent of the difficult children had developed behavior problems calling for psychiatric attention, while only 18 per cent of the easy children had such problems. The number of children in this study requiring psychiatric help seems high even for the easy children—10 individuals out of 56. Since all children in the study had highly educated parents, these parents probably sought the services of psychiatrists more frequently than other segments of the society would do. Be that as it may, the follow-up did reveal a relationship between the children's basic early temperaments and their later personalities and behavior problems. But the follow-up also indicated that the children's environments influenced their personality development. The implication of the observations is that each child is unique, and therefore that child-rearing practices should be geared to the particular temperament and needs of the child.

ETHNIC BEHAVIORAL DIFFERENCES IN NEWBORNS

Behavioral differences have been observed between Chinese-American infants and European-American infants when they were only 5 to 75 hours old (Freedman & Freedman, 1969). Most of the families of the Chinese-American infants had a Cantonese ethnic background, the European-American families a middle-European background. Eleven babies in each category were male, 13 female. The groups were very evenly matched, showing no significant differences in mean weight, heart rate, respiration, muscle tonus, and crying at birth. Nor did the ages of the mothers, medication during labor, mean hours of labor, or number of prior pregnancies vary significantly. When the babies were observed and tested shortly after birth, the groups showed similar sensory development, central nervous system maturity, motor development, and social interest and response. These two ethnic groups of babies were, then, very similar in many respects just after birth.

The infants did reveal significant temperament differences, however, in their responses indicative of excitability or imperturbability. The European-American infants moved back and forth more actively between states of contentment and upset than the Chinese-American infants, who were noticeably calmer and steadier. When a cloth was placed on the infants' faces, the European-Americans turned their heads and swiped at the cloth with their hands, while the Chinese-Americans lay still, with few responses. Similarly, the Chinese-Americans left their faces against the bedding when they were laid prone on their stomachs, while the European-Americans turned their faces to one side or lifted their heads. The Chinese-Americans were quickly consoled when they were picked up when they cried; the European-Americans tended to go on crying quite a while before they were soothed. The Chinese-Americans were thus less excitable and change-able, and calmed themselves or were consoled more readily than the European-Americans.

Such a small group—only 48 infants—is inade-quate as a basis for any general inferences, of course; many more subjects would be required to prove that other variables were not operative and that these were genuine differences of the two particular ethnic groups at birth. The study does suggest, however, that some basic early temperament traits may be innate—or possibly may result from different prenatal environmental conditions.

PHYSICAL MATURATION

In accordance with the principle of **maturational readiness,** an organism will not acquire a particular behavior until it is physiologically prepared to do so. Probably this is the reason that human infants exhibit various motor skills at about the same ages (see Figure 3-8).

The concept of maturational readiness is exemplified in the belief that you can't teach a child to walk until he is physiologically ready

to do so. That is, the nervous system must be mature enough to govern the movements, and the muscles must be strong enough to support the child's weight. Many experiments have shown that early practice of a motor skill does not accelerate motor development. For example, a study of the development of walking in Hopi Indian children showed that the age of earliest walking was not affected by an infant's opportunity to practice motor skills used in walking (Dennis, 1940). Traditionally, Hopi Indians wrap a newborn infant in blankets attached to a cradleboard in such a manner that movement of the infant's legs is severely restricted. The infants are restrained on the cradleboards for approximately nine months except when they are being cleaned and changed. When Hopi Indian infants who had spent nine months restrained on cradleboards were compared with Hopi infants who had not been restrained, there was no difference in the average age at which they first walked. Practice of motor skills seemed not to have affected the development of walking.

However, the assumption that no amount of

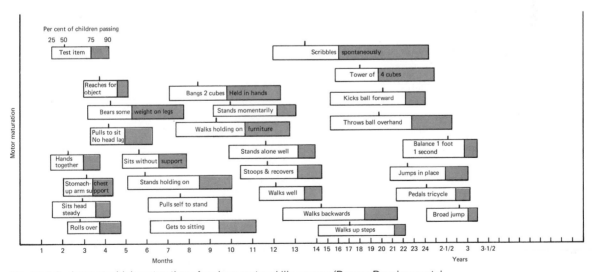

Figure 3-8 Ages at which maturation of various motor skills occurs (Denver Developmental Screening Test, 1970). For a discussion of the Denver Development Screening Test see Frankenburg & Hobbs, 1967.

stimulation prior to maturational readiness will facilitate the behavior has come under investigation in a study of the effect of brief daily exercise of the walking reflex in newborn infants (Zelazo, Zelazo, & Kalb, 1972). It has long been known that when newborns are placed on their stomachs, they will make spontaneous crawling motions with their diagonally opposed arms and legs—remarkably like the crawling of newborn puppies toward their mother's teats. Also, when they are supported by the body with their feet positioned on a surface, newborns from birth will begin to "walk," moving one leg before the other and placing their feet on the surface (see Figure 3-9). Normally such walking behavior weakens and disappears within the first month or two, to reappear later at about the age of 12 to 14 months, when infants begin to walk on their own. It has been assumed that infants follow the set developmental sequence of lifting the head, sitting up, making stepping movements, and then walking.

In the experiment conducted by the Zelazos and Kalb, six male infants were held by their parents so they could "walk" for four three-minute sessions a day from ages one to eight weeks. Six others were given passive exercise of their legs when they were lying on their backs for the same periods. Six more were given no exercises, though they were tested for walking at weekly intervals. A final group of six infants was not even tested. A great increase was found in the amount and quality of walking of the infants who were given the walking exercises. There were many indications that they were learning to walk during their practice sessions. They actually walked on their own at an average early age of 10.1 months, as opposed to 11.3 months for those passively exercised, 11.7 months for those only tested, and 12.4 months for those not even tested.

The investigators concluded that the first eight weeks may be a critical period for the development of the walking pattern. When the

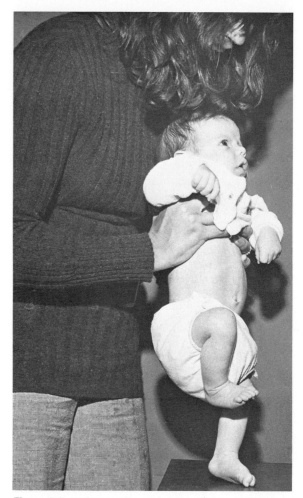

Figure 3-9 Walking reflex of the young infant. (Courtesy of Philip R. Zelazo)

pattern is practiced during that period, it will be retained and then transformed into spontaneous walking much earlier than usual. Without such stimulation, the pattern is lost entirely after about eight weeks, and reappears only much later. Furthermore, the study suggested that exercising an infant in walking may produce a beneficial early sense of competence in motor activities, thus supporting the infant's need to explore the environment and stimulating curiosity.

COGNITIVE DEVELOPMENT

Cognition is the process by which a person
acquires knowledge. You yourself have developed cognitively to the point at which you can
think and reason, argue and debate and
discuss all kinds of issues with other people.
You can solve many kinds of problems, acquire new knowledge, and change the ideas
you once thought unassailable. But how did
you attain this ability to deal cognitively with
all kinds of experiences? Somehow it developed during your childhood. The leading contemporary psychologist studying the cognitive
development of children is Jean Piaget. On the
basis of five decades of observing and experi-
menting with children of all ages, Piaget (1952)
has formulated a theory of cognitive development that emphasizes children's innate tendency to try to make meaning out of the world
in which they live.

Developmental Processes

According to Piaget, new information is added
to the child's existing knowledge by two processes: assimilation and accommodation. The
child acquires knowledge by adopting a
behavioral or cognitive structure for understanding information. When new observations
are consistent with the present understanding
or structure, the child assimilates the new information. **Assimilation** is the addition of new
information to the child's existing cognitive
structure. When there is a discrepancy between the new observations and the existing
cognitive structure, however, the structure
must be changed to fit the new information as

well as the old. **Accommodation** is the process of adjusting the existing cognitive structure to fit the new information. If children believe, for example, that all liquids taste good (for this may have been true in their limited experience), then they will be eager to drink new liquids. If the taste of an unfamiliar drink is enjoyable, they will assimilate the new information to the existing cognitive structure: "Liquids taste good." If the taste is not enjoyable, the child must accommodate the cognitive structure to fit the new reality: "Some liquids taste good, but others taste bad."

Development Stages

One of Piaget's main tenets is that intellectual development proceeds through a series of stages that are characterized by qualitatively different kinds of cognitive structures.

The first stage (birth to approximately two years) is called the **sensorimotor stage.** Infants in this stage acquire knowledge by physically interacting with the environment. Infants given a new toy will learn about the toy by picking it up, handling it, and inevitably putting it in their mouths. All of these acts provide information about the texture, weight, shape, and taste of the toy.

Piaget maintains that during the first two years of life an infant knows the world only in terms of sensory impressions and motor activities. Psychologist Jerome Kagan, on the other hand, believes that infants as young as eight to nine months old begin to acquire knowledge through cognitive activity or hypothesis testing that does *not* require sensorimotor activity. To support his position, Kagan cites evidence that infants at this age engage in mental activity when presented with an event that is inconsistent with the form with which they are familiar. In order to determine whether infants merely attend to a discrepant stimulus or think about it, Kagan (1972) conducted an experiment in which cognitive activity was measured by changes in heart rate

during the viewing of discrepant stimuli such as a mobile slightly different from a familiar one hanging over their beds at home. If an individual attends to a stimulus, heart rate decreases. If he thinks about the stimulus while attending to it, however, his heart rate increases. In Kagan's experiment, an increase in heart rate was observed in infants attending to discrepant events. It may be that infants try to transform mentally the discrepant event into the form with which they are familiar.

Later in the sensorimotor stage of development the child begins to use language, but does not use words symbolically to stand for objects and events. The child only names objects and events that are immediately present. Objects out of sight are out of mind—they seem to have no reality for a child in this stage. Of course, philosophers have questioned how anyone knows that objects continue to exist when we are not perceiving them. Is this just an unsupported assumption that we all make, or is there evidence for the continued existence of things in our ordinary perceptions of them? Older children learn that objects out of sight may reappear at a later time.

In the **preoperational stage** (2 to 6 years) the child is capable for the first time of using symbols and concepts. Words are used to stand for absent objects or events. The child may pretend that an object stands for something else, taking a folded piece of paper to be an airplane, for example. During this stage a large segment of the child's speech is self-directed. It is not uncommon to see children of this age in a group together, each talking volubly, but to themselves rather than to one another.

The next stage, the **concrete operational stage** (7 to 12 years), is marked by an advance in the child's understanding of logical relationships. The new understanding includes the ability to classify objects according to some dimension, such as color or shape; the ability to understand the relationship between subgroups and the whole; and the ability to un-

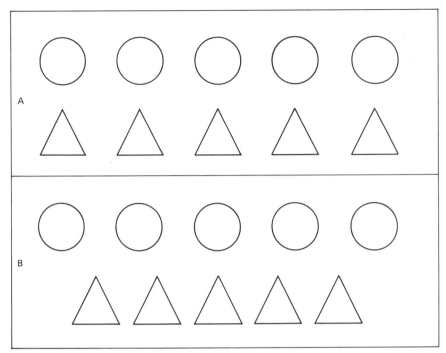

Figure 3-10 Conservation of numbers. A, the circles and triangles are evenly spaced and the child is asked whether there are more circles or triangles; B, the triangles are then placed close together and the child is again asked whether there are more circles or triangles.

derstand that properties like mass, number, volume, and weight remain constant regardless of changes in appearance. For example, changing the physical arrangement of a number of items in a set does not change the number of items. This principle is called the **conservation of numbers.** Before the concrete operational stage, the child does not correctly perform the task based on this principle illustrated in Figure 3-10. Because the row of circles in B is longer than the row of triangles, the preoperational child believes that there are more circles than triangles. Even if an attempt is made to explain to the child that the number of items in the row remains the same regardless of the placement, the child will not understand. The concrete operational child understands the conservation principle. Similarly, the concrete operational child understands that

if you pour liquid directly from a short fat beaker into a tall thin one, the amount of liquid is the same in both containers even though the level of the liquid is higher in the thin one (Figure 3-11). This principle is called the **conservation of volume.** The preoperational child does not understand the reciprocal relationship between width and height. Piaget has used these observations to support his view that qualitative changes take place in the cognitive structure as the child passes from one stage of development to the next.

The ability to make **transitive inferences** also characterizes the concrete operational child. Given the information that $A > B$ (the symbol $>$ indicates "is greater than") and $B > C$, the child can infer that $A > C$. According to Piaget, the preoperational child is unable to coordinate the two given items of in-

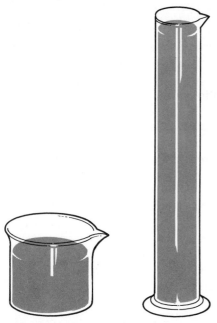

Figure 3-11 Conservation of volume. The child watches as liquid is poured from the short fat beaker into the tall thin one and is asked which holds more liquid.

formation in order to draw the correct conclusion. For instance, if children in the preoperational stage are asked which of two towers of blocks at a distance from one another is taller, they guess if the answer is not obvious. Concrete operational children, on the other hand, might measure the height of each tower with a measuring stick, realizing that if tower A is the length of the measuring stick, and tower B is shorter than the measuring stick, then tower A must be taller than tower B.

Piaget's conclusions about cognitive abilities that characterize children of the concrete operational stage of development have been questioned by other investigators. Children in the preoperational stage of development (2 years, 6 months through 3 years, 2 months) have been observed to perform correctly a task involving the conservation of numbers (Mehler & Bever, 1967). The children's responses were solicited in two ways: once by asking them to

indicate which of two rows of clay pellets contained "more," and a second time by asking them to take one of two rows of M & M candies to eat. As one would expect, older children in the preoperational stage (4 years, 6 months) also performed the task correctly. Interestingly, however, children of the intervening age group (3 years, 8 months through 4 years, 3 months) did not solve the problem. The investigators concluded that the temporary inability of the intermediate group to solve the problem was attributable to a period of overdependence on perceptual cues.

Preoperational children have been shown to be similarly overdependent on perceptual cues in conservation-of-volume problems (Frank, cited in Bruner, Olver & Greenfield, 1966). When children were presented with the typical task of judging which beaker contains more liquid when it is poured from a fat beaker into a thin one, the children performed correctly as long as they could not see the water levels in the two beakers. That is, they understood that if a given amount of liquid is poured from one container to the next, the volume does not change, regardless of the shape of the containers. In this experiment, misleading perceptual cues were eliminated by placing the beakers behind a screen with only the tops showing.

Under certain circumstances, preoperational children have been observed to make transitive inferences. In one experiment, children ranging from the ages of 4 years, 6 months through 6 years, 8 months were given extensive A > B and B > C training (Bryant & Trabasso, 1971). Specifically, they were taught that a blue rod was longer than a red one, and that the red rod was longer than a green one. The children could not see the actual lengths of the rods. When asked to indicate the relationship of the blue and green rods, these preoperational children made correct transitive inferences a large percentage of the time. The investigators attributed the success in this experiment to the children's retention of the information upon which the inferences were made. That is, these experimenters were careful to make sure that the children remembered the relative lengths of the blue and red rods and the red and green rods before asking them the relationship between the blue and green rods. The failure to demonstrate transitive inferences in similar previous investigations might have been due to the limited memory of children at this age.

The last stage of cognitive development, according to Piaget, is the **formal operational stage** (12 to 15 years). In this stage the adolescent develops the skill of complex logical reasoning. Adolescents are able to figure out the solution to a hypothetical problem by formulating alternative hypotheses and systematically examining the implications of each hypothesis. Adolescent reasoning is flexible and effective. Adolescents are also capable of reflecting on their own thoughts. In this period they question the integrity of their values and those of their parents, ponder their roles in life, and think about their futures.

The ages at which children pass from one stage of development to the next vary somewhat from child to child. Impoverished environmental conditions may retard a child's progress. Enriched conditions, however, do not necessarily facilitate progress. Piaget believes that children's learning cannot be accelerated beyond a certain rate because the necessary cognitive structure is not yet present. Unless children pass through a step-by-step understanding of new principles, they will not develop the cognitive structure necessary to acquire new knowledge; and even detailed step-by-step instruction in particular forms of thinking has limited value if a child's cognitive structure is not sufficiently mature to integrate the pieces of information that are taught.

Our understanding of the cognitive development of children remains incomplete, but the valuable work of Piaget has greatly contributed to the unfolding of information on this issue.

INTELLIGENCE

Like all abstract concepts, intelligence is difficult to define explicitly. Piaget describes intelligence as the ability to modify and expand cognitive structures through the processes of accommodation and assimilation. Does that definition clarify the meaning for you? Probably not. Luckily, intelligence is one of those you-know-what-I-mean terms, and there isn't much disagreement on its meaning. Many would define **intelligence** as the capacity of the individual to act purposefully, to reason, and to adapt to novel situations. David Wechsler (1975), author of the adult intelligence test that bears his name, points out four general criteria for defining intelligent behavior. First, the behavior must involve awareness or insight. This criterion has often been used to distinguish instinctual behaviors of some species from intelligent behavior. Although the bee engages in a very complex means of communication in the form of a dance, it is not given credit for being intelligent because the behavior is not based on an awareness of the reason for the behavior. Second, the behavior must be goal-directed or have meaning. Behavior that has no particular significance or importance is not valued as intelligent. Third, the behavior must be rational. Only behavior that involves an active process of reasoning is classified as intelligent. That is, the individual must have solved a problem or reached a conclusion. The act of going to the refrigerator and taking out a snack certainly involves awareness and goal direction, but it does not qualify as being intelligent because it requires no special cognitive skills. Finally, the behavior must have value or be esteemed by society. Acts of criminal violence, for example, are not generally considered intelligent, regardless of the complexity of reasoning involved in the act.

An important distinction should be made between the terms "intelligence" and "intelligent behavior." Although intelligence manifests itself through behavior, the term "intelligence" refers to the underlying capacity that makes the behavior possible. The distinction becomes important when the behavior is at variance with the underlying intellectual capacity. It is possible for people to be more intelligent than they act. For instance, an eight-year-old boy might be judged by his teacher to be not very intelligent because of the poor quality of his schoolwork. The child might be unhappy rather than a slow learner, however. His poor school performance could result from poor motivation to do the work or lack of attention. When intelligence is to be assessed, every effort should be made to assure that the individual being judged is performing under adequate conditions. Standardized intelligence tests are designed to meet this goal.

Intelligence Testing

Over the years, psychologists have devised a variety of standardized tests to measure many human characteristics against a common yardstick. Among these are intelligence tests, specialized aptitude tests, achievement tests, and personality tests. (A discussion of personality tests is found in Chapter 14.) In general, these tests are devised by administering a set of test items to a large sample of people representing the general population. The performance of the sample, called the **standardization group,** is recorded and summarized. (See Appendix: Statistics for methods of summarizing large bodies of data.) The performance of other people taking the test is compared with that of the standardization group.

Certain characteristics of standardized tests are important determinants of their usefulness. One is **reliability,** or the degree to which the test measures are consistent. Persons who take the same standardized test on two occasions should score about the same both times; those who take two sets of equivalent tests should receive similar scores. A test has low reliability when results are easily influenced by ordinary daily changes in mood, motivation, or attention of the people being tested.

A test should also measure what it is supposed to measure. The extent to which this is accomplished is called **validity.** Intelligence tests should measure the underlying intellectual capacity of the individual and not, for example, personality characteristics. One way to assess the validity of a standardized test is to compare its results with those of other standardized tests purporting to measure the same characteristic.

Intelligence tests are most frequently used to predict the degree of success that children will achieve in school or adults in a job. While intelligence tests are good predictors of school performance, they are less successful in predicting performance in most adult roles. People who perform well on intelligence tests are not necessarily more successful than average in their work. On the other hand, people who score very low on intelligence tests *are* usually less competent than average in a wide variety of tasks.

The Stanford-Binet Intelligence Scale

A standardized test frequently used in this country to measure intelligence in children is the **Stanford-Binet Intelligence Scale.** It is composed of a series of tasks, some performance and some verbal, of graded levels of difficulty. The tasks are administered by a psychological tester to one subject at a time (see Figure 3-12). One of the performance tasks requires the subject to put a wooden peg of a particular shape into a board with variously shaped holes, only one of which accommodates the peg. Another requires the subject to draw variously shaped figures from printed samples. Verbal tasks include naming objects, identifying pictures, demonstrating an understanding of word meanings, repeating lists of digits backward, and describing similarities between meanings of words.

Of course, older children would be expected to do better on the test than younger children. Therefore, each child's performance is com-

Figure 3-12 Stanford-Binet Intelligence Test materials.

pared with that of other children of the same age. The standardization group for this test consisted of a large sample of children of various ages ranging from 2 to 18 years. After the standardization group was tested and graded, each test item was classified according to the lowest age at which most of the children in the sample performed the task correctly. Separate age-level subtests were compiled for every six-month period for children 2 through 5, for every year for children 6 through 14, and for four adult levels. For example, a task classified as a 10-year-level item would be one that most 10-year-olds in the sample performed correctly but most younger children did not. Items classified within any one age level are considered of approximately uniform difficulty.

Testing begins at a level slightly below the expected ability of the subject. Thus a 10-year-old might be started at a level equivalent to the average nine-year-old's performance. The highest age level at which the child performs all the tasks correctly is called the **basal age.** Testing is continued until a level is reached at which the child fails in all the items. The child's performance, indicated as his **mental age,** is figured by combining his basal age with partial credit for items passed at higher levels. Partial credit for any one item is determined by the number of items at that level. If there are 12 items in one age level, the subject would get $1/12$ year or one month credit for each item passed. The subject's **intelligent quotient (IQ)** is defined as:

$$IQ = \frac{\text{Mental Age}}{\text{Chronological Age}} \times 100$$

Therefore, children whose mental age equals their chronological age have IQs of 100. Individuals whose mental age is greater than chronological age have IQs higher than 100, and those whose mental age is less than chronological age have IQs lower than 100.

The latest revision of the Stanford-Binet (in 1960) introduced a new procedure for figuring IQs. Instead of determining a ratio of an individual's mental age to chronological age, the psychological tester compares each individual's score with the scores of the individuals *of the same age* in the standardization group. A **percentile value** is computed by figuring the per cent of scores in a set that a particular score equals or exceeds. If a score has a percentile value of 84, that score is equal to or higher than 84 per cent of scores in the set. Table 3-2

Table 3-2 Relation of Deviation IQs to Percentile Ranks for the Stanford-Binet Intelligence Scale

Deviation IQ	Percentile Rank	Classification
148	99.9%	Genius
124	93.0	Very superior
112	77.0	Superior
100	50.0	Normal
88	23.0	Dull
76	7.0	Borderline
64	1.2	Mentally retarded

Adapted from Pinneau, 1961.

presents IQ scores, called **deviation IQs,** obtained from a ranking of scores of the standardization group. The average performance of the standardization group at any age level is arbitrarily assigned an IQ of 100. The statistical procedure used to determine deviation IQs above and below the average performance of 100 is discussed in the Appendix: Statistics. (The procedure involves transforming test scores from the sample to standard scores with a mean of 100 and a standard deviation of 16.) The same raw score is assigned different deviation IQs when it is compared with the scores of different age groups.

The change in scoring procedures increases the Stanford-Binet test's applicability to the measurement of adult intelligence. Before the modification, the test was applied to adults by using 18 as the chronological age for all adults. This was necessary because mental age does not change very much after this age. As presently scored, the test compares the performance of adults with that of standardization groups of several age groups, which do perform at slightly different levels.

Wechsler Adult Intelligence Scale

The standardized test used most frequently to measure intelligence in adults is the **Wechsler Adult Intelligence Scale** (WAIS). It differs from the Stanford-Binet in several respects. First of all, it provides separate verbal and performance IQs. Second, test items are administered differently. Rather than being grouped into age levels, all items are grouped into subtests according to topic and arranged in increasing order of difficulty within each subtest. The six verbal subtests and five performance subtests are shown in Table 3-3.

The standard procedure for administering the test is to present items from each subtest in order of increasing difficulty, beginning with a designated low-difficulty item. If the subject fails the first item, lower-ranked items are given. The subject is given credit for each item passed. Testing continues until the subject fails a set number of consecutive items, ranging from two to five, depending on the subtest.

Scores on the WAIS are compared with scores of a standardization group composed of 1700 adults in seven age groups. Each subject's score is compared with scores of his own age group: 16–17 years, 18–19 years, 20–24 years, 25–34 years, 35–44 years, 45–54 years, and 55–64 years.

As in the case of the Stanford-Binet, the average performance of each standardization age group for the WAIS is assigned an IQ of 100. Other scores are converted to IQs by determining their percentile rank in the set of scores of the standardization group.

Table 3-3 Subtests of the Wechsler Adult Intelligence Scale

Verbal Tests	Performance Tests
Information	Digit symbol
Comprehension	Picture completion
Arithmetic	Block design
Similarities	Picture arrangement
Digit span	Object assembly
Vocabulary	

Culture Fair Intelligence Test

Critics of intelligence tests contend that they test an individual's intellectual *achievement* rather than intellectual *ability*. The information subtest on the WAIS asks the subject questions like "How far is it from New York to San Francisco?" "At what temperature does water freeze?" "Where is Ethiopia?" Obviously the performance on this subtest depends upon the individual's exposure to the information. The basic assumption of the subtest is that most people in this country have had exposure to a general body of information, from which sample items are selected for the test. Similarly, the vocabulary subtest assumes that most people have had comparable experiences with the English language.

These assumptions are not entirely valid. In general, intelligence tests are biased in favor of white urban Americans. They have had more exposure to the type of information sampled by intelligence tests than other groups.

In an attempt to eliminate cultural bias in intelligence tests, R. B. Cattell developed the **Culture Fair Intelligence Test.** It is designed to minimize the influence of language, knowledge, and intellectual skills specific to any given culture. The Culture Fair test relies heavily on items designed to test logical relationships between objects, which are generally less biased by cultural differences than verbal items. Four example items from Cattell's Culture Fair Intelligence Test are presented below in Figure 3-13.

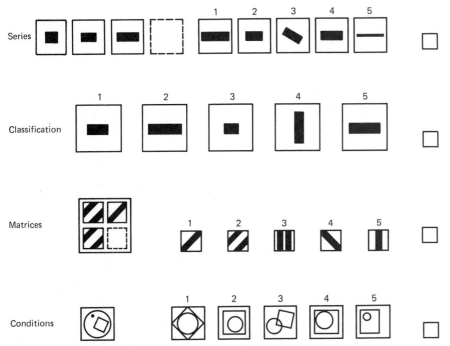

Figure 3-13 Example items from the IPAT Culture Fair Intelligence Test. In the series problem, select one of the five figures that best completes the series. In the classification problem, select the figure that is least similar to the others. For the matrix, select the figure that best completes the matrix. In the last problem, select the figure that best fulfills the conditions of the initial figure.

LANGUAGE

Perhaps the most important step in the cognitive and social development of the child is acquisition of language. After all, language is our chief, although not our only, means of communication. Body postures, gestures, and facial expressions also transmit a tremendous amount of information. Some psychologists, notably Piaget, are reluctant to say that cognitive development requires language. Evidence for this position is abundant. Deaf children, who have no systematic language, spoken or gestural, until about the age of six, show no marked cognitive impairment. Most psychologists agree, however, that adult cognitive activities, such as thinking, reasoning, planning, and remembering, are to some degree mediated and facilitated by language (see Chapter 11 for a discussion of verbal mediation).

Language facilitates social interaction by enabling people to organize a social system through such actions as giving commands, expressing feelings, and making plans for the future. Another great benefit of language is that it permits knowledge to be passed on easily from one generation to the next, without the distortions inevitably produced by lapses of memory and changing attitudes.

Language Acquisition

The study of the mental processes underlying the acquisition and use of language is carried on in a field of psychology called **psycholinguistics.** By six months of age a child begins to make well-differentiated utterances. The innateness of these utterances and the ways in which language learning occurs are described in Chapter 9. Infants comprehend their first words when they are about ten months old. **Receptive language** is developed earlier and remains more advanced than **expressive language.** That is, children under-

stand more words than they speak. Most children have learned to utter their first word or words by the age of 12 to 18 months. Nouns are usually the child's first uttered words, although some verbs may be used. Most psycholinguists believe that simple one-word utterances of the one- to two-year-old child are meant to express meanings that go beyond the meaning of the word alone (Bloom, 1970). "Mamma" may mean "Mamma, I'm scared" or "Mamma, give me the candy." Children continue to use one-word utterances until sometime during the second year, when they go on to two- and sometimes three-word utterances. This is an enormous advance because the child has begun to apply a few simple grammatical rules. **Grammar** is a set of rules by which words are combined into meaningful sentences. Naturally, the rules of two-year-olds are not always grammatically correct by adult standards, but the important point is that children use their own rules consistently. As they progress they learn the correct rules of grammar by listening to the speech of others, even though the language they hear is full of fragmentary and grammatically incorrect sentences. It is important to understand that children do not learn sentences merely by repeating those spoken by others, but rather learn rules enabling them to form sentences they have never heard before.

One of the child's first grammatical rules is that certain words can be combined into two-word utterances while others cannot. Table 3-4 indicates word pairs frequently used by children in one study. In this table any word in the left column could be combined with any word in the right. Another grammatical rule learned early is that of word order. The child consistently puts words in their correct order; that is, adjectives usually precede nouns, subjects precede verbs, and verbs precede objects. For example, the child might say, "See dog," "More cookie," "Daddy come." Children soon learn other rules: *s* indicates plural and *ed* in-

Table 3-4 Word-Pair Combinations Frequently Used by Two Children

want baby	all broke	more car	it ball
want car	all buttoned	more cereal	it bang
want do	all clean	more cookie	it checker
want get	all done	more fish	it daddy
want glasses	all dressed	more high	it Dennis
want head	all dry	more hot	it doggie
want high	all fix	more juice	it doll
want horsie	all gone	more read	it fall
want jeep	all messy	more sing	it horsie
want more	all shut	more toast	it Kathy
want page	all through	more walk	
want pop	all wet		no bed
want purse		pants off	no down
want rise	see baby	shirt off	no fix
want up	see pretty	shoe off	no home
want bye-bye car	see train	water off	no mamma

Adapted from Braine, 1963.

dicates past tense. As soon as regularities in speech are recognized, the child tries to apply them generally. Children at this stage generalize these rules to form word combinations they have never heard. They often say "goed" instead of "went" and "fishes" instead of "fish." The children are of course unaware that they are learning and making use of grammatical rules.

By the age of five children have learned most of the rules of language, although their vocabularies are limited. They have learned these rules by listening to the language of others and noting regularities in form. Parents often help their children learn words by repeating that this object is a "bottle" and that is a "car," but they don't explicitly teach their children grammatical rules. This training doesn't occur until children attend school, by which time they are already remarkably proficient in grammar. Since all of us learn language not by instruction but by "picking up" the language we hear, even as adults we often cannot express many of the rules we use in speech.

Psycholinguistic Theory

Noam Chomsky (1968), a leading psycholinguistic theorist, has proposed that the capacity for speaking and understanding language is innate. Furthermore, he holds that all spoken language results from the following basic process: Thoughts are translated from **deep-structure meanings** into verbal symbols that represent the meanings, and these meanings are overtly expressed through **surface-structure expressions** in particular spoken phrases or sentences. To get an idea of the difference between deep-structure meanings and learned surface-structure expressions, consider the following situation: The President makes a long statement in response to a reporter's question and is asked a few minutes later to repeat it. He is unable to repeat it exactly, but he can paraphrase it. Although he has not remembered the original surface structure, he has remembered the deep structure of what he wanted to say and can derive another surface structure from it.

According to Chomsky, the primary task

before the psycholinguist is to discover the characteristics found universally in all languages and to study the way in which environment influences particular aspects of language. Chomsky is hopeful that a study of innate language abilities and universal language characteristics will contribute to our understanding of the complex processes of the brain.

The Biological Roots of Language

E. H. Lenneberg (1967) has presented several convincing arguments that the capacity for language is part of human biological makeup: (1) The fundamental characteristics of language do not vary within the human species. Most languages are vocal, made up of about 40 different sounds, and generally employ agent–action–object relationships. (2) Children of all cultures seem to learn language in much the same way. They all start out with one-word utterances at about the age of one and gradually expand to more and more complex sentences by the age of five. (3) Language has a specific neurophysiological locus of control, since a particular part of the brain is involved in language behavior. Certain areas of the left frontal and temporal lobes are designated speech centers (see Figure 3-14). Damage to

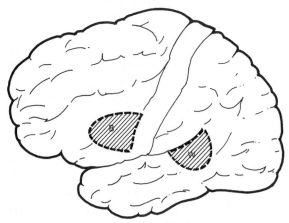

Figure 3-14 Speech centers in the left hemisphere of the human brain: B, Broca's area; W, Wernicke's area.

these centers results in language deficits. Damage to Wernike's area results in an impairment of receptive language. A person with damage in this area is unable to comprehend the meaning of spoken words, although self-generated, expressive speech is quite normal. A person with damage in Broca's area has difficulty with expressive language and may resort to one- or two-word utterances similar to the language of two-year-olds. Receptive speech is normal, however.

Before the age of about 11, children with damage in the speech centers are capable of recovering normal language abilities, whereas adults with the same damage are not. These observations have led to the belief that there is a "sensitive or critical period" in the biological development of language abilities during which the functions of the speech centers can be taken over by other areas of the brain, such as corresponding areas in the right hemisphere, in case of damage. During the sensitive period the brain seems to be maximally geared for the acquisition of language.

Traditionally language has been regarded as a uniquely human ability. Many attempts to teach language to other animals, such as chimpanzees, have failed. The early attempts to teach chimpanzees to talk were doomed to failure because chimpanzees lack the necessary vocal apparatus for the vocalizations of speech and because they are not tuned to the fine auditory distinctions required by spoken language. Later attempts to teach chimpanzees nonoral languages have met with greater success. Chimpanzees have been taught to name objects and events and to express concepts through American Sign Language (Ameslan).

The first chimpanzee to learn Ameslan was Washoe (Gardner & Gardner, 1971). She was about 11 months old when training began. Within 51 months her vocabulary had developed to include 132 signs. Washoe's language development proceeded in an order similar to that of human children. She first learned to name objects like "banana," "hat," and "dog." Washoe was taught signs by having her hands shaped or formed into the proper position for a sign and then was guided through the desired movement by the trainer. A correct unaided sign was rewarded by banana slices, candy, or other goodies. Next she learned to give one-word commands like "go," "tickle," and "come-gimme." Soon she was spontaneously combining words into two- and three-word sentences with the proper word order.

Washoe also learned to use signs that referred to concepts. For example, she learned the concepts "on" and "in." She would correctly respond to the instructions "Place the hat *on* the box" and "Place the hat *in* the box."

Since Project Washoe, several chimpanzees have been trained in Ameslan from birth (Gardner & Gardner, 1975). Chimpanzees Moja and Pili first used recognizable signs when they were about three months old. Within six months they had acquired vocabularies of 13 and 15 signs. It is hoped that the exposure to language from birth will facilitate language acquisition beyond the level achieved by Washoe.

Chimpanzees have also successfully been taught nonoral languages other than Ameslan. Sarah, for example, reads and writes with variously shaped and colored pieces of plastic, each representing a word (Premack & Premack, 1972). As you saw in Chapter 1, Lana reads and writes by punching appropriate keys on a large computer keyboard.

Knowledge gained from these research projects should provide us with a better understanding of the cognitive and linguistic abilities of nonhuman primates. Will chimpanzees be able to initiate conversations spontaneously with other chimpanzees about the weather, the dreams they had last night, or other common subjects? Will chimpanzees be able to teach other chimpanzees to speak? So far these more advanced skills have not been demonstrated, but the possibilities are mind-boggling.

SOCIAL DEVELOPMENT

As a mode of communication with others, language brings children into interaction with the people around them, so it is a most effective means of their social development. Socialization of infants has started much earlier, however, than their first use of language. From the moment of birth on, infants inevitably become involved with all the people around them, particularly their mothers, fathers, and other caregivers.

Attachment

The initial step in the socialization of the child is the development of attachment to the mother or other principal caregiver. **Attachment** first takes the form of physical closeness of the infant to another person and later represents a bond of affection between infant and caregiver. Feelings of affection for the mother, and of the mother for the child, are strengthened as the mother provides care and comfort. She provides food when the baby is hungry and warmth when the baby is cold. She is the infant's principal source of stimulation, and, as we saw earlier, infants seek sensory stimulation. The child learns through experience to associate the mother with pleasure and gratification, and therefore learns to enjoy her presence.

Recent evidence suggests that the initial formation of infant attachment to the mother may be a basic inborn tendency. One line of evidence for this belief stems from the now famous experiments of Harry and Margaret Harlow, in which infant rhesus monkeys were reared by various types of surrogate (substitute) mothers (Harlow, Harlow, & Suomi, 1971). All surrogates were inanimate forms roughly resembling monkeys, which varied in the amount of comfort they provided to the infant (see Figure 3-15). The infant monkeys formed an attachment (sought physical close-

Figure 3-15 Surrogate wire and cloth mothers used to rear young rhesus monkeys. The wire mother provides milk while the cloth mother offers only contact comfort. (Courtesy of Harry F. Harlow)

ness) to surrogate mothers that provided no comfort other than simple contact. An unexpected finding emerged from this study: Infants preferred a nonlactating cloth surrogate to which they could cling over a wire surrogate that provided milk. The implication is that infant monkeys have an innate tendency to form an attachment to a mother or mother-surrogate that is not based on the provision of nutritional sources of pleasure by the mother. This interpretation is further supported by the observation that an infant monkey rejected by its mother will repeatedly try to make contact with her, even after she has inflicted pain on the infant. Rejection of an infant often occurs when the mother herself was reared without a real mother.

Other investigators studying human infants have supported the view that the tendency of

an infant to form an attachment to the mother is innate. John Bowlby (1958) has described attachment as a species-characteristic behavior. The basic responses that serve to strengthen the bond between infant and mother —sucking, clinging, following, crying, and smiling—are universally seen in healthy infants. In terms of survival value for the species, it seems reasonable that the vulnerable human infant is endowed with relatively stable behavioral means of attracting and sustaining parental care.

INFANT CRYING AND MATERNAL RESPONSE

During the first 10 days after birth, infants cry perhaps 5 to 10 per cent of their waking time. Crying may be an innate behavior that promotes proximity or maintains contact with the mother or other caregivers. Crying is perhaps the most effective attachment behavior, for it arouses alarm or displeasure, followed by attempts to stop the crying, such as picking the baby up and fondling or feeding or talking to the child.

Two generations ago mothers were urged to use strict, not permissive methods in raising their children. Thus the U.S. Children's Bureau recommended not picking a baby up between feedings, for this would teach the child "that crying will get him what he wants, sufficient to make a spoiled, fussy baby, and a household tyrant whose continual demands make a slave of the mother" (U.S. Children's Bureau, 1924, p. 44).

A recent study (Bell & Ainsworth, 1972) has shown, however, that consistently and promptly attending to infant crying leads to a gradual decline in its frequency and duration. The investigators observed infant crying during periodic visits to children's homes during their first year of life. During the first three months the infants tended to cry most frequently when they were out of visual, auditory, or physical contact with other people and tended to be soothed best by close physical contact, as when they were picked up by their mothers and held. Mothers tended to respond to their babies' crying most frequently by picking them up, so the infant and maternal behaviors proved to be well adapted to each other.

By the last three months of the first year, however, the infants tended to cry more frequently when the mother was present, showing that they had become focused on the mother, were attached to her, and were using crying to communicate with her. Those babies whose mothers had been promptly responsive to them tended to cry less frequently than others. They were substituting other means of communication for the crying they had used so much in the first three months. The investigators concluded that responsiveness to crying did not make for spoiled babies. To the contrary, "the single most important factor associated with a decrease in frequency and duration of crying throughout the first year is the promptness with which the mother responds to cries" (p. 1183). Such studies suggest that mothers should respond to their babies' crying by soothing them and attending to their needs. That's what most mothers want to do anyway.

Initially the infant does not distinguish between the mother and other individuals. During the first months the infant normally responds positively to all people. Around the age of seven months the infant recognizes the mother or principal caregiver and shows a marked preference for her company. But at seven to nine months the infant may show distress at being held by a stranger (or even the father), or may cry intensely if the mother is briefly out of sight. As the child matures, attachments are formed to secondary caregivers, usually the father, siblings, and other relatives.

In recent years more and more mothers in this country are working outside the home and depending on others for partial child care. Psychologists agree that the principal caregiver for a child need not be the biological mother. Normal social and personality development can occur when someone other than the mother provides good and loving care. The question of interest is whether multiple-caregiver conditions lead to healthy social development. Do baby-sitters, nurseries, and day-care centers fulfill children's needs? Some psychologists have speculated that a situation involving multiple caregivers might result in impairment of the child's capacity to develop a close, meaningful relationship with another person in later life. The limited data available, however, suggest that this need not be the case. The critical factor in a child's development seems to be the giving of love, comfort, and stimulation by those with whom the child interacts. Obviously if a child is reared with serious neglect, whether by a paid caregiver or by the mother, social and emotional development will be retarded.

In this country most children are still reared in the home by their mothers. The effects of child rearing by day-care centers and other substitute caregivers have not yet been adequately studied. In Israel and Russia, however, where children are often reared in groups outside of the home, normal social and intellectual development seems to take place. In fact, the situation has some advantages: These young children quickly learn to interact with peers and to participate in group activities, opportunities that might not otherwise be available until they reached school age.

Self-Concept

A necessary condition for the development of social behavior is the child's understanding that he or she is a person, a unique individual with certain needs, goals, attitudes, and traits. This statement may seem too obvious to mention, but in fact infants do not possess a self-concept. They regard themselves and others as objects. Gradually they learn that certain objects—people—are agents that cause events to happen. Only then do they begin to differentiate between objects and persons. It is through experience that they begin to understand that they themselves are persons with special significance.

One index of children's self-awareness is

Figure 3-16 An infant's response to his mirror image.

pointed out several specific factors that determine identification. One of these is imitation: Children imitate the people with whom they identify, thereby increasing the similarity between them. You have probably seen a young girl try to hammer a nail when she sees her father do it or sweep the walk when her mother does it. That children readily imitate models has been shown experimentally many times. In one study, children around four years of age were exposed to an adult playing aggressively with a Bobo doll. Following this session the children were mildly frustrated by being prevented from playing with highly attractive toys and then were permitted to play with a Bobo doll like the one used by the aggressive model. These children showed more aggressive behavior directed at the doll than children who were not exposed to the aggressive model (see Figure 3-17). In fact, children who only viewed a film of the model acting agressively with the doll also showed more aggressive behavior than the control group.

Another factor contributing to a child's identification with another person is the child's tendency to share the emotions of that person. If a father is pleased about a promotion at work, his child may be vicariously proud. Or if the father is fired, the child may feel ashamed.

One final factor is the child's desire to possess the model's attractive attributes. A daughter may wish to be a good pianist like her mother, or a son may wish to be tall like his father. The average child identifies first with the mother, then with the same-sexed parent, and later with personal heroes or heroines, like an older child, a teacher, an athlete, or a television personality.

their reactions to their own mirror images (see Figure 3-16). Young infants do not respond to mirror images of themselves, although they may show immediate excitement at seeing their mothers' images. At the age of four to six months infants show interest in their images and treat them as playmates. By the age of six to seven months they attempt to relate the movements of the mirror images to their own movements. They may open and close their mouths or wave their hands while observing the movements in the mirror. Infants show true self-recognition at around one year of age (Ames, 1952).

As children mature, they constantly modify their self-concepts. One process through which this modification occurs is identification. Although the term has various theoretical meanings, **identification** is basically the process of perceiving similarity between oneself and another person. Kagan (1971) has

Another process influencing the self-concept is **gender** or **sex-role identification.** Children soon learn that some children are boys and some are girls, and they know to which of the categories they belong. And not only that; children between the ages of three

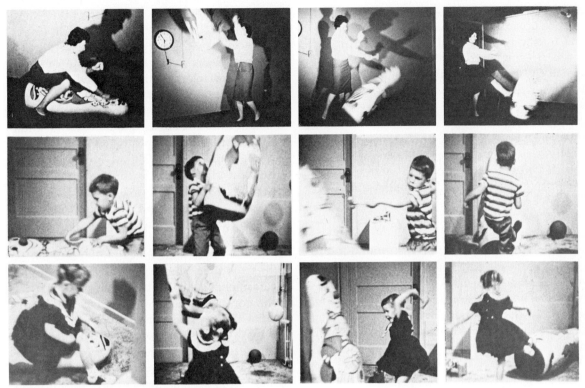

Figure 3-17 Children's imitation of aggressive behavior. In the top photographs, an adult model acts aggressively toward a large plastic doll. In the next two rows, a boy and a girl who have watched the aggressive behavior of the adult show similar aggressive behavior. (Bandura, Ross, & Ross, 1963)

and seven recognize that certain behaviors are thought to be appropriate to girls and others to boys. In our culture, children learn that boys should be strong, aggressive, and independent; girls, on the other hand, should be weak, passive, and dependent. Parents indoctrinate their children with guidelines like "Boys don't cry" and "Girls don't fight." Of course boys do cry and girls do fight, but these **sex-typed behaviors** have different consequences for girls than for boys, and both boys and girls soon learn to tailor their behavior to the sex roles they have been taught.

Whether the difference in behavior of men and women is entirely learned through pressures exerted by society or whether the difference is at least partly innate is a controver-

sial issue. In our culture the characteristics generally associated with men are viewed as superior, and women have long been second-class citizens. Advocates of women's liberation maintain that females are capable of being just as independent, occupationally successful, athletically proficient, and so on as men, if men would only stop telling women they are inferior, and if women would stop believing them.

If boys and girls were not taught sex-typed behaviors, would some differences still exist? Probably they would. Behavioral differences between the sexes can be seen in many species of animals. Other primates exhibit these differences. The male rhesus monkey or baboon shows more independence and aggressive rough-and-tumble play than the female. A difference in sex hormones between human male and female probably accounts, at least in part, for their differences in behavior. The *extent* to which the behavior is hormonally influenced, however, is unknown. And the necessary experiment is difficult to conduct. Even if parents treated their sons and daughters alike, other people would not. Teachers, peers, and relatives also help teach a child sex-role behaviors. If you observe a group of young children in a playground for an hour or two, you are likely to see expressions of gender identification in the children as well as gender indoctrination by caregivers.

A cross-cultural study of sex differences in socialization found that societies in North America and Africa tend to have large sex differences, while certain societies in Oceania, Asia, and South America tend to have small sex differences (Barry, Bacon, & Child, 1957). Small sex differences in some societies suggest the cultural rather than strictly biological nature of the differences.

Our society seems to be moving, at least for a period, in the direction of deemphasizing sex-role behaviors. Girls and boys now dress alike, have similar haircuts, and engage in sports and other activities together. This social change is bound to decrease a child's interest in being "masculine" or "feminine." It will be interesting, if this trend continues, to see the extent of change when today's children reach adulthood. Men may still be somewhat more aggressive and women somewhat more emotionally expressive. Differences of this kind, however, should not prevent men and women from assuming equal roles and responsibilities in society.

Child-Rearing Practices

Over the years people have practiced, and psychologists have advocated, many different child-rearing techniques. As knowledge about child behavior has increased, it has become obvious that no one particular child-rearing technique is best for all children. The important factors in child-rearing, regardless of the particular techniques used, are the existence of a loving relationship between parent and child, consistent enforcement of whatever disciplinary rules exist, and meaningful discipline. The child should see a direct relationship between behaviors and their disciplinary consequences. The instructions for discipline should vary according to the age of the child. A toddler around 18 months will understand only yes and no, but older children should be told why some of their acts meet disapproval.

Reward is a more meaningful disciplinary technique than punishment. Rewarding a particular behavior conveys the message that that behavior is desirable, whereas punishing a behavior, while it tells children that that behavior is undesirable, doesn't tell them what behaviors are acceptable. Children frequently proceed in a trial-and-error fashion until they come across a behavior that does not produce punishment. The difference between punishment and reward as techniques for modifying behavior is more complex than simply a difference in information value, however. Punishment produces anxiety, which also influences behavior. Although psychologists agree that reward is a more desirable technique of modifying behavior than punishment, child rearing requires both. In reality, some undesirable behaviors are bound to occur, and the child must be discouraged from repeating them. It is often helpful if the parent not only discourages the undesirable behavior, but at the same time directs the child's attention to an acceptable behavior.

TOILET TRAINING MADE EASY

The toilet training of young children has always presented problems for parents and often leaves children reacting negatively, sometimes with long-term problems like bed-wetting. No wonder many parents have followed a permissive approach to toilet training! The drawback is that children may not accomplish toilet training by themselves until they are three to five years old, although they are physically capable of controlling their sphincters by about 19 months. But a recent application of instrumental training has proved so successful that toilet-training difficulty should soon be a thing of the past (Azrin & Foxx 1974). Skeptical parents who had been sure the training would not work "characteristically expressed disbelieving pleasure" after trying the program.

Thirty-four normal boys and girls between the ages of 20 and 36 months were trained in this modification program, each in a single day at home or in a trainer's home. The time for complete training ranged, in accordance with age, from two to five hours. Parents and family members left for the day; toys and any other distractions were removed. The children were first instructed thoroughly in all the successive skills required for toileting, such as approaching the potty-chair, lowering the pants, sitting on the chair, urinating, raising the pants, and emptying the pot in the toilet. Frequent urination was stimulated by giving the children two cups of their favorite beverages per hour. The children were also given directed imitation with dolls, practicing all the toileting procedures with them between their own practice trials. At first each step in the process accomplished successfully was reinforced by many rewards: tidbits, verbal praise, smiles, hugs, caresses, applause. General reinforcements included telling the children how pleased their parents, friends, and heroes would be. Negative consequences included reprimands when a child's pants were wet, and practice was given in going to the potty-chair from 10 different locations in the house. Then the child was given time out for five minutes. As trials became more successful, rewards for each specific activity were given only intermittently, and finally were discontinued.

The children had had about six "accidents" a day before training. In the week following training, accidents had decreased by 97 per cent, to about one a week, and this near-zero level continued for a follow-up period of four months. All of the children reacted positively to the training, finding it a very pleasant experience and hugging and kissing the trainer. A few who initially rebelled and threw tantrums soon shifted to positive reactions as they received the training reinforcements. Parents were highly satisfied, although mystified, at how well the program worked compared with their own fumbling efforts. Perhaps we are near the end of conflicts created by toilet training.

Types of parental discipline may be categorized according to two major patterns: love-oriented versus power-assertive techniques and permissive versus restrictive techniques. **Love-oriented techniques** use praise or reasoning as positive approaches for modifying behavior, and threats of withdrawal of love, isolation of the child from the parent, or displays of disappointment for eliminating undesirable behavior. **Power-assertive techniques** use shouting and physical punishment. A review of the effects of various kinds of discipline (Becker, 1964) has shown that children whose parents use love-oriented discipline techniques tend to internalize their reactions to transgressions. That is, they have feelings of guilt, have a sense of responsibility, and exhibit cooperative social behavior. Children whose parents use power-assertive techniques tend to externalize their reactions to transgression. They are more concerned with avoiding punishment than with avoiding the behaviors that bring it about; they tend to blame the punisher rather than themselves, and are generally noncooperative and aggressive.

The success of love-oriented techniques is probably due to the fact that parents who reason with their children usually provide a clear explanation of why the behavior is undesirable (or desirable). The explanation provides the child with training in making explicit moral judgments. Too, the withdrawal of love is a powerful weapon. Children need their parents' love, and its withdrawal tells them more clearly than words that their parents do not find their behavior lovable. Because it is such a powerful weapon, it should be used in moderation. When it is used in excess, children may come to believe that it is they that are unlovable, not some specific unapproved behavior.

The relative failure of the power-assertive technique is probably due to several things. Power-assertive punishment tends to frustrate children, often leading to aggression. Parents who use this technique unfortunately provide models of aggression. Children hear their parents' shouts and feel their blows, and learn to shout and strike others themselves. Power-assertive parents often encourage aggressive behavior in children. They are likely to tell Johnny that if Fred hits him, Johnny should hit back. Since power-assertive techniques tend to be used by basically hostile parents, it is not clear whether the less desirable behaviors associated with this technique are due to the type of discipline or to the fact that the parents are hostile toward the child.

Restrictive techniques of discipline are those that attempt to force children to adhere to their parents' standards. **Permissive techniques,** on the other hand, tend to encourage children to adopt or formulate standards that fit them. In a study of individual differences in temperament at birth, Alexander Thomas and his associates (1970) suggest that "difficult" children usually respond better to rigid, clearly stated rules, while "easy" children usually flourish better with more permissiveness. Restrictiveness during the first three years tends to produce children who are more conforming and more dependent on adults, less aggressive, less dominant and competitive with peers, and less skillful in a variety of behaviors than children allowed more permissiveness. Restrictiveness later in development, however, particularly during adolescence, tends to result in boys who are more competitive and aggressive and in girls who are more passive and dependent, with less achievement mastery. Permissiveness during adolescence

fosters outgoing, sociable, and assertive behaviors with more intellectual striving.

Since each child is an individual, parents need to find the child-rearing technique that is most effective for each child, remembering always that it's no trick at all to turn an easy child into a difficult one by tense, hostile treatment. Most parents are successful by simply following common sense.

WHAT HAPPENED TO YOU?

■ Review the discipline patterns that your parents followed in raising you. Make a list of those discipline incidents that you can recall, starting with most recent ones and working back as far as you can. Early incidents you remember may have been extreme or traumatic. Do love-oriented or power-assertive patterns of discipline predominate, or was your disciplining a combination of the two? Was your disciplining restrictive or permissive, in general? What technique do you envisage that you might tend to use if and when you have children of your own?

Peer Relations

When children enter school they are exposed to an entirely new world. Instead of spending most of their time with their mothers and perhaps older or younger siblings, they are surrounded by other boys and girls of their own age. Peer relationships are easily established, probably because peers have much in common. They are physically very similar (about the same size and build) and they generally have similar interests. Young children play games together all day that would quickly bore adults.

Piaget has observed that children under the age of about seven are mainly aware only of their own needs and their own points of view. Piaget calls this inability to understand that others have outlooks different from one's own **egocentrism.** Children in this age period may be seen playing in a group, but close observation may reveal that each child is playing independently, ignoring the others. As children grow older they become aware of the interests and concerns of others and engage in more cooperative play.

Children around the age of eight or nine, sometimes younger, often have "best friends." They purposively select individuals they enjoy being with. At this age, however, there is a fairly rapid turnover of best friends. A child's best friend may change every two or three weeks. Not until adolescence are friends chosen on the basis of their personal qualities. These friendships are more enduring. During adolescence social relations reach a mature level. The many factors that influence social behavior are discussed in Chapter 17.

SUMMARY

Developmental psychologists study both the physical and psychological growth of the individual from conception to old age. During maturation, changes in behavior occur through the interaction of physiological growth and experience.

Prenatal development follows a regular pattern. By the seventh month of gestation, the human fetus has a chance of survival if it is born prematurely.

Newborn infants possess a wide array of behavioral skills. They demonstrate many inborn reflexes, such as rooting, sucking, and grasping, which have important survival advantages. They also have well-developed perceptual skills. They are born with the ability to see, hear, and smell remarkably well. In fact, they seem to have innate preferences for certain stimuli. Newborns also show individual differences in personality and temperament that tend to be stable characteristics throughout childhood and adolescence.

The principle of maturational readiness proposes that a certain minimum level of physical maturation is a necessary prerequisite for some behaviors. For example, infants cannot learn to walk until their muscles are strong enough to support their weight and their nervous systems have developed sufficiently to coordinate the movements necessary for walking. Stimulation or experience, however, may facilitate physical maturation.

Individuals develop cognitive skills in a relatively orderly sequence. Piaget has outlined four levels of cognitive development: sensorimotor (0–2 years), preoperational (2–6 years), concrete operational (7–12 years), and formal operational (12–15 years). At each stage children expand their cognitive framework through the processes of assimilation and accommodation. One of the principal theses of Piaget's cognitive development theory is that each successive level of cognitive development represents new, qualitatively different cognitive abilities.

Intelligent behavior generally has four characteristics: it involves awareness, it is goal-directed, it is rational, and it has value.

Intelligence is often measured by standardized psychological tests like the Stanford-Binet Intelligence Scale and the Wechsler Adult Intelligence Scale. Intelligence is calculated from these tests by comparing an individual's score on verbal and performance tasks with the scores of a large number of people comprising a standardization group. The results are used to predict the individual's performance in school or work.

Language acquisition begins around 10 months of age as the child begins to understand the meanings of a few words. Around 12 to 18 months the child begins to use several words meaningfully. By the age of five most children have learned most grammatical rules, although their vocabularies are limited. The rapid and orderly acquisition of language by children of all cultures has led to the belief that the capacity for language is a biological predisposition of humans. Chimpanzees have successfully been taught limited nonoral languages. Although their accomplishments have gone far beyond psychologists' expectations (and their maximum potential for language acquisition has not fully been explored yet), they do not possess an inclination to acquire language spontaneously, as human children do.

Among the processes that influence a child's social development are initial attachment to one or more principal caregivers; development of a self-concept, assisted by identification with an adult and by sex-role identification; reaction to discipline; and formation of peer relations.

NOW YOU'RE THE EXPERT

1. List the successive major developments you would expect to see babies make and the approximate age (month or year) at which they would occur.

2. Compare the development of the human being with that of some other kind of animal you know well, like a cat, dog, or bird. Is human development unique in any of the areas discussed in this chapter? In what areas do you find the most striking differences?

3. Do you think development research of the kinds described in this chapter is worthwhile? Why or why not? Which line of research seems most valuable to you and why? How would you suggest that it be pushed further? What experiments could you suggest?

4

Sensory
Processes

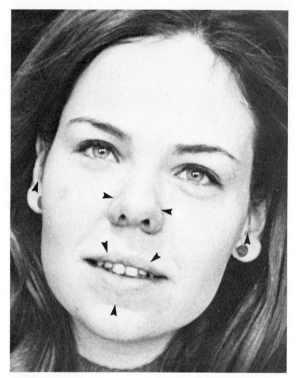

Figure 4-1 The particular areas of the face (arrows) in which long-lasting afterglow sensations usually can be stimulated in the skin. Afterglows may also be found just inside the lower part of the ear and on the lower eyelid.

AFTERGLOW SENSATIONS

■ Sensory systems are investigated by presenting physical stimulation of various kinds to subjects and observing their responses. A simple activity will familiarize you with the basic approach used in studies of all the senses. The activity involves a sensation called an **afterglow,** a tingling-tickling feeling that rises and falls in intensity and may last for a long time after stimulation. Very little is known about afterglows.

Afterglow sensations arise as a result of stimulating certain areas on the face (see Figure 4-1): either side of the nose in the creases between nose and cheek, the upper lip a half-inch or so from the midline and about an eighth of an inch below the lipline, and the chin just under the lower lip. Afterglows may also occur just inside the lower part of the ear, on the lower eyelid, in-

side the tip of the nose, and even on the back of the hand or on a fingertip.

A mirror, some dental floss or stiff thread, and a watch with a second hand are all the equipment needed for this activity. You can produce your own afterglows or have someone else produce them for you.

Poke the end of the floss or thread gently around the skin areas indicated in Figure 4-1, looking in the mirror if you are performing the activity on yourself. You have an afterglow when you feel a tickling-tingling sensation that grows in intensity and continues after the thread is removed. Once you have spotted a place that yields a good afterglow, poke the thread at it, take it away after two seconds, and time the duration of the afterglow. You may find that it almost fades away and then comes back strongly again.

Jot down the duration of the afterglow and repeat the process at the same or another spot 5 to 10 times more, provided you can stand the tickle! (Rubbing the spot will stop the afterglow.)

Now compare your afterglow times with those in the following table:

Afterglow Duration Intervals	Percentage of Subjects
Less than 12 seconds	33%
12 to 59 seconds	20
60 seconds or more	47

These figures were obtained in one of the few investigations of afterglow ever reported (Melzack & Eisenberg, 1968). The "60 seconds or more" group includes a few people who had afterglows lasting as long as 5 to 10 minutes. Some subjects reported afterglows on the sides of their faces opposite the spots poked. Afterglows following stimulation of the lips sometimes shifted position to a point closer to the center of the lips than the actual site of stimulation. And a few subjects reported that when the afterglow had entirely disappeared, a strange sensitive zone, or "zone of awareness," remained in that area of the skin.

Nerve endings in the skin may discharge nerve impulses for up to 10 seconds after stimulation ceases, but afterdischarges for as long as a minute have never been reported. Then how could some afterglows last 5 to 10 minutes? Since the skin regains its normal appearance as soon as the thread is removed, pressure from indented skin or changes in blood pressure caused by the thread do not account for persistence of the afterglows.

The investigators suspect that stimulation of the skin by the thread triggers prolonged activity in the central nervous system; that is, in the spinal cord or brain. The involvement of the brain would help to explain why subjects feel a longer afterglow if it is suggested to them that afterglows tend to persist. The conscious brain is capable of directing attention to specific sensations and is even able to "experience" anticipated, but not real, sensations.

Your awareness of the afterglow may keep returning, making you conscious of many weak sensations in the stimulated area of the skin that ordinarily would not be felt. Feeling itchy all over after one mosquito bite is perhaps similar to the afterglow effect.

ALL THE SENSES

Since the time that animal life first evolved, sensory processes were inevitable. To survive, all organisms, whether unicellular or human, must be aware of what is going on in their external environment. As multicellular organisms evolved, certain portions of the organism's zone of contact with the environment became specialized to receive information about different kinds of environmental events. Thus sense organs of a variety of types developed, their nature dependent on the kind of organism and the special information it needed.

Organisms respond to physical stimuli that reach them. To explain and eventually predict these responses, we need to understand how the sensory mechanisms work and how organisms abstract information from the complex patterns of stimuli they receive. From its very beginning as a science, psychology has been concerned with this problem. Wilhelm Wundt, who founded the first psychology laboratory in Leipzig, Germany, in 1879, specialized in the study of sensation and perception. Since that time probably more has been learned about sensory processes than about any other area of psychology.

The Human Senses

Human beings have at least nine sensory systems. The four most commonly remembered senses are *vision, audition, taste,* and *smell. Touch,* the perception of stimuli through the skin, is one of the **somesthetic (skin) senses,** along with *pain* and *temperature.* To these sensory systems can be added the *vestibular sense,* or the sense of balance, and *kinesthesis,* which is the sense of motion, weight, and position (see Figure 4-2).

Each of the nine sensory systems, called **modalities,** is most sensitive to one particular kind of stimulus energy. The preferred stimulus for the eye is light. A different physical stimulus, such as pressure on the eyeball, sometimes produces visual sensations. A boxer may "see stars" after a blow on his eye. Recent experiments by astronauts on space missions have indicated that cosmic rays, consisting of nuclear particles, sometimes produce brief light sensations as they pass through the eyes (Budinger, Bichsel, & Tobias, 1971; Pinsky, Osborne, Hoffman, & Bailey, 1975).

Sensory information cannot be processed in its original form, which is some type of physical energy such as light rays or sound waves. The primary function of the sensory system is to convert this original information into nerve impulses and to transmit these impulses to the brain. In the brain the impulses are processed and somehow translated into the experiences we call sensations and perceptions.

Each sensory system has a part that is sensitive to a certain kind or kinds of physical stimulation. This part is called the **receptor.** Receptors transform physical energy into neural energy through the process of **transduction.** Auditory receptors, for example, are cells that transduce the mechanical energy of sound waves into neural messages.

Figure 4-2 The sense organs for such modalities as vision, hearing, and kinesthetic and vestibular senses have become highly specialized, as seen in these dancers.

As early as 1826 a German scientist, Johannes Müller, suggested the theory of "specific nerve energies." In its general outline, the theory is still accepted today. According to this theory, sensory quality depends on *which type of nerve* is stimulated, not on the *means* by

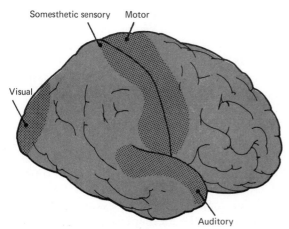

Figure 4-3 Right cerebral hemisphere showing localization of sensory and motor functions (hatched areas).

which it is stimulated. When receptors in the eye are stimulated, whether by light rays, pressure, or cosmic rays, the sensory quality is light. This constant relationship between type of nerve stimulated and kind of sensation experienced occurs because each nerve projects to a specific area in the brain that is responsible for only one kind of sensation. For example, visual sensations are produced by stimulation of receptors in the eye, creating nerve impulses that pass along the optic nerve to the visual area of the cortex. Differences in sensation between sensory modalities are thus determined by different functions of the areas in the brain to which the sensory pathways lead (see Figure 4-3).

Characteristics of Sensory Systems

One basic characteristic of all sensory systems is that they require the delivery of certain minimum stimulus intensities before a sensation will be evoked. This minimal stimulus inten-

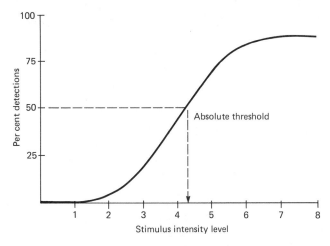

Figure 4-4 Absolute threshold determination. An observer is asked to judge the presence or absence of a stimulus of varying intensities. The absolute threshold is determined by dropping a perpendicular line from the threshold curve at the point on the graph where it passes 50 per cent detection. In this example, the absolute threshold is 4.25 stimulus units.

sity is known as the **absolute threshold** of the sensory system. The concept of absolute threshold does not mean that below a certain intensity the receptor is not activated at all; it simply means that lower intensities of the stimulus are not strong enough to arouse sufficient nervous activity in the receptor to evoke a sensation.

How are absolute thresholds measured? In a commonly used procedure called the **method of limits,** the experimenter alternately increases and decreases the intensity of a stimulus in small steps while the observer reports the presence or absence of a sensation. The absolute threshold is determined by measuring the minimum intensity level at which the observer detects the presence of the stimulus on at least 50 per cent of the presentations (see Figure 4-4). Notice in Figure 4-4 that the change from no detection to detection as stimulus intensity increases is not a sudden one. At threshold levels, a stimulus is detected on only some of its presentations.

Detection theory has shown that stimulus detection depends on several factors (Tanner & Swets, 1954). The theory assumes that a stimulus always occurs against a background of "noise"; that is, any sensations other than the signal. Noise arises from internal sources, such as spontaneous neural activity in the sensory systems, as well as from extraneous en-

vironmental sources. The intensity of noise varies from moment to moment.

When stimulus intensity is at or near threshold, a person is often unsure whether or not a signal has occurred. According to detection theory, the individual in this situation does not know whether to interpret the intensity of sensory neural activity as indicative of noise alone or of signal plus noise. Since the intensity of noise varies from moment to moment, this decision is not easy (see Figure 4-5).

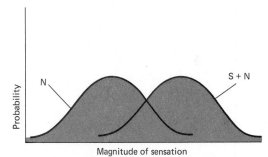

Figure 4-5 Hypothetical distributions of noise (N) and signal plus noise (S + N). The curves represent the probabilities of sensations of given magnitudes when only noise (random neural activity and extraneous stimuli) is present and when a signal is superimposed on noise. If the magnitude on the signal is, for example, 4 units, the S + N curve is displaced 4 units to the right of the N curve. At each observation an observer must decide whether the given magnitude of sensation represents noise (no stimulus) or signal plus noise (stimulus). (Tanner & Swets, 1954)

The greater the intensity of a signal in relation to the intensity of background noise, the easier the signal is to detect. Forced to make a decision, people sometimes say that they detect a signal when in fact the stimulus is not present. This error is called a **false alarm.** The individual mistakes the background neural activity for neural activity arising from the stimulus. A **hit** occurs when the individual correctly detects the presence of a stimulus.

Several cognitive factors may influence a decision on whether a signal is present or not. One important consideration is the *consequence of the decision.* If people have something to gain by correctly detecting a signal but nothing to lose by a false alarm, they may adopt a loose criterion for detection. That is, they may have a tendency to say that they detect a stimulus when only background noise exists. For example, a subject in an experiment is asked to indicate whether she detects a flash of light of threshold intensity in a series of trials in which the stimulus is presented during a random one-half of the trials. The subject is told that she will receive a quarter for every hit. She would be expected to adopt a loose criterion for detection and guess "signal" in some trials in which only noise is present. Naturally, the experimenter would hope that the subject would be honest and not guess "signal" in every trial. One way to eliminate this possibility is to restrict the number of times the subject can indicate a signal.

If, however, the consequence of a false alarm is undesirable, the subject may adopt a rigid criterion for detection. If she is told that the number of false alarms will be subtracted from the number of hits in determining her cash return, she will probably guess signals on fewer trials (see Figure 4-6).

A second cognitive factor that influences detection is *expectation of a signal.* The expectation that a signal probably will occur tends to shift the detection criterion in the loose direction. For example, a little boy afraid of being left alone at home may think he hears his

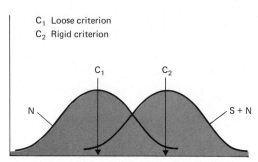

Figure 4-6 Hypothetical criteria for deciding between noise (N) and signal plus noise (S + N). The arrow indicates the minimum magnitude of sensation the subjects report as signal for each criterion. Criterion C_1 is extremely loose or reckless. Subjects maximize the number of detections, but also make a large number of false alarms. Criterion C_2 is very conservative. Subjects almost never make a false alarm, but they miss about half the signals present.

parents' car with every street noise that occurs.

All sensory systems also have a **difference threshold.** This is the minimum change in stimulus intensity that will make a subject report a difference in sensation, for example, "Sound B is louder than sound A." Difference thresholds are determined by measuring the minimum intensity *change* that is detected by the observer on at least 50 per cent of the presentations.

The study under controlled laboratory conditions of the relationship between changes in values of physical stimuli and changes in sensations is called **psychophysics** ("psycho" indicates mental sensations and "physics" indicates physical stimuli). The relationship between stimuli and sensations is of the greatest significance in penetrating the mysteries of the interplay between mind and body.

TESTING WEBER'S LAW

■ Any science attempts to state the relationship between the variables that it investigates, as you noted in Chapter 1. When such relationships hold uniformly and precisely for two or more variables, they are known as **laws.**

One of the first such quantitative laws in

psychology, Weber's law, was proposed in 1846. This law states a specific relationship between changes in intensity of a physical stimulus and subsequent changes in the sensations that result. Changes in the physical stimulus might be, for example, varying intensities of light, sound, or heat, or varying weights of stones. Changes in the resulting sensations would be increased or decreased brightness, loudness, temperature, or weight, respectively.

Weber's law states that a "just noticeable difference" (abbreviated jnd) in sensation intensity is a constant percentage of the intensity of the physical stimulus that produces it. The more intense the stimulus, the larger will be the stimulus change required to bring about a just noticeable difference in the observer's sensation. A stone weighing 1 pound may be noticeably different in weight from a stone weighing 2 pounds. A stone weighing 20 pounds, however, is probably not noticeably lighter than one weighing 21 pounds, even though the absolute difference in weight is the same in both cases. In the first case the increase in weight (from 1 to 2 pounds) was 100 per cent of the original weight, while in the second case the increase (from 20 to 21 pounds) was only 5 per cent. According to Weber's law, an increase in weight from 20 to 40 pounds should be as readily detectable as an increase from 1 to 2 because the change in intensity in both cases is the same percentage of the original stimulus.

You can check this variation in jnd's yourself with a set of small objects you can hold in your hand, like matchbooks or marbles. Hold one matchbook or marble in one hand and two in the other, and jiggle them a little. The difference in weight is easily detected. Then hold 10 in one hand and 11 in the other, and you will probably observe no noticeable difference. Better yet, try this comparison by having a friend place the items in your hands without telling you which hand has more. The foreknowledge might influence your judgment of the weights. Make it 10 against 12, then 13, and so on until you can just notice the difference. It is apparent that the larger or more intense the stimulus, the greater the jnd, although you have not used the method of limits here to discover the exact percentage.

Although Weber's law applies fairly well in the middle range of intensity for the various sensory modalities, it does not hold so well for extremes of low and high intensity. Furthermore, the precise relationship between stimulus intensity and magnitude of sensation depends on the particular kind of sensation being measured and the procedure for measuring it.

A second basic characteristic of sensory systems is that they adapt to constant stimulation. When a stimulus continues, the receptors respond less and less to it until partial or complete **receptor adaptation** has been reached. Some receptors adapt within a fraction of a second; others do not adapt for many hours.

VISION

TESTING THE ROLE OF VISION

■ You can check out the key role of vision and learn a little about its interconnections with the other senses by blindfolding yourself for 20 to 30 minutes. Try walking slowly around a room or rooms with which you are familiar (not across Times Square!). Try to find some small objects in the room. Then turn about several times in one spot until you have lost your sense of direction and try to find it again. Eat a meal, take a shower, water the plants—do anything you would normally be doing. How many of these activities are hampered or made completely impossible by your lack of vision? How much do you get out of a TV program without vision? What do you miss in conversations with others without your sight?

Through his study of the positions of the planets, the astronomer Johannes Kepler became interested in vision and came to some conclusions about it. He wrote in 1604 that "vision is brought about by pictures of the thing seen being formed on the white concave surface of the retina."

The French philosopher René Descartes experimented with this idea a little later in the seventeenth century. He scraped off the back outside layer of the eye of an ox to make it transparent and placed the eye in a hole in a window shutter. An inverted image of the outside view was cast on the retina of the ox's eye. Indeed, the eye does receive an inverted picture of the external environment on its retina. The picture is transduced into neural impulses and the complex neural activity reaching the brain is interpreted as a visual experience.

More neurons are concerned with processing visual information than any other kind of information received by the other senses. Let's take a trip through the visual system to see how it processes the information it receives. This exercise should demonstrate how the nervous system is designed to receive stimulation from the environment, code various properties of the stimulus, and translate the information into sensory experiences.

The Eye

The eye is a remarkable mechanism for transducing light. Light is a narrow band of radiant energy in the **electromagnetic spectrum,** which spans all wavelengths of electromagnetic en-

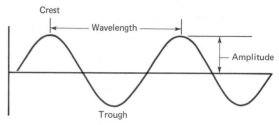

Figure 4-8 A sinusoidal wave showing wavelength and amplitude. Wavelength is the distance between successive crests or troughs. Amplitude is one-half the vertical distance between a crest and trough.

ergy (see Figure 4-7). Light can be pictured as consisting of waves with a peak-to-peak distance, called the **wavelength,** between successive crests or troughs (see Figure 4-8). The wavelengths of visible light range from 380 to 780 nanometers (abbreviated nm). One nm is one billionth of a meter. Within this range, differences in wavelength (physical stimulus) are sensed as differences in **color** (sensation). As shown in Figure 4-7, the visible spectrum ranges from the shorter wavelengths, which you see as blue, to the longer wavelengths, which you see as red. Just as wavelength determines the color of light, the **amplitude** of

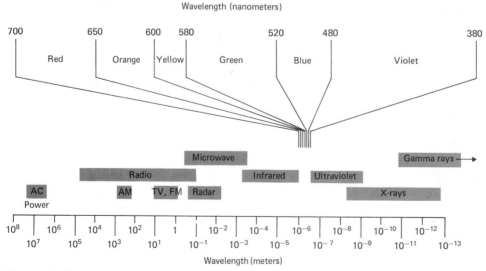

Figure 4-7 The electromagnetic spectrum. The visual portion is enlarged to show the relationship between wavelength and color.

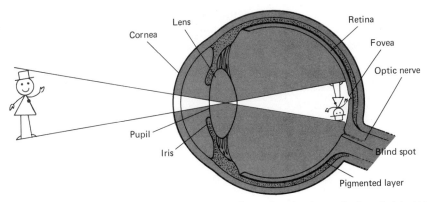

Figure 4-9 Cross section of the eye showing the major structures. An inverted image is projected on the retina.

the wave form, which is half the distance from trough to crest, determines the sensation of **brightness.**

The eye is nearly spherical in shape and is shown cross-sectioned in Figure 4-9. When light passes through the eye, it first passes through the transparent **cornea,** which protects the eye and also does the initial focusing of light. The amount of light entering the eye through the opening of the **pupil** is regulated by muscular expansion and contraction of the **iris.** The **lens** further focuses the light to give an inverted image on the **retina.** The black **pigmented layer** behind the retina prevents reflection of light within the eye. Albinos lack pigment in this layer and thus have poor detail vision because light entering the eye is reflected in all directions on the retina. Finally, in the spot where the nerve fibers pass out of the eye, there are no receptors. This is the eye's **blind spot.**

LOCATE YOUR BLIND SPOT

■ You can locate the blind spot in your left eye by closing your *right* eye and staring at the *right* circle in Figure 4-10. Hold the book about a foot and a half from your eye and move the book slowly back and forth. When the circle on the left vanishes, it is projected on the blind spot. Following the same procedure, locate the blind spot in your right eye. Close your *left* eye and look at the circle on the *left.* Now look at the circles with both eyes open. You are not ordinarily aware of your blind spots because one eye can usually see what falls into the other's blind spot.

The Retinal Transducer

Strangely enough, although they are not directly involved in vision, the tiny arteries, capillaries, and veins carrying blood to and from the retina are found near the surface of the inner side of the retina *on top of* the light re-

Figure 4-10 Locating your blind spot. With the book held about 18 inches in front of you, close your right eye and look at the right circle. Move the book from side to side until the left circle disappears. In this position, the image falls on the blind spot of the retina where the optic nerve leaves the eye.

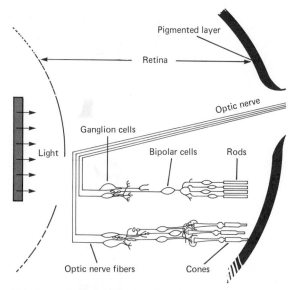

Figure 4-11 Schematized representation of the retina with its layers greatly enlarged. The rods and cones at the back of the retina are stimulated by light. Neural activity passes from the rods and cones forward in the retina to the bipolar and ganglion cells. Axons from the ganglion cells form the fibers of the optic nerve.

ceptors. (This makes the vessels of the circulatory system in the eye easily accessible for medical study. Their condition may be a clue to a wide variety of medical problems.) Light from the lens must pass through this system—as well as through the nerve fibers, ganglion cells, and bipolar cells in the retina—before striking the rods and cones next to the pigmented layer (see Figure 4-11). Fortunately, these layers do not greatly reduce the light-responding efficiency of the retina.

The **rods** and **cones** are the light receptors. These cells contain special light-sensitive pigments that decompose in the "twinkling of an eye" on exposure to light. The exact manner in which this photochemical process excites the rods and cones is unknown, but is under intensive investigation.

Rods and cones differ in a number of important ways. First, the rods are sensitive to very dim illumination, whereas the cones require more intense light to be stimulated.

Second, the cones respond differentially to different wavelengths of light and thus are color receptors. The rods respond equally to all wavelengths. Third, the cones are capable of transmitting more detailed information than the rods.

The ability to discriminate and transmit detailed information in the visual field is called **visual acuity.** The maximum visual acuity of the human eye is about 1.3 times the width of an average cone in the fovea (see below). This degree of acuity is like distinguishing two bright pinpoint spots of light as separate sources when they are 10 meters away and only 1 millimeter apart!

TEST YOUR VISUAL ACUITY

■ The finer the detail that can be seen, or the finer the points of light that can be separated, the greater is a person's visual acuity. Is your visual acuity great enough to separate the tiny dots that make up all the squares in Figure 4-12? Working from left to right, in how many of the photos can you see dots? If you don't see the dots in some of the squares, use a magnifying glass and you will.

Information from the rods and cones is sent to **bipolar cells** and **ganglion cells** in the retina. In general, multiple rods and cones are connected to each bipolar cell and multiple bipolar cells converge on each ganglion cell. On the average, 120 rods and 7 cones send information (through bipolar cells) to each one of the approximately 1 million ganglion cells in the retina. This means that one ganglion cell must pass on information from the approximately 127 receptor cells feeding into it. It does not pass on the summed activity of the many cells converging on it, but selects specific information from the activity of all the cells. In the retina, sensory information goes through a great deal of processing before it leaves the eye. The axons of ganglion cells make up the optic nerve connecting each eye with the brain (see Figure 4-11).

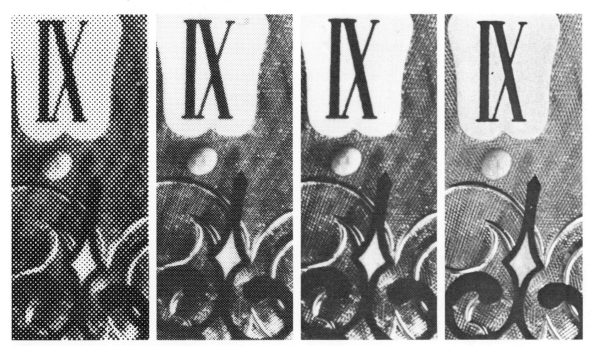

Figure 4-12 In how many copies of the photograph from left to right can you clearly see dots? The dots are beyond the limit of your visual acuity in those copies in which you fail to resolve them. When printed with small enough dots, photographs appear normal, for visual acuity is not sufficient to detect the separate dots.

The greatest visual acuity is obtained when light is focused on a small area of the retina directly behind the pupil called the **fovea** (see Figure 4-9). This small area, only 1.5 millimeters in diameter, produces vision of finer detail than the periphery of the retina does, primarily because the fovea is almost entirely composed of cones. The cones are densely packed, making high visual acuity possible because stimuli close together in space succeed in exciting different cones. Also, cones converge on bipolar cells with an optimum ratio (sometimes 1:1). Therefore, two cones close together in the fovea that are stimulated by light from separate sources send their information through different fibers (axons) to the brain. High visual acuity also occurs in the fovea because the inner layers of the retina—including ganglion cells, bipolar cells, and blood vessels—are displaced to one side of

the fovea so that light passes unimpeded to the cones.

Journey to the Brain

There is a systematic crossing of nerve fibers in the **optic chiasma** ("chiasma" is from the Greek word meaning crosspiece or crossing), where the optic nerves from each eye meet. At this point, fibers from the *left* half of each retina pass to the left **lateral geniculate body** of the thalamus, and fibers from the *right* half of each retina pass to the right lateral geniculate body. From here the left and right visual pathways project to their final destination in the **visual cortex,** lying mainly within the cleft of the occipital lobe that separates the two brain hemispheres. Pathways from the right and left geniculate bodies project to the right and left hemispheres, respectively. Trace out

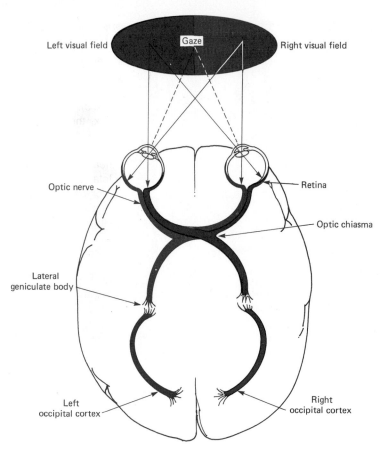

Figure 4-13 Visual pathways. With the gaze directed straight ahead, images of objects in the right visual field impinge on the left half of each retina; images from the left visual field impinge on the right half of each retina. Information about objects in either the left or right visual field is projected to the cortex in the opposite occipital lobe.

this crossing in Figure 4-13, from the right and left visual fields for each eye through the optic chiasma to the geniculate bodies and the occipital lobes of the cerebral cortex.

VISUALIZE THE OPTIC CHIASMA

■ To visualize the optic chiasma, try this: Place two small objects on a table, and draw them at the top of a sheet of paper. Then, below these drawings, draw your two eyes focusing straight ahead between the objects and indicate the pathways through which messages about the objects are carried to your lateral geniculate bodies and finally to your left and right occipital lobes. Refer back to Figure 4-13 only if you are stuck.

Each eye has its own visual field. The visual fields from both eyes largely overlap in the center, and corresponding images in the two fields are fused by the areas of the brain receiving information from both eyes. After all, you view one visual scene even though you use two eyes to do it. Is it a different visual scene from the one you see with one eye alone? Try it and see.

Every area of the retina sends visual information to a particular area of the visual cortex. Much more research is required, however, before the intricacies of the functions of cells in the visual system will be clarified.

Recordings of nerve impulses from single cells in the lateral geniculate bodies and visual cortex of monkeys have shown that these cells are selectively activated by particular patterns of light on the retina (Hubel & Wiesel, 1968). (To record from a single cell at any location in the brain, a thin wire, insulated except for the tip, is carefully passed through the brain to the desired location. This **electrode** picks up the neural activity of the cell at its tip and transmits it to electronic recording instruments to which the electrode is connected. Neural activity is often recorded on a paper chart. A deflection of the recording pen moving over the paper indicates that the cell has fired a nerve impulse.) For example, a cell in the visual cortex may be activated most (fire most nerve impulses) when a vertical slit of light shines across the retinal receptors that send information to that cortical cell. Another cortical cell may be activated most by a horizontal pattern of light on the retinal area. Since there is a direct correspondence between the *pattern* of light on the retina and activation of cortical cells, each visual stimulus produces unique cortical activity, which is somehow experienced as "seeing" that particular stimulus.

Total destruction of the human visual cortex seems to produce complete blindness. In other animals, the effects of such destruction are less clear. Following destruction of an animal's visual cortex, the animal can make simple visual discriminations, such as between two extreme levels of brightness, but cannot discriminate patterns. The animal may have visual pathways projecting to an area other than the visual cortex that can analyze simple visual information.

TOTALLY BLIND?

Even the firm belief that human beings are totally blind without the visual cortex has recently been challenged by an experiment with four human subjects (Poppel, Held, & Frost, 1973). With widespread injury to the visual cortex, the subjects could see only small portions of their visual fields. A light was flashed in an area where they could see it, followed at once by another light well outside this area, where they were totally blind. They were asked to indicate by motion of their eyes the location of the second light in relation to the first light. One subject demanded, "How can I look at something I haven't seen?"

Nevertheless, the subjects looked toward the correct location much more often than would happen by chance, even though they could not "see" the second light. The investigators suggest that some central visual mechanism may still be functioning in these subjects, despite their blindness. Perhaps lower brain centers, below the level of consciousness, were receiving information about both lights and governing the correct choice.

Visual Adaptation

Receptors in the eye, like all receptors, undergo sensory adaptation, reacting less and less to continuing stimulation. If the rods and cones of the retina receive constant stimulation, they gradually adapt, and the observer perceives an image of a formless gray field of light. In order to prevent this retinal adaptation, the eye engages in minute movements that shift the location of the image on the retina from 30 to 100 times *per second* (see Figure 4-14).

A second form of adaptation by the eye is called **dark adaptation.** This process involves an adjustment of the eye to low light intensity by an enlarging of the pupil, a buildup of visual pigments in the receptors, and a shift from cone vision to rod vision. Everyone has had the experience of entering a dark theater and being unable to see the rows of seats, the

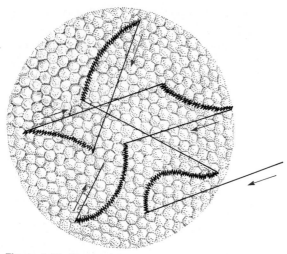

Figure 4-14 Types of tiny movements of the eye include (a) drifts, represented by curved lines, (b) tremors in the drifts, shown in the waviness of the curved lines, and (c) flicks, shown by the straight lines, moving back toward the center of vision as the arrows indicate. (Pritchard, 1961)

people, and the walls for a few minutes until the eyes have adjusted to the darkness. Under dark conditions, the visual pigments in the rods and cones undergo only a low level of decomposition. Thus larger amounts of visual pigments are available in the eye. The likelihood of light-initiated decomposition of pigments and activation of receptors is increased by the increased amounts of visual pigments that accumulate during dark exposure. The rods are capable of greater dark adaptation than the cones, as shown in Figure 4-15. When you leave a dark theater, your eyes are so sensitive to light that daylight is nearly painful until the buildup of visual pigments has been reduced by decomposition and the eyes have undergone **light adaptation.**

TEST YOUR LIGHT AND DARK ADAPTATION

■ At night, take a book from a brightly lighted room into a fairly dark room. It will help, too, if you have a watch or clock you can observe in the dark. Otherwise you have to estimate the time.

Look about you and at the open book minute by minute. Do you note the rapid dark adaptation during the first five minutes? Does adaptation begin to slow between 10 and 15 minutes, and then change very little? When you go back into the lighted room, how long does light adaptation take?

How Is Color Sensed?

As early as the eighteenth century it was known that all the colors of the visual spectrum could be created by mixing three primary colors in various proportions. In 1802 the English physician Thomas Young proposed a trichromatic theory of color vision that suggested that there are three separate color-sensitive mechanisms in the eye.

Today we know that the color-sensitive mechanisms are the visual pigments of the cones. As Young predicted, three different kinds of cones have been identified, each sen-

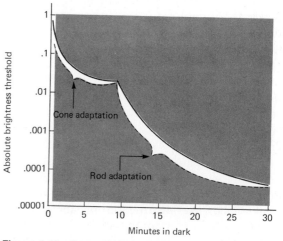

Figure 4-15 Curve of dark adaptation by the cones and rods. The subject looks at a light until the retina is fully light adapted. The subject is then placed in darkness and the eyes' sensitivity to flashes of light is tested. The curve represents the minimum light intensity that is detectable at various times in the dark. The initial part of the curve represents adaptation of the cones, and the second part adaptation of the rods.

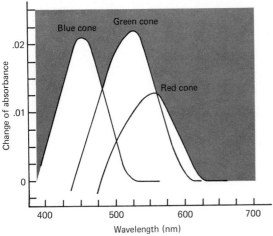

Figure 4-16 Sensitivity of cones to various wavelengths of light. The curves show light absorption (representing sensitivity) by the three color-receptive cones of the human retina. Each of the cone types is maximally sensitive to a different portion of the color spectrum. Although the "red cone" is most sensitive to yellow, it is the only cone type sensitive to the red portion of the spectrum. (Brown & Wald, 1964)

sitive to a different range of wavelengths (see Figure 4-16). Certain cones respond most to blue light, with an increased rate of nerve impulses, while others respond most to green and still others respond to red light.

Sensations of other colors result from stimulation of various ratios of the different types of cones. A blue-green light of 470 nm stimulates equally both blue and green cone types (see Figure 4-16). However, a blue-green light of 500 nm stimulates green-type cones more than blue-type cones. The 500 nm light appears greener than the 470 nm light because the green type cones are stimulated more by the 500 nm light. The sensation of yellow (570 nm) results from the stimulation of red and green cone types. The sensation of red (650 nm) results from stimulation of only red-type cones. Equal stimulation of blue, green, and red cones produces the sensation of seeing white.

Certain ganglion and lateral geniculate cells (and maybe cortical cells) respond to various wavelengths in an "opponent" manner, responding with excitation (greater firing of nerve impulses) to one wavelength and with inhibition (less firing) to another. These cells seem to be organized in the following opponent pairs: red-green, yellow-blue, and light-dark. For example, one cell may be excited most by red light and inhibited completely by green; colors similar to red produce a moderate amount of excitation, while colors similar to green produce less excitation. Or a cell may be excited by green and inhibited by red. Similarly, yellow and blue are linked to form an opponent system. The third opponent pair is a broadly sensitive light-dark system. Through opponent pairs, cells in the visual system are capable of complex coding of stimulus wavelength properties.

If you look steadily at a particular color for a while and then glance at a white surface, the **negative afterimage** is that of the complementary color. The afterimage is probably a result of light adaptation of certain cone types. Fixating on a red object, for example, causes decomposition of the pigment for red and buildup of the pigments for blue and green. Subsequently, looking at a white surface causes a blue-green afterimage, the result of relatively more stimulation of the blue and green cones, which now have more pigment available for decomposition.

TEST YOUR AFTERIMAGES

■ You can check the colors of your afterimages by focusing steadily on a small colored object for about half a minute and then switching your gaze to a sheet of white paper beside the object. Use plain, bright, solid-colored objects, and try the experiment with as many objects of different colors as you can find.

In **color blindness,** the normal sensitivity to the range of colors is altered. About 9 per cent of the population has some degree of color blindness, males 32 times more frequently than females. Complete color blindness, a relatively rare condition, results from the lack of functioning red, green, and blue types of cones. The person with this condition therefore sees the world only in shades of gray. More commonly, a single type of color cone is missing or functions abnormally. A person who lacks either red or green cones is said to be red-green color blind, since such a person is unable to distinguish changes in wavelengths between red and green. (Refer back to Figure 4-16 to see why this is the case.) Absence of blue cones, or blue color blindness, is rare.

Cortical Effects of Infant Visual Experience

Early visual experience can influence the organization of the visual system. Animals whose vision is blocked for several months after birth often develop permanent deficits in vision. Kittens that are permitted to see only horizontal or vertical bars after birth lack cortical activity when presented with bars at right angles to those previously shown them. Bars oriented like the ones to which the kittens had been exposed at an early age, however, do evoke normal cortical activity during testing (Blakemore & Cooper, 1970). There may be a sensitive stage in development during which the lack of a particular kind of visual experience leads to a *deterioration* of cells designed for a specific function. Also, visual experience at this sensitive stage may *stimulate* the development of highly specific anatomical and functional connections in the brain.

AUDITION

ACOUSTIC CONFUSION

■ Here is an activity that will show how closely related the senses of vision and audition are. Find a page from a newspaper or magazine with several columns of regular-size type. Sit down with it

Figure 4-17   Arrangement of materials for the acoustic confusion activity, including a newspaper, pen or pencil, and a watch (or clock) with a second hand.

at a table or desk and have a pencil and a watch or clock with a second hand ready (see Figure 4-17). You can do the timing yourself, although it is easier and likely to be more accurate if you have someone else keep time for you. Don't read anything on the page yet.

Now read down from the top of a column for four minutes, crossing out all the letter *e*'s as rapidly as you can. Get as much done as you can within the four minutes. *Do not read farther until you have done the experiment.*

Now you're ready to analyze your results. Count the lines in which you crossed out the *e*'s. Lines in newspapers and magazines vary in width and size of type, so anywhere from 25 to 50 should have been covered. If you've only done 10 to 15 lines, you have gone too slowly for good results.

Now read very slowly through the lines in which you crossed out the *e*'s. Look at each word. Circle any *e*'s that you missed. Unless you are very exceptional, or went too slowly and carefully, you will have missed quite a few. List the words in which you missed *e*'s and underline the *e*'s you missed in them. Look over this list of words. Do you notice anything in particular about the *e*'s you missed? What conclusion can you draw?

Do your conclusions about the *e*'s you missed agree with those of a British scientist (Corcoran, 1966, 1967) who has been studying such errors?

• The *e*'s that are missed are more likely to come at the end of words, or next to or close to the end, rather than at or near the beginning of words.
• The *e* in the word "the" is likely to be missed often. It comes at the end of the word, and the word is so common that we may not even notice it.
• The *e* is most often missed in words in which it is silent, that is, not pronounced. The *e* is silent in "are" and "pole," for example. The missing of such silent letters indicates the acoustic or auditory factor involved in this experiment.

Missing the silent *e*'s is one kind of **acoustic confusion.** As we read words visually, apparently we also read them or scan them acoustically. We hear them as well as see them. Do you recognize this silent saying of words to yourself as you read this sentence? Perhaps you even read some of the words aloud as you crossed out the *e*'s. Some people do. When the *e* or other letters in words are not heard because they are not sounded, they are more likely to be missed than letters that are sounded.

In many of our activities the sense of hearing is closely linked to the sense of seeing. Acoustic confusion is just one example of this linkage.

Sound Waves and Sound Sensations

Audition is called a "mechanoreceptive" sense, for the ear responds to mechanical vibrations caused by sound waves. A **sound wave** is a sequence of condensations (states of maximum pressure) and rarefactions (states of minimum pressure) of air molecules set in motion by a moving body (see Figure 4-18). The vibrating strings of a guitar create many sound waves, which we hear as music. In a similar manner, vibration of the vocal cords in the throat create sound waves. The tap of a pencil or the stamp of a foot will also create sound waves. These travel at about 1100 feet per second (750 miles per hour) in the air at sea level and 4.5 times faster in water. When you hear

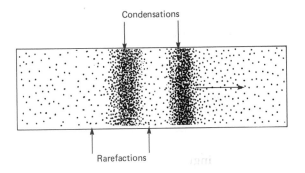

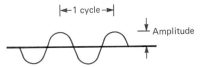

Figure 4-18 A sinusoidal wave showing the relationship between condensations and rarefactions of air particles and characteristics of a sound wave. The high points of the curve may be regarded as condensations, when the eardrum is pushed inward, and low points correspond to rarefactions, when the eardrum is pushed outward. One wave cycle is that portion of a regularly recurring wave that is completed once.

thunder crashing five seconds after the flash, you can figure that the lightning was about a mile away.

Like light waves, sound waves vary in frequency and amplitude. The **frequency** of a sound wave is the number of condensations (or rarefactions) that passes a given point in a second (see Figure 4-18). One condensation with its ensuing rarefaction is called one "cycle," and frequency is expressed in the unit of measurement called a Hertz (abbreviated Hz). A Hertz is one cycle per second. The human ear can detect frequencies of from 20 to 20,000 Hz. Frequencies below 20 per second are felt as vibrations, not detected as sound, and frequencies higher than 20,000 Hz are not audible to humans, although some animals, like dogs, can detect them. Dolphins are sensitive to sound with frequencies up to 150,000 Hz. The ear discriminates sounds of different frequencies as having different **pitch.** As you

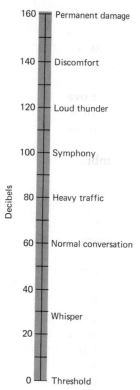

Figure 4-19 Intensities of common sounds expressed in decibels.

go up the scale on the piano the sound waves have higher pitches because of greater frequencies. Middle C on the piano has a frequency of 256 Hz.

The **amplitude** of a sound wave determines the loudness of the sound you hear (see Figure 4-18). Amplitude, measured in terms of pressure, represents the distance the sound wave makes the eardrum move. The unit used in measuring loudness is called the **decibel** (abbreviated db), which is a measure of the relative loudness of two sound intensities. As intensity or loudness of a sound increases, its decibel rating increases (see Figure 4-19). You can think of zero decibels as the sound intensity level at absolute threshold.

When many frequencies are combined randomly in one sound, the result is **noise,** a jumble of sounds in which it is difficult to distinguish individual pitches. Sounds differ in purity. A tuning fork gives rise to the sensation of a pure tone because it vibrates with a single frequency. Most sound sources (outside the laboratory) vibrate with more than one frequency. Take middle C on the piano, for example. Although the whole piano string vibrates at a frequency of 256 Hz, each half of the string vibrates separately at a rate of 512 Hz, each third at 768 Hz, and each quarter at 1024 Hz. These additional vibrations are called overtones, which are multiples of the basic frequency of a given sound. The overtones have less amplitude than the basic frequency and are important in our identification of sound sources, for they give sound its characteristic quality, or **timbre.** The overtones from a violin and a guitar playing notes of the same basic frequency are so different in timbre that you can distinguish them at once by their characteristic patterns of overtones.

PITCH, LOUDNESS, TIMBRE

■ Sound sensations have three primary characteristics. To distinguish these characteristics for yourself, take a wooden pencil and a plastic pen and tap them on a tabletop or some other hard object. Is there a difference in *pitch* between them?

Strike one harder than the other, to observe the difference in *loudness.*

When you tap them both in sequence, can you observe a difference in *timbre?* You might check this by having someone else tap them separately while you shut your eyes. Can you identify them correctly by their pitch and timbre?

The Ear

The complex structure of the ear (see Figure 4-20) looks like a science fiction contraption. But the ear is remarkably efficient in receiving sound waves, in discriminating their frequencies, overtones, amplitudes, and times of arrival, and in transmitting this mass of in-

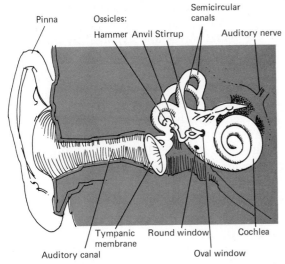

Figure 4-20 Cross section of the ear showing the major structures. The semicircular canals are involved in the sense of balance, not in hearing.

formation through the auditory nerve to the brain. The ordinary hi-fi system cannot compete with the human ear in transmitting auditory information. Hi-fi distorts many sounds, loses the full range of frequencies, and lacks delicate overtones easily picked up by normal ears.

The **auditory canal** acts as a resonator for the sound waves entering it, amplifying them by 5 to 10 db in the middle frequency range. The canal also protects the tympanic membrane from injury and from humidity and temperature changes that tend to distort the sounds. The **tympanic membrane,** with an area of about 60 square mm, is set in motion by the vibrations produced by sound waves. The vibrations are passed from the tympanic membrane to the ossicles.

The **ossicles** are three small bones of the middle ear, suspended by ligaments so that they transmit the vibrations to the inner ear. The **hammer,** attached to the tympanic membrane, makes the **anvil** vibrate, and this in turn vibrates the **stirrup,** which is attached to the oval window of the cochlea (see below). With this transfer of vibrations through the

middle ear, the ossicle lever system increases the force of the vibrations 1.3 times. In addition, the smaller surface area of the oval window, only about 3.2 square mm, as compared to the tympanic membrane, increases the force of the vibrations of the oval window. If it were not for this increase in force, about 98 per cent of the intensity of the sound wave would be lost through reflection of the sound waves from the tympanic membrane back into the air.

The **cochlea** is a coiled tube that contains the **basilar membrane** stretched throughout its length and suspended in a fluid. Inward movement of the **oval window** causes the fluid in the cochlea to move. It also increases the pressure in the cochlea and causes the **round window** to bulge outward. When this occurs, the wave of movement of the fluid makes the basilar membrane vibrate. The receptor hair cells in the **organ of Corti** on the basilar membrane are bent and stimulated by the movement of the membrane (see Figure 4-21). Stimulation of the hair cells in turn excites the **spiral ganglion cells,** which send nerve impulses along the **auditory nerve.** This nerve is composed of the axons of some 28,000 spiral ganglion cells.

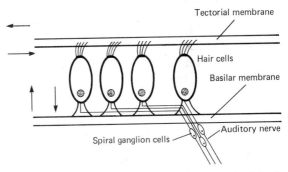

Figure 4-21 Schematized drawing of the organ of Corti within the cochlea of the inner ear. The hairs in the organ of Corti are bent by motion of the cochlear fluid and vibration of the basilar membrane. Up-and-down vibration of the basilar membrane causes a side-to-side movement of the tectorial membrane and a bending of the hairs embedded in it. The hair cells stimulate the spiral ganglion cells to produce nerve impulses.

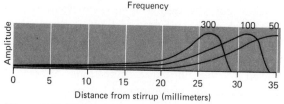

Figure 4-22 The points of maximum displacement of the basilar membrane are found at greater distances from the stirrup as the frequencies of the sound decreases. (Von Békésy, 1947)

As motion of the fluid in the cochlea travels along the basilar membrane, different parts of the membrane vibrate maximally at different frequencies of tone. Vibrations of high frequency cause maximum movement of a region of the basilar membrane close to its base at the oval window, whereas vibrations of lower frequencies cause displacement farther along the membrane (see Figure 4-22). The central nervous system identifies the pitch of an auditory stimulus on the basis of the activation of specific receptors along the basilar membrane.

The Auditory Pathway

Like a long-distance phone call that is transmitted through one microwave station after another, the auditory nerve passes through a number of relay stations before it reaches its final destination in the auditory cortex in the temporal lobe. The auditory pathway from each ear projects to both right and left temporal lobes (see Figure 4-3).

Cells in the auditory cortex are involved in an amazingly intricate analysis of stimuli. Some cortical cells are activated simply by tones of "best frequency" for them. Others respond to a very broad range of stimuli with more than one best frequency. Still others respond most to tones of constantly changing frequency. About one-third of the cells in the auditory cortex are so specialized that they can be stimulated only by such complex sounds as

voice tones. This organization is strikingly similar to that of the visual system, where cells in the visual cortex are activated by particular patterns of light on the retina.

When a person's auditory cortex is destroyed, almost total deafness results. However, cats whose auditory cortices have been destroyed not only can detect normal threshold sounds, but can even discriminate their frequencies. If destruction of the auditory cortices were indeed complete in these cases, somehow discrimination of tones must have occurred in lower brain centers.

OTHER SENSES

The Mystery of Taste

The way in which our taste sense functions is still a great mystery and is the subject of many conflicting theories. The vital function of the sense of taste, however, is clear: it allows organisms to discriminate various foods from nonfoods or poisons. Like a hen, which does not know how it lays an egg but does a good job of it, we can taste very well without being able to explain how we do it.

Taste buds containing the taste receptor cells are scattered around the soft and hard palates and in the upper throat, but are mostly concentrated on the tongue. Each of the 10,000 or so taste buds on the tongue contains about 20 **taste cells,** arranged around a minute taste pore (see Figure 4-23). Taste cells are "chemoreceptors," stimulated by chemical substances in the saliva when it reaches the several taste hairs protruding from each cell. But just how the chemicals excite the taste cells is basically unknown. Theories based on size, shape, weight, chemical group, and electric charge of the chemicals have been proposed. A characteristic that explains one type of taste may not explain another. While the electrical charge of sour things gives them their characteristic taste, sweetness seems to have something to do with the shape of the substance's molecules.

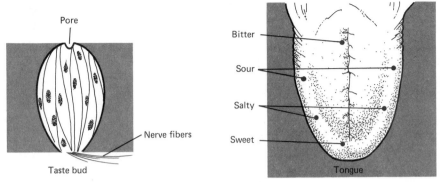

Figure 4-23 Simplified drawing of a taste bud and the tongue. Taste buds maximally sensitive to sweet, bitter, salty, and sour tastes have different locations on the tongue.

At least four primary taste sensations can be discriminated: bitter, sweet, salty, and sour. Probably a different type of receptor cell is associated with each of the four primary tastes. Other tastes may be composed of unique combinations of these primary sensations. Recordings of neural responses of single taste receptors have shown that most receptors respond preferentially to one type of stimulus, although they usually respond to a lesser degree to other stimuli. This property is similar to that of the retina's cone receptors, which have "best wavelengths" but respond to other wavelengths as well. Cells responding to sweet taste are located principally on the tip of the tongue; those responding to sour taste are on its two sides; and those responding to bitter taste are on the back of the tongue (see Figure 4-23). Salty taste is detected over the entire tongue. The final destination for the taste pathway is an area of the cortex in the parietal lobe.

Taste preferences probably result from differentiating mechanisms located in the brain rather than in the taste buds. In both humans and many other animals, food preference depends to some extent on the nutritional needs of the body. A rat with its adrenal glands removed would die in a week or two if it were fed a normal diet. The adrenal glands control the level of salts in the body. With an insuf-ficient amount of salt in its system, the rat will automatically select drinking water with a high concentration of salt in preference to plain water (Richter, 1942). Similarly, it has been shown that infants allowed to select their own diets from a "cafeteria" selection of foods will choose diets that may not be balanced on any given day but that are generally balanced over periods of a week or more (Davis, 1928).

Smell Is Primitive

The sense of smell is one of the most important sensory systems for many animals, but it is far less significant for humans than vision or hearing. The principal structures for smelling are shown in Figure 4-24. The receptors for the smell sensations are **olfactory cells** located in the olfactory membrane in the upper nasal cavity. Although this membrane covers an area only about the size of a dime, it contains about 600,000 such special cells. These cells have large numbers of olfactory hairs, which are stimulated by gaseous odors, consisting of substances in the air, given off by all kinds of odorants, from perfumed to decayed.

Like the other sense modalities, our smell receptors adapt to odors. If the olfactory cells are exposed to an odor for many minutes, the smell sensation becomes less intense and noteworthy. Adaptation of smell receptors

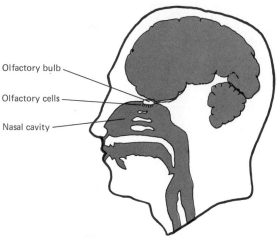

Figure 4-24 Cross section of the nasal passages showing the olfactory cells. Taking a large sniff causes air to pass the receptors.

may be frustrating if you are trying to detect the presence of leaking gas or smoke in your house.

A study of the sensitivity of olfactory receptor cells has shown that, like taste receptors, specialized smell receptors may be differentially sensitive to different types of odors. Many classifications have been attempted for the primary basic odors, from which combinations of other more complex odors may be built. One recent system identifies the primary odors as camphor-like, musky, floral, pepperminty, ethereal, pungent, and putrid, with the first five having characteristic odoriferous effects based on the shape and size of the molecules involved and the last two having distinguishable electric charges determining their characteristic effects on the nose. This system has led to the successful synthesis of more complex odors by combinations of these primary ones.

The sensory system for smell in mammals has several primitive characteristics. Unlike other sensory systems, each olfactory receptor sends an axon directly to its final destination in the brain without routing the information through any intervening cells. As a result, no processing of olfactory information occurs

along the sensory pathway. The final projection area is an old region of the cortex, the olfactory bulb. All other sensory modalities have final projection areas in the neocortex, the latest region of the cortex to evolve.

Receptors Crowd the Skin

The somesthetic (skin) senses include three senses activated by stimulation of the skin surface in a variety of ways: touch, pain, and temperature.

Receptors that detect touch are found most densely packed in the fingertips, lips, and other areas capable of spatial discrimination of pressure. (You worked with such receptors producing afterglows at the opening of this chapter.) Activation of the receptor is usually achieved by displacement of the skin in the region of the receptor. Vibration of the tissue, a form of touch stimulation, activates special receptors that are sensitive only to rapid stimulation. These receptors do not detect continuous touch, for they adapt to continuous stimulation within a fraction of a second.

Temperatures within the range of 30° to 45° C activate receptors for warmth in the skin, whereas temperatures in the range of 15° to 35° C activate receptors for cold. Notice in Figure 4-25 that cold receptors are stimulated by

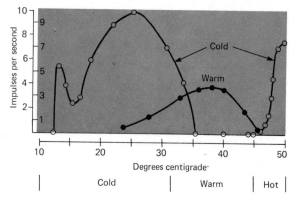

Figure 4-25 Frequencies of discharge of a cold receptor (open circles) and a warm receptor (filled circles) to temperatures between 10 and 50° centigrade. (Zotterman, 1953)

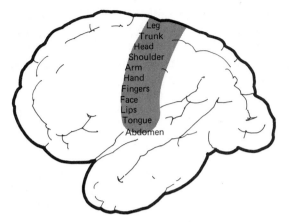

Figure 4-26 Representation of different parts of the body in the somesthetic sensory cortex.

very high temperatures as well as by low ones. This explains why high temperatures feel almost like freezing cold at the first instant of stimulation, an experience called **paradoxical cold.** Temperatures beyond the extremes of 10° and 48° C cause stimulation of pain receptors.

Although a variety of types of stimulation cause pain, the characteristic they have in common is that they produce tissue damage. Probably pain results from the release of a chemical, possibly histamine or bradykinin, from injured cells.

Somesthetic sensory pathways pass from the skin to the spinal cord, and from there to the thalamus and cortex on the side of the body opposite the site of stimulation. To a great extent, nerve fibers in the spinal cord are segregated according to modality. Thus damage to the spinal cord may result in a particular sensory loss while other types of sensation are unchanged.

The projection of nerve fibers to the somesthetic sensory area of the parietal lobe is orderly, so that each body region is represented in a specific cortical area (see Figure 4-26). The size of the cortical area representing any body region is directly proportional to the number of sensory receptors in that part of the body. Cortical damage in this area often produces little change in absolute sensory threshold for the part of the body represented in the damaged area. However, detailed and complex synthesis of sensory information, such as that involved in comparing two stimuli, is disrupted.

The somesthetic sensory cortex is responsible for perceived body image. Damage to this cortical area may result in curious disturbances in awareness of one's own body. A person affected with damage in the sensory cortical area representing the left arm not only loses sensory information from the arm, but also may have no awareness of that arm and may even claim that the arm belongs to someone else. Although severing all somatic nerves in an arm produces complete sensory loss for the arm, in this case the self-image of the arm is not lost. The role of the sensory cortex in determining body awareness remains an intriguing mystery.

The Vestibular Sense

The vestibular apparatus in the inner ear detects sensations concerned with movement and changes in orientation of the head. The major structures of the apparatus are the semicircular canals, the utricle, and the saccule (see Figure 4-27). They are very small. The canals, for example, are only one-hundredth of an inch in inner diameter.

The three **semicircular canals** are arranged

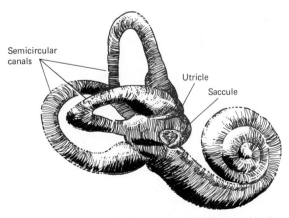

Figure 4-27 Drawing of the vestibular apparatus showing the semicircular canals, saccule, and utricle.

at right angles to each other. They detect the rotation of a person's head, or changes in the rate of rotation. The bending of receptor hair cells by fluid motion in the canals makes possible this detection. When the head begins to turn in any given direction, it stimulates hair cells of the particular canal that lies in the plane of the movement.

The function of the **utricle** is to detect changes in the position of the head with respect to the direction of gravity. When the head changes orientation, small particles in the fluid of the utricle move and bend receptor hair cells. The hair cells are oriented in several directions in the utricle so that varied positions of the head cause stimulation of different hair cells. The pattern of excitation of the hair cells allows the brain to identify the position of the head with respect to gravity. The **saccule** is probably nonfunctional in humans.

The vestibular pathway projects upward to the posterior portion of the temporal lobe. This area of the cortex is probably responsible for our awareness of the direction and speed of movement of our heads. A person who has lost the function of the vestibular apparatus manages to maintain equilibrium without much difficulty as long as the eyes are kept open. Visual cues, in addition to vestibular cues, may be used to establish balance.

The experience of "weightlessness" by astronauts in orbit about the earth sometimes has led to motion sickness. The fluids and particles in the inner ear are thrown out of kilter under weightless conditions, and sharp movements of the head may bring on nausea. Sensory adaptation apparently occurs in most cases, however. All three astronauts in the second Skylab mission experienced early motion sickness, but had adapted to it after a few days of their 60-day mission in space.

Kinesthesis

The term **kinesthesis** means the sense of orientation of the various parts of the body with respect to each other as well as the sense of rates of movement of the body parts. The **kinesthetic receptors** are located in and near the more than 100 body joints. They are stimulated strongly when a joint is suddenly moved, after which the discharge rate is a function of the speed and the extent of movement. Receptors in muscles, which detect the degree of contraction, also contribute to the kinesthesis.

Kinesthetic information is received by the posterior portion of the somesthetic sensory cortex of the parietal lobe. Without this information, you would be unaware of the position and movement of parts of your body and would have difficulty in maintaining posture and controlling voluntary movements.

THE PROBLEM OF SENSORY DEPRIVATION

Our need for receiving varied sensory information extends greatly beyond our need to be informed of details of our changing environment. It appears that varied sensory stimulation is necessary for maintenance of normal functioning of the brain.

In one of the first controlled studies of sensory deprivation (Bexton, Heron, & Scott, 1954), college students were paid to do nothing but lie comfortably on a bed with minimum sensory stimulation for as long as they cared to stay. Most subjects continued the experiment for three to six days. They wore translucent plastic visors that transmitted only diffuse light and cotton gloves with cardboard extensions to minimize touch sensations, and their heads rested on U-shaped foam pillows that masked low sounds (see Figure 4-28). Their only activities were eating and going to the toilet. Before and after the isolation, tests of simple arithmetic, anagrams, spatial block designs, speed of copying written passages, and so on were conducted on each subject. In almost every case, performance was poorer after the isolation.

The most striking results consisted of verbal reports of the experience obtained during post-isolation interviews. The subjects reported

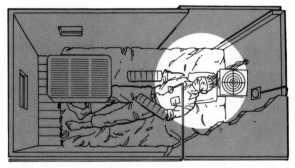

Figure 4-28 Sensory isolation chamber as seen from above. An air-conditioner is shown at the upper left and a fan at the upper right. In the center a microphone is suspended by which the subject could report experiences. The subject wore cuffs to prevent somesthetic sensations from the hands, a plastic shield over the eyes to prevent pattern vision, and a U-shaped cushion over the ears to reduce noise levels. Here the ear cushion has been removed so that EEG wires could be taped to the head. (Heron, 1957)

that they became extremely irritable or had mood swings from depression to giddiness and that they were unable to think coherently. Some experienced hallucinations (sensory experience without physical stimulation). One subject "saw" prehistoric animals walking about in a jungle. Another "heard" a music box playing over and over again. One subject reported that he felt as though his head were detached from his body. Recordings of brain wave activity before, during, and after the isolation period showed a slowing of brain wave frequency in the occipital region after 48 hours of deprivation. (See Chapter 6 for a discussion of brain wave activity.) The slowing persisted three hours after isolation.

Many later experiments have found similar effects of sensory deprivation. In one experiment (Zubek, Welch, & Saunders, 1963), subjects were isolated for 14 days. Recordings of brain wave activity showed that the slower frequency waves produced by isolation persisted for a week after isolation, with reports from the subjects of a lingering loss in motivation to engage in routine physical and mental activities.

Observations like these from sensory depri-

vation experiments have led to the hypothesis that the brain depends on continuous stimulus input for normal functioning. Without the arousal that results from continuous stimulation, brain functions become disorganized and behavior becomes abnormal. Some psychologists believe that several severe behavior disorders (schizophrenia and infantile autism) may be products of dysfunction of the brain's arousal system. (See Chapter 15 for a discussion of schizophrenia and infantile autism.) It seems that each of us is likely to experience mental disturbances under conditions of prolonged sensory deprivation.

SUMMARY

Organisms need to be aware of their environment in order to survive. Human beings have at least nine sensory systems: vision, audition, taste, smell, touch, pain, temperature, the vestibular sense, and kinesthesis. Each sensory modality responds preferentially to one kind of stimulus energy.

Sensory receptors transduce physical energy into neural activity. The sensation resulting from the neural activity depends on the part of the brain that has been stimulated by neural messages from receptors.

All sensory systems have thresholds. Detection theory predicts how cognitive factors, as well as stimulus conditions, can influence stimulus detection. Psychophysics is the study of the relationship between physical stimuli and the sensations they produce. Weber's law is an example of a psychophysical law.

Vision is one of our most important senses. Receptors in the eye, the rods and cones, are activated by energy from the electromagnetic spectrum, or light. Neural messages from the receptors are sent to bipolar and ganglion cells in the retina, from there to the lateral geniculate body in the thalamus, and finally to the visual cortex of the occipital lobe. The optic nerves from each eye cross in such a way that neural activity from the right half of each retina passes to the occipital cortex of the right hemisphere. The left half of each retina sends information to the left hemisphere.

Processing of sensory information begins in the retina itself. Ganglion cells respond selectively to patterns of light on the retina.

Sensory adaptation occurs when a receptor responds less and less to continuing stimulation. The eye engages in minute movements to prevent retinal adaptation by constantly shifting the location of images on the retina. Dark adaptation occurs when the eyes adjust to low levels of light intensity. Light adaptation occurs under reverse conditions.

The cones discriminate colors through their selective sensitivity to specific wavelengths of light. "Blue" cones respond most to wavelengths around 440 nm, "green" cones to 540 nm, and "red" cones to 590 nm. Sensations of other colors result from specific ratios of activity from the three basic cone types.

Visual experience during an early, sensitive stage of development may modify the function of cells in the visual system.

The ears respond to sound waves. Vibrations produced by sound waves set in motion the tympanic membrane, the ossicles, and the oval window of the cochlea. Movement of the oval window produces movement of the fluid in the cochlea, stimulating the hair cells of the organ of Corti on the basilar membrane. Excitation of the hair cells is transmitted to the spiral ganglion cells, and from there along the auditory nerve to the auditory cortex in the temporal lobe. The discrimination of pitch depends on what receptors are stimulated. High-frequency tones stimulate receptors on the basilar membrane close to the base of the cochlea; tones of lower frequency stimulate receptors farther along the basilar membrane.

Taste results from activation of taste cells on the tongue. Receptors for bitter, sweet, salty, and sour tastes are differentially distributed on the tongue. Taste preference is probably a phenomenon of the central nervous system, rather than of receptors.

Olfactory cells in the upper nasal cavity respond to gaseous odors. Olfactory information is sent to an old region of the cortex called the olfactory bulb.

Somesthetic receptors in the skin are activated by touch, pain, and temperature. The area of the cortex responsible for somesthetic sensations is the anterior part of the parietal lobe in the hemisphere opposite to the side of the body from which the nerve pathways arise. Within this sensory area, each body region has a specific representation.

The vestibular apparatus in the inner ear detects changes in the orientation of the head. This information is important for the maintenance of a sense of balance. The kinesthetic receptors, found in and around body joints, detect changes in positions of body extremities.

DO IT YOURSELF

1. Think of one or two of the most exciting situations you have ever experienced. What senses were involved, what sensations, and what was their intensity? Why was the experience so exciting for you?

2. Arm yourself with a pencil and paper, sit down anywhere, and make headings for each of your nine sensory systems or modalities. Then list the sensations involved with each modality, giving your attention first to one, then to another, and so on. Review the receptors involved for each modality, the physical stimuli, the sensory process in the receptor, the pathway to your brain, and the region affected there, leading finally to your actual sensations.

3. Think of an experience you have had in which you were extremely bored. What was the circumstance? What sensory stimulation was present? Do you think you had adapted to a monotonous sensory environment? Did you feel agitated?

5

Perception

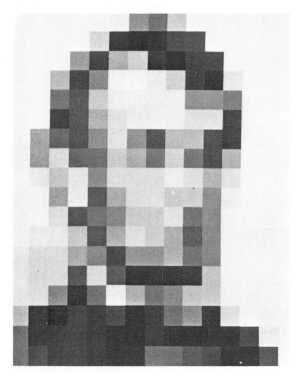

Figure 5-1 Probably from normal reading distance you can make nothing of this computer-processed block pattern of variously shaded squares. What does it become from a distance of several feet? At what distance do you find that it just begins to make sense visually to you? A variety of computer-drawn photographs of this kind have been used in investigating the factors that improve visual stimulus detectability or recognition. (Courtesy of L. D. Harmon)

The stimulation of sensory receptors produces nervous impulses in the central nervous system that are somehow transformed into sensations of all varieties that ebb and flow in conscious awareness. **Perception** is the experience of objects, events, or relationships obtained by extracting information from and interpreting sensations. (Although the term "perception" means understanding or comprehending in everyday usage, its meaning is different in psychology. To psychologists, perception means assigning meaning to sensory stimuli. Many simple perceptions occur automatically without the perceiver's comprehension.) Look at Figure 5-1. At a proper dis-

tance, your interpretation of the patches of light makes it into a meaningful picture for you. The relationship between sensation and perception is always direct; that is, sensory content or quality is always part of perception. Interpreting the meaning of sensory information, however, involves processes other than sensory content alone, processes like attention, expectation, motivation, and memory.

SENSATION VS. PERCEPTION

■ Open a book and stand it or prop it on a desk or table so you can view the open pages from a distance. Move 10 to 15 feet away from the pages and describe the way they look to you. Then move slowly closer, until you can make out some of the words. Move still closer until you can easily read sentences on the page. Describe the way the page looks to you now.

At the farthest distance from the book, you had visual perceptions of it as such — as an object you could identify as a book, or perhaps even as a particular book — but the page was simply a gray-black rectangular or trapezoidal shape against a background of white. These were your visual sensations of the page at that distance. When you came closer, you could visually perceive certain words, and when you came closer still you could perceive words grouped into sentences and read them as such. With your past experience in reading, you were able to interpret the visual sensations of the page as words and sentences. *Perception* occurred when you immediately interpreted your *sensations* of the words, recognized their meanings, and grasped what they were communicating.

One way to distinguish perception from sensation is to consider instances in which you perceive, or interpret, stimuli incorrectly so that your perception of the stimulus does not match the actual stimulus situation. Suppose you are in a large department store. Among the people shopping you spot your old friend Fred. You run up to Fred only to find that the person is not Fred at all. You have perceived Fred but he is not there. Such cases of mistaken identity occur when the person actually present resembles in some way the person perceived. Or suppose you are driving down the road on a foggy day and you think you see a dog run into the road. As you get closer you are relieved to find that it isn't a dog, it's only a piece of brown paper. Once again sensory information is interpreted as being something it is not.

A historical misinterpretation of sensations is the appearance of the motion of sun, moon, and stars through the sky from east to west. As you know, eventually it was discovered that this appearance is due in reality to the rotation of the earth on its own axis from west to east, making it look from our viewpoint on the earth's surface as if the bright objects in the heavens are moving. (*Actually* the moon moves eastward about 12 degrees a day in its orbit of the earth, but the earth's rotation makes the moon *appear* to move westward.) In the past, errors of perception led to doubts about the ability of human beings to know the world and helped to create the distinction between appearance and reality that underlies many Platonic Western philosophies and mystic Eastern religions.

PERCEPTUAL PROCESSES

Several perceptual phenomena have already been mentioned in Chapter 3. It was noted that infants seem to be able to perceive the distance of objects and to locate the source of a sound in space at a very early age. The following discussion of the perceptual processes behind these phenomena should make it clear why sensory information requires an interpretation on the part of the organism.

Distance Perception

Even though the retina of the eye is itself a nearly flat, two-dimensional structure, we perceive a three-dimensional world around us. The location of any object in the environment can be described in terms of three rela-

tionships to the observer: vertical position (up–down), horizontal position (left–right), and distance (near–far). You recall from Chapter 4 that images of the external world fall on specific areas of the retina in an upside-down, reversed position. An object in the observer's lower right visual field falls on the upper left side of each retina of the observer. Thus information about the vertical and horizontal relationships of an object is conveyed to the observer by the location of the activated receptors on the retina. But no retinal receptors respond to distance as such. Rather, a number of stimuli in the environment must provide information concerning the spatial locations of distant objects. What are these stimuli that serve as cues, or signs, of distance?

Take a moment to think of as many visual cues as possible that indicate distance. Visual cues for distance can be divided into two categories: those derived from vision with one eye, or **monocular vision,** and those that require vision with both eyes or **binocular vision.** The former condition, called **monocular distance or depth perception,** provides the most cues. Probably the most important monocular cue for judging the distance of a familiar object is *known size.* Images of objects located farther in the distance are smaller on the retina than those of objects close at hand (see Figure 5-2). This decrease in retinal image size is used as a cue for distance. Therefore, cars that seem like tiny bugs from an airplane because of their small retinal images are interpreted to be a long distance from the observer.

A second monocular cue is **interposition.** When two objects are in the same line of vision, the nearer object at least partially blocks the view of the more distant one. The object that occludes, or cuts off, the view of the other is judged to be closer (see Figure 5-3).

A **gradient** is a regular change in a property that occurs with changes in distance; for example, you feel a regular decrease, or gradient, in temperature as you move farther away from a fire in a fireplace. *Visual texture and density gradients* are other monocular cues for distance.

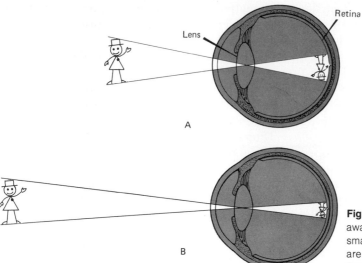

Figure 5-2 Retinal image sizes. The farther away an object is from the viewing eye, the smaller its retinal image. The figures in A and B are the same size, but the more distant figure in B produces a smaller retinal image.

Objects nearer to the observer are seen in more detail than objects located at a distance. Objects nearer the observer also appear larger. The way these cues may be used to judge depth is illustrated in Figure 5-4.

Another monocular cue that provides significant information about the distance of objects is **motion parallax,** the apparent motion of objects as the observer turns his head from side to side. The farther away an object is, the smaller its motion parallax.

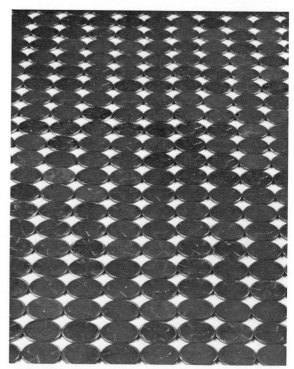

Figure 5-4 Texture gradient, implying depth. The coins in the foreground appear larger and more textured than the coins in the back.

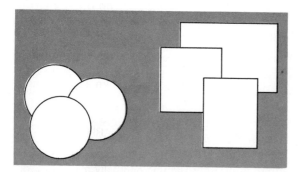

Figure 5-3 Interposition of circles and squares providing depth cues. The incomplete forms appear to be behind the full forms.

Still another monocular cue for distance occurs when the eyes focus the image of an object on the retina by means of a change in the shape of the lens, called **accommodation.** When an object in the visual field is near, the lens becomes thick to maintain a clear focus, whereas when an object is at a distance, the lens becomes thin. Since you are not aware of making the lens of your eye thicker or thinner, how does this take place? It all goes on without your conscious assistance. The eye muscles that control the thickness of the lens contain sensory receptors that detect muscular tension. Proprioceptive stimuli (stimuli arising from internal sources such as muscles or joints) from these receptors provide internal cues for the distance of objects within about 25 feet of the observer. When focusing on objects beyond this distance, the lens is relatively flat and does not change its accommodation shape.

The distance cues so far considered may be provided by one eye alone, in monocular vision. However, two cues for distance perception are obtained only with binocular vision, when both eyes are looking at an object,

giving **binocular depth perception.** The first of these cues is provided by proprioceptive feedback from eye muscles, as in accommodation. In this case, the eye muscles are those involved in **convergence,** the moving inward of the eyes toward each other when an object of fixation is within about 20 feet of an observer. Since the eyes are separated from each other by about 2.5 inches, they must move inward slightly when fixating on a near object. As you know, if you look at the tip of your nose, your eyes become crossed. Muscle activity controlling the convergence of the two eyes provides cues for judging the distance of objects. (Convergence can occur with monocular vision, but it does so less frequently because the observer usually adjusts his or her head to center the viewing object in front of a single viewing eye.) You can be conscious of stimuli arising from convergence, as opposed to accommodation. If you hold a pencil vertically about a foot from your eyes and then bring it in toward your nose, you can feel the pull of your eye muscles inward as you try to keep a focus on the pencil.

The second cue of distance obtained from binocular vision results from receiving slightly different views of the world from each eye. For all practical purposes, the visual field of the left eye overlaps completely, or is identical with, the visual field of the right eye when the eyes are focused on objects at a distance greater than 1000 to 2000 feet. At that distance the separation of the two eyes makes no difference in the visual world seen by each of the two eyes. Less overlap occurs, however, when the eyes are focused on objects nearer and nearer to the observer. The resultant difference between the views from the two eyes is known as **binocular disparity.**

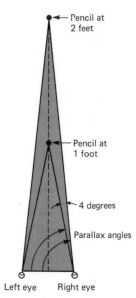

Figure 5-5 The parallax angle of a pencil viewed at a distance of two feet is greater by about four degrees than that of a pencil viewed at one foot. For this reason, the greater the distance of an object, the less the binocular disparity.

your fingers sc that the printing on the pencil can barely be seen on the left with your left eye. Hold the pencil steady, close your left eye, and open your right eye. The writing should not be visible at all from the right eye alone. Repeat the procedure, holding the pencil at arm's length. Do you notice that the two views of the pencil change less when it is at a greater distance? The reason is that the angles of the two eyes to the object, called the **parallax angles**, are larger the greater the distance of the object, as shown in Figure 5-5. The brain is able to interpret the difference between the views from the two eyes, or the binocular disparity, as a cue for distance. The smaller the discrepancy, the greater the perceived distance of the object.

Experiments in which the ability to judge distance is compared for the same subject under monocular and then under binocular conditions show that distance perception is superior with binocular vision, provided that monocular cues are weak. In these experiments, subjects are asked to judge the distance of an unfamiliar object in order to eliminate

Figure 5-6 Belvedere. (Engraving by M. C. Escher)

the effect of familiarity with the size of the object. Under dim illumination, which minimizes the influence of monocular cues, the increased accuracy obtained with binocular vision indicates that binocular cues provide particularly useful information for distance perception.

Take a look at the impossible house "Belvedere" in Figure 5-6. In this drawing, cues for distance are confusing. Can you identify the aspects of the drawing that are impossible?

INFANTS AND APES CAN DO IT

When they perceive two identical objects by vision and by touch, both adults and children as young as four years can recognize that they are

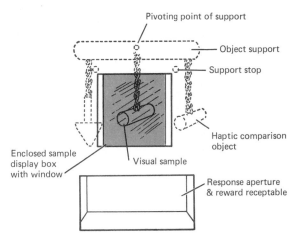

Pivoting point of support

Object support

Support stop

Haptic comparison object

Enclosed sample display box with window

Visual sample

Response aperture & reward receptacle

Figure 5-7 Apparatus for testing cross modality between touch and vision in apes. The apes could touch but not see the objects on left and right (dotted forms) and see but not touch the object in the center (solid form). (Davenport & Rogers, 1970)

identical (Blank, Altman, & Bridger, 1968). Such ability to recognize identity across sense modes, as from touch to vision, is called **cross-modal perception.** Cross-modal matching of objects has been explained by the hypothesis that the person gives the visual and tactile objects the same name, thereby using language to relate perceptions arising from two sensory modalities.

This language hypothesis has been cast into doubt, however, by an experiment in which five apes (three chimpanzees and two orangutans) were tested for cross-modality matching (Davenport & Rogers, 1970). The apes were trained to match objects in an apparatus (see Figure 5-7) that allowed them to see but not touch one object and to touch but not see two objects. One of the objects they could touch was identical to the object they could see; the other was a completely different shape. After feeling both objects, the apes were rewarded with a tidbit of food if they tugged down on the tactile object that matched the visual object, thereby matching across the modalities of touch and vision. The apes were perfectly capable of doing this task without the use of language, with an accuracy of 90 per cent or better. Furthermore, they were not simply learning to select matching stimuli on the basis of repeated experiences with the same set of stimuli.

Once they had learned the matching purpose of the task, they could select the matching objects in 40 sets of objects that had never been used before. Also, when they felt the object that matched the visual object first, they simply tugged it without bothering to feel the other object, further suggesting that they somehow had grasped the principle of "Match tactile *A* with visual *A*" without the use of language. Apes can even match an object that is felt with a photograph of that object on its first presentation (Davenport & Rogers, 1971).

Other researchers inferred that if apes had this cross-modal perceptual ability, then human infants should have it too (Bryant, Jones, Claxton, & Perkins, 1972). They tried a cross-modality problem on 120 infants, averaging eight months of age. The modalities were vision and touch, and the task used the two pairs of shapes shown in Figure 5-8, one ellipsoidal (A) and one cuboidal (B). One member of each pair had a large groove in one side so that it could be distinguished from the other member of the pair. As all parents know, infants are particularly attracted to objects that make a noise, so the experimenters rigged up bleepers within the objects so that they would bleep when tilted.

Each infant subject sat on the mother's lap in front of a table. First the infant was shown both objects of the pair, one with a groove in it and one without a groove. After the infant had looked at both, they were removed from view. Then, the experimenter took one of the objects and placed it in one of the infant's hands, covering it with his own, so the infant touched the object but never saw it. While the object was in the infant's hand, the experimenter made it bleep. Third, the experimenter removed the object without the infant's seeing it, then placed it with the other object of the pair on the table and moved the two objects to where the infant could reach them.

With most presentations of the ellipsoids (A), the infants reached for the ones they had felt and heard, indicating that they had been able to identify visually the objects they had touched. They displayed no significant tendency to reach for the cuboid objects (B) that had bleeped, perhaps because, as has been demonstrated, pairs of objects with straight-straight contours are very hard to distinguish either tactually or cross-modally.

These investigations with apes and human in-

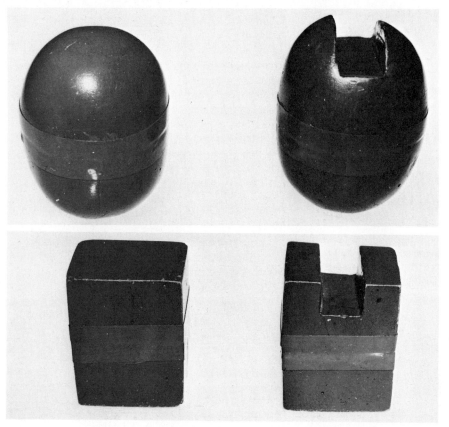

Figure 5-8 The "bleeping" ellipsoidal (top) and cuboidal (bottom) shapes, some with grooves and some without grooves, used to test cross modality between touch and vision in infants (Bryant, Jones, Claxton, & Perkins, 1972)

fants refuted the hypothesis that words or names are needed for cross-modal recognition. The infant experiment also showed that such cross-modal perceptual abilities are present at a very early age in perceptual development (eight months).

Sound Localization

By what means does a person accurately determine the location of a sound source? Suppose a young woman is quietly studying in a reading room in a library. Someone across the room drops a book on the floor and, startled by the noise, she looks up to see what happened.

She quickly turns her head in the direction of the noise. Somehow she must have received information from the sound source about its location. To some extent, loudness is a cue for distance of the sound source from the observer. In the example, a book hitting the floor near the woman would make a louder noise than a book striking the floor at a distance. But what characteristic of the sound source indicates its direction from the listener? Was the book to the right or to the left of the woman? This information is available because the two ears receive sound waves at different times and with different amplitudes from different places in space. Sound waves originating from the right side of the listener reach the right ear first and with slightly greater amplitude, or loudness, than in the left ear. The brain responds to the discrepancy in signals from the two ears as a cue for the direction of the sound source. The difference in signals is called **binaural discrepancy** ("binaural" meaning two ears).

You might question how this **sound localization** works because a sound coming from the right front of a listener would produce the same binaural discrepancy as a sound originating from the right back at the same angle. You may determine the front–back location of the sound by slightly rotating your head. If you turn your head to the right and the sound source is to the right in front of you, the discrepancy in arrival times for the two ears should *decrease*. However, if the source is to the right in back of you, a slight turn of the head to the right should *increase* the discrepancy in arrival times for the two ears. The vertical direction of a sound source may be localized by a similar method of slightly tilting the head at an angle.

Learning probably plays a role in our ability to judge the location of a sound source. Generally we tend to look down when we hear a crash, because experience has taught us that a crash often means that something has fallen. In the same way, we tend to look up when we hear a roar typical of an airplane. Although experience is an important factor in judging the location of a sound source, it is not sufficient by itself. A person deaf in one ear, and therefore lacking binaural discrepancy cues, has considerable difficulty locating sounds in space.

SOUND LOCALIZATION BY THE BLIND AND BY BATS

The remarkable ability of blind people to sense the location and distance of obstacles in their paths as they walk was a puzzle for many centuries. In 1749 a French scholar, Denis Diderot, studied a blind acquaintance and concluded that he judged the distance of obstacles by the pressure of air on his face, whose end organs and nerves must have become more sensitive than those of sighted persons. Other theories proposed over the years as observations gradually became more scientific included cues by air pressure on the eardrums or air temperature on the face, better discrimination and analysis of sounds, the effects of magnetic or electrical fields, and even the operation of the subconscious. Controversy persisted as a satisfactory explanation eluded investigators.

A series of experiments reported by psychologists at Cornell University in 1944 finally settled the issue of how the blind avoid obstacles (Supa, Cotzin, & Dallenbach, 1944). The subjects were two people who had been blind from their early years and two sighted people who were blindfolded. Various possible stimuli that might indicate the direction and distance of obstacles were eliminated. Thus in one experiment the subjects were seated in a soundproof room and provided with earphones through which they heard sounds picked up by a microphone carried by an experimenter as he moved toward one of the walls of another room. All of the subjects were able to judge quite accurately the distance from the experimenter to the wall by the sound of the experimenter's footsteps through the earphones. Generally the blind subjects did better than the sighted subjects, presumably because they had had more experience in trying to judge the location of obstacles from sounds. In this experiment, cues for location of objects provided by any sensory modality other than hearing were eliminated, since the subjects themselves were stationary. Auditory feedback from the experimenter's footsteps must have supplied the necessary cues. Since the microphone was held at a constant distance from the feet, characteristics of the sound arising directly from the footsteps did not change as the experimenter approached the wall. It must have been that sound waves reflected from the wall indicated its proximity to the experimenter. Reflections of sound waves occur more rapidly for nearer objects.

The way in which blind people tap their canes against the ground surface as they walk confirms this conclusion. Use of such reflected sounds to "place" objects is called **echolocation.** The phenomenon is similar to the way in which flying objects are located by radar. Pulses of long radio waves are transmitted, reflected from the objects, and picked up again at the radar instrument after a delay that indicates the distance of the objects.

A similar remarkable ability of bats to locate their tiny insect prey precisely and avoid obstacles while flying at night was found to be an example of echolocation (Griffin & Galambos, 1941, 1942). It was known that bats emit frequent cries at ultrasonic frequencies well above the range of human hearing. Elimination of sound stimuli from the cries, by gagging the bats or by plugging their ears so that they could not hear the cries, disrupted the bats' ability to locate objects. Evidently bats use the minute differences in the time required for the sound of their cries to be reflected from objects to determine their location.

But the bats' ultrasonic cries are strong and very frequent. Why do these cries not interfere with the hearing of the very weak sounds reflected back from objects to the bats' ears a few thousandths of a second later? The explanation for this was discovered in another series of experiments (Suga & Schlegel, 1972; Suga & Shimozawa, 1974). A rapid contraction of muscles in the bats' middle ears triggered by the cries dampens the hearing of their own vocalizations. In addition, vocal centers in the brain send inhibitory messages to the auditory pathway during vocalization that suppress the amplitude of its activity. The investigators speculate that there must be similar muscular and neural weakening of sounds from our own speech, which many of us never perceive to be disturbingly loud.

Perception of Motion

Motion pictures rely on the fact that whenever the same forms are exposed in a series of different positions at short intervals of time, the observer perceives apparent movement of the forms. Thus objects in movies appear to move when they occupy slightly different positions in adjacent still frames of a film. During *real*

movement of an object, successive areas of the retina are stimulated as the image moves across the retina. *Apparent* motion, on the other hand, is produced by stimulating one retinal area and then another without stimulating any of the receptors between the two.

A number of experiments have demonstrated a simple form of this phenomenon, called the **phi phenomenon.** Psychologist Max Wertheimer (1912) showed that if two short parallel lines of light are projected one centimeter apart in a dark room at intervals between 30- and 200-thousandths of a second, the light is seen as moving from one position to the other. At shorter intervals the lines are experienced simultaneously; at longer intervals the lines are seen as two independent lines.

Another fascinating perceptual phenomenon pertaining to motion is the apparent *lack* of motion of objects in some circumstances when their images move across the retina. When you move your head or eyes while looking at a stationary object like a chair, you accurately perceive that the chair is not moving even though its image moves across the retina as the head moves.

MOVING EYES AND OBJECTS

■ View the wall of a room while moving your eyes (or head) from side to side. The wall appears to be stationary, doesn't it? Now visually fixate on a finger held about a foot in front of you with the same wall in the background. Move your finger and your eyes (or head) together from side to side, still carefully fixating on the finger. In this case, the wall should appear to move with the movement of your eyes. Why does the wall appear to be stationary in the first situation and appear to move in the second situation? Can you explain the difference in cues in the two situations?

The difference between these situations is in the kind of eye movements involved. Looking at the wall while moving the eyes (or head) produces voluntary **saccadic,** or irregular flicking, movements of the eyes. On the other hand, fixating on the moving finger produces smooth, involuntary pursuit movements as the eyes follow the moving finger. Voluntary eye movements produce two kinds of cues that may be used for identifying a situation in which the eyes are moving but the object is stationary (Gregory, 1970). One kind consists of neural signals from the brain commanding the movement of the eyes, and the second kind consists of proprioceptive stimuli from the eye muscles controlling the movements. Either of these cues may cancel the cue for object motion provided by stimulation of a series of points across the retina; thus the object appears to be stationary.

A simple experiment distinguishes between the two possibilities. While viewing the same wall as in the previous demonstration, close one eye and gently push the other eye from side to side with your finger on the outside corner of the eyelid. The wall appears to move back and forth. The cues necessary for signaling a stationary object are lacking. Since passive (involuntary) movement of the eyes occurs without the neural signals from the brain that control voluntary eye movement, these neural signals may be the necessary missing cues. However, the other interpretation—that proprioceptive stimuli from eye muscles are cues for detecting a stationary object with moving eyes—cannot be eliminated completely. Passive movement of the eye muscles by pushing on the side of the eye does not produce exactly the same proprioceptive cues as active (voluntary) movement of the muscles.

PERCEPTUAL CONSTANCIES

A known object usually appears to retain its characteristic size, shape, color, and brightness regardless of the conditions under which the observer views it. This may seem surprising because changing the distance, direction, and illumination of the object in the viewing situation changes the visual information reaching the retina. This ability that we all have to perceive objects as relatively unchanged under different conditions of stimulation is called **perceptual constancy.**

Size Constancy

An object may be perceived to be of a constant size when viewed at varying distances from the observer, therefore manifesting **size constancy,** despite the fact that the size of the retinal image of the object varies with the distance of the object (refer back to Figure 5-2). The relationship between the perceived size of the object (C), the retinal size (R), and the distance (D) may be expressed as $C = R \times D$. If the distance of an object is known (through distance perception cues or otherwise), the perceived size of the object may be determined by the relationship given above, since retinal size (R) is, of course, "given." If the distance cannot be estimated, the observer has no means of estimating object size from retinal size. Then size constancy breaks down, and perceived size increases or decreases as retinal size increases or decreases, respectively, unless the observer knows from past experience what the size of the object really is. In such a case, when object size and retinal size are known, distance can be estimated by the relationship $D = C/R$.

Shape Constancy

An object viewed from varying angles appears to retain a constant shape regardless of the viewing angle. Suppose you look at a round wall clock. When you stand in front of the clock, the clock looks perfectly round. When you stand to one side of the clock, however, it actually looks elliptical even though you interpret the shape of the clock as round. In accordance with the principle of perceptual **shape constancy,** you perceive things around you as having their characteristic shapes, even though the images they cast on your retina will continually change in shape as you view the objects from different locations. Just as size constancy depends on cues for distance, shape constancy depends on cues for spatial orientation. However, it is more difficult to judge an object's spatial properties than its distance. As you might infer, shape constancy is not so reliable a feature of perception as size constancy.

ILLUSIONS

When a perception is an inaccurate representation of the real world, it is known as a **perceptual illusion.** Since perceptions are interpretations of sensory information, accurate perceptions depend on correct interpretations. Sometimes more than one perceptual interpretation may be suggested by sensory information. Illusions occur when we propose a perceptual hypothesis that is incorrect. At the beginning of the chapter, a situation of mistaken identity was described—a stranger was perceived to be your friend Fred. The person's stimulus characteristics suggested the hypothesis that the person was Fred, but this turned out to be wrong.

In forming perceptions, people are not aware that they are actually entertaining hypotheses about the meanings of sensations. The perceptual hypothesis is formed immediately and unconsciously. In fact, as possible explanations of a number of visual illusions are discussed, you will see that knowing a perceptual hypothesis to be false does not eliminate the illusion. The brain still accepts a false hypothesis even though it "knows" it is wrong. Let's examine several illusions.

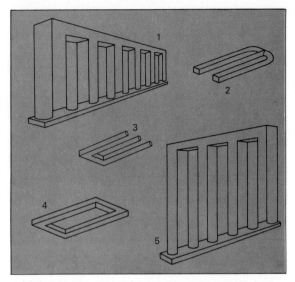

Figure 5-9 Inconsistent cues of shapes produce perceptual illusions in viewing these impossible objects. (Robinson & Wilson, 1973)

illusion comes from the completion of each pair of lines to make a cylinder at one end of the drawing and of three lines to make a square bar at the other end. The other drawings use similar inconsistencies to make a variety of impossible objects. If you draw some of these yourself, you will see how the inconsistencies arise.

The three illusions presented in Figures 5-10, 5-11, and 5-12 can be understood if it is assumed that they are based on false perceptual hypotheses suggested by the principle of size constancy. The illusions in Figures 5-10 and 5-11, called the Ponzo and Muller-Lyer illusions, respectively, may result because the observer regards the two-dimensional objects shown in the drawings as having three dimensions. In the Ponzo illusion, the top horizontal bar superimposed on the converging vertical lines appears to be larger than the bottom one because it seems to be farther away from the observer. Since the retinal-image size of the two bars is equal but perceived distance is unequal, the assumed real size of the two bars

IMPOSSIBLE OBJECTS

■ Many strange perceptual illusions called **impossible objects** can be created by providing inconsistent cues for shape and distance in drawings of objects. Some variations of impossible objects are shown in Figure 5-9 (Robinson & Wilson, 1973). Looking at drawing 3 in the figure, you can see that it gives you partial perceptions of two arms and of three arms, inconsistent with each other because of the way they are drawn. The inconsistency depends on the fact that a cylinder can be drawn with two lines, but a rectangular bar can be drawn only with three lines. The

Figure 5-10 Ponzo illusion. The two bars superimposed on the photograph are the same size. However, the top one looks longer because it appears to be farther away.

being longer. Since retinal size (R) is fixed, and distance (D) is presumed greater for the figure on the left, then perceived size, or length (C), has to be greater.

Similar perceptual mechanisms may underlie the moon illusion, shown in Figure 5-12. Kaufman and Rock (1962) concluded that it results from a size-constancy mechanism in which the cues for distance are different when the moon is high in the sky than they are when it is at the horizon. The distance of the moon at the horizon is estimated from cues from landscape features. Few distance cues are provided when the moon is viewed overhead; for this reason it may be perceived to be closer than it is. If this is true, size constancy would predict that the moon at the horizon, which is assumed to be a greater distance away, would be perceived as being larger.

Which circle is larger in Figure 5-13? Most people start out by declaring that they are the same size. But if they are *forced* to make a choice, the great majority of people say the right circle, outside the triangle, is larger. Both circles actually are the same size. Why does the right one appear to be larger? The size-constancy hypothesis can explain this illusion if we assume that the figure has *apparent* depth.

The depth cue involved in this figure is interposition. One way in which to interpret the figure is to postulate that a white triangle partially occludes the view of the black squares and black-line triangle. Although there is a tendency to perceive the figure in this way, the white triangle does not necessarily exist and therefore it is illusory. Interposition cues tell us that the white triangle is closer than the squares and black-line triangle. Therefore the circle on the apparent closer plane, that of the white triangle, should seem closer than the circle in the apparent background. The size-distance rule says that if two objects form images of equal size, the one seen to be nearer must also be judged to be smaller.

The Subjective Necker Cube illusion, shown in Figure 5-14, demonstrates nicely that per-

has to be different. Referring back to the formula relating apparent size to apparent distance, perceived size (C) is a function of retinal size times distance, or $C = R \times D$. The farther the perceived distance (D), the larger the size of the object (C) appears to be.

In the Müller-Lyer illusion, the vertical shaft of the outward-going arrow appears to be farther away than the vertical shaft of the inward-going arrow (see Figure 5-11). Even though the actual sizes of the vertical shafts of the two figures are exactly the same, the size-constancy formula would predict that the shaft that appears to be farther away would be perceived as

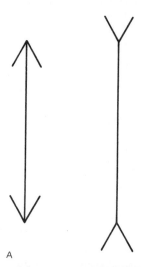

A

Figure 5-11 Müller-Lyer illusion. The vertical shafts of the figures in A are identical in length, but the second one appears to be longer than the first. One explanation is that the figures produce a corner effect. As seen in the photographs, the figure with outward arrows (B) suggests a corner that is farther away (and therefore larger) than the figure with inward arrows (C).

B

C

Figure 5-13 Both circles are the same size. However, the circle on the apparent white triangle appears to be a different size than the one beside it in the apparent background. (Coren, 1972)

Figure 5-12 Moon illusion. The moon at the horizon appears to be larger than the moon overhead.

a white cube against a dark background, looking through the white surface as if it were a piece of Swiss cheese? Try to see the figure both ways.

To make matters more complex, if you look at the cube for at least 10 to 15 seconds, it should appear to alternate between two orien-

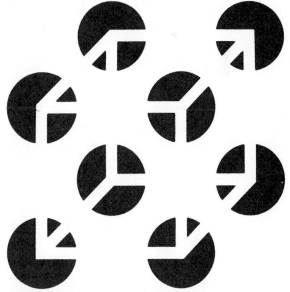

ceptions involve constructing an interpretation or hypothesis to account for sensory information. This figure may be perceived in many ways. It may be seen as a flat trapezoid figure interposed on top of eight black circles. More commonly the figure is perceived to contain a three-dimensional cube.

Do you see the cube in the foreground or in the background of the figure? That is, do you see a white, illusory or "subjective" cube interposed over the black circles and white background? Or do you see only the corners of

Figure 5-14 Subjective Necker Cube. Note that the illusory cube can be seen either as in front of the dark circles or behind the hole-filled white surface. Also, the orientation of the cube can shift from side to side. (Petry, 1975)

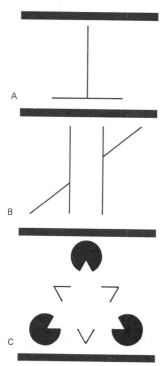

Figure 5-15 Difficult-to-explain illusions. In A, the horizontal line appears to be longer than the vertical one. Take a ruler and measure their length. B, the Poggendorff figure, consists of diagonal lines that appear not to meet if extended through the two parallel vertical lines. Align a ruler on the diagonal lines and see if they would meet if extended together. In C, the perception of a white triangle is illusory since no such figure physically exists. The white triangle appears to be brighter than the white background even though they are actually the same. (Kanizsa, 1955)

tations—front surface at the bottom left or front surface at the top right. The reversing of the cube orientation occurs because of ambiguous depth cues; either orientation could be correct. The many ways in which this figure may be perceived suggests that the brain may entertain any one of a number of hypotheses to account for the sensory information, and may even shift back and forth between competing hypotheses.

Some illusions are difficult to explain. Certainly many can be explained from theoretical orientations other than the suggestion that illusions result from faulty hypotheses about sensory information. A few of these are pre-

sented in Figure 5-15. Researchers are attempting to clarify their meanings. Some illusions may result from innate characteristics of our perceptual mechanisms.

A TOUCH ILLUSION

■ Perceptual illusions are by no means limited to the misinterpretation of visual stimuli. Get out a quarter, penny, or dime, and you can experience a touch illusion. Hold the coin on edge between the balls of your left thumb and forefinger, so the diameter of the coin is separating them. Then rotate the coin with the thumb and forefinger of your right hand, pushing with your thumb on one rim and then pulling with your forefinger on the other rim so the coin rotates around its vertical axis between left thumb and forefinger. As the fingers of your right hand come together on the surfaces of the coin, your right thumb slides back to engage the rim of the coin again and push it, while your forefinger slides along to engage the other rim again. Keep repeating this turning of the coin smoothly and fairly rapidly for 30 to 60 seconds. Do you notice that the coin seems to stretch out so its diameter feels longer to your turning fingers than to your holding fingers? This apparent elongation of the coin is the touch illusion. Almost everyone who tries it experiences the illusion, judging the turning diameter to be longer by from 10 to 50 per cent than the held diameter. The illusion grows over time for up to a minute, as you can see in Figure 5-16.

This recently reported touch illusion (Cormack, 1973) might be explained in several ways. One possibility is that the apparent flattening of the curved edge experienced by the holding thumb and forefinger is caused by adaptation to the continual pressure of the coin as it twists on the fingertips. Another possibility is that the turning fingers nearly meet across the thickness of the coin while the holding fingers are widely separated at the edges of the coin and that the differential adaptation of the fingers to these effects causes the illusion. A third possibility is that the sliding of the balls of turning thumb and forefinger along the coin makes the coin seem longer to the turning hand than to the holding hand. Although experiments with this touch illusion have not yet provided an explanation, it does illustrate well how we can misinterpret touch sensations.

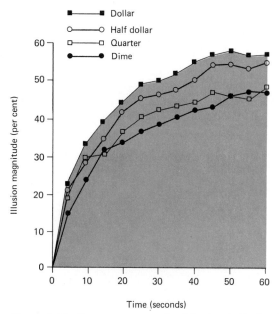

Dollar
Half dollar
Quarter
Dime

Figure 5-16 The average growth of the touch illusion for many subjects as they continued to turn various coins with thumb and forefinger. (Cormack, 1973)

PERSON PERCEPTION

Perceptual processes play a role in the interpretation of sensory information from animate as well as inanimate objects. **Person perception** refers to the interpretation of a person's intentions, emotions, and personality characteristics on the basis of nonverbal cues or sensory stimuli derived from the person. The concept assumes that some aspects of a person's physical features or nonverbal behavior have shared meanings that are understood by other people.

Perhaps the most important nonverbal cues for person perception are facial expressions. We usually know when people are happy, sad, or frightened by interpreting the meanings of their expressions. A number of facial expressions have been proved so universally consistent in their meanings that some scientists classify them as species-characteristic behaviors (see Chapter 2). People from all cultures tend to smile when they're happy and frown when they're sad. Even infants seem to be able to interpret the meanings of some facial expressions, and as we noted earlier, blind infants smile when they're happy even though they have no opportunity to see others smile.

Body expressions or **body language** also may convey information concerning an individual's emotional state. Wringing of the hands is a good index of anxiety. Tightly clenched fists usually indicate tension or hostility. Carefully observe expressive behaviors of those around you. Do you find meaningful such gestures as feet shuffling, head scratching, lint picking, and foot stomping?

When an audience responds positively to a performance by clapping, it is intentionally using body language to convey a meaning. But body language may also occur unintentionally, without the individual's conscious effort or control. It is often easy to tell when children are trying to conceal information because of their nervous behavior. Adults are more accomplished in controlling body language. For example, an adult being interviewed for a much-desired job may try to conceal nervous feelings by making an effort to act calm and confident. Sitting erect (but not rigid), tilting the head slightly upward, and steadying the hands by grasping something solid help convey the impression that an individual has self-confidence.

Most people use body language during speech to emphasize or specify the meaning of certain aspects of verbal communication. A host of these gestures has been discussed (Wiener, Devoe, Rubinow, & Geller, 1972). The position of the palms of a gesturing speaker expresses a general attitude about the communication or the person to whom the speaker is communicating. Palms up indicates uncertainty about what is being said: "It seems to me . . ." or "How should I know?" Palms down and out indicates certainty about the communication. The speaker is conveying the idea that what is being said is final and not open to question. Palms facing the addressee indicates "Don't interrupt" or "Stop right there." Circling gestures of the hands and arms are often used to indicate the generality of what is being said. The speaker may mean "This statement applies to all such cases" or "I am referring to the whole situation." The physical size of an object is usually indicated by holding the hands out vertically and moving the arms close together or far apart. Another gesture frequently used during speech is the rotation or oscillation of the hand back and forth three or four times. This gesture usually indicates "either/or" or "more or less" or "Yes, but . . ."

Although much of the meaning of speech gestures is redundant, merely emphasizing the verbal content of the message, we use the gestures extensively. In fact, some people have difficulty speaking when they are forbidden to use their hands.

Listeners also make expressive gestures, mostly facial (Wiener et al., 1972). If the addressees nod their heads up and down, this usually means that they approve or understand what is being said. If they maintain a blank, unexpressive look, they don't understand the communication. A shift of the eyes upward and to one side indicates that they are thinking about what has just been said. (This lateral eye motion is discussed further in Chapter 6.) A frown or shake of the head indicates disapproval.

A number of investigations have demonstrated that facial and body movements provide cues of personality characteristics. In one experiment, features of a schematized drawing of a face were systematically varied and subjects were asked to indicate their impression of psychological traits conveyed by the faces (Brunswik & Reiter, 1938). Slight changes in length of the mouth, nose, and forehead area greatly altered the subjects' impressions of characteristics like intelligence, mood, likability, energy, and age (see Figure 5-17). Facial features probably become perceptual cues for personality characteristics through an individual's experience of such physical and psychological traits occurring together in many people.

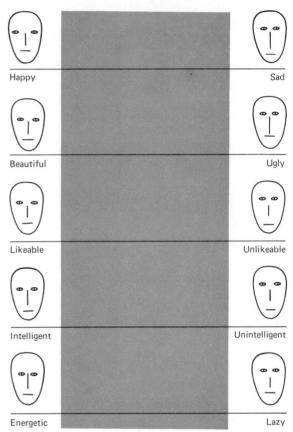

Figure 5-17 Schematized faces yielding extremely desirable and undesirable impressions. (Adapted from Brunswick, 1956)

FACTORS INFLUENCING PERCEPTION

Like other human processes, perception may work well or poorly, and there are individual differences in the accuracy and efficiency of perception. In addition to past experience, some of the principal factors that have been found to influence perception are attention, motivation, and expectation.

Attention

When people are focused on a source of stimulation in such a way that their awareness of the stimulus is heightened, we say that they are *attending to* the stimulus. **Attention** is an important influence on perception because it determines the objects or events that will be perceived.

A number of factors influence the attention we pay to stimuli. Some of these factors seem to be important for all organisms. One such factor is *stimulus intensity.* The more intense the stimulus, the more attention it attracts. It is difficult to ignore a crash of dishes in a quiet restaurant. But a less intense stimulus, like the sound of a fork hitting the floor, may not be noticed by anyone in the immediate vicinity.

A second attention-getting factor is *novelty.* Stimuli that are unfamiliar are more likely to receive attention than those that are familiar. You may remember from Chapter 3 that Kagan showed that very young infants tend to fixate longer on visual stimuli that are slightly different from stimuli with which they are familiar.

Stimuli that have *significance* are also more likely to receive attention than stimuli that have no significance for the organism. A dog, seemingly asleep, may be aroused by the approaching footsteps of its master returning home. The fact that the footsteps have special significance makes it more likely that they will receive attention. Much louder traffic noises coming through an open window may not disturb the dog's sleep at all. Have you ever been in a room where several conversations are going on simultaneously and heard your name mentioned in a conversation of which you were not previously aware? Hearing or reading one's own name is one of the strongest attention-getting factors. Naturally, a person's own name is a highly meaningful stimulus.

DRIVING AND MARIJUANA

Driving a car involves dividing attention between a *tracking task* (following the road) and *searching tasks* (picking up and recognizing other stimuli, like those from other cars, traffic signs, and lights). Some early studies reported no effect of marijuana on the driving skills of subjects being tested in a driving simulator. In 1973, however, another study was made of the effects of marijuana on subjects who had never smoked it before and on subjects accustomed to it (Casswell & Marks, 1973).

The subjects were asked to press a key whenever a central light missed a flash in its flashing rate of one per second, and to press another key whenever one of 15 lights on both sides of the central light flashed. The investigators believed this gave them a divided attention task similar to that involved in driving a car. Some subjects smoked control cigarettes that tasted and smelled like marijuana but did not contain it, while other subjects smoked cigarettes with either a high or a low component of marijuana. Each subject smoked one cigarette before the trial, holding each inhalation for 30 seconds. The results showed that subjects who smoked marijuana cigarettes, whether they were accustomed to them or not, consistently missed the gap in the center-light flashing and missed the flashing of the peripheral lights significantly more frequently than subjects who did not smoke marijuana. Furthermore, the higher dosage of marijuana led to more misses than the lower dosage. The investigators commented, "This decrement in performance on a divided attention task is similar to that found following alcohol intoxication, which is believed to be associated with the frequent occurrence of alcohol-related accidents" (p. 61).

You might question whether the divided-attention task in this experiment was really similar enough to the task of driving so that the conclusions would be likely to hold for driving. This criticism was answered in a different series of experiments with marijuana and driving under real-life conditions (Klonoff, 1974). Again the subjects smoked either a control or a low-dose or high-dose marijuana cigarette. Then they drove through a complex driving course with many curves, tunnels, and a funnel, or drove through a course on the streets of the city of Vancouver, British Columbia, with experienced driving observers. Both low and high doses of marijuana had detrimental effects on the subjects' driving, the high doses producing the more pronounced effects. The detrimental effects were greater in driving in city streets than on the driving course. A few subjects showed no significant decline in driving after smoking marijuana, possibly overcompensating for its effects by paying close attention. They may have been sedated by the drug and therefore not so nervous. But Klonoff warned that driving alone and driving at night or under other difficult conditions while under the influence of marijuana, or driving under relatively easy conditions after heavier dosages of marijuana than those tested, could produce even greater decreases in driving efficiency. He concluded: "Driving under the influence of marijuana should be avoided as much as should driving under the influence of alcohol" (p. 323).

Attention is also influenced by *motivation.* Let's say we handed you a picture of a crowd like the one shown in Figure 5-18 and told you that at the end of one minute we would take back the photograph and ask you questions about it. Your ability to answer the questions would probably be greater than it would be if you simply looked at the photograph but were not motivated to attend to it by having to answer questions about it. Now suppose we

showed you the photograph in Figure 5-18 and told you that at the end of one minute we would ask you to report the number of people in the crowd. Your report would probably be more accurate than if you had not been instructed to attend to the people. If you were asked to report instead the number of buildings in the photograph, then that aspect of the picture would receive the most attention. Attention may thus be voluntarily directed to different parts of the stimulus.

Although a person may concentrate on one or another aspect of a complex stimulus like a photograph, it is not possible to attend to many aspects of the stimulus at the same time. If a person has only limited exposure to a stimulus, attending to one aspect requires that attention not be paid to other aspects. If the person is instructed to report the number of people in the photograph, other aspects of the photograph will receive less attention. The process of directing attention to certain aspects of the environment and not to others is called

Figure 5-18 After briefly looking at a scene filled with a crowd of people, such as this photograph, you will recall very little specific information about it unless your attention is directed toward certain features.

selective attention. Selective attention has been explained by assuming that some kind of filter is interposed between our sense organs and that part of the brain responsible for perceptual awareness. It is not clear at what point selection occurs in the analyzing process, however. The restriction may be placed on the amount of sensory information the brain can receive at one time. Or the restriction may be further along in the perceptual process leading to awareness. Perhaps the limitation is in the amount of sensory information that can be simultaneously processed into memories.

ATTENTION-GETTERS

■ After you have collected the equipment for this activity, it will take you only a few minutes to complete it; if it took longer, it would be an imposition on your own and other people's auditory systems. Gather two or three radios and one TV set in a room and place them around you. With an open book in your hand, turn on all of this audio-visual equipment (tune them all to talk or discussion programs) and turn up the volume of each to the same moderate level. You've provided yourself with a situation almost as good as a cocktail party for observing your selective attention.

First, try to read a full page in the book as you sit in the chair with the sound coming from all sources simultaneously. Can you switch your attention from your auditory to your visual channels easily? Can you hold your attention on the visual material without interference from the auditory output, or does the noise crowd out visual reception occasionally?

Second, without turning your head, try switching your attention from one auditory source to another. Is your attention selective and strong enough to do this? Then put a finger in your left ear and try switching attention from an auditory source close to your right ear to an auditory source close to your blocked left ear. Can your right ear overcome the competition?

Third, turn your head to watch the TV screen and also listen to the TV sound. Does stimulation through both senses improve your ability to hold your attention on the TV sound?

Fourth, gradually turn down the volume of one of the sound sources, making it lower and lower. Does its volume reach a point at which the other, louder sounds keep bursting into your attention, despite the fact that the lower sound is still audible? Leave the volume at the point at which louder sounds interfere and turn off all the other equipment. Can you still make out the one sound source when you turn its volume still lower? What can you conclude from this?

Motivation and Expectation

Many experiments as well as everyday situations support the idea that motivation influences perception in ways other than through an attention mechanism. Motivation also influences the interpretation of stimuli. People have a tendency to hear what they want to hear, see what they want to see. One way in which this principle has been demonstrated in the laboratory is through a study of the perception of words presented very briefly on a screen to subjects. The presentation is so fast that the words are difficult to identify. Hungry subjects more accurately perceive words associated with food and have a tendency to label nonfood-related words as food-related. High achievers have a tendency to "see" success-related words.

A dramatic example of the way in which motivations and expectations influence perception is found in **pain perception.** You might consider pain to be a sensory experience so urgent that its perception would not be susceptible to modification. A vast amount of study and observation, however, indicates otherwise.

Cross-cultural comparisons have demonstrated the effect of cultural motivation on pain perception. In some cultures, childbirth, for example, is not regarded as an unusually painful experience. In these cultures women show low levels of distress during delivery (Melzack, 1961). In our culture, on the other hand, childbirth is regarded as an extremely painful experience. The "natural childbirth" indoctrination procedure used by some women in this country is designed to motivate women to think of the pain that they will experience during childbirth as nonthreatening, tolerable, and perhaps most importantly, in the best interest of the child, since the alternative of receiving an anesthetic may have a bad effect on the child. With this procedure, which combines muscle-relaxing exercises with training to adopt a nonanxious attitude toward childbirth, some women are more capable of tolerating pain than they would be otherwise.

Acupuncture anesthesia, used in the People's Republic of China, has been compared with "natural childbirth" in its use of motivation to reduce pain perception (Taub, 1974). People who undergo acupuncture anesthesia are socially motivated to withstand or to ignore pain, with the understanding that they will benefit by being conscious (many Chinese fear unconsciousness) and by avoiding the undesirable side effects of anesthetic agents. Acupuncture anesthesia is not widely used in China. Only those individuals who pass an initial pain tolerance test are candidates for its use.

The acupuncture procedure consists of inserting needles into skin areas determined to be appropriate for anesthesia of a given part of the body. Although the procedure *may* produce a blockage of pain stimuli in the nervous system, it is not clear at this time to what extent its effects are physiological or psychological.

Expectation of pain relief markedly reduces pain perception in some individuals given placebo medication. A **placebo** is a pharmacologically inactive substance that is described to the patient as being therapeutic, in this case in relieving pain. The placebo may produce complete relief of all signs of pain. It is important to understand that the pain relieved by placebos is real, not simply faked or imagined by the patients. A report sum-

marizing 10 studies of "placebo effects" involving a total of 831 patients stated that 35 per cent of patients with pain from surgery, angina pectoris (a kind of chest pain), cancer, and headache found relief from placebos (Beecher, 1960).

Factors other than expectation of pain relief also contribute to the placebo effect. Among these are confidence in the skill of the doctor, the patient's previous experiences with doctors and medicine, and the patient's personality characteristics, such as anxiety and dependency needs (Steinbach, 1968). The dentist's provision of music through headphones while drilling a patient's tooth has the advantages of masking the sound of the drill, thus reducing expectation of pain, and distracting the patient's attention to soothing music.

Expectation that pain *will* occur likewise increases pain perception. For example, volunteer subjects in one experiment were asked to judge the painfulness of electric shocks to the hand ranging from mild to intense, though not harmful to the subjects. The appearance of the word "pain" in the instruction caused anxious subjects to report as painful a level of shock that was not regarded as painful when the word did not appear in the instructions (Hall & Stride, 1954).

PERCEPTUAL THEORIES

Theoretical analyses of perceptual phenomena range from theories of simple stimulus detection, discussed in Chapter 4, to theories concerned with the perception of complex stimulus situations. You may remember that detection theory proposes that the simple detection of a stimulus depends on three types of factors: (1) the difference in intensity between the stimulus and background "noise"; (2) the consequences of the decision regarding detection; and (3) the expectation of the stimulus. Other perceptual theories emphasize different variables that affect perception.

Adaptation-Level Theory

Don't personal as well as situational variables influence perception? **Adaptation-level theory** states that all perceptions are affected by the organism's adaptation or adjustment to the specific conditions of stimulation (Helson, 1947). Stimuli determining an organism's adaptation level include the stimuli in the immediate focus of attention, contextual or background stimuli immediately present, and internal or residual stimuli representing the individual's past experience. Stimuli that differ markedly from an individual's adaptation level tend to elicit a perceptual response.

A simple experiment should demonstrate the concept of adaptation level. Subjects are asked to rate five weights, ranging from 200 to 400 grams in 50-gram steps, on a scale of 0 to 10, 0 being very light and 10 very heavy. Before the judging, subjects are asked to lift a standard weight to demonstrate the procedure. For half of the subjects the standard weight is 100 grams and for the other half it's 500 grams. Adaptation-level theory predicts that the judging of any weight in the series will be influenced by other weights in the series already judged (contextual stimuli) and the standard weight (residual stimulus). Subjects given the 100-gram standard weight would be expected to judge the weights as relatively heavier than subjects given the 500-gram standard. Predictions that adaptation level will influence perception have been confirmed in many studies of sensory modalities (for example, Harvey & Campbell, 1963).

From your own experience you probably are aware that perceptual judgments are influenced by present and past experiences. Often what makes college dining room meals taste so bad is students' adaptation to a much higher quality of food preparation at home. And after several months of college food, your adaptation level shifts downward, and your appreciation of a home-cooked meal goes 'way up. Similarly, you judge a person's attrac-

tiveness on the basis of your experiences with other people. The value of adaptation-level theory is that it makes explicit the relationship of contextual stimuli and past experience to perception.

Gestalt Theory

According to Gestalt psychologists, certain innate organizing principles govern perception. Two main organizing principles of **Gestalt theory** will be discussed here. The first principle states that the perception of stimuli is based on a tendency to perceive some aspect of the stimulus as **figure** and another aspect as **ground.** The ground is the less distinct setting for the figure. A person standing in a room may be perceived as a figure against the ground of the room. Sometimes stimuli may be perceived as figure and ground in several ways

Figure 5-19 E. G. Boring's ambiguous figure, which can be seen either as an attractive young lady (looking over her right shoulder) or as an old woman (left profile). (Boring, 1930. From *The intelligent eye,* By Richard L. Gregory. Copyright 1970, McGraw-Hill. Used with permission McGraw-Hill Book Co.)

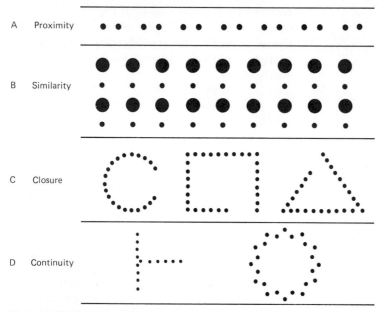

Figure 5-20 Arrangements of dots showing the major Gestalt principles of grouping. A, The top pattern is seen as pairs of dots. Points in close *proximity* are seen as "belonging" to one another. B, The series is seen as rows of dots rather than columns, even though the distance between rows and columns is equal. *Similarity* of dots in the rows influences the perceptual grouping. C, The three figures are seen as a circle, rectangle, and triangle. Incomplete forms tend to be seen as a whole, called the principle of *closure*. D, In these figures the tendency to organize patterns into continuous forms is stronger than grouping by proximity. The first figure is seen as vertical and horizontal lines of dots. The first dot that seems to belong to the horizontal line is actually closer to the vertical line. Similarly, the right figure is seen as two concentric circles although the dots in the inner circle are closer to adjacent dots in the outer circle than to one another.

(see Figure 5-19). Figure-ground relationships also occur in sensory modalities other than vision. When carrying on a conversation with another person, we hear that person's voice as a figure against a ground of extraneous noise. The figure is always the object of attention, and since attention is selective, it always occurs against a background of sensory stimulation that is being filtered from our awareness.

The second organizing principle concerns the tendency to group stimuli into patterns, called grouping. **Grouping processes** occur in such a way that we see patterns of stimuli in orderly relationships. Properties such as regularity, symmetry, simplicity, proximity, conti-

nuity, and closure influence our perception of stimulus patterns (see Figure 5-20).

A **gestalt** is a perceptual whole, and Gestalt psychology emphasizes that the whole of our perceptual experience is greater (more meaningful) than the sum of its parts. Thus in Figure 5-20 the circle seen as the result of the arrangement of dots in a circular pattern is more than the dots that compose it (the sum of its parts). It is the *pattern* of dots that gives rise to the circle. Gestalt psychologists emphasize that a perceptual experience cannot be analyzed by reducing the experience into its simple constituents. Rather, the gestalt or whole must be studied.

Gestalt psychology's major contribution to

perception theory is its emphasis on our innate tendency to make meaning out of new sensory experiences through figure-ground, grouping, and other organizational processes. If our perceptual abilities were based solely on our past experiences, we would be handicapped in making meaning out of each novel stimulus situation.

Cell-Assembly Theory

A physiological mechanism whereby perceptions are acquired on the basis of previous experience is proposed by the **cell-assembly theory.** According to this theory, perceptual organization occurs through the acquired organization of cells in the brain (Hebb, 1949). The simultaneous firing of a group of cells, called a *cell assembly*, in response to sensory stimulation leads to the establishment of a communication bond between the cells. Repeated activation of the cells in the assembly through repeated sensory stimulation strengthens the bond between the cells. When the functional strength of the assembly is well established, activation of only part of the cells in the assembly may be sufficient to activate the whole assembly, and this produces a whole perception. For an example, refer back to the cubist figure of Lincoln's face, Figure 5-1. Although much of the detail is missing and some sensory information is distorted, you can still accurately identify the picture. Your previous experience at viewing pictures of Lincoln has presumably caused an association between the activity of a set of cells stimulated by the picture and the label "Lincoln." Activation of some of these same cells by Figure 5-1 presumably is sufficient to activate the whole assembly and produce an accurate perception.

Experience does influence perception, as cell-assembly theory predicts. If you see one small edge of a newspaper lying beneath a stack of books, you can identify the paper as a newspaper. You form a perceptual concept of the whole object based on past experience.

However, the physiological aspect of the theory is too complex to test experimentally. There are billions of cells in the brain and the challenge of locating a cell assembly is overwhelming. However, a number of experiments have shown that communication between cells can be strengthened by experience (for example, Rosenzweig, Bennett, & Diamond, 1972).

EXTRASENSORY PERCEPTION

During the 1930s J. B. Rhine initiated his work on **extrasensory perception (ESP)** at Duke University. ESP is the perception of objects or events through means other than the known sensory modalities. Rhine believes that he and others have experimentally established the existence of a number of psychic processes, like **clairvoyance** (extrasensory perception of events), **precognition** (awareness of future events), and **telepathy** (the direct transfer of thoughts from one mind to another). All of these psychic processes, including **psychokinesis** (the effects of the mind on physical events, such as determining the fall of dice) fall under the heading of **parapsychology**, the scientific study of processes beyond ordinary human sensations and perceptions. Other psychic phenomena, like ghosts and communication with the dead, are also being studied by some investigators, although Rhine and most other parapsychologists do not believe they exist.

About 20 researchers in the United States are working full time on parapsychological projects, and many others devote part time to them. The Parapsychological Association reports more than 100 members here and abroad who hold a master's or Ph.D. degree in some field of science (Wade, 1973). A recent questionnaire survey of its readers by the British journal *New Scientist* resulted in 1500 returns. A quarter of the respondents indicated that they believed ESP was an established phenomenon and another 42 per cent reported that they considered it a likely possibility. More than half, however, thought that parapsychology was making "little if any progress." Many psychologists and other scientists point to the facts that no reliably repeatable ESP experiments have yet been reported, that ESP experimental conditions are often not rigidly controlled, that cheating has frequently been discovered in ESP research, and that the level of "better than chance" results has often been low. Furthermore, they point out that only significant ESP results tend to be published; the many experiments that yield no better than chance results may never be reported.

DOWSING EXPERIMENTS

Dowsers are among those people who claim to possess extrasensory powers. They believe that they are able to locate springs or running water underground to indicate where wells should be dug. Their usual method is to grasp the arms of a Y-shaped stick in their two hands and walk over the terrain, waiting for the stick suddenly to point downward with great force. Some dowsers also believe they can locate metals, stoneware, or archeological remains by this method, and a few even claim to locate water or other objects on *maps* of the terrain.

The abilities of many dowsers who claimed to be experts and were recognized as such by other dowsers have been tested experimentally (Foulkes, 1971). The British Army and Ministry of Defense permitted an area to be used to test whether these dowsers could locate buried metallic or plastic mines, as opposed to similar wooden or concrete dummies, and to test their findings where nothing at all was buried. For the British Army, accurate location of mines would, of course, be valuable. Wooden pegs were placed in the ground over 200 of these buried objects, and 22 dowsers were asked to dowse over each and to report whether a metal mine, a plastic mine, or nothing lay buried under the pegs. Their efforts were unavailing. Most hit very close to pure chance and only one obtained results much better than chance. In dowsing on maps, no dowsers managed to be better than chance. Similarly, in trials over water pipes and in dowsing for subterranean water flow where a boring was later made, no identifications significantly above chance were found. Foulkes concluded that he had found no real evidence of dowsing ability giving results better than chance or guessing.

As is often typical with ESP experiments, two later articles appeared on these same experiments (Merrylees, 1971; Smith, 1971). In one article, the statistician who worked on the analysis of Foulkes's experiment reported some errors in the original report and suggested that one of the dowsers may have (inconclusively) demonstrated some dowsing ability. Unfortunately, the dowser could not be retested. In the other article, one of the dowsers criticized the experiments and maintained that a deeper boring would have struck the subterranean water flow his dowsing indicated. He agreed that the mine experiment "was a failure although one man was successful far beyond the bounds of chance." Great difficulty is experienced in controlling ESP experiments so that rigorous conclusions can be drawn without the possibility of conscious or unconscious cheating by subjects, experimenters, or both.

Targ-Puthoff Experiments

Two physicists at the Stanford Research Institute have published a report of investigations that convinced them of the reality of ESP (Targ & Puthoff, 1974). They experimented in several series of trials with an Israeli magician, Uri Geller. Geller was placed in a steel room, thus shielded from any magnetic, electrical, or radio waves or transmissions. He was instructed to draw replicas of targets selected by senders outside the room after he had entered it. The targets and four of his more remarkable replicas are shown in Figure 5-21. Two independent judges were later asked to try to match the target drawings with Geller's response drawings and did so with no errors for the 11 trials made, a highly significant result. In other experimental series, in which Geller was to try to duplicate 100 target drawings placed between pieces of black cardboard and sealed in double envelopes, he tried some drawings but gave up on the series, overwhelmed by

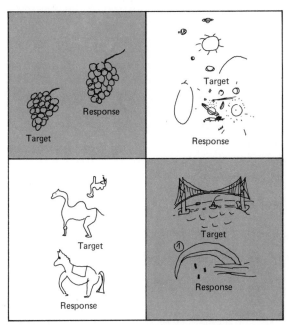

Figure 5-21 Target pictures selected by senders outside Uri Geller's steel-shielded room after he had entered it, and the drawings Geller made in response to them. (Targ & Puthoff, 1974)

such a large set of targets. When the drawings he made were compared with the targets, Geller had not done better than chance.

In still another try, an experimenter placed a ³/₄-inch die in a 3-inch by 4-inch by 5-inch steel box, shook the box vigorously, and then placed it on a table without permitting anyone to know how the die had fallen. Geller responded 8 times out of 10 trials and correctly indicated which face of the die was up all 8 times. The probability of so high a number of correct responses occurring by chance is one in a million times. But was there a cover on the box? Could the inner side of the steel box, if open, reflect an image that might have been seen? The report does not specify such conditions.

The referees who reviewed the *Nature* article that reported these and other experiments were critical of the way they were carried out and felt that "the details given of various safe-

guards and precautions introduced against the possibility of conscious or unconscious fraud on the part of one or other of the subjects were 'uncomfortably vague.'" Andrew Weil, author of *The Natural Mind,* spent some time with Geller and watched him perform various feats, apparently bending nails and keys by stroking them, starting watches that had stopped, and identifying names written on a blackboard while he kept his eyes averted (Weil, 1974). At first Weil was impressed with Geller's demonstrations. Then he learned from magicians how these and other feats can be brought off easily, by distracting the audience's attention, substituting bent nails and keys for straight ones, and using other sleights of hand. Whether sleight of hand or other natural methods were used in the Stanford trials, or whether they exhibited a genuine ESP ability, is a highly controversial question at the present time.

SUMMARY

Perception is the process of interpreting objects, events, or relationships on the basis of sensory stimuli. Visual distance perception depends on cues arising from a number of sources: known size of the perceived object, interposition, texture and density gradients, motion parallax, accommodation of the lens of the eye, convergence of the eyes, and binocular disparity. The last two sources of distance cues are provided only by binocular vision.

The localization of sound in space depends upon discrepancies in auditory stimuli reaching the two ears. When a sound source is anywhere but directly in front of or directly behind the perceiver, the ear closest to the sound receives the stimulus first and with a slightly greater intensity than the other ear. The brain uses these cues to identify the sound's location. The blind use echolocation to locate objects in space.

The perception of real motion occurs when successive points on the retina are stimulated by an image moving across the retina. The perception of apparent motion can occur if two points on the retina are stimulated in rapid succession without stimulation of the intervening points. Such is the basis of the phi phenomenon and motion pictures.

When stationary objects are viewed with moving eyes, the image of the object travels across the retina. The observer can correctly identify the object as stationary on the basis of several cues arising from eye movements. One possible cue is from neural signals from brain areas controlling the movements. The other is from proprioceptive stimuli from the eye muscles.

Objects appear to retain constant size, shape, color, and brightness when viewed under varied conditions. Perceived size of an object is a product of its retinal image size and distance.

Illusions occur when perceptions are based on inaccurate interpretations of sensory information. Illusions that seem to be based on inaccurate or ambiguous distance cues are the Ponzo and Müller-Lyer illusions, the moon illusion, and the Subjective Necker Cube illusion.

Interpretation of characteristics of people based on sensory information deriving from the people is called person perception. Cues for person perception are facial expressions, body gestures, and physical features of the face and body.

Many factors can modify or influence perceptions. Attention influences perceptions by determining which stimuli will reach an individual's awareness. Factors influencing attention are stimulus intensity, novelty, significance, and motivation.

A number of factors can influence the interpretation of sensory stimuli. Motivation is one such factor. Acupuncture anesthesia, for example, seems to rely, at least in part, on culturally motivated reduction in pain perception. Expectation of a stimulus also contributes to its perception.

Among the numerous theories dealing with variables that affect perception are adaptation-level theory, Gestalt theory, and cell-assembly theory. Adaptation-level theory proposes that stimuli that differ from an individual's adaptation level to stimulation tend to elicit a perceptual response. Stimuli to which an individual is attending, background stimuli, and residual stimuli from past experience all contribute to that person's adaptation level.

Gestalt theory emphasizes that certain innate principles guide perceptions. Among these principles are the tendency to perceive stimuli in terms of figure-ground relationships and the tendency to group stimuli into patterns that are regular, symmetrical, simple, and so forth.

Cell-assembly theory proposes that perceptions are learned responses to sensory stimulation. Experience with a stimulus leads to the formation of a cell assembly, whose activity produces a perception or interpretation of the stimulus.

Extrasensory perception is a perception of events or objects that is not mediated by any known sensory modality. ESP phenomena usually cannot be demonstrated under controlled experimental conditions.

NOW YOU'RE THE EXPERT

Look around you, wherever you may be. Attending to your various perceptions of things and events in your particular situation, see if you can answer all of the following questions:

What objects are occluded in your field of view? Which of them are closer to you, which farther away?

What visual texture and density gradients do you see that give you clues about distance?

Turning your head from side to side, what clues to distance of objects do you get from motion parallax?

What sound sensations do you have? Where are the sources located? What perceptions of objects and events do these sensations give you?

What perceptual constancies of size and shape of objects do you see in your field of view?

Can you identify features of your present perceptions that tie in with the adaptation-level and Gestalt theories of perception?

Have you yourself thought that you may have experienced extrasensory perception? Recall the experience and see if you can or cannot explain it in terms of ordinary perception, an illusion or hallucination, or on the basis of coincidence.

6

**States of
Consciousness**

TO DREAM OR NOT TO DREAM

■ Investigate your own dreams for several nights to provide yourself with firsthand observations about them. Keep a pencil and paper near your bed so you can record the content of your dreams as soon as you awaken, whether during the night or in the morning. If you wait until you are dressed or have breakfast, probably you will have forgotten most of your dreams. If you believe you rarely or never dream, make a special effort to try to recall dreams, searching your memory for them as soon as you wake up.

After you have noted the content of a number of your dreams, analyze their content, intensity, and emotional tone. Are they about past or future events? What roles do you or others play in your dreams? Do your dreams carry any symbolic meanings for you? What sensory experiences do dreams include? Do you experience color in dreams, or are your dreams in black and white?

An analysis of 1000 dreams reported by a group of adults has disclosed common dream material (Hall, 1951). The setting of most of these dreams was a familiar environment—a house, an automobile, a street or other outdoor area.

Although some people never recall color in dreams, 29 per cent of dreams in this study were experienced in color. As for the cast of characters, the dreamer was the only character in about 15 per cent of the dreams. When other persons appeared, they seemed to be strangers about half the time, and friends or relatives the other half. The emotional content of most dreams was negative. Apprehension was common, occurring 40 per cent of the time; anger, happiness, and excitement each occurred 18 per cent of the time; and sadness accounted for only 6 per cent of the dream emotions.

Many dream analysts believe that dreams supply a candid look at the way the dreamer views himself, the way others look to him, and his general attitude toward life. Yet dreams are so little understood at present that these views are only speculative. Dreams may merely represent a form of random thinking.

Can you exert control over your dreams? After you have recorded your dreams for several days, try focusing on some subject that stirs you for several minutes after you go to bed. It could be an old subject you feel strongly about or a new subject that arouses your feelings. Think hard about the subject, concentrate on various aspects of it, and express your feelings about it. When you wake up, try to remember: Did you dream about the subject? Could this kind of situation be one of the causes for your dreams?

■ CAN YOU ANSWER THESE?
Sleep and Dreams
What is the function of sleep, to which we devote about a third of our lives?
Does everyone dream, or are there some people who do not?

Hypnosis
What real differences, if any, exist between hypnotized and nonhypnotized persons?
What beneficial clinical applications have been found for hypnosis?

Meditation
What altered states of consciousness do meditators claim are involved in their experiences?
What actual physiological effects accompany regular meditation?

Psychoactive Drugs
How do the effects of stimulants differ from those of depressants?
Why is alcohol thought of as a stimulant when it is actually a depressant?

Two Spheres of Consciousness
Have you noticed how people shift their eyes sideways, to left or right, when trying to answer a complex question? What does this signify about them, if anything?

Many of the sensory and perceptual capacities of the normal awake and alert person have been discussed in the preceding chapters. These capacities contribute to the awareness of one's own private internal experiences, or **consciousness.** However, many **altered states of consciousness** are possible, quite different from the normal waking state. These altered states range from sleeping and dreaming through states of hypnosis and meditation to changes in consciousness induced by drugs.

Human beings have always been intrigued by altered states of consciousness and often have attempted to use them in various adaptive (and maladaptive) ways. Despite the great variety of altered states, they have many features in common (Ludwig, 1966). (1) Usually they involve cognitive changes due to alterations in attention, memory, thinking, or judgment. These cognitive processes are facilitated in some altered states, as in the case of states of alertness produced by stimulant drugs. However, cognitive processes are disturbed in most altered states of consciousness. Distinctions between cause and effect, appearance and reality, become blurred, as in dreaming. (2) The sense of time is affected, so that the passage of time may seem to stop, or be faster or slower than usual. Thus dreams may sometimes seem to occur in one flash or in slow motion. (3) A sense of loss of self or self-control, sometimes feared and sometimes desired, may accompany hypnosis, the use of drugs, and even just going to sleep. Meditators may seek the loss of self in a mystic experience that will reveal normally hidden realities or truths. The loss of self may be accompanied by changes in or loss of body image: a feeling of separation from the body, or weightlessness, or distortion of the body. (4) Loss of self-control is accompanied by increased suggestibility, so that people are more susceptible to their own repressed drives and desires; people under hypnosis are open to the suggestions of the hypnotist. (5) Emotional reactions, ranging from ecstasy to torment, occur with more primitive and intense expressions than usual. Drugs may produce "bad trips" as well as euphoria. Some dreams are delightful; others are fearful or depressing nightmares. (6) Hallucinations are frequent: Imagined events seem like reality. Sight, hearing, the sense of smell, and other modes of perception appear to be acutely sensitive. Mystics report vivid visual or other sensory impressions, as if they were experiencing the world in a new manner. (7) Often altered states of consciousness strike a person as extremely significant, leading to a rebirth of the self or a reinterpretation of reality with profound new insights, even though such experiences cannot be put into words or described. Because the experiences cannot be expressed, the uninitiated are often told that they cannot appreciate these states until they have experienced them themselves. Profound new truths acquired during altered states of consciousness tend to lack special significance when the individual returns to an ordinary state of awareness.

Consciousness normally undergoes changes every day. We all experience drastic alterations in consciousness when we pass from wakefulness to sleep.

SLEEP AND DREAMS

The normal states in which people are least aware of their environment are sleeping and dreaming. Only a comatose state, from which a person cannot be aroused, is lower than sleep on the continuum of levels of awareness or consciousness. Although we spend so much of our lives in sleep, 7 to 8 hours out of 24 on the average, we still know very little about its purpose.

Only recently has it been established that sleep is an active rather than a passive process. Although we frequently make statements like "I can't stay awake," implying that sleep is the absence of wakefulness, sleep is now known to be an independent state of consciousness that has its own triggering mechanism. The first such demonstration occurred when it was observed that electrical stimulation of numerous brain structures (through permanently implanted electrodes) caused alert cats to curl up and sleep (Hess, 1954). The triggering of sleep by brain stimulation suggests that sleep is an active process that may be "turned on" by certain conditions.

Since these initial observations, it has been shown that destruction of certain brain-stem areas causes insomnia, or inability to sleep,

just as destruction of another brain-stem area causes an animal to be permanently comatose. Normal wake-sleep cycles require the proper functioning of these brain-stem areas. Many other areas of the brain are also capable of modifying wake-sleep cycles.

Stages of Sleep

A normal night of sleep consists of a cyclic alternation between two main stages of sleep. One is the quiet stage, involving sleep as it is usually conceived. During this period, respiration is slow and regular, blood pressure drops slightly, heart rate is regular, and the **electroencephalogram (EEG),** a recording of brain electrical activity, is characterized by large-amplitude (high-voltage) slow-frequency waves that indicate a resting brain (see Figure 6-1).

The other sleep stage is physiologically more active. Blood pressure drops with brief periods of heightened pressure, respiration and heart rate increase and become irregular, muscle tone relaxes with occasional uncontrollable muscle jerks, and EEG recordings show small-amplitude fast-frequency waves characteristic of an alert brain (see Figure 6-1).

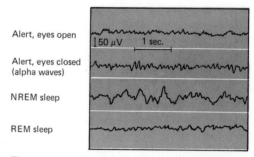

Figure 6-1 EEG recordings of electrical brain activity. Electrodes, attached to the scalp with tape, send spontaneous electrical activity of the brain to an amplifier and then to a paper chart recorder. The recordings presented here represent changes in amplitude (vertical deflections of the pen line) and frequency (number of deflections per second) of brain waves of a person during periods of alert wakefulness with the eyes open and closed, NREM sleep, and REM sleep.

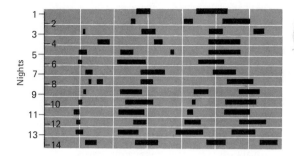

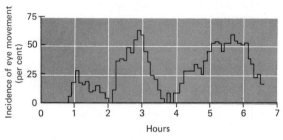

Figure 6-2 Rapid eye movements occurring during 14 consecutive nights of sleep for one subject. In the top graph, the presence of rapid eye movements during a seven-hour night of sleep is indicated by horizontal solid bars. The remainder of the sleep time was spent in the NREM stage. The histogram in the bottom graph shows the composite of the cycles of eye movements during the entire series of nights. (Kleitman, 1960)

Also readily observable during this stage are very rapid eye movements, 60 to 70 per minute, which may be seen under the sleeper's closed eyelids. Because the Rapid Eye Movements are the obvious feature of this sleep stage, it is called **REM sleep. Paradoxical sleep** is another name for it, because some physiological indices, like EEG, heart rate, and respiration, suggest an alert state, while psychological indices suggest that it is the deeper stage of sleep. As an example of a psychological measure, a person in the REM or paradoxical stage of sleep is more difficult to awaken than one in the quiet stage. This quiet sleep stage is often called **NREM or non-REM sleep.**

REM and NREM sleep are closely interrelated in their cyclic occurrence. As may be seen in Figure 6-2, NREM always precedes REM sleep, the latter occurring about three to four times a night at 80- to 120-minute intervals, each lasting from five minutes to over an hour. Approximately 20 per cent of total sleep time (or 1.5 hours) is spent in REM sleep nightly by adults.

Dreaming

Sleep researchers Nathaniel Kleitman and William Dement have determined that most dreams occur during REM stages of sleep. They asked volunteer research participants to spend a night of sleep in their sleep laboratory, where physiological measures could be made throughout the 7- to 8-hour period. The subjects were awakened at various times throughout the sleep period and asked if they had been dreaming. When the subjects were awakened during REM periods, they usually reported that they had been dreaming. Subjects rarely reported dreams during NREM periods.

Physiological changes that occur during dream periods seem to correspond with the dreamer's experience of participating in the dream activity. For example, a subject whose respiration and heart rate increase during a REM period may report upon awakening that she dreamed she was being chased, or a male subject who has a nocturnal emission may have dreamed of sexual activity. Fortunately, we are prevented from acting out our dreams at the motor level by an inhibitory mechanism that prevents full-fledged muscular activity. Sleepwalking cannot occur during REM periods, when muscular activity is blocked, but occasionally does occur during NREM periods, when muscle tone returns to its normal, uninhibited level.

Through objective observations of sleepers, a number of widespread notions have been discovered to be misconceptions. The first is that some people don't dream. Although some people are unable to remember dreams, all persons who have been observed sleeping have periods of REM activity nightly. Persons who claimed that they never dreamed nevertheless reported that they had been dreaming when they were awakened during REM periods of sleep. Although this finding does not surprise sleep investigators, such subjects are usually astonished when they find that they are indeed dreamers.

The second misconception is that dreams last only a fraction of a second. You have probably heard it said that dreams, no matter how intricate, occur in a brief moment of time. Reports from subjects awakened during dream periods, however, suggest that the time required to complete an action in a dream is about the same as it would take in the waking state, although some intermediary actions may be skipped, just as movies skip from one scene to another. Sleepers awakened a few minutes after a REM period begins report only the beginning of a dream.

The Function of Sleep

One of the long-unanswered questions about behavior is why animals sleep. Now that the existence of two distinct stages of sleep is known, another question emerges: Why two stages? Neither of these questions has yet been satisfactorily answered. The common assumption is that sleep provides needed rest for the body. But rest without sleep is not sufficient. If you have ever spent a sleepless night in bed, you know you feel tired rather than refreshed the next day.

Until recently, researchers have maintained that sleep is necessary in order to give the brain, rather than the body, a rest at the end of a hard day's work. EEG recordings, however, have shown that the brain is active during sleep, especially during the REM stage. Some areas of the brain are *more* active during sleep than during the waking stage (Evarts, 1967). Of course, certain critical areas of the brain may rest during sleep even though the brain as a whole does not.

One fruitful approach in attempting to discover the purpose of sleep is to look at the nature of sleep in the context of its evolutionary history. Since evolution selects adaptive characteristics, those processes that emerge during the course of evolution must have adaptive functions. Animals more primitive than reptiles (worms, insects, fish) do not sleep. Reptiles exhibit only NREM sleep, while higher animals show progressively more and more REM sleep. Evolutionary gain clearly suggests a functional significance for REM sleep, even if the precise nature of the function is still unknown.

Dement (1960) has shown that REM sleep is necessary for normal psychological functioning. His research approach was to deprive subjects of REM sleep by waking them each time physiological measures (eye movements and brain waves) indicated they had begun a REM period. By this method they were deprived of two-thirds to three-quarters of their normal REM sleep. Following a number of consecutive REM-deprivation nights, subjects were given several nights off to recover. Then they were given another series of interrupted nights that matched their first series in number of awakenings, although now they were awakened only during NREM periods. Following 2 to 10 nights of consecutive REM deprivation, subjects showed marked psychological disturbances: anxiety, irritability, difficulty in concentrating. None of these changes was seen following the period of NREM awakenings.

Subjects deprived of REM sleep seemed to try to make up the deficiency. The frequency of attempts to dream increased during REM deprivation. That is, subjects passed from NREM to REM sleep sooner than the usual one-hour interval after onset of sleep. REM-deprived subjects also spent a greater than normal percentage of sleep time in the REM phase during their recovery nights.

Speculations about the function of sleep, particularly the REM stage, have taken several forms. Giuseppe Moruzzi (1966) suggested that perhaps REM sleep is a period during which memories of the day's events are strengthened and put into permanent storage. (In Chapter 10, temporary and permanent aspects of memory are discussed. Briefly, some memories last only minutes or hours, while others last a lifetime. Permanent memory storage probably occurs through some relatively stable brain mechanism that consolidates short-term memories.)

Although Moruzzi's speculation is interesting, it is supported only by indirect evidence. First of all, the idea is compatible with the evolutionary development of REM sleep, since animals with more complex cognitive abilities do exhibit more REM sleep. Second, REM deprivation in humans does impair memory of events that occur during the deprivation period. Also, research has shown that recall of

learned information is better if a sleep period intervenes between learning and recall than if an equal period of rest or activity intervenes. Although memory consolidation may be going on during the intervening sleep period, the usual interpretation of this result is that sleep prevents intervening thoughts or activities from interfering with recall of the learned information.

William Dement and his associates have offered another interpretation of the purpose of sleep based on a study of its occurrence in the developing organism. Human newborns, as well as immature animals of other species, spend a greater percentage of sleep time in the REM stage than do adults. Figure 6-3 shows that newborns spend approximately 50 per cent of their total sleep time in REM sleep and that the percentage decreases as the individual matures. Dement suggests that perhaps REM

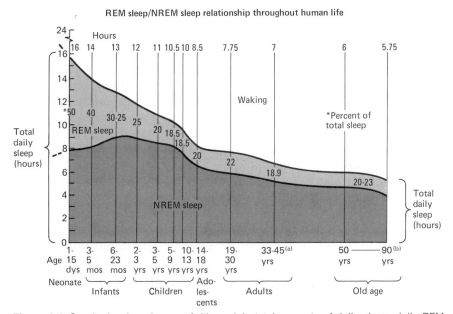

Figure 6-3 Graph showing changes (with age) in total amounts of daily sleep, daily REM and NREM sleep, and percentage of REM sleep (indicated in the light shaded area). Note the sharp diminution of REM sleep in the early years. REM sleep falls from 8 hours per day at birth to less than 1 hour in old age. The amount of NREM sleep throughout life remains more constant, falling from 8 hours to 5 hours. (Courtesy of Howard P. Roffwarg)

sleep serves a vital function of the immature organism. Specifically, it may serve to provide intense stimulation to the brain, thereby facilitating structural maturation. There is considerable evidence from other sources that stimulation of the nervous system enhances structural growth. Dement's hypothesis, if correct, would explain why infants need longer REM periods than adults and also why animals with more complex nervous systems require more REM sleep than those with relatively simple nervous systems.

It is hoped that further study will provide a better understanding of the purpose of sleep.

HYPNOSIS

"Is it real?" is the question most frequently asked about **hypnosis.** If "real" means that hypnosis is a highly suggestible subjective state that is uniformly experienced by hypnotized subjects and not faked, then the answer is yes. If, on the other hand, "real" means that hypnosis is a subjective state that may be clearly distinguished from the waking state, then the answer may be yes or no, depending on whom you ask. Some researchers who have studied hypnosis have concluded that it represents a special subjective state, the reported experiences and behaviors of which cannot be obtained by any other means. Hypnotized subjects, given appropriate suggestions, have been known to endure intense pain with no report of discomfort, to maintain fatigue-producing postures for extended periods of time, to report loss of sensory experience such as vision or audition and loss of memory, and to control various physiological responses that are traditionally (at least they were until recently) assumed not to be under voluntary control. Examples are changes in heart rate, pupillary diameter, and gastric acidity, and changes in skin vasodilation (diameter of blood vessels) that produce spots resembling burns or allergic skin responses. In a typical hypnosis experiment conducted recently, sub-jects under hypnosis were successful in simultaneously changing the skin temperatures of their two hands in opposite directions, while waking control subjects were not (see Figure 6-4).

Other researchers argue that hypnosis is a label applied to an extremely suggestible waking state that occurs under one or more of the following conditions: high motivation to please the hypnotist, expectation that certain experiences will derive from the hypnotic state (placebo effect), and extreme relaxation. According to this view, the hypnotic state is not unique, but rather a variation of the waking state that may be achieved by individuals with a positive attitude, high motivation, and expectancy toward the suggestions they are receiving.

Induction Procedures

Hypnosis may be produced by a variety of induction procedures in which the subject is told to relax and concentrate on suggestions by the hypnotist. Sometimes the subject is asked to stare at a stationary object until the eyes fatigue and close; sometimes the subject is asked to watch an object in rhythmic motion, such as a metronome. Most induction procedures are verbal, but some involve physical contact; a hypnotist may touch the subject's eyelids to make them close or otherwise physically signal a suggestion. Slow induction procedures involve a step-by-step relaxation technique that may take several hours, while some procedures take only a few minutes. Most induction procedures, however, require about 20 minutes. The more experienced in hypnosis a subject is, the less time is required for induction.

Controlled Experiments

One reason that researchers disagree about the uniqueness of hypnosis is that no objective or behavioral measure of it has been found.

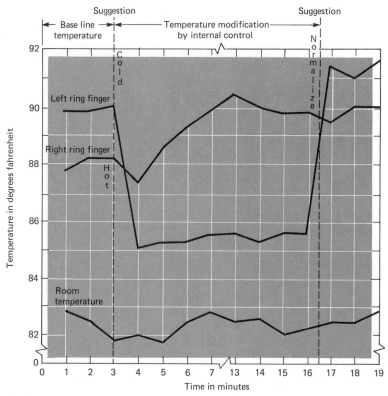

Figure 6-4 Simultaneous modification of skin temperatures in opposite directions in the right and left hands by one hypnotized subject. Following the suggestion to make the left hand colder and the right hand hotter, the subject rapidly regulated them in the appropriate directions. She reestablished the initial baseline temperature of the left hand as soon as she was given the instruction to normalize her skin temperature (in both hands). (Adapted from Maslach, Marshall, & Zimbardo: Hypnotic control of peripheral skin temperature: A case report, *Psychophysiology*, 1972, 9, 600–605. Reprinted with permission of the publisher, The Society for Psychophysiological Research)

Although hypnotized subjects have a characteristic trancelike appearance, this is not sufficiently unusual to infer that a unique subjective state exists. Objective physiological measures, including EEG activity, heart rate, and blood pressure, do not distinguish the hypnotic from the waking state.

Another reason for the lack of consensus about hypnosis is that well-controlled experimental investigations have only recently begun to be made. Early reports of successful hypnosis consisted of positive responses by

subjects to hypnotic suggestions, with no comparison of responses of alert controls. Subsequent controlled experiments have made this comparison. In many of these experiments, however, the experimental treatment of control subjects differed from that of hypnotized subjects in a number of important ways. First, of course, controls received no suggestion that they would go into a hypnotic trance. Then, when hypnotized subjects were told, for instance, "You will lose the hearing in your left ear," controls were often given no suggestion that any specific experience or behavior would occur. If controls were given some such suggestion, they received no instruction that would lead them to expect that they would be able to follow through with the suggestion, while hypnotized subjects were. Also, controls were not told that the suggested behavior was desirable, whereas hypnotized subjects were frequently told that they would please the hypnotist if they responded positively to the suggestion.

HYPNOSIS, DREAMS, AND THOUGHTS

A recent experiment explored relationships between a number of states of consciousness considered in this chapter: wakefulness, hypnosis, sleep, and dreaming and thinking during sleep (Barber, Walker, & Hahn, 1973). Seventy-seven female students between the ages of 17 and 22 slept in the laboratory for a night. Half of them were hypnotized before going to sleep and half were not. Some received authoritative instructions ("You will think and dream about the assassination of President Kennedy"); some received permissive instructions ("Try to think and dream about the assassination of President Kennedy"); and some received instructions with no special emphasis. One way or another, all of the subjects were asked to think and dream about the assassination of President Kennedy. The subjects were then awakened 10 minutes after they went to sleep, 10 minutes after the beginning of their first REM period of sleep, during a period of NREM sleep 45 minutes after the start of the first REM period, and during similar subsequent REM and NREM periods. When awakened, they were asked to tell what was going through their minds, whether they had been thinking or dreaming, what was the content of their thoughts or dreams, and how fast asleep they had been. When awakened at 6:30 A.M. the next morning, the subjects were asked to give any possible associations with the thoughts or dreams they'd had. All in all, it was a busy night. What effects did all these variations in conditions have on dreaming and thinking during sleep?

This experiment confirmed the conclusion of previous studies that thinking does not stop when we are asleep. Rather, a loose kind of thinking related to thoughts occurring during the day and just before sleep apparently continues much of the time we are sleeping. Slightly more thoughts (92) than dreams (85) were reported by subjects when they were awakened. Furthermore, the instructions given before sleep were found to influence the content of the *thoughts* of 42 per cent of the subjects and the *dream contents* of 25 per cent of the subjects. These subjects thought or dreamed about the assassination of President Kennedy. Hypnotism significantly increased the frequency of thinking about this subject, but the authoritative instructions had no greater effect than the permissive instructions on the thinking of the hypnotized subjects. Hypnotic induction did not affect dream content. Authoritative instructions, however, significantly increased the number of dreams on the specified topic for hypnotized subjects, while permissive instructions significantly increased the suggested dream content of nonhypnotized subjects.

These results leave us with perhaps more questions than we had before, a frequent consequence in scientific exploration of new fields. Why did hypnotized subjects have more thoughts about Kennedy's assassination than those who were not hypnotized, when hypnotism did not increase dreams about this subject? Why did the authoritative instructions affect the dreams of hypnotized subjects but not those of the subjects who were not hypnotized? Why were the subjects who were not hypnotized influenced by the permissive instructions but not by the authoritative instructions? The experimenters indicated that further research is needed to resolve these and many other problems arising from such studies of dreaming and thinking during sleep.

Were the results in your own dream activity in accord with the researchers' tentative conclusion that "subjects can learn to influence their own dreams by giving themselves suggestions before going to sleep at night. A potent effect on dream contents might also be produced if subjects purposively think about a particular topic immediately before going to sleep" (p. 426)?

T. X. Barber (1969) reported that he has produced suggested **analgesia** (inability to perceive pain), deafness, blindness, time distortion, hallucinations, feats of endurance, and amnesia as readily with task-motivated subjects (who were told they should try to accomplish and would be able to accomplish the suggested task) as with subjects given standard hypnotic induction. And there have been many other reports of positive physiological responses, comparable to those produced in hypnotized subjects, produced by suggestion in nonhypnotized motivated subjects. The response capability of nonhypnotized control subjects has surprised researchers and emphasizes the need for proper controls in all forms of experimentation. One commonly accepted definition of hypnosis specifies a psychological state in which suggestions from a hypnotist will elicit responses from the subject that are not ordinarily obtained from waking subjects, such as distortions of cognition, perception, or memory. Until the response limitations of awake, motivated subjects are determined, this definition has little value.

Martin Orne (1972) has suggested that certain real differences do exist between hypnotized and nonhypnotized subjects, even though their behavior cannot reliably be distinguished if the nonhypnotized subjects are motivated to follow the experimenter's suggestions. The main difference, according to Orne, may be the degree of *tolerance of incongruity.* Unlike nonhypnotized subjects, hypnotized subjects are not unduly troubled by suggested situations that cannot possibly exist in the real world. Orne reported as an example a situation in which subjects were told to hallucinate the presence of a particular person sitting in a chair. After the subjects reported that they "saw" Mr. X, the real Mr. X was brought in and the experimenter inquired, "Who is this?" Hypnotized subjects said something to the effect that there must be two Mr. Xs. Nonhypnotized subjects, who followed the instruction that they would be able to hallucinate the presence of Mr. X sitting in the chair, reported that the real and imagined persons could not be the same. Only the hypnotized subjects accepted the incongruent situation with minimum distress. Orne has pointed out that in this sort of situation the nonhypnotized subject does not know how to act hypnotized because he does not know how the hypnotized subject would react to that suggestion.

Susceptibility

All researchers agree that hypnosis, whether a highly suggestible waking state or a unique state of consciousness, occurs in varying degrees in different people. Most people can be hypnotized to some degree. Susceptibility data for 124 college students subjected to a standard induction procedure appear in Table 6-1. Fifty-five per cent of the subjects in this experiment were rated as having achieved a medium to high level of hypnosis, and only 6 per cent were judged to be unaffected by the induction procedure. A review of hypnotic susceptibility data shows the following: The optimum age for hypnosis is between 7 and 14 years; men and women are equally susceptible; intelligence is not a factor, given a minimum equal to elementary school level; and there is no typical personality of the hypnotically susceptible (Hilgard, 1967). Degree of imagination, however, does seem to be positively correlated with susceptibility.

Uses of Hypnosis

Unfortunately, hypnosis has traditionally been separated from the mainstream of psychologists' interests. Probably the factor contributing most significantly to the neglect of scientific interest is that throughout its history, hypnosis has been associated with witchcraft, spirit-rapping, clairvoyance, and trickery. Because hypnosis has no objective validation, charlatans have claimed great hypnotic powers as a gimmick to gain money or prestige. However, useful clinical and research applications

Table 6-1 Standardization Group Data for the Stanford Hypnotic Susceptibility Scale (SHSS) Obtained from 124 College Students

General Level	Raw Scores	Number of Cases		Per Cent of Cases		Percentile Rank
High	12	3		2		99
	11	6		5		95
	10	9	31	7	24	89
	9	5		4		84
	8	8		6		78
Medium	7	11		9		71
	6	10	39	8	31	62
	5	18		14		51
Low	4	13		11		38
	3	12		10		28
	2	13	54	11	45	18
	1	9		7		9
	0	7		6		3
		124		100		

Adapted from Weitzenhoffer & Hilgard, 1959.

of hypnosis, as practiced by trained hypnotists, clearly exist.

MESMERISM

The use of hypnosis is traced, historically, to Franz Mesmer, a medical student studying the causes of disease in Vienna in 1766 (Pattie, 1967). However, Mesmer's technique of inducing hypnosis, which he called "magnetic treatment," and his theories concerning its nature in no way resemble current practice and theories. Mesmer suggested that disease results from the unequal distribution of nervous fluid in the body, which normally ebbs and flows with atmospheric tides caused by gravitational forces of the sun and moon. He attempted to cure disease by giving patients medicine containing iron and then rhythmically passing magnets over their bodies to restore the natural flow of nervous fluid. His patients often underwent convulsions or crises during the treatment and later reported they could feel the swelling of nervous fluid with the passes of the magnet. Evidently they believed Mesmer's pronouncement that the treatment would be suc-

cessful—many reported a feeling of well-being following the ordeal.

Mesmer later found that the magnets were not necessary. He could simply pass his hands over the patients, thereby exerting the magnetic influence of his hands (although the magnetic field of all the rest of us is actually incredibly small). Mesmer was insulted by the suggestion that the beneficial effects of his treatment were psychological in nature. He firmly believed in the physical foundation of his treatment. Mesmer's later followers recognized the psychological basis of the phenomenon and initiated a relaxation-induction procedure similar to those used today in hypnosis.

Clinically, hypnosis is useful in the diagnosis and treatment of certain emotional problems. One of its most beneficial diagnostic applications is for **hysteric conversions,** a behavior disorder in which an emotional problem is converted into a physical symptom that has no physical base (see Chapter 15). As an example, a woman was recently admitted to a hospital with a sudden inability to speak. After a thorough examination uncovered no medical basis for her problem, a psychological examination under hypnosis was conducted. Under hypnosis the woman was told that she would be able to speak if she wanted to. The woman did speak and during the accompanying emotional release she said she was greatly troubled by her epileptic seizures. In such a seizure, periodic abnormal brain activity occurs together with loss of consciousness and muscular twitching. Fortunately, most epileptic patients can be successfully treated with drugs, but for a few who are not responsive to drugs and are incapacitated by the disorder, such as this patient, an operation in which the defective area of the brain is removed is the best hope of relief. The patient reported that she had been told by a neurologist that a corrective operation could not be performed in her case because the area of the brain causing the seizures was close to the speech center. An operation might leave her unable to speak. The psychiatrist who performed the hypnosis concluded that the woman had decided, probably unconsciously, that relief from seizures was more important than speech, and therefore had lost her speech so that there would be no reason for not performing the operation. Hypnosis used to relieve a symptom of hysteric conversion is not a treatment for the psychological problem. Unless the problem underlying the hysteria is resolved, the symptom may reappear, some therapists feel.

A second beneficial clinical application of hypnosis is as an aid to psychotherapy. Freud keenly observed that a suggestion given during hypnosis would often not be recalled upon awakening. He immediately realized the importance of the possibility that powerful mental processes could remain hidden from consciousness. Freud used hypnosis to make patients revert to the psychic state in which their mental problem first had appeared; in his words, he brought about **age regression.** Freud believed that if a patient's hidden problem or conflict could be brought forth during the hypnosis, the conflict could be resolved through understanding. Although Freud's use of hypnosis was instrumental in establishing its therapeutic usefulness, he eventually abandoned hypnosis for the technique of free association (see Chapter 16).

Currently hypnosis is used most frequently as a supplement to other forms of psychotherapy in cases in which clients are resistant to discussing or recognizing their problems. Hypnosis provides a setting in which individuals can relax and release their inhibitions by turning over control to the therapist. Also, hypnotic suggestions are used as a means of helping people break such bad habits as smoking and overeating. This works well for some clients, but not enough data are available to permit comparison of the technique with other behavior-modification procedures.

Interest in hypnosis has recently increased as a means of learning the limits of psychological control over physiological processes. Through self-hypnosis, people are being taught to control migraine headaches, hypertension, and other psychosomatic problems.

MEDITATION

Meditation is a procedure of inner withdrawal and concentration that has been developed in great detail by the leaders and disciples of various religious sects, particularly in the Far East. According to meditators, detachment from the finite self leads to attachment with the infinite being, the One, or Nirvana, variously described as perfect bliss or complete loss of consciousness.

Meditation Procedures

According to Hinduism, any number of paths may be followed toward union with the One. The way of jnana-yoga is through knowledge, of bhakti-yoga through love, of karma-yoga through work, of hatha-yoga through physical exercises. Raja-yoga maintains that the royal road to union is through psychological exercises. In following raja-yoga, the practitioner learns many principles of abstinence and self-discipline, learns how to sit in the proper relaxed posture (of which there are many), and learns how to regulate breathing and to withdraw from the senses to an inner world through concentration on one object. The final state of ultimate union with the One is achieved during half-conscious meditation, in which the mind is void of content and the distinction between subject and object is dissolved.

Transcendental meditation (TM) is a simple modern version of this meditation practice, developed by Maharishi Mahesh Yogi and taught by an organization of instructors personally qualified by him. As practiced in this country, it consists of 15- to 30-minute periods of meditation, usually two daily, in which the meditator sits in a comfortable position and attempts to focus attention on one source of stimulation to the exclusion of all others. The stimulus is a special sound, called the **mantra**, which the meditator repeats over and over. A mantra is selected for each meditator on the basis of individual personality. The goal is to contemplate this stimulus source so that all thought is banished save the bare percept of the mantra. Thus the meditator sits with eyes closed and perceives the sound, gradually arriving at its ultimate source so that it is experienced in a very basic manner, and all objective, analytical thinking is eliminated.

Another widespread type of meditation is practiced by followers of Zen Buddhism. Preparation is accomplished through realization of the weaknesses of logical thinking by trying to solve such inscrutable problems as "What is the appearance of your face before your ancestors were born?" or "What is the sound of one hand clapping?" Meditation is carried on in seated posture with eyes half closed and unfocused. This meditation eventually leads to the experience of **satori**, which the Zen Bud-

dhist finds difficult to describe. Life is viewed in this experience as completely good, with others' welfare as important as one's own. In satori, the meditator transcends pleasure and displeasure, good and evil, acceptance and rejection, to pass into an entirely blissful and eternal state.

All forms of meditation have certain features in common. Perhaps the most prominent is an experience of unity of one's self with the universe or God. The meditator also seems to transcend or rise above usual perceptions, moving toward perceptions that are more vivid than normal. Unique sensory experiences occur that are difficult to describe, as in many states of altered consciousness. These experiences are accompanied by a strong sense of ultimate reality.

MEDITATION AND PSYCHOLOGICAL STATES

If meditation is a condition of restful alertness distinct from the waking, sleeping, dreaming, and hypnotic states, then meditation, if practiced regularly, might have some effects on the psychological mood or personality of the meditator. In fact, some recent experiments have turned up such significant effects, although the number of subjects studied was not large.

In one series of experiments, the autonomic stability of meditators was compared with that of nonmeditators by presenting the subjects unexpectedly with a very loud noise at varying intervals of time, until they became habituated to it (Orme-Johnson, 1973). The subjects' reactions to this stress were measured in terms of **galvanic skin response (GSR)** The eight meditators, both men and women, had been meditating regularly twice a day for an average of 15 months. They habituated twice as quickly to the random noises as the nonmeditators, and showed many fewer multiple GSR responses to the first noise presented. Furthermore, these eight meditators (and another group of the same number of meditators) showed a much lower frequency of spontaneous GSRs both when simply resting and when meditating than a comparable number of resting nonmeditators. Meditators typically judge that they progressively gain more emotional stability and capacity to resist stresses, and this experiment offers evidence that supports their reports. Furthermore, many other studies have shown that quick habituation and low spontaneous rates of GSR are correlated with such indicators of good mental health as autonomic system stability, strong ego, low susceptibility to stress, and outgoingness.

Scores on a Personal Orientation Inventory of an experimental group of 15 subjects who had meditated regularly for two months and scores of a control group of 20 nonmeditators were compared in another experiment (Seeman, Nidich, & Banta, 1972). The inventory attempts to measure self-actualization. Apparently the meditation had good psychological effects, for meditators showed significantly more inner-directedness, an indication of self-determination. They also were more capable of expressing their feelings in spontaneous action, of accepting their own aggressive feelings, and of making intimate contacts.

Although the significant results of these and other experiments have tended to support the psychological benefits of meditation, these cannot be accepted generally as yet, for the numbers of subjects have been small and in the main they have been young college students, not typical of the general population. In addition, personality and emotional variables influence a person's decision to try meditation. The meditation experience might be expected to attract people who are inner-directed and capable of expressing emotions. People who are shy and lack self-determination are probably less likely to try meditation. Ideally, from a research design point of view, individuals should be randomly assigned to either a meditation or nonmeditation condition in experimentation. Self-selection by the individuals studied may result in bias that leads to erroneous conclusions about the data.

For some people, adverse side effects of meditation have been suggested, such as withdrawal from life, insomnia, and even hallucinations (Benson, Beary, & Carol, 1974).

Attempts to study the psychological characteristics of meditation have often been thwarted by the same problems that plagued Wilhelm Wundt in 1879 in his attempts to study conscious experience. Wundt hypothesized that all complex experiences result from a combination of basic experiences. He sought, through a method called **introspection,** to analyze conscious experiences into their component elements, much as a chemist would analyze water into two parts hydrogen and one part oxygen. Although Wundt established a rigorous scientific method, his goal was not achieved because the nature of the task was too difficult. Trained introspectors could not agree on the nature of their basic experiences. Any investigation that relies solely on reports from research participants has built-in problems of misinterpretation, distortion, and inaccuracy in the subjective reports. Mystic experiences reported by meditators have the same drawbacks, further complicated by the inability of most meditators to describe unusual aspects of their experiences in words. Given these inherent problems, however, reports of mystic experiences have been remarkably uniform in their major characteristics.

Researchers have not yet adequately tested the hypothesis that reports of meditation experiences are independent of such factors as preconceptions, preexpectations, and suggestions from the spiritual guide (Barber, 1970). Meditation may be a pleasant experience because the meditator expects it to be.

Meditation and Physiological Changes

The physiological changes that occur during meditation are in some ways dramatic, and indicate that meditation really is a state of consciousness different from the normal waking state. Research by Kasamatsu and Hirai (1971) has, in fact, shown that during meditation practiced by Zen masters and disciples, the altered state of consciousness is accompanied by distinct changes in the EEG. Even while the eyes remain open, alpha waves begin to appear and grow stronger as the meditation continues. **Alpha waves** are slow high-voltage patterns of electrical activity of the brain, occurring at a frequency of 8 to 12 cycles per second, which usually accompany states of wakeful mental alertness and relaxation when the eyes are closed. Moreover, the longer the disciples in the experiment had been receiving Zen training, and the more proficient they were considered to be, the greater the prevalence of alpha waves in the EEG record. While the occurrence of alpha waves cannot be said to *cause* the relaxed mental state, whatever one does to produce alpha waves may also be sufficient to produce a concomitant reduction of tension. But how can someone be taught to produce more alpha waves?

The pioneer of alpha brain wave research is Joe Kamiya, at this writing at the Langley Porter Institute in San Francisco. In the late 1950s, while Kamiya was engaged in dream and sleep research at the University of Chicago, he began to investigate the possibility that some brain functions, indexed by EEG patterns, might correlate with various states of consciousness. He became especially interested in whether people could learn to sense changes occurring in their EEG patterns while they were wide awake. In one of his earliest experiments (Kamiya, 1962), while his subjects were lying relaxed with their eyes closed, Kamiya would ring a bell several times a minute. About half the time, the bell would sound when the EEG apparatus showed the subject was producing alpha waves; half the time it was rung when no alpha was occurring. Kamiya instructed the subjects to guess whether or not alpha waves were being generated each time the bell was rung on the basis of the way they felt at that moment. Kamiya told the subjects whether they had guessed right or wrong. Can people tell when they're generating alpha waves? Kamiya's six subjects took from 50 to 500 trials to reach a level of 80 per cent correct responses. After a few hours of training, some subjects were correct 100 per cent of the time.

CONTROL OF ALPHA WAVES

Nowlis and Kamiya (1970) have investigated the psychological states associated with "turning on" and "turning off" electroencephalographic (EEG) alpha rhythms. Twenty-six subjects of both sexes participated, ranging in age from 21 to 30. Subjects were seated in a large reclining chair in a darkened, sound-deadened room. Electrodes on the subjects' scalps recorded their alpha waves, while earphones fed back tones to them when alpha waves were present. Then subjects were given two minutes to remain still with their eyes closed and become accustomed to the tone coming on and going off while the baseline levels of their alpha waves were measured.

Subjects were then instructed to see if they could figure out for themselves what made the tone come on and go off, and to tell the experimenter when they felt they understood what did. During this period, the tone indicated that alpha waves were being recorded in the EEG. After up to 15 minutes of this, subjects with eyes closed were given two minutes to keep the tone *on* with their alpha waves and another two minutes to keep the tone *off* by preventing the rhythms. Ten of the subjects with high alpha rates were then given similar trials with their eyes open. Most of the subjects succeeded in slightly increasing their alpha waves over their baseline rates, and all subjects had significantly more alpha during their "on" trials than during their "off" trials. None of the subjects showed inappropriate changes in alpha waves for either trial. Subjects did nearly as well with eyes open as with eyes closed. Given feedback, subjects were therefore largely able to control their alpha waves with eyes both open and closed. They were then asked in an open-ended interview how they accomplished this feat.

Although subjects reported that they controlled their alpha waves in many ways, these could easily be categorized in several major groups of methods indicative of their psychological states. Many kept alpha waves on, whether their eyes were opened or closed, simply by relaxing thoroughly, by a sense of letting go or floating, or by calling forth feelings of pleasure, security, or sensual warmth. They discontinued their alpha waves by being alert and vigilant, by tension or excitement, by visual attentiveness, or even by imagining seeing the room. Relaxation and tranquillity, then, seem to accompany alpha waves, and the rhythms disappear with tension and attentiveness. This finding is consistent with the observation that levels of alpha increase during the tranquillity of meditation.

Some researchers (Paskewitz & Orne, 1973) feel that control of alpha waves has not been demonstrated adequately in this experiment and related ones. Although most subjects slightly increased alpha activity during "turning on" periods over baseline rates with the eyes open, they may have been doing this by simply adapting to the experimental situation with the passage of time. Alpha control periods are usually compared with baselines obtained early in testing, perhaps before the subjects have adjusted to the testing procedure. Subjects in feedback experiments have been much more effective at decreasing rather than increasing their alpha activity, which accounts for most of the difference in alpha activity between "turning on" and "turning off" periods. But most people can decrease alpha activity by intense visual scanning without a change in subjective mood.

But what good is alpha? What will alpha do for you? How does it feel? Everyone seems to agree that, while in alpha, a person feels a general relaxation, a gentle calming of the mind. The person is not sleepy or drowsy, but remains quite alert. It's a good feeling, so good that Kamiya no longer has to pay subjects for participating in his experiments. Some are almost ready to pay him, and he has a long waiting list of people from all over the country.

The more probable benefits of systematic alpha training may lie in its usefulness in achieving a state of relaxation and in decreasing susceptibility to stress through reduced affective arousal (Nideffer, 1973). But relatively little is known about the long-term effects of alpha training, the best techniques for training people to control alpha, individual differences in control, and the underlying mechanism responsible for the results obtained.

Other profound physiological changes take place during meditation. In one experiment (Wallace & Benson, 1972), physiological measures from 36 transcendental meditators were taken before, during, and after a 30-minute meditation session. EEG recordings showed a marked intensification of "slow" alpha waves (eight to nine cycles per second) during the meditation period when compared with levels before and after meditation. In addition, significant decreases were observed in oxygen consumption, carbon dioxide elimination, levels of blood lactate (a substance produced in skeletal muscles during activity or stress), and respiration rates during the meditation session. Electrical resistance of the skin increased during meditation. All of these physiological changes are indicative of a restful, serene state. Moreover, the pattern of changes recorded during TM occurred more rapidly and, for some measures, were more pronounced than changes occurring during sleep. On the basis of these measures, meditation seems to be more restful than sleep. It also seems to be a conscious state clearly distinct from hypnosis, since physiological measures do not change between waking and hypnotic states. Figure 6-5 compares changes in oxygen consumption during meditation, hypnosis, and sleep.

A recent study (Pagano, Rose, Stivers, & Warrenburg, 1976) has shown that it is difficult to distinguish when people are meditating or sleeping, based on EEG measures. The EEG records of five advanced TM meditators showed that the subjects were asleep 40 per cent of their meditation time, on the average. The reports of the subjects themselves confirmed that they had been asleep during portions of their meditation sessions when sleep patterns appeared in the EEG. The prevalence of sleep during meditation led the investigators to conclude that "the range of states observed during meditation does not support

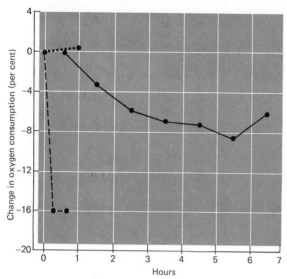

Figure 6-5 Oxygen consumption during a one-hour hypnotic trance (dotted line), a brief period of TM (broken line), and over six hours of sleep (solid line). Compared with sleep, meditation brings twice the reduction in a fraction of the time. No significant change occurs under hypnosis. (Wallace & Benson, 1972)

the view that meditation produces a single, unique state of consciousness" (p. 308), and to question "whether the beneficial effects reported for meditation . . . are due to the sleep that occurs during meditation or to some other feature of that process" (p. 309). We are still left with the evidence (Wallace & Benson, 1972) that other physiological processes, such as oxygen consumption, slow down more during meditation than during sleep. Unfortunately, the recent study that found no difference in EEG patterns did not report comparisons for other physiological measures.

PSYCHOACTIVE DRUGS

Many kinds of psychoactive drugs, or chemicals that affect the mind, exist: stimulants, depressants, hallucinogens, and mood modifiers. The first three classes of drugs, which primarily alter an individual's level of consciousness or alertness, will concern us here.

Drug use for the purpose of changing states of consciousness has increased dramatically in recent years. Although drugs have been used for this purpose since the beginning of recorded history, and probably earlier, only in the last two decades has a frequent use of drugs (other than alcohol and caffeine) become a way of solving problems or exploring new experiences in some Western subcultures. Americans spend over $30 billion each year for legal drugs that alter awareness or mood, an additional $18 billion on alcoholic beverages, and $1.5 billion on coffee, tea, and cocoa, all containing stimulants (Ray, 1972). Psychoactive drugs are extremely valuable for treating individuals with various forms of mental illness, but concern has arisen recently that the widespread use of drugs by the general population has reached the stage of drug abuse. The incidence of use of illegal psychoactive drugs is also high.

Many cultural conditions contribute to the present increase in drug use in this society: rapid technological advances producing feelings of social instability, the breakdown in both extended and nuclear family structure, a feeling of alienation or boredom by vast segments of the society, and many more. One very basic reason is availability. Drugs from natural sources, such as alcohol, are more efficiently distributed today, and new synthetic drugs are being developed at a rapid rate. About 70 per cent of all prescriptions written today are for drugs unknown 30 years ago (Ray, 1972).

All psychoactive drugs exert their psychological and physiological effects by altering the activity of one or more areas of the brain. A drug either increases, decreases, or disrupts ongoing neural activity. Most drugs affecting the central nervous system alter chemical transmission at the synapse, some by changing the amount of synaptic transmitter available and some by blocking or facilitating the release and transmission of the synaptic transmitter across the synapse to the appropriate receptor site (see Chapter 2). In general, stimulants increase synaptic activity and depressants decrease synaptic activity; the exact mechanisms of action of many of the hallucinogens is unknown. A few drugs, such as alcohol, alter the membrane properties of the entire cell and thereby interfere with the conduction of the nerve impulse along the axon. **Psychopharmacology** is the scientific study of the behavioral and psychological effects of drugs, including their effects on perceptual, emotional, and cognitive functions.

The psychological effect of a drug is to some extent dependent on the user's personality, past experiences, and expectancies. This is particularly true in the case of LSD. Some users have fantastic "trips," while others have nightmarish experiences from the same amount of the drug. Although LSD has a common physiological effect in all users, the individual's interpretation of the meaning of the induced effect determines the nature of the psychological experience. A drug may have a psychological effect even when it does not change in any way the physiological state of the user, provided the user expects a drug-induced result—the placebo effect.

Several psychopharmacological concepts are important in the evaluation of drugs. The first is **tolerance.** When repeated use of a drug produces a diminished drug effect, tolerance to the drug has been established. Tolerance may develop to one aspect of a drug effect and not to another. This is beneficial when tolerance develops to an undesirable side effect of a drug, but not to the desired effect. Thus, a constant dose of a drug may produce diminished side effects with time. Frequently, however, tolerance develops to the desired effect of the drug, requiring the user to take larger and larger doses to reproduce the initial drug effect.

The second important concept is **drug dependence.** When a drug user feels that a drug is necessary for the maintenance of an optimal state of well-being, the user is said to have acquired **psychological dependence** on the drug. Many people feel psychologically dependent on alcohol in times of social stress. In the extreme, psychological **drug addiction** may occur. That is, the drug user may develop a strong craving for a drug that leads to an overwhelming preoccupation with securing and using it.

When continued use of a drug is necessary to prevent a series of undesirable physiological responses, we say that **physical dependence** on the drug has developed. It is not known why people become physically dependent on some drugs. Presumably, the body makes physiological adjustments to the presence of the drug. Abrupt withdrawal causes a reversal to the predrug state that is so rapid that the body has difficulty adjusting. For example, drugs that generally depress the activity of the brain can produce sudden increased excitability with abrupt withdrawal.

Physiological responses to abrupt withdrawal of a drug produce the **withdrawal syndrome.** It may range in severity from mild discomfort to agonizing death, depending on drug, drug dose, and physical and mental state of the addict at the time of withdrawal. Although often related, psychological and physical dependence on a drug can occur independently. It is possible to be psychologically dependent on a drug without being physically dependent on it, and to be physically dependent without being psychologically dependent.

Stimulants

A **stimulant** is a drug that tends to increase alertness, reduce fatigue, and induce euphoria. In high doses it may induce irritability and anxiety. The most commonly used stimulant is **caffeine,** a natural constituent of coffee and tea and, in small amounts, of cola-flavored beverages. (See Table 15-3 for common sources of caffeine.) One cup of coffee has approximately the same amount of caffeine as two cups of tea or two 12-ounce bottles of cola beverage.

In regular caffeine users, one or two cups of coffee or their equivalent offsets fatigue and produces alertness, clear thinking, and a feeling of well-being. It is no wonder that a psychological dependence on the drug develops in many people. How many people do you know who feel they need the lift from a cup of coffee first thing in the morning before they start the day?

Although caffeine is a very mild stimulant, some noncaffeine users experience a nervous, jittery feeling from the amount of caffeine in one cup of coffee. With continued use, tolerance to the nervous feeling usually develops. Overindulgence in caffeine may produce undesirable effects such as sleeplessness, upset stomach, excess urine (polyuria), and even cardiac irregularities. These effects are sometimes mistaken for anxiety (see Chapter 15). Except for individuals with special medical problems (hypertension, peptic ulcer), moderate use of the drug, the equivalent of one or two cups of coffee a day, has no harmful physical effect. However, a drug can be classified as undesirable simply on the basis of its tendency to produce psychological dependence. Is caffeine an undesirable drug if you feel that you cannot get started in the morning without it? Many psychologists think the answer is yes.

Amphetamine, a more potent stimulant, was first used in the 1930s in a bronchial decongestant inhaler. Amphetamine misuse began almost immediately. People began sniffing (and even sucking) the inhalers as soon as it was realized that the effects counteracted fatigue and boredom and produced euphoria. Misuse spread throughout the world, especially during World War II, when soldiers were given amphetamine to combat battle fatigue. Following the war, overprescription of the drug was common in this country by "Dr. Feelgoods" who sought ways to give their patients a lift. In 1970 the drug was classified for restricted use by the Federal Drug Administration. The only legal uses now are for **narcolepsy** (a disorder that causes its victims to fall asleep frequently at inappropriate times during the day), **hyperkinesis** (a condition of overactivity in children; the drug has the paradoxical effect of calming them down), and weight control (amphetamine produces a marked reduction in appetite).

The Federal Drug Administration considers the drug to be dangerous for several reasons. First, and perhaps most importantly, its chronic use may produce a state similar to paranoid psychosis (see Chapter 15). This form of mental disturbance is characterized by delusions of persecution. Commonly, the chronic amphetamine user comes to believe that someone is out to get him or her, a condition that sometimes results in violence. The development of compulsive behaviors such as picking the skin is also common. A second reason for restricted use is that amphetamine may produce physical dependence. Debate over the issue of physical dependence continues, but abrupt cessation of the use of amphetamine does often produce depression and extreme fatigue.

Today many illegal users take another form of the drug, **methamphetamine**, better known as "speed." Taken intravenously in solution, this drug produces an initial "flash" of stimulation and euphoria described as sexually orgasmic in character. As with amphetamine, tolerance develops and some users increase the dose to obtain the desired effects. The major danger of the drug is that it too may produce a state of extreme paranoid psychosis. Stereotyped, repetitious behavior such as picking of the skin often occurs in users.

Another stimulant very similar to amphetamine is **cocaine.** It is popularly believed that cocaine gives a more intense euphoria, but no objective evidence supports this notion. Overdoses are extremely serious and may cause seizures and death from respiratory failure.

Depressants

A **depressant** is a drug that tends to decrease alertness and induce drowsiness. The most commonly used depressant and the most misused drug in our society is **alcohol.** Most people use alcohol because it produces a happy feeling, a "high," and because it reduces anxiety. Used in social situations to reduce tension, it allows the user to become more gregarious and maybe even to become the life of the party. Although alcohol acts as a depressant in the central nervous system, in moderate doses it seems to stimulate behavior. The explanation for this paradox may be that alcohol depresses areas of the cortex that normally inhibit emotional behavior. With the cortical check removed, unreserved emotional behavior is expressed. At higher doses, alcohol produces motor impairment, mental confusion, and impairment of judgment. Unfortunately, one of the judgments that is impaired is when to stop drinking.

An alcoholic is someone who uses alcohol regularly to an extent that interferes with day-to-day behavior. In the United States, as in Great Britain, France, and some other countries, alcoholism is a major medical problem. About 2.5 per cent of the total population of the United States, or over 5 million people, are estimated to be alcoholics (Ray, 1972). Alcohol use costs this country about $25 billion a year in absenteeism, accidents, and treatment costs. The most common medical hazards of chronic alcohol use are cirrhosis of the liver and brain damage (actually due to vitamin B deficiency, common in alcoholics).

Not only do alcoholics psychologically depend on alcohol to help them cope with anxiety and frustration, but they develop physical dependence on the drug. Withdrawal reactions from abrupt discontinuation of heavy alcohol use are extremely severe, sometimes resulting in death. The **barbiturates** are the second most commonly used depressants. This class of drug includes pentobarbital, secobarbital, and others. Aside from use as medical anesthetics, these drugs are primarily used to combat insomnia and anxiety. (Barbiturates also are sometimes used to raise seizure thresholds in epileptic patients.) Barbiturates produce a drowsy aftereffect over a period of days, possibly because they reduce the amount of time spent in the REM stage of sleep. As noted earlier in this chapter, REM sleep is an important part of the sleep process.

Barbiturates are frequently, perhaps too frequently, prescribed by physicians as sedatives. The user may initially take the drug as prescribed, but then increase the frequency of use. Tolerance develops rapidly, and the user must take larger and larger doses to get the desired effect. It has been estimated that the illegal market for barbiturates and related sedative-hypnotic drugs probably exceeds that of the narcotic drugs (Sharpless, 1970). Physical dependence on barbiturates develops, and sudden withdrawal can be extremely dangerous. Withdrawal from normal therapeutic doses is mild, but withdrawal from heavy use may produce seizures, delirium, and even death. An additional hazard of the barbiturates is that they are the "drugs of choice" for suicide through overdose, now accounting for about one-fifth of all suicides (Ray, 1972).

Hallucinogens

The **hallucinogens** produce distortions in cognition and perception, often including hallucinations.

Marijuana is a minor hallucinogen. Its primary effect is to produce euphoria, but it also yields distortions in cognition and perception. Users sometimes report visual experiences when their eyes are closed, though true hallucinations do not occur.

Marijuana has a long history of use. Like many of the hallucinogens, it has been used in religious and therapeutic practices in other cultures for centuries. Extensive use in this culture occurred for the first time in the 1960s. Marijuana is obtained from the female plant of Indian hemp, *Cannabis sativa.* The concentrated resin of the plant, known as hashish, contains the active ingredient tetrahydrocannabinol. In this country, marijuana and hashish are usually smoked.

Intoxication lasts two to four hours after smoking marijuana. The user usually reports a feeling of well-being, with flights of thought. Also common are reports of distortion of time, with a few minutes seeming like an hour; distortions of space; a sensation of flying or swimming; and a tendency to laugh. One well-documented effect of marijuana intoxication is a disruption of short-term memory (see Chapter 10). While intoxicated, the user has difficulty recalling information learned only a few minutes before. Also common is a phenomenon called **dissociation,** in which the user experiences a splitting of consciousness (see Chapter 15). That is, the user is at the same time both a doer and an observer. You may have experienced a form of dissociation in dreams when you were both a character in the dream and at the same time an observer ''knowing'' you were dreaming.

Frequently, an inexperienced user detects no effects of marijuana, but with repeated experiences the user somehow learns to recognize and enjoy the subtle effects. This effect is sometimes referred to as ''reverse tolerance.'' All in all, marijuana intoxication seems to have fewer negative features than alcohol intoxication. The marijuana high is mild enough so that the user can turn it off or control it at will, and no hangover follows.

The drug does not produce a physical dependency. Psychological dependency on the drug may occur, but does so less frequently than with alcohol (Grinspoon, 1969). Because of the marijuana boom, there has been considerable interest in determining whether the drug has any long-term potential hazards. The debate over these hazards is currently at full

tide. Most studies of long-term use in humans and other animals have found no harmful effects. A few studies, however, have suggested that marijuana may cause chromosome damage, disrupt cellular metabolism, cause impotence and temporary sterility, and result in brain damage (see Maugh, 1974). When marijuana is smoked regularly, it can cause irritation of the bronchial tract and lungs. (So will smoking anything else.) Marijuana cigarettes have more tar, the presumed carcinogenic compound in tobacco, than commercial tobacco cigarettes. Therefore, lung cancer is a potential hazard for marijuana smokers.

The Federal Drug Administration considers marijuana to be potentially hazardous, and classifies it as illegal, mainly because its safety is not firmly established. Certainly the hazards of chronic use of marijuana seem at this time to be much less severe than those from chronic alcohol consumption. The Federal Drug Administration does not control the use of alcohol simply because it cannot. Alcohol use was widespread before the existence of the regulatory agency. As you know, prohibition was tried and abandoned.

LSD (lysergic acid diethylamide) is a semisynthetic drug made from an extract of the fungus *Claviceps purpurea.* Its potent psychological effects were discovered in 1938 but were not made publicly known until 1943. In this country, LSD use, largely by the younger generation, reached a peak in the late 1960s. Since LSD produces primarily sensory distortions rather than euphoria, it is probably used most frequently by individuals who are seeking new adventures or are simply bored by life's routines.

Other psychological effects of an LSD ''trip'' are time distortions, an inner experience of self-discovery, difficulty in thinking, mood alternations that may swing from one extreme to the other, and dissociation. The overwhelming majority of users take the drug only a few times, perhaps because of the eventual loss of novelty of the experience, and because even on a "good" trip, dissociation is a frightening experience.

Frequency of LSD use has dropped in recent years. The major contributing factor may be the knowledge that LSD often produces bad trips. When intoxicated, some users panic, primarily because of a fear that they will not return to a normal state or because they feel they are disintegrating. Users often experience the inability to distinguish the boundaries of forms and may feel that they are blending into the environment. Sometimes LSD use leads to a psychotic reaction, often involving paranoia. The psychosis usually dissipates after the 12-hour intoxication period, but a few cases of permanent psychoses have been reported. Sometimes "flashbacks" of intoxication experiences occur weeks or months after use.

Physical dependence has not been observed in humans. There have been a few reports that LSD may cause harmful physiological effects such as chromosome damage, but the data are not convincing at this time. The severe psychological effects of LSD alone probably warrant its reputation as a hazardous drug.

TWO SPHERES OF CONSCIOUSNESS

Normally the cortices of the left and right hemispheres communicate by means of a large fiber tract that connects them, the corpus callosum of the brain (see Figure 6-6). The integration of function of the two hemispheres through the corpus callosum allows one to think, feel, and act as a unified person. When the corpus callosum is severed, the two hemispheres function independently. A small number of individuals have undergone operations to sever the corpus callosum for control of epileptic seizures. (Partial, rather than complete, severance of the corpus callosum is now used successfully as a surgical procedure for controlling seizures.) For these individuals, two independent spheres of consciousness exist within one person. Each hemisphere is completely unaware that the other exists.

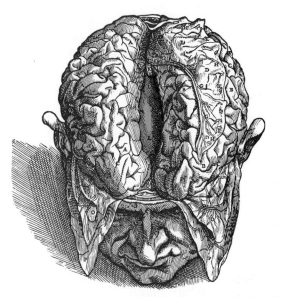

Figure 6-6 Hemispheres of the brain retracted to show the corpus callosum. Also see the corpus callosum in Figure 2-26.

The two hemispheres may have different sensory experiences in such "split-brain" patients. This difference occurs when sensory information is restricted to just one hemisphere. Visual information to the right of a person's fixation point is projected to the left visual cortex, and vice versa (see Chapter 4). Tactile stimulation from one side of the body reaches primarily the opposite-side hemisphere. Similarly, auditory information from one ear is more strongly projected to the opposite hemisphere. Because both eyes see largely the same visual field, both ears hear the same sounds, and so forth, the two hemispheres of a split-brain patient usually receive about the same information and function in unison.

Tests designed to restrict sensory stimulation to just one hemisphere demonstrate that the two hemispheres may function independently. One such test compared verbal reports of experiences when visual information was presented to the two hemispheres separately (see Figure 6-7). When a visual stimulus was briefly flashed on a screen to the right of the

Figure 6-7 Response to a visual stimulus tested by flashing a word or picture either to the subject's right or left visual field. The subject is asked to read the flashed word. The word must appear only momentarily to prevent the subject from having the opportunity to shift the eyes, thereby shifting the visual fields. (Gazzaniga, 1967)

patient's fixation point, thereby stimulating the left visual cortex, the patient correctly identified the visual object. When the same object was flashed to the left, the patient reported that he had seen nothing. Could this be true? Not really. When visual information was restricted to the right hemisphere, the left or "speaking" hemisphere was unaware and reported seeing nothing. Remember that language processes, verbal and written, are controlled by the left hemisphere in about 90 per cent of all people (see Chapter 3). In effect, the test had stimulated the right hemisphere and asked the left whether it had seen anything. Since the right hemisphere is "mute," it could not verbally report its experiences. When the test was repeated so that the patient could point at the object with his left hand (controlled by the right hemisphere), he correctly identified the object among a group of objects presented visually on the screen.

In similar experiments, when tactile stimulation was presented to the right side of the body, the left hemisphere could verbally report the experience. When stimulation was presented to the left side, the right hemisphere could nonverbally report the experience (see Figure 6-8). These tests showed that the right hemisphere probably possesses some small share of language comprehension, since it responded to verbal instructions given to the patient. The linguistic limitations of the right hemisphere have varied from patient to patient.

Are emotional as well as sensory experiences separated in the two hemispheres of the split-brain patient? Emotions are largely controlled by subcortical areas of the brain that are not isolated by this operation. At least one experiment, however, suggests that the two hemispheres can independently generate an emotional reaction. In this experiment a number of slides were flashed in the left or right visual fields of a split-brain patient. In

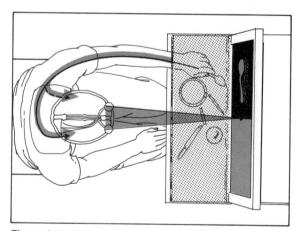

Figure 6-8 Visual-tactile association performed by a split-brain patient. The subject selects with his left hand from among a number of things spread on the table the object that is visually presented to the right hemisphere. (Gazzaniga, 1967)

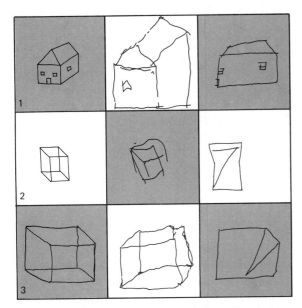

Figure 6-9 Visual reconstructions of three figures by a split-brain patient using his left hand and then his right hand. The first column shows the three figures presented to the subject; the middle column shows the responses of the left hand (right hemisphere); the last column shows the responses of the right hand (left hemisphere). (Gazzaniga, 1967)

the midst of the series, a slide of a nude woman was presented. When the slide was presented to the left hemisphere through the right visual field, the patient smiled and correctly identified the picture. When the slide was presented to the right hemisphere, she smiled and chuckled but could not explain why (Gazzaniga, 1967). Because reported experiences from the right hemisphere lack the sophistication of communication through verbal or written means, we may never fully unravel the mysteries of its nature.

Observations of split-brain patients have revealed that functions in addition to language are specialized in one hemisphere. In addition to language, the left hemisphere seems to be more adept at solving analytical problems. The right hemisphere, on the other hand, is superior in musical and spatial tasks. A comparison of responses by the left and right hemispheres

on a spatial task is presented in Figure 6-9. A split-brain man was asked to copy each of three drawings with one hand and then with the other. Even though the patient was right-handed, he was better able to reconstruct the figure with his left hand, under right hemispheric control.

LATERAL EYE MOVEMENTS AND PERSONALITY

■ When people are asked questions that require a little thought to answer, they usually shift their eyes to the right or to the left as they turn their attention inward, though sometimes their eyes may go up almost vertically and then shift left or right, and sometimes shifting is hardly noticeable. Some psychologists have recently concluded that this **lateral eye movement** is correlated with physiological, cognitive, and personality characteristics. To test this for yourself, try asking a number of people individually questions that will make them reflect, and see if they react with left or right lateral eye movements. You can use the following five questions, which psychologists have often used, or similar questions of your own:

1. Can you spell *society* backward?
2. How many letters are there in the word *anthropology?*
3. Can you multiply 13 by 14 in your head?
4. Repeat the following six numbers backwards: 1, 4, 7, 3, 6, 5.
5. Can you think of an English word that begins with *l* and ends with *c?*

Face your subjects, more or less, as you ask them the questions, so you can observe the way their eyes move as they first start to answer the questions. Keep a record of the movements. A left movement is toward the subject's left side, not toward yours. Don't insist on correct answers, for all you want to see is the eye movements. In one experiment (Sherrod, 1972) with 219 subjects, over 86 per cent of those tested tended always to move their eyes in the same direction. More were left-movers than right-movers, but the split was nearly even.

Psychologists have proposed that right and left

movements are related to the relative strengths of right and left hemispheric functions. Right eye movements indicate a more active left hemisphere and left eye movements a more active right hemisphere. Psychologists have found significantly more preverbal activity in left eye movers—such as greater imagery, hypnotizability, and alpha-wave activity—than in right eye movers. Tests have also indicated greater artistic and other creative abilities in left eye movers, greater focusing of attention on inner, subjective experiences, and greater reactions to persuasive messages, in either accepting or rejecting them. It has been found that left eye movers have more subjective and passive personalities, are more self-centered, and have less verbal and more mathematical ability. In another experiment, however, different observers quite often judged the eye movements of subjects to be in different directions, and the eye movements of some subjects changed from a first test to another test a week later (Templer, Goldstein, and Penick, 1972). This instability in lateral eye movements, and in the judgment of them, raises doubts about the conclusions that have been reached. Much more research is required before the conclusions can be verified or disproved.

SUMMARY

Cognition, perception, and emotional affect undergo changes when an individual passes from the normal waking state to an altered state of consciousness.

Sleep is an active process that consists of two principal stages, REM and NREM sleep, occurring in cycles through the night. The REM stage, during which dreaming occurs, is physiologically more active, but behaviorally deeper sleep than NREM sleep. Deprivation of REM sleep leads to psychological disturbances. The purpose of sleep, and particularly that of the REM stage, is little understood. REM sleep may function in storing memories of recent events or in providing for the maturation and growth of the brain.

Hypnosis is induced by relaxation and concentration on suggestions by the hypnotist.

Most people are susceptible to some degree of hypnosis, although they differ in the depth of hypnosis they attain. Differences between nonhypnotized and hypnotized subjects have not been adequately demonstrated, for with proper suggestions the former can accomplish feats comparable to those of the latter. One possible difference is that hypnotized subjects will accept incongruous situations with little, if any, question, while nonhypnotized subjects will not.

Hypnosis has been found useful in the diagnosis and treatment of various emotional problems and in helping people break bad habits through hypnotic suggestion.

An altered state of consciousness is attained through meditation, by the use of various procedures such as those of the yogas of Hinduism, the logical paradoxes of Zen Buddhism, and the mantra of Transcendental Meditation. Subjective reports characterize the meditational experience as vivid, tranquil, unique, but largely inexpressible. Physiological measures of the state have shown a predominance of alpha waves in brain rhythms; lowered oxygen consumption, blood lactate levels, and respiration rates; and increases in galvanic skin response, all correlated with the relaxed, serene state of meditators.

Psychoactive drugs (chemicals that affect the mind) vary in their effects on consciousness. Stimulants, like caffeine and amphetamine, increase alertness and produce a feeling of well-being; depressants, like alcohol and barbiturates, produce drowsiness and decrease anxiety; hallucinogens, like marijuana and LSD, produce distortions in cognition and perception. Drug users may become psychologically or physically dependent on drugs, or both.

Studies of split-brain patients have indicated that the two brain hemispheres have variant functions. The left hemisphere seems dominant for language processes and the solution of analytical problems, while the right hemisphere is superior in such creative processes as playing music and drawing.

NOW YOU'RE THE EXPERT

This chapter has described investigations of such varied altered states of consciousness as sleep, dreams, thought in sleep, hypnosis, meditation, and mystic and drug states. You have undoubtedly experienced some of these altered states, and you may not have experienced others. What have been your most striking and significant experiences with them?

The characteristics of altered states of consciousness have been described as:

Changes in attention, memory, thinking, or judgment.
Changes in sense of time.
Loss of self or self-control, or depersonalization.
Increased suggestibility.
Extreme emotional reactions, sometimes positive, sometimes negative.
Hallucinations.
Changes in interpretation of self or of external reality.

Consider each of your most striking experiences with altered states of consciousness in terms of these characteristics. Did your experiences show some or any of these characteristic changes?

Consider each of your most striking experiences with altered states in terms of beneficial or detrimental effects. Were these experiences adaptive or maladaptive for you and for others—did they have positive or negative effects on your well-being and that of others? Considering your judgments of the effects of your altered states on yourself and others, would you recommend them to a friend? Why or why not?

7

Conditioning

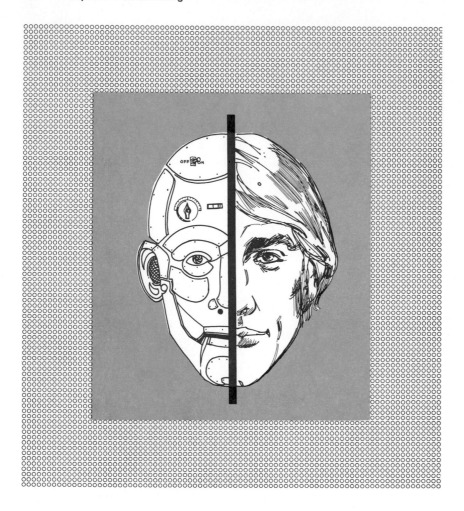

Consider for a moment the way you view yourself. Do you think of yourself as a knowing, willing human being, capable of initiating actions as you wish and choosing your own behavior? Or do you think of yourself as a terribly complex but machinelike system, reacting automatically and mechanically to events around you? Are your actions free or determined?

FREEDOM OR DETERMINISM?

■ The following activity should bring to light various factors involved in the way you shape your actions and should help you decide whether your actions are free or determined. Like most people, you have various decisions to make today. Whether they are minor or major decisions doesn't matter. Perhaps you have to decide whether to go shopping or not this afternoon. Or you have a choice to make between reading or going to the movies. Or between finishing some work today or leaving it till tomorrow. Or between going to bed or watching the *Late Late Show*.

Think of one or two of these decisions facing you. What things come to your mind as you make the decision? What gives you the inclination to decide one way or the other? Is it, for example, your needs or interests? Your feelings? The approval or disapproval of other people? Liking or disliking the effects of the decision? Other things? Mull over what is going on as you make the decision. Now answer this: Was your decision free, or was it determined by events outside or inside you?

Some philosophers and psychologists have said that following our own inclinations, or being internally controlled, gives us a sense of freedom, while following the expressed or known inclinations of others makes us feel determined, or externally controlled. A psychologist has even constructed a "locus of control" test to reveal whether people feel they are internally or externally controlled (Rotter, 1966). But does not control, whether internal or external, imply determinism rather than freedom?

Since psychologists want to understand and predict behavior, they too are inevitably drawn into the problem of freedom and determinism. Is observed behavior the outcome of some inner, voluntary process, or is it a reflex response to an external stimulus? Should we look for our answers in the mind or in the body?

The ways in which people have tackled this age-old problem have produced two great traditions of philosophical inquiry, and more recently of empirical psychological research. These traditions laid the foundation for the modern study of conditioning and learning, the branch of psychology that investigates the way people adapt and the way their behavior is modified.

THE HISTORY OF CONDITIONING

Although our discussion of the problem of freedom and determinism could be opened with an examination of ancient Greek and Roman lore, we shall start with the innovative ideas of René Descartes, who lived in seventeenth-century France. Descartes was skilled in both mathematics and philosophy. Perhaps

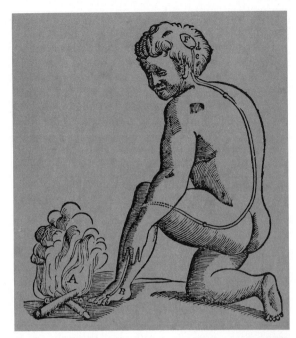

Figure 7-1 Descartes's explanation of the act of foot withdrawal as a purely involuntary, mechanical act. As the boy's foot touches the fire (A), the nerve (B) is set in motion. This motion is transmitted along the nerve "vessel" to the spinal cord and the brain (de), releasing "animal spirits" from a cavity (F). The spirits or vapors course down the same nerve, swelling the calf muscles, and producing reflex withdrawal. (Descartes, 1662, 1972)

this is why he distinguished between the human being as a machine running like clockwork and the human being as a rational creature, capable of choosing his own behavior.

Descartes's Mind–Body Split

Descartes thought that subhuman animals, unlike people, had only bodies, no souls. They could only react automatically to the sights and sounds around them. People too were in part constructed like machines, Descartes believed, in that they reacted with direct reflexes to the stimulation of their sense organs (see Figure 7-1). But the mind, or soul—a human being's distinctive feature—could both sense what the body was doing and cause it to act spontaneously. Descartes wrote (1642; 1934, p. 139):

. . . there is a vast difference between mind and body, in respect that body, from its nature, is always divisible, and that mind is entirely indivisible. For in truth, when I consider the mind, that is, when I consider myself in so far only as I am a thinking thing, I can distinguish in myself no parts, but I very clearly discern that I am somewhat absolutely one and entire; and although the whole mind seems to be united to the whole body, yet, when a foot, an arm, or any other part is cut off, I am conscious that nothing has been taken from my mind.

The dualism of Descartes's sharp distinction between mind and body had an enormous impact on the development of ideas. In this double skein, let's first consider the mind.

The Mentalistic Tradition

Descartes believed that certain ideas, such as "I think, therefore I am," and "God, an infinite Being," occur automatically and innately in all minds, regardless of the kinds of sense experiences people have. This doctrine of innate ideas was soon to be discarded, however, through the work of such empirical British philosophers as John Locke, George Berkeley, and David Hume in the seventeenth and eighteenth centuries. They argued that people have no inborn ideas, that the mind is like a "clean slate" at birth, and that all ideas are faint copies of our experienced sensations. Combinations of ideas derived from the senses may, of course, yield such unusual ideas as those of unicorns and mermaids.

The study of the mind soon turned to the ways in which simple sensations can combine, or be associated, to form more complex mental compounds in ideas. The explanation for the clustering of simple elements to form complex ideas was believed to be the frequency with which the elements were associated with each other. Elements could be associated by *contiguity*, or closeness to each other in space or time, or by *similarity*, or likeness to each other. Thus by association we form a complex idea of a rose out of a collection of such simpler ele-

ments as smell, color, size, and tactile quality, because these elements have been associated with each other in our experiences of roses. Similarly, association could account for a sequence of ideas. Thinking of the seashore reminds us of sand, shells, waves, and swimming on warm summer days, because we have frequently experienced these things in sequence.

In the minds of thinkers like James Mill and John Stuart Mill, Herbert Spencer and Alexander Bain, and in the laboratories of psychologists like Wilhelm Wundt, **associationism** flowered in the nineteenth century into an infant science of the mind. These men wished to explain how the sensations, ideas, and feelings that fill the mind combine to form our subjective experiences. The method consisted of analyzing our inner experience by introspection.

The Mechanistic Tradition

Another thread can be drawn out of Descartes's dualism. Descartes has been called the "father of physiology" because of his attempts to explain reflex actions, like the contraction of the eye pupil in response to a bright light and the jerking of the leg when it's struck below the kneecap. Actions of this sort, Descartes said, were functions of the body, not of the mind. He laid the groundwork for the reflexarc concept, in which a reflex is traced from the stimulation of a receptor to nerve impulses along afferent (conducting inward) sensory fibers to the central nervous system to the routing of impulses down efferent (conducting outward) motor fibers and finally to the contraction of muscles (see Figure 7-1.) Such actions are purely involuntary, although they can be adaptive, as when we jerk our fingers away from a hot object. Voluntary action, according to Descartes, could not occur without the involvement of the mind.

Nineteenth-century science had great difficulties with the Cartesian concept of volun-

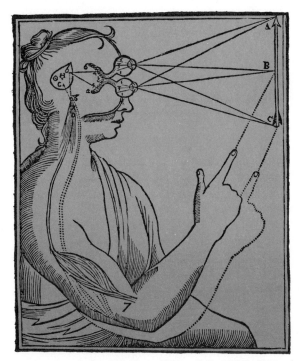

Figure 7-2 In Descartes's scheme of the interaction of mind and body, voluntary action is produced when the soul, or mind, inclines the pineal gland, which in turn causes a redistribution of animal spirits within the system of nerves, leading to the swelling of the appropriate muscles.

In the drawing, images of the arrow are conveyed from the two eyes by the optic nerves to the interior surface of the brain (6, 4, 4, 2), where they fuse together and radiate toward the pineal gland (H). Here the mind and body interact. The fused image of the arrow, projected upon the pineal gland, acts immediately upon the mind, producing awareness of the object.

The slightest movement in the gland greatly alters the course of animal spirits throughout the nerve-tube system of the body. By inclining the gland ever so slightly, this way or that, the mind can redirect animal spirits to produce any desired effect. In the drawing above, the mind has produced an upward movement of the arm and hand by inclining the pineal gland (H) so as to send animal spirits down the nerves leading to muscles in the upper arm, causing them to swell. (Descartes, 1662, 1972).

tary action. It was hard to explain how a mental or spiritual event, indivisible and ethereal, could produce a physical effect in the body, a material object. Descartes himself thought that this interaction occurred in the pineal gland, tucked away in the brain between the two halves of the thalamus. His idea of the way this worked is shown in Figure 7-2. Gradually Descartes's theory of the two-way interaction of mind and body gave way to other attempts to explain voluntary action. Some schemes, like the behaviorism of American psychologist John B. Watson, simply denied the existence of mental events entirely. They reasserted the claim of early Greek materialists, like Democritus, that all that exists is matter. More sophisticated scientists, impressed by the success of deterministic approaches in physical science, sought to account for voluntary action within a mechanistic framework. They tried to explain behavior that is called voluntary on the basis of reflex principles. One such scientist was Ivan Sechenov, the "father of Russian reflexology."

Inhibitory Reflexology

Sechenov realized that the distinction between voluntary and involuntary actions is not so sharp as it is usually assumed to be. He noted how acts that are initially voluntary can become involuntary with practice. Remember how purposeful your initial actions had to be when you were first learning to type or drive a car, and how automatically you can perform them now? Sechenov also observed that involuntary acts can often become voluntary. You have learned to blink voluntarily, and an actor can learn to cry on cue. Sechenov's solution was to interpret voluntary behavior as a special kind of reflex action.

The way Sechenov supported this conclusion involved some assumptions. He believed that the behavior of a living system is held in check by an inhibitory process in the central nervous system. Even a small external stimulus is capable of triggering inhibited energy, however, and when this happens, bodily movements will occur. You know how pepper or a small dust particle in the nose is sufficient to produce an explosive sneeze. According to Sechenov, the tiniest stimulus may be sufficient to produce a powerful reflex response.

Sechenov then speculated that even complex voluntary behavior might represent reflex response to imperceptible external stimuli, too faint to be noticed, but nonetheless effective in releasing the inhibition of gross motor reactions. In his book *Reflexes of the Brain* (1863) he proposed that even thoughts might be reactions of the brain to external stimuli that are **subliminal,** or below the threshold of conscious awareness. While some thoughts and actions *seem* to be under volitional control, they can in fact, argued Sechenov, be explained as reflexive events within a mechanistic framework.

SUBLIMINAL ADVERTISING

During the 1950s the matter of subliminal stimuli came up again with scare stories in the press about the possible use of below-the-level-of-consciousness messages from advertisers on movie and TV screens. Could people be unconsciously influenced with subliminal cues to rush out and buy the advertisers' products?

A psychologist tested the effect of subliminal flashes (1/200th of a second) of the word "beef" on movie screens during the showing of a film to an experimental group of more than 50 college students (Byrne, 1959). He showed the same film, without flashes of the word "beef," to 50 other students as a control group. "Beef" had not been implanted in the minds of the experimental group, apparently, for they showed no increase in references to it in several association tests, nor did they prefer roast beef sandwiches more than the students in the control group. However, those exposed to the word "beef" subliminally were hungrier than the students in the control group. Movie houses have tried flashing "Buy Popcorn" momentarily on the screen, but without noteworthy success.

The outcome of such experiments is not conclusive (McConnell, Cutler, & McNeil, 1958). Whether, and how, subliminal cues have an effect is simply not known. At any rate, Sechenov's theory is not supported by this investigation.

What an intriguing idea, that a person is a delicately balanced machine, ready to feed energy into behavior the instant some minor and often unnoticed event chances momentarily to disturb the inhibitory control system that holds everything in check! Sechenov was a highly respected scientist, a former student of Hermann von Helmholtz and of Johannes Müller in Germany (see Chapter 4), and a leading Russian physiologist. Yet his theory, novel and daring as it was, could not explain one very important attribute of human and animal behavior: The organism does not continue to respond in exactly the same way to the same stimulus. The machine system Sechenov envisioned was fixed and constant in its response to stimulation. Yet behavior is adaptive, flexible, even plastic. *We can learn.* Once we have reflexively withdrawn in pain from a hot stove, our behavior is permanently changed. But Sechenov's scheme did not allow for the modification of reflexes by experience. Can you think how the scheme needs to be changed to allow for this? Pavlov did.

CLASSICAL CONDITIONING

All great scientists base their scientific contributions on the work of others. Ivan Pavlov, another Russian physiologist already world famous for his study of digestive processes, was familiar with Sechenov's work. Strongly influenced by Darwinian thinking, Pavlov realized that organisms constantly adjust to their environments. An explanation of voluntary action based on the concept of fixed, inborn reflexes could not explain the obvious modifiability of behavior. Certainly the response of the new mother to a faint sound that may be her baby's cry is an acquired, rather than inborn, reflex. But how are such reflexes acquired? How does experience act to modulate our responsiveness to stimuli both strong and weak, increasing our sensitivity to some, canceling out our awareness of others, all in accordance with the changing demands of our daily experiences?

Pavlovian Reflexology

Pavlov concluded that there must be two kinds of reflex: A **biological reflex,** like the pupillary response to light or withdrawal from a painful stimulus, is simple and innate; an **acquired reflex** is conditioned by experience. When a previously neutral stimulus gains the capacity to trigger an innate reflex, the reflex is then said to be acquired (Pavlov, 1927). Pavlov's contribution was to show that, with the addition of the acquired reflex, Sechenov's reflexology could encompass even adaptive, learned forms of behavior.

As Pavlov developed more refined techniques for eliciting reflexes with previously neutral events, working mostly with dogs, he became more and more convinced that voluntary behavior, indeed all behavior, consists of complex combinations of simple conditioned reflexes. He developed this mechanistic explanation of behavior most thoroughly over a period of years, with many investigations in his laboratory.

TREAT YOURSELF LIKE A DOG

■ Put yourself in the position of one of Pavlov's dogs. Expose yourself to a conditioning procedure and see whether your own biological and acquired reflexes react in accordance with Pavlov's mechanistic theory.

The materials you need for this self-conditioning activity are some small pieces of a candy that you like and a glass or pan that sounds loudly when you strike it with a pencil, a bell you can ring, or a buzzer you can buzz. Also, have a glass of water on hand. The pieces of candy provide what Pavlov called the "unconditioned stimulus," and the glass, pan, bell, or buzzer furnish the "conditioned stimulus." You yourself will provide the reflex responses to these stimuli. (In actuality, of course, it's the response that's conditioned, not the stimulus, but these are the terms that are always used, so we'll have to go along with them.)

Put one piece of candy in your mouth, chew it, and taste it. (Limit yourself to one piece at a time, particularly if you happen to be on a diet.) Do you notice a reflex response or reaction—the supply of saliva in your mouth increasing? The salivary glands in your cheeks are reacting involuntarily to the candy by pouring saliva into both sides of your mouth. Pavlov called this an "unconditioned response"—it is inborn in all of us, like our other simple reflexes.

Now wait until the piece of candy is all gone. Have a sip of water if you wish to "neutralize" the taste in your mouth. When the taste is gone, pop another piece of candy into your mouth after you bang the glass or pan with a pencil, ring the bell, or buzz the buzzer.

When you have swallowed the candy, wash out your mouth again and repeat the banging or ringing or buzzing as you pop a candy into your mouth. Do this several times. After five or six times, see if you have conditioned yourself. How do you do that? Simply by banging or ringing or buzzing loudly, but putting nothing into your mouth.

If you are now conditioned, you should observe saliva flowing into your mouth after you bang or ring or buzz, even though you are eating no candy. Do you notice a considerable flow of saliva without any candy?

Classical Conditioning Procedure

Early in his research Pavlov discovered that the secretion of gastric juices in the stomachs of dogs occurred even when the animals only *saw* food; they did not have to eat it. Even previously ineffective stimuli, like the sight of a food dish, came to elicit secretions. If you own a dog, you are already familiar with its drooling as you prepare to feed it. So Pavlov turned from gastric secretion to salivary secretion as the principal measure of the effect of external events on the nervous system. In his scheme, the "mind" meant simply the brain and the nervous system. A study of the mind could thus be made objectively, by observing the effect of nervous activity on such observable indicators as the salivary response. The animal being tested came to learn that certain indifferent events, like the appearance of a food dish, signaled the imminence of food, which elicited a biological reflex. Suppose two external events (like the food dish and the food) occur together several times. This association is gradually recorded somehow in the central nervous system in such a way that eventually the food dish alone comes to elicit the same neurally mediated result, salivation, as did the food itself.

This casual observation is, of course, only the starting point of the scientific investigation of the conditioned reflex. Science strives for reliable, refined knowledge. This requires careful control of conditions and precise measurement of both causes and effects. Pavlov's laboratory was designed to isolate his experimental dogs from all distractions, so that they would be maximally attentive to the stimulus events the experimenter presented during a short span of time. These events were a neutral stimulus, like a tone or light (**conditioned stimulus** or **CS**), and a stimulus that elicited a biological response, like food powder presented to the animal (**unconditioned stimulus** or **US**). (See Figure 7-3.) The conditioned stim-

ulus (CS) became effective in eliciting the **response** only as a result of its repeated association with the unconditioned stimulus (US). For this reason the US is called the **reinforcing stimulus.** When salivation is elicited as a biological reflex by the US, the salivation response is called an **unconditioned response (UR).** When the response is elicited by a previously neutral stimulus like a tone, it is called a **conditioned response (CR).** Figure 7-4 shows the basic procedure, or paradigm, of Pavlovian or **classical conditioning.**

The response of salivation was measured by an intricate system that permitted Pavlov to record the behavioral effect in terms of (1) the number of drops of saliva, (2) the amount (volume) of saliva, and (3) the **latency** of the response, or the time elapsing between onset of the conditioned stimulus (CS) and the start of salivation.

Note how these procedures can be related to the discussion of dependent and independent variables in Chapter 1. An **independent vari-**

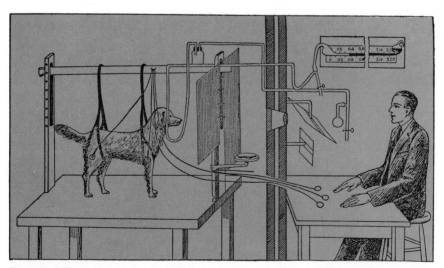

Figure 7-3 The setup for classical Pavlovian experiments in the conditioning of dogs. Tubes connected through the cheek to the dog's salivary duct measure salivation by recording both the pressure (right top) and the quantity (right center) of salivation. The food tray can be swung out toward the dog as some conditioning stimulus is presented. In this instance, the conditioning stimulus will be given to a foreleg or back-leg muscle to condition a leg jerk to the salivary response. (Pavlov, 1928)

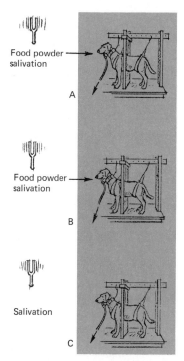

Figure 7-4 The way in which Pavlovian conditioning is established and then tested. (A) The vibrating tuning fork produces the tone that serves as the conditioned stimulus (CS) for the dog, and food powder serves as the unconditioned stimulus (US) for the unconditioned salivation response (UR). In conditioning, the CS is presented just before the US, after which the UR follows. The pairing of CS and US is repeated several times. (B) In one test for the establishment of conditioning, salivation (now the CR) starts directly after the conditioned stimulus (CS) is presented, and before the unconditioned stimulus (US) occurs. (C) In another test for conditioning, the unconditioned stimulus (US) is omitted entirely, but the response (CR) still occurs. (From *Introduction to Modern Behaviorism* by Howard Rachlin. W. H. Freeman and Company. Copyright © 1970.)

able is the event in an experiment that is deliberately and systematically manipulated in order to permit examination of its effect on the event under study, the **dependent variable.** In classical conditioning, some independent variables, many of which were studied by Pavlov, are the period of time separating the CS and US, the number of CS–US pairings, and the intensity of either CS or US. The number of drops, volume, and latency are all ways of

precisely measuring the dependent variable, the salivary response (CR). One independent variable, number of CS–US pairings, can be systematically increased to show regular unvarying changes occurring in the three dependent variables, as shown in Figure 7-5. The increase or decrease of both independent and dependent variables together is known as a **direct relationship.** When either variable increases as the other decreases, this is known as an **inverse relationship.**

When such relationships are repeatedly found between independent and dependent variables, a **uniform** or **lawful relationship** has been discovered. Such relationships are the lifeblood of science.

Laws of Classical Conditioning

Pavlov and his many collaborators established a number of reliable relationships between patterns of stimulation presented to the animals, on the one hand, and the dogs' resultant behavior on the other. These relationships constitute the major laws of classical conditioning. They may be regarded as statements of the way in which the nervous system adapts to certain environmental events that trigger expectations of the imminent occurrence or nonoccurrence of significant happenings. A flash of lightning sets off an emotional response in small children, for example, *after* they have learned that a frightful thunderclap is likely to follow. In the same way, the ringing of the ice cream vendor's bell produces pleasurable effects *after* the sound has come to signal the likelihood that ice cream will follow. In contrast, the boy who cried "Wolf!" too often finally realized that stimuli that arouse responses as a result of expectations of events to come eventually lose this capacity if the predicted events do not occur.

The laws of classical conditioning describe conditions that either strengthen a conditioned response (law of excitation) or weaken it (laws of inhibition). The **law of excitation** simply

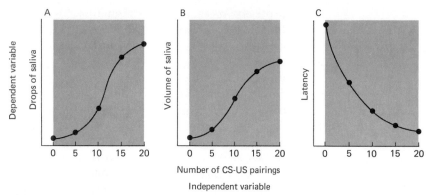

Figure 7-5 Relationships between the independent variable of number of pairings (trials) of conditioned stimulus (CS) and unconditioned stimulus (US) and the dependent variable, the conditioned response (CR), in terms of (A) number of drops of saliva, (B) volume (cc) of saliva, and (C) latency of salivary response, or time between stimulus presentation and start of salivation. The dependent variables undergo systematic changes as the number of pairings of CS and US increases, showing that independent and dependent variables are lawfully related to each other. Direct relationships are displayed in A and B, and C shows an inverse relationship between the variables.

states that pairings of CS and US increase the strength of the CR. The CS in such cases is sometimes called an **excitatory conditioned stimulus (CS+).**

The law of excitation is not so general that *any* response can be classically conditioned merely by arranging the appropriate CS–US contingencies. Some species, like rats and humans, readily form conditioned aversions to the taste of foods that make them feel sick. Birds, on the other hand, associate illness more readily with food color than taste. The law of excitation applies best to associations the organism is already prepared to make.

BRIGHT-NOISY WATER AND SAUCE BÉARNAISE

Organisms seem to be more ready to form some CS–CR connections than others. Moreover, associative connections get formed despite very long time gaps between CS and US. In a remarkable experiment, John Garcia and Robert A. Koelling (1966) exposed rats to X rays strong enough to produce radiation sickness (nausea and gastric upset) when they were drinking either sweetened water or "bright-noisy" water (plain water accompanied by a light stimulus and a clicking sound). The taste and the light-sound stimuli could be considered CSs, and radiation sickness the US–UR complex. After several treatments, the rats developed an aversion to tasty water but not to bright-noisy water.

Apparently an association between taste and nausea forms far more readily than one between external events like light and sound and nausea, despite the long time that elapses between exposure to the CS and the onset of sickness. You can see how a dog can develop a strong aversion to the taste of poisoned food (if it's lucky enough to survive), even though eating and feeling sick may come hours apart. Seligman's description of the "sauce béarnaise phenomenon" (Seligman & Hager, 1972) may remind you of a similar experience you may have had. Six hours after indulging himself on filet mignon covered with sauce béarnaise, Seligman became violently ill with the flu and vomited all night. From then on, he couldn't bear the taste of this sauce. The aversion was to a strong *taste*, and not to visual and auditory—that is, external—stimuli also present: his wife, *Tristan und Isolde* on the hi-fi, the china and silverware. Has something like this ever happened to you?

There are several **laws of inhibition,** and all predict a reduction in the strength of the CR. The simplest one, the **law of extinctive inhibition,** states that after a CR has been conditioned to a CS by repeatedly pairing the CS with a US, repeated presentations of the CS alone will lead to a reduction in CR strength. Dogs gradually stop salivating with repeated exposures to the CS alone. The CS is then said to become an **inhibitory conditioned stimulus (CS−),** as the process of extinction is continued. **Extinction** is the weakening and disappearance of a CR after the CS is presented repeatedly without a reinforcing US.

Pavlov made an important observation, however: "Extinguishing" a CR does not eliminate it. When dogs were returned to the experimental laboratory and reinserted into the harness one day *after* extinction had occurred, they demonstrated that the **extinction** procedure acts more to suppress the CR than to erase it. A series of nonreinforced trials had left the CS incapable of eliciting the CR, but when the CS was presented alone a day later, it immediately elicited a CR of considerable strength. This response was not so strong as the response that the CS could elicit at the end of a series of paired CS–US presentations, but certainly was far above the level produced at the end of extinction. Since this recovery of CR strength occurs without intervening conditioning trials, it is called **spontaneous recovery.** If further extinction trials are given, CR strength again declines, in fact at a faster rate than before.

The principle of **stimulus generalization,** or **irradiation,** states that a CR conditioned to one CS+ may also be elicited by other stimuli whose properties resemble those of the CS+. Thus, after Pavlov had conditioned his dogs to salivate to a high-frequency tone, he found that tones of higher or lower frequencies would also elicit some salivation. But Pavlov was interested in showing how the nervous system could detect small differences among environmental stimuli. On some trials he

would always follow the high tone with the US, making the high tone an excitatory stimulus, or CS+. On other trials, at various times throughout the conditioning session, he would present a lower tone, never followed by the US. The lower tone became an inhibitory stimulus, or CS−. This procedure obviously combines conditioning and extinction procedures and eventually leads to a good strong response to CS+ and a weak response, or no response at all, to CS−. At this point, a **conditioned discrimination** has been established. The second major law of inhibition, the **law of differential inhibition,** states that responses to stimuli resembling the CS+ will cease if such stimuli are never followed by the US, even though on interspersed trials the CS+ is *always* followed by the US.

The principal phenomena of classical conditioning and their conditioning determinants are summarized in Figure 7-6.

Behavioral Theory of Conditioning

How can the facts of classical conditioning, shown in Figure 7-6, be explained? Behavioral theories assume that every conditioning experience leaves some residual effects, and that such effects influence behavior. Consider diagram A in Figure 7-7, which shows that exposing the organism to paired presentations of CS and US leads after a few trials to the elicitation of the CR by the CS. At first not much can be said about the residual effect of these trials. Yet something must have happened to bring about the new CS → CR connection. Let's call that something "habit" (diagram B). (You could also call it X or Magrod or 437 or anything else you chose.) As the number of pairings of CS and US increases, habit should increase, and this increase should be reflected in behavior. And indeed it is.

Go back to Figure 7-5 and see how the amount of saliva and CR latency tend to change systematically with CS–US trials. Behavioral changes could be said to mirror

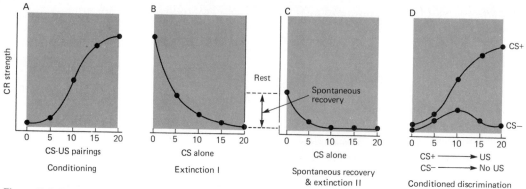

Figure 7-6 Basic phenomena of classical conditioning. Panels A and B show the acquisition and extinction of a classically conditioned response. If a rest period follows the end of the first extinction session shown in panel B, some spontaneous recovery of conditioned response strength appears at the beginning of the second extinction session, panel C. Note that conditioning proceeds at a faster rate in panel C. Panel D plots the formation of a conditioned discrimination, when one stimulus (CS+) is consistently followed by the US and a similar stimulus (CS−) is never followed by the US.

changes in the strength of the underlying process of habit. **Habit** ·is a theoretical construct devised to explain why repeated pairings of CS and US lead to progressive increases in the strength of the CR. Diagram B in Figure 7-7 shows that the construct intervenes between independent variables and behavioral consequences. (Of course, behavior depends on other things besides habit, as the difference between a hungry and a satiated dog will clearly reveal. Motivation, another important hypothetical process or construct relevant to behavior, is discussed in Chapter 12).

Figure 7-6 describes another fact that a behavioral theory must take into account: Repeated presentations of the CS without the US lead to extinction of the CR. Psychologists offer another theoretical construct, **inhibition,** to account for the facts of extinction, by assuming the arousal of an inhibitory factor that competes against the tendency of the CS to elicit the CR. It would be simpler to assume that extinction trials wipe out habit, but since in fact the CR reappears after it has presumably been extinguished, the introduction of a separate inhibition concept provides a more satisfactory

explanation (see Figure 7-7, diagram C). Most theorists assume that habit strength remains constant and that the performance changes resulting from extinction trials are due to the activation of a competing factor, inhibition. Whenever a nonreinforced response occurs, inhibition builds up, like habit. The stronger the inhibition, the lower the probability of a CR. When the strength of inhibition equals the strength of habit, the CS will no longer elicit a CR. The opposition of habit and ·inhibition is shown in diagram C in Figure 7-7. Inhibition built up during extinction is assumed to dissipate with rest. As time passes after extinction trials are over, inhibition weakens until it can no longer neutralize habit; then habit, now *relatively* stronger than inhibition, reveals itself in the regained ability of the CS to elicit the CR.

Everyday Classical Conditioning

Don't conclude from this discussion that classical conditioning is very remote from the everyday experience of human beings. The

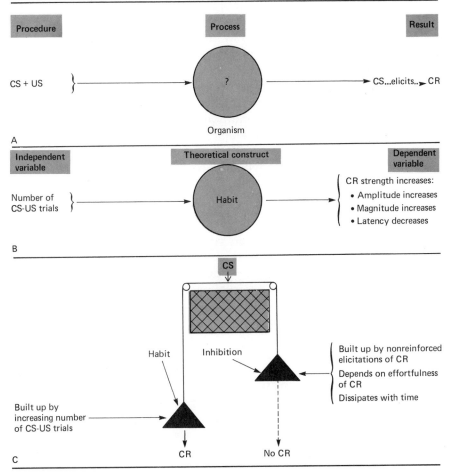

Procedure | Process | Result

CS + US } → ? → CS...elicits.. CR

Organism

A

Independent variable | Theoretical construct | Dependent variable

Number of CS-US trials } → Habit → CR strength increases:
- Amplitude increases
- Magnitude increases
- Latency decreases

B

CS

Habit   Inhibition

Built up by nonreinforced elicitations of CR

Depends on effortfulness of CR

Dissipates with time

Built up by increasing number of CS-US trials

CR   No CR

C

Figure 7-7 Ways in which behavioral theories attempt to explain the laws of conditioning. Panel A merely shows a lawful relationship between the independent variable (pairing the CS and US) and the dependent variable (an increased tendency for the CS to elicit a CR). In panel B, a theoretical construct, habit, is introduced to represent the hypothetical effects of the independent variable, that mediate changes in CR strength. Panel C explains the occurrence and strength of the CR as a resultant of two opposing hypothetical processes, habit and inhibition. (Panel C adapted from *Introduction to Modern Behaviorism* by Howard Rachlin. W. H. Freeman and Company. Copyright © 1970.)

principles of classical conditioning can be seen to operate across many species and at all ages within a species. They can be demonstrated both in the laboratory and in everyday life. They govern the acquisition of many kinds of behavior, principally glandular and visceral responses, which provide the biological basis of much emotional experience.

- Someone down the hall is using a power drill. You hear the racket and discover it raises goose pimples on your arms (a CR, the pilomotor reflex). It occurs to you that the sound resembles the whine of the dentist's drill (CS), which precedes some pain. Any stimulus that resembles the CS will also elicit the CR (stimulus generalization).

- After several months of not smoking, seeing and smelling a cigarette (CS) being smoked by another person no longer elicits the craving to smoke (CR). Extinction has occurred. One day, however, while sipping after-dinner coffee (a CS for smoking), you suddenly feel a great urge to smoke (spontaneous recovery).
- As you visualize the scene (internal CS) of your most embarrassing moment, your heart beats faster and perhaps you find yourself blushing (CR). Try it and see.

These examples suffice to show that Pavlovian laws don't apply only to dogs salivating a half-century ago in some laboratory in Russia. They permeate our everyday life and govern a great deal of our emotional behavior. The last example also suggests that humans have a special capacity for generating their own CS, merely by thinking about or visualizing some situation or event that once was associated with an effective US. Doubt this? Try to imagine putting a sour pickle in your mouth and see if you can avoid salivating. Try reconstructing in your imagination a detailed picture of your last accident, whatever it was, and note changes occurring in your breathing, pulse rate, and general emotional state.

Pavlov himself was convinced that conditioning was responsible, on the one hand, for the development of much pathological behavior, and on the other hand that it provided the basis for effective psychiatric treatment. Indeed, psychiatric applications of conditioning occupied the better part of his later years. Moreover, he felt that sound methods of education should be based on conditioning principles. His contribution was a major one, extending beyond psychiatry and education to the study of personality development, language, and complex learning. Most of all, however, he is honored for having provided an effective method for the objective study of behavior. The associationists' study of connections between ideas in the mind was, in his

hands, completely transformed into the study of the relationships between environmental events and behavioral consequences.

Think about the factors you found to be involved in the decisions you considered at the opening of this chapter. Now consider the factors that may be suggested to you by classical conditioning. What do you find to be the best explanation of these decisions? Are you now inclined to accept a deterministic or a free-will explanation for your decisions?

INSTRUMENTAL CONDITIONING

Whatever your conclusions, classical conditioning is only a part of the story. You now have the opportunity to go into another realm, that of instrumental conditioning, and check whether this, too, influenced your decision making.

TREAT YOURSELF TO SOME CONDITIONING

■ Give yourself firsthand experience with instrumental conditioning by conditioning yourself in this activity. The only materials you need are this book and a supply of small pieces of candy, like those you used in the classical conditioning activity.

Read along carefully in this book beyond this activity, paragraph by paragraph. When you have finished reading each paragraph, give yourself a reward of a piece of candy. In instrumental conditioning the candy is a **reinforcing stimulus,** or simply **reinforcer.** Another paragraph, another reward, and so on, until you have read through five or six pages.

Now review the way you reacted as you kept reinforcing your reading of paragraphs. Didn't you enjoy the reward and begin to look forward to it more and more expectantly? Did you wish the paragraphs were shorter or begin to hustle through them? Identify the elements of operant conditioning in your activity, according to the definition you encountered as you read ahead.

Another Kind of Learning

Although the importance of Pavlovian conditioning is widely acknowledged, it would be grossly inaccurate to suggest that these laws can explain the bulk of human and animal learning. After all, in the learning of many things our behavior does not consist solely of reactions of visceral organs. We learn our way around a new town; we find the movie theater, stores, and restaurants in accordance with our needs of the moment. We learn motor skills, simple ones like extracting a bottle from a soft-drink vending machine and complex ones like driving a car. We learn how to obtain interpersonal satisfactions in our relations with others. Unfortunately, we sometimes learn undesirable forms of behavior too, for example, using drugs or drinking in order to make ourselves feel more accepted by a particular group of people, or becoming overly dependent on another person to avoid the uneasiness of making our own decisions.

These examples reveal a kind of learning, called **instrumental conditioning,** that differs in important ways from classical conditioning: (1) The behavior in question involves the skeletal musculature, sometimes the entire body, rather than solely a glandular or visceral response like change in heart rate, salivation, and galvanic skin reflex (GSR); and (2) the behavior learned either produces some reward **(positive reinforcement)** or prevents from happening or terminates some unpleasant result **(negative reinforcement).** If the behavior in question *produces* an unpleasant outcome, the behavior will tend not to recur. Once a child receives a shock from sticking a finger into a light socket, the chances for repetition of that behavior fall drastically. Incidentally, you can now sense the meaning of the word "instrumental": The response is instrumental in producing some effect; if rewards are to come or if unpleasant events are to be stopped or avoided, some response must first occur.

Kinds of Instrumental Conditioning

Figure 7-8 compares classical and instrumental conditioning in detail. Instrumental learning is divided into two types: discrete-trial learning and operant or free-responding learning. In **discrete-trial learning,** the behavior that is learned always occurs as a response to some external stimulus; as soon as the response produces its desired effect, the incident is temporarily over. When the stimulus occurs again later, the response may occur again. For example, a child's learning to greet the ice cream vendor with a ready coin is a response to the bell signaling the vendor's arrival. When the response has occurred and the reward has been received, the behavior sequence is terminated until the vendor's signal occurs again the next day.

In contrast, consider an operant or free-responding learning situation: A child learns "cute" mannerisms because they bring rewards of approval and goodies from adults. The child will perform her tricks whenever she chooses, without waiting for external signals to initiate "cute" behavior. The frequency with which she "performs" is taken as a measure of the strength of the learning.

In **operant (free-responding) learning,** the organism is free to respond whenever it wishes; learning normally means an increase in the rate of responding. In a discrete-trial situation, learning means that the appropriate response occurs more promptly to a signal, which is no longer called a CS but an S^D (S-D), for **discriminative stimulus.** Such a stimulus is a signal that responding will be rewarded.

Discrete-Trial Learning

Note in Figure 7-8 that there are three types of discrete-trial situation in instrumental conditioning: reward, escape, and avoidance. For each one, try to keep a specific situation in mind to serve as a model. In **reward conditioning,** as in the case of the child and the ice

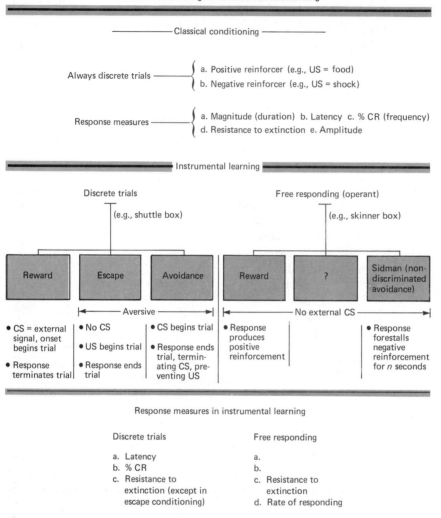

Figure 7-8 Classical and instrumental conditioning compared. Note that all classical conditioning consists of discrete trials, while instrumental learning sometimes occurs as discrete trials and sometimes takes the form of free responding. Many response measures apply equally to classical conditioning and to both forms of instrumental conditioning. But note that rate of responding applies only to the free-responding form of instrumental conditioning, and that latency and per cent CR measures apply only to the discrete trial-procedures, in either classical or instrumental conditioning.

Figure 7-9 In a shuttlebox, an animal like this rat must learn to jump the hurdle that separates the two compartments when a signal (a tone or light S^D) is turned on. In reward conditioning, the hurdle jump may be reinforced by a tidbit of food. In avoidance conditioning, crossing over within a brief, arbitrarily set time period prevents the occurrence of an aversive stimulus, like shock, and also terminates the S^D. If the animal fails to jump within the prescribed time, the aversive stimulus is presented until the animal escapes by crossing over. Both reward and avoidance procedures are examples of the discrete-trial form of instrumental conditioning. (Courtesy of Elliott R. Wald)

cream vendor, an external S^D occurs; if the "correct" response occurs in the presence of the S^D, the organism receives a reward, or positive reinforcer. When this type of learning is studied in the laboratory, a shuttlebox is sometimes used (see Figure 7-9). This is merely a large box with a barrier in the middle forming two compartments. An animal, say a rat, is placed on one side. If it jumps over the barrier when a light (S^D) comes on, it is positively reinforced, or rewarded, with a tidbit. If it jumps at other times, no reward.

Negative reinforcement occurs in **escape conditioning.** The rat is again placed in one compartment, but this time is given an electric shock through the grid floor. As you might expect, this US produces many URs, like jumping, squealing, and urinating. Eventually,

the rat hurls itself over the barrier and is immediately rewarded with the end of shock. On following trials, the moment shock starts the rat quickly jumps the barrier, for behavior that *terminates* negative reinforcement is strengthened. A child who learns to cry "uncle" while a bully is hurting him is practicing a form of escape conditioning. So are adults who take aspirin to cure a headache.

A distinction exists between punishment and negative reinforcement. Obviously both concepts deal with aversive stimuli. When a behavior produces an aversive stimulus, this is **punishment.** The pet that makes a "mistake" on the living room rug is thumped with a rolled-up newspaper: The pet's behavior produces an aversive consequence. Thus the punishment lowers the probability that the behavior will occur in the future. When a response terminates the effect of an aversive stimulus, this is **negative reinforcement.** Terminating discomfort will strengthen the response that brings relief. In other words, punishment means the response brings on discomfort or pain; negative reinforcement means the response reduces or eliminates discomfort or pain.

How is *escape* from aversive stimulation related to *avoidance* of aversive stimulation? All we need for **avoidance conditioning** is a signal, like a light S^D, preceding an aversive stimulus, and a system whereby a response made prior to the scheduled arrival of the aversive stimulus will prevent the latter from occurring. Note how this would work in the shuttlebox. Figure 7-10 shows how the naive (inexperienced) dog simply sits when the light goes on, then gets

shocked, and eventually escapes. Gradually, with repeated trials, he starts to jump in response to the light S^D before the shock actually comes on. By the tenth trial he no longer escapes, but avoids. In avoidance conditioning the correct response occurs in time both to prevent the occurrence of the aversive event and to terminate the S^D.

Does avoidance conditioning sound remote from your everyday experience? Consider how well you've learned to respond to the indicator on the gas gauge of your car, a good S^D. When it reads almost empty, you respond by buying gas. This avoidance response is reinforced because the aversive consequences of running out of gas are prevented from occurring. Your behavior also eliminates the warning (S^D) of the gauge. Of course, sometimes the correct avoidance response is not made in time.

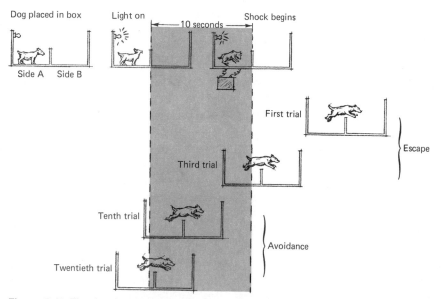

Figure 7-10 The development of avoidance conditioning. On the first trial the light S^D is turned on; since the dog fails to jump within 10 seconds, he receives shock until he escapes by jumping into the other compartment. On the third trial the dog is not avoiding shock, since he waits for the shock to arrive before he jumps. By the tenth trial we see a clear-cut avoidance response: The dog jumps after the S^D is presented but before the shock is scheduled to arrive. His avoidance behavior continues to improve: When the S^D is presented he makes a short-latency avoidance response. (From *Introduction to Modern Behaviorism* by Howard Rachlin. W. H. Freeman and Company. Copyright © 1970.)

The increasing strength of conditioning in discrete-trial situations can be measured in several ways. As training continues, the latency between the S^D onset and the occurrence of the avoidance response is reduced. As learning progresses, the likelihood increases that a correct response will occur on a given trial. For example, if 100 dogs are participating in an experiment involving a shock apparatus, a larger percentage of correct responses will be found among them on trial 10 than on trial 3. Finally, if the shock apparatus is completely turned off and the trials are continued, the dogs will continue to jump in response to the S^D for some time under these extinction conditions. However, resistance to extinction would be greater among dogs that have learned to avoid well than among those whose learning was poor. For this reason, **resistance to extinction** is another measure of the strength of instrumental conditioning, just as it is a good measure of the strength of classical conditioning.

Operant Conditioning

Free-responding forms of instrumental conditioning are known more simply as operant conditioning. In this form of conditioning it is often difficult to identify the stimulus initially responsible for the response. Rather, an increase is noted in the **emission rate** of responses that are followed by reinforcement. For example, a girl who is praised for her ballet dancing will be more eager to perform than one who is told she has two left feet. A suitor whose phone calls are greeted warmly will call more often than he would if the girl told him she couldn't go out with him because she had to wash her hair. While it is sometimes difficult to identify external S^Ds in operant conditioning, it is easy to see that the rate of responding increases when the responses are positively reinforced.

Note the rat in the operant chamber (sometimes called a "Skinner box," for its inventor,

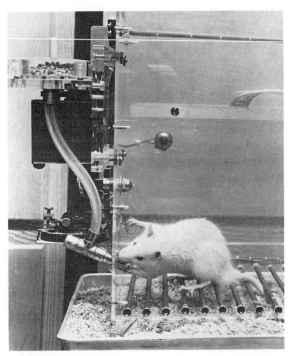

Figure 7-11 A trained albino rat presses a lever and checks the food-delivery tray for its reward. (Courtesy of Albert Weissman, Pfizer, Inc.)

B. F. Skinner) shown in Figure 7-11. The rat seems to act quite spontaneously when it first enters the chamber. It sniffs here and scratches there. Finally it happens to press down the lever that produces a food pellet. It's hard to say precisely what stimulus causes the rat to press the lever. The stronger the learning, however, the higher the rate of bar pressing.

Is it possible to operantly condition an organism to make an avoidance response when no external stimuli are present? Doesn't avoidance conditioning require some external warning signal so that the organism may know when to start avoiding? Yet Figure 7-10 does show that something called "Sidman avoidance" takes place in operant conditioning. Haven't you ever gotten up to do something in order to avoid some unpleasant outcome without any outside reminder? If you stay out at night after a certain hour, don't you start getting a bit

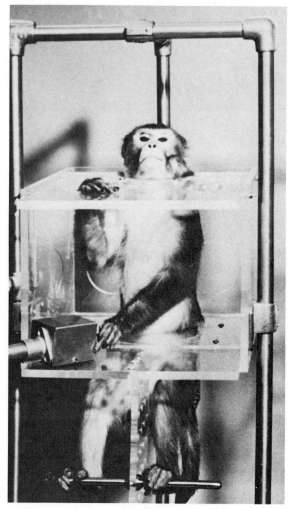

Figure 7-12 Both rats and monkeys, and humans too, are able to use internal time cues to achieve good avoidance behavior. In the photograph above, the monkey has learned to avoid shock by making a key or lever-pressing response before the shock is scheduled to arrive. With every avoidance response, the animal earns 20 seconds of shock-free time. Since this type of avoidance relies entirely on internal cues, it is said to be based on a temporal discrimination and is often referred to as "Sidman avoidance" because Murray Sidman first reported it. (Courtesy of J. V. Brady)

signal "Time is passing, better act if you want to avoid unpleasantness."

A famous experiment conducted by Joseph Brady made use of animals' reliance on internal time cues to maintain good avoidance responding (Brady, 1958). Brady had monkeys seated in a "monkey chair" like that shown in Figure 7-12. An electric shock was scheduled to arrive every five seconds. If the monkey pressed the telegraph key in front of it, however, the shock was delayed a full 20 seconds. You can see that a monkey with a good sense of time could avoid all shocks merely by responding once every 20 seconds. Actually, no monkey estimates time this well, but most were able to reduce the number of shocks to very low rates merely by maintaining a low but steady rate of key pressing. Apparently these animals formed a temporal discrimination on the basis of some perception of time elapsing since the occurrence of the last response.

Rats can form temporal discriminations too, as Murray Sidman showed in an earlier experiment (Sidman, 1953), although not so well as monkeys. And we know people can. When a certain amount of time passes since your last letter or phone call home, don't you start getting a bit uneasy about the consequences of your lengthening silence? Don't you immediately feel better the moment you mail your letter or complete your call?

Although it is difficult to determine the stimuli responsible for responding in reward and avoidance forms of operant conditioning, this doesn't mean that no stimulus control is possible. Once the animal has been reinforced for responding at a regular rate, it is easy to bring that response under control of an S^D, as was the case in discrete-trial procedures.

Suppose that a rat, now bar-pressing reliably and steadily for his pellet reward, suddenly finds that bar-pressing pays off, or is reinforced, only when a light is on, never when the light is off. This situation sets up the conditions for an **operant discrimination,**

uneasy about the consequences of not getting up on time the next morning? What is the warning signal? Your sense of time, perhaps. Well, then, in some cases the S^D for avoidance responding could be some internal cues that resembling the conditioned discrimination of classical conditioning. If "light on" and "light off" periods are alternated, always reinforcing a response in the presence of the light, the light becomes an S^D and the darkness becomes an S^Δ (S-delta). Stimulus control is demonstrated when the onset of S^D initiates and maintains responding, and when responding ceases during S^Δ. After all, responses made during S^Δ are not reinforced, and hence should extinguish.

Operant discrimination appears clearly in some everyday events. Tourists in Las Vegas will continue to put money into a "one-armed bandit," unless "Out of Order" is plastered on the machine. Such a sign is an S^Δ. It says that responding in its presence will not be reinforced. A small boy will continue to solicit candy and favors from his generous visiting grandfather (S^D), but not from his father (S^Δ), if the child has learned that only requests made to Grandpa pay off.

Similarities Between Classical and Instrumental Conditioning

Classical conditioning and instrumental conditioning differ sharply in (1) their use of visceral versus skeletal response systems, and (2) the relationship between the US and the response. In classical conditioning the response depends on the US; in operant conditioning the US depends on the response. Very important similarities between these two forms of simple learning must be acknowledged, nevertheless. In both, conditioning requires presentation of a **reinforcing stimulus,** either immediately after the CS (in classical conditioning) or after the response (in instrumental conditioning). In both types of conditioning, failure to present the reinforcing stimulus leads to **extinction** of the conditioned response. Following a time lapse after the termination of extinction, **spontaneous recovery** occurs for both classically and instrumentally conditioned responses.

Figure 7-13 shows the results of two experiments on auditory discrimination. Graph A shows a stimulus-generalization gradient based on classical conditioning of the eyelid response. The investigator, John Moore, first conditioned rabbits to make an eyelid-closing response (CR) whenever a 1200-Hz tone (CS) was presented; the US was a brief air puff to the eye (Moore, 1972). Later, when tones of higher and lower frequencies were substituted for the 1200-Hz CS, they too elicited the CR, but, as you can see, less and less effectively as the frequency of the test stimuli increased above or decreased below the frequency of the original CS.

Graph B in Figure 7-13 shows stimulus generalization following operant conditioning. Five pigeons were first reinforced for pecking a lighted disk in the presence of an S^D consisting of a tone of 1000 Hz. Pecking during silence (S^Δ) went unreinforced. Then test tones ranging from 300 to 3500 Hz were presented. As the graph reveals, each of the five pigeons responded most often in the presence of the original S^D, and as the frequency of test tones differed more and more from that of the original S^D, response rate fell off. Thus **stimulus generalization** is a basic phenomenon observable in both classical and instrumental conditioning.

The same can be said for **stimulus discrimination.** In classical conditioning, CS+ is always followed by the US, while CS− is never followed by the US. In operant conditioning the CR occurs to both CS+ and CS− in the beginning, since these stimuli are usually somewhat similar, and stimulus generalization therefore occurs. Later, however, the CR is elicited only by CS+ and not by CS−. Assume that a pigeon is rewarded with some grain whenever it pecks at an illuminated green key. When the key is red, key pecks go unreinforced. After a period of pecking the key at random, regardless of color, the pigeon will respond only when the key is green (S^D) and not when it is red (S^Δ).

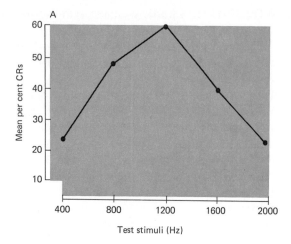

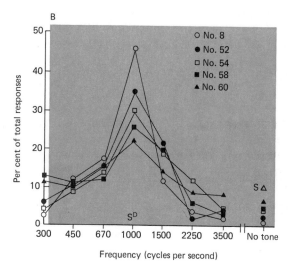

Figure 7-13 Results of experiments in auditory stimulus generalization. (A) After rabbits were classically conditioned to make an eye-blink CR to a tone CS of 1200 Hz, other tones also elicited the CR, but less and less effectively as test tones departed in frequency from the CS. (Adapted from Moore, 1972) (B) Stimulus generalization gradients obtained from 5 pigeons that had been reinforced for the operant response of pecking a disk in the presence of a 1000-Hz tone (S^D), but never during silence (S^Δ). As the frequency of test stimuli increased above, or diminished below, the 1000-Hz S^D, the response rate of each pigeon fell off. Stimulus generalization is a basic phenomenon in both classical and instrumental conditioning. (Jenkins & Harrison, 1960)

Schedules of Reinforcement

One of the most fascinating features of operant conditioning is that the less often an operant response is rewarded, the greater its resistance to extinction. It's strange that both people and animals work more for less. Years ago, B. F. Skinner demonstrated that if a rat was reinforced only after every fifth bar press, for example, its response rate would increase during conditioning (Skinner, 1938). Later, in extinction, this rat would continue to respond long after another rat, reinforced for every bar press, had stopped. Apparently *intermittent* reinforcement is a powerful determinant of resistance to extinction.

If it sounds unbelievable that animals should respond more to receive less, consider how hard it is to stop a child's begging for candy if the parent rewards begging behavior not upon each request, but only now and then. After several turndowns, the child's begging typically becomes more insistent. If the parent finally chooses to reward at *this* point, you can see that what would actually be rewarded would be vigorous and insistent begging.

There are many different patterns of **reinforcement schedule** through which reinforcements can be distributed in operant conditioning. These patterns fall into two major categories: **regular** or **continuous reinforcement,** in which every "correct" response is rewarded, without exception; and **partial** or **intermittent reinforcement,** in which only some correct responses are reinforced. Intermittent reinforcement is a general category that merely rules out reinforcement for every response. There are many patterns it can take.

RATIO AND INTERVAL SCHEDULES

In a **fixed-ratio (FR) schedule,** a fixed number of responses is required for each reinforcement. Such a schedule resembles the piecework wage system, in which people are paid for a specific number of work units completed. In a **variable-**

ratio (VR) schedule, the number of responses ~~required for reinforcement keeps changing unpre-~~ dictably. The Las Vegas tourist who just can't stop feeding the one-armed bandit knows full well the high resistance to extinction VR schedules can produce.

Another group of partial reinforcement schedules requires that a certain interval of time must elapse before a response gets reinforced. In a two-minute **fixed-interval schedule** (FI-2), for example, no responses are reinforced until two minutes have elapsed since the last reinforcement.

One of the most effective schedules for generating steady rates of responding and great resistance to extinction is the **variable-interval (VI) schedule.** Unlike the FI schedule, the VI schedule does not require a fixed interval of time to elapse before reinforcement becomes available. Intervals vary in length; sometimes very short intervals elapse before a reinforced response occurs, sometimes longer intervals occur. Thus in a VI-2 schedule, reinforcement becomes available every two minutes *on the average*—sometimes after intervals as short as 15 seconds, sometimes not until five minutes after the last reinforcement. Skinner (1953) has reported that a pigeon reinforced for key pecking on a VI-5 schedule emitted about two responses per second for a period of 15 hours. In another study by Skinner (1950), a pigeon emitted 20,000 responses in three hours and received only 36 reinforcements for all this work. Certainly this tremendous behavioral persistence is a stunning demonstration of the work that can be maintained by a VI schedule. Parents often complain that their growing children don't pursue a project to its conclusion, that they tend to show poor stick-to-itiveness. Rewarding their efforts on a variable-interval schedule would certainly be an obvious technique such parents might do well to try.

Behavior Shaping and Chaining

Everyone has seen, at a circus or on television, the remarkable feats animals can be trained to perform. Consider the dog trained to pirouette about on its hind legs at its master's command, and the elephant kneeling to allow its trainer to mount. How are these skills acquired?

The first temptation, of course, is to say that the animals do these things because they get reinforced for it. This is true as far as it goes, but it leaves too many questions unanswered. You'll remember that, in operant conditioning, reinforcement is response-contingent: no response, no reward. You also know that the correct operant response cannot be *elicited* from the organism, as can a Pavlovian UR; only after the organism has performed the desired behavior will reinforcement be given.

Now you can see the problem. If we wait for a dog to get up on its hind legs spontaneously before we reward it, we might well wait forever. Such a skill just doesn't happen automatically. Training must begin gradually, with naturally occurring responses, and those that *approximate*—ever so slightly at first—the performance we wish our subject eventually to attain must be systematically strengthened. Procedures based on conditioning principles can be used in **shaping** behavior into highly refined, precise skills, most of which involve the **chaining** of a number of separate responses into the desired complete pattern of behavior.

A practical application of behavior shaping was shown in a study that demonstrated that withdrawn children in a nursery school can gradually be taught to abandon their isolated play and turn to patterns of interaction with peers and teachers (Harris, Wolf, & Baer, 1964). Typically, withdrawn children who linger in a corner, refusing to play with other children, receive a lot of social reinforcement from teachers and aides. They express their concern about such children, and solicit their interest with entreaties to join the other children. But this study showed that selectively ignoring (nonreinforcing) the children whenever they displayed withdrawn behavior, and showing interest and encouragement when they merely looked in the direction of the group, tended to shape their orientation away from the corner and toward other children. As soon as the children took a few steps toward the group, that behavior brought attention, and mere looking was no longer sufficient to merit reinforcement. Gradually the requirements were raised so that the children received attention only when they were close to the others, and not at any other time. This step in the shaping process was very important, for it brought the children into contact with other, less deliberate, sources of reinforcement, especially those emanating from social interaction with their peers.

This sort of behavior shaping is nothing more than a kind of child training of a very specific sort: A final goal is identified (termination of maladaptive behavior, strengthening of behavioral interactions with others), and systematic extinction and reinforcement are applied, with the criterion for reward gradually increased. This method has been used to reduce the frequency of temper tantrums, and even the severely maladaptive and often self-injurious behavior (head banging, continuous biting of body parts) seen in autism, a form of childhood psychosis. Thus the principles of behavior shaping that are employed to train a circus animal for the amusement of children can also be applied to facilitate the social development of children, or to diminish the severity of their psychotic symptoms. Of course, behavior shaping also can be used to modify the behavior of adults.

Primary and Secondary Reinforcement

You first encountered reinforcement as the US in classical or Pavlovian conditioning. This form of reinforcement consists of a stimulus that reliably produces a biological reflex or UR in the organism, as food produces salivation and as shock produces foot withdrawal. Then, in instrumental conditioning, you saw that reinforcement may consist of the presentation of any stimulus that strengthens the preceding response, as food strengthens the response of key pecking. It may also consist of the removal of a noxious stimulus (a dog's hurdle-jump response is strengthened if it succeeds in turning off shock) or of the avoidance of a noxious stimulus (the dog jumps when the S^D comes on in order to avoid shock).

In all these cases, reinforcement seems to involve some stimulus event that, in Pavlovian language, has unconditioned effects on the organism. Food, shock, water, and sex are reinforcing from the start; they require no special training to acquire their reinforcing power. Therefore, this type of reinforcement is called **primary reinforcement.**

Reinforcement may also take the form of social approval—attention from other people, praise from parents, and the like. Such stimulation is not innately reinforcing; rather the reinforcing effect is *acquired.* When a stimulus acquires reinforcing properties, we call it a conditioned reinforcer. The use and effect of conditioned reinforcers is called **conditioned** or **secondary reinforcement.**

How does a stimulus that is not innately reinforcing, like a parent's smile of approval, become reinforcing? Reference to laboratory experiments provides the answer. It is by associating the stimulus with a primary reinforcer. A very famous experiment by J. B. Wolfe (1936) showed how even poker chips could acquire reinforcing value. Wolfe constructed a "chimp-o-mat," a kind of vending machine that provided a grape every time a poker chip was inserted. The machine was installed inside a chimpanzee cage, and the animals were trained to obtain grapes by inserting the poker chips. (One type of chimp-o-mat is shown in Figure 7-14.) This provided a splendid way of associating a poker chip (a neutral stimulus) with grapes (primary reinforcers), and the chips became reinforcing in their own right, as tokens. They became conditioned, or secondary, reinforcers.

It isn't sufficient merely to set up the conditions for secondary reinforcement. The reinforcing effect supposedly acquired by the chips should be demonstrable. If the chimps

Figure 7-14 Operating a chimp-o-mat, this chimpanzee inserts a poker chip (secondary reinforcer) and receives a food reward (primary reinforcer).

reinforcers from the moment of birth. Words like "good," money, cigarettes, good grades, and clothes are also generalized reinforcers, for their rewarding effect is not tied to a specific motivational state. The most powerful generalized reinforcers of all come from the behavior of other people. We all know how enormously rewarding we find the attention, affection, and approval of others, and to what lengths we will go to learn complicated interpersonal stratagems in order to obtain such reinforcers.

Generalized reinforcement is so important in interpersonal affairs that some consider it the most important factor holding a social group together, be it a family, a dating or married couple, a friendship group, or a social club. We like the people who reinforce us, and if we reinforce them, they like us too. We are not urging the deliberate use of generalized reinforcement for the purpose of exploiting or controlling others. We are saying, however, that whenever close and pleasant interactions occur among people in a group, you will usually find a constant flow of social reinforcements passing back and forth among the group members. Could generalized reinforcement be part of this thing called love?

WHAT IS LEARNING?

You've been considering age-old questions about the nature of human beings, and how human and animal behavior becomes modified as a result of encounters with orderly sequences of important environmental events. Along the way, you've learned a great deal about the nature of learning, probably enough to elaborate your own definitions of this process.

There is no general agreement among psychologists on the definition of learning. Some think of it as a change in expectancies: The subject comes to expect a US to follow a CS, or to expect that a particular response will be followed by reinforcement. Sometimes psychologists call this expectation a "preparatory

were now to learn a new response, using only poker chips as reinforcers, the acquired reinforcing effect of the chips would be demonstrated. Wolfe did just that. He showed that chimps would learn to press levers and pull strings, responses for which the only reward was a poker chip.

The poker chips in this experiment were associated with only one primary reinforcer, grapes. What if the chips were to become intimately associated with *many* primary reinforcers, such as various kinds of food, water, sex, and termination of aversive stimuli? If this were done, then a poker chip would become a generalized reinforcer. A parent's smile of approval is a generalized reinforcer, since it has been associated with so many primary set": getting ready to act in a certain way to receive reinforcement. Others view learning as the strengthening of a bond between a stimulus situation and a behavioral act, without necessarily including any conscious accompaniments. Some are satisfied to express the learning concept numerically, basing it on objective measures of, say, the number of reinforced learning trials. The concept covers such a vast variety of ways in which behavior is modified that it's no wonder there are so many different ways of conceptualizing learning. Yet it is possible to provide an objective, nontheoretical definition of learning that many psychologists would accept: **Learning** is a relatively permanent change in behavior resulting from reinforced practice.

Learning is a broad, generic concept that includes within it the more particular forms of both classical and instrumental conditioning. The definition leaves room, also, for far more complex forms of behavior change, like the acquisition of complex strategies in bargaining with an adversary, which are probably not reducible to simple classical or instrumental conditioning.

The definition is objective in that it specifies an observable outcome (a change in behavior) resulting from an observable antecedent (practice of some sort). The word "practice" should be taken broadly to include repeated exposures to sequences of stimuli, as a CS followed by a US. The term "reinforced practice" attempts to exclude extinction conditions, in which behavior certainly is modified in that the CR strength diminishes, but the response is repeatedly practiced without benefit of reinforcing stimuli. In observational learning, however, it is difficult to identify the reinforcing events. Learning to associate the Battle of Hastings with the year 1066, for example, seems to occur through sheer practice.

The restriction "relatively permanent" is important. It allows distinction between behavior change due to learning variables and behavior change due to many other factors.

When an infant begins to sit up without support, this change is due more to maturational changes than to learning (see Chapter 3). When visual sensitivity following entry into a darkened theater improves rapidly, this behavior change is due to reflexive photochemical changes taking place in retinal receptors (in rods, mainly), rather than to practice of some sort (see Chapter 4). Use of drugs like alcohol and marijuana will certainly produce changes in behavior, but these changes are reversible, and behavior returns to normal after the drug wears off. It is always possible to interfere with the results of past learning (witness extinction), but unlike the behavioral effects attributable to maturation, dark adaptation, and drug use, such interference usually requires a lot of practice and is nonreinforced to boot.

THE PERMANENCE OF CONDITIONED RESPONSES

What does "relatively permanent" mean for conditioned responses? It's hard to predict how long after acquisition trials are over a CS will still elicit a good, healthy CR. For one thing, the extinction opportunities the organism may have encountered in the intervening time are not always known. A good way to test the longevity of a CR is to use an unusual CS, which the subjects are not likely to meet again until they are retested some years later.

In an experiment with pigeons, Howard Hoffman and his associates (1963) did just that. After the birds had learned to peck at a lighted disk for food rewards, they were exposed to a 1000-Hz tone followed by a brief shock. Tone-shock pairings were repeated until key pecking practically stopped the moment the tone came on. This result means that the tone CS had acquired the capacity to elicit fear, and that this **conditioned emotional response (CER)** suppressed operant responding for food. This conditioned suppression of hunger-motivated and food-reinforced behavior also generalized to tones both higher and lower in frequency than 1000 Hz, as shown in Figure 7-15. Observe the solid-circle curve. Key pecking just about stops when the CS,

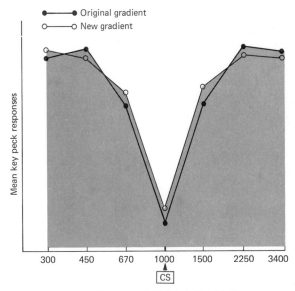

Original gradient
New gradient

Frequency of CS & test stimuli in Hz

Figure 7-15 Original conditioned suppression generalization gradient (solid circles) showing maximum suppression of the key-pecking response in the presence of a 1000-Hz fear CS and much less suppression to generalization test stimuli, and a generalization gradient obtained two and a half years later (open circles) from the same pigeon subjects. (Adapted from Hoffman, Fleshler, & Jensen, 1963)

a 1000-Hz tone, is presented, and the suppression effect weakens as the frequency of the test CS varies above and below 1000 Hz. The open-circle curve shows the amount of conditioned suppression to both the CS and the test tones by the same pigeons two and a half years later. The pigeons had spent their long vacation in their home loft far from shocks or pure tones. When protected from fortuitous exposure to tones, and thus from adventitious extinction, emotional conditioning seems to have held up very well across time.

The definition of learning says nothing about whether the behavior change is good or bad, desirable or undesirable, adaptive or maladaptive. People learn to smoke, drink, and take harmful drugs, yet this learning certainly would not be considered good. When we discuss psychopathology (see Chapter 15),

you'll see how certain behavioral disorders are learned. These are obviously undesirable consequences of learning conditions. We learn all sorts of things, it appears, and what gets learned depends not on our abstract value judgments, but on which behavior patterns have benefited from conditions propitious to effective conditioning.

Behavioral Laws and Individual Freedom

With all this talk about behavioral laws, conditioned reflexes, and determinants of behavior, you might get the impression that the psychology of learning explains the human being as a pretty standard, very predictable organism, one that is constrained to bend its behavior to the "laws of learning" and whose very individuality is lost in the universality of such principles. Nothing could be further from the truth.

Laws of learning determine *how* we learn, not what we *should* learn. The principle of reinforcement, for example, states that behavior immediately followed by reinforcement will be strengthened. It says nothing about what that behavior ought to be. Among the Arapesh of New Guinea, for example, massive amounts of social reinforcement can be obtained from adults and peers by the child who displays cooperative, noncompetitive behavior, while for a child of the neighboring Mundugumor people, the same rewards follow displays of aggressive, competitive behavior (Mead, 1935). The same principle of reinforcement guarantees a high prevalence of cooperative behavior in one society and a high prevalence of competitive behavior in the other.

Within our own country, from family to family and from one social class to another, many different types of behavior pattern are reinforced. One family may reinforce expressions of trust in and closeness to other people; another may punish when such feelings are expressed, and reward instead suspiciousness and domination of others. Hard work, striving

for success, and achieving independence are patterns far more often reinforced in middle-class homes than in lower-class homes. Since reinforcement is applied to the strengthening of different behaviors, the law of reinforcement not only allows for individual and group differences, but actually guarantees they will occur and predicts what they will be.

Finally, one hope for correcting and eliminating certain forms of undesirable and often tragic behavior, like neurotic and psychotic states, deficient academic performance, and inadequate interpersonal skills, lies in our ability to discover the determinants of behavior. If we can analyze the causes, we have a fighting chance of modifying the effects.

We all have some ideal goals for ourselves and our children. We like to think of ourselves and of them as self-confident, fully functioning, honest, and loving persons. Progress toward these goals will be difficult unless we can learn more about the conditions that foster the learning of such ideal behavior patterns.

THE WAY YOU MAKE YOUR DECISIONS

■ Perhaps now you can begin to draw conclusions of your own about the way you make your decisions. Go back to the decisions you considered at the beginning of this discussion of conditioning. What factors were present in them, in the light of what you have seen in this chapter?

Pavlov, Skinner, and a host of others have discovered a number of relationships in the conditioning of all animals, including humans. Laws express these relationships for both classical and instrumental conditioning. In the face of such laws, what play remains for freedom? Can there be anything but constraint between independent and dependent variables, necessary and inexorable causes and effects? If you choose freedom instead of constraint, what sources of hope remain for you?

Our unconditioned as well as conditioned responses to stimuli, governed by neurophysiological changes, seem completely reflexive and involuntary. Instrumental conditioning, governed by positive or negative reinforcers, and obeying similar laws, appears to offer little more flexibility, although operant conditioning can be called "free responding." But within the spontaneous, exploratory, evaluative behavior within which operant conditioning operates, and within the fluid situation in which decisions are reached, is there room for human freedom?

The relationships between the many variables involved in human decisions of what to do next, or what ideal to follow in the long run, have not yet been worked out. These kinds of situations will be described in more detail in Chapters 8 and 12. Meanwhile, perhaps you can begin to find your own answers to the questions with which this chapter opened.

SUMMARY

For thousands of years the notion of the human being as a free agent competed with that of the human being as a reacting organism. Mentalistic and mechanistic traditions were joined in Descartes's dualistic conception, in which a mind or soul substance interacted with the body. His physiological theories laid the basis for the reflex-arc concept, which much later was developed by the Russian reflexologists in an attempt to explain human and animal functioning in physiological terms. Sechenov viewed voluntary behavior as reflex action, and Pavlov introduced the concept of conditioning to explain the plasticity and modifiability of reflexes.

Classical conditioning procedures involve the pairing of an originally neutral stimulus (CS) with a biologically potent or reinforcing stimulus (US). The US elicits a biological reflex, the unconditioned response (UR). After several pairings of CS and US, the CS acquires the capacity to elicit the reflex, which is then called the conditioned response (CR). The strength of conditioning of the salivary response can be inferred by measuring the number of drops of saliva secreted, its volume, latency of the CR, and resistance to extinction.

The major laws of classical conditioning are the law of excitation and several laws of inhibition. If the CR is repeatedly elicited by presentations of the CS without the US, the CR will extinguish (law of extinctive inhibition); if the CR elicited by one CS is reinforced while the CR elicited by a similar CS is not, the CR to the second CS will extinguish (law of differential inhibition). Spontaneous recovery refers to the recovery of CR strength with the passage of time after the termination of extinction training, despite the lack of intervening reconditioning trials. Stimulus generalization is the elicitation of a CR by stimuli whose properties resemble those of the original CS. Conditioning theory assumes that with the pairing of CS and US, habit strength, a theoretical construct, increases; presentation of the CS alone on extinction trials increases the value of another theoretical construct, inhibition, which opposes the effect of habit.

Unlike classical conditioning, instrumental conditioning concerns learning in which the response is strengthened because it produces some reward (positive reinforcement) or avoids or terminates some unpleasant event (negative reinforcement). A response that produces an unpleasant event is said to be punished and tends not to recur. When the learning episode consists of a series of trials initiated by an external stimulus and terminated by a goal response, this is discrete-trial learning, of which there are three types: reward, escape, and avoidance. In operant or free-responding conditioning, it is difficult to identify the beginning and end of a trial, and rate of responding is used as a measure of the strength of conditioning. When the response rate has been increased sufficiently, stimulus control can be established by reinforcing operant responding in the presence of one external stimulus, S^D, but not in its absence, nor in the presence of a different stimulus, S^Δ.

The phenomena of classical conditioning (acquisition, extinction, spontaneous recovery, stimulus generalization, and discrimination) are also found in instrumental conditioning. In operant conditioning, schedules of reinforcement are important determinants of response rate. Ratio schedules require a fixed ratio (FR) or variable ratio (VR) of responses for each reinforcement; interval schedules require a fixed interval (FI) or variable interval (VI) of time between reinforcements of a response.

Complex behavioral acts can be learned by reinforcing better and better approximations of the desired behavior (shaping) or by reinforcing a number of sequential responses that together comprise a skill (chaining). Primary reinforcers are those whose effectiveness requires no special training. Events that acquire their reinforcing power through an association with a primary reinforcer are called conditioned, or secondary, reinforcers. A generalized reinforcer is a conditioned reinforcer that has been associated with many primary reinforcers and is not tied to any specific motivational state of the organism.

Learning is a broad generic concept, best defined as a relatively permanent change in behavior resulting from reinforced practice. The laws of learning apply equally well to desirable and undesirable forms of behavior change. While these laws may apply universally, the actual behavior that is learned in a given situation will vary, depending on which particular responses have been reinforced. Thus vastly different types of learned behavior patterns, varying from culture to culture and from family to family, may reflect the operation of the same laws of learning.

NOW YOU'RE THE EXPERT

Pavlov believed that sound educational methods should be based on his principles of conditioning, and Skinner has asserted that principles of operant or instrumental conditioning should guide the development of education.

Imagine that you are a psychologist observing all your current school activities.

1. Describe how you are now being conditioned classically or instrumentally in your various school activities, in terms of the concepts and principles of these types of conditioning.

2. Describe, in the same terms, the changes you would recommend to improve your educational activities.

3. What other educational changes might you recommend, if any, that go beyond conditioning principles?

8

Behavioral Technology and Self-Control

YOUR BAD HABITS

■ Think for a minute about some of your minor bad habits. All of us have a good many of them, actions that we do repeatedly but wish we didn't, either because we disapprove of them ourselves or because friends or relatives have demonstrated their disapproval. Such bad habits could be any of your activities that you dislike: driving too fast, arguing too much, being too early or too late for events, saying nasty things about others, biting your nails, whatever. Select one of these that seems worth pondering. How often do you do it? In what kinds of situations does it usually occur? What do you think really causes it? Why do you suppose you have failed to stop it? Do you have any ideas on how you might overcome it? Then go on with this chapter to see how some psychologists have been dealing with this sort of thing.

Human behavior is plastic and modifiable, not rigidly fixed and unchangeable. Every day of our lives we display a remarkable harmony with the external world around us, varying our behavior in accordance with changing events. If a farmer's efforts are more richly rewarded when he plants one crop rather than another, he will tend to stick with the first crop. (In fact, some farmers become one-crop specialists.) If a college student experiences intense discomfort in social situations, he may learn systematically to avoid them or seek to improve his social skills. If a businessman finds the stress of competition too great, he may develop a drinking habit or move into a less competitive field.

These examples indicate that change is the hallmark of behavior. They also suggest that, as responses to environmental problems, some forms of change are more beneficial than others. The shy college student who reduces her discomfort by becoming seclusive will not solve her problem in a way that will prepare her for community living; the businessman who learns to seek relief in four-martini lunches cannot be said to be making an adaptive adjustment to the stresses of life.

In recent years psychologists have deliberately sought to help people change in ways considered to be useful and beneficial through the systematic application of the principles of classical and operant conditioning. The gap between the experimental psychology of learning, carried out in laboratories under closely controlled conditions, and the psychology of behavior change, which seeks to assist people in achieving adaptive changes in their behavior, has narrowed enormously. The result is the new field of **behavioral technology**.

Certain principles of operant and classical conditioning are being systematically applied in medicine (to help people improve their physiological functioning), in education (to help young children, especially, learn efficiently), in psychotherapy (to teach individuals how to control their fears and anxieties), and in the general area of self-control (to train people to achieve control over such behaviors as overeating, drinking too much, and smoking). These applications sometimes reveal the nature of the interplay between the theoretical and the practical, between research performed to satisfy the need to know and research used to satisfy the need to change and improve.

BASIC BEHAVIOR-CONTROL PRINCIPLES

The field of behavioral technology is founded on a surprisingly small number of principles of behavior, based on the concepts of classical and instrumental conditioning. These principles fall into three broad categories: control by consequences, control by stimulus, and control by symbolic processes.

The Selection of Target Behavior

The target behavior one wishes to change, eliminate, or strengthen must be identified and described as objectively and completely as possible. Such behavior may be clearly observable to the naked eye of another person (nail biting); it may be detectable only with the aid of specialized instruments (high blood pressure); it may take the form of intense feelings (headache, acute anxiety) or mental images (obsessive imagery of a suffered rebuff or, more seriously, in hallucinations). The target behavior is usually recorded and analyzed in some detail in order to ascertain how frequent or how strong it is, under what conditions it arises, and what results it produces. A record of the target behavior gives a **baseline** for its occurrence, serving to show whether the behavioral techniques adopted are increasing or decreasing it as desired.

Control by Consequences

If the target behavior is to be eliminated or reduced in strength, the **law of extinctive inhi-**

bition (see Chapter 7) suggests that the situations in which the behavior occurs should be analyzed for evidence of reinforcing consequences that may be maintaining its strength. For example, teachers who give their pupils attention only when their boisterous behavior becomes excessively disrupting may be inadvertently reinforcing the very target behavior they wish to reduce. The law of extinction states that a particular behavior will occur less frequently if its positively reinforcing consequences are eliminated.

Behavior can also have negatively reinforcing consequences, however. Some behavior is so aversive to other people that it cannot be permitted to run the normal course of extinction. Consider the classroom bully who delights in hurting smaller children. It's hard to see how the target behavior (bullying) can be permitted to continue through one long, nonrewarded extinction schedule. To eliminate target behavior that is *intrinsically* positively reinforcing, a better tactic is to use punishment while reinforcing alternate incompatible behavior.

Punishment is a **response-contingent event;** that is, an event contingent on, or dependent on, a prior response. This means that the presentation or occurrence of an aversive, punishing event depends on the prior occurrence of the target behavior. Thus the young bully would receive punishment only for the undesirable target behavior. **Punishment** can be defined formally as the occurrence of an aversive event contingent upon the prior occurrence of a specified behavior. Shocking a rat for pressing a bar is punishment.

In the case of the bully (and people in general), the most frequently used form of punishment would not be painful stimulation, but **time out (TO)** from positive reinforcement. This means that whenever the bully performed the proscribed response, opportunities for obtaining *positive* reinforcement would be withheld for a specified period of time. This might take the form of denying the child who has misbehaved the fun of recess. Hyperaggressive children who are being taught to achieve self-control may be sent to an actual "time out" or "quiet" room for periods of ten minutes or more. Sidelining a basketball player for committing too many fouls is another example of the TO form of punishment, if we assume the ruling keeps the player from the enjoyment of playing the game and earning the adulation of the crowd. The denial of available positive reinforcement is considered to be punishing, as is the presentation of aversive stimulation.

The effects of punishment are very complicated, to say the least. Some investigators feel that punishment produces only a temporary reduction in the strength of the target behavior (Skinner, 1953). If so, the bully can be expected to be at it again soon. Others feel that the use of punishment merely encourages the clever child to learn to *discriminate* between those situations in which the behavior is likely to result in punishment (when adults are around) and those in which the transgression is not so likely to be detected (out on the playground). Still other investigators offer evidence that punishment, if traumatic enough, will *permanently* eliminate the target behavior (Solomon,

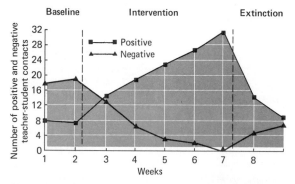

Figure 8-1 When students reinforce their teachers for positive behavior, positive contacts increase and negative contacts decrease. Good interactions require continued reinforcement: When student intervention stopped, positive teacher-student contacts declined. (Gray, Graubard, & Rosenberg, 1974)

WHO MODIFIES WHOM?

A generation ago a joke about behaviorists questioned whether they were conditioning rats to bar-press for food or whether the rats were conditioning the investigators to give them food by pressing the bar. Today, however, as behavioral technology develops, "Who is modifying whom?" has become a serious question.

Recent research has shown that junior high school students who have behavioral problems that disrupt their classes and their own learning activities can be taught how to modify the behavior of their teachers so that the teachers accept and praise them. As a result, the disruptive behavior ceases (Gray, Graubard, & Rosenberg, 1974). The behavior modification program modifies the students' behavior, true; but this in turn modifies the teachers' behavior, creating a constructive classroom situation that is reinforcing for all concerned.

For the first day of their modification program, students kept records of positive and negative contacts they had with their teachers to establish the baseline situation from which they started, as shown in Figure 8-1. Then, as they swung into action, still keeping their records, they offered positive reinforcements to teachers with smiles, praise, sincere efforts to learn, and talking with them before and after class. Students also discouraged negative teacher behavior with comments like "It's hard for me to learn when you're cross." Within a few weeks, as shown in Figure 8-1, this intervention program had reversed the character of teacher-student contacts. And when the students stopped their intervention, the number of positive teacher-student contacts quickly declined. Students had to continue the intervention longer in order to reorient the behavior of their teachers permanently.

Behavioral research has also demonstrated that with adequate preparation, junior high school students can modify the behavior of their friends and even their parents, as well as their teachers. Youngsters can be prepared to respond to unfriendly treatment by their peers by disregarding (extinguishing) the unwanted behavior like teasing, calling names, or provoking fights, and by expressing pleasure and approval of (positively reinforcing) friendly reactions. One girl selected her mother's failure to have meals on time and to wash and iron her daughter's clothes as the behavior to change, and successfully shaped her mother's behavior with praise and approval. Teachers and parents whose behavior is modified in these ways by youngsters react very favorably, although they contend that the projects have changed the youngsters' behavior rather than their own. But it hardly matters who modifies whom if the resultant behavior is gratifying and productive for all concerned. Students, teachers, parents, and friends all gain new self-respect, as well as increased awareness of the needs of others and of ways to bring all their needs into harmony.

1964). Punishment of such aversive intensity would not normally be found in behavior-modification programs.

Despite these diverse ideas, it is generally agreed that punishment used in conjunction with the **reinforcement of alternate behavior (RAB)** may be the most effective means of reducing the incidence of undesirable behavior. While merely punishing the classroom bully may only temporarily weaken his aggressive tendencies, a concerted effort on the part of teachers and even pupils to reward him when he behaves well will have longer-lasting consequences.

It is not only maladaptive behavior that may be weakened or eliminated; current systems of behavior change are also used to strengthen existing, though weak, components of adaptive behavior. This goal is usually accomplished by the systematic application of positive reinforcement. The shy, withdrawn child in a nursery school is rewarded at first with teacher attention and praise for even the slightest sign of interest in other children. Eventually, using the method of **successive approximations** (see Chapter 7), the teacher rewards only more tangible forms of interaction with other children. Finally the other children come to function as important sources of

reinforcement for maintaining the child's interpersonal contact.

The consequences of specific target behaviors can be manipulated to improve the adaptiveness of behavior or to reduce its maladaptiveness, either by withholding positive reinforcement whenever the undesirable behavior occurs, by applying negative sanctions, by positively reinforcing alternate behavior that can substitute for the proscribed behavior, or by strengthening weak but adaptive behavior by systematically rewarding stepwise improvements.

Control by Stimulus

Much behavior is directly elicited by external stimuli that are like the Pavlovian CS. The sight of a hypodermic syringe in the hands of a white-gowned person can frighten a child to tears. The visual stimulus of the syringe has, after all, been followed by an unpleasant sensation in past encounters with white-gowned adults. Seeing dad reach for the hairbrush also constitutes a potent fear-eliciting CS in children who have frequently experienced hairbrush and pain in close temporal and anatomical proximity. A stimulus situation like the view from the roof of a tall building or a reproving comment from a teacher may also be capable of triggering an internal response of great pleasure or discomfort. The elicited reactions may include both *physiological* components, like an increased heartbeat, sweating, and blushing, and *subjective* components, like feelings of dread, dizziness, an empty feeling in the pit of the stomach, and so on. Such respondent behavior is said to be under the control of Pavlovian stimuli. "The Telltale Stomach" (later in this section) describes a rare opportunity for observing simultaneous physiological and subjective reactions elicited in a human patient by external stimuli.

External stimulus events may also acquire powerful control over instrumental behavior. Smokers know very well how difficult it is to cut down cigarette consumption in an environment populated by heavy smokers. And all of us are aware that the beginning of a commercial during an evening TV program can stimulate an irresistible urge to raid the refrigerator. The sight of others smoking and the onset of the commercial have come to act like discriminative stimuli for the responses of lighting up and eating, respectively. The control these stimuli have over our behavior can be as powerful as the control exercised by the quitting-time whistle at an industrial plant. It would take a special kind of bravery (or foolishness?) to try to stop, or even slow down, the going-home behavior of 800 workers when the five-o'clock whistle blows. A great deal of our everyday behavior, desirable as well as objectionable, is under the control of discriminative stimuli, as discussed in Chapter 7. In Figure 8-2 we see how Dennis takes advantage of the control over his mother's dessert-making behavior that a little pointer on a dial can exercise.

We speak of **stimulus control** of instrumental behavior whenever the probability increases that a response will occur if a given stimulus is present. The acquisition of such control by a stimulus occurs, of course, through discrimination training: The plant workers may go off the job with no aversive consequences only after the whistle blows; the child is more likely to be rewarded for requesting an ice cream cone when the vendor's chimes are audible or the ice cream truck is in view; the obese person usually finds more pleasure when the eating situation excludes the presence of other people; the bravado of the young hoodlum is more likely to gain the gang's approbation when antisocial acts are carried out in the gang members' presence. The plant whistle, the appearance of the vendor, the departure of other people from the eating area, and the presence of one's peers all constitute stimuli (or stimulus situations) that are said to have acquired control because the

"MAYBE IF I TURN THE LITTLE WHEEL *THIS* WAY, SHE'LL START MAKIN' DESSERTS AGAIN."

Figure 8-2 Dennis has discovered his mother's behavior is also governed by the principle of stimulus control. (Copyright © 1975 by Field Newspaper Syndicate, T.M. ®)

behaviors described are more probable in their presence.

Some stimuli acquire control over undesirable behavior: nail biting, tantrums, antisocial acts, excessive eating and drinking, despondent and unproductive moods, poor study habits, and so on. Behavior modification techniques attempt to free the person from the tyranny of stimulus control by extinguishing the intense emotional reactions some stimuli have come to evoke, or by rewarding alternate and more appropriate forms of behavior in the presence of the controlling stimuli.

Control by Symbolic Processes

The final set of behavior-control principles is centered in the **symbolic processes** of the individual; that is, in such activities as thinking, imagining, and verbalizing, all of which are unobservable to others. It may seem somewhat unscientific to talk about behavior being controlled by subjective events, like an imagined threat or a private thought. Scientific rigor need not be abandoned, however, merely because the controlling events are less accessible to outside observers than are external stimuli like the sound of a fire alarm. As you will see in Chapter 13, although the feelings we have when we say we are "anxious" are certainly subjective, such private states can be objectively indexed by physiological signs (galvanic skin reflexes, changes in heart rate, sweating) and verbal reports.

Ideas and images can also be objectively indexed, mainly by the experiencing person's own verbal report. And ideas and images certainly do seem to have some stimulus control over behavior, as we have been defining the concept of such control: The probability of a given behavior will be changed by the presence or absence of some antecedent event. Think of the event as an image. If you visualize certain disgusting eating activities, you can definitely alter your eating behavior with respect to certain foods. The next time you start to eat yogurt, try to visualize the bacteria in the food that are responsible for its consistency and taste. How will this affect your eating behavior? Or as you reach for a cigarette, try to visualize a tiny mass of cancerous cells beginning to form in your lung. Pretty rough imagery, but it makes the point. Turning to another type of imagery and behavioral consequence, consider how long it's been since you called home, how little effort it takes to put a call through, and how good you'll feel for having pleased your family. Chances are this imagery will increase the probability of your telephoning (especially if you can call collect). The influence of symbolic activity on sexual behavior is well known: Masturbation by adult males is usually preceded and accompanied by vivid visual imagery. Shy people who wish to acquire effective social skills can be taught to reduce the tension of initial contacts with people by learning to imagine the positive consequences of such meetings before they take place.

Symbolic control has rapidly become one of the most important types of self-control training. Such training aims to teach people how to govern their own behavior through management of the variables that control it. Symbolic control is the keystone of self-control techniques for the treatment of such disorders as obesity and alcohol and tobacco addiction.

THE TELLTALE STOMACH

Attempts to correlate physiological and subjective reactions to external stimuli usually require sophisticated equipment, special conditions, and cooperative subjects. Some years ago, all the necessary ingredients came together in the case of Tom, a patient whose special problem allowed him to make an unusual contribution to scientific research: He was able to describe his subjective experiences to a variety of stimuli while at the same time affording the investigators a direct view of the inside lining of his stomach.

Tom's story begins with an accident he suffered as a child. He accidentally swallowed scalding clam chowder from a container, thereby producing so much scar tissue in his esophagus that it became permanently impossible for him to swallow food. A surgical operation was performed that created a fistula; that is, an opening leading directly through the body wall into his stomach. This made it possible for the investigators (Wolf & Wolff, 1947) to observe Tom's stomach activity directly under a variety of circumstances. For example, when Tom felt angry or resentful, as he once did when he was fired from his job for reasons he felt were unfair, his stomach mucosa became moist and engorged with blood, and gastric acid secretion increased. Tom also complained of stomach pain. It was noted that at this time the gastric lining was susceptible to pain and the tissue was easily damaged. Tiny ulcers could be made to form with ease. When Tom was able to calm down, the condition of the stomach lining returned to normal.

Interestingly, when some things made Tom feel afraid or depressed, the stomach lining became rather pale and dry, stomach movements decreased, and acid secretion diminished — just the opposite of the physiological reactions that accompanied the feelings of anger and hostility. Apparently different environmental situations can evoke at least two different types of gastric response.

As we all know, just talking with a person can produce feelings of anxiety and embarrassment. In a study by Mittelman, Wolff, and Scharf (1942), it was found that the discussion of a patient's psychological conflicts in a psychotherapy session produced increases in gastric secretions and stomach contractions. External situations can exercise control over both our physiological reactions and our subjective experiences.

OPERANT CONTROL OF INVOLUNTARY BEHAVIOR

Can you wiggle your ears? If so, can you wiggle one while keeping the other still? Can you will yourself to blush? Or stop a blush from developing? Can you tell your heart to speed up or slow down? Normally you have very little control over processes that go on inside your body, and until recently it was assumed that such "involuntary" processes could not be controlled. What if the cardiac patient could teach his heart to smooth out dangerous irregularities? What if the hypertensive person could be trained to keep his blood pressure within the normal range? What if the ulcer victim could learn deliberately to reduce the amount of acid secreted by his stomach during periods of stress? Such types of personal control could have vast medical implications.

In Chapter 2 you saw that many internal processes are under the control of the autonomic nervous system. The possibility of achieving operant control over visceral processes in humans received widespread attention after Neal Miller and his associates at Rockefeller University demonstrated that rats could learn to modify heart rate, urine production, intestinal motility, blood pressure, and other processes by making reinforcement (either rewarding brain stimulation or avoidance of shock) contingent on the occurrence of designated changes in the organ system in the direction desired. Thus if an increase in heart rate was desired, the rat would receive a brief burst of rewarding **electrical stimulation of the brain (ESB)** whenever the interbeat time got short enough to meet a specified criterion.

In these animal studies, the crucial elements involved in achieving operant control seem to be (1) precise specification and measurement of minute changes in the target response and (2) split-second timing in the delivery of reinforcement the instant the desired response change occurs. Thus if a decrease in heart rate is the target behavior, sophisticated electronic equipment is used to detect the instant the interbeat time increases to the preestablished criterion, then reinforcing electrical stimulation of the brain is delivered instantly. The electrical stimulation is delivered directly to a portion of the hypothalamus by means of permanently implanted electrodes. In order to prevent the animal from moving about (this would produce unwanted effects on the heart rate), it is usually kept in a state of paralysis of the skeletal musculature by the administration of a drug (d-tubocurarine chloride) that blocks impulses from the motor nerves from reaching the muscle fibers. Since the animal cannot breathe on its own, it is given artificial respiration by machine (see Figure 8-3).

Recently Miller and Dworkin (1973) reported increasing difficulty in producing heart rate changes through reinforcing ESB. Year after year the magnitude of the effect has been declining, and the most recent efforts to reproduce the phenomenon have failed. The reasons for the strange disappearance of this effect are very unclear. Yet Miller's original successes

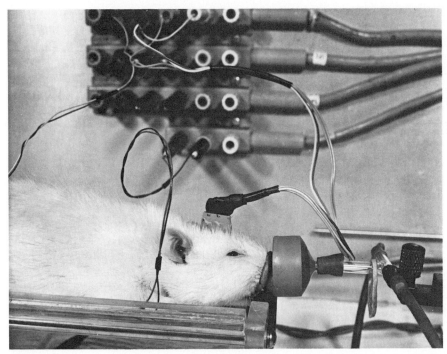

Figure 8-3 Artificial respiration administered to a rat during paralysis of the skeletal musculature. In this state, the effects of ESB as a reward for speeding up or slowing down heart rate can be observed, free of the influence of motor activity on heart rate. (Courtesy of Neal E. Miller)

have encouraged a great deal of research with human patients. It sometimes happens in science that the value of a new finding lies more in the direction and encouragement it gives to other researchers than in the durability of the original results.

Control of Human Cardiovascular Processes

At the Baltimore City Hospitals, cardiac patients of Bernard Engel have been learning to speed up, slow down, or stabilize their heart rates. Engel's **biofeedback** technique in conditioning these **cardiovascular processes** shows obvious similarities to Miller's techniques with rats. Patients lie quietly and watch a display panel on which are mounted three lights —green, red, and yellow. The green and red are instruction signals; patients are asked to make their hearts beat faster when the green light comes on, slower when the red is on. The yellow light is the reward or "reinforcer" light. It is crucial because the patients know that so long as the yellow light stays on, they are successfully controlling their heart rate in the direction required for the improvement of their medical condition. For seriously ill people, a signal that they are getting better can be a powerful reinforcer.

Specialized equipment monitors changes in heart rate by means of an electrocardiogram (EKG) machine coupled to electronic equipment, and these changes are reported to patients via the reward light. Feedback information, coupled with reinforcement, constitutes the essence of the biofeedback technique. Various clinical applications of this technique have been devised to help patients control cardiovascular functions.

Control of Cardiac Arrhythmias

Arrhythmias are irregularities in the pumping action of the heart. This can be a dangerous condition, for in some patients with heart disease arrhythmias may lead to cardiac arrest. One common type of arrhythmia is the premature contraction of the left ventricle of the heart, the chamber that normally pumps oxygenated blood into the arterial system. Normally the ventricle relaxes and contracts once a second. In a **premature ventricular contraction (PVC),** the contraction occurs a little sooner than it should. A sample EKG record showing the presence of PVCs is shown in Figure 8-4. Most patients are not aware when PVCs are occurring. Engel and Theodore Weiss, his colleague, wondered whether patients with this type of arrhythmia could be trained to control or eliminate PVCs if (1) they were strongly motivated to do so and (2) they could "see" PVCs occurring and could detect the results of their efforts to decrease the frequency of such irregularities (Weiss & Engel, 1971).

Motivation to engage in an activity that could prolong their lives was certainly strong in the patients. But how could appropriate feedback be provided? Whenever the sensitive electronic apparatus detected a PVC, the red light came on, followed immediately by the green light. This special signal told the patient that a PVC had occurred. The patient was also instructed to look for any internal sensations that might be accompanying the abnormal contraction. Only if patients could learn to spot any distinctive sensations that characteristically accompanied their PVCs could they hope eventually to wean themselves from the feedback signals provided by the apparatus. The goal, of course, was to increase patients' awareness of their own heart action until they could sense the abnormal contractions, and immediately try to eliminate them and stabilize the heart's pumping cycle.

By providing external visual feedback only during small portions of the sessions, Engel intermittently forced his patients to search for feedback among their own internal cues. Gradually some were weaned completely from apparatus-supplied feedback; not only could they report when PVCs were occurring, but they could also quickly restore the normal rhythm of the heart.

How does one "try" to speed up or slow down the heart? When successful patients were asked how they did it, there was no consistency in their reports. Some said they thought about peaceful, relaxing scenes; others visualized engaging in physical activities. One patient said she thought about arguing with her children and about running through a dark street. In short, no consistent strategy was employed by the successful patients. Simple muscular maneuvers like tensing the body muscles—or relaxing them—produced no reliable effects. Well, then, how do patients do it? Engel (1972, pp. 176–177) had this to say:

I have asked every subject whom I ever treated the same question: "What did you do?" "How did you do it?" And after ten years of this nonsense I finally recognized how silly those questions are. This year I decided to take up golf. . . . I asked myself on those occasions when I hit the ball well, "What did you do?" "How did you do it?" And the answer came back loud and clear: "I don't know."

If learned cardiac control is a form of motor

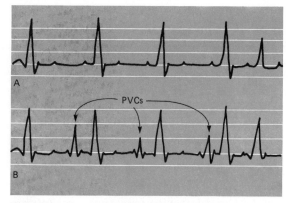

Figure 8-4 An electrocardiogram (EKG) tracing showing (A) normal cardiac action (B) a record containing premature ventricular contractions (PVCs).

learning, as I believe is the case, then why should someone be able to describe the details of his performance during the early stages of learning? . . . It is small wonder that I have not been able to find any consistency among the stories the subjects have told me. I am certain they do not know what they are doing, and that they are just making up stories to please me.

Engel has urged that more research be done to discover the variables that make cardiac control efficient, instead of continuing to hope that answers will come from the free associations of the patients.

You have seen how control over heart rate or its rhythmic irregularities can be achieved, much like any other skill, by rewarding small accomplishments at first, then by requiring better and better performance before the reward is earned. This special application of operant conditioning procedures does, however, involve the assumption that knowledge of results (either via biofeedback apparatus or, later, by discriminating internal sensations directly) is intrinsically reinforcing. Not all of Engel's patients were successful in achieving control. Not all were successfully weaned from the biofeedback equipment. Not all were able to maintain over time the control they had learned. While the foundation for a technology of cardiac control has been laid, much work still needs to be done before the structure is completed.

Control of Essential Hypertension

High blood pressure of unknown cause is called **essential** or **primary hypertension.** In the normal adult heart, as contraction of the left ventricle pumps blood into the aorta, the peak pressure of the blood against the arteries is sufficient to send a column of mercury to a height of 100 to 140 millimeters. This contraction phase in the blood pressure cycle is called the systole and is measured in terms of systolic pressure. Diastolic pressure, measured when the left ventricle is in the relaxed or diastolic phase, ranges between 60 and 90 millimeters. In the hypertensive patient, diastolic pressure fails to drop within the normal range, often remaining well above 100.

High diastolic pressure places a severe strain on the entire cardiovascular system and may also adversely affect other organs. Drugs that have the effect of reducing blood pressure are available, but often produce complicating side effects. The value of an operant conditioning technique that could enable hypertensive patients to be aware of a dangerous rise in diastolic pressure and to bring it back within the normal range is readily apparent.

David Shapiro and Gary Schwartz at Harvard worked on precisely this problem. Using normal college students, they first devised a method for accurately measuring diastolic pressure with a precision of ±2 millimeters of mercury. Such precision was required if small changes in blood pressure in the right direction were to be detected and reinforced. The feedback cue was a momentary light and tone signal. When the subjects succeeded in raising or lowering their blood pressure the required amount a number of times, they were rewarded with a chance to observe projected slides of landscapes or nudes, or were given monetary bonuses. Within 35-minute training sessions, reductions ranging from 2 to 10 millimeters were obtained. Subjects reinforced for increasing diastolic pressure achieved increases ranging from 2 to 18 millimeters. The fact that reinforcement could produce either an increase or a decrease in pressure rules out the possibility that the change in pressure was merely an unconditioned response to the reinforcers used. In young, healthy subjects, increases in pressure of the magnitudes obtained are not considered to be harmful.

Even more interesting results were obtained during a postconditioning phase, when the subjects were asked to continue trying to increase or decrease blood pressure *without* the benefit of either feedback signals or slide reinforcements. Under these conditions, subjects

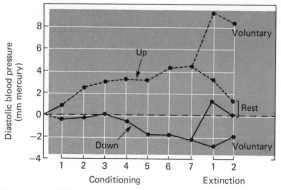

Figure 8-5 Mean diastolic blood pressure in two groups of human subjects reinforced for either increasing (up) or decreasing (down) their blood pressure. During extinction trials, half the subjects merely rested, while the other half were asked to continue the trials but without feedback or reinforcement. (Shapiro, Schwartz, & Tursky, 1972)

were still able to maintain control over diastolic pressure (Shapiro, Schwartz, & Tursky, 1972). These results are shown in Figure 8-5.

Research with hypertensive patients has demonstrated that these general procedures have some promise of effectiveness. In an average of 22 training sessions, six of seven patients decreased their systolic pressure an average of 16.5 millimeters pressure (Benson, Shapiro, Tursky, & Schwartz, 1971). It is still not known whether patients can continue to retain control in the absence of feedback. Gary Schwartz (1973) has raised other questions: Are positive results due to placebo effects? That is, is the positive expectation of success, rather than the training technique itself, responsible for the achievement of control? Is the novelty of the procedure a factor? What happens if expectation diminishes and novelty fades? How can patients be motivated to practice the desired skill? Can appropriate and effective incentives always be provided? How can patients be weaned most effectively from dependence on external feedback? Can they be taught to employ cognitive or postural strategies that can substitute for external feedback?

Following operant conditioning principles, then, people can acquire control over their car-

diovascular functions. This approach is still mainly in the research phase, however, and its techniques have certainly not replaced traditional medical or drug treatments. Nonetheless, the techniques do point up the relevance of principles of conditioning, abstracted from the animal research lab, to human beings. They also illustrate one feature of behavioral technology: the importance given to the goal of increasing people's control over their own innermost functioning.

EASTERN CONTROL TECHNIQUES

Indian mystics have long been known for their extraordinary feats of internal body control. In the past, Western scientists have generally disregarded these claims as unproven, or have attributed the control to surreptitious maneuvers. The assertion of several hatha-yoga practitioners in India that they could stop the heart or pulse was investigated by a team of American and Indian psychologists and physiologists in the late 1950s. Marion Wenger (1961) and his colleagues, using a portable polygraph apparatus, were able to demonstrate that while the yogis could indeed briefly weaken or even eliminate their heart *sounds,* the electrocardiograph (EKG) apparatus continued to show the normal contraction and relaxation activity of the heart muscle. What the stethoscope missed, the EKG did not. Still, how was the disappearance even of heart sounds to be explained?

One technique studied by Wenger and his team is called the Valsalva maneuver. The yogi builds up intrathoracic pressure by increasing muscular tension in the thorax and abdomen, while closing off the windpipe by pressing down the chin tightly against the chest. The resulting pressure, produced by contraction of skeletal muscles, not visceral effectors, has the effect of interfering with the return of venous blood to the heart. With little blood for the heart to pump, heart sounds diminish and the pulse becomes imperceptible. Only the EKG continues to bear witness to the fact that the muscular activity of the heart remains unaffected.

In one subject, however, direct control of the heart could not be discounted so easily. This subject, who had not claimed he could stop the heart, but only that he could slow it, was a yogi with five years of training. While engaged in several yogic postures, this subject was able to reduce his heart rate to about 24 beats per minute, *as monitored by EKG apparatus.*

Control Through Meditation

One form of yoga, raja-yoga, emphasizes philosophy, spirituality, and meditation more than the postural-muscular techniques of hatha-yoga. Marked mood changes, including a deep sense of mental and physical relaxation, are said to occur during **samadhi,** or meditation. Such yogis claim that while they become oblivious of external and internal environmental stimuli, their higher nervous system attains a state of "ecstasy" (Anand, Chkina, & Singh, 1961; see Chapter 6).

The practice of Zen meditation by experienced practitioners is also said to produce a changed state of consciousness, **(satori),** characterized by a heightened awareness of and responsiveness to events both inside and outside the body. How are we to understand this state of satori, or enlightenment? Erich Fromm (1960) likens it to being "completely tuned" to internal and external reality, to being open and receptive to the world. Such responsiveness must come, he feels, not from the brain alone, but from the awakening of the total personality.

Much current research will soon establish how useful Transcendental Meditation (TM) can be in clinical settings; for example, in helping patients reduce the effects of emotional stress in a variety of psychosomatic illnesses like ulcers and high blood pressure. As explained in Chapter 6, TM is a standardized technique developed by Maharishi Mahesh Yogi and taught by instructors personally qualified by him. Some attempts are already being made to use TM as an adjunct to traditional psychotherapy in the treatment of behavior disorders (Glueck & Stroebel, 1975) and as an alternative to drug use (Otis, 1972).

CONTROL OF HEADACHES

The "headache industry" is one of the most lucrative and competitive within the field of American patent medicine. Americans have many headaches, and they spend over half a billion dollars a year to treat them by means of various analgesic (pain-relieving) drugs. If we can acquire mastery over our brain waves, shouldn't we be able to conquer the common headache?

Unfortunately, there are several kinds of headaches, and each requires a different approach. The most common is the simple tension headache, which consists of a dull, aching pain on both sides of the head, mainly in the frontal area. Such headaches usually begin gradually in the morning and last all day. Sometimes they are triggered by a stressful incident during the course of the day, such as a missed appointment, an irritating encounter with a colleague, or a rebuff by a close friend. In the medical literature, the tension headache is generally attributed to prolonged contraction of the scalp and neck muscles (Ostfeld, 1962; H. G. Wolff, 1963). It is no surprise, therefore, that psychologists are now treating tension headaches by teaching their patients to relax their forehead and neck muscles with the use of the **electromyograph (EMG),** an instrument that detects electrical waves accompanying the activity of skeletal muscles and thus provides biofeedback for the relaxation of tension. The EMG apparatus converts muscular tension into a tone that varies in pitch: the greater the tension, the higher the pitch. Thus patients are provided with external, and very accurate, information about the state of

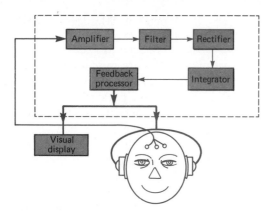

Figure 8-6 EMG biofeedback unit that detects contraction in the forehead muscles and converts muscular activity into sound signals varying in intensity. (Courtesy Biofeedback Systems, Inc.)

their muscles, and can actually "hear" themselves relaxing. Such methods, while still in the research stage, hold much promise. They amount to teaching a valuable skill that can be practiced, not only to eliminate headaches but also to control the tension that gives rise to them.

LISTEN TO YOUR HEADACHE GO AWAY

Thomas Budzynski and Johann Stoyva, psychologists at the University of Colorado Medical Center, have developed an interesting muscular feedback device that allows patients with tension headaches to "hear" just how tense their forehead and neck muscles are. The apparatus is diagrammed in Figure 8-6, which shows how electromyographic (EMG) electrodes on the surface of the scalp over the frontalis muscle of the forehead detect bioelectric signals indicating various degrees of contraction. The EMG signal is amplified, filtered, rectified, and integrated, and eventually converted into a fluctuating AC signal of varying intensity. Headphones then convey the signal to the subject as a constant volume tone that varies in pitch as the EMG changes. When the muscles are tense, the subject hears a high tone, which drops lower and lower as the muscles relax. The subject's task, then, is to learn to keep the tone as low as possible.

As the subject gets better at relaxing, the difficulty of the task is increased by requiring a greater degree of relaxation in order to maintain the same reduction in pitch. The subject is thus shaped, one step at a time, to reach ever deeper levels of relaxation.

Do the headaches go away? Initial reports are very promising. Budzynski, Stoyva, and Adler (1970) reported considerable success with five patients who received two or three 30-minute training sessions per week. All of the patients kept daily records of their headaches, rating them in accordance with the intensity of discomfort. Figure 8-7, which shows the combined results for the five patients across four weeks of feedback training (F1–F4), indicates a steady decline in headache intensity. Note that the diminishing headache level correlated with a progressive reduction in muscular activity.

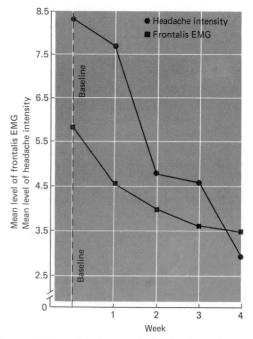

Figure 8-7 Mean tension headache levels and frontalis EMG for five patients. (Budzynski, Stoyva, & Adler, 1970)

Here is a description of the course of treatment for one patient:

Patient GA was a dynamic, middle-aged businessman who, ever since early adolescence, had suffered from frequent and severe tension headaches. He had previously received some training in deep relaxation while undergoing behavior therapy. Consequently, he had learned to relax his frontalis muscle very quickly and was able to maintain low EMG levels at all times during feedback training. Although his baseline headache activity was very high, it decreased rapidly during the second week of training and remained low for the duration of training.

After his fourth week of feedback training, the patient went on a 5-week vacation. Upon his return to work, his headaches also returned. Significantly, the patient had neglected his daily relaxation session. He reported he had to "get things back in order" after his vacation, and was in a state of high tension. He was then given two more feedback sessions and was strongly advised to schedule a period of relaxation practice every day. His headache activity then returned to low levels and has remained there for the rest of the 3-month post-training period [Budzynski et al., 1970, p. 209].

Not only does headache activity decline, but, as a bonus, beneficial changes also occur in the daily lives of these patients. They become more aware of rising tensions and more capable of reducing them. They also tend to overreact to stress much less often than before.

Migraine Headaches and Cool Hands

Migraine headaches require a different biofeedback approach. While this malady has been known for over 2000 years, and afflicts 5 to 10 per cent of Americans, no thoroughly acceptable treatment has been found. The most frequently prescribed medicines, ergotamine tartrate and methysergide maleate, are not free of serious side effects. One possible explanation of the migraine headache describes it as a form of stress reaction in which the blood vessels in the head become dilated. Another sign of stress is constriction of blood vessels in the hands, which acts to cool hand temperature as blood flow is reduced. Both effects—dilation of vessels in the head and cooling of the hands—are indicators of sympathetic arousal. The effectiveness of any procedure designed to teach a person to decrease excessive sympathetic activity could thus be measured merely by monitoring hand temperature: the warmer the hands, the greater the sympathetic relaxation, and, it is hoped, the elimination of the migraine headache due to constriction of head blood vessels.

At the Menninger Foundation in Topeka, Sargent, Walters, and Green (1973) devised a thermal biofeedback apparatus, the "temperature trainer," which permitted migraine patients to see at a glance the temperature difference between midforehead and right index finger. Patients were first taught to use a modified form of **autogenic training** (Schultz & Luthe, 1959), which involved learning to verbalize a series of statements ("My hands feel warm") while imagining the result. Then they were instructed in the home use of the temperature trainer. While noting the readings, patients would try to raise the relative temperature of their hands. The patients kept careful records, not only of temperature changes, but also of concomitant changes in headache severity. The investigators reported that significant improvement was achieved in 34 of 42 migraine patients over a 150-day period. Unfortunately, 19 per cent failed to benefit from the treatment. As with other techniques, individual differences in effectiveness abound. Research designed to enhance the effectiveness of these procedures is certainly in order.

Real Cures or Placebo Effects?

In medicine, a sugar pill that is given to satisfy a person but actually contains no drug at all is called a **placebo.** In Chapter 16 you will see how difficult it is to be really sure that it's the procedures used in psychotherapy that produce improvement, rather than placebo-like effects stemming from the attention that patients receive and their faith in the treatment. A clear-cut demonstration that therapeutic improvement results from the treatment that is applied, and not from other factors, is a necessary part of the systematic evaluation of any new technique. Otherwise, effects attributed to a new method may in fact merely reflect a placebo effect.

Moreover, a certain percentage of patients always improves or becomes "cured," even without receiving any treatment. Accurate measurement of the effectiveness of any technique, behavioral or otherwise, always requires knowledge of this **spontaneous remission** rate, against which the success level of the treatment in question can be assessed.

In the earliest stages of the development of a new treatment, great effort is usually made to demonstrate that people who receive the new treatment do indeed improve. Carefully conducted experiments, designed to control for the effects of placebo and spontaneous remission, come later. The effectiveness of some of the behavioral techniques discussed in this chapter has yet to be demonstrated in controlled experiments. However, the effectiveness of some other behavioral techniques, like those designed to reduce anxiety, can no longer be attributed to extraneous factors, as the studies described in Chapter 16 will indicate.

SELF-REGULATION OF ANXIETY STATES

The *experience* of anxiety, unlike the *construct* of anxiety (see Chapter 13), is a personal and private event. Any emotional experience is very difficult to define satisfactorily, since it will vary from person to person, and possibly from situation to situation. Nonetheless, many descriptions of intense feelings of anxiety have been offered:

Many lamentable effects this fear causeth in men, as to be red, pale, tremble, sweat; it makes sudden cold and heat to come all over the body, palpitation of the heart, syncope. . . . They that live in fear, are never free, resolute, secure, never merry, but in continual pain . . . no greater misery, no rack, no torture, like unto it; ever suspicious, anxious, solicitous, they are childishly drooping without reason, without judgement . . . [Burton, 1621, pp. 143–144].

You feel as if you were on the battlefield or had stumbled against a wild animal in the dark, and all the time you are conversing with your fellows in normal peaceful surroundings. . . . With this your head feels vague and immense and stuffed with cottonwool . . . and, most frightening of all, the quality of your sensory appreciation of the universe undergoes an essential change [editors of *Lancet*, quoted in Landis & Mettler, 1964].

In the grip of [an anxiety attack] the patient's heart pounds, his hands and lips tremble, he has difficulty breathing and perspires freely. There are also feelings of apprehension over some impending catastrophe. Often the patient may fear death is imminent, perhaps from a heart attack, but often there is no clear idea of why such a thing might be [Zax & Stricker, 1963, p. 138].

You can, of course, supply your own description of the feeling of anxiety, for no human being is entirely free of it. Anxiety has disruptive effects on our everyday lives, on the quality of our relationships within our families, on the ease with which we meet people and make friends, and on our effectiveness at our work. Fortunately, developments within behavioral technology now make it possible to bring under personal control the types of anxiety that are triggered by characteristic situations, people, or places. The anxiety-control techniques to be discussed here are all derived from laboratory research.

Learning-Based Techniques

Behavioral psychologists interpret anxiety as an emotional state conditioned to external situations containing either phobic stimuli (animals, open spaces, dirt), some potential physical danger (heights), or a threat to self-esteem (such as failure in social situations). The anxiety state may also be triggered by symbolic representations (thoughts, images) of anxiety-eliciting situations. In either case, anxiety, once elicited, acts like an intense drive motivating the person to seek relief from the experienced discomfort. Such **relief-seeking behavior** could be, for example, refusing a date in order to avoid interpersonal stress, climbing many flights of stairs in order to avoid riding the elevator, refusing invitations to visit friends living in the country for fear of encountering fear-eliciting insects and reptiles. As you can see, the anxiety-ridden do not merely stay put and suffer; they must actively work to avoid the things that terrify them. These avoidance responses are sometimes called symptoms. They are strongly reinforced whenever they succeed in temporarily reducing the intensity of anxiety. The eliciting conditions also produce sympathetic arousal, and the usual bodily indicators of anxiety also appear.

Figure 8-8 illustrates these ideas. They are largely based on O. Hobart Mowrer's (1947) two-factor theory, which assumes that classical conditioning governs the acquisition of fear, while instrumental conditioning underlies the learning of appropriate coping behavior. In exercising control over anxiety, the trick is either to countercondition some incompatible and more adaptive behavior to the conditioned elicitors or directly to extinguish the anxiety state itself. Let's look at counterconditioning first.

Counterconditioning

Counterconditioning is often referred to as **desensitization-relaxation therapy (DRT).** It was devised by Joseph Wolpe (1958), a psychiatrist, on the basis of laboratory experiments with cats. Wolpe's procedure involves teaching human subjects the techniques of deep muscular relaxation developed by Edmund Jacobson (1938). After individual subjects have learned to discriminate minute differences in their muscular tension and can voluntarily achieve a state of deep relaxation, Wolpe instructs them to visualize anxiety-inducing scenes from a hierarchy, or ranked list, of such scenes constructed by the subjects in earlier interviews. The least anxiety-inducing items in the hierarchies are presented first. The subjects are instructed to relax as deeply as they can while imagining their personal anxiety-inducing scenes. On the assumption that relaxation and anxiety are incompatible, Wolpe attempts to substitute one for the other in the presence of stimuli, real or imagined, that nor-

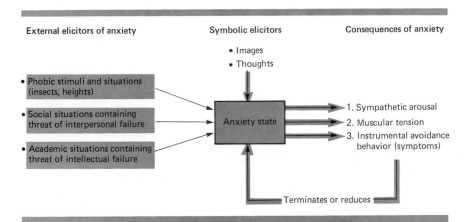

Figure 8-8 The anxiety state is conditioned to a variety of external and symbolic elicitors. The resulting behavior consists both of responses under autonomic control and instrumental behavior by which the person either terminates or avoids the elicitors, thus controlling the intensity of the anxiety state.

mally have functioned to elicit anxiety. As the individual becomes "desensitized" to scenes that evoke little anxiety, items evoking more anxiety are gradually introduced, and relaxation is counterconditioned in their presence. Wolpe also instructs the individual to practice relaxing in real-life anxiety-inducing situations. (Counterconditioning techniques are further discussed in Chapter 16.) The **counterconditioning** of relaxation responses in place of the anxiety state is analyzed in Figure 8-9.

An example of a hierarchy of items dealing with examination anxiety, representing the graded series of fears of a 24-year-old art student, follows (Wolpe, 1973, p. 116). Note that items are arranged in descending order of anxiety-inducing power, rather than strictly chronologically.

1. On the way to the university on the day of an examination.
2. In the process of answering an examination paper.
3. Standing before the unopened doors of the examination room.
4. Awaiting the distribution of examination papers.
5. The examination paper lies face down before her.

6. The night before an examination.
7. One day before an examination.
8. Two days before an examination.
9. Three days before an examination.
10. Four days before an examination.
11. Five days before an examination.
12. A week before an examination.
13. Two weeks before an examination.
14. A month before an examination.

More than one hierarchy is usually constructed for each subject, since most people have several different areas of anxiety. Some investigators are now questioning whether it is necessary to set up separate hierarchies, and suggest instead arranging all anxiety-inducing items into one heterogeneous hierarchy. Marvin Goldfried (1973, pp. 299–300) gives an example of a multithematic hierarchy constructed on the basis of interviews with a 17-year-old student whose fear reactions were rather pervasive. The procedure calls for starting desensitization with the least anxiety-inducing item, so in the following list the items are given in order of increasing anxiety.

1. With your boyfriend, sitting near a pond (pleasant scene).
2. Taking an English test, and not knowing exactly how to answer the question.

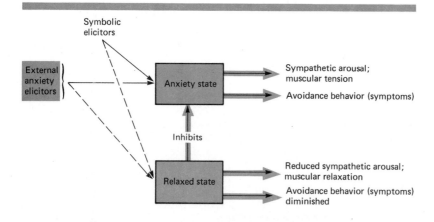

Figure 8-9 In desensitization-relaxation therapy, it is assumed that the anxiety state motivating "symptomatic" behavior is replaced by an antagonistic relaxed state, which itself becomes conditioned to the real or imagined anxiety elicitors. The dashed lines show the functional connections established during counterconditioning.

3. Sitting next to father, who is driving the car.
4. Sitting next to boyfriend, who is driving the car.
5. Driving car at night on highway, with boyfriend sitting in front seat.
6. Driving car alone at night on highway.
7. Standing on top of beginner's hill, about to ski down.
8. Walking into a girl friend's house for the first time.
9. Sitting in bar with boyfriend, and wondering if they will check proof of age.
10. Teacher is about to distribute questions for history test.
11. Baby sitting at night by yourself, watching T.V.
12. Helping father at work, and don't know where to find something he asks for.
13. Standing in a lobby, waiting for the elevator.
14. Walking into an elevator alone and pressing the button.
15. Girl friend tells you she doesn't like your hairstyle.
16. Standing in front of class, about to read a paper.
17. At home alone during the day, sitting in your room.
18. With boyfriend at train station, and he leans over to see if train is coming.
19. At beach during vacation, and walk over to a group of strangers your age to say hello.
20. Boyfriend on top of hill, calling for you to climb up.
21. Holding rail at skating rink, about to skate away from it.
22. Sitting in large auditorium, taking statewide exam.
23. At home alone at night, sitting in room, and thinking you hear noises.
24. Sitting in room, and hearing your parents and sister having a loud argument.
25. Sitting in living room with your father and sister, who are arguing.

While it is apparent how desensitization-relaxation therapy can reduce emotional over-reaction to things that have proved upsetting in the past, a number of investigators have reported that the anxiety-reduction effect spreads to areas completely unrelated to those included in the hierarchy and targeted for treatment (Paul & Shannon, 1969). This has led to the conceptualization of DRT as a way of teaching a general skill for the self-control of

anxiety. Goldfried (1971) sees it this way: We can't anticipate every anxiety-inducing situation an individual may encounter in the future, so desensitization as it is now practiced is limited to established anxiety elicitors. But why not teach people the skill of relaxing the instant they detect the weakest sign of anxiety, regardless of its source, whether it's externally or ideationally produced, whether the elicitor is new or of long standing?

Goldfried's method retains the general features of DRT, but places much greater emphasis on training the person in the skill of relaxing at the instant the slightest sensation of tension is detected, instead of attempting to condition relaxation responses to antagonize, or compete against, the anxiety state. Instead of replacing anxiety with relaxation, the person is taught to cope with anxiety by promptly activating a series of relaxing and calming procedures. The method also includes instructions for practicing these skills in everyday life situations, the moment the person begins to sense the onset of anxiety. Much research (described in Chapter 13) indicates that the ability to control anxiety results in substantial improvements in the quality of performance.

Cognitive Control

Wolpe's DRT theory relies heavily on the relaxation of the skeletal muscles as the crucial anxiety-reducing element. The theory considers relaxation an important sign that sympathetic activity is being inhibited. This "peripheralistic" interpretation of the real basis for improvement has not been widely accepted, in view of evidence that deactivation of the sympathetic nervous system in dogs does not substantially reduce the level of avoidance responding (Wynne & Solomon, 1955). While relaxation has been shown to be an important element in systematic desensitization (Davison, 1968), there is some evidence that the crucial processes may indeed occur in the central nervous system, perhaps in the form of a cognitive set. For example, Richard Lazarus and his colleagues (1962) have shown that fear induced by a frightening film can be reduced if the sound track encourages subjects either to intellectualize or to deny the upsetting content of the film. Cognitive reappraisal of a threatening event, rather than diminishing the muscular tension of sympathetic arousal, may be the key to anxiety reduction. Applied to systematic desensitization, this idea means that anxiety decreases as the subject perceives a lessening of muscular tension, leading to the conclusion: "I seem to be relaxed now, so I guess I must not be very anxious any more."

In other words, relaxation may work only when a person reinterprets the anxiety level in light of the observation that the body is more relaxed. Support for this cognitive view comes from a study by Stuart Valins and Alice Ray (1967) in which college students who were very frightened of snakes served as subjects. They were shown a slide bearing the word "shock" ten times, each time followed by shock. Intermixed with the "shock" slide were ten slides showing snakes. The subjects also heard what they believed to be amplified sounds of their own heartbeats, which increased during the shock trials but not during presentations of snake slides. (The heartbeats were not their own at all, but were specially contrived for the experiment.) We have here the elements necessary to test the idea that the amount of fear we experience may well depend on our "observation" or interpretation of the intensity of the fear our body processes seem to be indicating. If we note that our hearts begin to race when we expect shock to come, but not while we're looking at snake pictures, we may well conclude, "Gee, I'm really scared when I'm waiting for a shock, but snakes don't seem to bother me as much as I thought."

Valins and Ray reported that after the experiment was over, these subjects were able to approach a real snake more closely than control subjects who went through the same procedure but were not told they were hearing their own heartbeats. Apparently people's appraisal

of the effect of a situation on their internal processes may act to reduce their fear level, and consequently their avoidance behavior.

From a practical standpoint, however, it matters little whether relaxation techniques work because they directly antagonize the anxiety state or because they lead people to reinterpret their anxiety as being weaker than they had thought. The point is that they work.

According to the cognitive view, it should even be possible to reduce anxiety in people trained to tense rather than relax their muscles, provided they could be encouraged somehow to interpret increased tension as an indication of reduced arousal. Such an attempt has been successfully made (Sue, 1972). Snake-phobic college students were desensitized to a hierarchy of items dealing with snakes and were also trained either to relax or to tense their muscles. Both relaxation and tension subjects later showed less avoidance of snakes than did a no-treatment control group, but no difference was found between the tension and relaxation subjects. In fact, a greater reduction in subjective fear was reported by the tension group.

SELF-CONTROL IN EVERYDAY LIFE

Self-control procedures can be used by anyone to modify everyday habits. Actually, self-control is the ultimate goal of all systems of behavior change. Some have felt that the best answer to the charge that behavior-modification methods are insidious and manipulative tactics by which unscrupulous people acquire control over others is that the greatest personal freedom is acquired not by leaving behavior to be determined by chance or by someone else, but by training people to acquire mastery over their own behavior. This is what happens during the socialization process, as control over children by their parents gradually gives way to personal control. This is also what happens when the influence of teachers or counselors diminishes, and people take the reins for the management of their own learning and decision making. It would seem, therefore, that self-control means transfer of behavioral control from external sources (other people or situations) to the individual.

In the main, we speak of **self-control** (or willpower) whenever a person manages to (1) engage in behavior that immediately produces aversive consequences but holds out hope of future rewards, like studying for an exam, or (2) inhibit behavior that is immediately rewarding but carries delayed negative consequences, like overeating or smoking. Such behavior can be described as a problem in the postponement of gratification, and it's not an easy one to solve.

A Program for Self-Control

The behavioral approach does not urge us to use our willpower, to try harder, to be strong, or to feel ashamed for our lack of self-discipline. And it is usually insufficient simply to supply us with clear instructions as to how we *should* behave. Israel Goldiamond (1965, pp. 851–852) puts it this way:

Simple instructions often suffice, as when S cannot study because he does not have the assignment. On the other hand, S may not be able to study because he cannot allocate his time appropriately, because he daydreams at his desk, or because he engages in other behaviors which come under the general heading of lack of self-control. In these cases, simple instructions will not remedy the deficit since S himself knows what it is. He has often tried to instruct himself to behave appropriately but with little success. Indeed, the numerous jokes surrounding New Year's resolutions indicate both the prevalence of the problem and the ineffectiveness of its instructional solution, whether imposed by others or by one's self in self-instruction.

Instead, Goldiamond advises:

If you want a specified behavior from yourself, set up the conditions which you know will control it. For example, if you cannot get up in the morning by firmly resolving to do it and telling yourself that you must, buy and set an alarm clock. . . . The Greek maxim, "Know thyself," translates into "Know thy behaviors, know thy environment, and know the functional relation between the two."

Goldiamond reminds us that if a lawful relationship can be found between a specified behavior and a specified environmental condition, then when the environmental condition is introduced, the predicted behavior will be obtained. In an experiment, it is the experimenter who introduces the environmental condition in order to get the desired behavior. In the psychology of self-control, however, it is we ourselves who introduce the environmental condition in order to produce the behavior we desire.

Control of Overeating

All programs of behavioral control, even self-control, must begin by clearly specifying the target behavior we wish to bring under control. For example, if self-control is applied to overeating, we begin by setting up some specific goals to be attained, such as pounds lost, within a stipulated time period. The next task is to identify the variables that control overeating. Some controlling variables consist of the external stimuli that are S^Ds for eating, like the sight of rich desserts and the smells of the kitchen. Nearly all weight-control programs in current use urge dieters to confine their eating to one place in the house (the kitchen or dining room) and to one specified set of times (mealtimes) (Harris, 1969; Stuart & Davis, 1972). This way, stimuli in different places and associated with different times of the day lose their controlling power. Dieters are also advised to eat slowly, putting their utensils down between bites, in order to break the chain of responses that carry food from plate to mouth.

Other controlling variables are the reinforcements one obtains from eating—not only those inherent in ingestion, but also those acquired through years of associating eating with companionship, parental approval, rewards for good behavior, and denial of other pleasures.

Obesity-control methods usually include self-monitoring, a self-correcting procedure in which dieters keep careful records of the times and places in which eating occurs, together with an accurate count of the amount of food consumed. Self-monitoring enhances dieters' sensitivity to the factors that control their behavior and provides them with an accurate way of detecting progress toward their goals. It also allows them to apply positive reinforcements to themselves for avoiding temptation, such as buying and fitting of smaller clothes, stepping on the bathroom scale to enjoy the evidence of a weight decline, and visualizing their improved figures in bathing suits at the beach. Similarly, self-monitoring can be used to signal the need for self-administration of aversive stimulation for backsliding, such as visualizing themselves grown fat and ugly, imagining critical comments by friends, and recalling the increased probability of developing diabetes and heart disease. Thus, self-reinforcement can be used hand in hand with self-monitoring.

When behavioral analysis shows that overeating tends to be associated with feelings of anxiety or rejection, a form of desensitization-relaxation procedure is sometimes advised: These dieters are trained to "switch on" relaxation the moment these feelings arise. Finally, a procedure called covert sensitization is often used (Cautela, 1967), in which dieters are taught to associate the urge to eat with very aversive, nauseating imagery. The idea is the old one of punishing the response you wish to weaken, coupled with the notation of diminishing the incentive value of the proscribed behavior. Thus the urge to eat is followed by imagined aversive consequences, which terminate the moment the person turns away either from actual food or from thoughts of eating. People who wish to control their eating of rich desserts might be trained to follow this procedure:

I want you to imagine you've just had your main meal and you are about to eat your dessert, which is apple pie. As you are about to reach for the fork, you get a funny feeling in the pit of your stomach. You start to feel queasy, nauseous, and sick all over. As you touch the fork, you can feel food particles inching up your throat. You're just about to vomit. As you put the fork into the pie, the food comes up into your mouth. You try to keep your mouth closed because you are afraid that you'll spit the food out all over the place. You bring the piece of pie to your mouth. As you're about to open your mouth, you puke; you vomit all over your hands, the fork, over the pie. It goes all over the table, over the other people's food. Your eyes are watering. Snot and mucus are all over your mouth and nose. Your hands feel sticky. There is an awful smell. As you look at this mess you just can't help but vomit again and again until just watery stuff is coming out. Everybody is looking at you with shocked expressions. You turn away from the food and immediately start to feel better. You run out of the room, and as you run out, you feel better and better. You wash and clean yourself up, and it feels wonderful [Cautela, 1967, p. 462].

People who are tempted to eat dessert but resist the temptation should be reinforced for good behavior, wouldn't you say? These people would be instructed to obtain reinforcement in the following way:

You've just finished your meal and you decide to have dessert. As soon as you make the decision, you start to get that funny feeling in the pit of your stomach. You say, "Oh, oh; oh no; I won't eat the dessert." Then you immediately feel calm and comfortable [Cautela, 1967, p. 463].

What is being attempted here, of course, is to follow the response of self-denial with a rewarding sense of comfort and pride. Subjects receive homework assignments to practice covert sensitization several times a day, with the aim of transferring complete control over the developing aversiveness to overeating from the therapist to the subjects themselves.

The treatment of alcoholism requires extremely elaborate procedures, and so far no single treatment method has been satisfactorily effective. But one of the methods that is often incorporated into a total treatment plan is the same covert sensitization that has been effective with dieters, with beer substituting for apple pie. Sometimes it works, but there is little generalization of nausea from one alcoholic beverage to another. In order to build up an aversion to wine and whiskey and gin and the rest, the covert sensitization procedure should be carried out separately for each beverage, Cautela advises.

Control of Cigarette Smoking

Cigarette smoking has been classified as a health hazard by the U.S. Surgeon General's Office since 1964. In 1969 a report from the surgeon general carried this statement:

Additional evidence substantiates the previous findings that cigarette smoking is the main cause of lung cancer in men. Cigarette smoking is causally related to lung cancer in women but accounts for a smaller proportion of cases than in men. Smoking is a significant factor in the causation of cancer of the larynx and in the development of cancer of the oral cavity. Further epidemiological data strengthen the association of cigarette smoking with cancer of the bladder and cancer of the pancreas [U.S. Department of Health, Education and Welfare, 1969, pp. 3–4].

Despite this clear statement of the harmfulness of tobacco, total cigarette sales in the United States are still running over $8 billion a year, and per capita use by persons over 18 is about 4000 per year. Despite the fact that many Americans give up smoking without using any systematic psychologically derived techniques, most heavy smokers find it very hard to quit.

What can behavioral technology contribute to the smoker who wants to quit? Like overeating and alcoholism, smoking is difficult to control because gratification is immediate, while the ultimate aversive consequences to health are far in the future. Hence the important controlling consequence of smoking is positive reinforcement. To achieve self-control,

the chain of behaviors from the start of the craving for a cigarette to the positive reinforcement obtained from smoking it must somehow be broken. Self-control procedures can be viewed as a set of behaviors that the individual can interpose to interrupt the chain before the reinforcement from smoking can have its strengthening effect. What behaviors will interrupt the chain?

1. Do not keep cigarettes in your possession or in the house. This is one obvious way of lengthening the gap between the urge to smoke and lighting up.
2. If you must spend time with smokers, tell them of your goal and, if feasible, ask them to cooperate by not smoking in your presence. This will remove from your presence powerful cues for lighting up.
3. Ask close friends, especially if they are nonsmokers, to reinforce your abstaining behavior with praise, attention, and telephone calls. Conversely, really good friends may agree to withhold social reinforcements if relapses occur or if little progress is made.
4. Try to lengthen the amount of time you spend in areas in which smoking is prohibited, such as libraries, laboratories, certain classrooms, and homes of nonsmokers.
5. Eliminate from your living area every unnecessary item that is associated with smoking, like ashtrays and magazines containing many cigarette ads. Air out the area if someone has smoked in it recently—or better yet, don't allow smoking in your area.
6. When you feel the urge to smoke, use the covert-sensitization method to bring long-delayed aversive consequences of smoking out of the future and into the here and now, or to produce nauseous and repulsive imagery that can be counterconditioned to the urge to smoke and the smell of tobacco.
7. Strengthen thoughts incompatible with smoking (it causes heart disease and discolors teeth) by reinforcing them with pleasurable activities (drinking coke or chewing

jelly beans). This example uses ideational components of the Premack principle (Premack, 1965), which states that low-probability behavior is strengthened by making high-probability behavior contingent upon it. Thus if you wish to strengthen ideas antagonistic to smoking (low probability) whenever they occur, immediately follow them with some rewarding (high probability) activity or idea.

8. If you cannot stop smoking completely, confine smoking to one specific place and time; this will weaken the control that stimuli all over the environment have acquired over your smoking behavior. One investigator (Nolan, 1968) worked out a self-control program for his wife. She agreed to continue smoking as much as she pleased, but only in a particular chair, which was so placed that it made it hard for her to do the things she liked, such as conversing or watching TV. A record of cigarettes smoked indicated rapid acquisition of control (see Figure 8-10).

9. Analyze the situations that trigger smoking. Do you tend to smoke when you feel lonely and blue? When you are feeling a bit

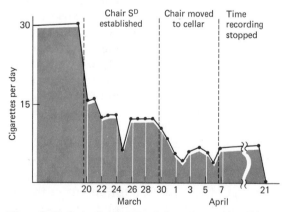

Figure 8-10 Reduction in rate of cigarette smoking. Prior to March 30, smoking was confined to the "smoking chair." Thereafter, the chair was made less accessible by moving it to the cellar. Smoking ceased entirely on April 21. A 6-month follow-up revealed no relapse. (Nolan, 1968)

uncomfortable in a social situation? If tension and anxiety seem to be controlling inner stimuli, learn some desensitization-relaxation techniques.

Other areas in which behavioral technology is being applied in everyday life are reduction of anxiety in social situations, control of speech anxiety, improvement of study behavior, and the improvement of marital relations. In Chapter 16, the application of therapeutic techniques for modifying the behavior of seriously disturbed individuals is discussed.

The Ethics of Control

To many people, control means coercion, and a technology that not only permits but capitalizes on coercion is repugnant. Any system of behavior change that allows one person to restrict the behavior of another, compels another person to act involuntarily, or exploits anyone is, of course, rejected out of hand by all professionals as grossly unethical. The success of behavioral technology, coupled with the appearance of movies like *A Clockwork Orange*, which depicted unspeakable experiences forced upon a criminal in the name of behavior modification, have aroused considerable interest in the development of a code of ethical conduct governing the application of behavioral principles. While behavioral technology, like any other powerful system of societal control, could be abused, the chances of misuse would be greatly reduced if certain ethical guidelines were followed. Ideally, techniques for behavior change should be applied only with the informed consent of the recipient. For example, there seems to be no great ethical problem arising in the case of an obese person who personally chooses to engage the services of a behavior-change specialist and who, after receiving a full explanation of the behavioral methods to be applied, freely agrees to begin the program of training.

A much more difficult ethical problem arises when informed consent cannot be taken for granted, because the person is too young or too disturbed to understand the implications of consent. Consider this hypothetical description of a seriously disturbed patient: A hospitalized psychotic boy of about 11 years has been treated with almost every therapeutic method possible in order to reduce his self-destructive behavior. All efforts to date have failed. The child's scalp frequently bleeds because he continuously pulls out his hair. His face and body are gouged by fingernail marks. Uncontrollable head-banging against the walls has left his head and face severely bruised. To alleviate some of the damage he inflicts upon himself, he is now made to wear boxing gloves and a football helmet, not as treatment but as a temporary measure while some new form of treatment is sought. It is finally proposed that aversive therapy sessions should be tried, during which he would receive moderately painful, brief electrical shocks, contingent on the occurrence of self-destructive behaviors.

This boy is obviously incapable of granting informed consent. Should the therapy proposed therefore be denied? Does the application of *any* kind of therapy require informed consent? Would behavior-control treatment be ethically acceptable if consent were granted by both the child's parents and the hospital medical supervisor? The application of aversive stimulation poses ethical questions in a most dramatic form. The majority of behavior-change procedures utilize positive reinforcement rather than aversive stimulation. Yet ethical questions persist. Consider a young offender, convicted for a series of petty crimes and misdemeanors, who is offered a drastic reduction in his sentence if he agrees to participate in a behavior-change program based on positive reinforcement for evidence of successful rehabilitation. The program attempts to modify antisocial attitudes and to strengthen prosocial behavior, through educative proce-

dures based on learning principles. Failure to participate in the program would require the offender to serve out his sentence. If he agrees to participate, can we assume he has exercised a truly free choice? Can one not argue that so long as the aversive alternative of a longer sentence hung over his head, he was hardly able to choose freely?

These questions are raised merely to point out that, despite the sincere efforts of well-intentioned people, ethical questions are not always easy to resolve. Two developments within the field of behavior technology raise our hopes for the future: First, an increasing awareness of ethical considerations is developing among professionals (the Association for the Advancement of Behavior Therapy now has a task force working on guidelines for the implementation of behavioral principles in the clinical field), and second, there is enormous interest in developing techniques of behavioral *self*-control. Such techniques are intended to teach people gradually to assume control over their own behavior, diminishing their reliance on the assistance of teachers, parents, therapists, and others and thus reducing undesirable forms of control exercised by external stimulus events. The significance of the question "Who controls?" is quickly reduced when it can be answered, "People control their own behavior." The interested reader is referred to Michael Mahoney and Carl Thoresen's book *Self-Control: Power to the Person* (1974) for a thorough analysis of self-control techniques.

SUMMARY

The field of behavioral technology applies the principles of learning to help people make useful and beneficial modifications in their behavior. The basic principles of behavior change involve the selection of a target behavior, modification of the strength of the target behavior by rewards and punishments, and manipulation of stimuli that have acquired control over the behavior. The target behavior should be objectively defined and records should be kept of its rate of occurrence throughout a behavior-change program. Undesirable behavior may be weakened through extinction, punishment, and reinforcement of alternate behavior. Stimulus control of maladaptive habits and emotions can be weakened by removing the controlling stimuli or by counterconditioning more adaptive behavior to the same stimuli. Adaptive behavior change sometimes requires a cognitive approach, since controlling stimuli may be images and ideas.

The operant conditioning of visceral responses in animals has encouraged the development of biofeedback techniques that enable human patients to improve heart functioning and reduce blood pressure. While it is difficult to specify precisely how patients acquire such control, necessary conditions include continuous information concerning the physiological response and strong motivation to achieve control. Meditational techniques can also produce control over physiological processes. Electromyographic feedback is being used to reduce headaches due to muscular tension; to control migraine headaches, patients are trained to increase the temperature of the hands relative to head temperature. These forms of biofeedback treatment are still in the experimental stage. Future research will determine how much of their apparent success is attributable to placebo effects or to spontaneous remission.

The control of anxiety has been achieved by a number of techniques based on learning principles. Counterconditioning methods, such as desensitization-relaxation therapy, attempt to condition relaxation responses to anxiety-inducing imagery on the assumption that relaxation is incompatible with anxiety. After patients are trained to relax, they visualize series of anxiety-inducing scenes, starting with the least anxiety-provoking of a hierarchy of such scenes. The desensitization-relaxation technique has been successfully applied to a wide variety of fears and phobias. Recent research suggests that the process of fear reduction is accompanied and may be caused by changes in cognitive processes.

The ultimate goal of all systems of behavior change is self-control. Self-control involves transfer of behavioral control from external sources, like other people or situations, to the person whose behavior is to be controlled. Programs of self-modification have been developed to assist people to acquire control over such behaviors as overeating, problem drinking, and smoking. These programs rely heavily on techniques for removing stimuli that elicit the undesirable behavior or counterconditioning other (incompatible) responses to the same stimuli; self-monitoring; self-reinforcement; soliciting social reinforcements for abstemious behavior; and covert sensitization, a method in which aversive imagery is associated with thoughts of indulging in the maladaptive behavior.

The success of behavioral technology has raised serious ethical questions. While there is general agreement that behavioral methods (or *any* methods) should not be applied without the informed consent of the person involved, the criterion of consent is not easily applied in the case of young children and seriously disturbed patients. In correctional institutions, an inmate's decision to participate in rehabilitative programs organized around behavioral principles, or any other theoretical approach, may not stem from a truly free choice if the consequence of noncooperation is a longer period of confinement.

Continuous study of ethical and legal implications by the profession and rapid development of techniques of effective self-control may be the best safeguards against unethical application of principles of behavior control.

PLAN A SELF-CONTROL PROGRAM

Sit down with a pencil and some paper. Go back to some aspect of your behavior of which you and/or others disapprove—the maladaptive behavior that you considered at the opening of this chapter. How can the various techniques discussed here be applied to change this behavior? Develop a program for self-control of the behavior, drawing as much as you can on approaches indicated in this chapter. Do you think the program would work? Why or why not?

9

Human Learning

MODIFYING VERBAL BEHAVIOR

By trying "Sample Your Own Learning," you can see that lists of words can be learned in relatively short order, somehow held together in a group that you can then recall. You already know the meanings of all the words in the two lists. These words, and thousands of others, make up your basic vocabulary. You use this vocabulary in your **verbal behavior,** your communications with others by means of spoken and written language. How do we all acquire this eminently human kind of behavior, which distinguishes us from other kinds of animals?

SAMPLE YOUR OWN LEARNING

■ Try a bit of learning. All you need are a pencil and a dozen slips of paper about 3 by 5 inches.

Read slowly down *once* through the following list of 10 words on the left:

1. Group	1. Beast
2. Word	2. Hoop
3. Five	3. Make
4. Learn	4. Circus
5. Mean	5. Tail
6. Effort	6. Snarl
7. Rain	7. Paws
8. Argue	8. Jump
9. Move	9. Order
10. Know	10. Ring

Then take one of the slips of paper and list the words you recall in whatever order they come to mind. When you have recalled all you can, total the number of words. Then turn back to the list, read down it again, and list the words you recall the second time on another slip. Continue this procedure until you've recalled all 10 words once. Then make up a graph of your "learning curve,"

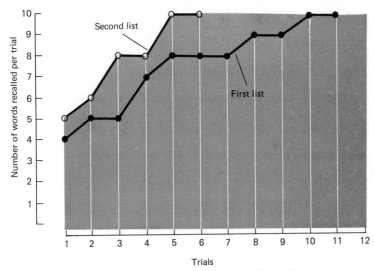

Figure 9-1 Sample graph displaying learning of two lists of words.

plotting number of words recalled per trial vertically and trials horizontally. Does your graph look like the one in Figure 9-1?

Repeat the same procedures for the second list of 10 words on the right, stop when you've recalled all 10 words once, and put the results on the same graph. How does the learning of the two lists differ? Can you explain the differences?

■ WHAT'S THE ANSWER?

Modifying Verbal Behavior

Why do you say the things you do and say them just that way?

What effects do other people have on the way you talk and what you say? Why?

Learning Motor Skills

Is learning of motor skills aided or hindered by verbalization during the learning?

Is it better to learn skills in single long sessions or in short sessions with breaks between them?

Transferring Training

Does learning of mathematics improve your reasoning ability?

Why is "learning how to learn" an important feature of education?

Acquiring Verbal Behavior

The way that human children learn to put words together in such a way as to form original, meaningful sentences was discussed in Chapter 3. Several ideas about the way children come to acquire the rules of syntax were examined. But where do the words come from? The answer to this question provides an excellent example of the way behavior results from the continuous interplay of hereditary and environmental factors. One of the most important environmental factors is the principle of operant conditioning.

The infant begins with a kit of inherited vocal responses—gurgling, cooing, grunting, and of course crying. Observation of any baby for a few minutes will show you how varied and frequent these responses are. The sounds infants make are being studied by means of sensitive audio equipment that analyzes them into their varied frequencies and producing graphic representations of the sounds called *sonograms* (see Figure 9-2). Among the many sounds that any human infant makes in the first year of life can be found all the sounds that appear in all known human languages.

Kilo HZ

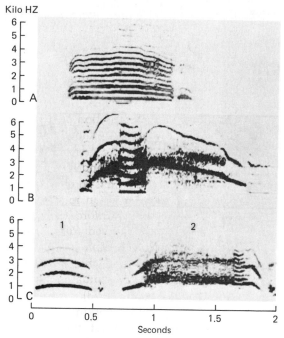

Figure 9-2 Sonograms displaying the differences in (A) the cry of a normal baby and (B and C) the cries of diseased babies. In B and C the wider spacing of the horizontal lines indicates "loss of control," with the pitch of the cry shifting momentarily to much higher frequencies. (Ostwald, 1972)

LISTEN TO SOME BABY TALK

■ If you have the opportunity, listen to the sounds a baby under the age of five months makes when awake, at the same time noting the behavior of the parent as the child vocalizes. Keep track of the different types of sounds the infant makes, tabulating them on a pad in such broad categories as the following:

1. Cries   / / / /
2. Grunts   / / / / /
3. Gurgles   / /
4. Moans   / / /
5. Coos   /

Do this for five two-minute periods, each period separated by about two minutes. Every time an utterance is followed by a positive response by the parent (cuddling, speaking, smiling, cooing), circle the mark you have made next to the sound the infant has made.

How many of the infant's sounds do you think you could imitate? Do some of them remind you of sounds heard in other languages?

Do you find that the infant tends to make more of one type of sound than others? Which kind appears more often? Which does the parent tend to reinforce most often or most strongly? Would you expect to find much correspondence at this age between the sounds the infant makes most frequently and the sounds reinforced by the parent?

By the age of three to four months the **babbling** stage begins, in which the infant repeats all kinds of meaningless sounds. Babbling does not occur in a vacuum. Attentive parents are often present. They can provide lavish reinforcements with cuddling, fondling, stroking, and gentle vocalizations. The first utterance the infant makes that even vaguely approximates a meaningful sound becomes a potent releaser of all sorts of reinforcement from the delighted parent. B. F. Skinner (1974) believes that the way people speak depends upon the practices of the verbal community of which they are members. Out of the common matrix of sounds that all infants can apparently make with ease, German-speaking people will selectively reinforce some sounds, French-speaking people others. A Chinese child will receive the same encouragement and attention while learning to speak that a Greek child receives. Reinforcements are dispensed with pride and joy by parents of all language groups; only the nature of the utterances that are rewarded is different. This does not mean that language acquisition merely involves the strengthening of discrete verbal responses by differential reinforcement (see Chapter 3), but it does show that operant conditioning principles play some role in determining verbal behavior.

Regardless of the manner in which the normal child acquires language, it is clear that operant conditioning principles can be used to teach rudimentary forms of speech to psychotic older children who have failed to acquire language. Ivar Lovaas and his associates have used operant techniques for a number of years to teach speech to psychotic mute children. Since no systematic studies had been published on ways to teach speech to a person who has never spoken, Lovaas and his group had to develop their own step-by-step procedure (Lovaas, Berberich, Perloff, & Schaeffer, 1966). Two of their patients were Billy and Chuck, six-year-olds whose verbalizations consisted only of a few vowel sounds, used mainly when they were throwing tantrums and without any apparent intent to communicate. Such sounds were the equivalent of the growls, snarls, and barks of dogs. Billy and Chuck were trained by the following four-stage procedure:

Stage 1. All of the children's vocalizations were rewarded, in order to increase any kind of vocal output. The children were also rewarded for paying attention to the teacher's mouth. Primary reinforcements were used, like spoonfuls of food or M & M candies.

Stage 2. To bring vocalizations under stimulus control, reinforcements were given only if the children vocalized within six seconds after the teacher spoke a word, like "ball." Any vocal response emitted within the six-second period was reinforced. This encouraged the children to pay careful attention to another person's speaking and to respond quickly in a vocal manner.

Stage 3. When the children had learned to vocalize actively in response to the teacher's words, reinforcements were withheld unless the child made a sound that matched that of the teacher. At first even a vague approximation, such as "ba" for "ball," was rewarded. The teacher helped each boy make the sound by holding the child's lips closed with his fingers and suddenly removing them when he exhaled. This type of prompting was gradually removed, or faded, after the child imitated words correctly on his own.

Stage 4. In the final stage, new and very different sounds were added to the program, interspersed between words mastered in Stage 3. To get a reinforcement, the child would now have to discriminate between different sounds the teacher made.

Billy's rate of word acquisition over 26 days of verbal imitation training is shown in Figure 9-3. Capitalizing on both children's rapid rate of imitative learning, Lovaas and his associates have developed new programs to teach autistic children functional, rather than merely imitative, speech. Thus food reinforcement might be given only if a child asked for a food by name, or later asked a question, made a comment, or generally used intelligible speech that was appropriate to the situation (Lovaas, Koegel, Simmons, & Long, 1973).

These procedures for working with psychotic mute children suggest the way that speech patterns in the normal child are shaped and guided by reinforcement probabilities controlled by the people who are themselves rewarded most intensely by the child's linguistic gains: the parents and other children in the family.

Modifying Adult Verbal Behavior

Just as reinforcement, selectively applied, can shape verbal behavior in children, so it can influence what adults actually say. Skinner (1957) has consistently asserted that verbal behavior, like any other kind of behavior, is controlled by its consequences. True, when we speak, the reinforcement must come only from other people, but Skinner argues that this is the only aspect of verbal behavior that distinguishes it from, say, learning to follow a trail back to a campsite or learning how to select a good cut of meat in a supermarket. After a person has learned, or internalized, certain norms of verbal behavior, these can guide future verbal behavior.

If verbal utterances are to be regarded like

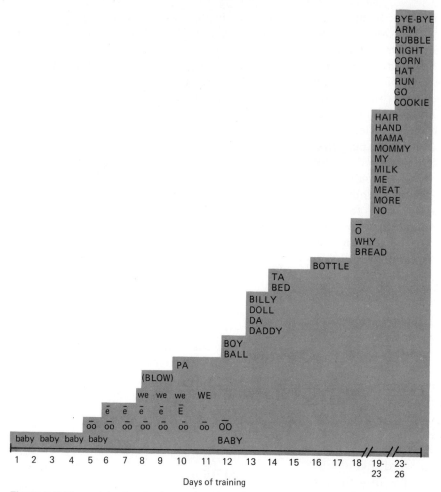

Figure 9-3 The variety of parts of speech and word sounds mastered by Billy during 26 days of verbal imitation training. Words and sounds are printed in small letters until the day Billy mastered them, after which they appear in capitals. Note that word acquisition starts very slowly, but rapidly accelerates just as it does in normal children. (Lovaas et al., 1966)

other responses whose probability of occurrence rises and falls in accordance with the consequences, an analysis of verbal behavior should involve a clarification of the **contingencies,** or probable relationships, between what people say and consequent reinforcements. Moreover, verbal behavior is under a remarkable degree of stimulus control. For instance, you would not ordinarily ask a farmer for help in solving a calculus problem or a mathematician how best to prepare the soil for spring planting.

Skinner's analysis of verbal behavior in terms of operant conditioning has stimulated many experiments designed to show the controlling effect of generalized reinforcements on what people say. In one of the earliest studies in verbal conditioning (Greenspoon, 1955), an experimental group of college students was merely asked to utter as many words as came to mind. But whenever a word happened to be a plural noun, the experimenter said, "Mmm-hmm." The result of this "reinforcement" was that the students emitted more plural nouns than did a control group that received no reinforcing comment from the experimenter. The reinforced subjects claimed no awareness of the connection between what they said and the experimenter's verbal reinforcement. Doesn't this situation resemble the free-responding operant paradigms described in Chapter 7?

In a more structured setting, like a discrete-trial form of instrumental conditioning, B. D. Cohen, H. I. Kalish, J. R. Thurston, and E. Cohen (1954) showed their subjects a series of 80 cards, on each of which a different verb was printed, together with the pronouns *I, we, he, she, you,* and *they.* The subjects' task was to make up a meaningful sentence for each card, using the verb given with any one of the six pronouns. Whenever a subject made up a sentence beginning with the pronoun *I* or *We,* the experimenter said, "Good," in a flat, unemotional tone. Did such verbal reinforcement selectively strengthen the particular verbal elements that it followed? Figure 9-4 shows the results of the experiment. Note that a control group of subjects who never received reinforcement gave about as many sentences using *I* and *We* as did the experimental group during the first block of 20 cards, when no reinforcement was given to anyone. The first stage can be considered the operant, or prereinforcement, level. From the second through the fourth blocks of 20 trials, however, subjects in the experimental group made up more and more sentences using the target pronouns, while little change occurred in the control group's use of these pronouns.

Are other types of verbal behavior in less artificial settings than the laboratory also controlled by reinforcements? Research has shown that the reinforcements we give each other, in the form of smiles and words of approval, exert a profound effect on the things we say. In one study (Hildum & Brown, 1956), Harvard summer session students were interviewed over the phone. A group reinforced with the word "Good" immediately following a positive comment yielded far more favorable

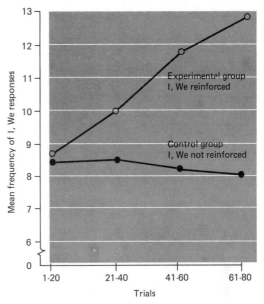

Figure 9-4 During the first 20 trials, no reinforcements at all were given. Thereafter, only the experimental group was reinforced for every sentence that began with the pronoun *I* or *We.* The use of the target pronouns by the reinforced group increased in frequency, and little change occurred in the nonreinforced control group. (Cohen et al., 1954)

opinions about the Harvard philosophy of general education than did another group similarly reinforced for negative comments. This is an important finding, for it shows how any results that might be desired could be engineered in a questionnaire survey. It also puts us all on guard against attempts by others to manipulate our behavior for their own purposes.

SKINNER IN THIS CORNER, CHOMSKY IN THAT

The American linguist Noam Chomsky has roundly criticized Skinner's explanation of spoken language, or verbal behavior, in terms of operant conditioning (Chomsky, 1959). Chomsky maintains that there is infinite variety in the utterances we speak, structured in accordance with a most complex syntax that is never, as such, taught to children. This fact is not adequately explained by reinforcement and motivational concepts. For example, how could operant conditioning principles enable anyone to predict how you would express yourself to your friend when you feel hungry at the end of an afternoon and conclude it is time to eat? You might say, "How about tying on the feedbag?" or "I'm going down to the Greasy Spoon" or "Are you as hungry as I am?" or "Feel like a pizza?" or a dozen other things. Your utterance might be a command, a question, an assertion, or simply an imaginative comment. Furthermore, each such utterance would have to be so organized and uttered that it agreed closely enough with the syntactical rules of your common language to be understandable to your friend. Chomsky suggests that at least the deep structure of utterances may not be learned, but possibly may be innate, in all humans, and that any language may be shaped by this innate structure as we use it, rather than being learned by reinforcement as we go along.

Perhaps it is too early in the scientific study of language to decide between these opposing theories; and besides, the controversies they stimulate have become very complex. The new branch of psychology called psycholinguistics is just beginning to make advances in our understanding of language. It is clear, however, that the theories of both Chomsky and Skinner have made valuable contributions that should be properly weighed and used as this understanding develops.

General Social Reinforcement

In the middle of a conversation about some controversial topic, have you ever found yourself beginning to see other people's point of view and gradually changing your views in the direction of theirs? Sometimes you change your mind simply because you come to appreciate that their arguments are better than your own. But at other times your views change because, unwittingly perhaps, other people behave differently toward you when you tend to agree with them than when you disagree. In a heated controversy, wouldn't you be more likely to show approval and encouragement if your opponents began to see things your way, even ever so slightly? And what effect would your approval have on them, in turn?

In a conversational situation, Paul Ekman (1959) succeeded in using the verbal reinforcer "Good" to condition negative opinions about capital punishment in college students. (Some students, however, showed reverse conditioning. Although they were reinforced whenever they made negative comments about capital punishment, the number of favorable opinions they expressed actually increased.) Even political attitudes have been shown to be affected by systematically applied verbal reinforcements. Women college students reinforced with "Good" or "Right" for answering items on a complex attitude scale in a prodemocratic direction gradually shifted their responses to a more liberal position (R. D. Singer, 1961). Moreover, the more liberal attitudes they acquired generalized to an entirely different attitude scale.

Such demonstrations of the power of **social reinforcement**—that is, the rewarding behavior of other people—to modulate the amount and content of another person's spoken behavior carry important implications. Whether the influence be unwitting or calculated, casual or deliberate, the ability to control the expression of other people's beliefs, attitudes, and opinions is a serious matter. Consider how unavoidable the opportunities are for interpersonal influence through verbal reinforcement. Any time two people are interacting, if the social approval of at least one person is significant to the other and if the approval is consistently applied following the emission of a given class of verbal behavior, the ingredients of control are present.

Such social control might operate in a psychotherapeutic relationship in which the client is anxious and miserable, and the therapist is perceived as an authority figure of considerable insight and knowledge. In such a situation, the approval and encouragement of the therapist can be a powerful reinforcer. In psychotherapy, clients' behavior is primarily verbal. What aspects of their verbal narration are most likely to receive reinforcement from the therapist? Here it must be remembered that the therapist is not exempt from the principle of reinforcement. Some things the client says are likely to be more reinforcing to the therapist than others. For example, a chain of associations that seems to lead to the supposed root of the client's problem, or the memory of a dream the therapist interprets as evidence for an already formed opinion on the dynamics of the client's underlying conflicts, are likely to make the therapist respond favorably.

Evidence that verbal reinforcement can alter the content of a client's report comes from a number of investigations. In an interview situation, H. Quay (1959) found that the types of early memories college students would report in conversation were influenced by such reinforcements as "Uh-huh." In one experiment (Heine, 1953), the types of insights achieved by clients in therapy were found to be more predictable from knowledge of the theoretical orientation of their therapists than from knowledge of the clients' own backgrounds and problems.

The characterization of the psychotherapeutic relationship as a social-influence situation does not necessarily diminish its value. In fact, a growing body of evidence supports the view that by rewarding the individual for verbalizing positive self-statements, like "I like my sense of humor" or "I can handle myself in most social situations," profound improvements in self-attitudes and belief systems can be achieved (Meichenbaum, 1973; Wolpe, 1973). Of course, some schools of therapy tend to recommend less directive approaches to their clients than others do (see Chapter 16). Still, modification of the client's verbalizations is not only inevitable but mandatory if the client is to profit from psychotherapy. Therefore, it may be less productive to argue about the issue of control of clients by therapists than to discover more effective ways

in which skilled and sensitive therapists can exploit their vast reinforcing power to help clients achieve beneficial changes in their feelings and behavior.

Awareness of Reinforcement Probability

To what extent does **awareness** of receiving reinforcement affect verbal behavior? Does it make any difference if you know that the other person will say approving things if, and only if, you make certain types of verbal responses? If too strict an analogy is made between reinforcing rats to press a bar and reinforcing human beings to increase their use of certain pronouns, for example, it really wouldn't matter whether the human beings were aware of the contingency between response and reinforcement. According to the principle of reinforcement, all that is necessary to strengthen a class of responses is to set up a contingency relationship between response and reinforcement. The rat need not be "aware" in order for the reinforcer to exert its strengthening effect.

Yet rats are not people; things are always more complicated for us. Let's see what part awareness plays in human verbal conditioning. You'll recall that in the Greenspoon (1955) and Cohen et al. (1954) experiments on the conditioning of subjects to use plural nouns and sentences beginning with *I* and *We*, it was claimed that the subjects had no awareness of the connection between the changes in their verbal behavior and the reinforcements uttered by the experimenter. But in this context "awareness" could have a number of meanings. It could mean that the subjects were conscious that the experimenter kept saying something, that they were conscious that they were using some words more than others, or that they realized that some relationship existed between the experimenter's behavior and their own. Furthermore, there could be different levels of awareness. In the earliest studies that reported conditioning without awareness, the subjects were generally asked a

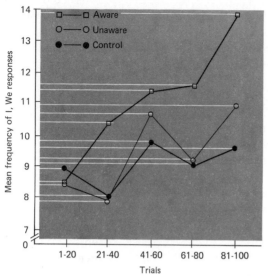

Figure 9-5 Mean frequency of *I* and *We* responses increases with reinforcement only in the group that is truly aware of the response-reinforcement contingency. The unaware group's performance is not statistically distinguishable from that of a nonreinforced control group. (Spielberger, 1962a)

few brief questions at the end of the experiment. Is it possible that the brief postexperimental interview was too superficial to identify clearly and then exclude subjects with some degree of awareness?

It is now generally accepted that the subject's awareness of the response-reinforcement contingency plays a very important role in verbal conditioning. This conclusion is based on the evidence that subjects who are judged to have been unaware only after very thorough and probing postexperimental questioning seldom show much verbal conditioning (Levin, 1961). Figure 9-5 shows that "truly unaware" subjects who were reinforced for using *I* and *We* conditioned little better than did nonreinforced control subjects. Even if people are aware that reinforcement is contingent on their emission of the target response, another ingredient is their desire for the reinforcer. Figure 9-6 suggests that even if subjects are aware, the ones who condition most are

those who want the experimenter's "Good" very much (VM); next are those who want it some (S); and last come those who say they don't care (DC).

Even more conclusive evidence of the role of awareness comes from a conditioning experiment in which subjects were asked to write down their "thoughts about the experiment" at periodic intervals during the conditioning trials. The idea was to spot the precise place at which subjects suddenly correctly verbalized

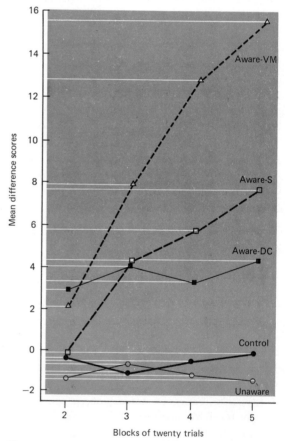

Figure 9-6 Difference between operant level and conditioning trials in the frequency of *I* and *We* sentences given by aware subjects who wanted the reinforcer either very much (VM) or some (S), and those who didn't care (DC). The performances of unaware and control subjects did not differ and showed no improvement. (Spielberger, Levin, & Shepard, 1962)

the response-reinforcement contingency and to note whether, at that point, their performance curves abruptly improved. L. D. DeNike (1964) examined his subjects' records of "thoughts about the experiment," which they had written after each block of 25 words in a word-naming task in which they were reinforced every time they said a word denoting a person, like *girl, doctor,* and *tailor.* Figure 9-7A shows that the behavior of subjects who remained unaware throughout acquisition did not differ from that of control subjects who received reinforcement for 10 per cent of their responses on a random basis—that is, not necessarily following "correct" responses. Aware subjects, on the other hand, showed a rapid rise in the percentage of noun responses. Even more sig-

nificant are the results shown in Figure 9-7B. These indicate that regardless of the precise points at which awareness was first verbalized, performance prior to that point was very poor, while performance following the verbalization revealed an abrupt and substantial gain. These data convincingly support the conclusion that the effect of social reinforcement on verbal behavior occurs abruptly, the moment people are able to perceive what they must say in order to obtain the approving behavior they desire from other people. What may be learned in a verbal conditioning situation is awareness of a response-reinforcement contingency that people can then act on to obtain reinforcement, if the reinforcer happens to be something they want.

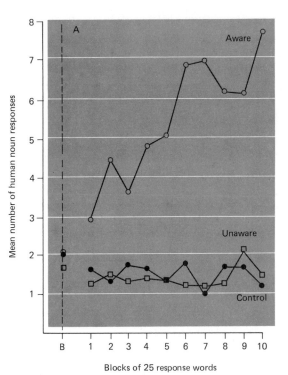

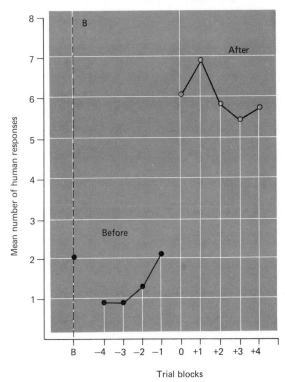

Figure 9-7 (A) Mean number of human noun responses emitted by aware, unaware, and control subjects before reinforcement, B, and across a series of 10 blocks of trials. Only the aware group shows an increase in performance. (B) Mean number of noun responses given by aware subjects on 4 blocks of trials before and after verbalization of the response-reinforcement contingency. (From De Nike, 1964)

LEARNING MOTOR SKILLS

Remember when you first learned to ride a bicycle? Play a musical instrument? Drive a car? The acquisition of such skills also falls within the psychology of human learning. Such behavior typically involves a series of muscular movements, all of them under a certain amount of sensory control. Thus, as you sense yourself tipping over too far while riding a bike, that sensory information leads to a correction movement that redistributes your weight in order to retain balance. It's harder to identify the sensory information that guides the fingers of skilled pianists, but they too respond to cues that tell them where their fingers are at any point in time. If you have learned to touch-type, you know how important it is to sense "home position" from time to time.

CAN YOU LEARN TO TRACE A LINE?

■ Following a line by tracing it with a pen is a motor skill. If you provide yourself with a few sheets of paper, a large paper clip, and a pen, you can see for yourself something of what is involved in learning a motor skill.

Open up a paper clip part way and trace along it to make its pattern 8 or 10 times on a sheet or two of paper (see Figure 9-8). Then place the paper on a desk, hold the pen as you usually do to write, and set the penpoint at one end of an inked pattern on the paper. Don't allow your fingers or hand to touch the paper at all and don't change the position of the paper. Trace with the pen around the pattern. Then make ticks on the tracing, as shown in Figure 9-8, for each error you made, indicated by white space between the pattern and your tracing of it. Go on to trace one pattern after the other with the pen, always starting at the same end of the pattern, until you have traced all 8 or 10. Count your errors for each pattern and make up a graph with number of errors on the vertical coordinate and trials on the horizontal coordinate.

What evidence do you find on the graph that you were learning this tracing skill? Recall what

went on from trial to trial. Did you try different ways of holding the pen and watch its point as it traced? Did you say or think anything to yourself (verbal behavior) like "It's better if I go slower (or faster)," "I need to keep my eye on the point," or "Now I'm really getting it"? Or did your improvement in tracing seem to come automatically, just an unconscious coordination of your muscles?

The Verbal Component of Motor Skills

Because motor skills include both sensory and muscular elements, they are referred to as **sensorimotor skills.** Playing golf and tennis are sensorimotor skills; so are running a machine lathe and making a macramé belt. While it is tempting to describe such behavior as nonverbal (in contrast to learning foreign languages, for example), it is more appropriate to say that verbal behavior plays a relatively

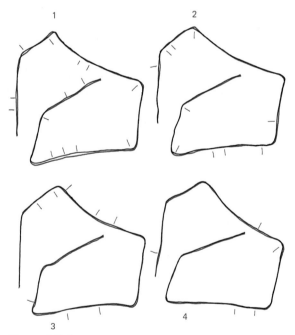

Figure 9-8 Open a paper clip up part way and draw around it 8 or 10 times to produce the lines (black) that you then try to trace in a different color (red). The ticks indicate errors of tracing, where white space shows between the lines.

small part in the performance of sensorimotor skills. Yet even this statement needs qualification. In the activity of tracing, some verbal behavior is involved, as well as cues from vision and touch in the muscular behavior of hand and arm. Consider how automatic are the responses in the chain of behaviors that begins with inserting the ignition key in a car as you prepare to drive away. Yet you may recall how much talking to yourself you had to do when you first began to learn these responses, and how much verbal rehearsal you engaged in the night before your driver's test.

The heavy involvement of verbal behavior during the acquisition of a sensorimotor skill is also shown by the continuous counting that youngsters do as they try to master the playing of a musical instrument. All youngsters who ever took piano lessons know how disruptive it is when someone tries to talk to them while they are desperately trying to count the time as they practice. As the sensorimotor skill becomes better learned, the verbal components that have served a useful integrating function during the earliest stages begin to drop out. Finally the skilled act occurs smoothly and automatically, with little or no conscious verbal control.

These considerations suggest that the distinction between motor and verbal learning is somewhat arbitrary. The difference between these types of learning is more one of degree than of kind.

Principles of Motor Learning

The variables that control motor learning stand most clearly revealed when a well-controlled experiment is set up. If you try to isolate the determinants of motor learning by watching people learn to bowl, drive a car, or type, you'll be so hopelessly overwhelmed by the complexity of the behavioral patterns rapidly unfolding before your eyes that you won't know what to look for and you'll easily miss crucial details. For this reason, psychologists create artificial situations—experiments—in which a very simple motor task can be acquired in a setting free of complicating factors—free, that is, except for the one condition whose effect is under study. You may recall (see Chapter 1) that the method of concomitant variations calls for systematically varying one condition and noting the effects of the manipulation.

To take an example, consider how often you may have wondered about the best way of spacing practice trials in learning a skill. Should you try for a limited number of long trials, in which **massed practice** is employed in a kind of marathon crash course? Or is it better to intersperse brief rests between short practice trials, a method called **distributed practice?** This question is not unrelated to the business problem of maximizing employee productivity and satisfaction through the judicious use of coffee breaks and other kinds of rest periods. The psychologist begins by posing the research problem: to determine the effect of varying the duration of rest periods on the acquisition and performance of a sensorimotor task. The task selected is important. It should be simple, require muscular effort and sensory involvement, and permit an objective, easily quantifiable measure of performance. One such "artificial" task is **mirror tracing,** which requires subjects to trace with a pencil the path between the lines that make up a star figure. They must do this as quickly as they can, all the while observing only a reversed mirror image of the star. An error is recorded every time the pencil touches a line (see Figure 9-9).

Another commonly used task for studying the effects of distributed practice is **pursuit-rotor tracking.** A pursuit rotor is shown in Figure 9-10. This task requires the subject to keep the metal tip of a hinged stylus in contact with a small disk on the surface of a platter rotating at a constant speed. As long as the tip stays in contact with the disk, a timer remains activated. The timer provides an objective measure of performance in the form of number of seconds "on target" during a practice trial of

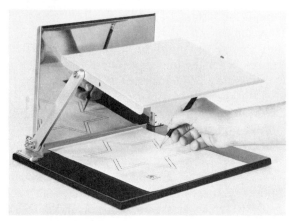

Figure 9-9 Mirror tracing of a star. On each trial, the task of the subjects is to trace between the double lines of the star as quickly as possible. While the subjects' view is blocked by the shield, they can observe a reversed image of the star by looking in the mirror.

fixed duration. As you might predict, time-on-target scores are quite low at first, but gradually improve with practice trials.

What does the pursuit rotor reveal about the role played by rest periods in motor learning? Figure 9-11 shows the results of an experiment in which all subjects received 20 practice trials. Each trial lasted 50 seconds, but the duration

Figure 9-10 A pursuit rotor used in studies of massed vs. spaced practice. The subject's task is to keep the metal tip of the hinged stylus in contact with the small disk on the rotating platter. An electric timer records the total amount of "time on target" during each practice trial.

of the rest pauses between trials was relatively long—70 seconds—for the distributed-practice group, and only 10 seconds for the massed-practice group. **Performance** on each trial was measured by adding up the number of seconds each subject kept the stylus in contact with the disk. The solid line in the graph shows the rapid and steady progress of the distributed-practice group, and the dashed line traces the slower improvement of the massed-practice group. Acquisition of a sensorimotor skill, then, improves more rapidly if practice trials are spaced, an important principle of learning a skill.

How can this principle be explained? One explanation is that responding creates **work inhibition.** During a rest interval the inhibition that builds up in a practice trial dissipates, so that subjects in the distributed-practice group start each trial without the handicap of a lot of built-up inhibition. The inhibition of subjects in the massed-practice group has less time to dissipate during their brief rest periods, so they carry stored-up inhibition into following practice trials. That's what hurts their performance, much as doing pushups gets harder and harder if you don't rest enough between them to let fatigue wear off.

Still, no one can actually *see* work inhibition. How can the assumption of such a condition be justified? Perhaps it is just a name dreamed up to label the difference between distributed and massed practice. However, scientists often theorize about processes or things they can't actually see, from electrons to emotions. One way to test the validity of the work-inhibition concept is to ask a question like this: If there were some process that (1) increased with responding, (2) suppressed performance, and (3) dissipated with time, what effects would one predict for a group of subjects who first received five massed-practice trials, then had a good five-minute rest, and then received 15 more massed-practice trials? Look at the dotted curve in Figure 9-11. During the first five

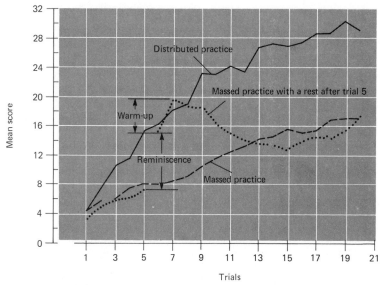

Figure 9-11 Performance curves of three groups in a pursuit-rotor task. The performance of the massed-practice group (dashed line) is impaired, presumably because work inhibition does not dissipate sufficiently during the very brief rest intervals between trials. Reminiscence, followed by warm-up, appears in the results of a group (dotted line) that practiced for five trials under massed conditions, then rested for five minutes before resuming massed-practice trials. (Kimble, G. A. & Garmezy, N., *Principles of general psychology*, Third Edition. Copyright © 1968. The Ronald Press Company, New York. Unpublished data of Marsha H. Graves)

massed trials, inhibition built up with little chance to dissipate. So performance was impaired just as much as that of the group that received massed-practice trials throughout (dashed line). The five-minute rest should allow all inhibition to wear off, and performance should jump to the level of the group that received distributed-practice trials throughout (solid line). The sudden improvement in performance following massed practice and a long rest is called **reminiscence.** Apparently subjects practicing with massed trials are learning every bit as much as those practicing under distributed-practice conditions; all they need in order to demonstrate this is a little rest, just enough to get rid of the depressing effects of work inhibition. But as massed practice resumes and inhibition builds up again, note how performance drops once more to the level

of the continuous massed-practice group (dashed line).

Finally, observe in Figure 9-11 the additional improvement between trials 6 and 7, right after the reminiscence effect. This additional spurt in performance is called the **warm-up effect.** Unlike improvement due to reminiscence, which requires nothing but rest, the warm-up effect results from the practice that occurs on the first trial following a rest interval. The subject needs to get into the swing of things again after a break from the task. This may require some readjusting of posture, reactivating of muscular sets, and getting into the rhythm of the revolving disk. While the theoretical properties of warm-up effects are not very well understood (Adams, 1961), they are very real indeed for the baseball coach who insists that relief pitchers practice in the bull pen before getting into the game. They also work for pugilists who shadowbox during the few seconds before the clang of the first-round bell, and even for students who straighten out their desks and arrange their books before settling down to a study session.

While (1) *distribute the practice sessions* is a powerful bit of advice for the person who is about to learn a motor skill, a few other practical principles should be mentioned. (2) *Analyze the task.* After ascertaining its component parts, practice on specific components, and then put the separate parts together into a smoothly integrated whole. Some piano teachers require their pupils, when learning a new piece, to practice the left-hand and right-hand parts separately at first. Only when each hand is able to play its part smoothly alone are the pupils permitted to start practicing the full piece as it is written, with both hands playing together. Pupils who object at first to the ban on even trying to use both hands together are delighted and astonished at the skill with which they play the music when, having learned to play the part of each hand separately, they bring the two hands together for the first time. (3) *Maximize feedback.* In parallel parking a car, for example, keep track of visual cues for continuous information about the way you are sliding the car into the space. People can also provide external feedback when they report to you how far you still are from the curb. After a while you can park almost "by feel." This means your behavior is guided by internal feedback. Experienced bicyclists have learned to shift the gears on their 10-speed bikes mainly by relying on internal feedback. (4) *Practice under varied conditions.* Performing a complex skill in a new setting is sometimes difficult. For that reason, a singer usually likes to practice in a new auditorium before a performance, and a pianist insists on practicing on an unfamiliar piano before playing on it in public. To do their best, cross-country runners or skiers need to be familiar with the course. It is helpful to practice a skill under the widest

variety of conditions, especially if we need to perform under varying conditions. This way, transfer of the skill to novel situations will be facilitated. The psychology of skill transfer is such an important area that it requires independent treatment.

TRANSFERRING TRAINING

Learning never takes place in a vacuum. The individual is always part of an environment. Whatever you learn, you do so by practice in the presence of certain stimulus conditions. It is hard to learn interpersonal skills, for example, if your environment provides few contacts with people. Once you've learned to respond appropriately in a given environment, it's easy to see how changing that environment, or key features of it, would confuse you and impair your performance. For example, your interpersonal skills would certainly need some additional practice if you had to get used to an entirely new set of people upon moving to a new city. The fact that you had already developed some social skills at home and in school, however, should certainly ease the making of friendships in the new environment.

Sensorimotor and Cognitive Skills

Some **transfer of training** usually takes place in learning situations, with the effects of previous learning carrying over to influence learning and performance in new situations. Whenever people meet new problems, they usually search their memories for similar problems they have learned to solve in the past. In a broad sense, the purpose of education is to train people in ways that will benefit them in the future. Thus high school students taking driving lessons often receive part of their training in mock-up trainers designed to resemble a car in simulated road conditions (see Figure 9-12). Such pretraining is presumed to make later stages of driving instruction faster

Figure 9-12 High school students receiving the initial stage of driving instruction using simulated road conditions and mock-ups of automobile controls. The effects of such training are assumed to transfer to actual road conditions, making learning in an actual car in motion faster and safer.

and safer. The astronauts learned to carry out a variety of tasks in conditions of simulated near-weightlessness here on earth, in preparation for the tasks they would have to carry out in space. Training pilots to fly 747 aircraft would be prohibitively expensive and dangerous if all their practice had to take place in the actual plane. Instead, visual simulators are used to provide, in a remarkably faithful way, all the qualities of an aircraft in flight. Using such a simulator is expensive, about $369 an hour, but it would cost $4329 an hour to train a pilot in an actual 747.

The effects of transfer are seen in verbal-cognitive skills as well as sensorimotor skills. Learning the vocabulary of a foreign language is easier when the words resemble words you already know in English. You can easily learn the German verb that stands for "to make,"

since the meaning of "make" transfers easily to *machen;* and if you've ever studied Latin, it might even have helped you learn some English words. It's a short jump from *nauta* to "nautical." British educators have tried to speed up the learning of the English alphabet by first teaching youngsters a longer alphabet, but one that is initially easier to learn because the letters correspond more closely to actual sounds in our language.

AN INITIAL TRAINING ALPHABET

English is a very difficult language to learn, foreigners say, because English words are often not spelled the way they are pronounced. The words "once," "iron," "through," and "muscle" come to mind, and you can add a host of others. But a 44-character alphabet has been devised that includes all the sounds of the English language, as opposed to our conventional 26-character alphabet, to help children learn to read and write (see Figure 9-13). With the phonetic alphabet, all words can be spelled just as they are pronounced. This **Initial Teaching Alphabet (ITA)** has been used experimentally in Britain and in the United States to teach thousands of children to read and write.

Since the characters in the ITA correspond to the sounds in spoken English, transfer from speech to reading and writing is accomplished more quickly and easily than when the conventional alphabet is used. Furthermore, children seem more confident in working with the ITA, need not depend so much on their teachers, show less frustration, and have a greater sense of achievement than when they must use the conventional alphabet. Finally, children seem to enjoy learning to read and write with the ITA. Later they shift to the conventional alphabet without difficulty. The research has indicated that ITA gives children an early lead, but not an assured final advantage, over those trained conventionally. Still, the spelling of words just as they sound apparently eases the processes of learning to read and write. Further research is required before the relative advantages of the two methods can be weighed with confidence.

Figure 9-13 The 44 characters of the Initial Teaching Alphabet (ITA). (Courtesy Initial Teaching Alphabet Foundation)

Positive and Negative Transfer

Positive transfer occurs when learning a prior task makes the learning of a subsequent task easier or the performance of it better. But you have undoubtedly found that sometimes having learned something earlier may interfere with later learning. The young son of one of the authors, while visiting in Italy, could not stop his bike in time to keep from colliding with a passing car. The boy tried to stop the way he had learned to stop bikes, by reversing the pedals. But European bikes can be stopped only by squeezing the handbrakes. The boy had not learned this braking adequately, and the result of this negative transfer was a fractured collarbone. In **negative transfer,** the learning of prior tasks makes the learning of subsequent tasks more difficult or less efficient. You may have experienced some elements of negative transfer the first time you tried to drive a manual-shift car, if you had previously learned to drive a car with an automatic transmission. Occasionally you hear of serious accidents due to negative transfer.

Negative transfer also occurs in verbal activities. A common example is the tendency to continue using last year's date long after the new year has begun. While, on balance, knowing one language well usually helps you learn a second, this is a net effect, the result of a lot of positive transfer mixed with some negative transfer. Students of French quickly learn to beware of *faux amis*, or "false friends." These are treacherous French words that sound like English words but mean something else entirely. Negative transfer is shown by the student who translates the French verb *rester* as "to rest," when the correct translation is "to remain." One of the authors, whose native language is Italian, once gave an embarrassing display of negative transfer when he announced to a large audience that the main speaker, an ambassador to the United Nations, was going to be "a little retarded." The Italian *ritardato*, which means "delayed," prompted emission of the English word "retarded"—a distressing case of negative transfer.

An Example of Transfer of Learning

Why does transfer of learning occur? Is there any basis for predicting under what conditions positive rather than negative transfer will take place? If you knew how to maximize the positive and minimize the negative, you would be able to facilitate future learning. Fortunately, a lot is known about the answers to these questions. In the following example, let's see how soon you can spot the working of a basic principle that was first discussed in Chapter 7. Miss Smith is a fifth-grade teacher. In April she marries Mr. Jones. The children in her class, despite their best efforts, find it very hard to call her "Mrs. Jones." When school closes in June they are still saying "Miss Smith." This problem of learning a new response to an old stimulus is shown in Figure 9-14. Let's think of Miss Smith as embodying a very complex set of stimulus features (S_1) to which the children have conditioned the response "Miss Smith" (R_1). This is like learning Task A. After her marriage, the children have to learn a new response, "Mrs. Jones" (R_2), to the same person. Learning a new response (R_2) to an old stimulus (S_1) is difficult because the old response (R_1) interferes with the new learning.

You can readily see that the principle underlying negative transfer is **stimulus generalization.** If a new response must be learned in Task B (see Figure 9-14), negative transfer will depend on the degree to which the old but now inappropriate response continues to generalize from the old to the new situation. Suppose, instead, that in April Miss Smith gets married and stops working, and is replaced by an entirely different-looking teacher whose name, by a rare coincidence, is also Miss Smith. This situation is diagrammed in Figure 9-15. Should you expect any negative transfer here? Hardly, since the old response is still correct and no other response is competing against it. All that's necessary is that it be associated with the new teacher. In fact, since the children don't have to learn a new name, some positive transfer would be expected. The

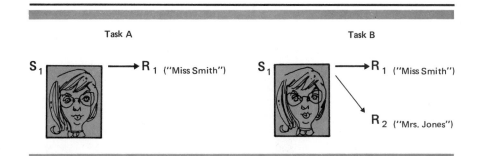

Figure 9-14 From September through April, the children learn to associate R_1 ("Miss Smith") with their teacher (Task A). By April the association is very strong. Although Miss Smith's appearance doesn't change after she gets married in April, the children now must learn to inhibit the old response, R_1 ("Miss Smith"), and build up the strength of a new response, R_2 ("Mrs. Jones"). This is labeled Task B. Because the new response tendency (R_2) must grow from zero strength to a point at which it surpasses the strength of the older tendency (R_1), you would expect negative transfer to occur.

Task A   Task B

S_1 ———→ R_1 ("Miss Smith") S_2 ———→ R_1 ("Miss Smith")

Figure 9-15 If the original Miss Smith left her job and was replaced by an entirely different teacher who also happened to be named Miss Smith, no negative transfer would be expected; there would be no old tendencies around to interfere with the attachment of the well-learned name (Miss Smith) to a completely new person.

children would immediately call the new teacher by her correct name.

Paired-Associate Experiments

These anecdotal accounts illustrate some of the principles of transfer of learning, but reliable knowledge about it must come from experimental research. In order to study how transfer effects depend on the relationships between new and old tasks, the stimuli and responses that comprise such tasks must be precisely identified and controlled. For this reason, experiments on transfer usually involve tasks that require a special type of verbal **rote learning** by simple repetition called **paired-associate learning.**

A paired-associate (P-A) list consists of a number of pairs of items, such as nonsense syllables, meaningful words, or visual forms. The task of the subjects is to supply the appropriate response term (R) when they are presented with the stimulus members (S) of the pair. Typically, subjects learn one P-A list (List A) to the criterion of one perfect recitation, just as you learned the list of words until you recalled them all once. Then they learn a second, or transfer, list (List B).

An **experimental design** in which the stimulus terms of List A appear again in List B,

although in List B the response terms have been changed, is shown in Figure 9-16. As you can now easily predict, a lot of negative transfer should be produced by such a design. What would happen, however, if the response terms were changed only a little bit? How much negative transfer would be obtained if, in going from List A to List B, the word "chunk" became "chink" and "preach" became "peach"? Much less negative transfer is most likely; in fact, the more similar the R_B terms are to the R_A terms, the more positive the transfer.

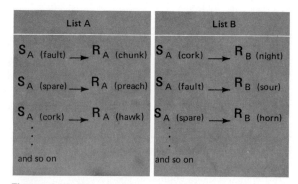

List A	List B
S_A (fault) ——→ R_A (chunk)	S_A (cork) ——→ R_B (night)
S_A (spare) ——→ R_A (preach)	S_A (fault) ——→ R_B (sour)
S_A (cork) ——→ R_A (hawk)	S_A (spare) ——→ R_B (horn)
⋮	⋮
and so on	and so on

Figure 9-16 Prior learning of paired-associate List A makes it harder to learn List B. Negative transfer occurs when new responses (R_B) must be learned to old stimuli (S_A).

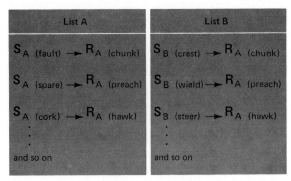

Figure 9-17 Positive transfer is expected in learning List B, for response terms (R$_A$) are already well learned and merely need to be attached to new stimuli (S$_B$).

Suppose, however, that the response terms are identical, but the stimulus terms in the two lists are changed, as shown in Figure 9-17. What transfer effects would you now expect to find? Again, according to the explanation of transfer, you should be able to explain why lots of positive transfer should be expected, since now already well-formed responses merely need to become linked to new stimuli, and there are no old associations around to make trouble.

All these predictions are fun to make, but the game is incomplete until they are em-

pirically confirmed. And just how do you go about measuring the effects of positive or negative transfer, in order to test the predictions? The most basic way is to use two groups of subjects, matched if possible for rote-learning ability. Subjects can be matched, for example, on the basis of the speed with which they learn a P-A list consisting entirely of nonsense syllables. Then each subject in the experimental group learns List A to a criterion of mastery and next practices List B, also to a criterion of mastery. The control group merely learns List B to the same criterion of mastery (Figure 9-18). If the mean number of trials required by the experimental group to learn List B is significantly greater (or smaller) than the number required by the control group, the difference can be attributed to the prior learning experience of one group and its lack by the other group. Thus negative (or positive) transfer would be demonstrated.

The left half of Figure 9-18 diagrams the design of the experiment just described. But couldn't the faster learning of List B by the experimental subjects merely reflect their extra general experience in learning by rote? To control for differences in learning experience, some designs require even the control group to learn a prior list. In that case, List A would

Standard design			Alternate design		
	Tasks			Tasks	
Group	A	B	Group	A	B
Experimental	Learns list A	Learns list B	Experimental	Learns list A	Learns list B
Control		Learns list B	Control	Learns unrelated list	Learns list B

Figure 9-18 Experimental designs used to measure transfer of training effects. In the standard design, both groups learn List B, but only the experimental group previously learns List A. The alternate design attempts to minimize differences in prior learning experience by requiring both groups to learn a prior list before learning List B; however, the first list learned by the control group consists of material entirely unrelated to the content of List B.

consist of content entirely unrelated to that of List B, such as stimulus–response terms consisting of nonsense syllables or of numbers. Such an alternate design is shown on the right side of Figure 9-18.

A summary of the ways transfer effects can carry over from one task to another is shown in Figure 9-19. Start in the middle of the diagram, where Task A is shown. The symbols S_A and R_A stand for specific stimulus and response elements that must be associated if the task is to be learned. Note that the amount and direction of transfer occurring in learning Task B depends on the similarity of stimulus and response elements in the two tasks.

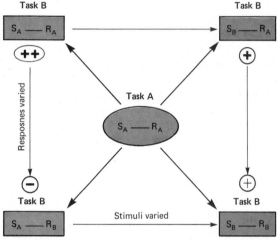

Figure 9-19 Summary of predicted transfer effects based on similarity of stimulus and response components of original and transfer tasks. Having learned Task A, with S–R terms symbolized as S_A–R_A, the subject learns Task B. The greatest amount of positive transfer occurs when S and R elements of Task B remain identical to those of A (Task B then merely consists of additional trials on Task A). Positive transfer is obtained even if stimuli are varied, so long as R_A responses are kept the same (S_B–R_A). When stimuli are kept identical and response terms change (S_A–R_B), negative transfer results. Note that in all these cases, stimulus and response properties need not change completely. When Task B involves a complete change in both stimuli and responses (S_B–R_B), transfer may be positive if subjects have benefited by acquiring *nonspecific* learning skills while learning Task A. (After Woodworth & Schlosberg, 1954)

Nonspecific Transfer

The transfer effects that occur when both S and R terms in Task B are altogether different from those of Task A (lower right of Figure 9-19) require additional comment. Some positive transfer may be expected, but how can this be if all elements are different? Inexperienced subjects often show positive transfer effects, for while practicing Task A they acquire a knack for learning this type of material. For example, they may try out different learning strategies, discarding those that don't work well and retaining those that prove to be efficient. Do you recall anything like this happening as you learned the first list of words in the activity? The acquisition of such skills is sometimes referred to as "learning how to learn."

Because these skills are not specific to the actual content of Task A, but can be applied in learning other types of lists by rote, this type of transfer is called **nonspecific transfer.** Nonspecific transfer has profound implications for philosophies of education that try to teach students how to approach problems, how to do research, how to study efficiently, how to submit beliefs to rigorous testing rather than making snap judgments. Probably you realize that a year from now you will have forgotten most of the factual content of the courses you are taking this year. However, you may take comfort in recalling that the goal of a college education is less the acquisition of facts than the development of a set of general motives, skills, and attitudes that should help you to organize and interpret future experience and enable you to confront the problems life has in store for you with a more informed and effective judgment.

What does it mean, anyway, to say rather vaguely that people learn skills, approaches, knacks, strategies, or, generally, that they "learn how to learn"—all terms that are often associated with the concept of nonspecific transfer? For several centuries the proponents of a "classical" curriculum argued for the inclusion of Latin, Greek, logic, and mathematics in young people's education on the ground that such studies "discipline the mind." This **doctrine of formal discipline** held that the mental "faculties" of reasoning, memory, attentiveness, and judgment would thereby be strengthened, much as a muscle becomes strong with exercise. The development of these general mental faculties would then later improve performance in specific tasks that required special reasoning ability or sustained attention to detail. Apart from having to put aside the discredited concept of "faculties," no empirical basis has been found for this particular notion of transfer. The study of Latin does not necessarily strengthen a general ability to reason. It may not even help a person's English vocabulary, unless the teaching of Latin deliberately stresses the derivation of English words from the Latin. Nor does learning geometry necessarily improve reasoning ability. So nonspecific transfer cannot be explained by postulating the growth of some particular mental faculty.

A clear example of nonspecific transfer in the form of a principle that carries over to facilitate performance in another situation comes from a study by G. Hendrickson and W. Schroeder (1941). These investigators found that teenage boys who were taught the basic principles of refraction of light by water were more accurate in firing their air rifles at underwater targets moved to varying depths than were other boys who did not receive refraction instruction. Apparently being able to verbalize a principle resulted in a more rapid adjustment of their aim toward the targets in the new locations.

Animal Transfer Experiments

Given extensive training, even some animal species will demonstrate the benefits of nonspecific positive transfer based on the learning of a principle. In a series of studies on discrimination learning in monkeys, Harry Harlow

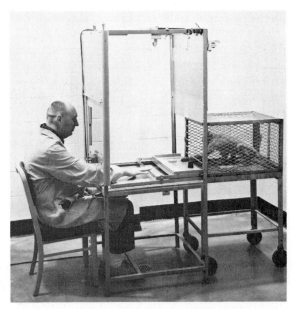

Figure 9-20 The Wisconsin General Test Apparatus. A trial begins when the opaque screen is lifted, allowing the monkey to select one of the two stimulus objects. The animal is rewarded only if it responds to the correct stimulus. Between trials, the opaque screen is lowered to block the monkey's view while the experimenter rearranges the left–right position of the stimuli in a random sequence. When the discrimination problem has been mastered, a new problem is begun, using entirely different stimulus objects.

(1949) showed transfer effects so powerful that they resembled the **sudden solutions,** occurring in a flash, that we often associate with the concept of creative insight. Harlow had his monkeys learn a series of discrimination problems, in each of which the animal had to select one of two objects it saw in the stimulus tray when a screen was raised. Harlow's apparatus is shown in Figure 9-20. In the first problem of the series, the animal might be rewarded only when it chose a cube rather than a cylinder. The left or right position of the correct stimulus would, of course, be varied randomly from trial to trial. When this problem had been mastered, the experimenter would present the next discrimination problem. This time, the rewarded stimulus might be a red circle, the nonrewarded stimulus a green triangle. As each problem was mastered, a new problem was presented. After solving hundreds of such two-stimulus discrimination problems, the monkeys had reached a superb level of performance. If by chance — for there was no other way the monkey could distinguish between rewarded and nonrewarded stimuli — the animal's response was correct on the very first trial of, say, the 300th problem, it never made an error on that problem. If the first-trial response happened to be incorrect, most animals switched to the correct stimulus object on the second trial and went on responding correctly after that. Figure 9-21 shows how, as different sets of problems were mastered, the monkeys showed more and more evidence of **instant learning,** or learning by sudden solution.

How is such sudden or instant learning of the final sets of problems to be explained? Cer-

tainly, learning that the correct stimulus on problem 299 was a star-shaped block could not possibly have helped the monkey achieve sudden mastery of problem 300, since the 300th problem used entirely different stimulus materials. Nothing that specific could have been transferred. But a principle could have been transferred, having been painstakingly repeated over the course of hundreds of problems. If monkeys had language, perhaps some thought process like the following might go on during the very first trial of each new problem: "I see a rectangle and a cross. I'll reach for the rectangle. If I get a reward, I'll always reach for the rectangle as long as they keep presenting me with these two stimuli. If I don't get rewarded, then the cross has to be correct, and I'll go for the cross from now on."

We can't assume that all this was going through the monkey's head, of course, but these contingencies can be restated in the objective language of operant conditioning. The first trial of problem 300 might be diagrammed as shown in Figure 9-22. When a rectangle and a cross are presented, let's assume the monkey chooses the rectangle. The response to the rectangle produces definite consequences. If the result is a reward (S^r), the reward itself comes to act like a discriminative stimulus (S^D) in the presence of which repeating the same response is reinforced. If the result is nonreward (S^{nr}), then the failure of reward to appear acts like an S^D in the presence of which switching the response to the cross produces reinforcement. Thus the principle is "Switch to the other stimulus if you don't get rewarded; otherwise, stick with the same one." The stimulus consequences of one choice acquire stimulus control over the next trial's choice.

Certain general conclusions can now be drawn about transfer effects:

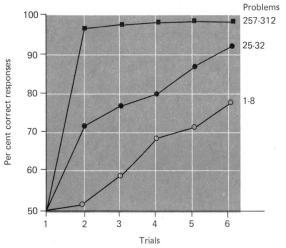

Figure 9-21 Learning curves for a group of monkeys learning a series of more than 300 discrimination problems. The average performance for the first six trials only of problems 1–8, 25–32, and 257–312 is plotted. Note that chance performance is 50 per cent, where all the curves begin. By the last group of problems, these monkeys are able to jump from chance responding to near-perfect performance on a new problem in only one trial. (After Harlow, 1949)

1. Past experience is not necessarily beneficial or harmful in learning; the effect of past experience depends on what it is that is transferred.

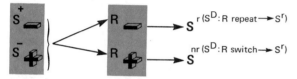

Figure 9-22 On the *first* trial of the 300th discrimination problem, the consequences of responding to either the positive stimulus (rectangle) or the negative stimulus (cross) are sufficient to determine successful responding on the second trial. Depending on the monkey's choice, reinforcement (S^r) leads to continued responding to the same stimulus; nonreinforcement (S^{nr}) becomes a cue for switching to the other stimulus.

2. Positive transfer can be enhanced by a search for similarities between the current problem and problems that have been solved in the past. ("Is this math problem in any way like other math problems I know how to solve?" "What did I do to resolve the interpersonal problem I created the last time I inadvertently betrayed a confidence?")

3. Positive transfer can also be facilitated by verbalizing some general principle that may apply to a wide variety of situations. ("In most lecture courses, it's better to listen carefully and jot down the main points than to try to write down every last detail.")

4. Negative transfer can be diminished by the discrimination of differences between old and new situations. ("Sure I didn't do well at my last job, but this situation is different. I'm better trained now, people have more reasonable expectations of what I can do, and I'm more highly motivated to work hard.")

SUMMARY

Operant conditioning shapes some characteristics of the speech patterns of infants through an interchange of reinforcements between parents and infants, leading through successive approximations of speech to cultural language norms. The degree to which talking is learned or innate behavior remains an open question. Operant techniques have proved effective in teaching speech to psychotic and retarded children. Generalized reinforcement also influences adult verbal behavior.

Many studies have provided evidence of the strength of social reinforcement in modifying verbal behavior. Awareness and acceptance of reinforcement for specific kinds of verbal responses, however, are important conditions for such social effects on verbal behavior.

Sensorimotor skills, like typing and tennis, are acquired with the help of language. Studies of simple skills like mirror tracing and pursuit-rotor tracking have pointed up the importance of work inhibition, reminiscence, and warm-up effect as variables influencing performance.

Short practice trials interspersed with brief rest periods have proved more efficient than massed practice in the acquisition of skills. Sensorimotor learning is also facilitated by analysis and practice of parts of complex tasks, accurate feedback, and practice under varied conditions.

The acquisition of verbal and sensorimotor skills may be influenced by both positive and negative transfer effects of prior training. Stimulus generalization from prior situations often underlies negative transfer. Paired-associate learning experiments have revealed the ways transfer of training works. When response terms remain identical although stimulus terms change, positive transfer occurs. But change of response terms produces negative transfer effects when the stimulus terms remain unchanged.

Nonspecific transfer occurs when the material learned can be applied to entirely different types of learning tasks, as in learning how to learn, how to study, how to approach problems, and how to do research. Nonspecific transfer does not imply the strengthening of some mental "faculty," as the doctrine of formal discipline held, but occurs when principles that are learned can be applied to new learning situations. Even monkeys have shown such nonspecific transfer effects in learning. Some types of nonspecific transfer can be understood as forms of discrimination learning in which reinforcement is contingent on response repetition following a successful trial and on switching to an alternate response following an unsuccessful trial.

Transfer of past experience can be either beneficial or detrimental in the learning of new skills. Positive transfer is facilitated by a search for similarities in the responses called for by new and old problems and by the verbalization of general principles applicable to many problems. Negative transfer can be diminished by discrimination between old and new problems, and the discarding of old solutions when they do not apply.

NOW YOU KNOW IT, APPLY IT

1. Review in your mind some of the new language that you have been learning in this course or in some other course you are taking. Without going back through the text, jot down as many of the new terms you have learned as you can. How have you been learning these terms? What aids to learning the terms are given in the text itself? Can you identify any transfer of your prior training that has helped you learn this new language? Considering the principles of verbal learning given in this chapter, how could you improve your learning of the language of the subject?

2. Suppose your right or left hand, whichever you use in writing, has become incapacitated. Make two 15-minute trials, with a half-hour rest between, of writing with your other hand. Though you may not advance very far in learning this complex motor skill, when you have finished the trials consider how the learning went on. Compare your first trial with your second trial. How much learning took place? What changes occurred as each of your trials progressed? How strong was the verbal component involved

in your motor learning? Did you think of any new strategies to use? Was there any transfer of training from the way you write customarily? Did you see any work inhibition developing toward the end of either trial? Was there any warm-up effect at the beginning of your second trial? How long do you judge it would take you to become proficient at writing with your other hand?

3. Recall your activities during the first few meetings after you joined a new social group or began to associate with one or two new friends. What instances of positive and/or negative transfer occurred from your learning of such associations in the past? Can you identify any nonspecific transfer that occurred? When faced with interpersonal problems or misunderstandings in these associations, did you experience any instances of sudden solution? Do any of the general conclusions about transfer apply to your association with a new group or new friends?

4. Do you type? If so, go to the typewriter and type the word "minimum." Your fingers traveled quite a bit, and the stroking load was assigned exclusively to the right hand. That's one of the problems with the standard typewriter keyboard: The letters are not efficiently distributed across the keyboard. Note, for example, how a letter that occurs frequently in English words, like *a*, is placed at the far left and assigned to a short digit, the "pinkie" finger. Figure 9-23 compares the standard keyboard and the American simplified keyboard (ASK). The ASK groups the most commonly used letters on the "home row," the second row up from the space bar, allowing 70 per cent of all typing to be done on this single row. Students who are first learning to type reach speeds of 60 words a minute in about the same time it would take to attain half that speed on the standard keyboard. Why doesn't everyone change to ASK?

Design an experiment to determine the

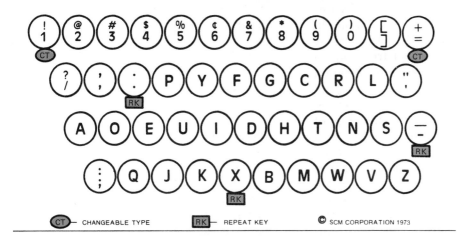

SMITH-CORONA AMERICAN SIMPLIFIED KEYBOARD

CT — CHANGEABLE TYPE   RK — REPEAT KEY   © SCM CORPORATION 1973

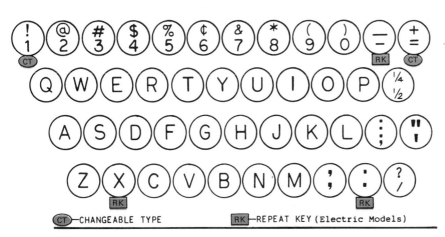

STANDARD KEYBOARD

CT — CHANGEABLE TYPE   RK — REPEAT KEY (Electric Models)

Figure 9-23 A simplified typewriter keyboard compared with a standard keyboard. Note that the simplified keyboard groups the most commonly used letters on the "home row." (Courtesy Smith-Corona Advisory Council)

amount of positive and negative transfer that would result if typists experienced with the standard keyboard suddenly began to learn the ASK. Would the amount of transfer vary with the degree of prior experience with the standard keyboard? Would the amount and direction of transfer change as the typists gained more experience with the ASK? How would you measure these effects? What controls would be necessary?

10

Memory

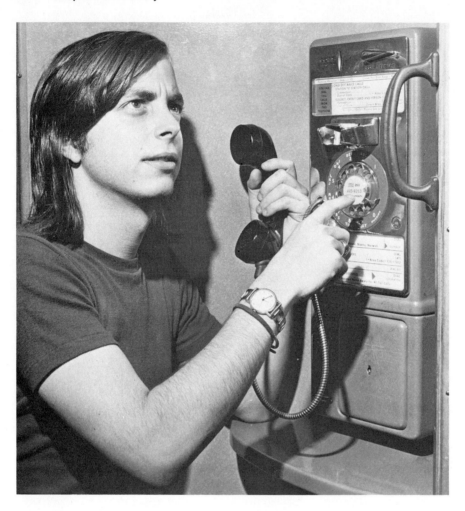

SAMPLE YOUR MEMORY

■ At least a day or two, and even up to a week or two, after you have sampled your own learning (see Chapter 9), turn back to the two lists of 10 words and relearn them, first the list on the left, then that on the right. Follow the same procedures that you used before, and make up a graph of your relearning. The differences between your first graphs and these second graphs provide a measure of your memory of the lists. Just what changes did take place? Can you explain these effects?

■ DO YOU KNOW THE ANSWER?

Remembering and Forgetting

Is memory something people have in varying degrees?

How would you propose to measure memory?

Are overlearned things (that is, things learned beyond the point of mastery) remembered better than underlearned things or vice versa?

Do you remember better materials you have thought about or materials you have just read carefully?

REMEMBERING AND FORGETTING

Everyone would like to have a better memory. How often do you hear comments like "My mind is like a sieve"; "I must be getting older, I keep forgetting things"; "He must have a photographic memory"; "If I could only remember where I left my glasses!"? But memory is not an object you can have or exchange; nor is it a "faculty" of the mind, as philosophers used to think; nor is it a muscle that can be made to grow stronger with exercise. **Memory** is a class of behaviors in which the individual is able to reproduce previously learned behavior—verbal or motor—or reexperience earlier images and ideas. The opposite of remembering is **forgetting,** the inability to reproduce previously learned behaviors. Of course, you can't conclude much about other people's memories unless the things they remember are expressed in the things they say or do. This doesn't mean that remembering solely depends on or consists of satisfying some objective behavioral criterion, only that the scientific study of memory requires it. The study of memory offers both theoretical and practical benefits. At the same time that you gain a better understanding of the process of forgetting, you can also learn how to minimize your forgetting.

Why Do We Forget?

Poor original learning is one of the main conditions for forgetting. How often have you blamed your memory because the day after a large party you can't remember the names of some of the people you met? The difficulty most people have remembering the names of those they meet is not caused by a poor memory but by poor original learning. In order to learn to associate any verbal response to an external stimulus, you know that the response must be practiced in its presence; that is, while attending to it. When people are introduced, especially at a party, they often don't fully attend to (or hear) the names that are spoken, perhaps because of social tension, because they are too busy thinking of something to say, or because of distractions in the room.

Principles for Less Forgetting

Whatever makes for good original learning also makes for less forgetting. Some ways of measuring how much of the original learning is retained are available. The most frequently used methods of measurement are described in "Applying a Yardstick to Memory." Let's take a moment to identify those principles that make for better original learning, and so for less forgetting: *Overlearn things you want to remember well.* Many years ago, it was demonstrated (Krueger, 1929) that retention of verbal material increases as the percentage of overlearning increases. **Overlearning** is learning beyond the point of mastery. If it takes 10 trials to master a paired-associate (P-A) list, and no more practice occurs, this is referred to as 0 per cent overlearning. If 5 additional trials are given, this is 50 per cent overlearning; 10 additional trials give 100 per cent overlearning. Figure 10-1 shows how the number of words re-

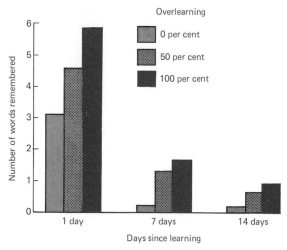

Figure 10-1 The greater the amount of overlearning, the better the retention of a list of 12 nouns. The advantages of overlearning persist over time. (Data from Krueger, 1929)

membered increases with overlearning. Notice that the superior retention of the 100 per cent overlearning condition is still apparent even after two weeks.

APPLYING A YARDSTICK TO MEMORY

How can you measure memory? If learning can be measured, so can memory. The basic idea is to measure the amount a person learns and then, at a later time, measure what is left of the original learning. Several methods can be used to measure what is left.

Recognition Method

All a person has to do under the recognition method is to identify—that is, to recognize—the correct responses, much like the task on a multiple-choice item in an exam. This method shows the greatest amount of retention.

Free-Recall Method

The free-recall method requires you to produce the correct responses without any cues, as in naming all the people you met at the last party you attended. You were using free recall in measuring your memory of the word lists in "Sample Your Memory," at the opening of this chapter.

Relearning Method

Suppose that when you were an incoming freshman it took you 10 practice trials to learn the names of the other students who lived on your floor in the dorm. Two years later you find you have forgotten some of the names. Fortunately, you find a list of them and give yourself enough practice trials to relearn the list. If you can relearn the list in fewer than the original 10 trials, you have saved some effort. Your **savings score** is computed as follows:

Number of trials to learn: 10
Number of trials to relearn: 4
Savings in trials   6

$$\text{Savings score} = \frac{\text{Savings in trials}}{\text{Trials to learn originally}}$$
$$= 6/10 = 60\%$$

Generally, as the time elapsed since learning increases, the greatest amount of retention would be shown on a recognition test, the least on a recall test, and an intermediate amount on a relearning test (Leavitt & Schlosberg, 1944). But there are exceptions to this rule. Leo Postman and L. Rau (1957) reported more retention two days after lists of syllables were learned when a free-recall measure rather than a recognition measure was used. Endel Tulving (1968) found better recall than recognition of the response terms of pairs of words. The recall test had subjects respond to presentations of the stimulus words of the pairs; on the recognition test, they had to recognize the response terms from among other words. How much you remember depends on a lot of things, and how you go about measuring memory is only one of them.

How much should you overlearn? This is a practical question. For a midterm quiz you may be satisfied to overlearn only enough to do fairly well; but if you're learning a part for a stage play, you'll want to overlearn far beyond the 100 per cent point, for nothing short of perfect retention is acceptable on stage.

Space your learning with occasional rest periods. The advantages of distributed practice, as opposed to mass practice, have been discussed in Chapter 9. Although the underlying mechanisms that make distributed practice more advantageous in learning verbal materials may not be exactly the same as those that operate in the performance of motor skills, the advice remains the same: When you sense your learning efforts becoming less efficient, take a rest or simply change to an entirely different activity.

Actively rehearse the material to be learned. Learning is an active process. It involves a dynamic interaction between the person and the material to be learned. Passively reading a section of your textbook may lead to some learning, but not as much as if you actively rehearse the key concepts, asking yourself questions about them, thinking of examples, and looking for connections with ideas presented earlier. In a classic study (Gates, 1917) students memorized a list of nonsense syllables. One group spent all its time silently reading and rereading the list. Four other groups spent 20 to 80 per cent of their time in self-recitation and the rest of the time in silent study. As Figure 10-2 shows, although the total amount of time spent in studying was the same, as the groups devoted larger percentages

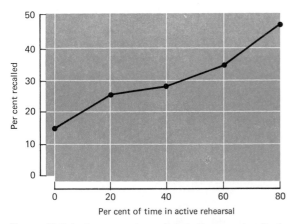

Figure 10-2 As the percentage of study time spent actively rehearsing a list of syllables increases, a larger percentage of items is recalled correctly on a test administered later. (Data from Gates, 1971)

of their study time to active rehearsal, recall after four hours steadily improved.

Make the material meaningful. The more meaningful the material, the more rapid the rate of learning. Meaningful material generates a richer complex of associations and images. A list of nonsense syllables takes more trials to learn than a list of meaningful words; a passage consisting of unrelated meaningful words is learned more slowly than a long prose passage; and poetry is learned most easily of all. In "Sample Your Own Learning" at the beginning of Chapter 9, you probably learned the second, more meaningful list of related words faster than the first list of unrelated words. The same principle applies to retention, as you may have found with your differential retention of the two lists of words. The moral is simple: Don't simply memorize material to be learned and retained. Rather, look for ways of relating the concepts you study to your own experiences; look for examples in your own life that illustrate the ideas you read about. Obviously, ways of investing your reading with greater meaning are not unrelated to the idea of active rehearsal.

These principles should enhance the strength and quality of the original learning and help protect what you've learned from conditions that produce forgetting. Let's assume original learning of some material is good and strong. People still forget some of the original learning. Why?

THEORIES OF FORGETTING

A number of theories have been proposed to explain why we forget. All except one are useful in accounting for, or integrating, some portion of the facts of forgetting. Since these theories came out of quite different intellectual traditions, they tend to emphasize different aspects of memory. Taken together, they provide a varied and fairly complete understanding of this aspect of human functioning. Let's examine some of the major theories.

The Theory of Disuse

The oldest theory of forgetting, and the layman's favorite, the theory of disuse can be dispatched quickly, for it's simply not sufficiently in accord with the facts. The **disuse theory** asserts that memory simply fades with time, much as an image on a photograph left in direct sunlight fades away. Time is the chief culprit, according to this theory. Appealing though the theory may be, it has trouble explaining why some things, like typing and swimming skills, are long remembered even though much time may pass. It also fails to account for the remarkably detailed memories older people have for events that occurred many years before, like the richness of Marcel Proust's recall in *Remembrance of Things Past,* while their memories for events that happened the day before may be weak. Why don't *all* images fade with time?

Interference Theories

Interference theories hold that forgetting occurs not because time passes, but because intervening events interfere with recall of what has been learned. For example, let's suppose you meet five new people at a party—A, B, C, D, and E—and that you meet them in that order as the evening progresses. The next day,

you find you have trouble remembering the name of A, but that the names of D and E, perhaps, come quite easily to mind. This is an example of a specific type of interference in which material that is learned after the original learning (the name of A) seems retroactively to weaken the traces of that original learning. Hence this type of interference is called **retroactive interference (RI).**

The effects of RI can be measured by use of a design like the one on the left side of Figure 10-3. In the typical RI experiment, subjects are assigned to experimental and control groups, and in Stage I are required to learn the same task; for example, a P-A list of nonsense syllables. In Stage II the groups engage in a second task, but the control group's task is entirely unrelated to the Stage I material. Reading a magazine is an example of an unrelated task. How much RI does Task B produce in the experimental group? To measure the amount of RI, after an equivalent amount of time has passed for both groups, they are given a retention test for the original (Task A) material. Often a recall test is employed, but the relearning method is also frequently used. The amount of RI produced by Task B is observed by comparing the retention test scores of the two groups in Stage III.

The RI and transfer of learning designs (see

Retroactive interference			Proactive interference			
	Stages				Stages	
Group	I	II	III	Group	I	II	III
Experimental	Learn task A	Learn task B	Test for retention of task A	Experimental	Learn task A	Learn task B	Test for retention of task B
	←— Transfer —→ ←— Retroactive interference —→				←— Transfer —→ ←— Proactive interference —→		
Control	Learn task A	Learn unrelated task	Test for retention of task A	Control	Learn unrelated task	Learn task B	Test for retention of task B

Figure 10-3 Experimental designs for measuring retroactive and proactive interference.

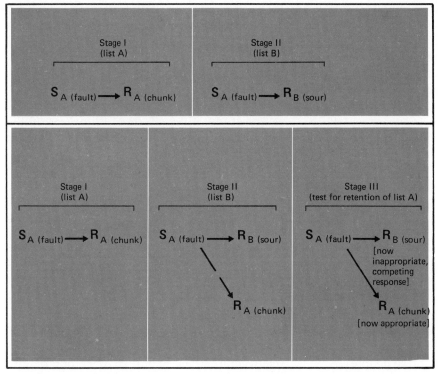

Figure 10-4 Experimental conditions that produce negative transfer (upper panel) also lay the basis for retroactive interference (bottom panel) when retention of List A is measured in Stage III.

Chapter 9) have some similarities. If you were primarily interested in transfer effects, you'd want to find out how learning Task A hinders or facilitates the learning of Task B. If RI is the target, then you'd ask how the interpolated learning (Task B) hinders the retention of content learned in Task A. RI always refers to forgetting.

Why does RI occur? Under what conditions does a little or a lot of RI develop? Can anything be done to minimize the effects of RI on retention? It's time for a little theory, so let's build upon the ideas that helped to explain transfer effects. Begin with a pair of items taken from the two P-A lists indicated in the upper panel of Figure 10-4 and originally appearing in Figure 9-16. The lists were designed to produce negative transfer, you'll recall. Now

let's add the retention test for List A and observe why RI occurs (lower panel of Figure 10-4). In Stage II, learning List B means building up the S_A–R_B connection to the point at which it's stronger than the S_A–R_A connection acquired in Stage I. But in Stage III, the correct association on the retention test is S_A–R_A. Unfortunately, because of the residual effect of Stage II learning, the subject's tendency is to respond with R_B when the stimulus S_A is presented. Thus it appears that RI occurs because associations acquired in the intermediate stage, which now are inappropriate, persist and interfere with the emission of the responses called for on the retention test.

Look at Stage II in Figure 10-4. There is some question whether Stage II learning merely builds up another association, S_A–R_B, which then competes with S_A–R_A in Stage III, or whether the S_A–R_A association actually gets unlearned or destroyed in Stage II. This is an interesting theoretical question that has generated many experiments. Some form of *competition* and some degree of *unlearning* are both involved in producing RI (Postman, Stark, & Fraser, 1968).

Have you wondered whether some types of interpolated learning will produce more RI than others? By now the principle should be obvious: When Task B requires the learning of new responses to old stimuli (the very basis for negative transfer), much RI will occur. The less relationship there is between Task B and Task A, the smaller the RI. Remembering a friend's phone number will be much easier if, in the intervening time, you have to memorize some poetry than if you have to learn five more phone numbers.

Now consider a little twist in the examples of forgetting through interference. At last night's party, you again met five people—A, B, C, D, and E—during the evening. (You'll have to imagine they were all equally interesting and that you spent an equal time with each.) The next day it's the *last* few people whose names you can't remember very well, even though not much name learning occurred after

that. Sometimes earlier learning "works ahead" to interfere with the recall of later learning. This type of interference is called **proactive interference (PI).** Stripped to its barest S–R essentials, the picture would look like that in Figure 10-5 if you were using P-A lists to study proactive interference.

The study of the effects of PI focuses on the retention of Stage II material (List B), the last material learned by the subject. PI will be strong and recall poor to the extent that the S_A–R_A association actively competes with the S_A–R_B response in the retention test. (The experimental design used to measure the amount of PI produced by prior learning is shown in the right half of Figure 10-3.)

A lot of evidence has shown PI to be a very powerful factor in reducing retention. Some years ago, Benton J. Underwood (1957) made the startling discovery that college students who were highly experienced learners of word and nonsense-syllable lists were unable to retain more than about 20 per cent of any given list overnight, despite their mastery of learning-how-to-learn skills. Inexperienced subjects, on the other hand, showed overnight retention scores of 75 per cent. The more lists the subjects learned, the poorer their recall of the last list. A survey of results obtained by

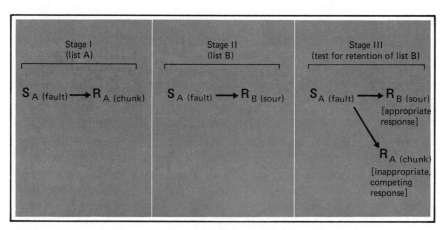

Figure 10-5 Experimental conditions for creating proactive interference.

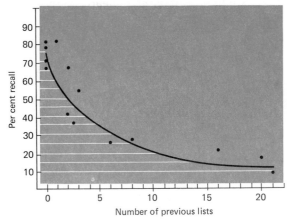

Figure 10-6 Data reported by many investigators indicate that recall of items in a list declines steadily as a function of the number of lists learned previously. (Underwood, 1957)

other investigators confirmed Underwood's observation (see Figure 10-6).

The poor recall of older people for recent events has already been mentioned. Is this caused by the effects of PI accumulated over a lifetime of previous learning? Possibly so, but this conclusion must remain conjectural. Real-life situations do not offer sufficient control over other factors that might produce the same result, such as biological effects of aging and more rehearsal of older memories than recent ones.

Why does PI occur? This question is still under investigation, but some researchers feel that prior learning (Stage I) may benefit from spontaneous recovery as time passes, coming back to wreak havoc on attempts to recall intermediate material (Stage II). Others feel that material from these two stages somehow crowds together, making it hard, for example, to think of List B items without thinking of List A items as well (Ceraso, 1967). Whatever the final answer may turn out to be, it is clear that some learning can come back to influence not only subsequent learning, but the recall of subsequent learning as well.

Organizational Theories

Organizational theories consider memory to be the result of a complicated process, analogous to the operation of a computer system in which information entering the nervous system is transformed, stored, and retrieved. By observing how people remember and forget within the controlled conditions of the laboratory, psychologists have concluded that there is not one memory system, but three different ones, each of which processes and stores information according to somewhat different rules and for different periods of time. Organizational theories explain forgetting as a result of the breakdown of one of these three memory systems.

Learning about these memory structures or systems must necessarily be indirect, for they are not directly observable. In a way, it's like trying to infer the laws of a strange country by restricting the observations to uniformities in the behavior of its citizens. The major components of systems for receiving, processing, and storing information are diagrammed in Figure 10-7. Material to be learned is received into sensory storage, passes into short-term memory (STM), then is either forgotten or coded for entry and storage in long-term memory (LTM).

Sensory storage—sometimes called *iconic memory* for visual storage and *echoic memory* for auditory storage—is more of a perceptual than a memory process. This storage is a very brief aftereffect of a stimulus on a sensory organ, lasting much less than a second. It is this aftereffect that fills in the gaps between the frames of a movie film, producing a continuous visual effect despite the small movements of the eyes, for example.

YOUR ICONIC MEMORY

■ If you wish to see sensory storage at work on visual sensations, hold up a pencil at arm's length in front of your eyes. Move the pencil back and forth slowly, and you will find that your eyes move

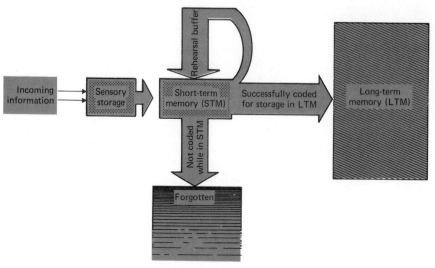

Figure 10-7 Incoming information is perceived and retained briefly in sensory storage. Information then enters STM, where, if rehearsed, it is coded for transfer to LTM for long-term storage. Material not successfully coded for transfer and storage in LTM is forgotten. (Copyright, 1971, by Harcourt Brace Jovanovich, Inc., and reproduced with their permission from *Introduction to Psychology*, 5th Edition, by Hilgard, Atkinson, & Atkinson.)

back and forth to track it. But when you move the pencil faster, your eyes cannot keep up with the motion, and since the images of the pencil endure, you begin to see a fan-shaped image before your eyes. This is your sensory storage at work. Investigations have shown that the images last about one-tenth to one-quarter of a second, the period of visual sensory storage (Haber & Hershenson, 1973).

Sensory storage occurs at the level of the sensory organ. In order for the information to be remembered, it must be encoded and passed into short-term memory. **Short-term memory (STM)** comes closer than sensory storage to what we call "memory," although its storage and retrieval of information is limited to between 10 and 20 seconds. It's a bit deflating to hear that the traces of things seen or heard decay completely within 20 seconds, yet if care is taken to prevent rehearsal of the information, this is exactly what happens. College students serving as subjects were pre-

sented with a single trigram (a nonsense syllable consisting of three consonants, like KRL), immediately after which they counted backward by 3s to keep themselves from rehearsing the trigram. After 18 seconds, as Figure 10-8 shows, recall of the single trigram had dropped almost to zero (Peterson & Peterson, 1959).

What can be done to keep information in STM from being forgotten so quickly? Consider what you normally do when you look up a number in a phone book in a restaurant and then wait for the phone booth to become available. You mentally rehearse the number. Figure 10-7 suggests that items can be kept active in STM in a **rehearsal buffer,** a process involving continuous rehearsal and hence reactivation of the memory traces. Apparently no more than about 7 to 9 elements can be actively rehearsed at one time. Try to rehearse two phone numbers, each composed of seven digits, at the same time!

The trick is to transfer information solidly from STM to LTM. For this transfer to be

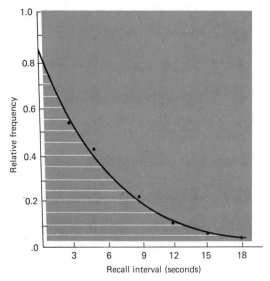

Figure 10-8 Short-term memory for a trigram as a function of time. Subjects were asked to recall a nonsense syllable from 3 to 18 seconds after it had been presented. Short-term memory decays very rapidly. (Peterson & Peterson, 1959)

made, the traces must be kept active long enough in STM for the necessary coding to occur. Rehearsal of STM material will do just that. But if rehearsal is prevented, as for example when someone asks you for the time while you're rehearsing a phone number, the information slips out of STM and is forever lost. Back to the phone book. New incoming information, it seems, will bump out content from STM. It has been suggested that this might constitute a simple explanation for the very rapid forgetting of dreams. We don't get a chance to rehearse them because the moment we awaken there is an immediate inflow of fresh information. It is not known whether rehearsal retards decay because it actively strengthens the traces of material already in STM, or because it keeps out new material and thereby reduces interference. Many investigators feel that the laws of proactive and retroactive interference, already discussed, also apply to information in STM.

Long-term memory (LTM) is what most people have in mind when they think of memory. LTM involves periods of retention ranging from a minute to a lifetime. The interference theories previously discussed, while they now can be shown to apply to STM as well, were originally developed in the context of LTM. There are two major questions about LTM: How is material successfully coded for transfer to LTM? Once material is stored in LTM, how is it retrieved?

Although it is not well understood how information is transferred from STM into LTM storage, a number of **coding strategies** can be described (Norman, 1969). One strategy is to reduce the number of elements to be stored into a small number of "chunks." The set of digits 1491625 is more difficult to rehearse and store than its coded form, 12345, obtained by taking the square root of each successively increasing set of digits: 1, 4, 9, 16, and 25. Not only is the overall number of elements reduced, but the coded form consists of elements taken from a very well-practiced dimension. The digits of a phone number, like 4421146, are easier to store if they are separated by a hyphen that groups them into two chunks, 442–1146. Generally, **chunking** is useful as a coding strategy when the total number of chunks is not greater than seven to nine. One theorist (G. A. Miller, 1956) speaks of "the magical number seven plus or minus two" to indicate the limits of the number of items or chunks of information that can be rehearsed and stored at any one time. Think you can juggle more than 8 or 9 digits in your rehearsal buffer? Try it!

Another coding strategy is use of the **mnemonic device.** Rhyming is a common mnemonic (memory-assisting) device, as in "Thirty days hath September . . ." Another mnemonic device is a single artificial word, each letter of which stands for a real word, known as an *acronym.* Thus VIBGYOR stands for the colors of the spectrum: violet, indigo, blue, green, yellow, orange, red.

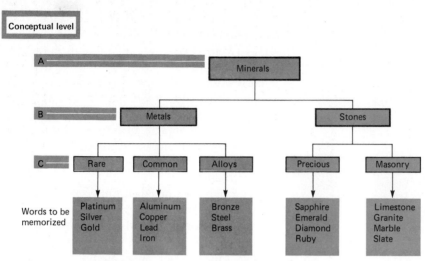

Figure 10-9 A hierarchical tree in which individual items to be learned or retrieved are clustered on the basis of categories based on similarities and differences (conceptual level C). Categories on conceptual level C are, in turn, subsumed under more abstract categories on levels B and A. (Bower, 1970)

Clustering the elements to be learned on the basis of conceptual similarities is often used as a coding strategy. In making up a list for grocery shopping, some people group the items by category: fruits and vegetables, household items like paper towels and scouring powders, meats, dairy products. If you had to learn such a list, it would be easier to do so if the items were clustered than if they appeared in random order. A more complex kind of clustering, in which categories are further arranged in hierarchical order, is the **hierarchical tree** shown in Figure 10-9. Gordon Bower (1970) has reported that the 18 words at the bottom of the tree were learned and retained better when the subjects could study the words as shown—that is, grouped within a hierarchical system of conceptual categories, or a classification system—than when the items were randomly arranged.

Once material is successfully stored in LTM, the problem is not over, as witness the man who finds a parking space for his car in the morning but can't remember its location when he leaves the office at night. The person who

successfully stores but cannot retrieve information has a serious problem. For that reason, psychologists have been very much interested in studying **retrieval strategies.** Many of the methods used to transfer information from STM to LTM can be used in reverse to retrieve information from LTM. Thus, after information has been coded into chunks and stored in LTM, retrieval involves decoding information into its original expanded form. VIBGYOR, easily stored, can be as easily expanded into the list of seven colors. The code 12345 can be converted into the phone number 149–1625.

In the same way, each of the categories at the lowest conceptual level of the hierarchical tree (rare, common, alloys, precious, and masonry) can, like a bin, be emptied of its contents. Isn't this what people often do when they get to the supermarket and discover they have forgotten to bring their shopping lists? ("Let's see now, what vegetable items were there? And what meat items?") For some reason, students often find it difficult to remember every course they took the preceding year. To help them retrieve the missing courses, an effective strategy is to ask them to inspect each of a number of bins or categories ("Was it an English course? History?"). The course is usually retrieved this way.

For thousands of years visual imagery has been used to help both store and retrieve information. Recent studies (Paivio, 1971) indicate that concrete words that can be recalled as images are likely to be remembered better than abstract words whose meaning is difficult to visualize. The **method of loci,** described in "A Mnemonic Device," goes back to ancient Greek times and was used by orators to help them remember, in order, the main points of their speeches. It calls, for example, for picturing a house with many rooms, with images of the main points "deposited" in different rooms. Retrieval involves visualizing a walk through the house, in the course of which the objects to be remembered are "encountered" in the various places in which they had been deposited.

A MNEMONIC DEVICE

The method of loci (places) is one memory device that anyone can use. Think of a series of locations with which you are familiar, like the houses you see as you walk down a street to your home, the rooms you see as you make a tour of your house, or the objects you see as you walk from your dorm across the campus to a distant building. Then you take the items you wish to remember, like a shopping list, and associate a vivid image of each item with the successive objects you pass on your mental tour. Thus you associate bananas with a banana peel on your doorstep, tomatoes with a red splash on the wall of the hallway, cat food with a tuna fish on the coffee table in the living room, cornflakes with rows of corn growing in the dining room, and steak with a thick cut sputtering in a frying pan in the kitchen. When you get to the supermarket, you walk up to your door in your imagination and see the banana peel, enter the hallway and bemoan the tomatoes, and so on through your list. You can use the same sort of tour for any other list or group of things that you

want to recall. Try this memory method the next time you have to learn a list of things, whether for a shopping trip or for a course, and see how well it works for you. A Russian memory expert used a walk down a street in Moscow to aid his memory, or made up highly imaginative stories in which to insert elements he wished to recall. Often his difficulty was not that he could not remember, but that he could not forget. Later he found he could forget specific memories by just telling his mind to erase them.

College students were asked in one study (Ross & Lawrence, 1968) to use 40 loci around the campus as bases for remembering 40 nouns. They were shown the nouns in a series and given 13 seconds for each noun. When the series was finished, they immediately recalled an average of 38 of the 40 nouns. The next day they still averaged recall of 34 of the 40 nouns in correct order. Clearly the method of loci can deliver staggering results.

Some insight into the nature of the retrieval process has come from a series of studies of the **tip-of-the-tongue phenomenon (TOT)** (R. Brown & McNeill, 1966). Try to name the object described by this definition: a navigational instrument used in measuring angular distances, especially the altitude of the sun, moon, and stars at sea. If you are unable to think of the target word right away, but feel sure that you do know it and that it's on the verge of coming back to you, you are in the tip-of-the-tongue state. In this state, can you guess the number of syllables the target word has? Can you guess the initial letter? Can you say what other words the target word sounds like? Or can you give another word that is similar in meaning to the target word? Subjects in a TOT state can usually provide some or all of this information as they struggle to retrieve the target word. Such findings are important, for they tell us that the process of retrieval is not as simple as finding the right storage "address" and discovering the complete word just sitting there calmly waiting to be found. Retrieval is not an all-or-none proposition.

Rather, people in a TOT state have accurate information about a number of features of the target word in the absence of complete recall; the closer they come to successful recall, the more accurate their information.

For readers still in the TOT state, the definition given above is for the word "sextant." In·the Brown and McNeill experiment, some TOT subjects gave words similar in meaning, like "astrolabe," "compass," and "dividers." Other subjects came up with words similar in sound, like "sexton" and "sextet." The initial letter of the word was guessed correctly 57 per cent of the time. Many subjects guessed correctly the number of syllables in the word.

TIP OF THE TONGUE?

■ If the definition for "sextant" failed to put you in a TOT state, try this definition: a skiff, used in the harbors of China and Japan, propelled usually with a scull. Remember, if you are sure that you don't know the word, you are no more in a TOT state than if you can give the word correctly. Not in a TOT state this time, either? Then try one of these definitions, or some other, on some of your friends until you find some true TOT subjects and then get them to tell you all they can about the word that is on the tips of their tongues. And if you can't bear waiting, check the answer at the end of this chapter.

Motivational Theories

Motivational theories are explanations for forgetting that depend on the general notion that people are motivated to forget things that make them anxious and emotionally upset. The concept of **repression** is a special type of motivated forgetting in which anxiety-arousing ideas are blocked from emerging into consciousness, and hence are forgotten. Freud's theory of the dynamics of the self is the most complete elaboration of the idea that a good deal of human forgetting occurs as a defense mechanism against anxiety (see Chapter 15). As you can see, repression is a kind of interference, but should not be con-

fused with the interference theories of forgetting described earlier. Interference theories attribute forgetting to conflicting S−R associations. Repression, on the other hand, is memory blocking reinforced by anxiety reduction. The most abundant examples of repression come from the clinical literature.

Amnesia is an especially dramatic form of repression, involving either total or partial loss of memory. Although sometimes the result of organic brain damage, amnesia also occurs as a form of hysterical neurosis. Such patients may retain their ability to read, write, travel about, and utilize their specialized professional skills, yet be unable to remember their names and addresses, or to recognize old friends or even members of their families. Sometimes amnesic episodes are accompanied by **fugue,** a state in which people try to escape the stress of their life situations by forgetting everything, and running away, and assuming new identities.

Attempts to study experimentally the conditions that cause repression have been only mildly successful. The general procedure is to create some unpleasant experience for the subject and to note whether events or ideas associated with the unpleasantness are later forgotten more than other, neutral elements within the same situation. Ethical considerations prevent the use of excessively unpleasant conditions, and this may be one reason why solid experimental evidence of forgetting due to repression is hard to come by. It is difficult, and undesirable, to create in subjects the intense trauma that drives the hysteric to seek refuge in an amnesic episode.

Nonetheless, it is interesting to note how some experimenters have gone about the task of producing forgetting by an apparently repressive process. Sam Glucksberg and Lloyd J. King (1967) had college students learn a paired-associates (P-A) list in which the stimulus terms were nonsense syllables and the response terms were meaningful words. Some examples of these pairs are shown in columns A and B of Table 10-1. After the P-A list had been mastered, the second, or shock, phase of

Table 10-1 Initial P-A List, Inferred Mediators, and Shock-Phase List

Paired-Associate List		Inferred Mediators	Words Associated with Shock or No Shock
A	B	C	D
cef	stem	flower	smell*
dax	memory	mind	brain
yov	soldier	army	navy
wub	wish	want	need
gex	justice	peace	war*

Source: Glucksberg & King, 1967.
* Items paired with shock in the shock phase of the experiment.

the experiment began. In this stage the subjects were presented with the words shown in Column D, one at a time. Note that the presentation of some words was accompanied by an electric shock. What the experimenters thought would happen was this: Fear is conditioned to the shock-associated words, then generalizes to words highly associated with the shock-associated words (*smell–flower*). In the third phase of the experiment, when subjects were given a retention test for the original P-A list, the presentation of *cef* not only should evoke a tendency to the response *stem,* but should also generate some fear, because of the preformed association between *stem* and *flower* (in column C), the inferred mediator of the shock-associated word *smell*. The investigators assumed that P-A list responses associatively linked with mediators of shock-associated words would be recalled with greater difficulty than responses linked with words unrelated to any shock experience, like *memory* and *soldier*. The results confirmed their assumption. Retention of responses associatively connected with the unpleasantness of shock was poorer than retention of other words in the P-A list.

Have you ever been interrupted in the middle of a task you were eager to finish? Did the interruption produce a feeling of tension, an urge to return to the unfinished task? This need for "closure" helps us remember uncompleted tasks. Better memory for uncompleted tasks is called the **Zeigarnik effect,**

after its discoverer. B. Zeigarnik (1927) had subjects engage in a number of tasks like naming 12 cities beginning with the letter K, stringing beads, and solving various types of puzzles. Sometimes she permitted the subjects to complete the tasks they were working on; at other times, the subjects were interrupted and prevented from completing the tasks. Later, Zeigarnik found, subjects tended to remember more of the tasks that they left uncompleted than the tasks they did complete. She assumed that this result reflected a form of psychic tension that persists whenever a striving for completeness is frustrated. This is much like the Gestalt notion that, in visual perception, we tend to close gaps and see incomplete figures as whole (see Chapter 5). Zeigarnik's subjects, however, were probably only mildly motivated to work on the tasks assigned. This effect is reversed when motivation is high and when the interruption is interpreted by the subject as indicating personal inadequacy. Then motivated remembering becomes motivated forgetting, and uncompleted tasks are remembered less well than completed tasks (S. Rosenzweig, 1941).

THE PHYSIOLOGY OF MEMORY

Another way to understand memory is to study the way the brain functions in storing information and retrieving it minutes, hours, or even years later. This sort of study must identify the areas of the brain that are involved in memory and the way they operate. Physiological approaches to studying memory are based on a mechanistic view of the nervous system, which assumes that a physical change of some kind takes place in the brain whenever new information is stored. The following analogy illustrates this assumption: Before your course in psychology began, you probably got a blank notebook intended for class notes. As the course progressed, you added more and more notes to your notebook, storing information in the physical form of writing on the pages. The pages of the notebook are like the areas of the brain that store memories, and the writing on the pages is like the physical changes in the brain by which information is stored.

Memory storage is only part of the total memory process. To be useful, a memory must be retrievable when needed. Are the areas of the brain that are involved in memory storage also involved in "reading" the stored information, or retrieval, or are different brain structures involved? How do these brain structures locate and activate specific memories? At this time, only crude answers to these questions are available.

Cortical Involvement

One of the first psychologists systematically to examine brain mechanisms during learning and memory was Karl Lashley (1929). He was particularly interested in determining what areas of the brain are involved in learning and memory mechanisms. Lashley agreed with most psychologists that complex mental activities, such as learning, memory, and reasoning, are functions of the cortex, since there is a strong correlation between ability to engage in these activities and amount of cortex in various animal species. Animals with very little cortex, such as reptiles, are extremely limited in their learning and memory abilities, while humans, with more cortex relative

to body size than any other animal, are most proficient in higher mental processes.

When Lashley began his investigations, around 1920, researchers knew that the cortex is organized so that sensory and motor functions are localized in specific regions. The remaining cortical area, called the "association cortex," was believed to play a primary role in complex mental activities. Lashley tested the hypothesis that memory traces, which he called **engrams,** are stored in the association cortex. His approach was to destroy surgically parts of the cortex of rats previously trained in tasks of various degrees of difficulty and then to observe the effect of this surgical destruction on recall of the task. If the destroyed area of the cortex contained the site of the engram, the specific cell or cells involved with it, or if the damage interrupted a specific neural pathway involved in the memory trace, then it would be expected that the animal would not be able to recall the learned task. Results showed that, aside from the particular sensory and motor areas directly involved with the task, the particular area of the cortex destroyed was not as important as the *amount* of cortex destroyed. Destroying 15 per cent of the parietal association cortex had about the same effect as destroying 15 per cent of the frontal cortex. If large amounts of any area were destroyed, recall of the task was lost. Similar results have been obtained in studies of monkeys and other animals. Most researchers today agree with Lashley's conclusion that there are no specific neural pathways or special cells reserved for storage of specific memories. Probably vast areas of the association cortex involving thousands or millions of neurons are involved with establishing a single new engram.

When damage occurs to a small cortical area, the remaining areas of the cortex usually function well enough to produce no observable behavioral changes. In humans, rather extensive damage of the association areas of the cortex produced by strokes, tumors, or other misfortunes often produces relatively little change in general intelligence or in learning and memory abilities of the afflicted individual. Most signs of damage to the association cortex are changes in mood, such as euphoria or facetiousness. These clinical results agree with laboratory results suggesting that memory engrams are not stored in specific locations in the cortex.

However, some fascinating observations by a famous neurosurgeon, Wilder Penfield, cast some doubt on the conclusion that there is no localization of memory function in specific cortical areas (Penfield, 1958). At the time of his observations, Penfield was engaged in brain surgery involving mild electrical stimulation of the surface of the cortex as a means of locating damaged tissue. Since the brain is not sensitive to pain, these operations could be performed with the patient completely conscious and capable of reporting the experience. Penfield found that electrical stimulation of specific sites of the temporal cortex triggered the recall of specific memories. Patients reported such memories as "I was on a street corner in South Bend, Indiana, corner of Jacob and Washington"; "I was listening to music from *Guys and Dolls*"; "I heard a mother calling her little boy somewhere—it was somebody in the neighborhood where I live"; "I just saw lots of big wagons that they use to haul animals in." Changing the location of the stimulus caused a different memory to come into the patient's consciousness (see Figure 10-10). The reported memories were similar to spontaneous memories except that they were more vivid. The patient reported that the memories were familiar, based on past experiences. In many cases, however, the evoked memories were not particularly significant to the patients, nor had they been current in their thoughts.

These findings suggest that the temporal cortex plays a special role in memory mechanisms, although our understanding of the nature of that role is incomplete. Memory traces

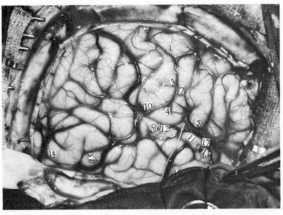

Figure 10-10 Exposed right cerebral cortex of surgical patient. Points 11, 12, 13, and 17 produced memories when simulated. (Penfield, 1958)

seem to be located either in the temporal cortex or in some other region of the brain that may be stimulated by the temporal cortex. Yet destruction of moderate-sized cortical areas, including the temporal lobe, does not interfere with the recall of specific memories.

Perhaps the most interesting question posed by these findings is whether we ever really forget anything we once experienced. Penfield's patients recalled scenes and events that they had presumably forgotten years earlier. Although they might have been unable to recall these distant memories voluntarily, the memories seem to have been permanently stored in their brains.

Hippocampal Functions

Another type of brain damage, this time in a region of the brain below the temporal cortex called the **hippocampus,** points to the importance of this region for normal memory function. When extensive hippocampal damage has occurred—for example, from strokes—severe disturbances in memory have resulted. Although the patients are able to recall memories formed before the hippocampal damage, they forget the incidents of their daily lives subsequent to the damage almost as fast as they occur. One such patient suspected that he had a problem because his wife left notes for him all over the house reminding him to do certain things. Although the patient's physician had explained his handicap to him, he was unable to remember the explanation or, for that matter, that he had been having difficulty with his memory (Victor, Angevine, Mancall, & Fisher, 1961). The hippocampally damaged patient seems to suffer from an inability to transfer information from short- to long-term memory. Memory retrieval mechanisms, however, seem to be independent of the hippocampus, since patients have no trouble in recalling previously established memories. Numerous animal experiments have confirmed that hippocampal damage produces a memory deficit. The extent of deficit is greater in primates than in lower animals like rats and cats.

Changes in Synapses

What kinds of changes might occur in the brain during memory formation? Many researchers today believe that the establishment of a memory trace in long-term memory involves some kind of permanent increase in the effectiveness of the synapses that interconnect the neurons participating in the storage of that trace. Facilitation at any given synapse during memory formation might occur in a number of ways. The amount of chemical transmitter released at the synapse might increase so that chemical excitation is more efficient, or the receiving cell may become more sensitive to the released chemical. A change in the structure of the synapse might occur. More or larger synapses might be formed, or the width of the synaptic gap between cells might be reduced so that the chemical transmitter more readily crosses the synapse. Data bearing on these hypotheses are difficult to obtain. The brain is a highly complex structure with billions of cells, and it is not known which ones are involved in the establishment of any given mem-

ory trace. Only very recently have microscopic photographs of brain tissue been obtained with the detail needed to observe ultrastructure changes in neurons and their synapses.

Since looking for neurons participating in the storage of a specific memory trace is like looking for that well-known needle in a haystack, some investigators have attempted to observe brain changes in animals that have had drastic differences in experience (Rosenzweig, Bennett, & Diamond, 1972). If the long-term memory of an experience consists of a permanent modification of neural pathways in the brain, then comparing the brains of animals having many or few different kinds of experience should reveal some differences in brain structure and chemistry. To this end, some rats were reared in enriched environments, cages furnished with an ever changing variety of objects with which to play. Other rats were reared in impoverished environments—solitary confinement in bare cages equipped only with food and water (see Figure 10-11). At the end of the experimental period (which lasted up to several months), the rats were sacrificed and their brains compared. Both anatomical and chemical differences were found in the brains of the two groups of rats. Rats with enriched experiences had a heavier cerebral cortex, greater thickness of cortex, larger cortical neurons, larger (but fewer) synapses per neuron, and greater total activity of acetylcholinesterase, a chemical involved in the metabolism of the synaptic transmitter, acetylcholine.

The lives of these experimental animals differed in more respects than variety of activity, however. Animals in the impoverished environments were less active, were handled less by the experimenters, and were more likely to have suffered isolation stress. It is possible that any one or all of these factors caused the observed brain differences, rather than learning and memory factors. The investigators tested this possibility by comparing animals that differed with respect to each factor: high

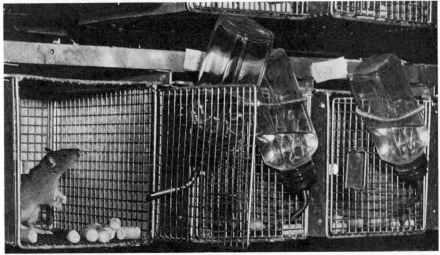

Figure 10-11 Enriched (top) and impoverished (bottom) environments that produce physical differences in brains of litter-mate rats. (Bennett, Diamond, Krech, & Rosenzweig, 1964; courtesy of Mark Rosenzweig)

activity versus low activity, intensive handling versus no handling, and social (several animals per cage) versus isolation conditions. None of these factors alone produced brain change. The investigators concluded, therefore, that the brain differences observed in the original experiments must have been due to differences in the number and complexity of the learning experiences of rats in enriched versus impoverished environments.

Another line of experimentation has shown that drug-induced changes in the amount of chemical transmitter at the synapse produces a change in memory. Giving animals drugs that block transmission at synapses utilizing acetylcholine produces a deficit in retention of previously learned behaviors (Deutsch & Deutsch, 1973). In these experiments, rats were trained to escape electric shock in the initial segment of a Y-maze by turning into the lighted arm of the maze. If the animal made an incorrect response by choosing the darkened arm of the maze, it received another shock. At a specified interval following learning of the discrimination, animals were injected with the drug and tested for retention of the correct response. Presumably the drug, absorbed into the brain after the injection, reduced chemical transmission at all acetylcholine-type synapses, including any that may have been involved with the established memory trace.

The use of other drugs that alter acetylcholine transmission demonstrated consistently that increasing acetylcholine transmission to an optimum level facilitates retention of previously learned behaviors, while decreasing transmission impairs retention (Deutsch & Deutsch, 1973). The researchers concluded that memory mechanisms involve an increase in the amount of transmitter available at acetylcholine-type synapses or an increase in sensitivity to acetylcholine in the neurons composing the engram. This animal research is consistent with the clinical observation that the acetylcholine-blocking drug scopolamine produces what used to be called, with great inaccuracy, "twilight sleep," characterized by no loss of consciousness or sensation but little retention of events occurring during the time the drug is effective.

Nevertheless, progress in this area of research has been slow. There are numerous chemical transmitters in the brain, and full understanding of the way they might be involved in memory has not yet been achieved. Perhaps the most surprising result has been the observation that learning and memory frequently are *unimpaired* by gross alterations of chemical transmitters known to be important for normal brain functioning.

Functions of Giant Molecules

Another current hypothesis concerning the physiology of memory is that memories are stored in the giant molecules of ribonucleic acid (RNA) or protein in neurons. You may remember from Chapter 2 that DNA is the genetic material of a cell that carries hereditary information. Structural and behavioral traits characteristic of a given species, called species memories, are coded in the sequence of fractions of the DNA molecule, or four-letter alphabet, described in Chapter 2. RNA in the cell serves the intermediate function of translating the genetic instructions from DNA into specific cellular activities. DNA guides the formation of RNA with a matching sequence of letters of the genetic alphabet. The specific RNA formed determines the synthesis of specific proteins. Proteins govern the specialization and activity of the cell by regulating all its chemical processes.

Although DNA itself is generally believed to be unchanged by the particular experiences of a cell, there is evidence that RNA may change. Several experiments have reported an increase in amount of RNA and a change in the ratio of fractions, or letters, of the RNA molecule, producing "new" RNA, following training in animals. Rats reared in enriched environments have more RNA than rats from impoverished environments (Rosenzweig et al., 1972). In another study (Hydén & Egyházi, 1964) rats were forced to reach for food in a narrow tube using their nonpreferred paws. After the rats had repeatedly used their nonpreferred paws for several days, an analysis of the rats' brains showed an increase in amount of RNA and a change in its composition in the learning cortex—that is, the motor cortex in the hemisphere opposite to the trained-paw side of the body—compared to the control cortex, the same cortical area in the other hemisphere.

Interference with protein synthesis by the administration of appropriate drugs to animals prevents the retention of previously learned behaviors (for example, Agranoff, 1967). Yet the way these observations relate to memory mechanisms is still not clearly understood. Perhaps RNA and protein alterations govern changes in the cell's synaptic relationship to other cells. This possibility ties in with the previously discussed idea that memory involves an increase in the effectiveness of synapses involved in the memory trace. Other possibilities exist, however. For example, Holger Hydén suggests that proteins may serve the critical role of determining whether a given stimulus or input to the neuron will cause release of that cell's chemical transmitter (Hydén, 1967). Presumably the protein would allow transmitter release only when the same meaningful input to the cell that corresponded with past experience occurred (see Figure 10-12). This model postulates that memory storage is mediated by protein-controlled release of chemical transmitter at selective synapses involved in the memory trace. It does not require the assumption that a physical change takes place at specified synaptic locations.

Memory Consolidation

The formation of a memory involves a labile (unstable) period, varying within the range of several minutes to several days, depending on the situation. During this period the **consolidation** of the experience into permanent or long-term memory is susceptible to disruption from external sources. It was first noted that severe blows to the head frequently produced amnesia (lack of recall) of events immediately preceding the blow, but not of earlier events. Presumably the blow momentarily disrupts ongoing brain activity. **Electroconvulsive shock (ECS),** a brief electrical shock to the brain of an intensity producing convulsions, also disrupts memories of events immediately preceding the shock. ECS is used for the treatment of some severe mental disorders (see Chapter 16).

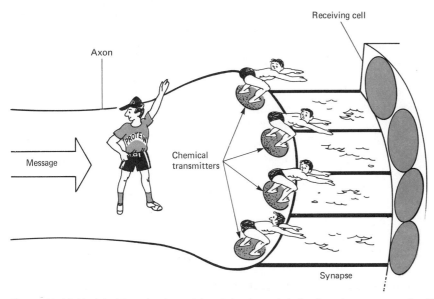

Figure 10-12 Model of the role of special proteins formed during learning on neuronal activity. Proteins may direct the release of chemical transmitters when a previously experienced input reaches the cell.

Laboratory experiments with animals have demonstrated that ECS, **hypothermia** (reduced body temperature), **hypoxia** (reduced oxygen to the brain), and certain drugs, all of which disrupt ongoing brain activity, impair memory in animals when the procedure occurs during a critical interval following learning. In a typical experiment, Carl Duncan (1949) trained rats to avoid shock to the feet in a shuttlebox. The animals received one trial per day for 18 days, and each experimental animal received ECS following each day's trial. The time interval between the training trial and ECS ranged from 20 seconds to 14 hours for the 8 experimental groups. Testing occurred at a constant interval following training for all groups. Rats given ECS 20 seconds, 40 seconds, 4 minutes, or 15 minutes following each trial learned to avoid the foot shock more slowly than did rats not given ECS at all, and also more slowly than rats given ECS 2 to 14 hours after each trial.

What is going on during the critical interval following learning that makes memories so vulnerable to disruption? Donald Hebb (1949) has suggested that following an experience there is a continuing reverberation of neural activity in the areas of the brain stimulated by the experience. "Reverberation of neural activity" is a concept that assumes that neural activity in a closed loop of cells excited by a stimulus continues to circulate or bounce around for a brief period after stimulation. Repetition of the neural activity is somehow necessary for memory of that experience to be stored as a physical change in the brain. If the neural activity is disrupted—by ECS, for example—the memory will not be consolidated into a permanent form.

As previously mentioned, the hippocampus seems to be important for the consolidation of memories from short-term to long-term memory. Destruction of the hippocampus produces a deficit whereby memories are retained only a few minutes, never to be transferred to the long-term form. It is hoped that answers to the question of how the hippocampus functions during consolidation, and other equally important questions like how the brain locates specific memories, will be forthcoming with continued research.

SUMMARY

Memory is the ability to reproduce previously learned verbal or motor behaviors, and forgetting is the loss of this ability. Memory is measured by recognition (identifying the correct responses), free recall (producing the correct responses), or savings in relearning the original responses. The degree of remembering (or forgetting) varies with the method of measurement used.

The more material is overlearned beyond the point of mastery, the better the material will be remembered. Distributed practice in learning makes for better remembering than massed practice. Self-recitation (or active rehearsal) of material, thinking about concepts and examples, and looking for interconnections among ideas aid memory more than merely learning by rote. Making the material personally meaningful and associating it with familiar material also retards forgetting.

The disuse theory of forgetting is inconsistent with evidence that people clearly recall experiences of long ago and that well-learned skills require only brief exercise to regain former levels of proficiency. There is greater evidence in favor of interference theories of forgetting, which hold that memory is impaired because of interference between the effects of materials learned at different times. "Retroactive interference" refers to the disruptive effect of material learned after the original learning. "Proactive interference" refers to the forgetting of recently learned material as a result of the interference produced by earlier learning.

Organizational theories of forgetting, based on information processing models, distinguish between brief sensory storage, short-term memory in which constant rehearsal is required for recall, and long-term memory processes. Various coding strategies are used in transferring material from short-term to long-term memory, such as chunking, clustering, and making hierarchical trees in accordance with classification systems.

Some coding strategies are used in reverse order in retrieving memories. Mnemonic devices, like acronyms and the method of loci, are also very effective as aids to retrieval. The tip-of-the-tongue phenomenon has shown that retrieval of memories is an active, complex process.

Motivational theories of forgetting postulate an active process in which anxiety-arousing ideas are kept from entering consciousness by such defense mechanisms as repression.

Actual physiological traces of memories, or engrams, in the cortex have not been identified. In fact, large areas of association cortex may be involved in memory, although the temporal cortex appears to be a key memory area. The hippocampus plays a role in the consolidation of long-term memories.

Drugs blocking synaptic transmission affect the retention of previously learned behavior. Drugs that block protein synthesis also interfere with retention. One hypothesis is that RNA molecules or proteins produced by RNA are involved in memory. Changes in brain RNA have been measured following training in animals. Electroconvulsive shock to the brain seems to prevent the consolidation of recent events in long-term memory, perhaps by interfering with reverberation of neural activity in closed loops of nerve cells. The specific physiological processes accompanying storage and retrieval of memories, however, have not yet been discovered.

NOW IT'S UP TO YOU

1. Discuss the questions with which this chapter opened in the light of your current understanding of learning and memory.
2. Think of some group of items, concepts, or principles that you learned for a course or for some other reason during the last week or two. Without referring back to your source, jot down as many of these items as you can right now. Using the free-recall method of measuring your memory of the group, check back with the source to see what proportion of the group you recalled now. Then relearn the group of items, counting the time or the number of times or trials you use to do so. To get a rough estimate of your savings score, compare the time or trials you spent relearning the items with the time or trials you probably used originally. Does the relearning method give you a better score than the recall method?
3. Try the method of loci to memorize the following hypothetical shopping list:

Nails	Steak	Pencils
Gum	Cookies	Newspaper
Tomatoes	Aspirin	Bread
Napkins	Pincers	Soup
Potatoes	Shoes	Asparagus

Immediately after you have identified the items on the list with loci, recall the list. Try recalling it again tomorrow. Do you make out as well as the students in the experiment described?

Answer to the tip-of-the-tongue problem in the activity box on p. 284: sampan.

11

Mediation,
Problem Solving,
and Creativity

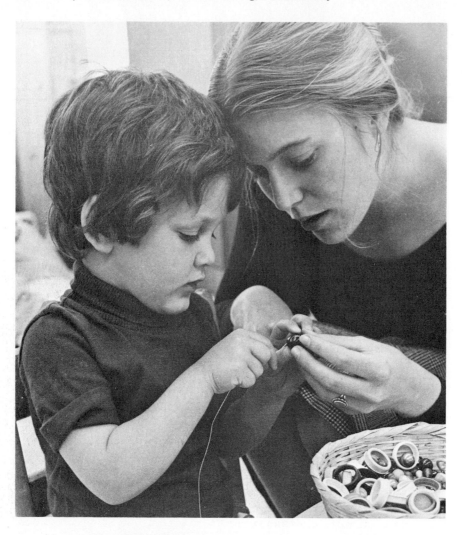

OBSERVE LANGUAGE AT WORK

■ You can have immediate contact with the content of this chapter by responding to a few words. Take the word *cow* as a stimulus word, and note all the other words that come to your mind at once in association with it. Somehow you have a whole series of other words, thoughts, images, and feelings associated with the word. Probably you even think of events or stories related to cows.

Now if you are female take the word *man*, and if you are male take the word *woman*. Write the word on a sheet of paper and then list all the other words that come to your mind. When this **free** **association,** as it is called, starts to slow down, go back to the original word, *man* or *woman,* and start over again on another line of free association. Probably you have myriad associations with these words, some expressing thoughts, some images and feelings, some attitudes or even prejudices about men or women. Whether you are black or white, you can look into your emotionalized attitudes or prejudices by taking the words *blacks* and *whites* as they relate to people and seeing what positive and/or negative associations you have with them. Compare your lists of associations. What do they have to tell you?

With the aid of language and other symbols, images, and feelings, you carry on covert, private processes of thinking and imagining within yourself. How would you suggest they should be studied?

■ **CAN YOU ANSWER THESE?**

Mediational Processes

What is the meaning of meaning?
How do organisms use meaning?
How are meanings involved in prejudices?

Problem Solving

What are problems and how are they solved?
What factors are likely to increase or decrease the efficiency of problem solving?

Creativity

Is creativity an innate talent with which some people are endowed, or does everyone have it?
Think of as many unusual uses for newspapers as you can. Are you being creative?
Have you found that you become less or more creative year by year?

Mediation by symbols, problem solving, and thinking creatively are all processes that seem to go on inside us somehow. The phrase "A penny for your thoughts" indicates that the other person's thoughts are not immediately observable. These inner thought processes are called **covert processes** to distinguish them from **overt processes,** or responses or activities that are observable by everyone. The thoughts you are having now are covert or private, known only to yourself, but if you express them by speaking them to someone else they become linked to overt, public behavior. As you will see, language plays an important role in symbolizing, problem solving, and thinking—even in the development of prejudices.

MEDIATIONAL PROCESSES

Processes like thinking, planning, and problem solving are called **mediational processes** because they mediate between environmental stimuli and observable responses, serving as a means of guiding or selecting the appropriate responses to the given stimuli. In earlier chapters the relationships between external (overt) unconditioned and conditioned stimuli and responses have been discussed. Here we turn to the covert processes that sometimes occur after an external stimulus has been presented and before an overt response occurs.

Suppose that you have taken several cans of food in your knapsack on a long mountain hike. Hungry, hot, and weary, you build a fire, take out the cans, and search the knapsack and your pockets for the can opener you customarily carry. It isn't there. You look for a knife, a hatchet, but still find nothing. Won't you go into some rapid covert activities to mediate an adequate response to the situation in which you find yourself? Such internal cognitive activities are part of what we call "thinking." Any description of human behavior that was restricted solely to overt responses and failed to take into account these mediational processes would be enormously limited. You have seen how transfer and retroactive and proactive inhibition can be explained in large measure by simple mechanisms of habit competition between stimuli and responses. Something more is obviously needed, however, to explain the mediational processes in which language and other symbols are usually involved.

Secondary (Mediated) Stimulus Generalization

Primary or **stimulus generalization** occurs in both classical and operant conditioning, as you have seen in Chapter 7. Thus children apply the word "dog" not only to the family pet, but also to other similar creatures, large and small, black and white and brown, particularly when they hear the animals bark. If children's relations with dogs have been friendly, they are prepared to respond by patting any dog they see; the same responses—speaking the word "dog," moving closer to pat the dog—have generalized to many slightly different stimuli. Certain physical similarities between the stimuli underlie this type of stimulus generalization.

Another kind of stimulus generalization can be demonstrated by an experiment with words and mild electric shocks. K. E. Diven (1937) gave his subjects a shock whenever he presented a stimulus word like *cow*. The shocks caused an unconditioned galvanic skin response (GSR). After a few pairings with shock, the word *cow* became a conditioned stimulus for the GSR. Then came the interesting part of the experiment. When other "rural" words were presented to the subjects—*barn, milk, farm*—these words also elicited a GSR (see Figure 11-1). The original conditioned response to the stimulus *cow* had somehow generalized to other words usually found in rural contexts, not simply to other physically related or physically similar stimuli. This process, called secondary or **mediated generalization,** is based upon a similarity in the meaning of stimuli; that is, what they stand for or represent. The stimuli are semantically related.

Mediated generalization was confirmed in another, more elaborate study of college psychology students (M. T. Mednick, 1957). The students were divided by means of an anxiety test into low- and high-anxiety groups. Then they were individually conditioned to the word *light,* paired with a loud, raucous noise transmitted to the subjects via earphones from a tape recorder. Soon the word *light* elicited the GSR response in the subjects. Word-association tests have shown that people most frequently associate the word *light* with the words *dark, lamp, heavy,* and *soft.* Sure enough, when these words with closely associated meanings were presented to the subjects, they responded with elevated GSRs, just as they had to the word *light,* although the generalized responses were weaker. The high-anxiety group responded more strongly to each of the associated words than did the low-anxiety

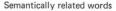

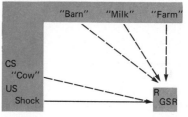

Figure 11-1 The stimulus of the word "cow" rapidly becomes a conditioned stimulus (CS) for a galvanic skin response (R$_{GSR}$) when paired with the unconditioned stimulus (US) of a shock. Words with similar meanings then tend to arouse the same response, illustrating secondary, or mediated, stimulus generalization.

group, but neither group responded with GSRs to unassociated words like *square.* They had generalized the response to words with associated meanings, even though the physical properties of the words—that is, the way they sounded—were quite different.

Other experiments have shown that similar meanings, rather than similar sounds, of words account for mediated generalization. In one experiment, Gregory Razran (1939) conditioned subjects to salivate at the sight of the words *style, urn, freeze,* and *surf.* He found that they generalized the salivary response more to the sight of the words *fashion, vase, chill,* and *wave,* words with similar meanings, than to the sight of words that sound similar: *stile, earn, frieze,* and *serf.* Razran (1961) also reported a Russian experiment in which the generalization of conditioning of normal schoolchildren to the Russian word *koshka* (cat) was compared with that of mentally retarded children of about the same age. The normal children generalized their conditioning only to semantically related words, like *sobaka* (dog) and *zhivotnoye* (animal), while very retarded children generalized only to words having similar sounds, like *dryshka* (cover) and *kroshka* (crumb). Less seriously retarded children showed a little mediated generalization, but not as much as the normal children.

Apparently, then, the mediational processes are more highly developed in normal than in retarded persons and vary in degree. The most common form of generalization in language is this secondary mediated variety between stimuli that have the same or similar meanings or associations. But what does "meaning" mean? Must we fall back upon subjective or introspective psychology in trying to describe the representation or symbolization involved in meaning? Perhaps, but before we succumb to this expedient, let's see what some other experiments have to offer.

Delayed or Mediated Reactions

You have seen how mediational processes often occur between overt stimuli and responses. In 1913 an American psychologist, Walter Hunter, developed a **delayed-reaction experiment** to see what would happen when the time between stimulus and response was lengthened (Hunter, 1913). He placed hungry rats in an enclosure within a box having a grid floor for shocks and several exits with light bulbs that the rats could see (see Figure 11-2). Then a light went on before one exit. The rat found food if it chose the lighted exit, but was shocked if it chose one of the other exits. Soon the light became a discriminative stimulus (S^D) for the correct response (R), running to the lighted door. Then the light at one of the exits went on and off, but the rat was confined to the enclosure and could not approach the exit. After a delay, the rat was freed from the enclosure. Hunter found that rats would choose the exit that had been lighted even after a delay of up to 10 seconds between stimulus and response.

Further studies showed that raccoons still could choose the exit that had been lighted after delays of up to 15 seconds, while dogs could be delayed up to three minutes, and five-year-old children could make correct

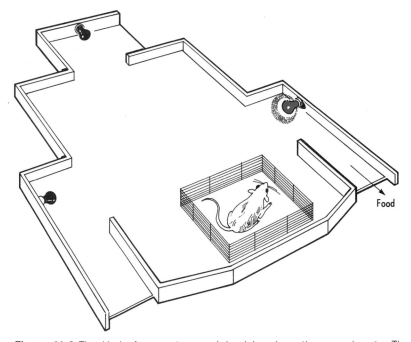

Figure 11-2 The kind of apparatus used in delayed-reaction experiments. The animal placed in the release box (lower center) can see the lights at the three exits from the apparatus. One of the lights is turned on and then off, and after an interval of time the animal is released. (Hunter, 1913)

choices after delays of 20 minutes or more (Munn, 1950). What was going on during the delay? Why were some subjects capable of dealing with longer delay than others?

Hunter figured that some intermediary process must have occurred during the delay. He noted that the rats responded correctly only when their heads and bodies were kept oriented during the delay toward the exit that had been lighted. Apparently this directional posture was a response (r) that provided rats with continuing kinesthetic, or proprioceptive, stimuli (s), to which they responded by moving toward the correct door when they were freed from the enclosure. **Proprioceptive stimuli** indicating posture and movement of the limbs come to the central nervous system from the joints and muscles. These postural responses (r) and the proprioceptive stimuli (s) they generate must then have been the implicit mediating processes for the rats. The overt stimulus of the light (S^D) evoked the postural response (r), which was maintained until the rat was freed, setting off proprioceptive stimuli (s), which produced the final overt response (R) of running toward the door that had been lighted. The development of the postural mediating mechanism is shown in Figure 11-3.

But raccoons and dogs did not need to maintain a fixed directional posture in order to choose the correct exit. And children could move about and turn around freely during the delay after seeing the light and still go eventually to the correct exit. The higher animals and human children must have used implicit processes or intermediaries (r → s) other than postural behavior and its associated cues to cover the delay between stimulus and response.

In further investigations, Hunter and others used **double-alternation mazes** that require some sort of mediating element (see Figure 11-4). The correct solution of this maze requires two right turns (RR) from the starting point followed by two left turns (LL) before the reward is obtained. On the second right or left turn, subjects simply retrace their course, so

Training conditions:

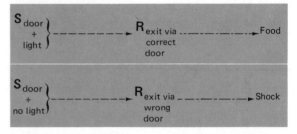

Result of training:

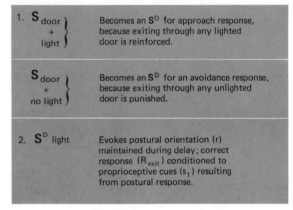

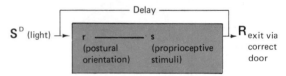

Figure 11-3 A hypothetical postural-mediation mechanism in a rat in the Hunter delayed-reaction task.

there is no external cue in the maze itself that tells the subjects which way to turn next. Somehow they have to run through an RRLL pattern (or even more complex courses like RRLLRR or RLRRLR). Only a few rats can solve the simplest of such mazes (RRLL), even after an extensive series of trials. Raccoons manage to solve RRLL, however, and monkeys can handle several more alternations. Human beings can solve much more complex combinations by learning a set of verbal cues, such as saying, "Right, right, left, left," thus keeping in mind just what alternations have to be made.

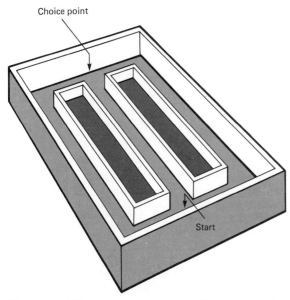

Figure 11-4 The arrangement of the double-alternation maze. In an LLRR task, the animal starts up the middle lane, turns left at the top, goes around and up the middle lane again, turns left a second time at the choice point, going counterclockwise again, then makes two clockwise runs by executing two right turns at the choice point. (Hunter, 1931)

These delayed-reaction and double-alternation experiments have shown that the mediating process can be, as in rats, some sort of proprioceptive response (r) that in turn provides a stimulus (s) that eventually produces the correct response. In higher animals the mediating process is more likely some central nervous system activity that symbolizes, or represents, the location of the previously lighted exit, or the number of left turns already completed, or a set of instructions for driving through a city. The symbolic process retained in raccoons, dogs, and monkeys may perhaps be some sort of image. And we know that symbolic language processes are used by human beings in solving such problems by retaining words or other symbols that stand for stimulus and response events and then letting the words cue appropriate behavior.

Human beings can also use images, as well as verbal processes, and can retain them over long periods of time. Suppose your uncle gives you directions for getting to his new home: "Turn left at the stoplight and then make a right just after you pass a big red barn." You might retain these instructions verbally, "Left at stoplight and right after barn," or you might use an image of a road going left at a stoplight and another road branching right beyond a red barn. Experiments have shown that human subjects use both types of intermediaries in delayed-response tasks requiring mediating processes. The main point is that we don't simply record the effects of external stimulation; we also elaborate on them, retain them in coded or symbolic form, modify them, and add the effects of other symbolic processes to the input from stimulation. Then these mediational processes affect our eventual overt responses (see cartoon).

THE GIRLS   Franklin Folger

"Now you don't want a parfait—it's loaded with calories. But I only had one piece of toast with my breakfast and hardly any butter. Well then, go ahead."

Acquisition of Meaning by Conditioning

Delayed-reaction and double-alternation experiments imply that implicit covert responses and their stimulus properties are critical for understanding complex mediational processes. The variety of response-produced stimuli or cues that can be used has been demonstrated in many experiments. In one experiment with human subjects (N. E. Miller, 1951), a visual stimulus consisting of the presentation of the letter T was paired with shock, producing a galvanic skin response (R_{GSR}). After the GSR had been conditioned to the sight of T, hearing someone pronounce the letter T produced the same GSR. It is assumed that the visual conditioned stimulus (CS) triggered an internal process (fear? tension?) mediating the GSR reaction; the internal process must have had something in common with the internal process triggered by the sound CS, for the latter also elicited the GSR. (Hearing other letters spoken did not produce a GSR.) To go one step further, having the subjects merely think of or visualize the letter T also produced a GSR. Images or thoughts of other letters did not. Obviously, the internal processes mediating the GSR—whether triggered by an external visual stimulus, an auditory stimulus, an image, or a thought—must have shared some common property, some similarity in "meaning." Similarity in mediated generalization is not in the instructions either ("Think of T" or "Imagine T"), but in the implicit response processes.

With this explanation in mind, you can now go back to Figure 11-1, which showed that after the GSR had been conditioned to the word *cow*, the conditioned response (CR) also generalized to other farm words. You can now see that semantic generalization occurs because of similarities in the properties of implicit responses aroused by the conditioned word stimulus (*cow*) and by related test words (*barn, milk, farm*). The implicit responses may consist of farm-related images, thoughts, or even feelings, or any combination of these. Why do certain groups of sights and sounds come to yield similar implicit responses? Presumably because various past experiences have taught the subject that there is a strong relationship between cows, barns, and milk, and many other rural things as well.

You may wonder whether it is proper to invoke past experience with a class of objects, and the words referring to them, in order to explain mediational processes. Are we not assuming a great deal about an unknown factor, past experience, when we suggest that implicit mediational processes come to develop similar properties because they have been associated in the past? This assumption could be proved, however, if we could experimentally control associations and show that a previously neutral stimulus can acquire a property common to other words through experience. Such an experiment has actually been carried out (Staats & Staats, 1957). You will recognize that certain words, like *beauty, healthy,* and *happy,* have a pleasant meaning, while other words, like *thief, poison,* and *fear,* have an unpleasant meaning. On the other hand, nonsense syllables like *yof* and *xeh* are more or less neutral, without any meanings for you. They arouse no pleasant or unpleasant reactions. As diagrammed in Figure 11-5, *yof* was paired with many words that arouse pleasure. In some trials the subject experienced *yof* paired with *beauty,* in others with *healthy,* and so on. It was assumed that all the pleasant words would function like unconditioned stimuli, each producing a pleasant implicit response (r_p). Through a procedure resembling classical conditioning, the nonsense syllable *yof* also came to elicit the pleasant implicit response (r_p)—that is, it acquired a pleasant connotation. Conversely, the nonsense syllable *xeh* was repeatedly paired with words that arouse displeasure (*thief, poison, fear*). Again, *xeh* became conditioned to evoke an unpleasant implicit response (r_u) common to the words

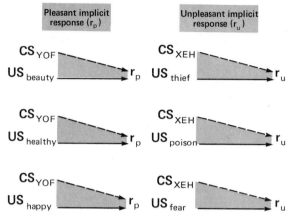

Pleasant implicit response (r_p)   Unpleasant implicit response (r_u)

CS_{YOF}
US_{beauty} ⟶ r_p CS_{XEH}
US_{thief} ⟶ r_u

CS_{YOF}
$US_{healthy}$ ⟶ r_p CS_{XEH}
US_{poison} ⟶ r_u

CS_{YOF}
US_{happy} ⟶ r_p CS_{XEH}
US_{fear} ⟶ r_u

Figure 11-5 One way in which pleasant or unpleasant meanings are conditioned to nonsense syllables by associating them with words that produce pleasant or unpleasant implicit responses. (Staats & Staats, 1957)

with which it had been paired. In a later study it was shown that the amount of pleasant or unpleasant meaning acquired by these originally neutral syllables depended on the number of times they were paired with words that normally arouse pleasure or displeasure. The greater the number of paired presentations, the more they picked up the pleasant or unpleasant implicit responses to the original words.

If a classical conditioning process can thus explain how words derive their meanings, then the same process should be applicable to the meanings of sentences. A Russian experiment, reported by Gregory Razran (1961), showed this very process at work in sentences. A 13-year-old boy named Yuri was conditioned to salivate profusely to the Russian word *khorosho* (well or good) and to differentiate it from the word *plokho* (poorly, badly, or bad). After this conditioning, he secreted 14 drops of saliva to the sentence *Khorosho uchenik otvechayet* (The student answers well) and only 3 drops to the sentence *Plokho vorobey poyot* (The sparrow sings poorly), so he had clearly discriminated between the meanings of the words in his response. The conditioning was effective, even when the stimu-

lus words were used in sentences. Then Yuri was tested with sentences that had good or bad meanings but that did not actually include the word *khorosho* or *plokho* (see Table 11-1). Yuri secreted much saliva when the meaning was good ("The enemy army was defeated and annihilated," trial 24), and very little saliva when the meaning was bad ("My friend is seriously ill," trial 23). Different sentences with entirely different objective meanings still evoked a common overt response when they had the same emotional meanings, which had generalized from the originally conditioned meanings of *khorosho* and *plokho*.

The meanings that words acquire through mediated generalization are called their **connotative meanings,** as opposed to the external stimulus objects or events to which words refer, called their denotative meanings. Thus the word "teacher" denotes any person who works in the teaching profession, while it connotes a certain complex concept that you have developed over the years as you have gone to school. The connotation of "teacher" may include such characteristics as friendly, helpful, wise, just, and informal, or it may include unfriendly, difficult, unjust, and ignorant. But how could you measure the connotations that various words like this actually have for many people? The meaningfulness of words has been measured in many ways, such as determining the number of associations aroused by a word in a given period of time, and the number of people who can give an association to a word in three seconds or less. The words normally associated with a given word can also be investigated to determine the meaning of words. It was in this way that the strong association between the word *light* and the words *dark, lamp, heavy,* and *soft* was determined.

Such methods are used to study the quantitative properties of meaning. The qualitative aspects of meaning have also been investigated, however, through a method called the semantic differential (Osgood, Suci, & Tannenbaum, 1957). The **semantic differential**

Table 11-1 Salivation of 13-Year-Old Boy to Various Words and Phrases After He Had Been Conditioned Positively to the Word *Khorosho* (Well, Good) and Negatively to the Word *Plokho* (Poorly, Badly, Bad)

Trial No.	Time of Experimentation		Words or Phrases Tested	Test No.	Saliv. Dps. in 30 Sec.
	Date	Exact Time			
1	6/26/52	11:20′00″	*khorosho*	47	9
2		11:25′15″	*Uchenik prekrasno zanimayet-sya* [The pupil studies excellently.]	1	14
3		11:29′15″	*Deti igrayut khorosho* [The children are playing well.]	1	19
4		11:31′15″	*plokho*	11	2
5		11:32′45″	*khorosho*	48	15
6		11:37′00″	*Sovet-skaya Armiya pobedila* [The Soviet Army was victorious.]	1	23
7		11:42′00″	*Uchenik nagrubil ychitel'nitse* [The pupil was fresh to the teacher.]	1	0
8		11:45′15″	*khorosho*	49	18
9		11:49′45″	*Pioner pomogayet tovarischu* [The pioneer helps his comrade.]	1	23
10	7/31/52	10:10′00″	*khorosho*	50	18
11		10:14′00″	*plokho*	12	1
12		10:17′00″	*khorosho*	51	16
13		10:21′00″	*Leningrad — zamechatel'ny gorod* [Leningrad is a wonderful city.]	1	15
14		10:24′30″	*Shkol'nik ne sdal ekzamen* [The pupil failed to take the examination.]	1	2
15		10:26′00″	*khorosho*	52	15
16		10:29′30″	*Brat obizhayet sestru* [Brother is insulting sister.]	1	1
17	8/1/52	11:20′00″	*khorosho*	54	12
18		11:25′30″	*Rybaky poymali mnogo ryby* [The fisherman caught many fish.]	1	18
19		11:31′30″	*Sovet-skaya konstitutsiya — samaya demokraticheskaya* [The Soviet Constitution is the most democratic (of all).]	1	17
20		11:36′30″	*Fashisty razrushili mnogo gorodov* [The Fascists destroyed many cities.]	1	2
21	8/1/52	11:40′30″	*Uchenik razbil steklo* [The pupil broke the glass.]	1	2
22		11:41′30″	*Sovet-sky narod lyubit svoyu Rodinu* [The Soviet people love their Motherland.]	1	17
23		11:45′30″	*Moy drug tyazhelo zabolel* [My friend is seriously ill.]	1	2
24		11:47′30″	*Vrazheskaya armiya byla razbita i unichtozhena* [The enemy army was defeated and annihilated.]	1	24
25		11:51′30″	*Uchenik sdal ekzamen na posredstvenno* [The pupil passed the examination with a mediocre grade.]	1	10

measures the qualitative feeling tone of words on seven-step scales of contrary adjectives, like "active–passive," "small–large," "good–bad," and "fresh–stale" (see Figure 11-6). Up to 50 bipolar scales of adjectives can be used to express the qualitative meanings of words in profiles like those shown in Figure 11-6 for the words *polite* and *burning*. Here a rating for both words of about 4 on the bipolar scale for "angular" and "rounded" shows that they are about neutral for this meaning, while at a scale value of 2 *polite* is very "good" and at a scale value of 5 *burning* is rather "bad." The ratings of many words on such semantic scales have revealed certain clusters of meanings of words around scales that express activity (active–passive), potency (strong–weak), and evaluation (good–bad). These three scale clusters represent significant dimensions of connotative meanings of words in a great variety of languages.

Divergent and Convergent Hierarchies

Verbal associations, clusters of words with similar meanings, and mediational generalization all point toward the great complexity of relations between words and the enormous flexibility that words give to behavior. When a word has been associated through implicit cue processes with some given response, there is a tendency for that word to elicit other similar and related responses. This tendency is called *response generalization,* as opposed to the stimulus generalization that we have been discussing. For example, the word "Fire!" or the sound of a fire-alarm bell in a school can lead to a whole series of responses that have been related to it by previous fire-drill training, such as standing up, forming a line with other students, and marching outdoors (see Figure 11-7). According to our analysis, the cry of "Fire!" produces a characteristic internal process (r_{fire}) whose cue properties (s_{fire}) are quite different from those of other internal states, like those set off by a lover's sigh or a rude

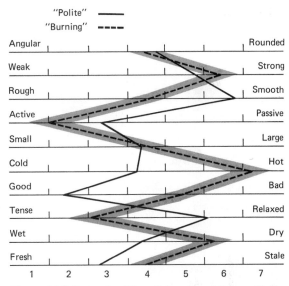

Figure 11-6 Semantic differential profile of the qualitative meanings of the words *polite* and *burning*, based on 10 bipolar adjective scales. (Osgood, 1952)

remark, for example. It is to these cue properties (s_{fire}) that appropriate behaviors, like orderly progress toward an exit or going to a lifeboat station aboard ship, are conditioned.

Since the same verbal stimulus gives rise to a number of associated responses, whether these are evoked separately on different occasions or in a series on one occasion, this is called a **divergent hierarchy** of responses. If a new word, like the Italian *incendio* or the French *feu*, is attached to the implicit cue process involved with "fire," then it immediately can assume command over the already established hierarchy of effective responses to "Fire!" No separate conditioning is necessary and great economy is achieved. Similarly, it's an easy matter to condition the implicit cue process to a nonverbal stimulus like a fire gong or bell. Only the single mediating process, not the many overt behaviors, needs to be conditioned to a new external signal.

Many general terms, like "ship," "car," and "airplane," can serve to evoke a large and divergent hierarchy of implicit response cues, or

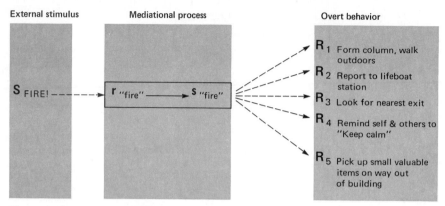

Figure 11-7 A divergent response hierarchy showing how the tendency acquired by an external stimulus (S_{fire}) to evoke any of a series of appropriate behaviors (R_1–R_5) is mediated by an internal process (r_{fire}) that has cue properties (s_{fire}).

meanings, depending on one's current circumstances and past experience. Although these hierarchies will vary from person to person, still they will have many characteristics in common. Ideally, if definitions are sound, they distinguish the objects referred to from all other objects of a similar nature.

The tendency for verbal stimuli, acting through a mediational process, to acquire control not only over a single response but also over a cluster of similar or related responses may help to explain the way in which prejudices function. For example, some people have strong prejudices against people on welfare or receiving public assistance for one reason or another. The stimulus of a person on welfare, or even the thought or discussion of such people, can then arouse an internal state to which many attitudinal responses concerning people on welfare are conditioned, as shown in Figure 11-8. Without objective evidence, those receiving welfare funds are often said to be lazy, to refuse work, to scheme for something for nothing, to be ignorant and childish, to be dishonest, and finally to be immoral in raising large (usually fatherless, it is assumed) families. But notice that, with perhaps a few variations, these characteristics are also frequently attributed by prejudiced people to members of racial or ethnic minority groups. These people too are often thought of as lazy, ignorant,

scheming, and dishonest, and treacherous besides. Such restricted and rigid clusters of standardized characteristics form the oversimplified images known as **stereotypes,** which often accompany emotionalized attitudes, or **prejudices,** toward members of various groups. Turning again to Figure 11-8, note how little it would take to attach the mediational process, and the host of prejudiced behaviors it controls, to an unknown person being introduced for the first time. If people have already been conditioned to respond negatively to people on welfare or to members of a minority group, all that is necessary is for the new person, S_2, to be perceived as a member of group S_1. Once the newcomer is identified with S_1, note how this person too evokes the mediational response.

Often prejudices against a minority are accompanied by the attribution of a cluster of physical characteristics to the minority, even though the objective study of many members of the minority group may reveal no such characteristics. Divergent hierarchies of responses to stimuli can then have disadvantageous and misleading functions as well as advantageous and genuine ones.

Convergent hierarchies of stimuli generalized to evoke the same response have already been dealt with in discussing the acquisition of meaning by words. We speak of a **convergent**

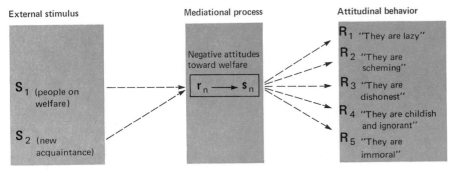

Figure 11-8 A divergent hierarchy showing how members of an economic or social group (people on welfare) evoke a negative internal state that mediates a variety of prejudiced (verbal) behavior. To the extent that a new acquaintance seems to share some of the properties of the original group, that person will mobilize the entire system of internal and overt prejudiced behavior.

hierarchy when a number of external stimuli become equally capable of acquiring control over the same mediational process and the response conditioned to it. Convergent hierarchies as well as divergent hierarchies operate in the expression of prejudices. A convergent set of stimuli that might evoke a person's dis-

approving responses toward young people of a rejected group, hippies, and a convergent set that might evoke the same person's approving responses toward youths of accepted groups are shown in Figure 11-9. The stimulus properties characterizing the hippie have usually been experienced together many times. Thus

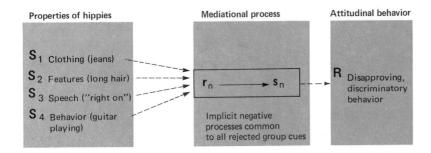

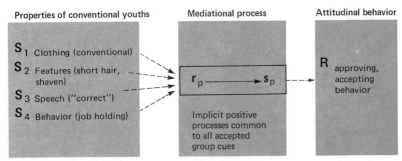

Figure 11-9 Two different convergent hierarchies of stimuli (S_1–S_4) evoke mediational processes that determine disapproving or approving responses (R) toward various youth groups.

any one of the stimuli characteristic of hippies could trigger the same implicit mediational process (r_h). Cues (s_h) associated with this process in turn evoke disapproving behavior. The lower portion of Figure 11-9 shows how any one of the several properties of conventional young people can, when encountered, take over, triggering a different, positive mediational process and approving or accepting behavior.

In recent years some customs formerly associated with hippies have spread widely among young people in our culture, and have even been adopted by many older people. To the dismay of barbers, many men over thirty wear their hair longer now, and let their beards grow. Still, many older people are unable to change their stereotypes, and have simply broadened their discriminatory reactions in a sweeping condemnation of most young people and a lot of older ones too.

An investigation of prejudice among some college students has shown how common stereotyped attitudes toward minority groups in general directly affected their judgments of the personal qualities of specific members of such minority groups (Razran, 1950). In the first stage of the investigation, the students rated 30 girls' photographs on five-point scales for beauty, intelligence, ambition, and character. In the second stage, two months later, the same students rated the same photographs, but this time fake surnames had been added, some of them Jewish (like Rabinowitz and Finkelstein), some Italian (like Scarano and Grisolia), and some English (like Adams). The general liking and beauty ratings for girls pictured with Jewish and Italian names went down and the ratings for ambition and intelligence of the girls pictured with Jewish names went up. Incidentally, some evidence indicates that the more prejudiced people are against Jews, the better they are able to distinguish between Jews and non-Jews (Allport & Kramer, 1946). Students identified as anti-Semitic on the basis of a prejudice scale were definitely more successful in distinguishing

Jewish from non-Jewish students in photographs. It must become important to anti-Semites to distinguish Jews, seeking out stimuli that are relevant to their prejudice; and the same process surely holds for people with other prejudices.

The mediation process, then, explains a great deal about our use of language and even helps to explain instances in which prejudiced responses emerge the moment a label or stimulus for membership in a minority group is identified, whether correctly or mistakenly. But perhaps the greatest role played by mediational processes is in problem solving.

PROBLEM SOLVING

Usually your behavior runs along smoothly as you perform a series of actions, complete them, and turn to others. Occasionally, however, you stop what you are doing, you hesitate, you begin to feel confused, your behavior becomes indecisive, and you don't know what to do. You are in a **problem situation.** You may have been asked a question that you can't answer. You may be thwarted from doing what you want to do. You may be confronting a new situation in which you don't know how to act. You have a problem, and you must set about solving it. How do you solve problems? Simply by subjective thinking or reasoning? What kinds of behavior or processes are involved in problem solving?

CAN YOU SOLVE THESE PROBLEMS?

■ Try solving the following problems in order to see how you behave when you are solving problems. If you are already familiar with one of them, turn to another. The important thing to observe is what happens to you and how you behave as you go at problem solving, not the solutions of the problems as such. They are rather difficult problems for most people, and usually they are not solved very quickly, although they are definitely soluble.

A. Nine dots are arranged in a square, as shown in Figure 11-10. Can you figure out how to connect all the dots by drawing just four straight, continuous lines without lifting your pen or pencil from the paper?

B. Six matches, shown in Figure 11-11, all of the same length, must be arranged together to form four congruent equilateral triangles, each side of which is formed by one match. Can you so arrange them?

C. You have the following information:

1. There are five houses.
2. The Englishman lives in the red house.
3. The Spaniard owns a dog.
4. Coffee is the drink in the green house.
5. The Ukrainian drinks tea.
6. The green house is immediately to the right of the ivory house.
7. The Camel smoker owns snails.
8. Kools are smoked in the yellow house.
9. Milk is the drink in the middle house.
10. The Norwegian lives in the first house.
11. The man who smokes Chesterfields lives next door to the man who owns a fox.
12. Kools are smoked in the house next to the house where horses are kept.
13. The Salem smoker drinks orange juice.
14. The Japanese smokes Parliaments.
15. The Norwegian lives next door to the blue house.

Each man has one house, one pet, one type of smoke, a different nationality, and a different drink. *Problem:* Who owns a zebra, and who drinks water?

After you have solved one of the problems or worked on one or two of them for a while, describe what your problem-solving behavior was like, what processes you used, and how you reached a solution, if you did. (The answers to these problems are given at the end of the chapter.)

Figure 11-10 Can you draw the required single line through these nine dots?

eses that can be investigated in terms of overt behavior. A scientific account of problem solving need not consist of a description of the subjective thought processes or patterns involved, any more than a theoretical account of learning must concern itself with neurophysiological processes. In the same way, as you have seen, an account of the meaning of words need not be given in subjective terms. Suppose we accept the fact that the purely subjective and private aspect of a person's thinking cannot be objectively studied by outside observers, and turn instead to explore the publicly observable behavior that occurs in problem-solving situations. (This behavior might offer a set of the operations performed in problem solving that would provide an **operational definition** of its nature.) If problem solving can be defined as a special class of behavior with objectively stated properties, then the situations that elicit this class of behavior can be arranged, the conditions can be systematically varied, and the effects of these variations can be observed.

The Nature of Problem Solving

Historically, introspective accounts of the thinking or reasoning processes that occur during problem solving have been found to be both unreliable and unverifiable. However, such accounts may serve as sources of hypoth-

Figure 11-11 Can you arrange these six matches to form four equilateral triangles?

Let's see what can be learned about problem solving in this manner.

First, problem-solving behavior occurs in situations in which normal behavior is blocked in some manner or for some reason. You have a problem, for example, when, having loaded the groceries into the trunk of your car in the supermarket parking lot, you slam the lid shut, locking up both groceries and the key case you had laid—for only a second, you thought—inside the trunk. You first try a normal response: You press the button to release the catch so the lid will open. The lid does not open.

Second, you try to think of other ways that might work. You've gotten the lid open before, when it was stiff and frozen, by tugging abruptly and jerking hard. This doesn't work either.

So far you have been behaving much as you did when you first attempted the dot problem or the match problem: You simply went ahead in your usual manner, and found that it did not work. In the same way, when dogs, monkeys, or children are presented with an Umweg problem (*Umweg* is German for "way around"), their natural behavior does not work. In an **Umweg problem** the subjects are placed in the middle of a length of fence or other obstruction, with a goal object like food or a toy near them on the other side (see Figure 11-12). They try to get to the goal object directly, through the fence or obstacle, but this does not work. The obvious, direct behavior is inadequate. Going around either end of the fence or obstacle does not occur to them at first.

What happens then in the problem-solving situation? *Third,* you try out one possible solution after another, using trial and error to find a way that will solve the problem. You look in your pockets to make sure the keys are really not with you—and also check inside the car, in the ignition, on the seat. No luck. Even though you have a mental image of placing the keys inside the trunk, you repeat the search responses. Similarly, you probably tried a variety of ways to draw the lines through the dots and to rearrange the matches, and you discarded one incorrect approach after another. You probably tried some things more than once.

Fourth, you begin to use covert symbolic or verbal behavior in dealing with the problem that is presenting such difficulties. Thus you might sit down and try to think of some way the lock might be picked, of some person (the

Figure 11-12 The baby (A), the hen (B), and the chimpanzee (C) were all faced with Umweg problems, but only the chimpanzee has solved it. (B and C adapted from Munn, 1957)

auto dealer?) who might have a master key, or of a locksmith who might help. You talk to yourself, if you will. You may have used an implicit mediational process to figure out new and unusual solutions to the dot and match problems too. Obviously the problem-solving process involves much detailed verbal activity in the case of some problems, like the one about the houses: Who drinks water and who has a zebra as a pet? Manipulations of symbols is a much more efficient way to solve problems than overt trial-and-error behavior. You can construct an entire situation in terms of visual or verbal symbols that stand for actual physical objects or events, and then manipulate these symbols in many ways to discover the best or the correct solution. Thus you can map out several moves ahead in a game of chess or checkers, planning your overall strategy as well as immediate tactics. The use of visual or verbal symbolic mediational activities short-circuits actual trial and error and makes problem solving much more efficient.

Fifth and finally, the solution of the problem occurs to you suddenly. As your thoughts center around the theme of other keys that may fit this lock, you may suddenly say, "Aha!" as you remember that a duplicate set of car keys is kept in a secret place in your garage at home, in case some other family member wants to use the car. This is only a partial solution, for the extra keys are at home and you can't drive your car to get there. Another "Aha!": You visualize riding home in another car, a cab. You run to the pay phone in the store and call for a cab, which takes you home for the keys and back again to the supermarket lot. Problem solved!

Such an **"Aha" experience** is very common in the solution of problems and has been dignified with the term of **insight.** The solution to the dot or match problem may have come to you in a flash in the same way. Cartoonists depict the "Aha" experience with a lighted bulb. Often problem solution requires that you see things in a new and different light, which

may swiftly occur to you after you have become deeply involved, have not succeeded, and are casting wildly about for any possible solution. Somehow you have to go beyond the customary set solutions you've used before. Once you have found the solution to a tough problem, you usually retain it in memory very well. When you approach similar problems later, merely verbalizing the principle used in solving the original problem and observing the similarity between the original and the current problem usually are sufficient to facilitate **sudden solution.**

Problem solving, then, is behavior that occurs in situations in which normal responses are blocked; immediate set solutions do not work; a variety of trial-and-error solutions are attempted, often with the assistance of symbolic mediational behavior; and solutions are sometimes discovered in a flash of insight. Psychologists have found that they can easily develop tasks that will arouse this problem-solving behavior in subjects. By systematically varying the conditions for these tasks, they can observe how these variations affect the character of the problem-solving behavior and the ease of solution.

Insight or Trial and Error?

The sudden insight with which many tough problems are solved, often in combination with covert, mediational processes, raises an immediate question about problem-solving behavior. As you have seen, most learning processes appear to be gradual, and the curves that represent learning trials are smooth, without the sudden jigs and jags that might indicate insight. Yet when learning seems to take place in one trial as a consequence of symbolic or verbal behavior, this suggests that insight may also be involved in learning, through a flash of understanding.

At the turn of the century, the psychologist E. L. Thorndike did a series of experiments in which he placed hungry cats in **problem boxes**

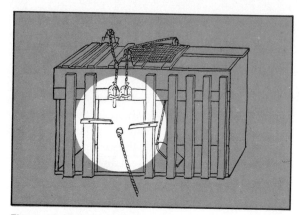

Figure 11-13 A Thorndike problem box for cats, arranged so that the animal inside it had to step on the treadle to release the door. (Thorndike, 1898)

outside of which they could see food (Thorndike, 1898; see Figure 11-13). The doors of these boxes could be opened only by pulling a string, depressing a lever, or moving a catch. The cats bit, clawed, squeezed, and pushed in a variety of actions that Thorndike labeled **trial and error**, finally opening the doors by chance movements. The next time they went through the same activities, but in this and succeeding trials they gradually learned the behavior that set them free, until they could get out quickly and efficiently. Thorndike suggested that this trial-and-error behavior was a paradigm of all learning.

Then, during World War I, the Gestalt psychologist Wolfgang Köhler concluded from experiments with chimpanzees that something more than blind trial-and-error behavior was involved in learning (Köhler, 1925). He suspended a banana from the top of the cage above the reach of a chimpanzee and placed several boxes at a distance in a corner of the cage. Typically the chimpanzee would try to jump higher and higher, but could not reach the banana. During a pause in this frantic activity, however, the animal would see the boxes and suddenly grasp the solution to the problem. Dragging the boxes under the banana, the chimpanzee would place one upon

another and then climb up on them to reach the banana. Köhler proposed that the solution came as the chimpanzee surveyed the whole situation and suddenly discovered the pattern of piling boxes and standing on them to bring himself closer to the banana.

Köhler claimed that insight occurred in the solution of many other problems he set for his chimpanzees (see Figure 11-14). They could suddenly realize that a banana outside the cage could be reached by fitting two short sticks together to form one long stick, for example. Or they could pull in a long stick outside the cage with a shorter one at hand, and then use the longer stick to reach the banana. According to Köhler, chimpanzees, as well as human subjects, eventually see situations as organized wholes in solving problems, grasp the relationships involved between the elements, and reorganize them in a flash of insight.

Is there any way to put the Köhler and Thorndike conclusions together for a full explanation of the way that learning, including problem solution, takes place? Or does learning work sometimes by trial and error and sometimes by insight? Sudden solutions of problems do occur, it's true. Often solutions depend on a rearrangement of the elements in a situation so that relationships can be easily perceived and manipulated. When there is a sudden solution in this way, it is called insight. Still, invoking the term "insight" does not really explain the process of sudden solution; it only labels the process to be explained. It is more appropriate to ask what conditions facilitate insight or sudden solution.

If sudden solution requires some perceptual rearrangement of the elements in the situation—that is, "seeing" new relationships among the elements, such as perceiving that two short sticks can be arranged together to make a longer stick—then experience in handling these elements may help. Experiments have shown that past experience with the elements involved in the problem does indeed

Figure 11-14 Chimpanzees have proved capable of solving many problems by using boxes or sticks as aids in ways demonstrated here. Does this strike you as involving genuine cognitive ability or insight?

facilitate the occurrence of such rearrangements (Birch, 1945a). Herbert Birch gave sticks to four-year-old chimpanzees and placed food just beyond their reach outside their cages. Only one of them solved the problem by using a stick as a tool, and this one had previously become acquainted with sticks. Then the other chimpanzees were allowed to play with the sticks for three days. After this experience, in which they learned to shovel, pry, and poke with the sticks, even touching objects beyond their reach, they were able to solve simple stick problems fairly well. So the sudden solution may not come automatically, even if all the elements required for solution are present and visible (as Köhler thought). Rather, in-

sightful behavior seems to require some prior learning experiences. The foundation for it must be acquired; it is not simply "given."

Similar experiments with tool problems given to nursery school children showed that they first solve problems by trial and error. Such behavior only gradually gives way, with more relevant experience, to sudden solutions. On this basis, insight can be explained in terms of **response set,** a relatively permanent tendency to respond in a certain way to given stimulus situations or in the solution of problems.

Response sets are learned ways of tackling problems that have been acquired through past experience and are later applied to the solution of an immediate problem. Although you may not always be aware of the role that past experience has played, the "Aha" experience may occur when a principle or strategy devised for solving problems in the past is suddenly perceived to be appropriate for solving the current problem. The sudden insight perhaps has a forgotten history behind it. Thus a student who grasped the solution of the match problem within a few seconds, having a sudden insight that the matches should be placed in the four-faced shape of a three-dimensional tetrahedron, realized afterward that she had been able to solve the problem because of past experience. She had previously studied the tetrahedral shape of some crystals and learned that each of their four faces is an equilateral triangle. She had then immediately transferred her knowledge of crystals to the solution of the match problem. Insight accompanied problem solution, but her past experience had made insight possible.

RATS HAVE BEEN MALIGNED!

Comparative psychology, the study of the behavioral similarities and differences of various species of animals, was turned topsy-turvy recently by the unusual results of a new experiment on the learning-to-learn, or learning-set, capacity of rats (Slotnick & Katz, 1974). Prior experiments over many years had indicated that of all animals, primates, including monkeys and humans, are most capable of establishing learning sets that can be transferred to the solution of similar problems, with solution in one trial that looks remarkably like insight. Some carnivorous animals, like raccoons, could solve the problems only after many more trials. Even after hundreds of trials, rats have not been able to duplicate the learning-set achievements of the "higher" animals.

Learning-set experiments with rats had previously employed visual or auditory tests, but now researchers gave their rat subjects olfactory problems to solve. The rats had to learn to press a button for a drink of water in the presence of one odor, such as that of a rose, and not to press the button when a slightly different rose odor was present, one odor at a time being presented in an airstream through a test chamber. Then the rats were presented with a large series of choices between two entirely different odors. Soon they learned to stay with their choice of the first odor when it was rewarded with water, but if the first odor was not so rewarded to switch on the next choice to the second odor. In other words, they quickly adopted the learning-set strategy of "win-stay, lose-shift," with which such problems could be correctly solved in a single trial.

Most rats learned to solve such problems virtually without error within a series of 5 to 8 of the problems, and all rats could do it within a 16-problem series. When using smell stimuli—the stimuli most appropriate for them—the rats showed they could achieve the sets much faster than primates and carnivores, who required hundreds of trials (see Chapter 9). The researchers concluded: "The present results are notable not only because they demonstrate that rats can acquire a learning set for odor stimuli comparable to those achieved by primates in response to visual stimuli, but also because of the rapidity with which the learning occurs" (p. 798). They also made this observation: "Stimulus variables having particular relevance for the organism may be as important as phylogenetic status or cortical development in determining performance in many standard laboratory tasks" (p. 798). Perhaps humans have given too much significance to the great development of the cortex in themselves and other primates.

Variables Affecting Problem Solving

Perhaps it will be easier to understand the conditions that affect problem-solving behavior if that behavior is reduced to its barest essentials. Problem-solving behavior occurs in situations in which the most direct approach, the running off of previously learned responses, simply doesn't work, and consequently some new approach must be taken. This simple statement covers problem solving whether by animals or by people, and it applies equally to tasks requiring motor skills or intellectual activities in which the responses are symbolic. Any conditions that *inhibit* the automatic running off of old, now incorrect, responses will tend to facilitate problem solving, and any conditions that *strengthen* dominant, but now incorrect, responses will tend to retard problem solving. Discovery of a correct solution requires a flexible approach, the ability to abandon well-learned behavior when such behavior clearly does not work. The clue, then, is to identify those conditions that strengthen the rigidity of behavior, keeping it in the same groove, so that the range of varied attempts at solutions is constricted. If such conditions can be identified, we have a chance to eliminate them and free the problem solver to try more novel approaches.

Strength of motivation has proved to be one of the most important conditions determining problem-solving effectiveness. This may seem obvious, for people generally assume that the more motivated you are to solve a problem, the quicker you'll solve it. But motivation does not act as you might expect it to. In a study of motivation and problem solving in chimpanzees, Herbert Birch (1945b) deprived the animals of food for varying periods of 2, 6, 12, 24, 36, or 48 hours to produce varying intensities of hunger drive. Then he presented each chimpanzee with a variety of stick problems; correct solutions were rewarded with food. Some problems required the animals to use a stick, located within reach just outside the bars of the cage, as a tool to rake in food a little farther away. Sometimes the stick was located inside the cage, but on the side away from the food. In one problem, a short stick inside the cage had to be used to reach a longer one outside the cage, and the food raked in with the long stick.

Chimpanzees with low hunger drive were easily distracted from the food by other things and happenings. But chimpanzees with intense hunger drives concentrated on the food to the exclusion of everything else, as do animals in the Umweg experiment. The starving chimpanzees often screamed with frustration and flew into a rage when stereotyped activities like reaching through the bars did not gain them the food. Moderately hungry chimpanzees solved the problems most effectively, because they were not driven to concentrate on the food to the exclusion of stick-using behavior that would gain it for them. They were hungry enough to keep at the task, however, trying one method of solution after another. Birch reported, "Their behavior was characterized by both direction and flexibility of response" (Birch, 1945b, p. 316). So low motivation permits distractions, high motivation strengthens overly rigid responses and restricts flexibility, and moderate motivation, the best for problem solving, encourages the emergence of initially weak but novel responses that eventually lead to the solution of problems.

You've seen children so eager to open their birthday presents that they can't untie the knots in the strings around the packages. You've read of hundreds of people dying in burning night clubs and stadium riots, all pressing so hard toward the exits that they trample each other and can't get through the doors. Scientists, too, may sometimes be so eager to confirm their theories that they fail to notice errors in their experiments. So human beings suffer inefficiencies all the time because their motivation in solving problems is too intense. You may have noticed such inefficiency yourself in struggling with test questions under severe time limitations, although the answers occurred to you later when you had the time and the pressure was off. In Chapter 13 you will see how intense anxiety, acting like a state of strong motivation, can impair human performance. Moderate motivation, neither too high nor too low, is best for human problem solving, just as it is for other animals. Moreover, the more difficult the problem, the more disruptive the effect of high levels of motivation (Yerkes & Dodson, 1908). Now you can easily see why management-union negotiations, made under increasing pressures, often break down without arriving at solutions of all the problems involved. Strong pressures result in rigid, stereotyped responses.

Some problems require the use of objects for their solution, as when you need to tighten a screw but can't find a screwdriver. In such problems, stereotyped, erroneous activities interfering with problem solving often result from **functional fixedness,** the tendency to think of objects as useful only for their usual function and to ignore other ways to use them. Thus it is difficult to think of a coin as a screwdriver, if you've never used one that way before. One of the authors was stuck with a flat tire on a country road without discernible traffic. He found the bolts on the wheel to be taken off rusted tight and unturnable with the only wrench available. A search of the car revealed no oil cans to loosen the bolts. Until functional fixedness was overcome, he did not think of using the oil from the oil stick in the engine, for that is *engine* oil—but it worked fine.

Functional fixedness has been studied in a candle experiment in which subjects were shown three candles, boxes, matches, and thumbtacks on a table (Adamson, 1952; see Figure 11-15). The problem was to mount each of the three candles on a vertical wooden screen standing on the table. One group of subjects was given the arrangement shown in panel A, with the candles, matches, and thumbtacks all in their respective boxes. For the second group, the candles, thumbtacks, and matches were simply grouped on the table outside of the empty boxes, as in panel B. The first group demonstrated the effects of functional fixedness in persistently thinking of the boxes as containers. Only 41 per cent of the subjects in this group were able to solve what seems to be a very simple problem by the method shown in panel C in the time allotted. Not fixed on thinking of the boxes as containers, 86 per cent of the subjects in the second group solved the problem within the same

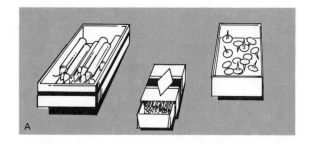

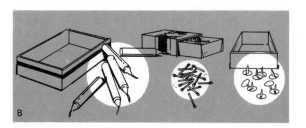

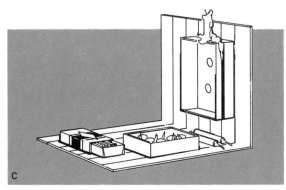

Figure 11-15 When subjects are presented with the materials arranged as shown in panel A, they take much longer to solve the problem of mounting the candles on the screen than when given the arrangement shown in panel B. The solution is shown in panel C.

time limit. How many times do you ignore an object directly under your nose because its normal function is different from that required in solving the problem at hand?

The effect of strength of motivation on problem solving was well demonstrated in another experiment with this candle problem (Glucksberg, 1962). One group of subjects was highly motivated to solve the problem by the offer of a prize of $20 for the quickest solution and $5 for being among the top quarter of the group in solution time. Another group was asked to solve the same problem but no money was promised them. Both groups were given the problem in its hardest form, with the materials all in their containers. Two-thirds of the low-motivation group managed to solve the problem, averaging only seven minutes to reach the solution. Although half of the highly motivated group managed the solution, they averaged a long 11 minutes in attaining it. While both groups were handicapped by their functional fixedness, the higher motivation made it more difficult for one group to abandon the dominant perceptual tendency to see a box as a container. Under conditions of lower motivation, it was easier to inhibit the dominant tendency and to "see" new uses for old objects.

When two other groups of subjects similarly motivated with high and low incentives were shown the problem with the materials *outside* of the boxes, what do you think the results were? Functional fixedness should be much lower, of course, since the boxes could more easily be perceived as shelves. In addition, the experimenter subtly suggested the solution, thereby giving a welcome boost to what would normally be a very weak, but correct, perceptual response. In this case, all those in the highly motivated, prize-seeking group solved the problem, taking an average of less than four minutes, while only four-fifths of the less motivated group reached the solution, and they required an average of five minutes. When the problem is really easy to solve—that is, when the correct response is already dominant—high motivation can be more effective than low motivation.

Response set is another factor that affects problem solving. As previously mentioned, "set" is a relatively permanent tendency to respond in a given way. You have perceptual sets, for example, to perceive things in certain ways in accordance with such Gestalt princi-

ples as wholeness, togetherness, and belongingness (see Chapter 5). Tending to perceive or react in the wrong way because of a set prevents the solution of a problem from occurring to you, just as does functional fixedness. The problem of connecting the nine dots with four continuous straight lines, for example, is made more difficult by a set or tendency to perceive the nine dots as forming a square and trying to solve the problem within those confines (see Figure 11-10). Similarly, forming four equilateral triangles with six matches is made more difficult because of a set tendency to construct all triangles in the same plane, even though this requirement is not indicated in the instructions. Lying on the table, or as shown in the drawing (see Figure 11-11), the matches are all seen in the same plane, reinforcing a set to treat them this way.

The similarity between perceptual set and functional fixedness must be apparent to you. Both are strongly influenced by habitual ways of doing or seeing things, and they can be very detrimental to problem solving. In considering the effect of habitual modes of response on problem solving, Martin Scheerer wrote, "There is truth to William James's statement that habit is the 'flywheel of society' but one might add that habit can also be the flypaper of society" (Scheerer, 1963, p. 128).

TRY SOME WATER-POURING PROBLEMS

■ The purpose of this activity is to permit you to experience for yourself one of the variables that affect problem solving. Suppose you have three pitchers that hold different amounts of water when full, as shown in Figure 11-16. For each problem you are to obtain the required volume of water in a jar by measuring out water (which is unlimited) using various pitchers. Suppose, for example, that you have to obtain a volume of 20 pints with a 26-pint and a 3-pint pitcher. You would first fill the 26-pint pitcher, then fill the 3-pint pitcher twice from the 26-pint pitcher, leaving the 20-pint volume you wanted. Now go on and solve the eight problems in Figure 11-16, obtaining the volumes required as efficiently as you can. Do not read any further till you have solved the problems.

This activity shows how quickly a set becomes established through practice, just like any habit, and how powerfully it interferes with the solution of problems. Did you solve problems 6 and 7 by filling pitcher B, filling pitcher A from B, and then filling pitcher C twice from pitcher B, leaving the required volume in pitcher B (B–A–2C)? This is the way most people solve problems 6 and 7, for they get the set for solving the problems in this way from the first five problems. But there is a much easier way to solve problem 6: Fill pitcher A and simply pour off enough water into pitcher C to fill it. Problem 7 can be solved by filling both pitchers A and C, and then pouring the contents of both into pitcher B. Probably the set you established in doing the first five problems prevented you from at once seeing the simpler solution. And how about problem 8? There is only one way to solve this problem: Fill pitcher A, then pour from it to fill pitcher C. Many people who establish the B−A−2C solution by first working on problems 1 through 7 are unable to solve problem 8 when they get to it. Did you? Did you feel the power of the old set? What did you do to overcome it?

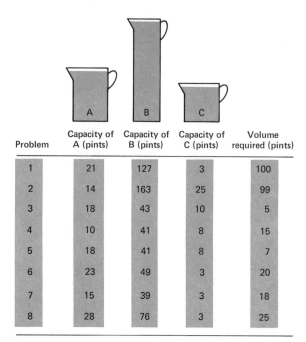

Problem	Capacity of A (pints)	Capacity of B (pints)	Capacity of C (pints)	Volume required (pints)
1	21	127	3	100
2	14	163	25	99
3	18	43	10	5
4	10	41	8	15
5	18	41	8	7
6	23	49	3	20
7	15	39	3	18
8	28	76	3	25

Figure 11-16 Problems: Obtain the required volume of water by using the three jars. The capacity of each jar, shown in the table, is changed with each problem. (Luchins, 1942)

The set you quickly developed to solve the water-pouring problems reinforced persistent use of the same method. Since you were reinforced for using the same approach so often, it became a habitual, stereotyped response. You are also likely to try the same kind of solution first when you are later presented with problems that strike you as similar to the water-pouring problem. In other words, sets based on well-practiced, reinforced habits tend to transfer, on the basis of stimulus generalization, to many other problems that may look the same but require different solutions. When a tendency toward one sort of problem-solving behavior is strengthened, a rigid, inflexible approach persists, and a fresh approach has to struggle hard to emerge. Perhaps you are familiar with the puzzle of taking apart two spikes that are intertwined with each other.

Once you have solved one such spike problem, say, by arranging the spikes in a certain pattern and then sliding one spike off the other, you may tend to transfer this solution to any other spike puzzles you encounter. But not all of them are solved in the same manner, and the transfer of set training in this instance leads you astray.

Another variable that determines problem solution is the way in which you verbalize the problem, the way you (or the instructions) state the problem. The instructions you are given, or give yourself, often lead to incorrect methods of attacking a problem. Consider the following problem: Two trains traveling toward each other are 100 miles apart. The eastbound train moves at 40 miles per hour and the westbound train at 60 miles per hour. You, yourself, start flying east in a helicopter from the eastbound train, traveling at a rate of 80 miles per hour. When you reach the westbound train, you turn around and fly back until you reach the eastbound train. You continue to fly back and forth between the trains until they meet. How many miles will you have traveled in the helicopter when the two trains meet each other? (Assume no decrease in your rate of flying when you turn around.)

Following these instructions, most people will figure how many miles they will travel to reach the westbound train, add to this the miles traveled to return to the eastbound train, and so on. But this solution requires high-grade mathematics. A much easier solution is to realize that the two trains meet in just one hour (60 miles + 40 miles = 100 miles), and you will have flown just 80 miles in your helicopter in that hour. The way you construe the problem, in this case because of the way the instructions were given, often determines the speed with which you solve the problem.

Problem-solving processes, then, are not basically different in kind from other forms of human behavior. You have seen that problem solving follows many of the principles of learning, especially the transfer of training (at the root of which, you may recall, lies the process of stimulus generalization). Problem solving is also affected by motivation, by the way the situation is perceived, and by habit competition and set. The persistence of sets, the persistence with which the problem solver continues to apply unproductive methods in seeking solutions, tends to slow down problem solving, if not to prevent it entirely. How can greater flexibility and freedom be gained in solving problems, increasing the probability that the new, unusual, but often initially weak kind of response needed to solve a problem will occur? How can we become more creative?

CREATIVITY

"To create" means "to make or bring into existence something new." When you think of creative activity, perhaps the work of highly tal-

ented or creative geniuses comes to mind: the creations of great sculptors, dancers, composers, painters, writers, scientists, mathematicians, inventors. At one extreme are gifted people such as these, whose work may change the course of civilization or the character of an art; at the other extreme is the vast majority of people who follow the customs of their culture faithfully, rarely acting in an original manner. From this viewpoint, some people are highly creative but most are highly uncreative. Yet surely even uncreative people act every now and then in original ways. Whether you believe you are creative or uncreative, think back over your activities this past week. Don't you find a number of situations in which you acted in an original, creative way? It could have been the way you did a bit of work, things you expressed in conversations with friends or strangers, something you wrote, or arrangements you made.

CREATE SOMETHING OF YOUR OWN

■ Think of some artistic activity that you enjoy very much. It could be anything from flower arranging or room decorating to writing, painting, cooking, or some other art or craft. To give yourself perfect freedom in this imaginative activity, assume that money is no object. Then go ahead and indulge yourself freely and easily in this imaginative activity, sketching out in your mind or on paper how you would do it. Although you may think of the creations of others that you have known and admired, don't copy such creations—they would not be your own. Loosen yourself up and don't judge or evaluate what you are doing. Let yourself go and simply express your own ideas and draw on your own feelings. One idea or imagination may give way to or lead to another, until you create something for yourself that is truly satisfying.

After you have created for a while, sit back and recall how you did it. Surely everyone can be creative, but what does it mean to be creative—what is involved and how does it work?

Descriptive Approaches to Creativity

Psychologists view **creativity** as a characteristic that all people display, to a greater or lesser degree. For psychologists, creativity is a human characteristic—like intelligence, humor, or aggressiveness—that follows a continuum from very uncreative to very creative. They do not find a sharp dichotomy dividing people who are uncreative from people who are creative. Rather than being black or white in this way, creatively we are various shades of gray.

A traditional description of the creative process has been based on what very gifted and creative people, both scientists and artists, have had to say about the way their great creations were brought forth. First developed by the renowned scientist Hermann von Helmholz, who made many discoveries in both physics and psychophysics, this description of the **creative process** is divided into four stages:

1. *Preparation.* The person is immersed in all the details involved in a problem, searching out its elements and becoming completely involved in trying to fit them together and arrive at a solution—to no avail.
2. *Incubation.* The problem is set aside as at least temporarily insoluble, or other activities intervene. During this time all the earlier ideas seem to be dwelling in and worked upon by the unconscious mind.
3. *Illumination.* Suddenly the person has an insight into the answer, it all seems clear, and the way to the solution is open.
4. *Verification.* The solution is formulated in a series of ideas or principles, whether they pertain to an artistic creation or a scientific theory. The solution is tested and its fruitfulness is evaluated.

Although these stages of creativity may describe the process as great thinkers and artists have experienced it, they are based on retrospective self-reports, sometimes made long after the events themselves, rather than on direct observations of creative behavior itself. Therefore, in recent years psychologists have been studying creative people and attempting to identify and measure their traits in comparison with those of others. Comparable developments have taken place in the attempt to study and understand human personality (see Chapter 14).

How would you set about finding creative people in any field—writing, architecture, music, the visual and performing arts, the physical and social sciences? In any sphere of activity there are people who act, dress, and talk as if they were very creative in their work, but who never seem to accomplish anything. In order to identify those who are most creative in a field, psychologists have turned to the judgments of people who work in that field or to the judgments of people who are well known as experts in the activity. People thus judged to be highly creative by their peers can then be observed and tested to see how they differ from others who are simply unselected representatives of the field, or who are actually judged to be less creative.

Intensive studies of creative writers, architects, and mathematicians selected in this manner were made at the University of California at Berkeley (Barron, 1965). Although no simple, single type of creative personality has been discovered, it has been inferred from these and other studies that creative people are relatively more individualistic and genuinely unconventional than the less creative. With their individualism goes considerable self-centeredness and moodiness. They are independent in their judgments. Their ideas run counter to those of their peers, their teachers, and others; they can ignore pressures toward conformity. They seem to be more impulsive and expressive than others, and seek to uncover relationships between forms and ideas that are not ordinarily associated. On artistic tests they tend to prefer complexity and asymmetry in drawings rather than symmetrical designs. They are flexible and can tolerate ambiguity or even chaos in their work as they try to reach their own understanding or expression of it.

Extreme creativity, at least in the form of genius, has often been associated in people's minds with a touch of madness. Highly creative people do tend to rate higher than average on tests like the Minnesota Multiphasic Personality Inventory (see Chapter 14) that measure psychopathological tendencies, such as hypochondria, hysteria, and depression. But these tendencies are countered by greater ego strength than the average person has, with sure self-acceptance and self-confidence, strong ego defenses, and greater personal effectiveness. On occasion they may seem arrogant and impatient, but they do in fact stand out from the ordinary run of people and "have bite." Furthermore, although studies of outstandingly creative people show that they are often above average in intelligence, this need not be the case, and some very creative persons have below-average intelligence test scores. In other words, there is no necessary correlation between creativity and intelligence. Good grades in school, which often depend to a great extent on the capacities measured by intelligence tests, do not imply talent or creativity, and creative people often disregard grades or other indices of good performance in conventional pursuits.

COMPARE YOURSELF WITH CREATIVE PEOPLE

■ Copy the following traits on a sheet of paper. Which of these traits would you say apply to you? Give a trait one check when you feel it is *fairly* representative of yourself, two checks when it is *very* representative:

Appreciative	Inventive
Artistic	Logical
Dependable	Moderate
Determined	Practical
Enthusiastic	Progressive
Good-natured	Responsible
Independent	Sincere
Individualistic	Tolerant
Industrious	Understanding

Eighty per cent of a group of architects judged to be highly creative checked the nine items listed at the end of the chapter (Barron, 1965). Eighty per cent of a group of architects judged to be less creative checked the nine remaining traits. How do you come out with your own checks and double checks? Total the number of high-creative and low-creative traits you checked and also the total number of checks for each set of traits and compare your totals. Does this suggest that your traits tend to be like those of low-creative or highly creative architects, or are they somewhere in between?

These descriptive approaches to creativity, which attempt first to identify creative people and then to describe their creative activities, are valuable. They constitute a beginning in the observation and study of this aspect of behavior, although there is a very long way to go. Furthermore, these approaches have begun to indicate how creative people can be identified early in life, so that their educational experiences can be enriched to encourage a full achievement of their potential. One of the critical periods in the development of creativity seems to come between the ages of 8 and 10; during this period many children may be "turned off" by the increasing pressures on them to conform at school, with their playmates, and at home.

Experimental Approaches to Creativity

Some recent studies of creative behavior have been made in the stimulus–response (S–R) tradition. In these studies, the character of creative behavior is defined, a criterion for degree of creative behavior is selected, various techniques for affecting this behavior are applied to experimental and control groups, and differences or changes are observed.

One of the tests for creativity that has been developed, although it is not claimed that it measures the whole range of creativity, is called the **Alternate Uses Test (AUT)** (Christensen, Guilford, Merrifield, & Wilson, 1960).

Subjects are asked to state unusual uses to which various common things, such as buttons, chairs, eyeglasses, and automobile tires, could be put. The greater the number of the uses and their relevance to the conditions, the higher the score on the test. This test indicates originality, surely one of the features of creative behavior.

DO TEACHERS AFFECT STUDENT CREATIVITY?

Hundreds of young research psychologists and chemists across the country, some creative and some not so creative, were asked to nominate those college teachers who, in their judgment, had most stimulated and most inhibited their creative work (Chambers, 1973). The young research scientists then evaluated these teachers as they had known them both in the classroom and out, and described those incidents with the teachers that they felt had been most influential in stimulating their creativity or in inhibiting it. This investigation indicated that college teachers significantly affect creativity in their students and revealed surprising unanimity in the students' judgments of the qualities of stimulating and inhibiting teachers.

The stimulating teachers tended to be informal in the classroom, well prepared, and less frequently relied on assigned text material than the inhibiting teachers. The stimulating teachers asked student preferences on topics to be covered, welcomed class discussion and contradictory views, and tended to reward student initiative and originality. Students saw the stimulating teachers as hard-driving leaders, very intellectually demanding of students. Although they seldom made students dependent on them, they encouraged class-related contacts outside the classroom, and the more creative students gained most from such interactions.

The inhibiting teachers discouraged class discussion, could not accept student disagreement with their views, and had great difficulty admitting ignorance on any subject. They were more concerned with memorization of assigned materials. Little involved in their subjects, they tended to discourage independent study. They used sarcasm and cynicism to control students and rarely displayed any originality themselves. Finally, the inhibiting teachers rarely interacted with students outside of class, struck their students as lacking knowledge of their subject areas, and spent little time doing research work of their own.

While all teachers were not solely stimulating or inhibiting, enough of them were so to lend significance to these pictures of the two types of teachers. While the teachers evaluated in this investigation had their greatest influence on the creativity of students in their graduate work, very similar results have come from studies of stimulating and inhibiting teachers in secondary school and undergraduate college work. Teachers can and often do strongly affect creative attitudes and activities of their students.

Creativity has also been defined as the ability to form new associations between conceptual elements that are remote from each other. Poets do this regularly in making the striking associations of metaphor; for example, "the lion's ferocious chrysanthemum head" (from Marianne Moore's poem "The Monkey Puzzle"). On the basis of this approach to creative thinking, a **Remote Associates Test (RAT)** has been developed (S. A. Mednick, 1962). The assumption of this test is that a creative person can generate associations with any word or concept rapidly and can identify the common or mediating elements between words even though these associations may be remote. Thus when given the words "rat," "blue," and "cottage," the creative person will quickly see that the word "cheese" is associated with or mediates between them all—"rat cheese," "blue cheese," and "cottage cheese"—even though this link may be somewhat remote. Again, the association mediating between "surprise," "line," and "birthday" is "party," even though you can see that this association is much more likely to hold for "birthday" than for the other words.

Only 30 items in the RAT test need to be answered in 40 minutes, so it is a relatively easy test to administer. But is this a valid test for creativity? Does it measure what it is supposed to measure? Creativity ratings given by a faculty of architects to their students correlated fairly well with RAT scores in one measure of the test's validity. In another measure of validity, high and low creativity ratings of psychology graduate students by their faculty research supervisors corresponded well with their high and low RAT scores: 6 of the 8 students rated high in creativity had high RAT scores and 6 of the 7 students rated low had low RAT scores. On the other hand, the correlation of RAT scores with college grades of students was negative, although the high RAT scorers received higher grades from teachers rated flexible than from teachers rated dogmatic. Finally, high RAT scorers held more liberal views on sexual morality and on women's rights (S. A. Mednick, 1962).

A number of studies have investigated differences between people varying in RAT scores in experimental situations. In one experiment, high and low RAT scorers were asked to read one of a pair of words, one a noun and the other a nonnoun (Houston & Mednick, 1963). The experimenter would respond with improbable associations when the subjects read nouns and stereotyped associations when they read nonnouns. The preference of the high-scoring subjects for unusual or improbable associations was demonstrated by an increase in the frequency with which they chose to read nouns, while the low scorers showed a decrease in choice of nouns under these circumstances.

Creativity, on the basis of high versus low RAT scores, was again treated as an independent variable in experiments that investigated differences in the ability to generate associations to word stimuli. In Mednick's view (1962), people with low RAT scores can be expected to have a strong tendency to give a small number of stereotyped associative responses to word stimuli, and to exhaust their reservoir of associations rather quickly. People with high RAT scores should continue to emit a slow but steady stream of associations long after the low scorers have stopped, and their responses should be less stereotyped. In an experiment devised to test this interpretation (Desiderato & Sigal, 1970), high- and low-creative subjects, distinguished on the basis of the RAT test, were asked to associate to each of 10 words for periods of three minutes each. Some concrete words, like "child," "plant," and "water," were used, as well as abstract words, like "hope," "thought," and "friend." It was found that the high-creative group had a greater associative productivity than the low-creative group, producing more associations and taking longer to exhaust their associative reservoir. Moreover, the associative output declined faster for concrete than for abstract words, and the associations became less common as time passed for both the high- and low-creative groups. Therefore, this experiment did not support the idea that the associations of the high-creative group were less stereotyped, but did suggest that RAT performance may be related to the number of associations that can be produced per unit of time. Still, it may be that the ability to generate associations in quantity is different from the ability to produce original and nonstereotyped responses, and that the RAT test may not be indicative of the latter.

Our society sorely needs as much creative talent as we can possibly find and nourish, and some of the current research is directed toward this need. Henry David Thoreau, in *Walden,* offered this suggestion to the creative individual: "If a man does not keep pace with his companions, perhaps it is because he hears a different drummer. Let him step to the music which he hears, however measured or far away." And on the basis of his research in creativity, particularly with children, Paul Torrance (1962) gives the following advice: Creative people should recognize the value of their own talent and try to avoid its exploitation by others and not fall prey to their ridicule. They should learn to accept the inevitable restrictions on the overt expressions of their talent imposed by their social environment, such as parents, schools, and communities. They should try to develop the minimum skills needed to enter situations in which they can express themselves, and search for opportunities to do so. If one avenue is cut off by circumstances, others may serve as well. Creative people should develop their own values, strengthen their purposes, and believe that these are worth great effort. They should learn to cope adequately with hardships, failures, and anxieties, and avoid depression, retreat, and isolation from others. They should learn that although they are "different," this does not imply that they are mentally ill. They should not equate rebellion with delinquency, or be led to extreme opposition to society because it does not accept all of their ideas at once. Creative people should learn to accept the blend of characteristics that make them the unique individuals that they are, and not sacrifice feelings or their expression to masculine–feminine sex stereotypes. Although creative people are bound to be abrasive to others on occasion, they should restrain some of the behavior that others find obnoxious. All of this is a tall order, but unfortunately development and expression of creativity in our society are still largely left to the creative themselves.

SUMMARY

Mediational processes, like thinking and problem solving, intervene between environmental stimuli and observable responses by selecting or guiding the responses made. Mediated, or secondary, stimulus generalization, involving the meanings of words as opposed to their physical properties or sounds, is basic to such mediational processes. Proprioceptive cues, images, or verbally expressed thoughts may serve as the mediating elements.

Classical conditioning experiments have shown that words, as well as sentences, derive their connotative meanings through mediated generalization. Semantic-differential techniques have been used to measure the qualitative or feeling-tone properties of words.

Response generalization explains how a word acquires control over a divergent hierarchy of responses. A convergent hierarchy results when a number of external stimuli acquire control over the same mediational process and the response conditioned to it.

Problem-solving behavior, in situations in which habitual responses are blocked, also involves mediational processes. Trial-and-error attempts are made in problem situations, with the assistance of symbolic mediational behavior, and the solution is often suddenly reached. Sudden solutions have been interpreted as insight, resulting from perceptual rearrangement of the elements of the problem and grasping of their relationships. However, learning sets, principles, and strategies derived from past experiences seem to explain sudden solutions of problems as resulting from "learning to learn."

Efficiency in problem solving may be affected by motivation. Since weak motivation permits distraction and strong motivation inhibits flexibility of approach, moderate motivation is best in most cases. Efficiency is also affected by functional fixedness, or the perception of objects only in terms of their usual functions, and by response set, or the tendency to perceive or verbalize a problem in just one way.

The solution of problems often requires creativity, or original behavior producing something new. The creative process has been described in a general way as passing through the states of preparation (accumulation of a great deal of information), incubation (assimilation of the information in the unconscious mind), illumination (sudden creation of the new idea), and verification (testing the fruitfulness of the novel solution).

Studies have shown that creativity is not a particular talent belonging to one type of person, but is instead a capacity that all persons have to a greater or lesser degree. Very creative people, however, tend to share such traits as individualism and independence, impulsiveness and expressiveness, ego strength and self-confidence, and flexibility, with toleration of ambiguity.

Tests constructed to measure creativity include the Alternate Uses Test, asking for unusual uses to which things may be put, and the Remote Associates Test, requiring unusual or farfetched associations between words. Although the adequacy of these and other creativity tests is questionable, studies based on them have revealed that creativity can be modified by reinforcement. Situations enriched to encourage creativity have helped to develop it in individuals.

NOW YOU'RE THE EXPERT

1. How would you solve the problem of the missing can opener described at the beginning of the chapter? One natural and feasible solution requires that you overcome functional fixedness, as you might expect.

2. All of us belong at least occasionally to groups against which others have prejudices and direct discriminatory behavior. Pick out a "minority" group to which you sometimes or always belong. It could be anything—being tall or short, fat or skinny, a teenager, a student, a woman, a foreigner (when on a trip), black, yellow, red, brown, or white, a southerner or northerner, a Catholic or a Presbyterian or an atheist, rich or poor or middle class. Analyze the discriminatory behavior that has been directed at you, and the divergent and convergent hierarchies of response that prejudiced individuals have toward you. Can you find a satisfactory explanation for this prejudice?

3. Identify recent situations in which you have demonstrated stimulus generalization, delayed reaction, symbolic mediation, divergent and convergent hierarchies of response, an Umweg problem, an "Aha" experience, learning sets, functional fixedness, and creativity.

Start

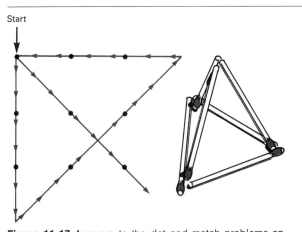

Figure 11-17 Answers to the dot and match problems on p. 309.

Answer to the activity box on p. 321: The following traits were checked by highly creative and less creative architects:

Highly Creative Architects	Less Creative Architects
Appreciative	Dependable
Artistic	Good-natured
Determined	Logical
Enthusiastic	Moderate
Independent	Practical
Individualistic	Responsible
Industrious	Sincere
Inventive	Tolerant
Progressive	Understanding

Answer to the problem on p. 309 of who owns a zebra and who drinks water:

House:	Yellow	Blue	Red	Ivory	Green
Nationality:	Norwegian	Ukranian	Englishman	Spaniard	Japanese
Drink:	Water	Tea	Milk	Orange juice	Coffee
Smoke:	Kools	Chesterfields	Camels	Salems	Parliaments
Pet:	Fox	Horses	Snails	Dog	Zebra

12

Motivation and Emotion

YOUR OWN MOTIVES

■ What motives or emotions do you suppose the people in Figure 12-1 are expressing? Probably it's rather hard to tell. But it's easy for you to produce two very different, immediate examples of your own motives against which you can test some characteristics of motivated behavior that will be proposed.

1. Take a good deep breath and then hold it as long as you can. Observe what happens as you go on holding it. When the stress becomes great, after half a minute or a minute, stop holding your breath and observe what happens then. Describe the events as fully as you can.
2. Your behavior right now is working with this book; that is, reading or studying it. Consider for a few minutes why you are behaving in this way. What are your reasons for doing so? List your reasons as they occur to you. If you find you have a number of reasons for reading this book, rank them in order of the significance or value they have for you. How else could you describe this behavior besides giving the reasons for it? Does it have any other characteristics?

Why introduce concepts like motivation and emotion into psychological descriptions of behavior? Is it possible, for example, to describe your behavior in holding your breath and in reading this book (see "Your Own Motives") without resorting to such concepts as determinants of your behavior? It is true that the terms "motivation" and "emotion" are difficult to define explicitly, because they often refer to subjective experiences or internal states of an organism that are inferred from behavior. For example, when one little boy hits another, can you be sure that he is angry? Might he not be frustrated or jealous instead? You could ask the boy how he feels, but would you be able to rely on his answer? You know how *you* feel when you are angry, but do you know how someone else feels?

In spite of these difficulties, most psychologists have found the terms "motivation" and "emotion" useful in describing factors that influence behavior. These concepts are used to account for the possibility that an organism may respond differently in a given situation on two different occasions. Suppose you deprive a rat of food for a day and then make the opportunity to eat contingent on a response like running a maze, pressing a bar, or turning in circles. The animal will do what is necessary to obtain food. However, if the same experi-

Figure 12-1 What emotions are these people feeling?

ment is repeated several days later after the animal has had free access to food, it probably will not perform. The concept of motivation, in this case hunger, is used to explain why the animal behaves one way when it is deprived of food and another way when it is not. Similarly, emotions can act as determinants of behavior.

MOTIVATED BEHAVIOR

A few general characteristics are present in all motivated behavior. **Motivated behavior** is behavior that is aroused, that persists, and that is directed toward a goal. When motivated, a person is aroused or energized into action to obtain a specific goal. When students are motivated to do well in a class, they will read books, write reports, and engage in other activities that lead to good performance.

Motivational States

We have proposed that motivated behavior is behavior that is aroused and directed toward a goal. The degree of arousal, or intensity, of the motivation is a function of two factors: (1) the situational factors that lead to the motivational state and (2) the attractiveness of the goal.

Motivational states, called **motives** or **drives,** are usually thought of as arising from needs. A **need** is an internal state involving a deficit. In our example of the hungry rat that performs the task required of it in order to get food, the lack of food for a day is the situational factor leading to the need for food. The longer the animal is without food, the greater is its need for food, and the more it will be aroused to seek food (until abstinence from food leads to physical weakness). Thus an animal that is deprived of food for 22 hours will run faster to obtain food than one that has been deprived of it for only 3 hours (see Figure 12-2).

The goal toward which behavior is directed is called the **incentive.** Food is an incentive for a hungry rat, a good grade-point average is

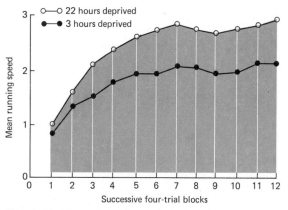

Figure 12-2 Very hungry rats (deprived of food for 22 hours) learned to run down an alley for a food reward faster than a less hungry group (deprived of food for 3 hours). The difference in running speed was maintained throughout the experiment. (From *The Motivation of behavior* by J. S. Brown, copyright 1961. Used by permission of McGraw-Hill Book Company. From data by N. C. Fredenburg, 1956)

an incentive for an ambitious student, and money is an incentive for a wage earner. The magnitude of an incentive also influences the degree to which motivated behavior is aroused. Rats will run faster to get two pellets of food than one, students will study harder for a final examination than for a quiz, and salespeople will tend to sell more if their income consists of commissions on sales rather than fixed salaries. In some cases, an attractive incentive can lead to motivated behavior even in the absence of a need. No one *needs* a weekend in Las Vegas, but many companies have found it very profitable to offer such incentives to their sales force for extra productivity.

Associated with each motivational or drive state there is a distinctive set of internal stimulus conditions. The behavior that is appropriate for satisfying each motivational state is quickly conditioned to the stimulus conditions generated by that state. Thus when rats have learned that by turning right in a T-maze they will come to food and that by turning left they will get to water, they will eventually learn to turn right when deprived of food and left when thirsty (Bolles & Petrinovich, 1954). Each drive has its own stimulus conditions to which successful instrumental behavior becomes conditioned. When you are intensely motivated by a need for sleep, you discriminate such a state from a state of hunger, and retire to your room rather than to McDonald's.

Types of States

When you considered why you are reading this book, you may have come up with any number of reasons. Perhaps because this reading has been assigned by your instructor, because you are determined to get at least a B in psychology, because you are intrigued by what motivates people and stirs their emotions, because you are bothered by conflicts and wonder how serious they are, because you'd like an easy life financially and feel a college diploma will help make it possible, or because you'd like to know how to influence and control other people, to name a few. Motives are so various and numerous that many different classifications have been proposed to group similar motives together or to identify basic motives underlying the others.

Human motivational states can be roughly classified as follows:

1. *Biological motives or drives,* such as hunger, thirst, sex, respiration (like your breathing in "Your Own Motives"), excretion, and maintenance of normal temperature.
2. *Safety motives,* such as avoidance of things, events, people, and places that produce fear, anxiety, or discomfort.
3. *Personal motives,* like self-esteem and self-respect, achievement, creativity, and establishing personal identity and one's own set of values.
4. *Interpersonal motives,* including gregariousness or affiliation, need for power and prestige, and independence as well as dependence.

All of these motives conform to the criteria proposed for motivated behavior, since they all lead to the arousal, persistence, and goal-directedness of behavior.

BIOLOGICAL AND LEARNED MOTIVES

Some basic drives originate from the biological state of the organism. Historically, the concept of instinct, an innate force that predisposes an organism to act in a goal-directed way, preceded the concept of biological motives or drives. In Chapter 2, instincts were described as highly specific nonlearned behaviors of a fixed form characteristic of a species. In addition, some theories of instincts assume that the energy for instinctive behavior is stored in the nervous system as action-specific energy. Thus the presence of the sign stimulus for an instinctive behavior triggers the action-specific energy, giving the organism energy for the instinctive behavior. The concept of action-specific energy has an obvious parallel with the concept of biological drive. In this chapter, motivational tendencies sometimes described as instincts, such as sexual instincts, are described as **biological drives.**

Internal Conditions

Many biological drives are aroused by changes in the organism's internal (body) environment away from an optimum state. Within this category fall drives like hunger, thirst, respiration, and temperature regulation. **Homeostasis** is the body's tendency to maintain a constant optimal internal environment. Drives that arouse behavior designed to restore the body's optimal internal environment are called **homeostatic drives.** Slight deviations in either direction from optimal conditions are fed back to a "regulator" that sets into action both automatic physiological mechanisms and overt behavior designed to restore balance. If you are cold, mechanisms causing shivering are automatically triggered, and shivering increases your body temperature. In addition, you seek warmth by putting on more clothes or retreating to a warm shelter. If you become too warm, other physiological mechanisms and behaviors help to reduce your body temperature to its optimal level.

Some biological drives govern behavior that is not essential for the maintenance of a physiological equilibrium. Such **nonhomeostatic drives** include the sex drive and parental drives. Sexual and parental behaviors are necessary for the survival of the species, but not for the survival of the individual.

The theory that certain stimulus conditions can induce in an organism a motivational state that energizes and directs behavior has led to such physiological questions as what areas of the brain are involved in biological drives and what stimuli activate them. In recent years a model of motivational mechanisms of the brain has been established. Basic biological drives, homeostatic as well as nonhomeostatic, are regulated by a subcortical region of the brain called the **hypothalamus** (see Figure 12-3). Changes in the neural activity of the hypothalamus produce dramatic changes in motivated behavior. A large body of evidence suggests that various drives are regulated by separate areas of the hypothalamus.

Experimental evidence demonstrating the importance of the role of the hypothalamus in the regulation of motivated behavior comes from animal studies in which an electrode, a thin wire electrically insulated except for the tip, is lowered into the hypothalamus. The wire is guided in place by an instrument that provides an accurate indication of the location of the electrode in the brain. By using the coordinates appropriate for locating the electrode in the hypothalamus from an atlas or map of the animal brain, the researcher can carefully direct the electrode to this position with minimum damage to the rest of the brain.

When brief pulses of weak electrical current are passed through the electrode, the tissue at the electrode tip is artificially stimulated. By stimulating certain areas of the hypothalamus and observing behavioral changes that follow, the researcher can study the relationship between activity in that area of the hypothalamus and a particular motivational state. Conversely, the passage of a constant electrical current of greater strength through the electrode destroys the tissue in the immediate area of the electrode tip, and thus the behaviors of the animal before and after destruction of a discrete area of tissue can be compared. If the destroyed tissue is somehow involved with the animal's motivational state, a change in motivated behavior should be observed.

Hunger

Most adult animals, including humans, maintain a constant body weight from day to day and year to year. Since the body needs a fixed amount of calories for the maintenance of physiological functions and for energy, expendable through activity, the body must have a finely tuned mechanism that regulates the amount of food that is eaten.

Hunger is the biological motivational state produced by food deprivation. Presumably a person feels hungry when certain nutritional deficits exist, like low sugar or fat levels in the

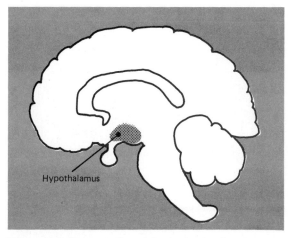

Figure 12-3 Cross section of the brain showing the location of the hypothalamus.

Hypothalamus

bloodstream. Other factors such as stomach pangs (caused by contraction of the stomach) and temporal conditioning (eating about the same time every day) are also hunger signals. A stop-eating, or satiety, mechanism is probably similarly signaled by the presence of a certain level of nutrients in the blood, stomach distension, and perhaps cues from receptors in the mouth.

The **hunger center,** or region of the hypothalamus that seems to control hunger, is called the **lateral nucleus.** (A **nucleus** in this case is a cluster of cell bodies in the central nervous system having a similar function.) When the lateral nucleus of the hypothalamus is artificially activated by electrical stimulation, an animal will readily eat if food is available. Normally, hunger signals probably initiate activation of the lateral hypothalamus.

Does electrical stimulation of the hypothalamus make the animal feel hungry, or does it simply trigger the behavior of eating without triggering the underlying motivational state? A good deal of evidence suggests that the hunger drive is stimulated. Animals not only eat upon hypothalamic stimulation, but will readily perform a response that leads to a reward of food. This motivated behavior occurs even if the animal has eaten a full meal immediately before the electrical stimulation.

Destruction of the lateral hypothalamus (on both sides of the brain), on the other hand, causes the animal to stop eating (and drinking). Such an animal will starve to death in the midst of food unless it is force-fed. After several days of force-feeding, the animal will gradually begin to eat voluntarily, but only very palatable food. As it resumes eating, it begins to gain weight, but the weight will level off much below the normal body weight.

In addition to having a hunger center, the brain also seems to have a separate **satiety center** that indicates when enough has been eaten. Electrical stimulation of the **ventromedial nucleus** of the hypothalamus will cause a hungry animal to stop eating. Similarly, stimulation there will inhibit a hungry

animal from responding for food reward. As you might expect, destruction of the ventromedial nucleus produces an effect opposite to stimulation. The animal overeats until it achieves a body weight of two or three times the normal weight (see Figure 12-4). But even though the satiety center has been destroyed, the animal does not continue to gain weight indefinitely. After its weight reaches a certain level, it stabilizes there (Hoebel & Teitelbaum, 1966). These animals do not seem to be more highly motivated to obtain food than others. They will not work harder for food reinforcement, but merely continue eating food available to them longer than normal animals. The overeating seems to result from the absence of a finely tuned stop-eating mechanism.

Obesity is a major medical problem in this country. If we have such a sensitive hunger-satiety mechanism, why is it that some of us are

Figure 12-4 Obese rat in which the ventromedial nucleus of the hypothalamus was destroyed. (Courtesy of Neal E. Miller)

overweight? Although overeating is a complicated problem that may result from many psychological factors, research suggests that most overweight people are not responsive to the internal cues that should regulate food intake. For example, researchers have demonstrated that eating habits of overweight people are strongly influenced by the incentive value of food. In one experiment (Nisbett, 1968a), fat and lean people were asked to sample and rate the flavors of various ice creams. The fat subjects ate large amounts of good flavors and very little of bad flavors, while lean subjects ate only a small amount of each. In general, overweight people tend to respond to the incentive value of food and eat good-tasting food even when they are not hungry.

Other research has shown that overweight people do not readily respond to satiety cues. They tend to continue eating long after the hunger feeling has subsided. In an experiment designed to demonstrate this tendency, subjects who performed a "monitoring task" were offered lunch following a morning of testing (Nisbett, 1968b). When they were given large meals, the overweight subjects ate everything they were served, while the lean subjects left part of their meals uneaten. When they were served small meals, the overweight people did not eat more than the lean people, nor did they accept an invitation to go to the refrigerator for seconds. The results suggest that overweight people will habitually eat everything they are served in a typical meal.

If you are overweight, you might ask yourself if you tend to clean your plate or eat delectable food even when you are not hungry. If so, an attempt to respond to internal hunger cues rather than external cues may favorably change your eating habits.

Thirst

Thirst is the biological motivational state aroused in an organism by lack of sufficient fluids. The lateral hypothalamus plays an important role in thirst as well as hunger mechanisms. Stimulation of this region of the brain will cause an animal to drink as well as eat, and surgical destruction will cause an animal to refuse liquids. Although both the thirst and hunger centers seem to reside within the lateral hypothalamus, they may be selectively stimulated by chemical means. The chemical transmitter **norepinephrine,** when applied to this region through a small tube inserted in the brain, causes an animal to eat. **Acetylcholine,** another transmitter, stimulates the lateral hypothalamus to initiate drinking (Grossman, 1960). Two subgroups of cells in the lateral hypothalamus, each using a different chemical transmitter, seem to mediate separate hunger and thirst mechanisms.

Injections of concentrated salt solutions into the hypothalamus causes an otherwise nonthirsty animal to be thirsty (Anderson, 1971). That is, the animal will drink if given an opportunity or will respond in order to receive water as a reward. It has been proposed that cells in the hypothalamus detect the body's need for water and activate the hypothalamus to control the motivational state. These cells are stimulated by dehydration, or cell shrinkage, produced by high concentrations of a number of substances in the blood, primarily salt. Concentrations reach an excess, and cells are stimulated, when an animal loses fluids through perspiration, excretion, and respiration. The animal then feels thirsty, drinks, and replenishes its body's supply of water. Other conditions that seem also to influence thirst are a decrease in volume of body fluids and a dry mouth.

There is no evidence that a separate thirst-satiety center exists within the hypothalamus. Then what causes the organism to stop drinking when it's had enough? Thirst satiation may come about when cells in the thirst center are no longer activated by dehydration. All evidence suggests, however, that animals stop drinking long before the water is absorbed from the stomach and cells in the thirst center are rehydrated. It seems likely that receptors in the mouth signal thirst satiety.

Sex

The hypothalamus also plays a major role in the sex drive. The exact locations of regions of the hypothalamus that mediate sexual behavior vary across species. Electrical stimulation of these regions of the hypothalamus elicits vigorous sexual behavior in animals (Vaughan & Fisher, 1962). In addition, the injection of the male sex hormone **testosterone** into the hypothalamus of male rats stimulates male sexual behavior, such as mounting of females, thrusting of pelvis, and intromission with ejaculation (Fisher, 1956). The injection of **estrogens,** female sex hormones, into the hypothalamus elicits female sexual behavior in cats, making them receptive to mounting males (Michael, 1962). In many animals such as rats and cats, sex hormones circulating in the bloodstream stimulate the hypothalamus, activating the sex drive. In females, levels of sex hormones fluctuate in a cycle. The female is sexually receptive only during a stage of the cycle when hormones are at an optimum level. In males, sex hormone levels are steady and the male will engage in sexual behavior whenever a receptive female is present. Although, in general, male sexual behavior is induced with testosterone and female sexual behavior is induced by estrogens, the behavioral distinction between the two is not clear-cut. Under certain circumstances, testosterone may activate female-type sexual and maternal behaviors in both males and females, and estrogens may elicit components of male sexual behavior.

The presence or absence of testosterone at an early stage in development determines the later sensitivity of the hypothalamus to male and female sex hormones (Levine, 1966). In the male rat, the testes secrete testosterone into the bloodstream during a brief period of about 10 days following birth. The sensitivity of the hypothalamus to circulating testosterone in the mature rat is dependent on this early "priming" or exposure to testosterone. If the male rat is castrated (testes removed) at birth, he does not exhibit normal male sexual behavior as an adult, even if testosterone injections are given throughout adulthood. By comparison, if the animal is castrated at a later time, say one month after birth, and is given testosterone as an adult, he will exhibit normal sexual behavior. On the other hand, if a male rat castrated at birth is given estrogen during adulthood, he will exhibit female-type sexual behavior, complete with receptive posture.

If the female rat is given testosterone injections during the first few days after birth, her hypothalamus does not develop its normal sensitivity to estrogen at sexual maturity, developing instead a sensitivity to testosterone. When the female rat is given testosterone shortly after birth and again as an adult, she will exhibit male-type sexual behavior, with mounting of other females and thrusting of the hips. The presence of estrogen following birth is not necessary for later hypothalamic sensitivity to the hormone. It seems that the hypothalamus in *both* males and females automatically develops a sensitivity to estrogen unless testosterone is present during a critical stage of development.

Similar results have been obtained with rhesus monkeys (Goy, 1970). One major difference between sex differentiation in rats and monkeys is that for the monkey the critical period during which the hypothalamus may become masculinized, developing a sensitivity to the male sex hormone, is during an embryonic or fetal stage of development.

It is not known to what extent the mechanism of sex differentiation of the hypothalamus operates in human beings. In higher animals, particularly humans, situational or psychological factors exert greater control over sexual behavior than hormones. In fact, sexual behavior in human adults usually continues indefinitely after castration. Therefore, sex hormones are not necessary for human sexual behavior, and normal fluctuations in hormone levels bear little relationship to the intensity of sexual motivation.

Nevertheless, the implications of the sex differentiation data for variant human sexual behavior are impressive. The data suggest that at least some cases of homosexuality may result from physiological causes, specifically hypothalamic sensitivity to the sex hormone of the opposite sex, rather than psychological causes.

Although a controversy currently exists regarding the extent to which the hypothalamus is divided into anatomically separate regions that control specific motivations, there is no doubt that this small subcortical region is the primary motivational center of the brain. Other subcortical areas of the brain within the limbic system (see Figure 12-5) also influence motivated behavior, but their role is less direct (Robinson, 1964).

Primary and Secondary Motives

The classification of human and subhuman motives suggests that many needs or motives exist beyond the **primary motives,** the physiological drives like hunger, thirst, and temperature control, which maintain homeostatic conditions. **Secondary (acquired) motives** are based on primary motives and are derived

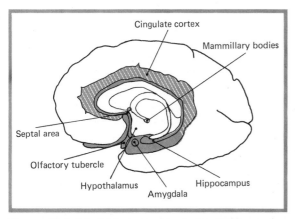

Figure 12-5 Principal structures of the limbic system showing the hypothalamus, olfactory tubercle, septal area, cingulate cortex, hippocampus, mammillary bodies, and amygdala.

from them. Experiments with rats in avoidance training demonstrate how fear, based on the primary drive of pain avoidance, can become a powerful drive itself (N. E. Miller, 1948a). Placed in a white box with a grid floor, the animal is shocked until it escapes into an adjacent black compartment by turning a wheel. Even when shock is no longer given, the rat continues to run into the black compartment. By associating the white walls of the shock compartment with the shock, the animal has come to fear the white compartment. Its fear is learned, and now serves as an acquired drive motivating escape behavior. Wheel turning is a response that is quickly learned, for it leads to reinforcement in the form of an abrupt reduction in the fear drive as the rat enters the safe black compartment. For many people, some persons, places, or activities act like conditioned stimuli for fear or anxiety, and motivate them to escape into their own black boxes.

Certain acquired human motives seem to be traceable to primary motives in this manner, as fear may be based on pain. Thus a child may learn to fear dentists and doctors, as well as hospitals, because of the pain involved or anticipated. Sigmund Freud believed that a great many of our actions, like dreams, slips of the tongue, and selective forgetting, can be traced back to the operation of a generalized sexual motive, the libidinal drive, as will be discussed in Chapter 14. However, it has been very difficult to trace back many so-called secondary motives to primary, biological motives. The **attraction,** or love, of a baby for its mother is a case in point. Early explanations of this attraction assumed it to be a learned motive, based upon the many times the infant experienced the mother in close association with the satisfaction of primary drives like hunger, thirst, and relief of discomfort. Experimental manipulation of infant affections in human babies cannot be performed, of course, but investigations with infant monkeys have turned up surprising results. As discussed in Chapter

3, infant monkeys develop an attachment for surrogate mothers that provide no comfort to the infant other than simple contact. Whether or not affection of human babies for their mothers is a primary drive in its own right, it probably is not derived from the satisfaction of such primary motives as hunger and thirst. The current thinking is that complex human motives—such as gregariousness, the need for prestige, and the need for achievement—are indeed learned, but probably not through any direct connection with primary, physiological motives.

Abraham Maslow developed a hierarchy of human motives according to the extent to which they express a fundamental need for **self-actualization** (Maslow, 1954, 1962). Motives located at the bottom of the hierarchy appear earlier in human development and are more biological in nature. Maslow holds that people must satisfy their lower motives before their behavior reflects the influence of the higher motives. Here is his hierarchy of motives, from lower to higher:

1. *Physiological needs,* such as hunger, sleep, and thirst.
2. *Safety needs,* like avoidance of discomfort and seeking of security and stability.
3. *Belongingness needs,* like affection, love, and identification with others.
4. *Esteem needs,* such as the need for the approval of oneself and others.
5. *Self-actualization needs,* actualizing all of one's capacities creatively.

Over and beyond these basic needs, Maslow recognizes **metaneeds,** like desires for beauty, goodness, justice, order, and wisdom, which have no hierarchical order like the basic needs, but are striven for as the individual's talents and circumstances permit. When these are not fulfilled, **metapathologies** may develop, with alienation and cynicism, a lowering of esteem for oneself and others, and a lessening of self-actualization. As people advance in self-actualization, Maslow suggests they have more

peak experiences, characterized by feelings of wholeness, self-sufficiency, beauty, richness, simplicity, perfection, spontaneity, harmony with others, and creativity.

THE ROLE OF MOTIVATION IN LEARNING

Early in this century, Edward Thorndike stated a law that he thought governed learning, or the acquiring of new or modified behavior. According to this **law of effect,** those responses in a situation that lead to satisfaction will be repeated when the situation occurs again, while those responses that do not give satisfaction will not be repeated. Immediately you can see that this law can be stated in terms of instrumental conditioning: Behavior that is positively reinforced will be learned, while behavior that is not reinforced will be extinguished. According to the **drive-reduction theory of reinforcement,** when behavior reduces a drive of some kind, that behavior is reinforced and is learned. This theory is thus tied in with learning. The motivational process involved in such **drive reduction** is diagrammed in Figure 12-6.

Drive-Reduction Theory

Drive-reduction theory can be seen to apply to many behavioral situations. After heavy exercise, like a game of basketball or a modern-dance session, you are thirsty. Water lost during your strenuous activity is an **instigating condition** that yields a **drive state,** the discomfort and tension of thirst, with dry mouth and parched lips. Your **instrumental response** is to get a drink, downing one glass after another of the **reinforcing goal,** water. You find your tension easing and your thirst reduced with drive reduction. Soon you have had enough to drink and you feel satisfied. The drinking behavior, which has thus reduced thirst many times in the past, is positively reinforced. In another situation, you

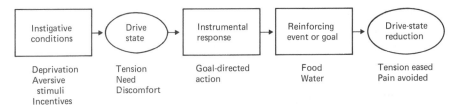

Figure 12-6 The elements involved in drive-reduction theory, from instigative conditions for the drive state through to the reduction of the drive state.

look at your books on your desk one evening and the sight of one text gives you a feeling of great tension. You haven't looked at that book for a week, and any day now you're likely to have a quiz sprung on you. Tension resulting from your lack of preparation acts like a drive, motivating you to study. You sit down and try to cover all the latest assignments. After an hour or two of cramming, your goal-directed behavior has reduced your tension. You have the good feeling of being satisfactorily prepared, so you can now visit friends or turn on the TV with good conscience; your behavior may now turn to the reduction of other drives.

Whether or not all learning involves drive reduction in this manner—which is questionable, as you will see—this model of motivation seems to make a good deal of sense. When any organism loses homeostatic equilibrium, it is goaded by a tense and uncomfortable drive state to seek relief. We don't seek pleasure or satisfaction as such, as much as relief from uncomfortable internal stimuli. This implies that we are pushed by tensions or drive states toward incentive goals because of the tension relief they can provide, not pulled toward them because of their intrinsic properties. By analogy, a lover is driven to escape the pangs of unrequited love, not inspired to pursue the joys of love. If you've noticed that the drive-reduction view of motivated behavior is more like escape conditioning than reward conditioning (see Chapter 7), you're very observant. You have probably also concluded that this drive-reduction theory of motivation is perhaps too narrow.

Limitations of Drive Reduction

As your favorite activity may have shown you, and probably did show a majority of your classmates, people often seek *increases* in stimulation, excitement, satisfaction, gratification, or pleasure, rather than strive for reduction of a drive and a tranquil, quiescent state. It is true that sometimes people have drive reduction as a goal. Yet even then excitement or pleasure may be intrinsic to the behavior they engage in. On other occasions, it is difficult to see anything but sheer excitement and pleasure resulting from the activity. Is mountain climbing, for example, or a ride on a roller coaster best explained in terms of drive reduction? What drives do these activities reduce? Don't they seem to intensify, rather than reduce, stimulation? Some experiments have indicated that the drive-reduction theory is limited in its explanatory power and that reinforcement sometimes appears to result from an increase in excitement and drive rather than from the quiescent state that accompanies drive reduction.

Minimal reward studies with hungry rats and monkeys have demonstrated that they will press levers, run alleys, and solve problems for tiny pellets of only a twenty-fifth of a gram of food. The pellets hardly offer significant hunger-drive reduction, and the activities seem to arouse the animals rather than reduce their drives. Saccharine, a synthetic sugar, does not reduce a hunger drive but does taste sweet. Hungry rats rewarded with saccharine for running mazes are reinforced by it although it does not reduce any drive (Sheffield & Roby, 1950).

You have seen in Chapter 3 how some species of animals, like birds, become imprinted to their mothers or other moving objects during certain critical periods of their infancy and will thereafter follow those objects faithfully. What drive reduction is manifested in these responses?

In an experiment with rats (Sheffield, Wulff, & Backer, 1951), sexually inexperienced but mature males increased their speed in runways when their goal was access to receptive female rats. Their copulation was incomplete, however, for they were not permitted to reach ejaculation. Since it is ejaculation that presumably provides tension reduction in the copulating male, these rats should have experienced no drive reduction. Nevertheless, their running response was strongly reinforced. Teenagers who engage in heavy petting without release might testify to the same kind of reinforcement, although tension is markedly increased, not reduced.

An additional argument against the drive-reduction theory of reinforcement stems from

the discovery that an animal will press a lever in order to receive a mild electrical stimulation to certain areas of the brain. (A fuller discussion of self-stimulation of the brain is presented later in the chapter.) Electrical stimulation of the brain seems to be intrinsically and powerfully reinforcing and is not easily explained in terms of a drive-reduction theory of reinforcement.

Still other kinds of stimulation have been revealed to have the effect of reinforcing the behavior of organisms despite the absence of any obvious drive reduction. Visual exploration often seems to be a reinforcing activity in its own right, for example. Rats will choose that arm of a Y maze that leads to a still more complex maze, rather than the arm that leads to a blind alley (Montgomery, 1954). When enclosed within a box, monkeys will learn to press that panel which opens to give them a view of an electric train, other monkeys, or people in the laboratory, as shown in Figure 12-7 (Butler, 1953). Similarly, human babies prefer to explore complex visual patterns to simpler ones, even in their first year of life (see Chapter 3). Such experiments seem to reveal a powerful reinforcing effect deriving from

Figure 12-7 What reinforces this monkey for pressing a panel to get a peek at a moving toy train? (Courtesy of Harry F. Harlow)

interesting stimulation. Human infants, as well as young chimpanzees, show manipulative tendencies in touching and handling objects. On successive days, W. I. Welker presented chimpanzees with new objects for six minutes each day (Welker, 1956). He gave them chains, lights that could be switched on and off, and variously shaped pieces of wood. Although the chimpanzees showed a decrease in playful manipulative behavior over the six-minute periods and also from day to day, still they demonstrated that novel stimulation can be enormously rewarding. These kinds of experiences hardly seem to be drive reducing. One could, of course, invent a drive that the specified behavior would presumably be reducing, like a drive to look at electric trains or a drive to handle pieces of wood or chains. But such a strategy seems like an unnecessary effort expended merely for the purpose of preserving the integrity of the drive-reduction theory. To many psychologists, it seems more accurate to say that organisms are simply motivated to seek some amount of stimulation, will work to get it, and are reinforced by it.

Sensory deprivation studies, like those referred to in Chapter 4, have shown that human subjects soon need adequate stimulation when placed in isolated situations designed to reduce stimulation from all the senses. Subjects in such investigations cannot take the sensory deprivation for more than two or three days without becoming very disturbed, susceptible to hallucinations and panic, and unable to sleep. If stimulus input is reduced too far, disorganization occurs. Again, this does not square with the idea that drive and tension reduction can explain the whole range of motives. The current emphasis in motivation research stresses the tendency of organisms to seek information, stimulus novelty, and complexity, and to increase arousal and stimulation rather than simply to reduce it (White, 1959). Furthermore, behaviors like exploration, curiosity, stimulus variability, competence in dealing with all kinds of things in our environment, and solving the problems they sometimes present hardly seem to derive from physiological drives. They seem to be important motivational states in their own right.

No one theory of the nature of motivation is currently generally accepted. Perhaps investigations will gradually lead to some other, more comprehensive theory of motivation, capable of explaining all the evidence now emphasized by the various competing theories.

PERSONAL AND INTERPERSONAL MOTIVATION

In our own personalities, as well as in interactions with other people, we encounter many complex motives beyond those drives, needs, and incentives already discussed. Your personal actions may often be guided by needs or motives to be creative, to conform, to value or respect yourself, or to achieve or accomplish as much as you can. Your interactions with others may often reveal to you a strong affiliation motive—that is, a desire to form a close association with them—or a desire to cooperate or compete with them, or a desire to influence and control them in order to gain power over them. Such general, overarching motives have often been selected and emphasized by political, religious, and economic ideologies. Laissez-faire economic systems stress individual achievement; Judeo-Christian religions concentrate on affiliation; and Machiavellian or Nietzschean political systems emphasize power. Whatever our ideologies, we often turn to such needs or motives in trying to explain our own actions or those of others. Psychologists have recently devoted many investigations to such motives as achievement, affiliation, and power.

WHY DID YOU DO THAT?

■ Make three headings, "Achievement," "Affiliation," and "Power," at the top of a sheet of paper. Then go back in your memory day by day for the past week, as far as you can reconstruct events. Recall your specific personal and interpersonal actions during these days and list those that fit fairly well under three headings. (Much of your behavior may not fit under any of these headings.) In this small and possibly unrepresentative sample of your activities, which of the three motives appeared to dominate? Examining some of the actions you listed, would you say they were probably based on needs for achievement, affiliation, or power, or that they probably were derived from or were instrumental to other, more basic needs? Do some of your activities seem to reflect a combination of these different motives? Under what headings would you put your activities that do not seem motivated by a need for achievement, affiliation, or power? Can you discern other motives involved in these other activities?

Ask a friend to evaluate the extent to which your behavior seems to be based on needs for achievement, affiliation, and power. Is there a discrepancy between the way your friend rates your behavior and the way you rate your own? If so, try to find out the reason(s).

Figure 12-8 An example of the type of picture used for measuring the need to achieve. What do you think is going on here?

Achievement Motivation

Achievement motivation is a personal motive to excel, to do well in reference to some personal standard of excellence. Tests for the strength of achievement motivation were developed and used by David McClelland and his colleagues (McClelland, Atkinson, Clark, & Lowell, 1953). These tests were based on people's reactions to selected **Thematic Apperception Test (TAT)** pictures showing a person or people in scenes that could be interpreted in many ways, depending on the subjects' fantasies, or more or less unconscious emotional and motivational reactions (see Figure 12-8). Subjects were asked to write brief stories about what had led up to the situation shown in the picture, what was going on in the scene, who was thinking what, and what would happen as a result. Subjects were treated differently, to arouse their **need for achievement (n-Ach)** more or less strongly before they wrote their stories. Some were told the stories

they were to make up would be a test of leadership and intelligence; some were led to believe the test had little importance; and others took the test under neutral conditions. It was found that the first, or achievement-oriented, group produced stories with greater achievement imagery. Thus n-Ach can be deliberately aroused and tested. N-Ach tests have been thoroughly developed and standardized, and many investigations have been made both of conditions that strengthen need for achievement in individuals and of the different behavioral characteristics of individuals with varying levels of achievement motivation.

The American cultural roots of the need to achieve have been traced back to such religious values as the emphasis on worldly success as a sign of spiritual grace, the Protestant ethic of self-reliance and hard work, and the competitive frontier spirit of "every man for himself and the devil take the hindmost.'' Such attitudes embedded in cultural traditions and institutions may provide a general background for the reinforcement of achievement-oriented behavior.

Parental attitudes may also be instrumental in instilling n-Ach, providing the bottom rungs of the ladder of success that youngsters are encouraged to climb. One study revealed a strong relationship in eight-year-old boys between n-Ach and their mothers' early expectations that their boys would become independent. Such demands involved standing up for their own rights, going out alone to play, knowing their way around the neighborhood, and trying to accomplish difficult things by themselves (Winterbottom, 1958). Another study tended to confirm the effects of cultural background on n-Ach, for it showed that Protestant and Jewish parents expect their children to exercise independence and self-reliance earlier than do Catholic parents (McClelland, Rindlisbacher, & DeCharms, 1955). Furthermore, more highly educated parents demand earlier development of independence than do the less educated.

Situational factors also affect the strength of the achievement motive, and consequently they influence achievement-related behavior. Whether male or female, you yourself can easily recall all kinds of competitive situations in which you have been placed, even in your early years. As you became involved in such situations, whether it was a competitive sport of some kind, an attempt to be outstanding in some way, or a drive to achieve success according to your standards or those of society, you may have found your desire to achieve becoming stronger.

Many investigations have shown that n-Ach does act as a motive in the sense that high levels of n-Ach are associated with greater work output, although on occasion the effects may be complex. Given scrambled-word and arithmetic tests, college men who tested high on n-Ach performed these simple tasks more

quickly and efficiently than did subjects who had low n-Ach scores (Lowell, 1952).

Think of some people you know who strike you as having very strong n-Ach as opposed to others with n-Ach too low to discern or arouse. Can you identify any personality traits that distinguish those with low and high need for achievement? A number of traits are fairly reliably related to strength of the achievement motive (McClelland, 1971b). High need achievers tend to be persistent, working long and hard to meet the standards they set for themselves. They seek advice and help from experts or those superior to them in the field of their activities, rather than from friends with whom they may be competing. They exhibit considerable self-esteem and self-confidence, but do not set unreasonable goals for themselves or take immoderate risks (which further raises their probability of success).

After graduation, high need achievers tend to become entrepreneurs, working independently. One study (McClelland, 1965) revealed that 15 years after college, 83 per cent of those in entrepreneurial positions had high n-Ach scores while in college, but only 21 per cent had low n-Ach scores. High n-Ach people tended to save more money and invest more in the economy than low n-Ach people. Those with high n-Ach also proved to be more upwardly mobile than those with low n-Ach, with nearly twice as many moving up from their fathers' socioeconomic classes. Ethnic background also tended to distinguish low and high n-Achievers. Thus, Italians, who had lower n-Ach on the average, were not so upwardly mobile as Jews, who had higher average n-Ach.

If it is true that minority groups with high n-Ach can rise above other groups economically, it seems to follow that a whole nation might develop more rapidly within the family of nations if it were strongly achievement oriented. The achievement levels and trends of various cultural groups and nations have been analyzed and compared in an extension of the studies of achievement motivation (McClelland, 1971b). It has been found that countries, and even entire civilizations, do differ in the general level of achievement motivation, as inferred from such diverse bases as achievement themes and imagery in literature, visual artistic productions, folktales, and children's primers. McClelland further reported that while the level of achievement waxes and wanes across the history of any given nation, increases in n-Ach tend to precede periods of economic growth and decreases tend to forecast periods of decline. The strongest n-Ach imagery in Spanish literature, for example, occurred just prior to Spain's period of overseas expansion and New World conquests; achievement imagery had begun to decline before the defeat of the Armada by the English and Spain's subsequent decline as a world power. Looking at a more recent period, McClelland finds that achievement themes in children's stories predicted differences in economic growth among Western and Middle Eastern countries through the first half of this century. High national levels of n-Ach are to be found in the Soviet Union, among the Ibo of Nigeria, and in Ethiopia.

Avoidance of Success

Investigations of the achievement motive in women has turned up surprising results. In one study, the need for achievement of male and female students was pitted against their **need for affiliation (n-Aff),** or need for close association with others. Each subject brought a friend to the experiment, and both the subjects and their friends were asked to unscramble anagrams (Walker & Heyns, 1962). If subjects slowed down to help their friends, as they were permitted to do, their own chances to excel were diminished. Most of the male subjects, all of whom had high n-Ach, tended to concentrate on their own solutions, ignoring pleas from their friends. Nearly all of the female subjects, however, slowed down to help their partners, and those few who did not had high n-Ach and low n-Aff scores. It was concluded that many women may experience strong conflicts when their n-Ach is aroused.

Further studies have shown that women in particular tend to have a strong **motive to avoid success or achievement (M₋ₛ),** which is often in conflict with their n-Ach. The M_{-s} is not to be confused with a need to fail, however. Matina Horner (1972), who has carried out much of this research, explains:

The presence of a "will to fail" would . . . imply that they [most women] actively seek out failure because they anticipate positive consequences from failing. The presence of a motive to avoid success, on the other hand, implies that the expression of the achievement-directed tendencies of most otherwise positively motivated young women is inhibited by the arousal of a thwarting disposition to be anxious about the negative consequences they expect will follow desired success [p. 159].

The motive to avoid success is also measured by responses to TAT cards, this time in the form of stories showing conflict about success, the anticipation of bad consequences from success, or denial of responsibility for success or effort to achieve it. When shown pictures indicating male success, over 90 per cent of men revealed strong positive reactions; but when shown pictures indicating female success, 65 per cent of women were troubled or confused. Women anticipated such consequences as "loss of femininity, social rejection, or personal or societal destruction or some combination of the above" (Horner, 1972). (See Figure 12-9.)

Higher M_{-s} has been found in college women than in high school girls, and the greater their n-Ach, the greater the conflict with M_{-s}. Perhaps a measure of the stress that such conflicts produce, heavy use of drugs was reported by more women (54 per cent) with high M_{-s} than by those with low M_{-s} (8 per cent).

Figure 12-9 Would you say the young woman (right) or the young man beside her (left) seems to manifest a greater need for achievement? Does your perception of the girl possibly involve a stereotype of "the female student"? Can you see how such a stereotype might cause conflicts in women?

Not surprisingly, the performance of high M_{-s} women is impaired in competitive situations, especially in mixed-sex situations. Many students change their majors while in college, but high M_{-s} women change their majors in the direction of traditionally feminine careers—toward the humanities, for example, as opposed to the sciences—more than low M_{-s} students do. As you might expect, students with a combination of high n-Ach and high M_{-s} tend to have bitter and hostile feelings.

Males with M_{-s} tend to be found in non-traditional settings, such as social work. When men show a motive to avoid success, the reason is quite different from women's fear of social rejection: These men seem to fear commitment to a life of materialistic and shallow values, which they attribute to most forms of "success" in our culture. It is hoped that further research on the motive to avoid success in both sexes may help us to find means by which we all can work to counter the strong

tendencies of many people to inhibit their potentials for growth—a tragedy for themselves as well as a loss for society.

The Need for Affiliation

The need for affiliation (n-Aff) has also been investigated by the analysis of affiliative imagery in stories written about TAT pictures. The n-Aff is a concern for friendly, affectionate interactions with others. In one study the n-Aff of subjects was aroused over a 20-minute period by having them rank the traits that make people likable, describe these traits as they appear in themselves and others, and identify at least three people as close personal friends (Atkinson, Heyns, & Veroff, 1954). When this arousal was followed by a TAT test, the subjects revealed much more affiliation motivation in their stories than a control group that merely worked for the 20 minutes on anagram solutions.

Persons with high n-Aff have been found to

pay more attention to faces than to other visual objects. They tend to seek approval from their peers and are, perhaps surprisingly, especially egocentric. Their school grades are higher in classes with friendly, informal instructors, and when the approval of the instructor is an important incentive. They do not appear to be more conforming than others, although their friends (but not strangers) can persuade them to conform.

Firstborn children tend to have higher n-Aff than later-born children, perhaps because first-borns receive more direct attention from their parents and become more dependent on them, giving rise to a need to be close to others (Dember, 1964). Other experiments, however, have not supported this birth-order relationship, so this finding is not conclusive. Persons with high n-Aff but low n-Ach have been found to choose friends as partners in work, while those for whom the reverse is true choose work partners on the basis of their competence rather than their friendship.

What factors give rise to the need for affiliation? Surely the need for attachment and affection, sometimes developing into love, is one such factor, initiated by the infant's interactions with the mother and reinforced by associations with other members of the family and with peers. Another factor that has been found to arouse n-Aff is the need to overcome anxiety or apprehension by associating with others, thereby clarifying and reducing these feelings by social comparison.

A recent experiment has yielded significant conclusions bearing on the relationship between anxiety and n-Aff (Teichman, 1973). High general anxiety was aroused in some undergraduate male subjects by telling them that they were to be placed in a self-disclosure situation with two strangers, in which unfortunate personal traits would be revealed. Other subjects were told separately that they would have to suck objects representing oral gratification, such as baby bottles, pacifiers, breast

shields, and lollipops. These instructions were intended to arouse high specific anxiety in these subjects. All subjects were then told they would have to wait their turn for the experiment, but could choose whether to wait with other people or alone. Most of the subjects in whom high general anxiety about self-disclosure had been aroused chose to wait with others (a high degree of n-Aff had been aroused in them), while those in whom specific anxiety had been aroused chose to wait alone, in order to avoid revealing their embarrassing situation (their n-Aff had not been aroused). Anxiety, then, does not always lead to n-Aff, but sometimes leads instead to a need for isolation, depending on the circumstances.

The Power Motive

The philosopher Bertrand Russell and the psychoanalyst Alfred Adler have viewed the need for power as a central and dominant human motive. Comparative psychologists have emphasized dominance–submission patterns in apes and monkeys, but psychologists have barely begun to investigate this motive in human beings. Perhaps this is because the **need for power (n-Pow)** — the need to control others or to influence their decisions — seems to be intertwined with the need for achievement in many situations, as well as with the aggressive drive, so that n-Pow is sometimes hard to distinguish from them. Nevertheless, a projective measure has been developed and used for the study of the need for power (Veroff, 1957). Surely you are familiar with situations that develop into power confrontations, when you cannot agree with someone else and both of you strongly desire to impose your own point of view or determine the outcome. These situations can turn into bitter battles, involving psychological and sometimes physical violence.

College students with high n-Pow have been found to argue more frequently in class

Figure 12-10 People with strong need for power tend to be argumentative and eager to bring others around to their point of view.

and to try to convince others of their point of view more often than those with low n-Pow scores (see Figure 12-10). They are also more interested in becoming leaders in whatever jobs they are doing as opposed to gaining satisfaction from working with others. High n-Pow fathers have been found to treat their sons more affectionately than those with low n-Pow, perhaps using affection to increase influence. In a nationwide survey, members of socially deprived minority groups and those with low socioeconomic status were found to be higher in n-Pow than those with higher social status (Veroff, Atkinson, Feld, & Gurin, 1960). If n-Pow is as prevalent as many believe, and if it is clearly distinguishable from other needs and not solely derived from them, it deserves more attention than investigators have given it.

Such motives as the needs for achievement, affiliation, and power are often accompanied by strong emotions as we experience these needs, strive for situations that will satisfy them, and sometimes bask in their consummation. How are the emotions related to these and other needs and drives?

EMOTIONS

An **emotion** is an aroused state of an organism that has both physical and affective components. An **affect,** or **feeling,** is the qualitative aspect of sensations, awareness, or consciousness, and when feelings are strong, we have emotions. Emotions, like joy, love, hate, anger, fear, and contempt, to name just a few, arouse and direct behavior *and* have personal significance: They are either pleasant or unpleasant. When you are angry, you experience an unpleasant feeling. Still, don't feelings of pleasantness and unpleasantness, emotions of joy and sorrow, love and hate, seem to be difficult to put your finger on, or to describe? In investigating them, psychologists have tried to approach them within the contexts, or situations, in which they occur, and to describe and observe them in terms of the internal and external behavior in which they appear.

As you might have concluded, the differentiation between emotions and motivations is not always clear. But we usually make statements like "I'm thirsty" and "I'm hungry" about our motivations, and statements like "I feel angry" and "I feel sad" about our emotions. Although these ways of speaking about motives and emotions do not always distinguish them, they do express a difference we recognize between them.

Features of Emotions

A number of basic features of emotions that psychologists have investigated bring us closer to their characteristics:

1. Emotions often arise in response to certain typical situations in which people find themselves. When you have an accident, or your security or safety is threatened in some other way, you experience fear. When you see someone else in an accident, you feel alarm, horror, or sorrow. When someone thwarts you or treats you unjustly, you feel anger. As you celebrate a victory like winning a game, you experience exhilaration and joy.

2. The situations in which people become emotionally involved attract their attention, make them keenly alert, and beyond this, stir arousal. Some psychologists have suggested that such arousal is the main defining feature of emotions. With arousal, people say they are "stirred up" and, with extreme arousal, may feel "out of control."

3. A whole series of physiological reactions accompanies arousal, and such reactions may be part of what we mean by "emotionally stirred up."

4. Emotions are accompanied by a variety of overt expressive reactions. These include verbal statements, like "I love you" or "You're disgusting"; a great variety of gestures, postures, and movements of the body; and facial expressions, like smiling and laughing, frowning and pouting.

5. Emotions are generally pleasant or unpleasant, and therefore can serve as reinforcement for behavior that produces them. A theory of motivation based on these hedonic features is described in "Every Cloud Has A Silver Lining."

EVERY CLOUD HAS A SILVER LINING

A new theory of motivation has been proposed which points out that extremely pleasant or unpleasant experiences elicited by a stimulus or situation seem to be followed by the opposite type of affective response when the stimulus is terminated (Solomon & Corbit, 1974). According to this view, there are systems in the brain that operate to reduce all deviations from an optimum (called hedonic neutral) level of operation, whether the deviations be in the direction of pleasure or displeasure. Significant departures from equilibrium automatically cause an oppositional reaction in the nervous system that gradually returns to neutral baseline level (see Figure 12-11). For example, if a person is forced by circumstances to do something unpleasant, like driving through hectic rush-hour traffic, the termination of the unpleasant situation will automatically be followed by a temporary pleasant feeling. Gradually the pleasant afterreaction decays and the individual returns to the neutral affective level. A similar interpretation might explain why some people become trapeze artists and bullfighters. Presumably the intense aversiveness of the feat is followed by an extremely pleasant feeling of exhilaration. The idea of this **opponent-process theory of motivation** is expressed in the statement "The nice thing about hitting yourself in the head with a hammer is that it feels so good when you stop."

If the first reaction to a situation is pleasant, the afterreaction will be an unpleasant affective state. Solomon and Corbit use love as an example of this situation. When two lovers are together, they experience excitement and happiness. When they separate, there is an immediate feeling of loneliness. With time, the unpleasant feeling of the departure subsides.

The theory has several interesting implications. First, it suggests that **masochistic behavior** (behavior that is injurious to oneself) is a natural consequence of the opponent-process system. Individuals may engage in behaviors that initially have aversive consequences, but which are followed by intensified pleasure. Second, the model suggests that there probably are psychological stresses caused by pleasurable stimulation just as there are stresses caused by aversive stimulation. That is, when a pleasant experience is repeatedly followed by aversive aftereffects, the experience itself may become aversive. Consequently, there may be emotional disorders resulting from both kinds of stress.

The opponent-process theory is young and therefore not adequately tested at this time. It will be interesting to see if implications of the theory are supported by research data; many predictions about behavior are exactly the opposite of those of more traditional theories of motivation.

Psychologists have tried to get a handle on emotions by investigating all of the five features mentioned above. Emotions are complex reactions that probably involve various combinations of all these factors. At any rate, knowledge of emotions has been advanced by many investigations in each of these areas. Some of the most significant studies have been those of the physiological reactions to emotion-stimulating situations.

The Physiology of Emotions

The physiological reactions to emotional situations are largely under the control of the sympathetic division of the autonomic nervous system (see Chapter 2). As the term "autonomic" suggests, these reactions are automatic, or occur without conscious, voluntary assistance. The sympathetic division generally prepares the body for an emergency through its control over the body's **visceral organs,** like the heart, blood vessels, stomach, and bladder, and its glands, like the salivary and adrenal glands. You are probably well aware of the physiological reactions produced by the sympathetic nervous system. Think of the first time you had to speak, or otherwise perform, before a large group. Didn't your heart start pounding, your stomach feel jittery, your mouth feel dry? Perhaps your hands became moist from perspiration. (You surely retained control over your bladder, but children sometimes don't in emotional situations.) All of these are **visceral reactions** of the organs and glands, governed by the sympathetic nervous system. Sympathetic arousal is largely mediated by activation of the adrenal glands to produce the hormone **epinephrine** (also called adrenaline). Epinephrine acts directly on the heart and glands to produce emergency-type reactions.

Physiological reactions not only accompany emotions but also contribute to the *experience* of an emotion. It may seem strange to think that emotional responses precede emotional

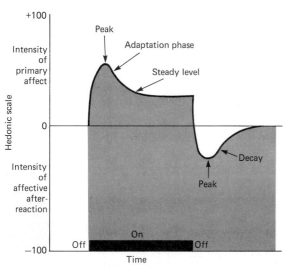

Figure 12-11 Affective reactions during (horizontal solid bar) and after the presence of an emotion-arousing stimulus. Following the sudden introduction of either a pleasurable or aversive stimulus, an affective or hedonic reaction begins and quickly rises to a peak. It then slowly declines to a steady level, where it remains if the stimulus quality and intensity are maintained. At the termination of the stimulus, the affective reaction quickly gives rise to a qualitatively opposite type of reaction that has its own peak of intensity and slowly decays with time. (Solomon and Corbit, 1974)

experiences—that you are afraid because you run away, rather than the other way around. But this is exactly what William James (1884) proposed. In essence, his theory of emotions was that emotional experience results from an awareness of physiological reactions to external situations. A physiologist, Carl Lange (1885), later modified the theory by specifying that the important physiological reactions giving rise to emotions are vasomotor reactions, dilation or constriction of the body's blood vessels. An important implication of the James-Lange theory is that each emotional experience that can be discriminated from all others arises from a unique set of visceral responses. However, evidence that the many diverse emotional states have detectably unique visceral responses is lacking.

Although we do not believe today that visceral reactions always precede emotional experience, there does seem to be an element of truth in the James-Lange theory. A series of experiments by Stanley Schachter and others has shown that visceral reactions can contribute to emotional experiences.

In one study (Schachter & Wheeler, 1962), college students who volunteered for the experiment were asked to watch a film of a slapstick comedy. Subjects in one experimental group were given an injection of epinephrine shortly before viewing the film. Ephinephrine produces feelings of accelerated heart rate and other internal upsets. Subjects in another experimental group were injected with chlorpromazine, a tranquilizer that produces a physiological reaction opposite to that of epinephrine. Finally, subjects in a control group were injected with saline, a salt solution that produces no bodily changes. In order to mask the purpose of the experiment, all subjects were told that they were being given an injection of a vitamin to test its effect on vision.

You probably have guessed the hypothesis. The researchers wanted to learn if the epinephrine-injected subjects would feel more emotional—that is, think the movie was fun-

nier—than the chlorpromazine or saline-injected subjects. Two response measures were taken: (1) emotional expressions of each subject during the film, and (2) verbal reports of the funniness of the film by the subjects. The epinephrine group did show more emotionality and rated the film as funnier than did the chlorpromazine group. The response of the saline group was midway between those of the other two groups. Therefore, the emotionality of the subjects was positively related to the degree of arousal produced by the drugs.

In order to test further the hypothesis that visceral reactions can contribute to emotional experience, another experiment was conducted (Schachter & Singer, 1962). Epinephrine-injected subjects were either correctly told to expect a feeling of arousal from the drug, misinformed (told they would experience numbness, headache, and itching), or not informed as to the effects the drug would have. Saline-injected subjects were given the same treatment as the epinephrine uninformed subjects; namely, they were told that the injection was mild and harmless. It was hypothesized that correctly informed subjects who could identify the arousal they experienced as resulting from the epinephrine would not feel more emotional than the subjects given saline. The incorrectly informed subjects and the uninformed epinephrine-injected subjects, not expecting the physiological reactions, should have interpreted their arousal as originating from emotional sources, as did the subjects in the previous experiment.

Following the drug injection, a potentially emotional situation was created by having each subject wait for the experiment to begin in a room with a confederate of the experimenter. For half the subjects, the confederate acted very euphoric, throwing wads of paper at the wastebasket and sailing paper airplanes. For the other half, the confederate acted very disgruntled at having to fill out forms for the experiment.

The experimental results turned out as predicted. The misinformed and uninformed epinephrine-injected subjects showed more emotionality than ephinephrine-treated subjects informed as to the physiological effects of the drug and were also more emotional than the saline-treated subjects. Subjects who had no explanation of the arousal they experienced following epinephrine injections tended to be more euphoric when exposed to the euphoric confederate and more angry when exposed to the angry confederate, in comparison with subjects in the other groups. The researchers concluded that situational stimuli can alter cognitive appraisal of one's visceral reactions, and thus one's emotional experience. In this experiment the epinephrine subjects informed as to the effects of the drug could say, "I can feel myself getting excited, but that's because of the drug, not because of what's going on here." It might be pointed out that visceral reactions to epinephrine did not produce specific emotions. The epinephrine provided arousal, but situational factors determined the form the emotion would take.

Because experiments designed to study brain mechanisms that underlie emotions are conducted with animals, *emotional behavior* rather than *emotional experience* has been the focus of study. It is possible that other animals have emotional experiences similar to ours, but we have no way of determining whether that is true. Most studies of emotions in animals have investigated aggression. **Aggression** is behavior intended to threaten or to inflict injury on another or to destroy property. Aggression seems to be a universal response of all animals. It is favored as an emotional behavior to study because it is easy to elicit and identify.

Research has demonstrated the importance of a predominantly subcortical area of the brain, called the limbic system, in the production of emotional behavior. The **limbic system** is the group of interconnected structures illustrated in Figure 12-5. Electrical stimulation and surgical destruction of most regions of the limbic system produce changes in emotional behavior.

John Flynn and his associates have attempted to clarify the role of various structures of the limbic system in the expression of aggressive behavior in cats (Flynn, 1967). Feline aggressive behaviors include fighting, snarling, hissing, and crouching. The experimenters permanently implanted electrodes in a specific region of the limbic system by securing them to the animal's skull with cement. (The electrodes may be kept in place for an extended period of time, even years, without producing any noticeable change in the animal's behavior or capabilities.)

The cat and a rat (not a mouse) were placed together in a cage. Normally the cat and rat remained together quietly, but aggressive behavior was elicited when certain areas of the cat's limbic system were electrically stimulated. The cat attacked the rat as soon as the stimulation began and stopped as soon as the stimulation was terminated (see Figure 12-12). The regions that elicited aggressive responses when stimulated were certain sites in the hypothalamus, midbrain (brainstem) and thalamus. Electrical stimulation of certain other sites within the limbic system modified ongoing aggression. Areas within the amygdala, hippocampus, thalamus, and midline reticular formation (brainstem) facilitated or inhibited aggression elicited by simultaneous stimulation of the hypothalamus. Stimulation of these sites alone did not produce aggressive behavior. Electrical stimulation of the cortex does not produce aggressive behavior (Fangel & Kaada, 1960; Sano, 1958).

Surgical destruction of discrete regions of the limbic system also produces changes in emotional behavior. Damage to some regions makes animals more emotionally reactive, while damage to others makes them less reactive. The behavioral role of each of the structures in the limbic system is, however, far from understood at this time.

Figure 12-12 Aggressive behavior in a cat elicited by electrical stimulation of the hypothalamus. *Top,* stimulation of one area causes attack behavior accompanied by a display of rage. *Bottom,* stimulation of another region elicits a quiet biting attack. (Flynn, 1967)

Extensive destruction of the cortex produces a highly emotionally reactive animal. This observation has led to the belief that the cortex normally moderates emotional expression initiated by the limbic system (Bard & Mountcastle, 1948). The cortex probably also plays an important role in the interpretation of emotional stimuli, both external and internal, and in the conscious experiencing of emotions. A proposed model of the relationship between the cortex and limbic system in the control of emotions is presented in Figure 12-13.

Pleasure and Displeasure

Most emotions include a feeling of either pleasure or displeasure. Therefore, emotions can serve as reinforcements of behaviors that produce them.

Approximately twenty years ago it was accidentally discovered that electrical stimulation of certain areas of the brain in animals is a powerful reinforcement of behavior. James Olds and Peter Milner observed that animals would learn to perform any response that produced brain stimulation, whether it was running through mazes or pressing levers. The animals seemed to enjoy it. In fact, they acted as though it were the ultimate pleasure. In one experiment, rats with electrodes inserted in an area of the hypothalamus could give themselves brief electrical stimulations with the arrangement shown in Figure 12-14 (Olds & Milner, 1954). Some rats attained bar-pressing rates as high as 7000 an hour, or an average of 2000 per hour over a waking period of 48 hours. Human terminal-cancer patients with electrodes implanted with their permission in the "pleasure centers" reported that they had pleasurable sensations and increased alertness (Sem-Jacobsen & Torkildsen, 1960).

It has also been shown that electrical stimulation of certain other sites is aversive (Delgado, Roberts, & Miller, 1954). Rats will readily learn to press a lever to turn off stimulation in these areas. About 35 per cent of the brain may be classified as pleasure centers, only about 5 per cent as punishment centers. These areas are almost all within the limbic system. Most of the brain, including the cortex, is hedonically neutral (Olds, 1961).

A British physiologist, H. J. Campbell, has tested the suggestion that stimulation of the pleasure centers is ordinarily brought about by the action of the sense organs and other receptors throughout the body, which pour stimulation into them (Campbell, 1968). To test this hypothesis, he rigged up electrodes vertically in one corner of an aquarium so that fish could swim between them, with a photoelectric eye to trigger a weak current between the electrodes when the fish interrupted the beam of light (Figure 12-15). The current stimulated the peripheral receptors of the fish. They acted to keep the current flowing, just as rats and other

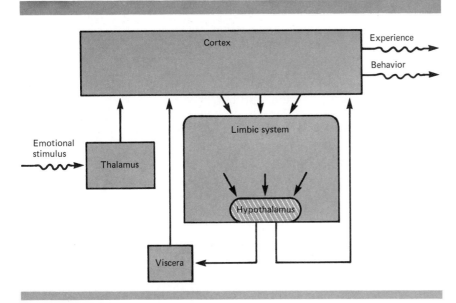

Figure 12-13 Proposed model of the physiological basis of emotions showing the relationship between the cortex, hypothalamus, limbic system (structures other than the hypothalamus), and viscera controlled by the autonomic nervous system. External emotional stimuli are sent to the cortex by way of the thalamus. The cortex interprets the emotional meaning of the stimuli and sends this message to the limbic system. The output from the limbic system is by way of the hypothalamus. Visceral reactions produce stimuli that the cortex interprets. Overt behavior and emotional experience are controlled by the cortex.

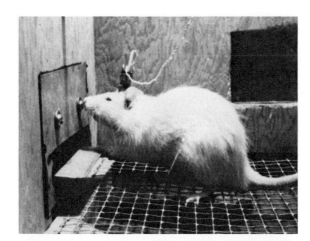

Figure 12-14 A rat with an electrode implanted in its brain pressing a lever to produce pulses of mild electrical stimulation to a small subcortical region of the brain. (Courtesy of James Olds)

Figure 12-15 These fish constantly swim back and forth between the vertical electrodes in their aquarium. A photoelectric cell triggers an electric current stimulating their peripheral receptors. (Courtesy of H. J. Campbell)

animals bar-press constantly to stimulate the pleasure centers in their brains. The fish quickly learned how to stimulate themselves and keep the stimulation going 75 per cent of the time. Campbell concluded: "From these results it would seem that self-stimulation of the peripheral receptors may function as a reward in a manner not yet distinguishable from direct self-stimulation of brain regions" (pp. 104–105).

These results may also explain why stimulus variability is such a strong need for human beings and why sensory deprivation has such devastating effects. Self-stimulation of the pleasure centers becomes compulsive in many laboratory animals, a stronger drive than eating, drinking, or mating.

As we have seen, brain stimulation has also been employed as a means of producing pleasure in humans. In the early 1950s, some years before the cancer patients volunteered to participate in the brain-stimulation experiment, Robert Heath of Tulane University implanted electrodes in the brains of a few individuals suffering from severe emotional disturbances that would not respond positively to any form of treatment. At the time Heath began this work, "pleasure" and "punishment" centers in the brain had not yet been discovered in animals. Heath had another use for brain stimulation: He believed that certain areas of the limbic system, primarily the septum, were inhibited by some unknown suppressing influences in people suffering from schizophrenia. He hoped that stimulation of these areas would produce an excitatory reaction that would correct the aberration.

Patients began to report that brain stimulation in certain regions evoked pleasurable sensations and produced an elevation of mood that lasted for several days. Heath then began to use brain stimulation for activating pleasurable reactions. Others followed his lead and tried brain stimulation as a means of treating individuals with severe emotional disturbances not amenable to other forms of treat-

ment. These patients too reported feelings of comfort, relaxation, joy, and intense satisfaction from stimulation of different sites in the brain. As might be anticipated from the animal research, stimulation of other sites produced feelings of fear, anxiety, instability, depression, and horror.

Heath eventually abandoned brain-stimulation treatment of schizophrenics because they were less responsive to the treatment than other types of emotionally disturbed patients. Those suffering from intractable pain or extreme anxiety or depression seemed to benefit most.

The use of brain stimulation for treatment of the emotionally disturbed is extremely controversial. Opponents say that the risk involved with surgically produced deficits (or death) or stimulation-induced damage to brain tissue is much too great to warrant its use over more traditional forms of therapy. They also argue that the idea of push-button pleasure has undesirable mechanistic implications. Patients, they argue, should be taught to adjust to daily stresses and to try to exercise control over their own life circumstances. The use of brain stimulation might temporarily reduce the symptom, but surely would not remove the underlying cause of the disturbance.

THE PHYSIOLOGICAL ROLE OF HEDONIC FEELINGS

Stimulation of our sense receptors and nerve endings sets off nerve impulses that go to the brain and somehow are translated into sensations of varying qualities and intensities, like loud and soft sound sensations and hot and cold skin sensations. But these sensations also have an affective, or feeling, quality of pleasantness or unpleasantness, although on occasion they may be neutral. Investigations reveal that these feeling tones or **hedonic qualities** of sensations can be affected by the internal motivational state of the organism (Cabanac, 1971).

When subjects immersed in water in bathtubs

dip their hands into basins of water of varying temperatures, they report the pleasantness or unpleasantness of the water in the basin to be dependent on the temperature of the water in the tub. When the body temperature of the subjects is raised above normal by raising the temperature of the water in the tub, the subjects report basin water colder than the tub water to be pleasant and warmer to be unpleasant. (The heat or cold is kept below the threshold of pain.) But if the tub water is cold, they report warm basin water to be pleasant and still colder basin water very unpleasant, as shown in Figure 12-16. Thus the hedonic quality of these sensations is affected by the homeostatic imbalance of the subjects. Basin water that helps to restore homeostatic balance of the body temperature is preferred.

The same kind of relationship between the pleasantness and unpleasantness of stimuli and homeostasis holds for taste and smell stimuli as well, as shown in Figures 12-17 and 12-18. A sweet taste remains pleasant for hungry subjects when the sweet liquid is not swallowed. But if it is swallowed, relieving hunger, the sweet taste soon becomes neutral and then unpleasant. An orange smell is pleasant for fasting subjects, but after they receive sugar the smell quickly becomes neutral and then unpleasant. Somehow internal physiological states, like hunger, must modify the hedonic qualities of sensations produced by receptor stimulation. Thus these motivational states help to regulate what we ingest and thereby help to maintain homeostasis.

Facial Expressions

Human infants seem able to feel and express emotions almost from the moment of birth, though in the first few weeks their repertoire is limited. In alert wakefulness they may lie quietly, reacting to stimuli impinging on their various sense organs, with occasional puckering of the face and smiling and sucking with the lips. In distress they squirm about, kicking legs and flinging arms and crying. Very early they begin to exhibit delight, with cooing and smiling. Over the following months of their first year, infants' emotions

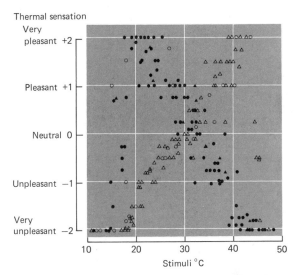

Figure 12-16 The variations of pleasantness and unpleasantness of a 30-second thermal sensation on the hand of a subject from a stimulus that varied from cold (10° C) to hot (50° C). Open symbols represent the reports of the subject with a below-normal body temperature in a cold-water bath, and closed symbols represent the reports of the subject with an above-normal body temperature in a hot-water bath. (Cabanac, 1971)

become more differentiated (see Figure 12-19). Delight becomes identifiable as affection for the mother and others or as elation, and distress is distinguishable by the mother and those who know the infant as anger, fear, or disgust (Bridges, 1932). By the close of the first year, then, infants have a battery of basic emotions, accompanied by many of the facial expressions and vocal behavior that one sees in older people.

The early behaviorist John Watson concluded from his observations of infants that three emotions were basic and probably inborn: fear, anger, and delight or love (Watson, 1928). Contrary to Bridges—who concluded the newborn is capable of only a calm emotional state or "generalized excitement"—Watson described how his infant subjects reacted with *fear* to loud noises and to loss of support when they were dropped a few inches or jarred by

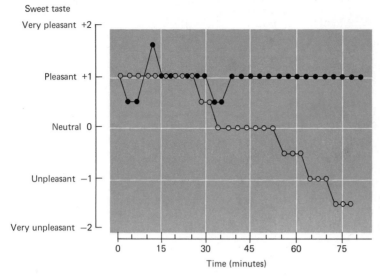

Figure 12-17 The pleasantness and unpleasantness of a sweet taste reported by a fasting subject. When the subject did not swallow the samples (filled circles), the pleasantness of the taste continued. When the subject swallowed the samples (open circles), relieving hunger, the taste soon became unpleasant. Have you noticed the pleasantness of sweetness varying in this manner? (Cabanac, 1971)

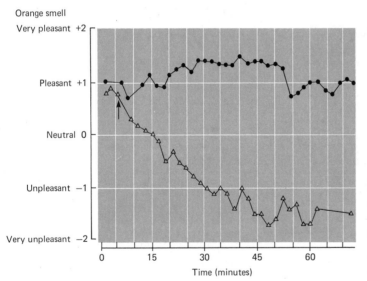

Figure 12-18 The pleasantness and unpleasantness of an orange smell reported by a fasting subject. The pleasantness continued when the subject had no sugar (filled circles), but changed to unpleasantness (open triangles) after the subject had 100 grams of sugar in water at the time shown by the arrow. Have you noticed the pleasantness of food odors changing in this way? (Cabanac, 1971)

the twitching of the blanket on which they were lying. Their fear responses included a tensing of muscles, crying, and trying to move away. They showed *anger,* Watson reported, when head, trunk, or legs were held immobile, crying, and struggling to get free. *Love* or *delight* appeared with stroking of the skin in such sensitive areas as the lips, the ears, the

back of the neck, the nipples, and the sex organs, which stopped their crying and caused them to lie quietly or to coo and smile.

Facial expressions of adults have been studied by showing subjects pictures of people in the throes of a variety of emotions and asking them to name the emotions expressed. Sometimes this is difficult, particularly when the

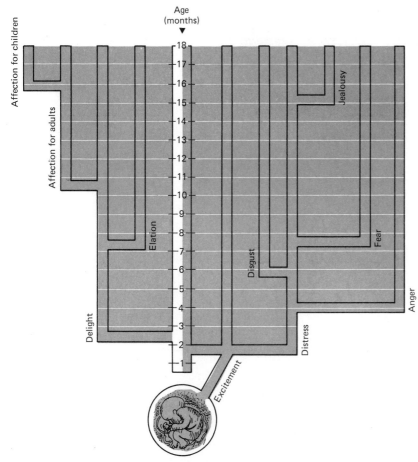

Figure 12-19 The way in which infant emotions are gradually differentiated during the first 18 months of life, from original excitement to delight and distress during the first months and then to a variety of emotions, according to K. M. B. Bridges. (Adapted from Bridges, 1932)

emotions expressed are not strong or when very similar emotions like anger and determination are involved. Robert Woodworth, however, found that subjects could fairly consistently judge the meaning of certain facial expressions (Woodworth & Schlosberg, 1954). His subjects could normally distinguish mirth and suspense, fear and suffering, anger and determination, disgust and contempt in the facial expressions of people in photographs. On the basis of these ratings Woodworth compiled a scale of emotional expressions, with similar emotions placed next to one another.

In later investigations, Harold Schlosberg found that the emotions at the ends of this scale, mirth and contempt, were often confused with each other. This finding prompted him to rearrange the scale in the form of a circle, around which were located two basic emotional dimensions: (1) pleasantness and unpleasantness, and (2) attention and rejection (see Figure 12-20). Later, he and his associates added a third dimension of sleep and tension, or inactivation and activation, vertical to the other dimensions (Engen, Levy, & Schlosberg, 1958). With these dimensions, they felt that the

Figure 12-20 A circular scale of emotions in accordance with Schlosberg's dimensions of (1) pleasant (P) and unpleasant (U) and (2) attention (A) and rejection (R). The additional third dimension of activation and inactivation can be imagined as vertical to the page. (Adapted from Schlosberg, 1952)

whole range and variety of emotions could be placed in a logical and natural set of relationships. Recently N. H. Frijda (1970) has suggested on the basis of further experiments that the three emotional dimensions should be called pleasantness and unpleasantness, attention and disinterest, and certainty and uncertainty. Frijda holds that the strength of emotions is better expressed as certainty or uncertainty than as sleep or tension.

LISTEN TO DIMENSIONS OF FEELINGS

■ In the nineteenth century the "father of scientific psychology," Wilhelm Wundt, proposed the theory that feelings are tridimensional, an idea very similar to Schlosberg's and Frijda's. Wundt said that feelings range along the dimension of pleasantness–unpleasantness, relaxation–tension, and calm–excitement. Wundt was an introspective psychologist and held that these feeling dimensions, or elements, can be distinguished in any experience, even in the feelings aroused by listening to a series of beats. Get a pencil or pen and see if you, too, can experience Wundt's dimensions introspectively.

Tap the pencil or pen rhythmically on a book or a table. Do slow beats give you a calm feeling and faster and faster beats a sense of excitement? Doesn't slow music yield tranquillity and isn't fast music exciting? When you tap out the beats very slowly, doesn't the wait between the beats arouse tension, and a sense of relaxation or relief as the beats occur? For the third dimension, try a series of random beats for unpleasantness and a rhythmic combination of beats for pleasantness. Also, some rhythms may be very pleasant and others, with less discernible pattern, unpleasant. Wundt believed that these three dimensions provide the basis from which all more complex feelings are developed.

SUMMARY

Motivated behavior is aroused, persists, and is directed toward a goal. Emotions are aroused states with a strong feeling component that often accompany motivation. Motives or drives may arise from needs, internal states involving a deficit. Incentives are goals toward which behavior is directed. Human motivational states include biological drives, safety motives, and personal and interpersonal motives.

Homeostatic drives, like hunger and thirst, are directed toward restoring the body's optimum internal environment, the condition of homeostasis. Nonhomeostatic drives, like the sex and parental drives, are necessary for the survival of the species but not for the survival of the individual.

A hunger center in the lateral nucleus of the hypothalamus and a satiety center in its ventromedial nucleus control the hunger drive. These centers are probably activated by nutritional conditions in the bloodstream, as well as by stimuli from stomach and mouth. Similarly, the hypothalamus contains a thirst center, although a thirst-satiety center has not been found. The hypothalamus has also been found to mediate sexual behavior in response to male and female sex hormones. Human sexual behavior is largely under the control of psychological rather than hormonal conditions.

Secondary or acquired motives are sometimes based on primary motives, as fear can derive from pain. However, certain secondary motives, such as the attraction of an infant to its mother, are probably not based on satisfaction of primary drives.

According to drive-reduction theory, an instigating condition, or need, results in a drive state that directs responses toward a goal that produces drive reduction. However, drive-reduction theory does not explain the powerful reinforcing effects of exploration, stimulus variability, and excitement, which do not appear to derive from the reduction of basic drives.

Personal and interpersonal motives studied by psychologists have included the need for achievement (n-Ach), the motive to avoid success (M_{-s}), the need for affiliation (n-Aff), and the need for power (n-Pow). Thematic Apperception Tests designed to measure these motives have shown that they vary in intensity from individual to individual. Cultural norms and parental attitudes influence the development and expression of an individual's personal motives.

Emotions, which often accompany personal and interpersonal needs, have both arousal and affective components. They are accompanied by a variety of visceral reactions that may contribute to the emotional experience.

Emotional behavior is initiated by a predominantly subcortical area of the brain called the limbic system. The cortex moderates the emotional expression of the limbic system. The cortex probably also plays an important role in the interpretation of complex stimuli and in the conscious experience of emotions.

Pleasure and punishment centers have been identified in the brain, mostly in the limbic system. Electrical stimulation of these centers in animals produces behavior indicative of pleasure and pain. Pleasure has also been reported from brain stimulation in humans. Sensory stimulation may normally bring about stimulation of brain centers controlling the experiences of pleasure and pain. Three basic dimensions of emotions seem to be pleasantness — unpleasantness, attention — rejection, and activation–inactivation.

INVESTIGATE IT YOURSELF

Pick out a situation, or several situations, over the last few days in which you were strongly emotionally motivated. See if you can answer the following questions about the situation or situations:

Was a biological, safety, personal, or interpersonal motive involved?

Was the motive primary or secondary, learned or unlearned?

How well does the drive-reduction theory explain it?

Were achievement, affiliation, or power motives involved in it?

What emotion(s) did you have as the motive was satisfied or unsatisfied?

What situational, physiological, and behavioral features accompanied the emotion(s)?

Did your emotion(s) change in nature or strength as the situation developed and was concluded?

How would you conclude emotions and motives are related?

13

Anxiety, Frustration, and Conflict

thoroughly as you can and write a detailed description of it.

Now write another description, this time about the anxiety state itself. Describe your feelings in the situation and any other physical or behavioral manifestations of your anxiety that you can. How did you feel and react in the anxiety-producing situation?

The two descriptions together make up a case history on anxiety to which you can check back as you work with the discussion in this chapter.

In Chapter 12 you saw how motivation provides the "push," the activation, for the behaving organism. Generally, but not always, this results in behavior that has the goal of relief of tension. In this chapter, the ways in which three specific motivational states, anxiety, frustration, and conflict, can be studied and possibly controlled are examined. Since it is virtually impossible to avoid all of these conditions in everyday life, the content of this chapter has obvious relevance to our lives. Indeed, some students can legitimately claim to be past masters of one or more of these conditions, if frequency of experience is any criterion.

ANXIETY

If only neutral terms like "alpha" and "gamma" could be used to refer to psychological processes, people might be less likely to invest such terms with their own personal—and very different—sets of meanings, as usually happens when a scientific vocabulary contains words taken from everyday life. So it is with anxiety: All of us have our own definitions for this term—fear, dread, worry, the "creepies," inner discomfort. Most such definitions tend to be of one type: They refer to some qualities of inner experience, as does the definition from Webster. While psychologists are crucially interested in inner experience, they are more prone to go beyond the experiential referents for the term, seeking to

REMEMBRANCE OF ANXIETY PAST

■ Undoubtedly you have quite a good notion as to what anxiety is. Your notion may be rather well expressed in a dictionary definition of anxiety: "a state of being anxious or of experiencing a strong or dominating blend of uncertainty, agitation or dread, and brooding fear about some contingency" (*Webster's Third New International Dictionary*). Before going further into the anxious state, however, let's look at a specific instance of it.

Recall a situation in your past that aroused in you great anxiety, dread, or apprehension. It could have been something you or someone else did, some emergency or danger that aroused you, some serious situation in your family in childhood. It could have been a situation that happened only once, or it may have continued for some time or happened intermittently. Recollect the situation as

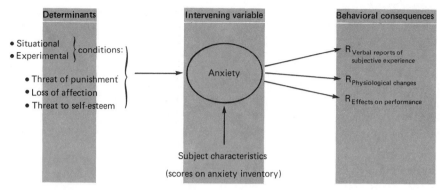

Figure 13-1 The concept of anxiety, showing operational linkages to objectively definable determinants and behavioral consequences.

relate it to determining conditions on the one hand, and to behavioral manifestations on the other. As you examine Figure 13-1, you can readily see how the logical status of the concept of anxiety resembles that of other intervening variables, like habits and drives, with which you are already acquainted. **Anxiety** can be defined as a complex motivational state that can be aroused in everyday life or in a laboratory setting, whenever the person is threatened with an extremely painful or aversive event ("You will receive a very intense electric shock"), with the loss of affection or companionship, or with a blow to self-esteem ("Your performance on this task places you among the poorest group of college students we've tested").

In addition to the fact that some situations can arouse more anxiety than others, people differ widely in their tendency to become anxious in the face of the same threatening condition. Some people always seem to feel anxious about something or other; for others, worlds could crash around them without making them bat an eye. These differences among people are assumed to reflect differences in an anxiety trait or traits. A **trait** is a relatively enduring and rather general predisposition to display certain behavioral tendencies and can be estimated by the use of a variety of psychological tests, as you will see

in Chapter 14. For the moment, assume that test scores on a valid anxiety scale correspond to levels of this strange motivational state called anxiety.

Anxious Behavior

Now that you know that environmental conditions can generate different levels of anxiety, and that people vary in their tendency to react anxiously to such conditions, you may still wish to know, "What is anxiety?" A complete answer requires at least brief mention of the behavioral consequences: The anxious person makes characteristic statements like "I'm petrified!" or "Oh, my God, I'm scared!" These reports are presumed to correlate with inner experience, although psychologists are always prepared for the possibility that people may have good reason for concealing what they privately feel. Both people and nonverbal organisms may show systematic changes in physiological patterns that correlate with exposure (or threat of exposure) to aversive events: Heart rate may go up, blood pressure rise, and skin resistance fall. In fact, some evidence suggests that when people are made anxious, the adrenal medulla secretes increased amounts of epinephrine (adrenaline), while a state of anger seems to produce increased secretion of norepinephrine (noradrenaline)

(Breggin, 1964). Furthermore, anxiety appears to be correlated with increased systolic blood pressure and heart rate, while anger tends to be associated with increased diastolic blood pressure and not so great an increase in heart rate (Martin, 1961). So, at least for these two rather basic conditions, anxiety does seem to manifest itself in ways different from those of anger. The overt behavior of anxious and non-anxious people is also different, either in the form of gestural or postural behavior, in the performance of interpersonal skills, in academic performance, or even in such things as voice quality.

Anxiety, then, is a hypothetical state that can be aroused more or less readily by specifiable external conditions, and manifests itself by characteristic verbal reports of private experience, by patterns of physiological change, and by interference with complex intellectual and social skills.

Fear and Anxiety

Most experimental psychologists tend to use the terms "fear" and "anxiety" rather interchangeably. Some psychologists, especially clinical psychologists, distinguish between fear as a realistic apprehension, proportional to a real threat (you are afraid while driving a car known to have defective brakes in hilly terrain) as opposed to anxiety as a state of unreasonably high tension, disproportionate to any real threat (you avoid riding in cars because there may be an accident someday). Others distinguish between the two concepts on the basis of the recognizability of the source: Fear has a known, easily identifiable source (you are afraid of the rising flood waters, or of being attacked while walking alone late at night in a high-crime area), while events that trigger an anxiety state are often obscure ("All of a sudden, while I was sitting in the library, I felt overwhelmed by an enormous sense of dread"; "For no reason at all, I sometimes start to sweat and tremble, and feel terribly fright-

ened"). But following the usage of experimental psychologists, we shall use the terms "fear" and "anxiety" interchangeably.

ANXIETY AND ANGER

Both interpersonal stresses and stresses arising from the physical environment can arouse strong emotions and lead to behavior disorders. Recently the relation between physical stresses and anxiety and anger has been investigated in studies that showed at least some of the differences between these emotions (Russell & Mehrabian, 1974). Subjects were given a series of verbal descriptions of physical situations to read, asked to imagine themselves in these situations, and then asked to rate the emotional states of anxiety or anger that they felt, on the basis of nine-point semantic-differential scales. For example, one of the verbal descriptions read:

From a nearby hill you can see a raging brush fire in progress. Clouds of black smoke billow up until the sky is darkened. The flames are a contrasting bright red and you can hear them crackling. They seem to be spreading quickly and the brisk wind helps them to leap from one spot to another. The sound of sirens can be heard in the distance [p. 80].

Imagine yourself in such a situation for a minute. How would you feel about it? The anxiety or anger aroused by such situations had certain dimensions in common, the researchers found, similar to the dimensions of emotions discussed in Chapter 12. Both anxiety and anger could be described as involving varying degrees of displeasure on a pleasure–displeasure dimension, and varying degrees of arousal on a low-to-high–arousal dimension. The main distinction between the two emotional reactions, however, appeared on the dimension of dominance–submission: Anger was rated high on dominance and anxiety high on submission. While social situations may call up more intense feelings of dominance and submission, these could also be aroused by physical situations, such as noise, crowding, pollution, danger. In this case, dominance was expressed as power to control events, and submission as weakness or inability to control events. Displeasure was found much more important than arousal in the makeup of anger, while displeasure and arousal were equally significant components of anxiety. Furthermore, evidence showed that chronically anxious people generally feel unhappy, aroused, and submissive, and it is such persistent anxiety that is characteristic of many of the neurotic behavior disorders.

Anxiety and Human Performance

In Chapter 12 you learned that anxiety acts like a powerful drive, motivating behavior and reinforcing whatever responses have the effect of reducing the strength of the anxiety state. The rats in Neal E. Miller's (1948a) experiment were made anxious when they were confined to the white box in which they had been shocked, and they quickly learned to turn a wheel or press a lever to get out of the white box and into the safe black box, the escape response presumably reinforced by anxiety reduction. Thus anxiety provided both a powerful drive and a drive-reduction motive for the learning of escape behavior. Some theorists characterize the anxious person as one whose total motivational level is chronically high, because of the contribution of the anxiety state to the general motivational system, and as one who spends a lot of time learning behaviors (symptoms) that serve to reduce (at least momentarily) the sharp edge of anxiety, and which are therefore strongly reinforced. The strange symptom called a hand-washing compulsion seems to involve intense feelings of guilt and anxiety that abate only when the hand-washers wash their hands; the consequent and immediate relief experienced by these people strongly reinforces the hand-washing symptom. The assumption that anxious people have a generally high total drive level leads us to a number of predictions concerning their behavior. Kenneth W. Spence (1958) argues this way:

1. Behavior (B) results from the interaction of habits (H) and drives (D), or $B = H \times D$.
2. In simple response situations, in which the "correct" response does not have to com-

pete against other habit tendencies, the higher the drive, the more vigorous the performance.
3. If anxious people have a higher drive than nonanxious people, they should display more vigorous behavior in simple response tasks.

Everyday observation immediately suggests some examples. The little boy being pursued by a big bully runs faster the more frightened he is (provided, of course, he knows where to run—that is, provided one direction does not have to compete with other, equally strong directional tendencies). To make a more reliable test of this notion, we could observe how rapidly high- and low-anxious people learn a very simple response, like blinking in a classical conditioning experiment. You know how to set up an experiment to condition the eyelid response (puff of air on the eye as the US, a weak light for the CS), but would you know how to identify people differing in anxiety level? Let's detour at this point to consider some fundamentals about the measurement of anxiety.

The Measurement of Anxiety

Like the measurement of other psychological traits, the measurement of anxiety is only a refinement of everyday observation. After all, you have a pretty general idea who, among your friends and acquaintances, are very anxious people, and you can also think of people who are exceptionally calm. In both cases, with a little effort, you can probably enumerate the behaviors that serve as the stimuli responsible for your discriminations. Psychological measurement merely tries to spell out more fully and clearly what the distinguishing behaviors are, and tries to increase the objectivity of our judgments, so that our assessment of another's anxiety level won't vary with our own moods and tensions.

Measurement of anxiety takes many forms, all of which involve the observation of a person's behaviors by another, or a self-report of the person's own behavior. Accordingly, you could assess anxiety by long-term observation of large segments of a person's behavior (as in a hospital setting), by sampling behavior in a structured interview situation, by observing the person's physiological responses to a variety of mild or disturbing stimuli, or by asking the person to fill out a self-report inventory.

An **anxiety inventory** usually consists of a number of statements concerning behaviors and feelings, to each of which subjects respond by indicating whether or not each statement

---

Table 13-1 Sample Items Taken from Various Anxiety Scales

A. *Taylor Manifest Anxiety Scale* (TMAS)*

I am often sick to my stomach.   (True)
I worry quite a bit over possible troubles.   (True)
I do not have as many fears as my friends.   (False)
I am a very nervous person.   (True)
I am very confident of myself.   (False)

B. *Test Anxiety Questionnaire* (TAQ)†

If you know that you are going to take a group intelligence test, how do you feel *beforehand?*

|	|	|
Feel very confident	Midpoint	Feel very unconfident

When you are taking a course examination, to what extent do you feel that your emotional reactions interfere with or lower your performance?

|	|	|
Do not interfere with it at all	Midpoint	Interfere a great deal

C. *Achievement Anxiety Test* (AAT)‡

Items measuring *facilitating* anxiety (AAT +):

I work most effectively under pressure, as when the task is very important.

1	2	3	4	5
Always				Never

Nervousness while taking a test helps me to do better.

1	2	3	4	5
It never helps				It always helps

Items measuring *debilitating* anxiety (AAT −):

In a course where I have been doing poorly, my fear of a bad grade cuts down my efficiency.

1	2	3	4	5
Never				Always

The more important the examination, the less well I seem to do.

1	2	3	4	5
Always				Never

* Taylor, 1953.
† Sarason & Mandler, 1952.
‡ Alpert & Haber, 1960.

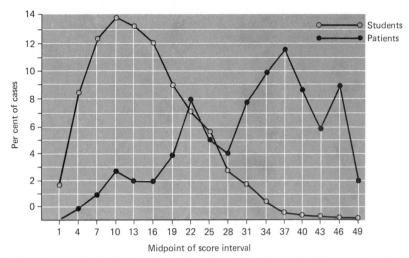

Figure 13-2 Distributions of Taylor Manifest Anxiety Test (TMAS) scores obtained from a sample of 1971 college students (open circles) and a sample of 103 psychiatric patients (filled circles). (Taylor, 1953)

applies to them and, in some tests, to what degree it applies. Sometimes the statements from which the final items of the scale are selected are taken from descriptions of behavior considered to be good symptoms of anxiety by expert psychiatrists and psychologists working in clinical settings with patients known to be anxious. One scale, the **Taylor Manifest Anxiety Scale,** or **TMAS,** consists of items selected this way, to each of which subjects respond by writing "T" or "F" to indicate whether the description is generally true for them or not. Table 13-1 shows some items from the TMAS. As the items suggest, this scale attempts to measure a *predisposition* to behave anxiously, not the subject's immediately experienced emotional state. The score depends on the total number of items to which the subject has given the anxious response. Figure 13-2 compares the distribution of TMAS scores of a large group of college students and of a group of psychiatric patients known to be anxious. The scale has a rather high reliability index, since correlations for test–retest scores obtained anywhere from 3 weeks to 18 months

apart range from 0.81 to 0.89 (see Appendix: Statistics).

But is the TMAS valid? You may recall the definition of "validity" in Chapter 3. Certainly the TMAS scale has **face validity,** for a glance at the items is sufficient to establish that they deal with anxiety rather than with other states, like anger, for example. More important, however, is a demonstration of the scale's **concurrent validity**—its ability to discriminate between groups known to differ in anxiety. Figure 13-2 shows that college students and neurotic patients do indeed get different scores on the TMAS: The median score for the college group is 13, while that of the patients is 34. About 95 per cent of the scores of the college sample lie below the patients' median score. It is also interesting to note that TMAS scores correlate rather well with tests measuring neuroticism, which is another way **of** saying that neurotic disorders tend to invo**lve** a high anxiety component.

A final measure of validity, construct validity, takes us back to the main road after our detour: People with high and low anxiety should

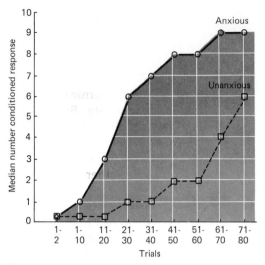

Figure 13-3 Anxiety, like other motives, energizes habits. Hence the conditioning of a simple eyelid response is facilitated. (Taylor, 1951)

behave differently in the acquisition of a simple noncompetitive response, like eyelid conditioning. If high anxiety contributes to drive level, the more anxious person, having greater drive strength, should condition better than a less anxious person. **Construct validity** refers to the degree to which predictions based on the *theoretical* properties of the concept being measured are confirmed. Figure 13-3 shows the results of one experiment (Taylor, 1951) in which a group of subjects with high TMAS scores and another group with low TMAS scores were given classical eyelid conditioning. Note that high-anxiety subjects showed better conditioning than less anxious subjects, demonstrating that anxiety acts like other drives to facilitate performance in simple tasks in which only a single response is elicited by the CS.

The apparent advantages of high levels of anxiety may be difficult for many students to appreciate, however, for who among us has never felt self-confidence withering and performance falling apart as anxiety rises and undermines the foundations of a well-prepared performance? If anxiety facilitates performance, why do our tongues thicken and our heads feel full of tapioca when, in the middle of an interview, or an extemporaneous talk or an important exam, we suddenly feel anxious? The answer to this paradox is to be found in the principle that anxiety, acting indeed like a drive, energizes *all* habit tendencies, even the tendency to say foolish things or make wrong responses. To see how this works, think of the effects of hunger-drive level on T-maze learning: Assume a rat is mildly hungry and must learn to turn right at the choice point, since food is to be found only on the right side. A rat with a slight tendency to turn left instead of right has a problem; it must learn to overcome a competing wrong tendency. Now, what if the rat were *terribly* hungry? Its tendency to turn left—that is, to respond incorrectly—would be even stronger, and it would have even greater difficulty learning to overcome this tendency and turn right instead. Increased levels of motivation will impair performance whenever competing tendencies to make incorrect responses exist. The stronger, or more dominant, the incorrect response tendencies, the more an increase in motivation will raise their relative strength, and the more performance will suffer.

High and Low Anxiety

If you've ever arrived at your front door and heard the phone ringing inside, you probably remember how difficult it was to find your keys and to use them quickly and efficiently to turn the lock so you could get inside and run to the phone. The greater the anxiety, the more you fumbled, dropped your keys, or tried to insert the wrong one. *High anxiety interferes with complex behaviors*, unless the correct responses are highly dominant. That's why troops in basic training are repeatedly drilled to drop to the ground at the first sign of danger. This protective response is so well practiced that it becomes by far the most dominant response tendency in combat. When danger triggers anxiety, the response of sprawling on the ground occurs automatically. Social situations often arouse anxiety, and we certainly do not have all the correct verbal responses on the tip of the tongue. In such cases, anxiety may trigger a well-practiced verbal amenity that unfortunately may be terribly out of place. A young man who went to pay his last respects to the father of a friend encountered the widow as he was leaving the funeral home. She thanked him for coming, and the young man replied courteously, "Don't mention it, the pleasure was mine." Anxiety tends to convert our most dominant response tendencies into behavior.

PANIC AND SURVIVAL

A very high intensity of anxiety, spurred higher by immediate threat to life, can lead to panic, in which instincts for survival overcome all thought and judgment and screaming fear predominates. Thus in 1974 during a fire at Gulliver's Restaurant, a basement discothèque in Port Chester, New York, 24 young people were trampled to death as all the patrons tried to get out the same way they had come in, in their panic ignoring three emergency exits. In a similar fire at the Club-Cinque in St.-Laurent, France, in 1970, 145 young dancers died, piled six feet high against an inner turnstile and the main door. During the past century, panics in 17 such fires in places of public assembly have killed nearly 5000 people.

When faced with such threats to survival, most people tend to become extremely anxious and to panic, following the crowd without thought as to the best way to save their lives. Only if the appropriate escape behavior is dominant, well learned through much practice, can some individuals resist the pull of "crowd psychology" and keep from rushing to do what everyone else is doing. If successful escape activities are well rehearsed, so that they will be performed almost without much conscious effort, panic reactions can be avoided. This is the reason for fire drills in schools and lifeboat drills on ships. When you are at any public gathering or sleeping overnight in an unfamiliar building, it's a good idea to spot the available exits, particularly the exit nearest to you, so that the tendency to go out that way will be aroused automatically if an emergency occurs. This is the best way to avoid panic.

As you might expect, there have been many experimental demonstrations of the complex effects of anxiety on behavior. Ernest K. Montague (1953) found that high anxiety impaired the serial learning of a difficult list of nonsense syllables (Chapter 9), in which error tendencies were presumed to predominate. By contrast, anxious subjects learned an easy list faster than did less anxious subjects, perhaps because correct responses in an easy list quickly become dominant. In another experiment, Charles D. Spielberger and L. J. Smith (1966) reasoned that high anxiety should impair learning a difficult serial list the most during the *early* trials, when correct responses have not yet acquired enough strength to predominate over incorrect response tendencies. On the other hand, anxiety should facilitate performance *late* in learning, as correct responses have gained in relative strength. These investigators found that when the subjects (college students) were additionally stressed by being told that speed of learning was strongly related to intelligence, the performance of high-anxious subjects was indeed poorer early in learning, but superior late in learning, relative to that of low-anxious subjects.

Do you think anxiety impairs *your* performance? Let's take academic performance, since you are quite familiar with that type of situation. At this point, you know that the answer to this question has got to be "It depends." Sometimes you find anxiety impairs your performance, sometimes it facilitates it, and sometimes it doesn't seem to influence it much one way or the other depending on a number of factors. But it depends especially on the complexity of the performance, how anxious you are, and how well you know the material. Consider a single item on a multiple-choice exam:

Pavlov was a famous: philosopher
chemist
physiologist
psychologist

What effect will different levels of anxiety have on a student attempting to choose the best alternative? The effect will depend on how well the student has learned the correct answer. Think of the stem of the item ("Pavlov was a famous . . .") as the stimulus term. If the student has really learned the correct response very well, the tendency to select R_3, "physiologist," will be much greater than that of even a close competitor like R_4, "psychologist," and high anxiety should, theoretically, facilitate selection of the correct response. For a less well-prepared student, however, the R_3 and R_4 tendencies might be much closer in strength, or R_4, the incorrect tendency, might even be the stronger. High anxiety will certainly not facilitate correct responding if an incorrect tendency predominates.

This analysis makes it easy to understand the results obtained in a study by Wilbert J. McKeachie and his colleagues. Students taking regular course examinations of the multiple-choice type were encouraged to write any comments they wished about the test items on the examination sheet. It was assumed that items difficult to answer are likely to increase anxiety, but that the chance to comment gives the student a way of discharging tension. Students encouraged to comment made significantly better scores than did a comparable group that took the exam in the conventional way (McKeachie, Pollie, & Speisman, 1955). This procedure has been found to be especially effective in improving the test scores of students who are exceptionally anxious to begin with (Smith & Rockett, 1958).

Relating anxiety levels to competing response tendencies becomes much more difficult, if not impossible, when the test is of the essay type. Such a test requires the student to produce a number of thematic elements on his own, and then to assemble them into a coherent structure. Since at various points during an essay exam you are faced with many attractive alternative directions and choices, you might well expect that high levels of anxiety would seriously impair performance. Perhaps this is one reason students often prefer a take-home

exam; it would seem that performance on a take-home essay exam would be less influenced by the student's anxiety level than an essay exam taken in class.

Perhaps the most complex measure of academic performance is the **grade-point average (GPA),** which assesses the quality of academic behavior over the period of one or more semesters. While a lot more than anxiety factors influence one's GPA, it seems plausible to assume, from our discussion thus far, that high anxiety would be associated with a lower GPA. Quite a number of research studies have found such an inverse relationship between anxiety and measures of academic performance, among both college and high school students. In one of the most interesting studies (Spielberger, 1962), the relationship between anxiety and GPA was examined in college students who varied greatly in academic aptitude. Male college students scoring in the upper or lower 20 per cent of the TMAS distribution were designated as high-anxiety (HA) or low-anxiety (LA) subjects. Each anxiety group was subdivided into five levels of scholastic ability, on the basis of total scores on the ACE test, a measure of scholastic aptitude. Figure 13-4 compares the GPA of HA and LA students at five levels of scholastic aptitude. In the middle ability range, where the bulk of the college population is to be found, HA students obtained poorer grades than LA students. Anxiety level made no difference in the GPA of students whose aptitude for college work was either very high (Group V) or very low (Group I). Thus anxiety affects the academic performance of middle-aptitude students most of all.

Anxiety level was also related to dropout rate. Only 8 of the 138, or 6 per cent, of LA students involved in the study dropped out of college because of academic failure, compared with 26 out of 129, or 20 per cent, of HA students. In the lowest aptitude group (Group I), the dropout rate for HA students compared with LA students was 2 to 1. While Figure 13-4 suggests that students of the highest aptitude

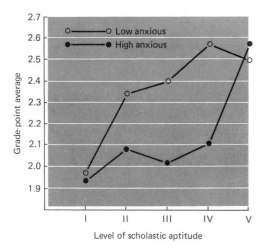

Figure 13-4 Academic performance of HA and LA college students, grouped according to scholastic aptitude level. (Spielberger, 1962b)

(Group V) do excellent academic work regardless of anxiety level, a more detailed analysis indicated that high anxiety may actually have facilitated performance. For the students with the very highest aptitude scores (above the 96th percentile) within Group V, the GPA of HA students was 3.01, compared with 2.70 for LA students of comparable aptitude. Spielberger concludes that for students of the very highest aptitude level, anxiety may act as a spur to greater effort.

ANXIETY AND MEMORY?

A number of investigations have revealed that being "nervous," "apprehensive," or "anxious" affects remembering in a surprising way, hindering memory over a relatively short period but facilitating long-term memory. In a recently reported experiment along this line, 240 women students in an introductory psychology course served as subjects (Geen, 1974). Some were told that the learning of a paired-associates list in which 6 nonsense syllables (*tov, cef, qap, jea, laj,* and *dax*) had to be associated with the digits 2 to 7 was being used to evaluate their intelligence, and others were told that the list was being tested to see how some stimuli are recalled better than others. Some were watched by the experimenter during the test and others were not watched. After the presentation of the list, the subjects were given a checklist on which to indicate whether they felt relaxed, fearful, jumpy, or carefree during the learning trial. Then the subjects' recall of the list was tested at intervals of 2, 15, and 45 minutes after the learning session.

Those students who thought their intelligence was being evaluated indicated they felt relaxed much less frequently than those who thought it was only a list of items that was being tested. Differences between subjects who were and were not observed during the presentation of paired associates were not significant. However, the recall of the paired associates by those who thought they were being evaluated, and who were therefore apprehensive during the presentation, was significantly different from the recall of those who thought the list was being assessed. Short-term recall (after two minutes) of the evaluated group was much poorer than that of the nonevaluated group, but the long-term memory (after 45 minutes) of the evaluated group was much better. Apprehension aroused by the thought of evaluation reduced short-term recall and improved long-term recall. Why memory should be affected by anxiety in this manner is still an open question.

Look back at the sample of items from the TMAS in Table 13-1. They seem to deal with anxiety in general, and not specifically with test-taking situations. Such a test is called a **general anxiety measure.** A number of investigators have found it more useful to work with tests that measure anxiety in specific situations, most often in test-taking situations. An example of such a **specific anxiety measure** is the **Test Anxiety Questionnaire,** or **TAQ** (S. B. Sarason & Mandler, 1952). The TAQ consists of 35 items dealing with one's reaction to taking an examination or an IQ test. As shown in the sample items in Table 13-1, each item is answered by marking a point on a 15-centimeter line that represents a dimension with a neutral midpoint and two extreme opposite positions. The score for each item is then obtained by measuring with a ruler along the scale from the left to the subject's mark. A true–false 17-item version of the TAQ, which is much easier to score, has also been devised (I. G. Sarason, 1958), as has a scale specifically designed to measure test anxiety in schoolchildren, the TASC (S. B. Sarason, Davidson, Lighthall, Waite, & Ruebush, 1960).

As we have seen, anxiety tends to impair academic performance, except possibly among students at the very highest aptitude level and at the very lowest. Yet occasionally students seem to feel that anxiety actually makes them perform better. Actors and musicians often claim that a certain level of tension gives their performance an extra brilliance. On the assumption that anxiety may *facilitate* the academic performance of some students, Richard Alpert and Ralph N. Haber (1960) developed the **Achievement Anxiety Test (AAT),** designed to measure both debilitating and facilitating effects of test anxiety. The test consists of 9 facilitating anxiety items and 10 debilitating anxiety items. Each item, as can be seen in the samples shown in Table 13-1, is answered by circling the appropriate number on a five-point scale. As is generally true of tests of specific rather than general anxiety, scores obtained on the AAT tend to be fairly good predictors of academic performance. In one study (Desiderato & Koskinen, 1969), college women with high debilitating anxiety had lower GPAs than women with high scores in facilitating anxiety. Moreover, the debilitating-anxiety students were also shown to have poorer study habits than the facilitating-anxiety subjects. It's hard to say whether high levels of debilitating anxiety lead to poorer academic grades because anxiety disrupts performance during examinations, because it makes effective studying difficult or onerous, or both.

Reduction of Anxiety

What can be done to help students whose anxiety level keeps them from realizing their potential in their studies? One approach has been to provide anxious students with a chance to reduce their anxiety levels through group counseling (Spielberger, Weitz, & Denny, 1962). On the basis of anxiety tests administered at the beginning of their college career, anxious freshmen who were having academic difficulties were invited to participate in a voluntary program that included weekly group counseling sessions. Of the 56 volunteers, 28 began their counseling in the middle of their second college semester. The other 28, matched for academic aptitude, had their counseling delayed one semester; they served as a control group. Counseling sessions revolved around methods of study, dormitory experiences, personal goals, and relationships with teachers, and no attempt was made to explore personal problems in any great depth. Figure 13-5 shows the improvement in GPA between midterm and the end of the semester, comparing the gain achieved by the counseled students against the change in GPA achieved by the noncounseled group. Note that the ben-

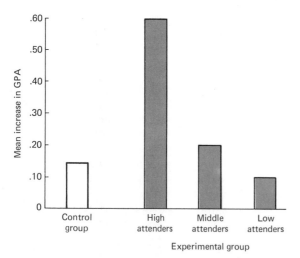

Figure 13-5 Improvement in the academic performance of anxious college freshmen participating in different numbers of counseling sessions. (Spielberger, Weitz, & Denny, 1962)

efits of counseling were greatest for students who attended nearly all sessions. The GPA of spotty attenders improved much less.

More direct methods for reducing anxiety in college students involve the application of systematic **desensitization** and **relaxation** techniques, described in Chapter 8. For example, Richard Cornish and Josiah Dilley (1973) have reported on a method specifically designed to help college students combat examination anxiety. First, students are trained in the fundamentals of progressive relaxation. Following the systematic desensitization procedure of Wolpe (1973), they learn to relax while imagining faintly anxiety-arousing scenes concerning some aspect of examination taking. For example, they imagine being informed that an examination has been scheduled two months in the future. As relaxation responses replace the mild anxiety responses that such imagery evokes, more upsetting imagery is gradually introduced; for example, of an exam being announced for the next class, or—the all-time champion panic rouser—the snap quiz. While desensitization-relaxation techniques have only recently been applied to the reduction of test anxiety, results so far are quite promising and increasing use of this method seems probable. The trend, in fact, is toward the use of both desensitization and group counseling. This combination has been successful not only in reducing the level of test anxiety, but also in improving academic achievement (Mitchell & Ng, 1972).

A RELAXATION RESPONSE

A relaxation response that can be learned by self-instruction in an hour is under investigation and may prove useful in dealing with anxiety and tension (Beary, Benson, & Klemchuk, 1974; Benson, Beary, & Carol, 1974). Ten females and 7 males with a mean age of 24 years served as subjects in the experiment. All the subjects taught themselves the relaxation technique, quite similar to that of Transcendental Meditation (see Chapter 6),

for an hour before the experiment started. During the experiment, various physiological data were collected while the subjects, for 12-minute periods, simply (a) sat quietly and read, (b) sat quietly with closed eyes, or (c) sat quietly inducing a relaxation response in accordance with the following instructions:

1—Sit quietly in a comfortable position. 2—Close your eyes. 3—Deeply relax all your muscles, beginning at your feet and progressing up to your face. Keep them deeply relaxed. 4—As you breathe out, say the word "One" silently to yourself. For example, breathe In . . . Out, "One," In . . . Out, "One." 5—Continue until told to stop. Do not worry about whether you are succeeding in achieving a deep level of relaxation. Maintain a passive attitude and permit relaxation to occur at its own pace. If distracting thoughts do occur, ignore them and continue to repeat "One" as soon as you become aware of them [Beary, Benson, & Klemchuk, 1974, p. 116].

The data showed that during the relaxation period (c) oxygen consumption decreased 13 per cent, carbon dioxide production decreased 12 per cent, and respiratory rate diminished significantly, in comparison with the period of sitting quietly and reading (a). Period (b), sitting quietly with eyes closed, did not produce any such significant changes. The investigators suggest that the relaxation response "results in generalized decreased sympathetic nervous system activity," the opposite of the fight-or-flight response, in which the sympathetic nervous system is stimulated and excited. They conclude that "regular elicitation of the relaxation response may be of therapeutic value in diseases characterized by increased sympathetic nervous system activity," such as hypertension, or high blood pressure, and are making studies of its use by subjects suffering from headaches, drug abuse, psychoses, and anxiety neuroses. This relaxation technique might also be useful in connection with Wolpe's systematic desensitization procedure, described previously.

Whatever the final outcome of relaxation-response research, the contrast between the goal of final absolute union with the One sought by mystics over periods of many years and the goal of physical relaxation sought by concentrating on the word "One" is amazing to contemplate.

You have seen how anxiety, an extremely significant motivational concept, is a much more complicated business than our everyday, casual use of the term would suggest. And you now know how very important it is to separate, in your thinking, definitions of anxiety that refer to precipitating conditions, to subjective states, to physiological processes, and to behavioral consequences. These differentiations give you a better basis for predicting what the effects of anxiety on behavior are likely to be and how you can acquire greater control over this state.

FRUSTRATION

Like the study of anxiety, the study of frustration is an aspect of the study of motivation. In general terms, **frustration** occurs when a motivated organism, striving to achieve a desired goal, is blocked or impeded in its progress toward that goal. Figure 13-6 displays these basic ingredients of a frustrating state of affairs. Does the sketch remind you of another concept you read about? It should. Turn back to Figure 11-12 and see if you can distinguish between the basic elements of frustration and problem solving. In both cases, the organism's progress toward a goal is blocked. The difference is that the psychology of frustration stresses the effects of *thwarting*, usually as expressed in some form of aggressive behavior; the study of problem solving focuses more on the way the organism finally gets to the goal or its discovery of a solution. Moreover, in problem-solving studies, the thwarting is usually temporary, for a solution is possible in most cases.

Nevertheless, the organism may indeed feel frustrated before it finally solves the problem, and if we chose to study both responses to thwarting and the emergence of a solution, we'd be investigating the psychology of frustration and the psychology of problem solving together. Maybe psychologists should be this broad in their studies, but they aren't. In this

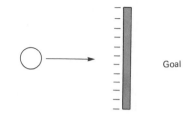

Figure 13-6 Frustration occurs when a motivated organism is blocked from achieving its goal.

case, they tend to investigate *either* problem solving *or* frustration. So here we'll be mainly concerned with frustration, but without losing sight of its close association with problem solving.

What Brings On Frustration?

Thwarting of goal-directed behavior instigates frustration. But the barriers that keep people from attaining their goals vary enormously, and so do the effects of encountering these barriers. The most basic distinction between barriers is that some are internal and others are external. **External barriers** are conditions in the environment that block goal attainment, while **internal barriers** are within the individual. The situation shown in Figure 13-6 represents an external type of barrier. A car that won't start when you're late for an appointment, a mother's insistence that her daughter straighten her room before she goes out to join her friends, the lack of funds that prevent the purchase of good hi-fi equipment—all these are external barriers preventing progress toward a goal; without them there would be no frustration.

While external barriers may be just as effective as internal barriers in keeping the organism from its goal, the intensity of the frustration effect is usually stronger when the barriers are internal. The teenager who yearns for a sexual experience but is thwarted by a sense of guilt, the suitor who can't bring himself to propose for fear that marriage may cost him his independence, the college student whose shyness prevents active participation in social events—all of these people are being thwarted by barriers within themselves. They carry their conflicts with them wherever they go. Clearly conflict is a major source of human frustration.

Frustration that occurs after many successful pursuits of a certain goal is more intense than frustration experienced without a history of prior reinforcement. The first firm "No!" that a previously meek and submissive wife manages to utter in response to her domineering husband's demands will produce much greater frustration in him than he would feel if he had encountered a negative response before. Children used to having their own way all the time will be much more frustrated when they are denied something than will children who have frequently encountered nonreinforcement. Experimental research has amply shown that the emotional effects of nonreinforcement are much stronger when they follow a history of continuous, rather than intermittent, reinforcement (Amsel, 1962). This finding can be turned into a principle of considerable practical importance: If you want to build frustration toler-

ance in a child, let the child experience frustration (nonreward) now and then; let that goal, whatever it is, remain out of reach some of the time. (But be sure the goal that is intermittently attainable does not consist of undesirable behavior, for partial reinforcement may also strengthen the very behavior you wish to extinguish.)

Delayed reinforcement also produces frustration. For some, it is tantamount to no reinforcement at all. The innocent man who desperately wants an early trial so he can prove his innocence may well feel that "justice delayed is justice denied." One can learn to reduce the emotional effects of delayed reinforcement, like those of nonreinforcement, by rewarding people who can "stick it through." In *Walden II* (1948), B. F. Skinner described how hungry children rushing in to dinner can be taught to endure frustration by having them pause and wait a bit while standing before the soup bowls placed before them, instead of immediately sitting down and digging in.

A FRUSTRATED CAT

In these times of food shortages around the world in the face of rapidly expanding populations, we Americans are fortunate in that most (though not all) of us have enough to eat. And psychologists do not, in their experiments, severely deprive their human subjects of nourishment in order to investigate the human hunger drive. They do, however, find that hunger is a convenient drive to study in other animals, in order, they hope, to reach conclusions that will prove beneficial for people. This is the story of a hungry cat, frustrated in its drive for food.

The cat, a male, was thoroughly trained to press a button that made a light come on, followed by the ringing of a bell, then by a tidbit of breaded salmon that dropped into his food box (Masserman, 1950). Nearly all cats love salmon, and this cat did; and for several months he routinely worked for his food in this manner. Then one day the cat received a harmless but disagreeable blast of air against his nose when he lifted the lid of his food box to obtain his reward. The cat dropped the food and jumped away from the box. He wandered about the cage, obviously hesitant to approach the switch or the food box, yet wanting to do so—a conflict situation. When the cat became so hungry and frustrated that he finally followed his routine again, no air was introduced for several feedings. Then he experienced the blast again. This blast came on intermittently from two to seven times a day for a week. The cat could not become accustomed to it, and developed a definite conflict, with symptoms similar to those of some human neuroses. He perspired, his heart beat irregularly, he trembled at the blast. He was startled at slight sounds and became fearful of harmless lights, closed places, air currents, and food itself. He had asthma attacks and stomach troubles, and became sexually impotent. He paced about restlessly, became aggressive, and lost his dominance over other cats, regressing to dependence and helplessness. All these results from a disagreeable blast of air!

By experimentally producing conflict-related frustration in many cats and other animals, investigators have learned a great deal about the variables involved in frustration, anxiety, and conflict, and techniques for overcoming such states in human beings.

Having examined some of the conditions that produce frustration, let's turn to the *consequences* of frustration. What are the behavioral reactions to frustration and what theoretical properties of the internal state of frustration can be inferred from such reactions?

Intensification of Behavior

Thwarting of a previously reinforced response usually leads to an intensification of the behavior, even though the response is no longer effective. Everyone has seen the vigorous plunger-pulling that occurs when the cigarette or candy machine takes the money but refuses to deliver. A door that usually opens easily but one day is stuck tight evokes an impressive amount of tugging. The laboratory rat that has learned to bar-press on a continuous reinforcement (CRF) schedule increases the vigor of its pressing when the extinction schedule goes into effect.

Some researchers have suggested that frustration acts like a drive, much as anxiety does, to intensify ongoing activity. In the experiment (Amsel & Roussel, 1952) described in Figure 13-7, rats were first trained to run down a straight alley to a goal box for a small food reward, and then to continue down an additional alley to a second goal box for a second food reward. After 84 training trials, 36 test trials were administered. Eighteen of the test trials were just like the training trials, with food present in each goal box. But the researchers intermixed 18 more test trials on which the first goal box was empty, producing frustration. What are the effects of frustration? If you wanted and expected a reward in goal box 1 and didn't find any when you got there, do you think you'd hurry on to goal box 2 at a faster clip than if you had found your usual reward in the first goal box? Rats certainly did hurry on to goal box 2 at a faster speed on those test trials in which nonreinforcement occurred at goal box 1. Figure 13-7 shows the difference in running time, which supports the view that frustration acts like a drive, intensifying the organism's goal-directed behavior. The young man who, despite his optimistic expectations, receives only a polite "Thank you" when he returns his date home may find himself exceeding the speed limit by more than the usual amount as he drives away feeling frustrated. Just as anxiety energizes behavior, so too does frustration!

You've seen how fear can be classically conditioned so that a previously neutral stimulus, like a tone, can elicit it. Can a state of frustration also be classically conditioned so that a previously neutral stimulus can elicit it? Theoretically, if a person happened to hear the words "feel frustrated" a number of times on

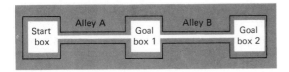

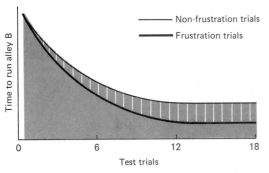

Figure 13-7 By comparing the speed with which rats run through alley B to a reward in goal box 2, after having been rewarded or frustrated in goal box 1, the motivational effect of frustration can be measured. The graph shows that after experiencing frustration in goal box 1, rats run faster in the second alley. (Amsel & Roussel, 1952)

an occasion when, indeed, he *was* actually being frustrated by something-or-other, later on it should be possible to produce the frustration state by merely telling him to "feel frustrated." Such stimulus control has not been demonstrated in humans, but something like it may have been found in animals. Helen B. Daly (1969) frustrated rats by rewarding them for running down a runway, first with 15-pellet rewards and then abruptly shifting to one-pellet rewards. The shift to the skimpy reward presumably produced frustration. Daly paired a light CS with the presentation of the small, "frustrating" reward. On the assumption that the state of frustration is aversive to the animals, the rats should be reinforced for leaving a place in which they feel frustrated. Daly's rats learned to jump a hurdle to escape the previously neutral light. Only if the light had acquired the capacity to elicit frustration (and only if frustration is an aversive state) would the animals have been reinforced for making the hurdle-jump response. Apparently frustration, like fear, can be conditioned.

As you might expect, a lot of factors will affect the intensity with which frustration energizes behavior. Generally, the stronger the motivation to achieve the thwarted goal, the more vigorous the response to frustration. Similarly, the closer the subject is to the thwarted goal, the more intense the reaction. Mothers who do not plan to buy their children candy when they go shopping would do well to notify them of this fact before leaving the house, rather than wait till the child comes within touching distance of the goal. Also, the greater the number of thwartings, the more vigorous the response. The child who continues to interrupt a mother's phone conversation for trivial reasons may elicit a far more vigorous response after the sixth interruption than after the first.

Aggressive Reactions

One of the most basic reactions to frustration is an attack on the barrier that blocks access to the goal. Direct attacks on frustrating obstacles often occur among young children. A child who forcefully confiscates another child's toy is likely to elicit an aggressive reaction. Aggressive reactions may take many forms. If direct attack on the instigator of frustration tends to pay off, either because the frustrated person is strong or clever enough to avoid punishment for aggressive behavior, overt aggressive behavior will become a habitual response to frustration. Bullies, having been reinforced often for expressing their frustrations physically, are not easily converted to more peaceable ways of coping with frustration.

If aggressive reactions are often and severely punished, direct attack upon the source of the frustration may be displaced to safer targets. The child whose capricious demands are blocked by a firm parental stance may have learned that aversive consequences follow aggressive responses directed toward the parent. In such cases, the aggressive response may be redirected toward an innocent younger sibling or a pet. In a study by Neal E. Miller and B. R. Bugelski (1948), workers at a summer camp were frustrated by being compelled to complete a number of long tests, thereby missing a chance to get to the theater in town in time for a lottery drawing. Both before and after this frustration, they filled out questionnaires measuring their attitudes toward Japanese and Mexicans. One result of the frustration was that aggressive responses that could not be safely directed against the experimenters were displaced toward these two ethnic groups in the form of more negative attitude scores. Some consider **displacement** to be the basis for **scapegoating,** in which aggressive forms of prejudice are directed away from the primary agents of frustration and shifted toward people who are neither responsible for the frustration nor able to defend themselves against the aggressive display. The most frequently cited example is that of the Jews in Nazi Germany, who were made the target of the German people's reactions to the hardships they had suffered after their defeat in World War I.

Sometimes the target for displaced aggression is anyone who happens to be around when frustration hits a peak. You've already seen the emotional behavior displayed by an animal at the start of extinction following training on a CRF schedule. Pigeons start flapping their wings and vigorously pecking at the response disk when the reinforcement for pecking is suddenly cut off. If another pigeon happens to be present in the same cage, the frustrated bird will soon shift its aggressive attack toward the innocent bystander (Azrin, 1967).

In one experiment, rats learned to turn off shock on the grid floor of their cage by standing on their hind legs and fighting each other. If one rat was removed and a celluloid doll inserted in its place, the remaining rat generalized the attack response to the doll

(Miller, 1948b). If your friend or roommate snaps at you tonight "for no reason at all," it may be nothing personal. You may simply be an available target for displaced aggression originating in some frustrations your friend has experienced during the day.

Frustration so often seems to lead to aggressive behavior that a group of psychologists at Yale was led to propose the **frustration-aggression hypothesis** (Dollard, Doob, Miller, Mowrer, Sears, Ford, Hovland, & Sollenberger, 1939). This hypothesis asserts that frustration *always* increases the tendency for the organism to respond aggressively. The hypothesis is rather well supported by the evidence, provided the definition of aggressive behavior is broadened to include indirect, nonovert forms of hostility, such as verbal comments, increases in prejudice, and rough handling of objects (kicking an empty can). When you include such indirect signs of hostility as may be inferred from a person's interpretation of a TAT picture (see Chapter 14), or from hostility "turned inward toward the self," you can see how it can be very difficult to test the hypothesis once and for all. A more contemporary interpretation is that frustrating conditions may indeed set up some distinctive internal state (anger?), but that any consequent aggressive behavior depends on a wide variety of other factors. Albert Bandura (1971), for example, stresses the *consequences* of aggressive behavior: If the frustrated person observes another also frustrated person (the "model") reacting aggressively and with impunity, the observer is more likely to respond aggressively also. Further, if aggressive behavior is reinforced, it is likely to be learned as a habitual response to frustration.

Some have considered aggressive behavior to be an instinctive, unlearned component of human nature. Konrad Lorenz (1966), for example, thinks of human aggression as an instinct gone wrong. While other animals have built-in inhibitory mechanisms that keep members of the same species from fighting to the death, humans have somehow lost this innate inhibition and must rely on social organization to control their aggressive tendencies. Freud, too, believed that aggression was basic to human makeup, thinking of it as an instinct. On this basis, he felt the chances of ever eliminating institutionalized forms of aggression, like war, were slim indeed.

Withdrawal Reactions

Persistent frustration over long periods of time leads to diminished aggressive behavior and often to renunciation of the original desired goals. Ghetto children who encounter different customs, a different kind of language, and expectations they may not be able to meet in a school system organized around middle-class values will experience repeated frustrations in their striving for the reinforcements contingent on academic achievement. Persistent failure eventually gives way to withdrawal and the pursuit of other, more easily attainable goals. Sometimes people turn from the frustrations of real life to goal attainment in **fantasy.** We all engage in a certain amount of daydreaming, in which our handicaps vanish, we enjoy the admiration and envy of others, and win all sorts of success. The frustrated suitor, and the young woman who watches him from a distance and wonders why he never notices *her*, are well practiced in overcoming their frustrations in their daydreams. While daydreaming can be very useful in providing us with a chance to plan and rehearse our attack upon personal or social problems, excessive reliance on obtaining goals in fantasy may reduce the motivation to strive for them in real life. Despite the prevalence of daydreaming, little serious research had been done on this type of behavior until recently (Singer, 1974).

Prolonged intense frustration, especially when it is coupled with economic privation, can produce a kind of **apathy,** or depression, in which people are helpless to initiate activity. They simply stop trying. The concept of

learned helplessness (Seligman & Maier, 1967) arose from experiments in which it was found that dogs given a series of brief but intense inescapable and unavoidable shocks were later incapable of learning a simple escape conditioning task. The "normal" dog in a two-compartment shuttlebox quickly learns to jump over a hurdle from the shock compartment into the safe compartment. Dogs given prior exposure to inescapable shock, however, simply don't learn to escape; they merely stand and whimper and take the shock. They seem to have learned that nothing they do matters, so why do anything? Dogs that were pretreated with the same amount of shock but could terminate it by making the proper response showed no signs of helplessness on subsequent tests.

It seems paradoxical that, under certain conditions, repeated frustration can lead to perseverance rather than to helplessness or withdrawal. For example, in Chapter 7 you learned that intermittent reinforcement leads to great resistance to extinction. That is, the organism performing on a partial reinforcement schedule is frustrated on every nonrewarded trial, yet builds up enormous perseverance. Responding may continue long after all reinforcement has stopped. Critical conditions for perseverance in the face of frustration may include (1) failure to achieve positive reinforcement rather than failure to escape an aversive stimulus, and (2) the intermixing of rewarded and frustrated experiences early in the organism's learning history.

The apathy observed in chronically economically deprived people, in some schizophrenic disorders, and in some forms of depression may reflect the effects of a history of repeated, systematic failure of attempts to achieve or retain crucial goals.

While **suicide** has sometimes been interpreted as aggressive behavior turned inward upon the self, in many cases the victim seems less motivated by aggressive feelings than by feelings of acute unhappiness, hopelessness, futility, and despair. Viewed in this light, suicide may be interpreted as an extreme form of withdrawal. This ultimate "solution" is far more prevalent than most people imagine. While 9 out of 10 suicide attempts fail, that leaves 25,000 Americans who succeed each year. By this time tomorrow, 60 more people will have killed themselves in this country. Suicide ranks third, after accidents and cancer, as the major cause of death among college students.

Fortunately, suicidal people do give clues. A large majority do voice their intention to commit suicide, and such warnings or threats should always be taken seriously. Suicide occurs more often among single than married people, twice more often among whites than blacks, and three times more often among men than women. The three-month period of "improvement" following a suicidal crisis, strangely enough, is the time when other—and often successful—suicide attempts are made. As more is learned about the clues that suicide-prone people give, it may be possible to provide them in time with appropriate psychological attention (Schneidman, Farberow, & Litman, 1970).

Regressive Behavior

Intense frustration can sometimes cause people to adopt behavioral patterns more appropriate to an earlier stage of life. The husband whose reaction to a spat with his wife is to sulk and brood, hoping she will feel sorry and come to comfort him, displays behavior that was probably reinforced by his mother when he was a child. When a student at school begins to have more problems than she can cope with, a surge of homesickness may send her home, where she can count on the sympathy and support of her family.

In more serious cases, behavior may regress until the individual adopts the dress and speech patterns of childhood. In a famous case of **regression** described by Jules H. Masserman

(1946), a seventeen-year-old girl displayed a variety of childish behaviors: giggling, childish speech, bed-wetting, and unwillingness to feed herself. Her parents had begun to quarrel when she was four, and after a violent marital history had separated when the girl was thirteen. Her mother retained custody of the child. There were episodic regressions to childish behavior, and serious difficulties appeared when, at the age of sixteen, she witnessed a violent scene between her parents on a visit to her father. In the period that followed, marked by numerous tantrums, the patient found a photograph of herself taken at the age of five. This prompted her to cut her hair and assume the posture of the child in the photo, possibly in an unconscious attempt to recapture a relatively peaceful period in her life before the turbulent parental quarrels destroyed the security of her existence. Figure 13-8 shows how the patient looked just before she found the picture of herself, and how she later tried to resemble the way she had looked as a child.

In a famous experimental study of regression, Roger Barker, Tamara Dembo, and Kurt Lewin (1941) set up a play situation that clearly contained the defining features of a frustration situation. Children were allowed to play with a standard set of toys, and the "constructiveness" or developmental level of their play activity was rated. Then they were allowed to play with a far more interesting set of toys. Finally the exciting toys were removed and the children were left with the less interesting toys to play with. In this last phase, the exciting toys could still be seen behind a wire screen, but could not be reached. The investigators wanted to know what would happen to the constructiveness of the children's play with the standard toys as a result of the frustration they were experiencing. The results indicated a sharp drop in constructiveness ratings, which, when converted to mental-age equivalents, suggested a regression equivalent to 17.3 months of mental age. The investigators concluded that frustration sharply reduced the cre-

Figure 13-8 An example of regression to an earlier stage of life. The patient is shown (left) just before she found a photo of herself (center) taken when she was five, and after she changed her appearance (right) to resemble the old photo of herself. (Masserman, 1946)

ative level of play behavior. If you have found that, after one or a series of sharp frustrations, the quality of your thinking or creative effort loses some of its recently acquired refinements or skills, you may well be experiencing a form of frustration-induced regression in yourself.

CONFLICT

Remember when it came time to get up this morning? You may have felt motivated to get up for breakfast, or for a class. But chances are you were also motivated to get in those additional 40 winks. Did you eat more than you wanted to last night at dinner? Or couldn't you decide whether the enjoyment of the mashed potatoes and rich dessert was really worth the extra calories you'd be consuming? You may have had a conflict. If you are a smoker but are not smoking this minute, do you want to light up right now, or are you trying to cut down, or even quit? Caught between the desire to smoke and not to smoke, you are in conflict. These are examples of easily resolved conflicts: Sooner or later you will either eat the dessert or leave the table, you will either get up or go back to sleep, either light up or not (probably the former). In short, these conflicts are of brief duration. They may recur (every morning, or every meal), but each time the conflict is broken and we get on with the business of living.

Not so with all conflicts. Some last for years, taking their toll of human health and happiness. Some are so intense as to produce behavioral disorders, lead to alcoholism or drug abuse, or result in psychosomatic disorders. If we could better understand the dynamics of conflict, we might be better able to resolve them and thus dissipate the terrible frustration they can produce. Since conflict is so often at the root of neurotic disorders (see Chapter 15), such understanding might help us head off the development or reduce the intensity of such conditions. But there are various approaches to the psychology of conflict and various types of conflict situations.

The Nature of Conflict

The study of conflict, like the study of anxiety and frustration, is also an extension of the study of motivation. But for the first time, you now have to consider what happens when a tendency to approach a positive goal (or to avoid a negative goal) is matched in strength by an opposing tendency. That's what **conflict** is all about: Opposing response tendencies are pitted against each other, thus blocking the person from acting one way or the other. Recall the cat, its food, and the blast of air. You can see why conflict and frustration go together. In conflict-produced frustration the barriers are *within* the organism in the form of competing but incompatible motives, and not in the external situation. Around this basic notion of competing tendencies several approaches have been developed.

The Freudian Model

As Chapter 14 describes in detail, conflict is a most important element in Sigmund Freud's theory of normal and neurotic development. Briefly, Freud assumed that in infancy people all start out with instinctive—and very powerful—biological drives, and that the course of development hinges mainly on the way they come to terms with the fact that, in a civilized society, their basic urges cannot always be directly and immediately satisfied. The drives of the infant, libidinal (sexual) in nature, soon come into conflict with social prohibitions, for they are directed toward a parent and hence are unacceptable. In the male child, for example, the expression of libidinal urges for the

mother brings about fear of retaliation from the father. This **Oedipus conflict** between striving for sexual expression and inhibition due to fear leads to all sorts of stratagems. The boy acquires various defense mechanisms that basically are strategies for reducing his anxiety over the terrible consequences, such as castration, which may befall him if his sexual yearning for his mother continues. Girls, Freud assumed, experienced similar conflicts in their relationships with their fathers (the **Electra conflict**).

One mechanism, **repression,** helps reduce anxiety by distorting reality. The individual denies these unacceptable urges, but they enjoy a continued existence in the unconscious. When such repressive tactics fail, the urges seek gratification in the form of neurotic symptoms. The Freudian conception of conflict is much more complex than this brief mention suggests, and includes mechanisms for coming to terms with both external reality and social morality (see Chapter 14).

The Phenomenological Model

The most influential basis for subsequent research in the psychology of conflict was developed many years ago by Kurt Lewin (1935). Lewin conceptualized a person in a conflict state as a point in space, acted upon by forces (vectors) that exert pressure toward positive objects or activities and away from negative ones. The term "valence" was applied to the positive or negative features. Since Lewin had in mind psychological rather than physical forces, acting within the life space (or the perceived rather than physical world) of the individual, his conception is called a **phenomenological model,** a term indicating that the conscious experience of the individual is the focus of the analysis. Examples of the application of Lewinian concepts to two conflict situations are shown in Figure 13-9.

Given some knowledge of the valence of the incentives and the strength of the vectors, it

 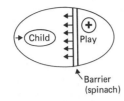

A college student in conflict: Becoming a premedical student is a very attractive goal, but a great deal of hard work acts as a barrier, keeping the student away from a psychologically valued region of her life space

A six-year-old in conflict at the dinner table: Play is a positively valenced activity, and a strong vector directs the child toward this incentive; finishing the spinach on his plate is negatively valenced and he is repelled.

Figure 13-9 Two conflict situations that illustrate the Lewinian concepts of positive and negative valence, vector, barrier, region, and life space.

should be possible to predict the behavior of an individual in a conflict situation. Resolution of the conflict would depend on the relative strength and direction of these components. And how can one obtain this information? There's the rub. Unfortunately, since vectors, valences, and everything else in the person's life space must be approached in terms of phenomenal reality, you have no way of mea-

suring these determinants of behavior save by asking the person to introspect for you or by inferring them by watching what the individual does. If the college student drops her premed ambitions and decides to major in a much easier field, you might infer that the relative strength of the negative valence was stronger than the positive valence. But by that time it's too late: The conflict has been resolved by then, and instead of prediction, all you'd have is a reasonably good explanation of a past event.

The Behavioral Conflict Model

Neal E. Miller (1959) used objectively defined determinants in developing a conflict model that nonetheless closely resembled some of the main features of Lewin's approach. Miller's scheme begins with simple facts: Some objects, places, people, or events motivate a person to move away from them, while others motivate movement toward them. Now note in Figure 13-10 how many different ways the tendencies to approach and withdraw can be combined.

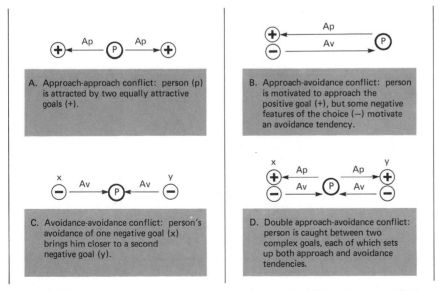

Figure 13-10 Four types of conflict situation, based on combinations of approach (Ap) and avoidance (Av) tendencies.

1. The tendency to *approach* (Ap) a (+) goal or *avoid* (Av) a (−) goal increases the closer one gets to the goal.

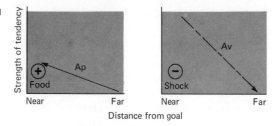

2. In a conflict situation involving *both* a (+) and a (−) goal, the avoidance gradient is steeper.

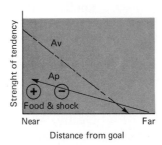

3. Raising or lowering the drive to approach (by increasing hunger) or avoid (by increasing shock level) raises or lowers the entire gradient; the slope remains unchanged.

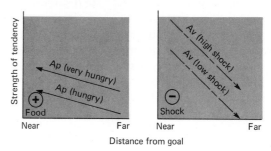

4. Whenever two incompatible tendencies are in conflict, the stronger of the two prevails. For example, in Ap-Av conflict, near the goal the avoidance tendency is the stronger; far from the goal, the approach tendency is stronger.

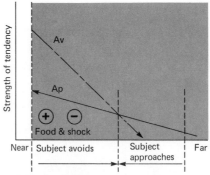

Figure 13-11 Four basic assumptions on which Miller's behavioral model of conflict is based. (Miller, 1959)

These constitute the main conflict situations psychologists have studied.

To these two basic tendencies of **approach** and **avoidance** Miller added a few assumptions, based on experiments with rats conducted by himself, Judson S. Brown (1948), and others. The best way to understand Miller's conflict model is to study carefully some of his main assumptions, one by one. To help you visualize each one, imagine a simple runway with food, the positive goal (+) at one end, and a rat learning to race to it trial after trial. A negative goal (−), shock, can also be introduced in the alley, setting up an avoidance tendency. The strength of approach and avoidance tendencies could be measured at any point in the runway by seeing how hard the animal would try to get to (+) or away from (−) the goal. Miller's assumptions are depicted in Figure 13-11. Armed with these assumptions, drawn admittedly from animal experiments, let's see whether they help in the analysis of some human conflict situations. If the assumptions are adequate, they should help to explain why some conflicts are easily resolved and some last for years, and how some conflicts might be resolved.

Approach–Approach (Ap–Ap) Conflicts. The simplest, least stable conflict involves two equally strong approach (Ap) tendencies pitted against each other: Shall I go to the drive-in tonight or to the theater in town (same film at both)? Shall I have pie or ice cream for dessert? Shall I take the elevator or the escalator? There's no need to belabor the point that such conflicts are quite trivial in significance and very unstable. But why? Figure 13-12 shows that, starting from a point of indecision, movement toward one goal is immediately accompanied by a drop in the relative strength of the tendency to approach the opposite goal. If the two goals are equally attractive—and this is a crucial condition—the slightest move toward one goal will resolve the issue. If you find yourself locked into a conflict situation involving two positive goals and simply can't resolve it ("Shall I go out with Lee or with Leslie?"), the chances are that there are some penalties—that is, some negative features—associated with each goal, and you are probably struggling with a double approach–avoidance conflict.

Incidentally, behavioral tendencies need not necessarily involve moving through space, as

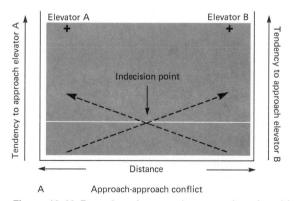
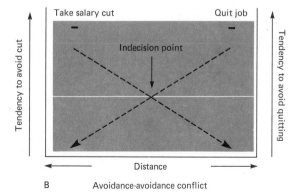

Figure 13-12 Examples of approach–approach and avoidance–avoidance conflict. In *A*, a person standing in the lobby when two empty elevators arrive simultaneously quickly resolves his Ap–Ap conflict: Movement toward elevator A is accompanied by a decline in the tendency to go toward elevator B. In *B*, the employee who backs away from the idea of taking a salary cut finds the tendency to avoid quitting gets stronger; but if the person backs away from quitting, the aversive features of a salary cut loom larger. The avoidance–avoidance conflict is more stable than the approach–approach conflict.

in running toward an elevator or an escalator. You can think of conflict resolution as involving movement through *psychological* space, as when you feel you are leaning toward one solution rather than another, on the verge of deciding between two alternatives. Freud, as mentioned previously, believed in the importance of conflict in either repressing certain thoughts or admitting them into consciousness. And certainly the almost ubiquitous hostile and affectionate ambivalence of young people toward their parents in our society is not necessarily expressed in spatial terms.

Avoidance–Avoidance (Av–Av) Conflicts. Caught "between the devil and the deep blue sea," the person locked into an avoidance–avoidance conflict finds it much more difficult to resolve than an approach–approach conflict, and, depending on the intensity of the aversion to the negative goals involved, also much more stressful. As the Av–Av conflict depicted in Figure 13-12 shows, the two negative goals set up incompatible avoidance tendencies such that an increase in the tendency to avoid X only leads to an increase in the relative strength of the tendency to avoid Y. Consider the employee who is told, "Take a cut in salary or quit," or the couple living in a deteriorating neighborhood who must decide whether to sell their house now at a loss or risk seeing it continue to decline in value, or the student who desperately wants to attend a special party but must decide whether to accept an invitation from an unattractive escort or risk not getting a date at all.

Consider the severe conflict faced by the soldier in combat who, though terrified, must either follow the order to advance toward the enemy or be shot for refusing. Every infantry soldier who is likely to see combat realizes he may have to face such a conflict. Indeed, some recruits are disturbed by this problem even during their basic training. But that far from the time of decision, the amount of stress the foreseen conflict produces is generally quite low. This follows from the fact that the avoid-

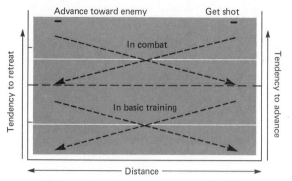

Figure 13-13 The amount of stress produced by an Av–Av conflict depends on the strength of the intersecting tendencies. While a conflict about killing or being killed may be active as early as basic training, the same conflict produces far more stress when it is activated in combat.

ance tendencies are rather weak in the relatively benign setting of an army training camp. Accordingly, the point of indecision, shown in Figure 13-13, occurs rather low on the vertical scale. When the conflict is encountered on the front lines, however, the avoidance tendencies intersect at high levels of relative strength, and the stress experienced is much greater.

How do people react to Av–Av conflicts? If at all possible, the individual will do everything possible to escape the conflict rather than resolve it. Leaving the field is the most common attempted solution to Av–Av conflicts. Place yourself in this picture: You are in the middle of a large open pasture. From the east an angry bull starts to come toward you; movement away is quickly discouraged by a large snarling dog approaching you from the west. Assuming equal distances to safety, chances are you will "leave the field" by moving either north or south. More than one combat soldier has left the field by "accidentally" shooting himself in the foot.

Such oblique solutions to Av–Av conflicts can be stopped only by placing barriers in the field to prevent the individual from leaving. Walls around a penitentiary serve this function. Humans, being rather resourceful organisms, can leave the field in very imaginative

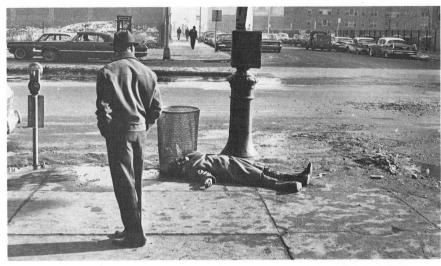

Figure 13-14 Alcoholism provides an immediate and profound escape from the stress of intense conflict.

ways. They may rely on fantasy, which has already been described as one of the reactions to frustration. Students trapped in a classroom with a droning teacher and a sluggish clock on the wall can (and do) leave the field for the more interesting blandishments of reverie. In the case of severe stress-inducing conflicts, regression serves to ease the person from the field. Combat soldiers under great stress sometimes cry like children, whimpering and pleading for protection and, in extreme cases, reverting to baby talk. While such regressed behavior often occurs without the deliberate intent to use it as an excuse for release from active duty, it nonetheless has in fact considerable instrumental value: It is usually reinforced by removal of the soldier from the scene of conflict, greatly reducing his anxiety.

A frequent reaction to the stress of severe conflict is drinking. Alcohol is a remarkably effective stress reducer, a fact that may partially account for its ranking position as the source of this country's most serious and most costly drug problem (Chafetz, 1967). Alcoholism may be viewed as a habitual withdrawal reaction, reinforced by immediate anxiety reduction

when the alcohol is consumed in moderate quantities, and by complete psychological escape — temporarily — if a person drinks enough of it (see Figure 13-14). Some of Masserman's cats placed in conflict had gotten to rather like spiked milk, and preferred it to regular milk, as the duration of conflict stress was prolonged (Masserman & Yum, 1946). The development of alcoholic addiction in animals subjected to stressful conflict situations has now been experimentally established (Casey, 1960).

Hysterical disorders, in which people suffer loss of sensation (blindness, loss of feeling in the hands or feet) or of motor function (paralysis of legs or arms), also occur as reactions to stress that facilitate leaving the field (see Chapter 15). These disorders are purely functional; they are not the result of any known organic condition. A case of hysterical paralysis was described by Roy R. Grinker and John P. Spiegel (1945): An artillery soldier, resting during a lull between periods of enemy shelling, was heavily shaken by three shells that fell nearby as the enemy resumed its attack. Half an hour later he found himself unable to remove his right hand from his trouser pocket. In the hospital he was calm, displayed no residual anxiety, and regained control over his hand. When it came time to return to his unit, tremors developed in both arms. Such disorders are not the result of conscious, deliberate attempts to deceive. They reflect unconscious mechanisms that serve effectively to control anxiety.

An extremely effective, and serious, "solution" to intense and prolonged conflict is **amnesia.** As discussed in Chapter 9, amnesia is always a condition of selective forgetting: Amnesia victims may forget their names, their addresses, their places of work, and their telephone numbers, but not how to read and write, to do arithmetic calculations, or solve problems. In short, what seem to be forgotten are those elements that would consciously link them to those portions of their lives in which they suffered intense conflict. Amnesia, then, is an extreme form of repression and may be accompanied by a **fugue,** or actual escape from the scene of conflict.

All of these reactions represent ways of coping with severe conflict. While they have been presented as reactions to intense avoidance–avoidance conflict, severe and prolonged approach–avoidance conflict may also bring them on. These behaviors are called ways of coping because their function is to reduce or control anxiety. They do not necessarily involve faking or malingering, but tend to reflect unconscious processes.

Approach–Avoidance (Ap–Av) Conflicts. When approach and avoidance tendencies intersect, the conflict is also a stable one. Consider some examples, and note the similarities and differences with Av–Av conflicts: A baseball player wants a raise but is afraid he may be traded if he demands one; a teenager feels a strong urge to smoke, but also has a great fear of cancer; a virginal college student wants to have sex but is inhibited by fears of pregnancy, sexual inadequacy, or a sense of guilt. Unlike Av–Av conflicts, in which the individual is

reinforced for attempting to leave the field, Ap–Av conflicts have a built-in barrier that discourages escape: the powerful attractive effect of the goal.

Let's take the example of a sex-versus-fear conflict in an attractive college woman who has both strong sexual urges and strong moral inhibitions. Figure 13-15 presents the conflict from her viewpoint (rather than her partner's), and shows how, in her relations with a partner, her petting behavior stops at a certain point in lovemaking and further progress is inhibited. As attempts are made to go further, the avoidance tendency becomes stronger than the approach, and she will draw back further from the goal. If she returns to the stage of social conversation, however, the inhibition is now weaker than the approach tendency, and heavy petting may resume. As in the case of Av–Av conflict, movement in any direction away from the point of indecision tends to set in motion a counterforce that acts in the opposite direction.

Not every virgin experiences this conflict. In some, the moral inhibition may be so powerful (Av-2 gradient in Figure 13-15) that it never intersects the approach gradient. The lifelong virgin may have powerful sex urges, but even stronger avoidance tendencies. She may experience yearnings but no conflict. Should something happen one day to increase her approach gradient enough for the two to intersect (attentions from an exceptionally attractive man or an unusually romantic setting), interesting problems might develop. Visualize an Ap gradient high enough to intersect gradient Av-2, above the letter B. The woman would now be indeed in a state of conflict, and since the strength of the urges and inhibitions at the point of intersection would be very intense, the amount of anxiety experienced would be correspondingly high. Reassurance or counseling might well reduce the Av-2 gradient to the level of Av-1; in that case, there would still be a conflict, but a more manageable one.

Alcohol is known to reduce the fear gradient

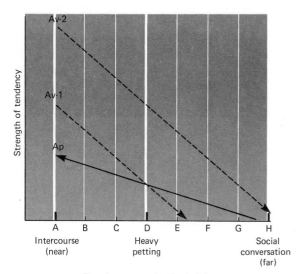

Figure 13-15 When the sexual urge (Ap) and inhibitory tendencies (Av-1) reach equal levels of strength at a point in the petting sequence short of intercourse, progress toward intercourse may be blocked. If the inhibitory tendency is very strong (Av-2) relative to the approach tendency (Ap), no conflict and no sexual activity will occur.

without affecting the approach gradient. When a person is more boldly affectionate following three martinis, this behavior may reflect a reduction in the height of the inhibitory gradient. Whether anything further will happen depends on whether, and where, urges and inhibitions intersect—and on the notorious ability of alcohol to impair sexual performance in the male!

The present example is, of course, quite simplistic, for it does not take into account the behavior of the partner, or, more properly, the interaction between partners. Mutual stimulation will obviously alter expressive and inhibitory gradients in each partner. The figures shown are, therefore, representations of simple motivational processes at one point in time, like frozen sections of a dynamic process that is always fluid, always changing. Nonetheless, the discussion at least identifies the most basic conceptual tools that analysts of human conflict often employ.

PARACHUTING CONFLICTS

Many sports and stunts, like parachuting, ski jumping, rock climbing, motorcycle stunting, and exploring, present dangerous but still exciting situations that involve approach–avoidance conflicts. A series of investigations has been made of this Ap–Av conflict in sport parachutists. In one study, 33 inexperienced parachutists (1 to 5 jumps) and 33 experienced chutists (over 100 jumps) were asked after a jump to rate the intensity of their approach and avoidance feelings on a scale from 1 (minimum) to 10 (maximum) at various points before and after the jump (Epstein & Fenz, 1965). The parachutists' ratings on the night before the jump, on reaching the airport, and so on up to the point of jumping and the opening of the chute are shown in Figure 13-16 for both the inexperienced and the experienced chutists.

Note how the *approach* ratings of the inexperienced parachutists decreased until they were in the plane and waiting to jump, in contrast to the gradual increase in the approach ratings of experienced men. The *avoidance* ratings of the inexperienced chutists increased until the "ready" signal, then decreased until they nearly matched approach ratings at the point of jumping. Perhaps only their commitment to jump, and loss of face if they didn't do so, enabled the inexperienced men finally to jump. On the other hand, approach feelings rose and avoidance feelings decreased for the experienced parachutists after they reached the airport, and they were strongly inclined to jump when they reached that point. Note how the crossover between approach and avoidance tendencies occurred much earlier for the experienced parachutists than for the inexperienced jumpers, for whom the crossover was at the point of jumping. Somehow experienced jumpers learned to keep their avoidance reactions inhibited and under control more than the novices, so that, with experience, the point of maximal avoidance occurs prior to reaching the airport.

If you have been involved in any sports like this, you might rate your own approach and avoidance feelings at points leading up to the final action and see how your ratings compare with those of parachutists.

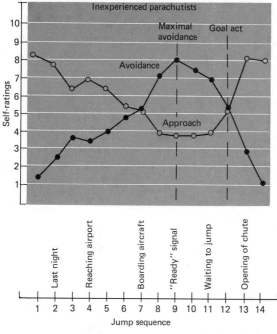

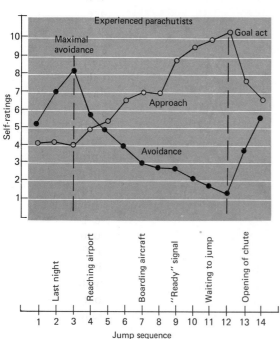

Figure 13-16 Inexperienced parachutists show a maximal tendency to avoid jumping right up to the time of the "ready" signal; by contrast, for experienced parachutists the tendency to avoid jumping occurs most strongly much earlier in the sequence. (Epstein & Fenz, 1965)

Double Approach–Avoidance Conflicts. You've already been warned that an Ap–Ap conflict that is prolonged and even mildly stressful is probably a **double approach–avoidance conflict.** The woman who receives a marriage proposal from two very attractive suitors does indeed have more than an Ap–Ap conflict, for marrying Peter means (usually) giving up Paul. Since positive and negative consequences attend whatever choice is made, the conflict tends to be stable: The closer a person comes to deciding in favor of one alternative, the stronger becomes the avoidance tendency, since it is aroused by the loss of the other alternative.

Conflict Resolution

What can be done about resolving conflicts? The analysis of conflict behavior yields a number of useful suggestions.

1. Competing motives must be identified. In everyday situations, it is helpful to begin by asking yourself what the various alternatives are and what it is you want—or wish to avoid—most. Making a list of positive and negative consequences associated with each of two alternate courses of action is useful, for this often lets you see that the alternatives are not really equally attractive or repelling after all.

2. If the alternatives still look pretty well balanced, you can try to change the environment in which the conflict occurs. A student with very strong academic motives that compete with powerful social needs may wish to consider transferring to a college with somewhat less rigorous academic requirements. In a different setting, it may be far easier to satisfy both motives. This is a way of reducing the incompatibility of motives. If the real environment can't be changed, the *perceived* environment can sometimes be altered. Some conflicts are based on faulty perceptions of conflicting goals. The student who can't decide between a career in medicine and one in physiological research should try to obtain as much information as possible about the kind of life patterns, daily routines, intellectual and physical demands, and general conditions that distinguish the two professions. Additional information about alternative goals often reveals them to be not at all equivalent in their attractive or aversive qualities.

3. You can work at reducing the strength of certain tendencies. Women who find suspicious lumps in their breasts are sometimes in great conflict about seeking immediate medical attention. They fear that a surgical examination may be necessary, that the growth may be found to be malignant, and that disfiguring surgery may have to be performed. Such thoughts, inducing intense anxiety, set up avoidance tendencies that then compete with tendencies to secure appropriate and possibly reassuring medical attention. The avoidance tendency can be weakened in such cases by observing that other women who did act promptly earned an increase in survival probability. Exposure to data indicating that most such growths turn out to be benign also reduces anxiety. Fear that surgical intervention might make the woman less desirable to her mate can be reduced through discussion between the partners, or through counseling.

4. When conflict stems from inadequate skills, reeducative procedures are desirable. People who are in conflict about interacting in social settings often react by withdrawal, becoming solitary and lonely. Their avoidance of social contact is often based on an accurate appraisal of their deficient social skills, not knowing what to say or how to behave. Current individual and group counseling procedures, sometimes called **behavioral rehearsal,** are being used with increasing frequency to teach the socially inept person useful social competence skills (Wolpe, 1973).

This discussion of the dynamics of conflict should leave little doubt that conflict resolution is less a matter of willpower than a matter of careful analysis of the underlying competing tendencies, followed by deliberate attempts to modify the properties of the alternate goals.

SUMMARY

Anxiety is a complex motivational state aroused by threat of pain, loss of affection, or threat to self-esteem. The trait of anxiety is usually measured by means of psychological inventories, and varies in strength from person to person. Observable indices of anxiety include subjective reports, increased heart rate and blood pressure, decreased skin resistance, and complex effects on performance. High anxiety tends to facilitate the performance of simple tasks but impairs performance of complex tasks.

Anxiety scales are self-report inventories. The Taylor MAS is a scale of general anxiety that attempts to measure the predisposition to behave anxiously in a wide variety of situations. It has been shown to possess high levels of concurrent and construct validity. High levels of anxiety impair academic performance, especially in students of average scholastic aptitude. Tests of anxiety in academic situations have been devised to measure both facilitating and debilitating effects of anxiety on academic performance. Counseling and desensitization-relaxation techniques can reduce anxiety and improve performance.

Frustration is defined as the thwarting of a motivated organism striving to achieve a desired goal. While the study of problem solving stresses the search for successful responses, the study of frustration focuses on reactions to the blocking of goal-motivated behavior. Progress toward a goal may be blocked by external or internal barriers; the latter usually produce greater distress. Reactions to frustration include intensification of goal-directed behavior, aggressive attack on the instigator of frustration or on available scapegoats, and withdrawal reactions such as fantasy, apathy, regression, and even suicide.

The study of conflict, like that of frustration, is an extension of the study of motivation, since conflict involves the opposition of two or more incompatible motivational tendencies. The Freudian model of conflict postulates the opposition of instinctive biological urges and the constraints of social and moral reality. The phenomenological model of Lewin, which stresses the relation between perception and behavior, sets the basis for behavioral models by conceptualizing conflict in terms of forces acting upon the individual. Miller's behavioral conflict model is based on the notion of gradients of approach and avoidance that characteristically have different slopes.

Approach–approach conflicts involve two equally strong but opposing tendencies to approach positive goals, and are easily resolved. Avoidance–avoidance conflicts are more difficult to resolve, since the avoidance of one negative goal brings the organism closer to a second, equally aversive goal. A person prevented from escaping an avoidance–avoidance conflict may attempt to leave the field through fantasy, regression, alcoholism, development of hysterical disorders, or amnesia. Such reactions reflect unconsciously motivated attempts to cope with severe conflict-induced anxiety.

Approach–avoidance conflicts are also difficult to resolve. A built-in barrier, the powerful attraction of the positive goal, prevents escape, despite the negative consequences that goal attainment also entails. In a double approach–avoidance conflict the person is caught between two incompatible goals, each of which has both attractive and repellent features.

Conflict resolution requires some understanding of the dynamics of the incompatible response tendencies. Reliance on willpower is a poor substitute for the development of methods of conflict resolution. Such methods include training to identify the competing motives in a conflict, changing the environment responsible for maintaining the strength of one or more of the motives, acquiring information that controls the positive or negative intensity of the opposing goals, and improving goal-attainment skills.

TRY IT YOURSELF

Consider several of the conflicts, weak or strong, in which you recently have found yourself enmeshed. What evidence of anxiety and frustration do you find involved in each one? Can you determine what type of conflict each one was? Can you diagram it in accordance with the behavioral model of conflict? How have you, or how could you, deal with each conflict in order to weaken or resolve it?

Consider the conflict represented in Rembrandt's etching of the biblical story of Abraham's sacrifice (Figure 13-17). According to the book of Genesis, God ordered Abraham, the first of the Hebrew patriarchs, to slay his only son, Isaac, and to offer him up as a burnt offering. Abraham must have been torn between love for his son and his obedience to God. How would you describe this type of conflict? Abraham proceeds toward a resolution of the conflict by moving to kill his son. What dynamic changes in the conflict process might be occurring at this point? Fortunately, at the last moment the angel of the Lord releases Abraham from the terrible command, and Abraham sacrifices a ram in place of Isaac.

Figure 13-17 As Abraham moves to sacrifice his only son in obedience to God's command, his hand is stayed by an angel sent by God. (Rembrandt)

14

Personality

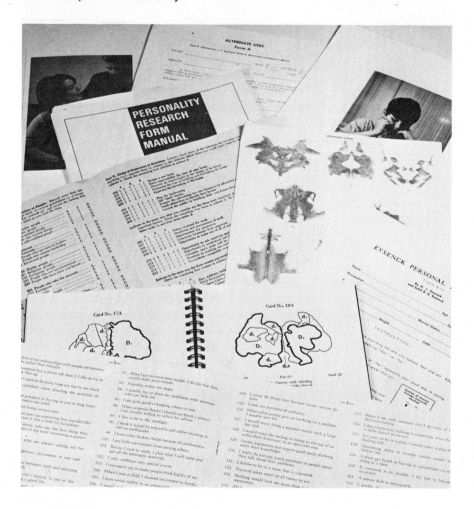

YOUR OWN PERSONALITY

■ Like "learning," "intelligence," and "motive," the term "personality" is hard to define. But let's hypothesize (1) that you know quite well what "personality" means, at least in a general, common-sense sort of way, and (2) that you know quite well what your own personality is like. How can you test the truth or falsity of these hypotheses? You can test them by using one of the measurements that psychologists have often employed to test all kinds of things from attitudes to interests—a rating scale. On a **rating scale,** the particular quality or degree of any property or characteristic possessed or manifested by a person or thing is checked along a scale representing a series of degrees. Copy the characteristics and scales shown in Figure 14-1 on a sheet of paper. Group A consists of a set of opposed characteristics often used to describe persons, and Group B is a similar set of characteristics, a few of those picked out by Aristotle nearly 2500 years ago, which range from one extreme through a mean to the other extreme.

Rate yourself by placing an X along each scale for Group A and Group B characteristics, thus indicating the extent to which you consider you have these characteristics. It helps to think of the way you generally behave in situations in which these various characteristics are manifested. You might even think of a number of occasions in the past in which you have manifested these various characteristics. Using a straight edge, connect the Xs with straight lines to create a "profile" of yourself. Now, using a pencil of a different color, also rate a friend whom you know pretty well on the characteristics in Groups A and B, and connect the Xs to obtain your friend's profile. To what extent do your ratings of your friend differ from your ratings of yourself?

The characteristics in Groups A and B are settled ways of behaving called **personality** or **character traits.** While these are only a few of many human traits, you can recognize that they are deeply involved in personality, verifying hypothesis 1, that you have a good idea of what "personality" means. Furthermore, in rating both yourself and a friend on these traits, you have supported hypothesis 2, that you have a good idea of what your own personality is like, as well as that of your friend. Investigations have verified that people do have fairly extensive, implicit concepts of personality traits, as well as ideas about what traits often go together (Stricker, Jacobs, & Kogan, 1974). (See Chapter 5.)

Group B characteristics reflect Aristotle's theory that **virtues** are the golden mean between extremes of habits. Thus modesty is the virtue to be found between the extremes of bashfulness and shamelessness. Although the mean traits given represent only a few of Aristotle's virtues, how do you come out on them? Do you tend to fall in your ratings toward the vice of deficiency or excess, or toward the virtue of the mean? Do you seem to have a generally favorable or unfavorable view of yourself? Since the days of Aristotle and earlier, people have been wondering what characteristics really constitute human personality and how it can be explained.

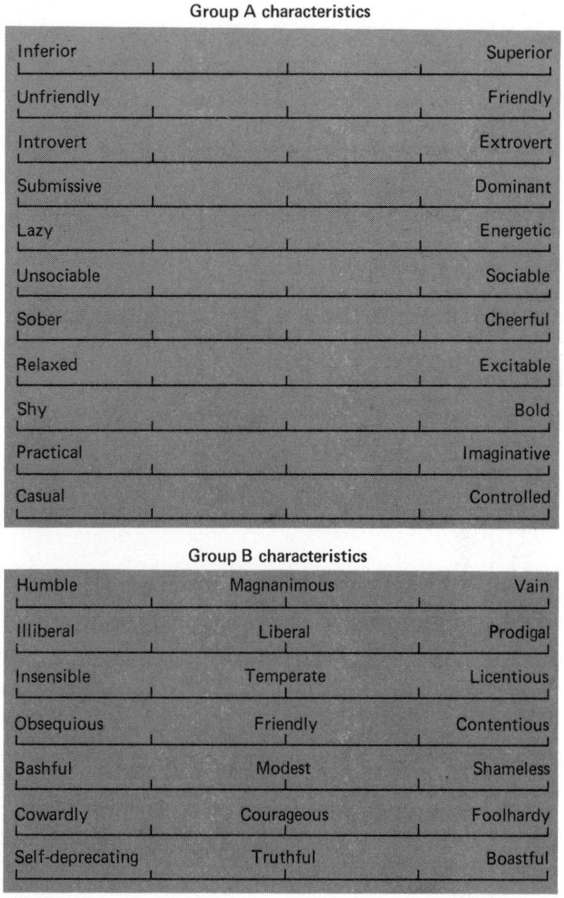

Figure 14-1 Rating scales of Group A: some general bipolar, or opposed, personality characteristics; and of Group B: extremes of some personality characteristics with Aristotle's "golden mean" between them.

An inventory of the human features or processes that have been discussed up to this point includes the genetic constitution and development of human beings, their receptors, effectors, and central nervous system, their sensory and perceptual processes, their learning, memory, thinking, motivation, and emotions, and the anxiety, frustration, and conflicts to which they may fall prey. All of these processes are but part and parcel of the total human being, the whole person. All of these processes must function together somehow in individual personalities as we know them, in ourselves and others. What is personality, how have psychologists studied it, and what have they discovered about it?

■ WHAT'S YOUR ANSWER?

Investigating Personality
- What is personality, if anything, beyond the ways a person usually behaves under various circumstances?
- Can you change your personality if you really want to?

Personality Assessment
- Can you depend on your own evaluation of yourself, or others' evaluations of themselves?
- Can personality really be measured accurately and reliably?
- How good are personal interviews in assessing personality?

Personality Theories
- Can most people be grouped under a few personality types?
- Does astrology help us understand personality?
- Is the sex drive the predominant human motive?

Traits and Situational Determinants
- Do outer events or inner controls dominate your decisions?
- Is your self-esteem a stronger motivating incentive than social approval?
- Are your personality traits consistent, or do they vary with the situations in which you find yourself?

INVESTIGATING PERSONALITY

One limited but common meaning of "personality" is the social skill or effectiveness that a person manifests in interaction with other people. People who feel socially inept sometimes enroll in personality courses to learn how to become more effective as persons and to "win friends and influence people." Such social skills, however, constitute only one aspect of the whole personality.

Another incomplete meaning of "personality" is the single principal impression that a person creates—a boastful personality, a friendly personality, a cheerful personality. This meaning, too, selects only one characteristic or trait as essentially descriptive of the whole personality, but does not provide an adequate definition of it. It's true that a door-to-door salesman or a sales clerk in a store may strike you as having a very aggressive personality, but this is only one trait, and one that may have been learned; the salesperson may exhibit quite different traits in other situations. And even though one trait or a set of traits may be predominant in some people, are these traits not interrelated with a variety of others?

The Nature of Personality

A simple working definition of **personality,** then, is the complex of stable behavioral characteristics, patterns, or traits that distinguishes one person from another. A whole mosaic of traits or behavioral patterns is involved in each individual personality, making each of us unique. These traits delineate the kind of persons we are, developing out of the multitude of genetic and environmental factors that influenced us as we grew. You may remember from Chapter 3 that individual differences in personality seem evident in newborn infants. Furthermore, these behavioral characteristics are fairly stable, changing only very slowly, if at all, over the adult years. Look back at some of the traits in Figure 14-1 on which you rated yourself. Would you rate yourself last year, or years ago, in much the same way on most of these traits? With a radical and prolonged change in living conditions, or by association with different people over a period of years, some of these behavioral traits may change. A long-term psychoanalysis, a behavior modification program, or the influence of encounter groups or conversions may also have their effects on behavioral characteristics, sometimes long-lasting, but often all too temporary (see Chapter 16). At any rate, these personality patterns are fairly stable and difficult to change. Such patterns are involved in our **life styles,** the typical essential attitudes and behavior associated with our ways of living, which remain very consistent, as opposed to superficial styles, such as hair style, adornments, and the cuts of clothing we wear. A personality, then, is a mosaic of behavioral traits with which we characteristically express ourselves and interact with others as we try to cope with life's incidents and emergencies.

Personality Theory

In rating your own personality characteristics, you saw that all of us have simple, common-sense conceptions of what personality is and what characteristics are included in it. Psychologists start from such common-sense ideas, of course, make many observations and studies, and build up their theories of personality on the basis of the evidence they have found. They study individual differences in many traits. A **personality theory** attempts to select and state a set of principles or regularities that relates all of the basic, as well as superficial, behavioral patterns that compose the mosaic of personality. As you will see, there are many theories of personality, ranging from Freudian to stimulus-response and existential approaches. Clinical psychologists usually work from a theory of personality that has seemed fruitful to them as they apply its principles to the explanation and prediction of the way individuals behave in real-life situations. They also try to assist individuals in the resolution of personal difficulties that have arisen when their particular patterns of traits produce inner conflicts or conflicts with other people. Personality traits may be adaptive or maladaptive for people in their real-life situations, depending on the circumstances.

Personality theories are concerned not only with habitual patterns of behavior, but also with the underlying entities or constructs involved in personality and the processes by which these entities interact. For example, Sigmund Freud's theory of personality involves several constructs, as you will see, each with its own nature and interactions, leading to

characteristic behavior patterns. Such theories attempt to explain what people are like and how they got that way. In formulating these answers, theorists make inferences about the dynamic interaction of underlying cognitive and emotional processes in particular persons, as well as the way heredity, upbringing and other cultural factors, and their own unique experiences have affected those processes so that these people now behave in certain characteristic ways. But before we go into all these different ways of explaining personality, the means by which personality is observed, measured, and evaluated need to be considered, for these methods of **personality assessment** tell a great deal about what is being assessed.

PERSONALITY ASSESSMENT

All of us evaluate and judge other people's personalities every day, and often make judgments about our own personalities as well. Thus a man may feel let down or even betrayed when a friend refuses to loan him money, because he had judged that friend to be a very generous person. Or a woman may be surprised by the conversation of a fellow worker because she had always seemed very "down to earth" and practical, but now she proves to be a very imaginative person as well. And after many classes with your instructors, you can undoubtedly describe their personalities in some detail—at least their classroom personalities, which you suspect may be quite different from their personalities when they leave the campus.

EVALUATE A PERSONALITY

■ Select a person whom you know fairly well and write a brief description and evaluation of that person's personality. What are the general traits of the person, and which of these traits seem to be most basic, influencing many of the person's actions? What are the strengths and weaknesses of this person? That is, which traits or characteristics enable the individual to interact smoothly and successfully with others and which traits plunge the person into problems or conflicts? Build up as complete and well-rounded a thumbnail sketch of this person as you can in a reasonable time. This is your common-sense assessment of a person, the kind of assessment you make of all those people you interact with very frequently. How accurate and reliable an assessment do you think this is? How would you go to work to fill in missing parts or to make it more accurate? Was your evaluation too subjective? If 100 other people turned in their own evaluations of the same person, would their evaluations be more objective than yours? Or would they still be subjective? This question suggests that objectivity may be increased if you can devise an evaluative procedure that yields a high degree of agreement among observers.

Personal Interviews

Psychological observations and assessments of personality have to be more systematic and detailed than everyday, informal observations, if comprehensiveness and accuracy are to be achieved. One step toward fulfilling such criteria is the **personal interview,** in which the interviewer asks a series of questions and the interviewee answers them. Job interviews, for example, are often conducted on a more or less haphazard basis, although they are aimed at finding out whether the interviewee has the occupational qualifications and personality characteristics presumably required for a position. Impressions obtained in unsystematically conducted interviews are undependable predictors of a person's subsequent performance (Mayfield, 1964). Clinical or psychiatric interviews, on the other hand, are sometimes structured to reveal personality traits by a series of prearranged and standardized questions. Indepth interviews may probe even more deeply into an individual's personality, with detailed

questions about various facets of behavior or conflicts.

Although the more structured interviews are more useful than the informal ones, interviews have severe limitations as they are normally conducted. Specific interviewers and interviewees may vary greatly in rapport, so the results can be very different. Those being interviewed have different attitudes toward such examination, which may strongly affect the results. Interviewers may tend to develop stereotyped judgments on the basis of their first reactions to interviewees, or the answers to initial questions may create a **halo effect,** influencing either positively or negatively many other judgments the interviewer makes. Furthermore, interviewer reliability varies widely; various interviewers may come up with very different assessments of the same person.

The **reliability** of a method of assessment or a test is the degree to which it gives the same results later that it gave the first time it was used. Interviewers are reliable, for example, when they obtain the same result in interviewing the same person a second time. A test is reliable when a person gets nearly the same score on it two or more times, a month or a year apart. Like any methods or tests, personality assessment should be as reliable as possible. The **validity** of a method of assessment or test is the degree to which it actually measures what it is designed to measure (see Chapters 3 and 13). Validity may be determined in a number of ways, such as by showing that employment-test results are correlated with actual proficiency on the job, or that achievement-test results compare well with actual performance in school. With a good relationship between test scores and criterion or performance scores, the test is actually measuring what it sets out to measure, and has high validity. Personal-interview assessments often prove weak in both reliability and validity. For example, many people placed solely on the basis of brief personal interviews do not actually work out on the job, and others who are rejected go on to do excellent work for other firms.

Situational Measures

Behavioral sampling, placing people in typical situations and seeing how they react, is another way of testing personality characteristics. For example, students in a police academy basic training course may be sent on a simulated police patrol, to test their behavior in a number of emergencies for which they have been trained. The information provided by such patrols has been found to predict success fairly accurately when the students actually become full-fledged policemen. The most famous behavioral sampling was developed by the Office of Strategic Services (1948) during World War II for its trainees in intelligence work. In one of its tests, candidates were given 12 minutes to develop a cover story explaining why they had been discovered with top-secret papers in a government office in Washington. Then they were interrogated roughly for 10 minutes in an attempt to tear down their cover stories. In another test, candidates were encouraged, and in fact strongly pressured, to break OSS security regulations. Candidate reactions to the stresses created by such tests facilitated the selection of successful intelligence operatives. Situational measures, however, are predictive only to the extent that the test situations and real-life situations are truly analogous in most respects. Simulated test situations may have a stamp of unreality about them, and if subjects realize that they are only being tested, they may not behave just as they would in real-life circumstances.

Rating Tests

Rating tests consist of rating scales of behavioral characteristics similar to the scales you used in evaluating a few of your own personal

characteristics. When the scales are divided into equal segments or units, these rating scales permit quantitative judgments of the degree of the trait a person has. Figure 14-2 shows how the general characteristic of introversion or extroversion might be judged on such a scale. With **absolute rating scales,** the rater assigns a score to each individual on each trait on the basis of comparison with a standard for each trait (see Figure 14-2.) When several people must be rated in relation to each other, **relative rating scales** are used in which the rater ranks each subject in relation to the other subjects on each trait. Rating scales are used in many measures of personality and other behavioral traits. For example, they are employed in industry and in education for the merit rating by supervisors of employees and teachers. Evaluation of teachers by students may use some form of rating scale. And these scales are even used in asking people for recommendations about people whom they know.

The reliability of rating tests is improved when thorough behavioral descriptions are assigned to the points on the rating scales and when the judgments of several raters are averaged out, for stereotype and halo effects can influence the judges using rating scales. If the judge has a **stereotyped judgment,** or preconceived notion, of the characteristics of people in a given profession—librarians, for example—this can influence the ratings of a person who happens to be a member of that profession. If the judge finds a person high (or low) on the first trait rated, then the halo effect may operate, and the judge may tend to rate the person high (or low) on other traits. You may suspect that your grades on essay tests or

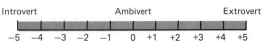

Figure 14-2 A quantitative scale for rating the degree of introversion or extroversion manifested by a person.

term papers sometimes reflect a stereotype or halo effect. Ideally, raters should be from about the same social group as those they rate, for the judgments made by raters of superior status have been found to be of low validity and reliability. This finding raises doubts about ratings of employees by supervisors, of students by teachers, and of teachers by students. This weakness, however, is at least partially overcome when judges have had a long and thorough acquaintance with those whom they are rating. Still, interviews, situational tests, and rating tests do not have the validity and reliability that can be attained by other measures of personality characteristics.

Personality Inventories

The answers to a series of set questions or statements in **personality inventories** indicate the interests, attitudes, or traits that people have and thereby reveal something about their personalities. Personality inventories are paper-and-pencil tests, usually self-administered and sometimes self-scoring. They are called **structured tests** because they consist of a series of statements to which subjects give brief answers—"Yes," "No," "Don't know." **Unstructured tests** allow subjects to respond with stories or statements of their own, which may reveal more about their personalities. Inventory statements in structured tests are selected because they do discriminate between people who display a given trait and those who do not. For example, more depressed people answer the statement "I sometimes tease children" with "No" than do people who are not depressed. This statement, then, would be included among a group of statements that have been shown similarly to differentiate between people who are generally depressed and those who are not. Such a collection of statements could be organized into an inventory to measure the trait of depression.

PERSONALITY INVENTORY ITEMS

■ You can see how personality inventories work by answering "Yes" or "No" to the following statements, indicating whether they seem to apply to you generally. List your answers with the numbers of the statements on a separate piece of paper. This is a set of selected statements that has been used in personality inventories to indicate two personality characteristics (Cohen, 1969).

	Check One	
	Yes	No
1. I like quiet rather than exciting amusements.	—	—
2. I often avoid unpleasantness by running away.	—	—
3. I can change my opinions easily.	—	—
4. I am generally satisfied with myself.	—	—
5. I would rather be by myself most of the time.	—	—
6. I often have the feeling of being a burden to others.	—	—
7. I would rather save money than spend it.	—	—
8. I never feel left out of things.	—	—
9. I dislike thinking about myself.	—	—
10. I sometimes have the idea that people are watching me on the street.	—	—
11. I act on suggestions quickly, before stopping to think.	—	—
12. I worry a great deal about my attire when attending a social affair.	—	—

Having listed your "yes" and "no" answers to the statements, you can now score yourself on the two traits. The scoring for these traits is given at the end of the chapter. (This is just a sample of an inventory, so don't regard your score as a valid or reliable measure of the traits in question.)

As you can see, personality inventories are scored very objectively, without permitting any scorer bias to effect the final measure of the traits, as it can in the interpretation of behavior observed in interview or situational measures. Subjects supply the information about themselves, as you did in answering the statements in "Personality Inventory Items." Did you find yourself tempted to give "good" or socially acceptable answers to some of the statements? Although the implications of the answer to "I sometimes tease children" are not obvious, the implications of a "yes" answer to "I often have the feeling of being a burden to others" are generally negative, and subjects may avoid a "yes" if they are trying to create a favorable impression of themselves. Thus people applying for sales positions would be bound to agree with "I enjoy meeting people" if they really wanted a job. Many of the personality inventory tests, however, have been so constructed that they contain indicators of whether a person is answering truthfully. Personality inventory items must also be kept up to date, as you can see from item 12.

Personality inventories have been widely developed and, when carefully constructed and properly standardized for large populations, serve as fairly valid and reliable measures of many personality characteristics. Psychologists

like L. L. Thurstone, R. Likert, and L. Guttman have developed more than 100 tests for measuring attitudes of approval or disapproval, antagonism or protagonism in regard to a variety of subjects, such as patriotism, war, ethnic minorities, and government. Gordon Allport, Philip Vernon, and Gardner Lindzey (1970) have made an inventory measuring attitudes toward values, on the ground that an important component of personality is well manifested in the interests and intentions, or values, that people hold. Their *Study of Values* inventory is based on six ideal personality types proposed by Edward Spränger (1928), with predominantly theoretical, economic, aesthetic, social, political, or religious interests and values. The profiles on these values for male and female students appear in Figure 14-3.

Another widely used inventory is the **Strong-Campbell Interest Inventory,** indicative of interest in many specific occupations. This inventory is based on the responses of hundreds of people happily employed in the various occupations. Their average responses are compared with those of others who take

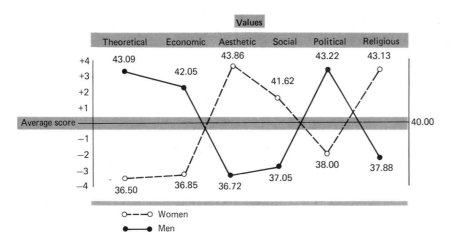

Figure 14-3 Mean value scores on the Allport-Vernon-Lindzey scale of values for male and female college students compared with the average scores. Women tend to score higher than men on aesthetic, social and religious values, and the men tend to score higher on theoretical, economic, and political values. (Allport, Vernon & Lindzey, 1970)

Basic interest scales

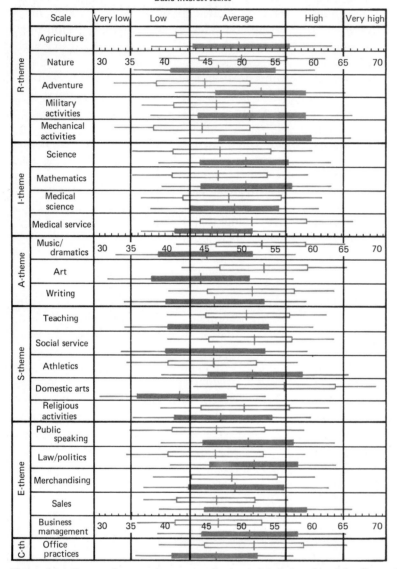

Figure 14-4 Scores of men and women on the basic interest scales of the Strong-Campbell interest inventory, grouped under the realistic (R), investigative (I), artistic (A), social (S), enterprising (E), and conventional (C) themes of general occupational interest. The open bars indicate the middle 50 per cent of female scores, the solid bars the same for male scores. The mark in the middle of the bar is the average and the extended thin line indicates the middle 90 per cent of the scores. (Campbell, 1974)

the test. Figure 14-4 summarizes male and female scores on basic interest scales in a variety of occupations. These occupations are grouped under several general themes, like the realistic (R) theme, which covers the occupations of agriculture, nature, adventure, military activities, and mechanical activities (Campbell, 1974).

Another inventory that helps to reveal vocational interests as well as personality traits is the *Personality Research Form* (PRF), developed by Douglas Jackson (1967). This form uses 22 scales for various personality characteristics. Scores on these scales are put together in significant personality patterns on a profile, and these patterns are correlated not only with variant personalities but also with vocational interests. When you think of the personalities of people you know in various occupations, do they seem to vary enough to support the idea of a relationship between personality and vocation? Are salesmen *really* more aggressive than most other men? Are women engineers *really* more masculine than most other women? These tests help us to find answers to such questions.

It has been suggested that it is easy to "fake good" on some personality inventories. A good example of an inventory designed to overcome this shortcoming is the **Minnesota Multiphasic Personality Inventory (MMPI).** The MMPI (Hathaway & McKinley, 1951) consists of more than 550 statements to each of which the person being tested answers "True," "False," or "Cannot say." It is used sometimes to diagnose personality disorders, since it measures traits that, if present to an extreme degree, would characterize behavioral disturbances. Statements known to be true of various types of psychiatric patients, as opposed to people in cross sections of the normal population, make up the groupings of items measuring the ten major traits in the inventory.

The objectivity of subjects taking the MMPI is indicated by their scores on several groups of statements that are included. A high "Cannot say" score indicates evasiveness. The L group, for example, tends to reveal a subject's tendency to lie. Answers of "True" to the statements "I have never been late for an appointment" and "I have never disobeyed the law" raise the L score and indicate lying, since every one of us has been late or broken some law at one time or another. An F group of statements indicates whether people are trying to fake the inventory or are being very careless in their responses. A high F score is obtained by giving a "True" response to such statements as "I believe it is perfectly all right to steal." A high score on a K group of statements means that the subject is defensive or unwilling to admit weaknesses, and a low score indicates that the subject is extremely self-critical or trying to fake poor answers. So these L, F, and K scores indicate whether a person's inventory results can be trusted, or whether they cannot because of the subject's attempts to mislead, or uncooperative attitude.

The MMPI is widely used; more than 1200 research papers have been based on its use and it has been translated into more than 17 languages. The test is scored on 10 basic scales indicating various abnormalities of personality, as well as on the "Cannot say," L, K, and F scores. The scales indicate hypochondriasis (Hs), or preoccupation with physical symptoms although no organic disease exists; depression (D), general hopelessness and pessimism; hysteria (Hy), or functional physical disturbances due to frustrations and conflicts; psychopathic deviation (Pd), false beliefs of persecution; masculinity-femininity (Mf); paranoia (Pa); psychasthenia (Pt), obsessive-compulsive thoughts; schizophrenia (Sc), coldness and withdrawal; hypomania (Ma), disturbed, excited emotions; and social introversion-extroversion (Si), uneasiness in social situations. An abnormal MMPI profile appears in Figure 14-5, compared with a normal profile. This also shows the scores of the "Cannot say," L, K, and F groups of statements. Many MMPI sec-

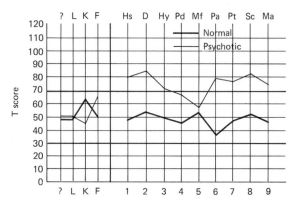

Figure 14-5 Profiles of a psychotic patient and a normal adult on MMPI scales, including "Cannot say" (?) and the L, K, and F scores. (Adapted from Gough, in A. Weider (Ed.) CONTRIBUTIONS TOWARD MEDICAL PSYCHOLOGY, Volume II. Copyright © 1953, The Ronald Press Company, New York)

ondary scales have also been developed for such characteristics as dominance, brooding, delinquency, alcoholism, emotional immaturity, hostility, altruism, neuroticism, originality, role playing, shyness, social status, and tolerance. In several investigations, interpretations based on the MMPI have proved as good as the judgments of experienced clinicians, if not better (Meehl, 1954).

ANTARCTIC-WINTER PERSONALITIES

Arctic and Antarctic explorers have in the past reported such personality or experiential disorders as delusions and hallucinations resulting from isolation, lack of sleep, starvation, and fear of the elements. A recent study has compared the personalities of a group of 15 scientists and support personnel who were wintering at the American South Pole Station with those of a control group of typical male college students in the United States (Butcher & Ryan, 1974). Although conditions at the underground South Pole station are not so severe as they used to be in Antarctic exploration, still the men have to undergo eight months of winter isolation from March through September. They live under cramped, boring, stressful, and potentially hazardous conditions,

with only radio contact with the outside world. The explorers were given the MMPI and the PRF at the beginning of winter, in midwinter, and at the end of the period.

The highly selected and somewhat older explorers had a normal configuration of characteristics on the MMPI, and they were generally better adjusted than the college students. The explorers showed significantly less anxiety (psychasthenia and anxiety), less bodily concern (hypochondriasis and hysteria), less alienation and more conventionality (psychopathic deviation and schizophrenia), and greater ego strength than the student control group. They also were more achievement-oriented, more serious-minded and self-sufficient, and revealed less tendency to play and to seek love, advice, or protection from others. Neither the student control group nor the Antarctic explorers showed any significant changes in their scores over the eight-month period. Although the explorers had experienced headaches and minor symptoms of depression and irritation through the winter, these were not strong enough to affect their basic stable personalities as measured by the MMPI and the PRF.

Projective Tests

Projective tests are unstructured personality tests, in that they present stimuli that are so vague and ambiguous that subjects being tested have to use their imaginations in interpreting them, and thus their underlying personality characteristics are given full play. One projective test, the **Rorschach test,** was designed by a Swiss psychiatrist, Hermann Rorschach, in 1921. It consists of a series of 10 inkblots of varied vague shapes, both black and white and colored (see Figure 14-6.) Subjects are asked what they see in the inkblots, what they might mean to them, and what they make them think of. Later, subjects are asked to point out the locations on the blots that gave rise to the images they saw in them. All their responses are scored and interpreted on the basis of standards that have been established. Although the Rorschach has proved

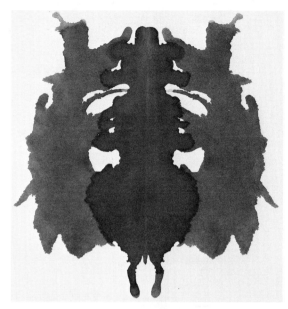

Figure 14-6 Inkblot similar to those used in the Rorschach test. What do you see in this inkblot? What might it mean to you? What does it make you think of?

to be of questionable validity and reliability, some clinicians claim to find it useful, particularly in diagnosing personality difficulties. Most users of the test place less emphasis on precise scoring rules than on general impressions of subjects' reactions to the total testing situation, their defensive or competitive style, or their personal standards of performance. Obviously this type of test depends heavily on the clinician's sensitivity, insight, and capacity for acute and objective observation.

Another projective test in widespread use is the **Thematic Apperception Test (TAT),** to which we have referred earlier. Published in 1935 by the American psychologist Henry Murray, this test consists of 19 ambiguous pictures capable of being interpreted in a host of ways, thereby revealing a great deal about subjects' personalities and the dynamics underlying them (see Figure 14-7). Subjects are asked to make up a story about each picture, what is happening in the scene, what led up to it, and how the story will come out (see Figure

14-8). Wishes, conflicts, fears, repressions, and a variety of defense mechanisms may be displayed in subjects' stories about the scenes. Different pictures are used for men, women, and children, with some overlap. Not only do these tests provide a picture of peoples' personalities; they have also been scored to measure their need for achievement or affiliation, for example. Although the validity and reliability of the TAT are just as low as (if not lower than) for the Rorschach (Murstein, 1963), both of them have proved very useful in probing the personality for information that other tests can verify. Other, simpler projective tests include word-association tests, sentence-completion tests, and tests based on the building of models, the drawing of pictures, and the acting out of roles, all manifesting various facets of the subjects' personalities. Any projective test depends to a considerable degree on the skill and objectivity of the testers. None has yet been standardized to the same degree as personality inventories, nor have any attained the latter's solid levels of validity and reliability.

Figure 14-7 A picture of a type used in a Thematic Apperception Test. Tell what is happening in this picture, what led up to it, and how it will come out. Do you see how your story may manifest some of your basic reactions or conflicts? (Courtesy Henry Murray)

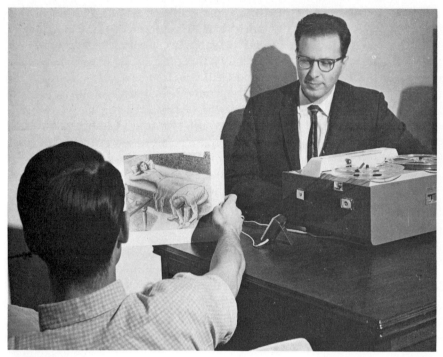

Figure 14-8 A subject's reactions to a picture in a TAT series are recorded, then later transcribed and analyzed.

PERSONALITY THEORIES

You have seen how methods of observing and investigating personality have gradually developed, starting from people's common-sense observations of the predominant ways in which human beings act, and gradually becoming more objective with interviews, rating scales, and finally the various forms of personality inventories and projective tests. Along with the ways of observing and measuring personality, theories of personality and its development have evolved. Some personality theories concentrate on the *structure* of personality, identifying and describing the fundamental traits descriptive of people's behavior. Such theories classify personalities into a series of types, or classify the basic traits that make up personality, so they are called type and trait theories, respectively. Other theories stress the *functioning* of personality, concen-

trating on the processes and their interactions as personality develops. These are called dynamic theories of personality, and are addressed to such questions as how people react to inner or outer conflicts, how they handle stress, and what processes, like defense mechanisms, they use in dealing with their conflicts. The earliest ideas about personality were expressed as type theories; trait and dynamic theories of personality followed.

Type Theories

One of the first recorded views of personality in Western society was expressed in the fourth century B.C. by the Greek physician Hippocrates. He believed there are four types of human temperament manifested in people's personalities: sanguine, choleric, melancholic, and phlegmatic. A sanguine person is wide-awake and cheerful, with agreeable emotions. Great vigor in action and strong emotional reactions typify the choleric person. The melancholic type tends to be withdrawn and depressed, and the phlegmatic type is slow, stolid, and inattentive. Hippocrates' types of personalities, so simple yet so all-encompassing, were given wide currency by the Greek physician Galen, who practiced and wrote medical treaties in Rome in the second century A.D., and were influential during the Middle Ages and down to modern times (see Figure 14-9). For a time Alfred Adler, one of the early followers of Freud, even used the four Hippocratic types in his "individual psychology."

Through the ages from earliest recorded times, **astrology** has offered a more complex set of personality types, founded on the presumed influence of the sun, moon, stars, and planets on the ways in which people act. Astrologists claim that personalities are determined by the position of the sun and planets in 12 principal constellations of stars along the band of the zodiac, which sweeps across the sky in a circle. The zodiac is a ribbon of sky on the line of the ecliptic, along which the sun appears to march from month to month with the actual motion of the earth around it. The zodiac was divided into 12 parts by the ancients to correspond with months of the year. Each of the 12 portions of the zodiac is iden-

tified by a particular constellation, or pattern, of bright stars, like Aries (the Ram) and Aquarius (the Water Carrier).

Astrologers claim that each person has the personality that goes with the sign of the constellation that dominated the zodiac at the time of birth, modified, of course, by the positions of the sun, moon, and planets at the exact hour and minute when the person was born. The chart in Figure 14-10 shows the astrological signs of the zodiac and their names, and briefly describes the dozen basic personality types that presumably are manifested in people born under them. Astrologers have developed these zodiacal personality types in great detail. Taurus (the Bull), for example, is a bright constellation to be seen sparkling in the night sky to the south during the winter. Taurus stands for all the forces that produce stability and permanence in the universe. Those born under its sign, between April 20 and May 20, are said to work with and conserve the resources of the earth. They are builders, practical, kindly people who never act without reflection in the light of their experience. The sign of Aquarius, on the other hand, represents the ideal relationship between all things. Those born under it, between January 20 and February 18, are supposedly dedicated to the search for true knowledge and seek through cooperation to achieve universal brotherhood.

Figure 14-9 The four principal character types as pictured in phrenological literature of the nineteenth century. These types were probably strongly influenced by Hippocrates' four temperament types.

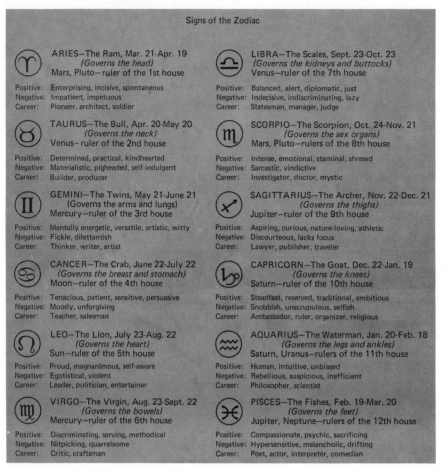

Figure 14-10 The ancient astrological signs of the zodiac and thumbnail sketches of the personality types under each sign. Would you say that the positive and negative character traits under your sign are descriptive of your personality?

Astrological analyses of personality and their predictions are made in such vague terms that they are difficult to verify or refute. The notions of the 12 different types of personalities have yet to be tested in any empirical manner. Recent personality research has not pointed toward or uncovered these kinds of personality. One unusual correlation between a trait and period of birth is described in "Femininity and the Zodiac?" But as it stands, astrology is an ancient notion unsupported by empirical tests. Astrologers do not fall over

each other in a rush to verify or refute their theory by scientific investigation.

FEMININITY AND THE ZODIAC?

Recently an attempt was made to check astrology's claim that people born under different signs of the zodiac have different personality characteristics. A personality inventory was administered to college students born under the 12 signs of the zodiac. Then the investigator (Pellegrini, 1973) checked to see whether there was any correlation between their traits as revealed by the inventory and their signs of the zodiac. The subjects were 144 men and 144 women, with 12 males and 12 females born under each sign of the zodiac. The California Psychological Inventory was used, an inventory arranged with scales to reveal 18 personality traits, such as dominance, tolerance, intellectual efficiency, responsibility, sociability, flexibility, femininity, and self-control. Although the scores on communality, socialization, and flexibility showed some relationship to sun-sign groups, it was the trait of femininity that turned out to be significantly correlated with half of the zodiac groups—Leo, Virgo, Libra, Scorpio, Sagittarius, and Capricorn. Students born under these six signs scored distinctly higher on the femininity scale than did those born under the other six signs. Note from Figure 14-10 that the signs of the zodiac related to high femininity cover an unbroken six-month period from July 23 to January 19.

Pellegrini observes:

The powerful effect on the femininity variable is very puzzling. It would require an almost absurdly conservative approach to data interpretation to attribute to chance a relationship of such magnitude. And yet, to the writer's knowledge, there is just no way to explain it in terms of established principles of any orthodox theory of personality. On the assumption that the effect on the femininity variable is a reliable one, the problem of how to account for it is challenging indeed. Why should people born at different times of the year differ in *any* dimension of personality? [p. 27].

Can you suggest any natural events or combination of events that might tend to create such an effect?

A type theory of personality very popular during the nineteenth century in Europe and the United States moved back from the stars to the human body, in this instance the bumps on the head (see Figure 14-11). The "science" of **phrenology,** which claimed that four character types can be identified by means of the size and shape of the skull, has been exploded as based on no justifiable evidence. And during the 1920s and 1930s a German psychiatrist, Ernst Kretschmer, and an American anthropol-

ogist, W. H. Sheldon, worked out three personality types based on many measurements of body build. The endomorphic type of person has a roundish body build, large digestive and other body cavities, and often fat deposits, but is weak in bony and muscular development. Endomorphs, said Sheldon, are relaxed and enjoy eating. They are sociable and need other people when troubled. The mesomorphic type is athletic, with large bones and muscles, broad shoulders and narrow hips, and a squarish build. Mesomorphs are energetic, competitive, and action-oriented. They love adventure, take risks, and are generally noisy, needing action when troubled. Ectomorphic types have a linear build, with long, slender arms and legs, small body cavities, and lack muscular development. Ectomorphs tend to be intellectual, antisocial, sensitive, and secretive. They have rapid reactions, may be anxious and inhibited, and want solitude when troubled. The trouble is that correlations between such body types and personality traits have turned out to be very low and undependable.

In fact, none of these type theories of personality has proved sound under investigation. Such theories assume that everyone will fit into a limited number of classes, an oversimplification. Sheldon finally found himself with some 70 different types of body build as he worked further with his theory, and at that point they simply related much too tenuously to personality traits. Furthermore, a type description tends to imply too much about a person. Once people have been pigeonholed as being submissive types, for example, all of them are then presumed to have all the characteristics associated with this type and no other; but the determinants of personality are much too numerous to produce such homogeneous and simple types. Finally, type theories are generally associated with outmoded conceptions of personality, conceptions that neglect external cultural or internal motivational influences. Few personalities fit under ideal stereo-

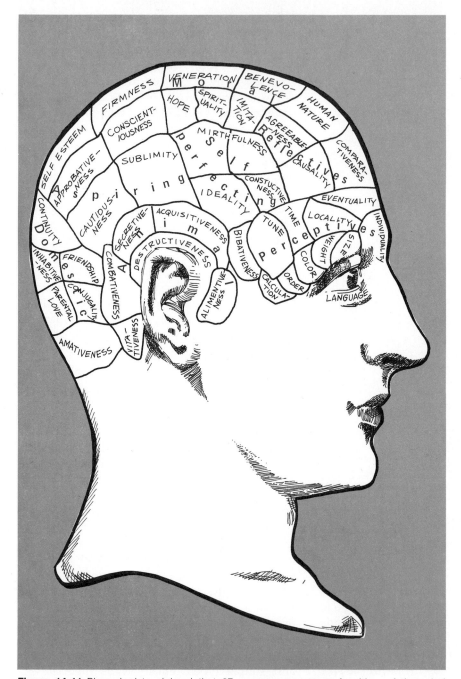

Figure 14-11 Phrenologists claimed that 37 or more organs, or faculties, of the mind, displayed in the shape of the head, indicated the extent of development of such traits as cautiousness, amativeness, hopefulness, self-esteem, and benevolence.

types proposed by type theories. Somehow it seems personality must be investigated in a more basic and complex manner than is called for by these type theories.

Trait Theories

With the development of personality tests and inventories, as well as projective tests, many characteristics of persons can be identified and described. When such characteristics persist, manifesting themselves in many people and not changing over periods of time, and are expressed in behavior in a variety of situations, they are called **personality traits.** Thus you display, to some degree, a trait that ranges along a dimension of shyness or timidity at one extreme to boldness or adventurousness at the other extreme. Presumably people have a vast number of persistent and consistent ways of behaving, which can be referred to as submissiveness, honesty, self-esteem, and intelligence, to name only a few. If people's behavior can be measured, or inventoried, for a variety of different and significant dimensions, perhaps these inventories would provide a good picture of their personalities, a picture made up of the most significant traits. A problem arises, however, in that hundreds of traits have been distinguished by rating scales and inventories. How are those traits that are basically significant for personality to be sifted out from others that are superficial? How can a group of traits composing the basic structure of personality be selected objectively?

In recent years, psychologists have begun to use a statistical technique called **multivariate factor analysis** in analyzing and selecting personality traits. R. B. Cattell and J. P. Guilford have been particularly active in this field (Cattell, 1950; Guilford, 1959). In this technique, scores representing many personality traits are correlated with each other, each trait with every other trait, to see the extent to which they "hang together." This turns up certain traits that tend to appear together; these are called **surface traits.** For example, Cattell found a high correlation (r) of 0.81 between assertiveness and aggressiveness (see Figure 14-12). A perfect correlation is indexed as 1.00, and no correlation at all as 0.00. Thus 0.81 shows a pretty strong relationship (see Appendix: Statistics). Furthermore, several traits may be intercorrelated in clusters, like thoughtfulness, austerity, and wisdom, or their polar opposites, as illustrated. And when they do group in this manner, the combination might be called disciplined thoughtfulness (versus foolishness). Again, honesty (versus dishonesty), loyalty (versus fickleness), and fair-mindedness (versus partiality) form another cluster of traits that might, together, be called integrity (versus dishonesty) or dependability (versus undependability).

Cattell worked with about 170 traits, derived from life records, self-rating inventories, and laboratory situations. Grouping traits that correlated with each other with an r of 0.60 or better, he found many correlated and clustered traits. He then went on to isolate and identify 15 to 20 source traits, using mul-

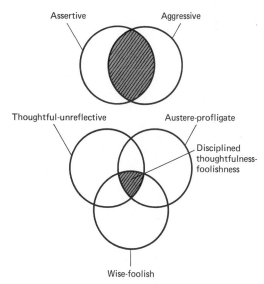

Figure 14-12 The correlation and clustering of surface traits in accordance with Cattell's theory of personality.

Table 14-1 Terms and Descriptions of Some Primary Source Traits Found by Factor Analysis of Life-Record Data

Schizothymia Obstructive, cool, reserved, cautious	*Cyclothymia* Easygoing, warmhearted, expressive, generous
Unintelligence Unintelligent, unreflective, quitting	*Intelligence* Intelligent, thoughtful, conscientious
Low ego strength Emotional, worried, changeable, undependable	*High ego strength* Emotionally stable, unworried, steadfast, dependable
Low excitability Deliberate, self-controlled, demanding	*High excitability* Overactive, changeable, emotionally immature
Submissiveness Unsure, frank, timid, obedient	*Dominance* Confident, reserved, adventurous, willful
Desurgency Pessimistic, seclusive, dull, taciturn	*Surgency* Cheerful, sociable, witty, talkative
Low superego strength Fickle, frivolous, indolent, neglectful	*High superego strength* Determined, responsible, ordered, attentive
Threctia (threat reactivity) Shy, aloof, hostile, inhibited, lacks confidence	*Parmia* Likes meeting people, genial, friendly, impulsive, self-confident
Harria Tough-minded, self-sufficient, practical, logical	*Premsia* Tender-minded, dependent, gregarious, intuitive, imaginative
Alaxia Trusting, introspective, composed, understanding	*Protension* Suspicious, crude, awkward, withdrawn, jealous
Praxernia Conventional, anxious, narrow interests	*Autia* Unconventional, complacent, cultured interests
Artlessness Forthright, natural, sentimental	*Shrewdness* Shrewd, calculating, worldly
Confidence (untroubled adequacy) Self-confident, self-sufficient, accepting, tough, spirited	*Guilt-proneness* Worrying, lonely, suspicious, sensitive, discouraged

Source: Cattell, 1957.

tivariate factor analysis to see what clusters of traits correlated highly with each other but poorly with other clusters. The description of source traits must be derived from the groups of traits composing them. These source traits seemed to have a deeper unity than surface traits, manifesting more basic aspects of personality. **Source traits** are thought of as general personality factors from which specific traits are derived, much as Charles Spearman and L.

L. Thurstone proposed that there is a general intelligence factor from which specific abilities like verbal fluency and numerical ability derive. One listing of Cattell's source traits, with his brief descriptions of them, appears in Table 14-1. With primary source traits like these and the results of many other studies dealing with personal attitudes and roles, for example, Cattell felt that the basic constitution of the individual personality could be understood.

A difficulty with trait theories like Cattell's is that the results of the factor analysis depend on the original data used, such as rating scales and biographical records. Using self-inventories, Thurstone obtained only seven source traits with factor analysis, and Guilford identified two basic kinds of traits, motivational needs and temperamental characteristics. These varying results raise the suspicion that personality may be so variable, dependent to such an extent on each individual's experience, particularly in early life when the personality is being formed, that trait theories cannot adequately depict it. Although trait theories may give a good X-ray or cross-sectional picture of the dominant characteristics in personality, still this approach represents the piecemeal identification of the components of personality, and does not show how the pieces are organized and how each develops. For adequate recognition of such dynamic elements in personality, we have to turn to psychoanalytic and other theories of personality.

Psychoanalytic Theories

During the first third of this century, Sigmund Freud (1856–1939) developed a new and comprehensive theory of personality that greatly broadened its boundaries and changed its interpretation. Freud was led to this dynamic theory by his careful observation and analysis of his patients' dreams and unconscious slips of the tongue, and by using a technique of **free association,** in which patients spontaneously talk about whatever comes directly to mind. These revealed to Freud the operation of new elements and processes in personality.

Freud proposed the existence of the **id,** an unconscious, infantile reservoir of psychic energy. The unconscious furnishes the motive power for all our conscious experiences and behavior through the **libido,** the sexual drive or motive, and for other basic motives like hunger and thirst. The id follows the **pleasure principle,** simply driving for the gratification of instinctive wants and the avoidance of pain. Conscious experiences themselves compose the **ego,** which exists to satisfy the id by mediating between its needs and the environment. The ego follows the **reality principle,** channeling the libido and guiding behavior until objects that will provide wish fulfillment for the id have been secured. The ego thus serves to mediate between the libidinal drives and the outer world, maintaining the life of the individual and reproducing the species. As children grow, learn to walk, and begin to satisfy their own drives, however, they soon discover from their parents that some behavior is approved and other behavior disapproved. They internalize these attitudes, creating the third basic element of personality, the **superego,** or conscience. The superego serves to inhibit the instinctive, pleasure-seeking drive of the id, particularly its sexual and aggressive drives. Sometimes Freud thought a **death instinct,** destructive of the self, was opposed to the libidinal drive, or **life instinct,** directed toward maintenance of the individual and reproduction of the species. The superego, part of which becomes unconscious, is divided into conscience, yielding guilt feelings to control behavior, and ego ideals, yielding pride in behavior that competently satisfies drives.

The elements of the person, or whole self, are roughly diagrammed in Figure 14-13. Id, ego and superego sometimes function smoothly in reducing the tensions of drives, but often they conflict with each other. When this happens, **anxiety** is aroused. Reality anxi-

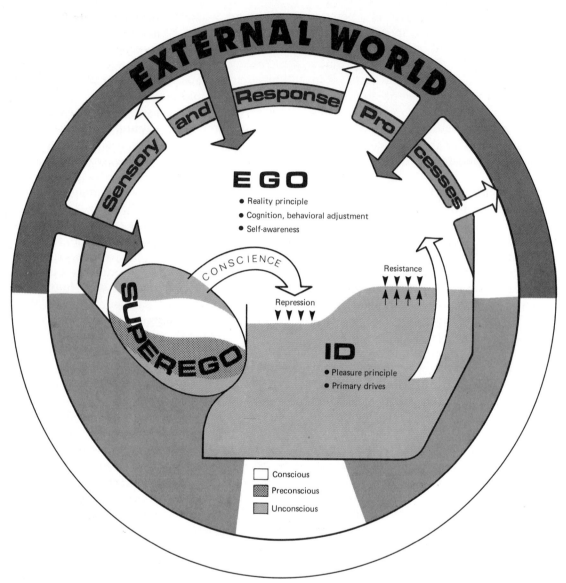

Figure 14-13 A schematic diagram of the three Freudian psychic areas of the id, ego, and superego.

ety is soundly based on real threats or dangers to the satisfaction of drives from the realities of the objects and other people around us. Neurotic and moral anxieties, however, are fears that drives will get out of control and lead to pain or punishment, or to guilt and shame created by the superego. In order to avoid conflicts and the anxiety they produce, the ego uses many **defense mechanisms.** One such mechanism is **repression,** used to force back unacceptable wishes or feelings into the id or the superego, or to prevent them entirely from coming to consciousness **(resistance).** Another defense mechanism is **displacement,** by which the ego, when it is blocked, finds other objects for the satisfaction of libidinal drives. For example, Freud believed that children at three or four years of age are blocked by social taboos from gratifying their libidinal desires toward the parent of the opposite sex, and eventually have to displace these desires to socially acceptable mates. The boy's sexual love for his mother is called the **Oedipus complex,** and the girl's love for her father is called the **Electra complex.**

Personalities develop gradually through the expression and satisfaction or the blockage of these drives, and through the defense mechanisms and complexes that the interaction of id, ego, and superego produces in dealing with the drives. Development progresses through a series of stages. In the **oral stage,** during the first year, libidinal pleasure is obtained largely through the lips and mouth with suckling and eating, while aggressiveness may be manifested in biting or spitting out. In the second and third years, the **anal stage** leads to concentration on excretory functions. Toilet training aims to control these functions, and it is here that the child first faces intense cultural pressure and that anger-anxiety conflicts arise. The anal stage is followed by the **phallic stage,** from three to five years, during which sexual and aggressive feelings are associated with the genitals. In this stage the mother becomes a sexual object for the boy and the father for the girl, bringing them into the conflicts with their parents that create the anxieties of the Oedipus and Electra complexes. The repression of these conflicts leads to the **latent stage,** from 5 to 10 or 11 years of age, in which children find playmates of the same sex outside the home and displace their drives in learning skills at school and in play. The **genital stage,** during adolescence, gradually leads to the discovery and acceptance of socially approved mates.

Sometimes the sexual drives are satisfied in part as well by another defense mechanism, **sublimation,** in which love of achievement in any area of life — economic, artistic, or re-

ligious, for example — may substitute for sexual satisfactions. Sometimes the personality may be driven by extreme anxiety to **fixations,** in which the self does not develop beyond a given stage, like the oral or anal stage, or it may use the defense of **regression** against anxiety, dropping back to an earlier, simpler stage of development. Fixation at the early oral stage may produce oral-sadistic personalities — for example, people who are prone to biting sarcasm, ridicule, strictness, and cynicism. Fixations may also produce the anal-expulsive character, fixated at the anal stage and given to persistence and generosity. On the other hand, the anal-retentive character may be obstinate, stingy, and over orderly, constipated in more ways than one. According to psychoanalytic theory, malfunctioning personalities lead to all kinds of maladaptive behavior, expressive of mental disorder (see Chapter 15).

Developed early in the twentieth century, Freud's theory of personality has had a great impact on the conceptions of human nature in the Western world. His influence ranged from psychology, in which Freud had many followers, to history, anthropology, philosophy, and religion. In literature, for example, the plays of Eugene O'Neill express many Freudian concepts. Among Freud's lasting contributions are his emphases on the importance of infant and childhood experiences and on unconscious motivations. The great significance that Freud attributed to the sex drive has been criticized, however, as probably a consequence of the extreme sexual repressions of his time and culture. Furthermore, he and his early followers depended on case histories rather than on objective, controlled studies through which predictions from his theory could be checked. Finally, the effectiveness of Freudian psychoanalytic techniques for dealing with behavior disorders has been challenged in recent decades (see Chapter 16). Nevertheless, Freud made a profound and lasting imprint on psychology, to say nothing of modern civilization.

Carl Jung (1875–1961), one of Freud's early

followers, broke away in 1914 and created his own dynamic theory of personality, although he remained greatly influenced by the master. Jung also identified the source of vital or psychic energy as the **libido,** although he thought of this as a generalized life force rather than a solely sexual drive. Jung also accepted from Freud the concept of the ego, or the conscious mind, to which Jung gave the functions of perceiving, feeling, thinking, and intuiting. With intuition we sense the deeper significance of events, whether in the world around us or deep within ourselves in mystical experiences. The ego may adopt one of two opposing attitudes, oriented in the main toward the external world with **extroversion** or toward the inner, subjective world with **introversion.** Furthermore, within each person dwells a personal unconscious, made up of once-conscious experiences that have been forgotten, repressed, or ignored. At this unconscious level many **complexes** are found, organized nuclei of strong feelings, thoughts, and perceptions, such as the mother complex we all have, in part derived from the infant's maternal experiences and in part arising from a deeper level still, the **collective unconscious.** This unconscious consists of latent memories, called **archetypes,** which are inborn in each and every one of us as residues of human evolution. These **archetypes** are similar predispositions, like fears of the dark and of snakes, that early people developed under primitive living conditions. Another such predisposition is to recognize and respond to a mother; still another is to recognize and react to the life-giving sun, an archetype that Jung believed had led to sun worship and the gods of certain religions.

Physiologically, both men and women have both male and female sex hormones, with a preponderance of those of their sex. Psychologically, Jung believed that men have a female archetype he called the **anima** and women a male archetype, the **animus.** These archetypes are implanted by men's experience with women and vice versa over the millennia of evolution. They assist the sexes in understanding and responding to each other. Jung calls another archetype the **shadow,** an inborn vestige of human beings' animal instincts, which include many predispositions to act in socially or religiously tabooed ways. From the shadow, as from Freud's id, come destructive thoughts or feelings that may be repressed in the personal unconscious. Still another archetype is the predisposition to strive for unity and **actualization,** which gives rise to the **self,** seeking self-realization, and such values as were embodied in Christ, Buddha, Mohammed, and other great religious leaders. Thus all people must find their own individual ways to wholeness of self and realization of their potential, according to Jung.

In describing the development of personality, Jung suggested that the four functions of the ego—perceiving, thinking, feeling, and intuiting—combine with the two basic opposing attitudes of introversion and extroversion in various ways. Thus varying degrees of introversion and extroversion may be expressed through the functions. Usually a person develops one of these functions predominantly, and tends to ignore or repress the others into the personal unconscious, which may develop the functions to compensate for their lack in the conscious ego. Conflicts result from the opposition of the various functions, the attitudes, and the systems of the ego, personal unconscious, and collective unconscious. Yet these oppositions can be transcended and the personality unified with the integrating function of the self. Jung's conception of the dynamics of personality is thus more optimistic than that of Freud.

Another disciple who broke away from Freud was Alfred Adler (1870–1937), who developed his own personality theory in what he called **individual psychology.** Adler did not accept the existence of the unconscious or the id as Freud conceived them. Rather than being driven by libidinal urges, Adler thought, people are attracted by goals. It is the goals or ends for which they seek, rather than unconscious drives, that shape people's actions. Adler first expressed our predominant goal as **power** and later called it **superiority,** or self-assertion. He believed this goal of superiority to be innate, a part of life itself, carrying people on from stage to stage as their personalities develop. Normal people strive for superiority in achieving goals that are primarily social, although neurotic people strive for egoistic goals like self-esteem and fame.

Within the personality, **inferiority feelings** may be aroused by any imperfections or failures, physical or psychological, that are experienced. People attempt to overcome such inferiority feelings at the same time that they strive to attain superiority. Although all have the same goal, they may seek it in innumerable ways, and each person has an individual **life style,** influenced by feelings of inferiority but also manifesting methods of achieving superiority. We perceive, learn, and remember what fits into our life style, and overlook everything else. In molding our own personalities, we strive for a creative self that will integrate our behavior and make it consistent. The creative self offers our final goal, which really gives meaning to our lives. Adler thus presented a humanistic and idealistic conception of human personality, the opposite in many ways of Freud's.

A number of other psychoanalysts have depended heavily on the thought of Freud, but have developed **neoanalytic personality theories** so far as they have departed from him. Thus Erik Erikson has stressed the attainment of **ego identity** as children pass through developmental stages quite similar to those of Freud, organizing a strong sense of self that gives a person stability within and continuity in dealing with other people. **Group identity,** the ways in which groups regularly organize

experience for their members, also must be developed for its effects on the individual members as well as the continuity of the group.

Karen Horney (1885–1952) held that basic anxiety is produced by anything that disturbs a child's security, creating feelings of helplessness. Children seek to protect themselves by forming an **idealized image** of themselves, as opposed to the **defaced image** produced by insecurity. We have basic impulses to move toward, away from, or against other people, which affect the development of our personalities. We attempt to match our actual self to our idealized image and escape from our defaced image, but the real need is to create a genuine self that expresses and satisfies our genuine needs.

Erich Fromm holds that human beings feel lonely because they have become separated from nature and isolated from each other. As children gain freedom from their parents, they become lonely and insecure. We can resolve this problem by either constructively immersing ourselves in shared activities with others or destructively by simply conforming to society and submitting to authorities. People have distinctively human needs for relatedness, for transcendence, for rootedness, for identity or a sense of permanent self, and for a frame of orientation. Like Jung's archetypes, these needs have developed through human evolution and are innate. So far as people develop healthy, constructive ways of genuinely satisfying these needs, their lives are well balanced and significant for them. If they try to "escape from freedom," however, rather than taking advantage of it, they develop conflicts and disorders. Fromm points out various types of personality prevalent in modern society: the receptive, exploitative, hoarding, marketing, and productive types. Recently he has added the **necrophilous** (death-loving) **type** and **biophilous** (life-loving) **type.** Only the productive and biophilous types of people are actually able to lead free and satisfying lives. Although human society has often hindered the development of constructive personalities, Fromm believes, it may still be possible to create a kind of society in which our real needs can be freely and abundantly fulfilled.

Social-Learning Theories

The cultural matrix of personality development was emphasized by Harry Stack Sullivan (1892–1949). Sullivan (1953) was influenced by the anthropologists Ruth Benedict and Margaret Mead, and by the social orientation of Karen Horney and Erich Fromm. Sullivan held that the human being differs from all other animals in cultural development, which is not based on instincts or drives, but on interpersonal tenderness, first manifested between mother and infant. "The activity of an infant which arises from the tension of his needs produces tension in the mothering one which is felt by her as tenderness." Sullivan based his interpersonal theory of personality on such situations. According to Sullivan, your personality consists of your customary interpersonal behavior as you interact with other people. As a person you do not and cannot exist except in such interactions. All psychological functions—perceiving, remembering, thinking, dreaming—are interpersonal in character.

The habitual behavior of individuals in relations with other persons, whether overt like talking or covert like imagining, consists of patterns of energy transformations that Sullivan calls **dynamisms.** Most of these dynamisms are goal-directed, aimed toward the satisfaction of needs. The infant's cry, for example, is a complex behavioral pattern designed to overcome hunger, discomfort, or need for bodily contact. The satisfaction of these or any other needs gives rise to euphoria and a sense of integration, self-esteem, and security. When the mother feels anxious, this feeling is transmitted to the infant by em-

pathy. Such basic anxiety creates tension and is disintegrating, leading to lack of self-esteem and insecurity and interfering with the satisfaction of needs.

Security arises, then, from meaningful and satisfying interpersonal relations, and insecurity arises from the lack of them. A self-system develops with many dynamisms based on the insecurities experienced by children, and this system defends them against anxieties. As they grow, individuals construct **personifications,** or images of themselves and other people. A baby's personification of a good mother derives from her care, while experiences with her that arouse anxiety personify her as a bad mother. Eventually these personifications of the mother are combined with others that are formed by the infant's interactions with her into a complex image or concept of the mother. Similarly, infants create personifications of themselves from their satisfying "good me" and anxious "bad me," and these also combine into the self-system, through which they gain security and try to ward off crippling anxieties and disorders.

John Dollard and Neal Miller (1950) formulated a theory of personality derived from the principles of stimulus–response learning (Chapter 7) and motivation (Chapter 12). Personality, according to the Dollard-Miller theory, consists of complex systems of habits that link environmental and internal stimuli to behavior. Energized by primary or secondary drives and motives, and reinforced by rewards, these habitual goal-directed behaviors are gradually established in accordance with generalization and discrimination principles. With the use of language, social rewards and punishments become very effective. Thus a mother uses "yes" and "no" in encouraging or inhibiting the actions of an infant who is able to crawl about. Words not only facilitate generalization or extinction of responses, but they can also arouse drives and facilitate their satisfaction or reduction in socially approved behavior. Eventually, through the guidance of their parents, children develop the vast interwoven sets of social habits that constitute their personalities.

Dollard and Miller identify several critical situations in the early lives of all individuals that greatly influence the development of their personalities. These situations are the *infant feeding* situation, toilet or *cleanliness training*, training in the expression and control of *anger*, and early *sex training*. The relative success with which children learn to deal with these situations and to adjust to the social restrictions placed on them determines to a great extent the development of adaptive or maladaptive interpersonal relations. Infants who are fed at once when they cry from hunger find that their crying and other efforts lead to drive reduction, and thus establish a particular pattern for effectively dealing with the environment and satisfying their needs. If infants are left alone to "cry themselves out," however, they may well begin to adopt apathetic and anxious reactions, mistrust their ability to deal with the environment, and fear being alone—learned reactions that establish the foundation for maladaptive patterns of motivation and behavior. Dollard and Miller conclude that parents should try to keep children's drive stimuli at a low level, promote their adaptive behavior, and extinguish fear or anxiety responses by appropriate gratifying drive reduction. They also emphasize that parents should not make learning demands before children are adequately equipped to deal with them. Thus, until the maturation of sphincter control at the age of 18 months to two years, clean pants should not be demanded of infants.

Psychologists like Dollard and Miller suggest that the concepts of psychodynamic theories of personality like Freud's can be explained in relatively objective S–R terms, applied not only to observable environmental and behavioral events, but also to covert processes like anxiety and images. The defense mechanism of repression, for example, is interpreted as the avoidance of certain thoughts, images, or feelings. People learn such avoidance in accordance with S–R principles, just as they learn any other behavior. Not thinking or not feeling about certain things produces drive reduction and is reinforced as a result. Thus repression soon becomes a matter of habit. If the thought of snakes, for example, has come to produce fear in an individual, avoiding the thought prevents the fear from arising. But the original fear reaction is not extinguished, only repressed, and may arise automatically in other, similar situations and become generalized as a phobia. According to the S–R view of personality, explanations of other defense mechanisms can be constructed on the basis of such learning processes, without the need to postulate a set of complex entities like Freud's ego, id, and superego.

Humanistic and Existential Theories

In recent years, humanistic and existential psychologists have formulated their own theories of personality with a strong emphasis on the concept of the self. These psychologists have felt that in dealing with specific objects or processes in their experiments, investigators have entirely overlooked the initiating and guiding functions of the self, key to the understanding of the whole person.

SEARCH FOR THE SELF

■ The idea of the self is illusive, without doubt. It is difficult to grasp just what the term means. Surely "self" does not mean a tiny person inside you somewhere who makes your decisions and guides your behavior. This activity may help to direct you toward what the term "self" refers to.

Think about what you will do after you finish your study session with this book. Do you already have a clear idea of what you will do next? If you do, then think of other possibilities, and evaluate them against your current idea. If you haven't decided yet what to do next, think of various possibilities that are feasible for you and evaluate them in any way that occurs to you. After thinking it over for a few minutes, decide what you will do after finishing your session with this book.

When you've reached a firm decision, recall what was involved in your coming to it. What was the "I" or "self" that was doing all this thinking, imagining, weighing, evaluating, and deciding? You can say, "I thought," "I imagined various activities," "I judged them in relation to each other," and "I chose to do such-and-such." To what did this "I" refer as you did these things? Can you describe or define your "I" or "self"? Is it an agent, like your body, that carries on various covert activities? Is it anything more than the totality of the activities themselves? Is it your identity as a person, the common element that accompanies all your activities? Or what? Psychologists are by no means agreed on the nature of the self.

As a result of his client-centered or "nondirective" method of psychotherapy, Carl Rogers (1961) has developed a humanistic theory of personality based on the concept of the self. In **nondirective therapy**, therapists make every attempt to accept and value their patients as they are and to encourage them to express their feelings and conflicts freely, thus gradually building up greater self-acceptance and regard and actualizing the real self. Rogers found that his patients tended to talk about their problems in terms of their selves, and made the self the basic element in his view of personality. For Rogers, the I, me, or **self** is the organized pattern or structure that gives a consistent form to a person's perception of his relationships with others, to all the events going on within and outside of him, and to the values he attaches to these events. In these terms, your self as you experienced it in "Search for the Self" was the personal structure that gave form to the alternative actions that you imagined and evaluated, and thereby produced the decision to which you came. The self or structure is available to your awareness, although you may not always be conscious of it when you are attending strongly to your perceptions or thoughts themselves. Furthermore, your self is fairly flexible and may change as your personality develops, Rogers believes. All individuals thus have their own unique structure or self, their characteristic ways of dealing with life. Each self strives for consistency as well as for adequacy, trying to maintain and actualize itself.

Each person acts as a whole, fairly permanent being or self in interpersonal relations, Rogers holds. Our selves need to be positively regarded and accepted by others, and also need positive self-regard. These selves direct us toward goals considered to be worthwhile and thereby increase our own sense of worth. We derive some of the values we use to direct our activities from others, and some we develop for ourselves. Our selves are adequate and well adjusted when they enable us to assimilate our social and environmental experiences in ways consistent with our own concept of ourselves. When we clearly perceive events as they really are and find that, as conceived, they assist the actualization of our own self-concept, our behavior will be adaptive and worthwhile.

American **existential psychologists** like Rollo May (1969) and Adrian Van Kaam (1966) have really just begun to elaborate theories of personality. They have been influenced by such European *existentialists* as Jean-Paul Sartre and Albert Camus, as well as by so-called *phenomenologists* like Martin Heidegger and Karl Jaspers, who sought to get down to the "givens," or phenomena presented in immediate experience. Existential psychologists attempt to perceive the basic phenomena of experience directly and immediately, without preconceived notions, and thereby grasp its significance and understand it correctly. Existentialists claim that such immediate experience discloses that causal or deterministic explanations of human behavior are inadequate, for these explanations miss the role of the self and its values in freely deciding our future behavior. According to the existentialists, our immediate experience of our self, of our existence, and of our free exercise of choices creates our essence, or what we will become as consistent human personalities. Suppose the door of your room is standing open, and you look at it, get up, and close it. A causal explanation of the pressure of your hand exerted in a certain direction on the door bringing about the effect of the door's swinging shut is not adequate to an understanding of your behavior. You experienced a cold draft through the open door, you wish to keep warm, the room will be likely to warm up if you shut the door, so you decide to get up and close it. Your motives, thoughts, and predictions, as well as values, were involved in your decision to perform this action. They were the phenomena of your existence that then created your behavior through your own volition and decision. The human self is free, creative, and responsible for its own choices and actions as it gradually builds up typical ways of acting and develops its own personality or essence, the existentialists maintain.

People often feel the absurdity of their existence or the nothingness of their experience, particularly when they are severely frustrated or defeated. Life is absurd, existentialists hold, as long as people are simply reacting to the events crowding in around them. Until they exercise their free will, play active roles in guiding the emergence of events, and make of themselves what they have chosen to be, life is bound to be meaningless to them. But the existentialists point out that freedom also entails responsibility. You cannot have one without the other. You are absolutely responsible for your freely chosen acts and eventually for the character that all of your acts make of you. You are by that very token responsible for the effects of your actions on other people. The type of personality you develop has, in fact, consequences for the whole human race. Therefore, people must consider the effects of their actions on others and make their decisions as if they were representing all of humanity.

What seems on first view to be an individualistic doctrine turns out to be sensitive to the social roles that people inevitably play in realizing the vast possibilities inherent in them.

TRAIT AND SITUATIONAL DETERMINANTS

The degree to which personality traits actually determine individual behavior has been questioned. For example, you may have a certain general tendency to be dominant in your relations with other people. Yet you recognize that dominance may be actually expressed in your behavior to a greater or lesser extent, depending on the situation. When you are with a group of your peers, an objective observer might judge you to be markedly dominant, tending to assume a leadership role; yet when you are in company with your professors or your superiors at work, an observer might judge you to be somewhat submissive, tending to accept statements or orders without question and acting forthwith on them. Variations of this kind have led some psychologists to the conclusion that situational factors play a large role in determining behavior, and many investigations have supported this position (Mischel, 1968).

Locus-of-Control Effects

Expectancy-value theories of behavior indicate that the probability that a person will perform a certain action depends (1) on the person's level of expectation that this action will bring certain rewards, and (2) on the value that those rewards have for the person, in comparison with the value of rewards attainable by other actions. You can see how this expectancy-value analysis of behavior places less emphasis on traits of the individual involved than on factors in the situation, the rewards it has to offer, how much the person wants those rewards, and the *perceived* chances of getting them by acting. These expectancy-value theories have been supported by locus-of-control experiments. A **locus-of-control scale** has been devised (Rotter, 1966) that measures the extent to which a person's locus of control is perceived to be external or internal. Pairs of statements in the scale are indicative of the locus of control. Thus, accepting the statement "In my case getting what I want has little or nothing to do with luck" indicates internal locus of control; the statement "Many times we might just as well decide what to do by flipping a coin" implies external locus of control.

The use of this scale in many investigations has shown that people who are internally oriented and controlled tend to conform less to group pressures than externally controlled people and are less influenced by persuasive communications toward changing their attitudes and beliefs. When internally controlled people are given the task of persuading others of beliefs they do not accept themselves, however, they are more likely to change their own beliefs by thus participating actively in the process than those who are externally controlled (Sherman, 1973). Changes in attitudes are apparently likely to be self-induced by people whose locus of control is internal. In any event, factors in the experienced situation, whether these factors are external to the individual, like propaganda, or internal, like the individual's values, do play a large role in determining behavior.

Situation and Trait Interactions

Investigations have brought to light other significant situational determinants of behavior, such as the need for social approval and the need for self-esteem. You can recall how you have talked on one side of an issue in company with people who favor that side, but tended to swing to the other side of the issue, or not to express your own views strongly, when associating with people who favor the other side. Desire for social approval, or desire

to bolster self-esteem, also influence our behavior in many situations. Yet strong personality traits surely also affect the way we act. The tendency in recent work on personality has been to recognize that behavior results from the interaction of situational and trait factors, rather than from one to the exclusion of the other. As expressive of the whole character of a person, personality is perhaps the most complex as well as the most significant set of variables in determining behavior.

SUMMARY

The whole person, or personality, is expressed in the complex of enduring traits that are apparent over a period of time in the ways an individual tends to behave, both overtly and covertly. These traits involve an essential life style rather than simply social skills or the predominant impression the person tends to make.

Personality is measured and evaluated by means of many psychological techniques, like personal interviews, situational measures, rating scales, personality inventories, and projective tests.

All of these measures have their weaknesses, reflected in measures of validity and reliability. With the exception of personality inventories, personality measures depend heavily on the tester's objectivity, avoidance of halo and stereotype effects, and ability in interpreting the results. Situational measures are usually more successful than interviews, and structured personality inventories are better than rating scales and projective tests.

Personality theories offer a set of principles, often referring to underlying constructs, to explain the complex of behavior patterns involved in personality. In grouping all personalities together in a few classes, type theories, like those of Hippocrates and Sheldon, tend to oversimplify the richness and variety of personalities and neglect the multiplicity of factors in their development. Oversimplification is also characteristic of trait theories, like those of Cattell and Guilford, which concentrate on the predominant behavioral patterns through which personality is expressed.

Psychoanalytic theories, like those of Freud, Jung, and Adler, emphasize the internal entities, like Freud's id, ego, and superego, that are felt to determine the dynamic development of personality through a series of stages. Social-learning theories, like that of Sullivan, derive the personality from the effects of social interactions from infancy onward. S–R theories depend on stimulus-response learning to explain the complex systems of habit patterns constituting personalities. Individual behavior is energized by primary and secondary drives or motives. The resultant goal-directed behaviors, greatly affected by social rewards and punishments, develop the individual's personality.

As opposed to social theories, humanistic theories, like that of Carl Rogers, and existential theories, like that of Rollo May, base personality on the initiating and guiding functions of the self. Each of us is considered largely responsible for the personality we eventually develop, as we freely choose our activities in interaction with others.

Other theories, like that of expectancy value, point to the varying locus of control, which tends to be either internal or external. They point to such basic needs as self-esteem on the one hand and social approval on the other. These are viewed as strong determinants of the extent to which individuals will express traits or patterns of behavior in given situations. Personality is variable and flexible, according to these views, dependent on many situational and trait factors interacting with each other.

NOW YOU'RE THE EXPERT

1. Do you agree or disagree with the arguments presented against the various type theories of personality discussed in this chapter? What evidence can you present yourself for and/or against these theories?

2. Rate yourself on Cattell's source traits shown in Table 14-1, using a rating scale of 5-4-3-2-1-0-1-2-3-4-5 between the low and high poles of his traits. After you have completed the rating, consider whether (a) these source traits seem basic to your personality and are frequently expressed in the ways you behave, and whether (b) you can think of other source traits not appearing here, yet frequently expressed in your behavior.

3. Think of a fairly recent situation in which you found yourself in a serious and lengthy conflict with another person or persons. Consider all of your behavior in the conflict. Then try applying various personality theories discussed here to explain your behavior. Is your behavior best explained by (a) one of the psychoanalytic theories of personality, (b) a social-learning theory, (c) a humanistic or existential theory, or (d) some combination of trait and situational determinants?

The odd-numbered statements in the sample of a personality inventory in the activity box "Personality Inventory Items" on p. 398 are indicative of the trait of introversion or extroversion; the even-numbered statements are indicative of security or insecurity:

Items	Introversion	Extroversion
1	Yes	No
3	No	Yes
5	Yes	No
7	Yes	No
9	No	Yes
11	No	Yes

Items	Insecurity	Security
2	Yes	No
4	No	Yes
6	Yes	No
8	No	Yes
10	Yes	No
12	Yes	No

15

Behavior Disorders

was disordered? Similarly, which symptoms have to be very acute or intense before they mean "mental illness" to you? Is mental illness or behavior disorder all just a matter of degree, intensity, or repetition? At what point, then, for these symptoms, would you draw the line between health and illness, order and disorder? Are there some symptoms, like having hallucinations or being irrational or violent, for which it is easy to draw the line? And are there others, like fear, depression, anger, anxiety, suspiciousness, for which it is difficult to draw the line?

■ CAN YOU ANSWER THESE?

Criteria of Behavior Disorders

- Can a line be drawn between normal and abnormal behavior?
- Are behavior disorders a sickness or a problem in living?

Neurotic Disorders

- Can one be neurotic part of the time and well adapted the rest of the time?
- Are the multitude of phobias all based on the same mechanisms?

Addictive Disorders

- What is the difference between physiological and psychological dependence on drugs?
- Can anyone become an addict?

Psychotic Disorders

- What is the difference between psychotic and neurotic behavior?
- Have any physiological causes for psychoses been identified?

Personality or Character Disorders

- When and how do personality disorders usually develop?

Organic Behavior Disorders

- What behavior disorders are based on organic conditions?

YOUR OWN CRITERIA?

■ All of us absorb from our own culture and our experiences and standards certain criteria or norms by means of which we distinguish between disordered and ordered behavior, mental illness and mental health. Take a few minutes to review your own experiences and concepts, and make a list of those symptoms or characteristics that strike you as identifying behavior disorder or mental illness. You'll probably find that the longer you think about it, the longer your list becomes.

Now look over your list of behavior disorder symptoms. If I exhibited a symptom only once or on rare occasions, would you say my behavior was disordered or that I was "mentally ill"? Which behaviors have to be repeated, or chronic, before you would say the person who displayed them

People with "behavior disorders" or "mental illness," call it what you will, are always with us. Altogether too many are afflicted, as our newspapers indicate every day. Rough es-

Table 15-1 Estimated Total Number of People with Major Behavior Disorders in the United States, 1970

Type of Disordered Persons	Millions
Neurotics	10.0
Alcoholics	9.0
Hard-drug abusers	1.0
Psychotics	2.0
Emotionally disturbed children and teenagers	5.5
Antisocial personalities	4.0
Persons in prisons or arrested for serious crimes	2.0
Mentally retarded	6.5
Total	40.0

timates of the number of people in the United States in 1970 suffering from principal behavior disorders are shown in Table 15-1. Although these figures are probably underestimates of the number of persons whose behavior causes serious troubles for them and for others, the total of 40 million men, women, and children represents 20 per cent of the whole population. One out of five people is in behavioral difficulties, according to this estimate.

CRITERIA OF BEHAVIOR DISORDERS

The identification, definition, and classification of behavior disorders has always been a problem. Crime, or violence to people or their property, is not so difficult to identify. But other behavior disorders do not yield so easily to identification. Where do you draw the line between "mental health" and "mental illness," for example? What makes you think that one person is crazy and another sane? Hostile behavior that is tolerated or even admired in one culture will be rejected and punished in other cultures, or in the same culture during a different period. What distinguishes ordered from disordered behavior, the normal from the abnormal?

Abnormal or Maladaptive?

The terms "abnormal" and "maladjusted" are often used in the attempt to define behavior disorders. These terms are highly ambiguous, however. "Normal" can mean the perfect personality, functioning at an optimal level in all respects, which makes all of us "abnormal." Or "normal" can be taken to mean the persons who conform to the customs of their own society and "abnormal" those who reject some of these customs. Or "normal" can mean average behavior of any type, as opposed to the two extremes—no anger under any circumstances on the one hand and outbursts of rage at anything at all on the other—either of which is "abnormal." Definitions based either on ideas of conformity or statistical averages, however, are enduring only in a culture that is unchanging or in which there is little variability. Furthermore, some persons who conform may be so compliant or dependent that we would tend to classify them as neurotic, and "average" behavior may be quite maladjusted under certain circumstances. Some have tried to resolve the problem by distinguishing between adaptive and maladaptive behavior. Behavior is said to be **adaptive** when it is effective in maintaining a person's well-being or survival and good interpersonal functioning. Behavior that impedes progress toward these goals would be termed **maladaptive.** A **behavior disorder** would then be behavior that tends to be maladaptive. Would prejudiced behavior then be interpreted as maladaptive and therefore abnormal, although statistically it is probably "normal"? Perhaps it should be. The people who display prejudices might live quite normally in other respects, even though their prejudiced behavior is tragically maladaptive for them, for other people, and for society as a whole.

The Medical Model

In the past, behavior disorders have often been conceived and treated as if they were a kind of disease, and referred to as "mental disease" or "mental illness." This approach follows that of medicine, which has advanced by the identification and understanding of all kinds of physical diseases. Thus it was found that various groups of symptoms were indicative of the malfunctioning of certain organs or of the attack of certain bacteria or viruses. Once the causes of the diseases could be identified, effective treatments could often be devised. It was quite natural, then, that medical men and psychiatrists should follow this **medical model** of disease in working with behavior disorders. And it is true that a number of diseases of the brain and central nervous system were identified and are now treated, more or less effectively, by following this medical model. When known physiological conditions produce aberrant behavior, we speak of **organic behavior disorders,** and these are discussed later in this chapter. Although the search has been intensive and persistent for similar organic or physical causes for the remaining behavior disorders, it has not yet been successful. Such disorders, for which no organic conditions have been found, are known as **functional behavior disorders.** Thus brain concussions and hardening of the arteries may cause organic behavior disorders, but no physical causes have been discovered for most of the neuroses, psychoses, and personality disorders. Except for schizophrenia and depression, for which organic determinants have been identified, the medical model of behavior disorders as mental diseases has been largely discarded.

SANITY IN THE MIDST OF INSANITY

Wouldn't it seem that the professional personnel in psychiatric or mental hospitals, including psychiatrists, clinical psychologists, social workers, nurses, and psychiatric attendants, should be able to distinguish sanity from insanity most efficiently? After all, they are surrounded by the insane and treat them constantly. This proposition was tested recently by eight pseudopatients who entered 12 psychiatric hospitals on the east and west coasts (Rosenhan, 1973). The three women and five men, all quite normal individuals, included three psychologists, a psychology graduate student, a pediatrician, a psychiatrist, a painter, and a homemaker. Each called the hospital for an appointment and at the admissions office complained that they had been hearing voices that seemed to be saying, "Empty," "Hollow," and "Thud." The voices were of their own sex, they said, but unfamiliar to them. These were artificial "existential symptoms," similar to those the existentialists claim arise in people who are overcome by the realization of the emptiness and meaninglessness of life. Actually such existential symptoms are not reported in psychiatric literature, so they should have aroused suspicion. The pseudopatients also gave incorrect names, vocations, and employment, and beyond this told the truth about their life histories, so far as these were explored by hospital personnel. As soon as the pseudopatients were admitted to a psychiatric ward, they began and continued to act just as they normally would. Many of them had never visited a mental hospital before, and at first they were a bit nervous. Since the experiment required that they get discharged entirely on their own, their fears were justified to some extent.

Although these pseudopatients acted entirely normally, even openly taking notes on everything that happened to them, not one of them was ever suspected of being normal by the hospital personnel. Many of the mental patients, however, told these pseudopatients that they must be sane, and guessed they were journalists or professors, since they were taking such profuse notes and acting so normally. No hospital personnel asked to see the notes, but all labeled the writing as pathological behavior. Because of the symptoms reported, like hallucinations, all the pseudopatients but one were classified as schizophrenic. All were given various tranquilizers and other medications (which they did not take). Eventually they managed to get discharged from the hospitals after stays averaging 19 days and ranging from 7 to 52 days. They were discharged with the diagnosis of "schizophrenia in remission."

Once these people were diagnosed psychotic,

their quite normal behavior was not sufficient to cause the hospital staffs to change this label. Their fairly normal life histories were interpreted by the professionals who interviewed them in such a way as to fit the schizophrenic labels they had firmly in mind. When these pseudopatients asked questions of professionals in the halls, they were generally ignored. In fact, the admissions interview, ward meetings, and meetings with psychiatrists, psychologists, and physicians averaged only seven minutes a day. The pseudopatients felt entirely depersonalized, for the professionals rarely made eye contact or talked with them; they treated them, in fact, as if they were not human. One nurse, for example, unbuttoned her uniform and adjusted her brassiere in the view of a whole ward of male patients. She was not acting seductive; she merely acted as if they didn't exist. Staff members were often verbally or physically abusive of patients, except in the presence of superiors. The study demonstrates how difficult it is sometimes, given the existing stereotypes and treatment, for sanity to be distinguished from insanity.

Interpersonal Models

In recent years a number of critiques have been made of the medical model of mental illness. Thomas Szasz has maintained that this model is responsible for continuing a myth, the tradition that behavior disorders are a kind of disease. Functional behavior disorders reflect the difficulties and conflicts of living, not the presence of a bodily or mental "illness," he claims (Szasz, 1960). O. H. Mowrer has argued along similar lines, attributing the functional behavior disorders to a lack of moral responsibility and inability to make crucial moral decisions as to proper courses of action (Mowrer, 1960). These men and many others believe that the medical model encourages the confinement of many persons to a hospital environment in which they become depersonalized and are often allowed to vegetate. Only those few inmates who tend to be violent and may do injury to themselves or others should be hos-

pitalized, according to this view; the others should be treated in intensive care or community health centers in which they can be quickly helped to move back into the stream of normal activities.

Various **interpersonal models** have been proposed as alternatives to the medical model. As you saw in Chapter 14, Harry Stack Sullivan proposed that the development of individual personality and the self are entirely based on the interactions of the infant and child with the mother and other people. Sullivan saw a social basis for behavior disorders as well. Other predominant models for behavior disorders are the Freudian dynamic structure of personality and the behaviorist learning model, such as that proposed by Dollard and Miller. The general principles of these models of human behavior have been given in Chapters 13 and 14. They will be applied here in the description and explanation of behavior disorders.

Anxiety and Defense

Did you list such conditions as anxiety, fear, conflict, anger, or depression among the symptoms of behavior disorders? As you have seen in Chapter 13, anxiety, frustration, and conflict occur in many situations that people meet from day to day. These emotional reactions and emotionalized behaviors can be aroused to a normal degree in threatening or thwarting events that happen to everyone. You become anxious when you don't know what the outcome of a situation will be, for example, or depressed when the remarkable results you expected from your efforts do not materialize. A normal degree of anxiety arouses us for quick and effective action, leads us to review the possibilities that can be expected, and readies us to deal with whatever happens—the "fight or flight" syndrome. But anxiety may become exaggerated, far more intense than the circumstances warrant. It may also become chronic or persistent in highly stressful circumstances from which a person finds no escape. These anxiety conditions may seriously affect one's enjoyment of life and relations with other people. Then the anxiety or other emotional reactions become antisocial and are characteristic of a variety of behavior disorders.

A LIFE-EVENTS INVENTORY

■ A **life-events inventory** of the serious and stressful situations in which people may find themselves appears in Table 15-2. These principal psychosocial stressors were gathered from the responses of a variety of patients in a mental hospital and were then rated on a scale of 1 to 100 by psychiatrists, psychologists, mental-hospital patients, and university students for the amount of turmoil, upheaval, and social readjustment that these judges thought the events would cause, with 100 standing for maximum disruption (Cochrane & Robertson, 1973). Then the ratings of these judges were averaged for each of the items to give the mean scores on stress or turmoil. The mean ratings made by 75 students are given in the table.

You can get an idea of how stressful your own life has been during the past year by noting the scores for those items that have happened to you and totaling them for your overall score. Items with scores over 50 are particularly stressful, of course, and items under 50 less stressful. The number of items you check and their stress scores should indicate how much anxiety you have experienced during the last year. They do not give any idea, however, as to how adaptive and maladaptive your responses to these stressful situations may have been.

According to the Freudian psychodynamic theory, infants experience **primary and basic anxiety** or distress when they feel strong hunger, pain, and discomfort, when they hear loud noises, and when they are roughly handled, since they are helpless to deal with the situations. They express their anxiety or hostility and discharge their tensions in crying and struggling, which usually bring their mothers to satisfy their needs or correct the distressful conditions. Gradually infants become less helpless. With the aid of their parents they learn how to satisfy their own needs and resolve the conflicts that arise from the demands of the unconscious id. Their egos and superegos develop as they pass from one stage of life to the next, from oral to anal and phallic levels. At each of these levels, typical anxiety-generating conflicts must be resolved. But in infants and children, separation from others or loss of their love can arouse extreme anxiety, as can children's conflicts about their parents at the Oedipal stage. Children and then adults build up such ego defenses as identification, projection, repression, and denial against their conflicts (see Chapter 14). But when the stresses are too great, they regress to earlier stages of development and become enmeshed in behavior disorders.

Learning theories of behavior disorders are based on classical and operant conditioning principles. Behavior disorders result from failure of children or adults to learn all the adaptive behaviors necessary for the satisfaction of their drives. Disorders may develop from the learning of maladaptive behaviors, or from conflict situations in which people do not feel capable of making the adequate and necessary discriminations or decisions that will reduce their drives. Thus when infants have not learned to overcome their wariness of strangers appropriately toward the end of the first year, they may develop anxiety and a sense of inadequacy in dealing with other people, always turning toward and depending on their mothers. Later, when they are placed in situations demanding independent decisions in dealing with others, making friends or carrying on social affairs, their dependence, particularly under stress, may result in maladaptive, socially unacceptable behavior accompanied by extreme anxiety and dread. Whether a psychodynamic or learning model is adopted, anxiety and some of its extreme manifestations in fear, dread, anger, insecu-

Table 15-2 A Life-Events Inventory to Measure the Amount of Stress That Has Been Present in a Person's Immediate Environment During the Preceding Year

Events	Ratings	Events	Ratings
Section 1. All		28. Period of homelessness (hostel or sleeping rough)	51
1. Unemployment (of head of household)	66	29. Serious physical illness or injury requiring hospital treatment	63
2. Trouble with superiors at work	39	30. Prolonged ill health requiring treatment by own doctor	48
3. New job in same line of work	29	31. Sudden and serious impairment of vision or hearing	58
4. New job in new line of work	50	32. Unwanted pregnancy	70
5. Change in hours or conditions in present job	28	33. Miscarriage	65
6. Promotion or change of responsibilities at work	40	34. Abortion	63
7. Retirement	52	35. Sex difficulties	58
8. Moving house	41	*Section 2. Ever-married only*	
9. Purchasing own house (taking out mortgage)	40	36. Marriage	50
10. New neighbors	16	37. Pregnancy (or of wife)	49
11. Quarrel with neighbors	23	38. Increase in number of arguments with spouse	52
12. Income increased substantially (25%)	35	39. Increase in number of arguments with other immediate family members (e.g., children)	43
13. Income decreased substantially (25%)	60		
14. Getting into debt beyond means of repayment	67	40. Trouble with other relatives (e.g., in-laws)	28
15. Going on holiday	27	41. Son or daughter left home	46
16. Conviction for minor violation (e.g., speeding or drunkenness)	20	42. Children in care of others	54
17. Jail sentence	72	43. Trouble or behavior problems in own children	49
18. Involvement in fight	31	44. Death of spouse	83
19. Immediate family member starts drinking heavily	63	45. Divorce	70
20. Immediate family member attempts suicide	66	46. Marital separation	65
		47. Extramarital sexual affair	56
21. Immediate family member sent to prison	56	48. Breakup of affair	47
		49. Infidelity of spouse	70
22. Death of immediate family member	67	50. Marital reconciliation	53
		51. Wife begins or stops work	31
23. Death of a close friend	54	*Section 3. Never-married only*	
24. Immediate family member seriously ill	55	52. Breakup with steady boy or girl friend	51
25. Gain of new family member (immediate)	42	53. Problems related to sexual relationship	54
26. Problems related to alcohol or drugs	59	54. Increase in number of family arguments (e.g., with parents)	43
27. Serious restriction of social life	45	55. Breakup of family	77

Adapted from Cochrane & Robertson, 1973.

rity, or depression are singled out as characteristic of behavior disorders that become chronic and debilitating.

NEUROTIC DISORDERS

When anxiety reactions become very intense, continue too long, or are present most of the time, they result in abnormal behavior. Anxiety reactions are widespread in a group of behavior disorders called neuroses. In a **neurosis,** the person experiences and expresses anxiety directly, or may control it at an unconscious level by means of various defense mechanisms and be distressed by symptoms of anxiety like fear, depression, or obsessions. Still, neurotics are aware that their behavior is maladaptive and that they are not functioning properly; **psychotics,** on the other hand, are often unaware of the peculiarity of their condition and reactions. In **chronic anxiety,** strong tensions are felt continuously for long periods. These may be interrupted by acute anxiety attacks or **panic,** with extreme, almost unbearable tension in which the person is helpless to deal with the anxiety.

Anxiety Neurosis

A typical case of chronic neurotic anxiety was displayed by a man named Carl when he finally sought relief from a psychiatrist (Cameron, 1963). Carl's symptoms had developed to such a point that he feared he was going insane. For a number of years he had noticed attacks of weakness, dizziness, blurred vision, and unsteadiness. In recent years he had been distressed by nervous tensions, frequent fatigue, irritability, insomnia, and nightmares. He had become very restless, overworked, began to drink during the day and take sleeping pills at night. He experienced anxiety attacks in which he had queer sensations in his head, his heart pounded, his breathing was labored, he sweated profusely, and he had a terrible fear of dying. He felt surrounded by nameless terrors and dreaded insanity as the

attacks became more frequent. Talking with the psychiatrist sometimes panicked Carl too, and he would berate the psychiatrist for not calling in a heart specialist. During such anxiety attacks, Carl would lean forward and make rhythmic mouth movements that he said seemed to relieve his tension. They were reminiscent of those of an infant nursing, and the psychiatrist thought Carl's behavior indicated a regression to an oral stage of helplessness.

Carl had a kind of behavior disorder called an **anxiety neurosis,** characterized by great sensitivity to tension-producing conflicts and a tendency to react with diffuse anxiety, dread, or fright accompanied by bodily organic disruptions. Chronic anxiety reactions go on more or less continuously over long periods of time. The anxiety is frequently present in only slightly stressful circumstances and is not restricted to the specific objects or situations that would normally arouse anxiety in other people. In chronic reactions, anxiety spreads a pall over everything the individual does and says, with little letup. In people subject to acute anxiety attacks, on the other hand, anxiety may occur less frequently. Such attacks may be accompanied by a number of the bodily symptoms reported by Carl, including restlessness, heart palpitations, dizziness, nausea, vomiting, labored breathing, and extreme sweating. Urgency to urinate or diarrhea may develop. In such attacks, people may tremble and walk unsteadily. They may fear death, heart failure, insanity, or some unnamed disaster, asking those around them for help and insisting they are in grave shape.

ANXIETY OR CAFFEINE?

A 23-year-old nurse came into a medical clinic complaining that for the last three weeks she had felt lightheaded, trembly, breathless, and headachy, and frequently had irregular heartbeats. Her "spells" occurred as often as two or three times a day. She was given a full clinical examination with many laboratory tests, in the course of which she admitted to being apprehensive, especially during her "spells." The evaluation turned up no physical difficulties and she was referred to a psychiatric clinic with the notation "Acute anxiety reactions, probably secondary to the fear that her affair with an older man is breaking up." The nurse refused to accept this diagnosis. Instead of going to the psychiatric clinic, she searched for 10 days for a dietary cause, and then found that her attacks were correlated with excessive coffee drinking—10 to 12 cups of strong black coffee a day. Cutting down the coffee cut out her "spells."

Recently it has been emphasized that excessive doses of caffeine, found in many beverages and medications sold over the counter today, will mimic the symptoms of anxiety neurosis, even of acute anxiety reactions (Greden, 1974). Excessive caffeine gives rise to nervousness, headaches, agitation, irritability, tremulousness, heart palpitations, nausea, vomiting, diarrhea, and occasional muscle twitching, as well as insomnia, ringing in the ears, and even visual flashes of light. A diagnosis of anxiety should be made only after the effects of drugs like caffeine have been ruled out. Common sources of caffeine and the amounts they contain are shown in Table 15-3. Amounts over 250 milligrams of caffeine per day are considered large, likely to result in some of the symptoms noted. Two cups of coffee, two cola drinks, and a couple of headache or aspirin tablets can easily total 500 milligrams a day, as you can see from the table, with long-term results ranging all the way from the jitters to hypertension or ulcers.

Greden calls this constellation of symptoms **caffeinism** and suggests that its prevalence in the population should be surveyed. "From the clinical perspective," he says, "many individuals complaining of anxiety will continue to receive substantial relief from psychopharmacological or hypnotic agents. For an undetermined number of others, subtracting one drug—caffeine—may be of greater benefit than adding another."

Table 15-3 Some Common Sources of Caffeine and the Amounts They Contain

Source	Approximate Amounts of Caffeine per Unit
Beverages	
Brewed coffee	100–150 mg. per cup
Instant coffee	86–99 mg. per cup
Tea	60–75 mg. per cup
Decaffeinated coffee	2–4 mg. per cup
Cola drinks	40–60 mg. per glass
Prescription medications	
APCs (aspirin, phenacetin, caffeine)	32 mg. per tablet
Cafergot	100 mg. per tablet
Darvon	40 mg. per tablet
Fiorinal	40 mg. per tablet
Migral	50 mg. per tablet
Over-the-counter medications	
Anacin, aspirin compound, Bromo-Seltzer	32 mg. per tablet
Cope, Easy-Mens, Empirin, Midol	32 mg. per tablet
Vanquish	32 mg. per tablet
Excedrin	60 mg. per tablet
Pre-Mens	66 mg. per tablet
Many cold preparations	30 mg. per tablet
Many stimulants	100 mg. per tablet

Source: Greden, 1974.

Anxiety neuroses may develop from all kinds of unresolved conflicts of childhood or adolescence. Carl, for example, had been reared very strictly by his parents and taught to fear sin. When he was fifteen, his parents were divorced, and although he continued living with his mother, he could not forgive either of his parents. He thought them hypocrites and believed all women were untrustworthy. Although as an adult he had affairs with several women, he found them all unsatisfactory. He felt guilt and tremendous anxiety when he found that his co-workers knew of his most recent affair, and his acute anxiety attacks set in. With the breakup of this affair, his symptoms increased.

People with anxiety or other neuroses know that their confusion, their maladaptive behavior, and their anxieties are injurious to their own well-being and that of others, but they feel irresistibly impelled to behave inappropriately. They have not learned how to deal effectively with conflict, or they have learned maladaptive responses to conflict. Their increasing helplessness and anxiety precipitates anxiety attacks time after time. Often they are not able to deal constructively with their neuroses on their own, and require the objective and understanding assistance provided by some kind of therapy (Chapter 16).

Depressive Neurosis

Neurotic depression, called the "common cold of psychopathology," is a behavior disorder caused, according to one theory, by aggression or anger turned inward against the self. The neurotically depressed show excessive dejection, self-depreciation, bodily complaints, and feelings of inferiority, hopelessness, and worthlessness. When depression appears in an extreme form with little reality contact, and is difficult to correlate with external causes in the life of the person, it may be a psychotic condition (see Table 15-4). Neurotic depressions may be brought on by the withdrawal of love

or emotional support, the loss of a loved one, or personal or economic failures. One kind of depression that comes with new responsibilities is known as promotion depression: Recognition of success or achievement may make people who derogate themselves and want to be dependent on others actually reject offered promotions or feel extremely depressed about them.

All of us experience temporary setbacks or difficulties and, with them, depressions in which we lose self-confidence, feel inferior, and become critical of ourselves. These depressions are soon resolved, however, as we go on to new successes in our daily activities or receive love and reassurance from others. In neurotic depressions, however, worry, self-blame, and dependence on others increase. Depressed persons may complain of backaches, poor sleep, continuous fatigue, headaches, all kinds of physical disorders. They lose interest in their normal pursuits, have no initiative, and become irritable and lonely. They continually demand support of their self-esteem from others. Sometimes they claim they are no good, failures, defeated. Life seems absurd and meaningless to them and they feel helpless, with no control over their fate, feelings that have been emphasized by existentialists (see Chapter 14). They also frequently complain of inability to concentrate, to remember, or to think clearly. When their families and friends become tired of denying their inferiority or failure and express their irritation at this despondency, the depressed persons are driven into quarrels with them and then to even greater depression. A vicious cycle is established in which their lack of interest and inability to think clearly lead to inability to perform as they used to, producing even greater depression.

Freudians claim that, although neurotically depressed people do not always know it, they always come to hate themselves. The Freudians go on to interpret this as evidence that a strong superego is rejecting and attacking

Table 15-4 Frequency of Clinical Symptoms in Neurotic Depressive Reaction (NDR) and Psychotic Depressive Reaction (PDR)

Clinical Symptom	Symptom Present		Symptom Present to Severe Degree	
	NDR, % (N = 50)	PDR, % (N = 50)	NDR, % (N = 50)	PDR, % (N = 50)
Sad face	86	94	4	24
Stooped posture	58	76	4	20
Speech: slow, etc.	66	70	8	22
Low mood	84	80	8	44
Diurnal variation of mood	22	48	2	10
Hopelessness	78	68	6	34
Conscious guilt	64	44	6	12
Feelings of inadequacy	68	70	10	42
Somatic preoccupation	58	66	6	24
Suicidal wishes	58	76	14	40
Indecisiveness	56	70	6	28
Loss of motivation	70	82	8	48
Loss of interest	64	78	10	44
Fatigability	80	74	8	48
Loss of appetite	48	76	2	40
Sleep disturbance	66	80	12	52
Constipation	28	56	2	16

Source: Beck, 1972.

the regressed and infantile ego. Depressed persons regress from the normal, adult ego and become as dependent as children on the support of others. They despise themselves as they originally felt their parents despised them for being disobedient or disappointing children.

Learning theory, on the other hand, interprets neurotic depression as a form of "learned helplessness," the behaviors that result from the loss of strong sources of reinforcement, like the withdrawal or death of a loved one, or the inability to control important events in one's life. As a result, depressed people lack the normal motivation to carry on their daily activities or initiate new projects (Seligman, 1972, 1975). Moreover, the attention and sympathy from others that they often receive reinforce their helpless and dependent behaviors.

MULTIPLE FACTORS IN DEPRESSION?

Two psychiatrists have suggested that all forms of depression may be products of many combined genetic, biochemical, and psychosocial factors (Akiskal & McKinney, 1973). They point out that experiments in learned helplessness with dogs and the separation of infant monkeys from their mothers produce effects very similar to human depression. Thus dogs shocked repeatedly with no way to escape from or avoid the shocks simply become inert and helpless, like depressed people, until they are dragged to the safety of an adjacent compartment; after that the dogs eventually, but slowly, become less helpless (Seligman & Maier, 1967). Hopelessness and helplessness, produced by the experience that one's efforts have no effect on important events, take the form of passivity, apathy, the lack of any motivation to work for rewards—in short, depression. In other investigations, the separation of infant monkeys from their mothers and juvenile monkeys from their peers throws the isolated animals first into a state of agitation and search, followed by huddling in despair and self-clasping. These behaviors are very similar to those of human infants who are separated from their mothers after a strong attachment bond has been formed (Harlow & McKinney, 1971).

The excited protests caused by separation may in turn lead to strong arousal and excitability of the neurons involved in the centers of reinforcement and punishment of the brain. This may disturb the proper functioning of the brain which may be vulnerable to such disturbances through genetic inheritance. Furthermore, this disturbance may diminish the concentration of biochemicals called amines (such as catecholamines and indoleamines) in the brain, whose depletion has been shown to be associated with depressions. Thus depressions have sometimes been triggered in hypertensive patients who have been treated for their high blood pressure with an amine-depleting drug such as reserpine. These biochemical effects on the brain could lead to further inadequacies in arousal, which would increase the depression.

Pulling all this evidence together, Akiskal and McKinney conclude that depression is

a psychobiological state that is the final common pathway of processes involving interpersonally induced states of mind in which the individual sees himself as losing control over his fate (hopelessness); increased psychic turmoil; depletion of biogenic amines; impairment of the neurophysiological substrates of reinforcement; further decrements in coping mechanisms; and a vicious cycle of more hopelessness, psychic turmoil, and neurophysiological impairment.

Obsessive-Compulsive Neurosis

We experience our own compulsive behavior and that of others very often in our culture. For example, people carry charms on their persons or in their cars to ward off evil or to bring them good luck. Youngsters watch each other at their games, like hopscotch or "giant step," to be sure each step in a ritual series is fol-

lowed exactly. Adults feel they must strictly follow certain customs, like opening the bedroom window at night even if the thermometer registers zero, or perform certain rituals, like repeating specific prayers at specific times, word for word. In superstitious behavior we go through all kinds of absurd and fixed routines, like rapping on wood, tossing spilled salt over the shoulder, and avoiding crossing the path of a black cat. When people develop *their own* magical rituals and are driven to repeat them time after time, then they display behavior characteristic of an **obsessive-compulsive neurosis.**

People with an obsessive-compulsive neurosis find that they have to repeat apparently useless words, thoughts, or actions over and over in order to reduce their anxiety. With these behaviors, according to Freudians, they either imagine themselves doing something forbidden, protect themselves from indulging in something forbidden, or punish themselves for wanting to indulge in something forbidden. Thus a mother may have repetitive thoughts of harming or killing her infant. It is not always easy, however, to trace a compulsion to anything forbidden. A workman may avoid looking at his boss for fear that he will die, a child will avoid every crack in a sidewalk for fear of untold consequences. The variety of such compulsive behaviors is tremendous, and those who succumb to them sometimes realize they are magical and absurd when they think about it but they cannot stop, and frequently elaborate them. Repeated thoughts of this kind are called **obsessions,** and repeated actions or words **compulsions.** Most of us occasionally repeat actions compulsively, such as looking at a stove to be sure it is off or checking to be sure a door is locked. Such actions may be minor and unimportant, but they can become so widespread and acute that they cut down people's efficiency and affect their lives.

Obsessive-compulsive activities have been found to serve a number of functions. They are considered by psychoanalysts to be neurotic attempts to discharge strong tensions and anxiety through regressions to a childish or infantile magical level, to displace current conflicts with infantile conflicts, or to eliminate anxiety or other emotions by concentrating on simple, repeated actions. When normal repressions have failed, the neurotic, overcome by anxiety, then tries to escape through regression to magical infantile reactions or other compulsive actions. Unless they are interfered with, these actions do reduce the tensions, at least in some measure. Many neurotics of this kind are perplexed and often ashamed of their behavior, but although they realize its odd character, they cannot overcome it and require therapy of some kind to deal with it.

Compulsive behavior strongly resembles the persistent responding of monkeys in a nonsignaled avoidance task. In Chapter 7, Sidman avoidance was described as a situation in which every response postponed shock for a fixed though brief segment of time. Uninformed observers might well wonder at the monkey's "compulsive" key pressing, since they would detect no external reason for the behavior. They would observe, though, that as seconds elapsed since the last response, the monkey would show increasing signs of restlessness until it pressed the key again, after which it would calm down. Isn't this much like the behavior of compulsive hand-washers who periodically become very agitated for no apparent reason until they perform their ablutions? In the case of the monkey, we know about the aversive event the compulsive behavior is warding off. In the case of human compulsions, the catastrophic events that the compulsive acts are warding off have been lost to consciousness.

Other Neurotic Disorders

Phobias are intense, irrational fears of certain objects, like lightning, guns, spiders, or snakes, or situations, like enclosed or high

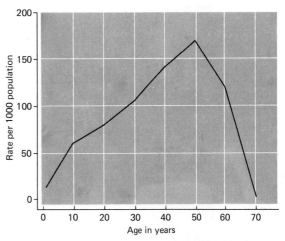

Figure 15-1 Prevalence rates for phobias within the general population by age. (Adapted from Agras, Sylvester, & Oliveau, 1969)

places, or to the contrary, wide-open or low places. The prevalence of phobias in the general population by age is shown in Figure 15-1. Although phobic neurotics realize that these things offer no real danger in any circumstances in which they are likely to encounter them, their extreme fear may be experienced as faintness, heart palpitations, fatigue, nausea, perspiration, or even panic when they encounter these objects or situations. According to psychoanalytic views, phobias may develop from sexual excitement aroused by some persons or events, which phobic people unconsciously deny because the sexual impulse is unacceptable to the superego. They then displace the impulse onto some other object or situation. After this original displacement, the anxiety becomes bound to the phobic object, and any other situations similar to the original one may then arouse it again. Thus one may appear to love or fear a person, animal, or object because it serves as "surrogate," representing the original loved or hated person. Freud's case history of "Little Hans" involved a young boy's conflict of love and hate for his father. According to Freud, Hans displaced his hatred for his father to a horse, and then devel-

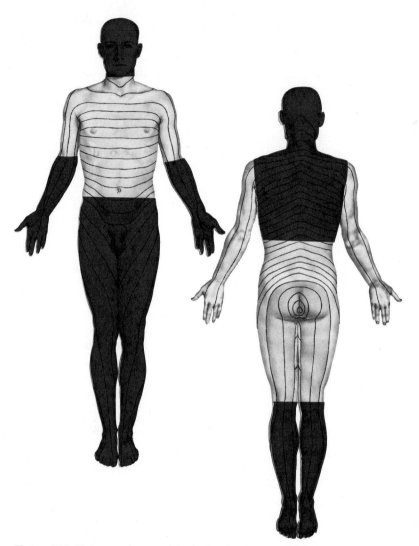

Figure 15-2 The unusual areas of the body affected by functional hysterical anesthesias (in color) can be distinguished from the areas that would be affected by organic neurological disorders (along the lines) because of the arrangement of the nerves. (© Copyright 1953, 1972 CIBA Pharmaceutical Company, Division of CIBA-GEIGY Corporation. Reproduced with permission from the *CIBA Collection of medical illustrations* by Frank H. Netter, M.D. All rights reserved)

oped a neurotic fear of horses. Often the objects of phobias represent the parents of the neurotic. Neither reassurance nor logical reasoning alone is usually sufficient to overcome a phobia. Phobias are thus often assumed to help neurotics conceal unconscious conflicts and emotions from themselves. This Freudian interpretation is not as widely accepted as it used to be.

How do phobias get started? Most learning theorists have concluded that the simpler phobias result from classical conditioning in which the (future) phobic stimulus, like the sight of an angry dog (CS), is paired with a painful experience (US), like being bitten. Some phobias even may be based upon second-order conditioning. This is a form of classical conditioning in which a neutral stimulus comes to elicit a CR as a result of being paired not with a US, but with an already established CS. For example, a child who has already been conditioned to fear dogs may also come to fear places and objects associated with dogs, like kennels, dog leashes and collars, canine excrement, and even dog stories and movies.

An experiment by Ross Rizley and Robert Rescorla (1972) may help explain why phobias based on second-order conditioning are so persistent. Rats were conditioned to fear (CR) a tone (CS) because it always preceded shock (US). Then, with the shock turned off, a flashing light was paired many times with the tone, making the light an effective second-order conditioned stimulus now also capable of producing fear. In the next phase, fear of the tone was extinguished by repeatedly presenting it without shock. In the last phase, both tone and light were tested for their fear-eliciting effect. The tests showed that the second-order CS, the flashing light, had retained its fear-eliciting power. This experiment suggests that in human phobias, while the original CS may have long ago lost its frightening power, secondary stimuli may have escaped the effects of extinction and persist in producing apparently irrational fear.

A **hypochondriacal neurosis** consists of preoccupations with the body and intense and growing fears of diseases in various organs. Although there are no actual diseases or organic losses in function, hypochondriacs may firmly insist that they are ill despite reassurances to the contrary. Bodily complaints are more general in neurasthenia or **neurasthenic neurosis,** in which people become weak, easily and constantly fatigued, and sometimes completely exhausted. Neurasthenic neurotics are usually distressed by their condition, as are hypochondriacs, but they do not make any particular gains from their condition except so far as it gives rise to momentary attention and sympathy from others. Both of these neuroses differ from **hysterical neurosis,** in which the neurotic seems to lose the function of an organ, such as vision or hearing, or arms or legs become paralyzed in what is called a **conversion reaction** (see Figure 15-2). The loss of function is psychogenic having no physical basis. Hysterics are said to discharge unbearable anxieties or tensions through these conversions, which may relieve them of unpleasant responsibilities. In **dissociation reactions,** on the other hand, the state of consciousness or identity is altered, and neurotics may walk in their sleep **(somnambulism),** fail to remember who they are **(amnesia),** or exhibit a number of different personalities in **multiple personality neurosis.** All of these kinds of neurosis manifest various ways of dealing with extreme anxiety or intolerable conflicts when the ordinary ego defenses have failed to protect a person. They are clearly distinguishable from **psychosomatic disorders,** disorders in which psychological conditions lead to malfunctioning of the autonomic nervous system, and from **malingering,** or consciously pretending illness in one form or another in order to gain attention or avoid responsibilities.

A WAY OUT BY CONVERSION

Lester F., a middle-aged businessman with a family, suddenly found himself open to prosecution for fraud as a member of the board of directors of his firm (Cameron, 1963). His associates in the company had made illegal deals that brought financial ruin to many in his small-town community. Although innocent of the fraud, Lester was technically guilty as a director and was offered immunity from prosecution if he would testify against his associates. This placed Lester in a severe conflict, torn between loyalty to himself and his family and loyalty to his associates. After he agreed to testify for the prosecution, his associates tried to beat him up in the street, shouting that he had thrown them to the wolves.

Passers-by rescued Lester, but he had suddenly become completely mute.

Referred to a psychiatric hospital, Lester was thoroughly examined and his speech apparatus was found to be completely sound. His mutism, undoubtedly a hysterical conversion reaction beyond his control, continued in the hospital until the trial was over, although otherwise Lester seemed to be in good spirits. Then speech gradually returned. The mutism had saved him from testifying against his associates, and his acceptance of immunity prevented his prosecution. Since he could not resolve his conflict consciously, he had done it unconsciously. The conversion prevented him from accusing the associates publicly and also punished Lester himself for his proposed treachery to his friends, since he could not openly clear his own reputation. But the trial did that, and after the mutism served all of its several purposes, it disappeared.

ADDICTIVE DISORDERS

Throughout history and undoubtedly even in prehistoric times, human beings have used fermented drinks containing ethyl alcohol, as well as many other drugs, for a vast variety of purposes, including altered states of consciousness, euphoria, and a sense of increased power, and as a part of religious rituals. The effects of these drugs on consciousness have been discussed in Chapter 6; here we shall consider the disorders to which addiction leads. **Drug addiction** is the chronic or continuous use of drugs to the extent of physical and/or psychological dependence on them.

Alcoholism

The American Psychiatric Association (1968) recognizes the following types of alcoholism: episodic excessive drinking, in which enough alcohol is consumed to impair coordination, speech, or other behavior at least 4 times a year; habitual excessive drinking, in which a person becomes intoxicated more than 12 times a year or recognizably under the influ-

ence of alcohol more than once a week; and **alcohol addiction,** with such dependence on alcohol that the person is unable to go one day without drinking or has been drinking heavily for three months or more. Recently it has been estimated that 9 million or more Americans are addicted to alcohol and that addiction has been growing much faster among women than among men (but in overall numbers there are still more male than female alcoholics). Statistics on alcoholism for a number of countries are given in Table 15-5.

Alcoholics usually show personality disturbances before addiction, with unsatisfactory or inadequate relations with other people. Often their adjustments within their families, at school, or at work have been poor, and they rarely reach their goals. Their marriages disintegrate more frequently than those of nonalcoholics. Investigators have been impressed with the self-destructive character of alcoholics. Although they are as likely as nonalcoholics to marry, their ties with other people both in and out of marriage tend to be insubstantial, and they tend to be rigid and aloof in these relationships. Often they are hostile, depressed, and unable to achieve adequate sexual relationships.

Psychological and perceptual tests and clinical evidence in one study of 46 male alcoholics (Zwerling & Rosenbaum, 1959) indicated that most of them exhibited a basic character disorder combining dependence, depression, passivity, aloofness, hostility, and sexual immaturity. Such a combination of traits constitutes a heavy burden. The alcoholics manifested their passive dependence in demanding care and security from others. Their locus of control was external; they tended to await passively the fates that external events dealt out to them. Although many put on jolly and humorous masks, they were depressed and sad, sometimes to the extent of attempting suicide. They held themselves aloof from others, and at the same time felt superior to them. Extreme hostility often was expressed, particularly during

Table 15-5 Annual Per Drinker Consumption in Liters of Absolute Alcohol, Estimated Rates of Alcoholism, and Rates of Death from Cirrhosis of the Liver

Country	Per Drinker Consumption (1966 or 1967)*	Estimated Rates of Alcoholism per 100,000 Population Aged 15 and Older†	Rate of Death from Liver Cirrhosis per 100,000 Population Aged 15 and Older (1963, 1964, or 1965)
France	25.9	9405	45.3
Italy	20.0	5877	27.3
Portugal	19.5	5652	42.7
Spain	17.1	4635	24.3
Austria	16.0	4212	35.0
West Germany and West Berlin	16.0	3978	26.7
Switzerland	15.8	3901	19.7
Luxembourg	12.5	2988	34.2
Hungary	12.4	2952	12.9
United States	12.0	2198	18.4
Czechoslovakia	11.4	2655	13.1
Canada	11.1	2272	10.0
England and Wales	10.9	1946	3.7
Republic of Ireland	10.9	1946	4.5
Denmark	9.4	1848	10.2
Belgium	9.3	2052	12.9
Poland	9.0	1752	8.6
Sweden	8.4	1515	7.9
Netherlands	7.7	1456	4.9
Finland	5.9	945	4.6
Norway	5.9	945	4.7

Adapted from de Lint & Schmidt, 1971.

* In liters of absolute alcohol.

† Alcoholics are defined here as drinkers of daily averages in excess of 150 milliliters of absolute alcohol.

intoxication. Their sexual immaturity was manifested especially in failure in masculine identification, with inadequate sexual behavior or homosexual relationships, though none of the alcoholics was completely homosexual. Although this combination of characteristics and the maladaptive behavior expressing them appear to combine neatly in a type of personality, as you have seen in Chapter 14, personality types tend to be oversimplified. This sort of categorization does nothing to explain how this combination of traits happens to be associated dynamically with each other in many alcoholics.

A great variety of theories have been proposed to explain the dynamics leading to and maintaining alcoholism, but none of these theories has proven satisfactory enough for general acceptance and fruitful use in treating alcoholics. Freud believed that alcoholism was caused by strong oral influences in infancy and childhood, providing a change in mood and relaxation of inhibitions that permitted regression to irrational, infantile levels with an escape from the stresses of reality. Karl Menninger emphasized self-destructive drives as the main cause of alcoholism, and believed such drives derive from children's feeling of betrayal or rejection by their parents, arousing strong fears as well as extreme rage. Physiological theories of susceptibility to alcoholism have attributed it to genetically transmitted metabolic defects of the adrenal glands, to vitamin or hormonal deficiencies, and to a masked allergy to alcohol, which acts as an unrecognized poison and supports self-destruction. Sociological theories have emphasized the stresses and tensions produced by cultures on their members, cultural attitudes toward drinking, and the acceptance of drinking as a way of overcoming tensions or of substituting satisfactions. Learning theories have suggested that the use of alcohol yields a temporary reinforcing reduction in anxiety, fear, and conflicts. However, the use of alcohol is followed by a miserable "hung-over" state at its withdrawal, and alcoholics are driven to more drinking to avoid withdrawal symptoms. Alcoholism, like depression, probably develops through the interaction of many factors, psychological, cultural, and physiological, which will have to be brought together before an adequate explanation will be found.

Narcotics Addiction

The illegal narcotic drugs include opium and its derivatives, primarily heroin, morphine, and codeine. These drugs quickly produce **tolerance,** requiring larger and larger doses for the same effects, and leading to physical and psychological dependence. Withdrawal effects can become extreme unless withdrawal of the drugs proceeds gradually, with substitution of a less addictive drug. Usually the effects of the drugs are euphoric, although they may be accompanied by vomiting and pallor. Sexual desire is decreased, although some addicts report sensations within the abdomen like orgasm after intravenous injection of the drug. Some investigators believe that an opiate may become attractive to people principally because it reduces such basic drives as relief from pain and other physical discomfort, sexual urges,

and hunger. On the other hand, alcohol and some other drugs do not reduce such drives, but release the inhibitions on that behavior that is directed toward directly satisfying these and other needs. However, others add that opiates create a new organic drive, the reduction of which is pleasurable and thereby reinforcing. This new drive, for more opiate itself, forces addicts into activities directed toward obtaining more of the drug, and thus induces a vicious and compulsive cycle in their behavior from which they find it very difficult to escape.

Not too much is known about the personality and other factors that may lead to narcotics addiction. Freudian theorists describe the behavior of addicts in terms of regressions to pregenital or oral levels of psychosexual development and fixation at these infantile levels. Profiles of addicts based on the Minnesota Multiphasic Personality Inventory (MMPI) show significantly high levels of hypomania (Ma), schizophrenia (Sc), psychopathic deviate (Pd), and depression (D) scales, but these profiles do not differentiate addicts from juvenile delinquents and alcoholics (Farina, 1972). (See Chapter 14.) Other investigators have emphasized the passive dependence of narcotics addicts, who tend to deal with anxiety and stress by indifference and withdrawal; but as we have seen, passive dependence also characterizes the alcoholic. Although the majority of narcotics addicts is found in metropolitan slum areas, with very disturbed relations between the parents and between parents and children, still the majority of ghetto inhabitants do not become addicts and social environment cannot be the whole explanation. Probably the major factors leading to opiate addiction will eventually be found in the effects of the drugs and the personalities of the addicts, interacting within a framework of disturbed and depressed social conditions. Investigators are still far from such an adequate explanation, however, and no altogether successful method of treatment has been developed, though limited success has been claimed for several methods.

PSYCHOTIC DISORDERS

People with **psychotic disorders** are less able than neurotics to distinguish reality from unreality. Their disorder so impairs their functioning that they often cannot meet the ordinary demands of life. Their perceptions may be distorted with delusions and hallucinations. **Delusions** are fixed beliefs held strongly by a person even though they do not correspond with physical or social realities, such as the belief that "I am the President." Speech and memory may be severely affected and shifts in mood and feeling may be extreme, so that psychotics lose their grasp on situations. Although some psychotic disorders have been found to be associated with organic conditions, it is difficult to say whether these biochemical factors are the cause or the result of the disorder.

Schizophrenia

Up to 50 per cent of the patients in public mental hospitals have been diagnosed as schizophrenic (Farina, 1972). **Schizophrenia** includes a group of disorders that have common characteristics of disturbances in thinking, mood, and behavior. The reactions of schizophrenics are often bizarre and incomprehensible, including hallucinations, delusions, and a private system of speech incomprehensible to others, known as a "word salad." They display flat or weak emotions or emotions inappropriate to the situation, such as laughing on learning that someone has died. Often their reactions are ritualistic and repetitive, and they are extremely withdrawn from other people.

Many subtypes of schizophrenia are distinguished on the basis of variations in these basic symptoms. **Hebephrenic schizophrenia** is marked by regressive behavior and shallow and inappropriate emotions, with unpredictable giggling and hypochondriacal complaints. **Simple schizophrenia** reveals increasing loss of interests and attachments to other people, withdrawal and apathy, mental deterioration, and a childish level of functioning. The victim of **catatonic schizophrenia** is either excited, showing violent behavior and frenzy, or withdrawn, characterized by stupor, negativism, or a kind of "waxy flexibility," in which limbs remain in the same position for long periods of time or body position remains unchanged. **Paranoid schizophrenia** involves delusions of persecution or of grandeur, often accompanied by hallucinations, and by aggressive behavior in accordance with the delusions, projecting to other people the personal difficulties the paranoid cannot accept. Patients can shift from one of these types of schizophrenia to another, and the types are not mutually exclusive. Probably they do not represent separate conditions. More research has been done on the causation, condition, and treatment of schizophrenia than on any other behavior disorder, for it is one of the most serious and disabling of the disordered conditions.

SCHIZOPHRENIC EYE TRACKING

Progress has been reported in an eye-tracking test that may help to distinguish people with schizophrenic disorders from other psychotics and from normal people (Holzman, Proctor, & Hughes, 1973). This test consists of the tracking of a pendulum swinging back and forth about a yard in front of the subject, whose eye movements are recorded on a tracing. Normal subjects show smooth pursuit patterns with only occasional brief interruptions by small movements of the eyes known as **saccades.** Abnormal subjects show jagged curves with many interruptions caused by **eye arrest,** or momentary complete cessation of eye movement.

Twenty-one schizophrenic patients were given tracking tests, as well as 4 manic-depressives, 8 with personality disorders, and 33 normal controls. Sixteen of the 21 schizophrenic patients displayed significantly more eye arrests than any of the other groups of patients and nonpatients.

The eye-pattern differences were not caused by differences in attention or motivation, the researchers found, but were involuntary, reflecting some kind of malfunctioning of the fine regulation of neuromuscular activity required for eye tracking. They concluded that the impairment of visual perception in schizophrenic patients "may be associated with the impaired and idiosyncratic reality appraisal typical of these patients, inasmuch as visual perception is a central factor in reality contact, involves the organization of the entire perceptual system and requires effective motor response and feedback for its adaptive tasks." In a follow-up study, similar eye-tracking impairment was found in parents and siblings of the schizophrenic patients, but not in these close relatives of those in the other group. The eye-tracking impairment may then be indicative of a genetic difference between schizophrenics and others.

What can cause such a varied group of disturbances in behavior as those exhibited in schizophrenia? Many investigations have pointed to a genetic origin of schizophrenia (Kallman, 1959). The genes inherited by a schizophrenic, according to this theory, cause abnormal biochemical processes that lead, for example, to improper metabolic activities in such organs as the brain and liver, which then bring on the disordered behavior of schizophrenia. Some studies of the high incidence of the disorder in children whose parents have it, as well as in twins, have pointed to such a genetic component of the disorder, although much lower incidences have been found in other studies (see Chapter 2). The finding of a higher incidence of schizophrenia in identical twins that were brought up together than in separated identical twins indicates that environmental factors must play some part in the development of schizophrenia. It seems likely that a genetic factor establishes a susceptibility to schizophrenia, which then usually requires adverse environmental factors for its development.

Many investigators have looked for a specific biochemical cause of schizophrenia, genetic or otherwise. Great claims have been made of the discovery of abnormal chemicals like a protein substance, taraxein, in the blood of schizophrenics but not in that of normal persons. Taraxein is assumed to interfere with physiological activities in specific parts of the brain. When these claims were tested by others, however, they have not been found to hold (Snyder, Banerjee, Yamamura, & Greenberg, 1974). Such biochemical differences may be the effects of schizophrenia rather than its cause, or they may be products of the diets, the drugs given, the lack of exercise, or other conditions in the mental hospitals that house the schizophrenics. Although it would be most convenient if a biochemical source of schizophrenia could be isolated, this has not yet been accomplished. On the other hand, certain drugs, like the amphetamines (see Chapter 6), have been found to produce schizophrenia-like symptoms in those who take them in quantity, often bringing on a psychosis that looks like acute paranoid schizophrenia. Other drugs, like phenothiazines, have been found to be more effective than sedatives in alleviating the basic symptoms of schizophrenia, a great boon to those who have the disorder. The biochemical effects on the brain of both pro- and antischizophrenic drugs are being investigated intensively to find out how they produce these effects and thus to learn more about the biochemical causes or concomitants of schizophrenia (Snyder et al., 1974).

Learning theories of the causation of schizophrenia select a variety of conditions in the experiential history of schizophrenics as fundamental to the development of their disorder. Many investigations have claimed to identify conditions always present in the families of schizophrenics. Some point to a domineering and unperceptive mother coupled with a submissive and detached father as the combination that produces schizophrenia. Yet it would seem that neurotics and normal people often have parents like these also.

Others point to the **double bind** as a condition productive of schizophrenia (Bateson, Jackson, Haley, & Weakland, 1956). If a mother wishes to appear loving and accepting of her son, for example, but basically rejects him, she can "prove" that he is "impossible" by engineering situations in which it is literally impossible for him to do anything right. "Come sit on my lap," she may say, but her tone of voice makes it clear that she does not want him there at all. She is conveying two messages to the boy, one verbal and one indirect, and since they are contradictory, no appropriate response is possible to him; no matter what he does, he's wrong. For a true double bind to exist, there must be a third message, usually unexpressed but nevertheless clearly communicated, forbidding the victim to leave the field: He is required to choose between two possible responses, both wrong. Prolonged exposure during the formative years to this confusing pattern of contradictory messages is thought to play a large part in the development of the irrational and disorganized behavior of schizophrenia. Although the double bind has been shown to have been operative in the childhoods of many schizophrenics, studies of letters written by mothers to their schizophrenic children have not consistently revealed an identifiable double-bind characteristic (Ringuette & Kennedy, 1966), nor have studies of the verbal behavior of mothers of schizophrenics (Mishler & Waxler, 1968). The double bind may also be found in the backgrounds of people who do not become schizophrenic. It thus may be a contributing factor but not a necessary factor in the development of schizophrenia.

Another family condition that has been related to schizophrenia is that in which one or both parents are disturbed or potentially psychotic and make a scapegoat of a child by unconsciously encouraging that child to be psychotic. Such families may seem to be quite normal superficially, but when studied in depth reveal repressed and unduly intense emotional conflicts that may be focused on one particular child, placing the victim under stress and susceptible to the development of schizophrenia. This **scapegoat theory** would tend to explain why only one child in a family may become schizophrenic while siblings raised in the same home do not. It would seem, however, that this family condition might lead to many neurotic and other psychotic conditions, not just to schizophrenia alone.

Psychodynamic theories consider schizophrenia to be an extreme defense reaction that has disintegrated into deep regression and fixation at an early infantile stage. Schizophrenics, according to this view, almost completely lose contact with reality through their egos, are unable to distinguish fantasy from fact, and fall prey to delusions and hallucinations that seem just as real to them as do events in the outer environment. With no longer any clear separation between the conscious mind and the unconscious, they give way to primitive processes of feeling and thinking that dominate their conscious experiences (see Figure 15-3). Such extreme regression may be caused by the loss of their principal sources of security or satisfaction, by a sudden extreme release of previously repressed erotic or hostile impulses, or by situations greatly increasing their guilt. Normal mechanisms of defense crumble under such conditions, according to psychodynamic views, and the schizophrenic picture of a completely withdrawn, infantile, and deluded person is the result.

The intensive investigations to which schizophrenia has been subjected have not yielded an adequate explanation of its causation but have resulted in many improvements in dealing with it. The use of electroshock therapy and of drugs, such as the phenothiazines, has enabled many more schizophrenics than in the past to leave mental hospitals and return to living in the community, and to prevent the conditions of others from

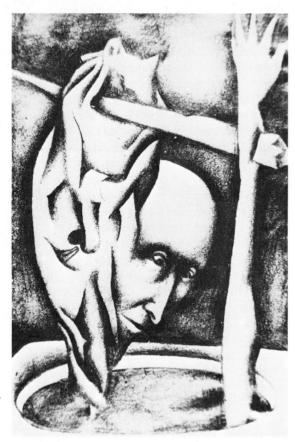

Figure 15-3 This painting and the one that opened this chapter were made by a young patient with temporal-lobe epilepsy, and they manifest anxiety in relation to aggressive and sadistic reactions. (Roubíček, 1969)

deteriorating. If schizophrenia is treated early enough, psychotherapy in various forms has proved fruitful, and it can often be cured, if "cured" is defined as ability to live outside an institutional setting (Cameron, 1963). Such effective treatments counter the widespread belief that schizophrenia is hopeless and almost always leads to complete deterioration and helplessness.

Other Functional Psychoses

Several kinds of disorders are known as **affective psychoses,** for they involve extreme moods or emotions that dominate a person and result in loss of contact with reality. Also known as **manic-depressive psychoses,** these may be marked by severe shifts in moods that have a tendency to disappear for a time and then reappear. Manic reactions consist of extremely elated moods; the person is very active and talkative, with flight of ideas, shifting quickly from one subject to another. Depressive reactions include severe despondency, with great anxiety, fear, and fatigue, and such mental and motor retardation that these patients may approach total stupor. Illusions and delusions may occur with manic reactions; delusions are common in psychotic depression. Manics may have delusions of grandeur, with great self-assertion and self-aggrandizement, making impossible claims. In the rare bipolar type of manic depression, at least one episode of mania and one of depression occur, swinging from one to the other, sometimes in a regular cycle.

Usually psychotics of either manic or depressive type have met with profound losses of love, personal security, or self-esteem. They find it impossible to cope with such losses by means of their customary defenses. After periods of deepening worry, anger, and depression, they then become typically manic or depressed. In mania, they make a sweeping denial of their losses and reconstruct their world in terms of grandiose delusions. They become so hyperactive and changeable that they lose all contact with other people and can accomplish nothing, often going without eating, sleeping, or taking any other care of themselves. Their actions are typically childish in denying themselves and their losses. In their extreme regression and denial, they become as helpless as babies. In their delusions, they often identify with the people who they believed have caused their difficulties, acting out all kinds of aggressive and outrageous impulses, which may be harmful to those around them.

Paranoid reactions are psychotic disorders in which persistent delusions are built up, usually involving persecution, but sometimes jealousy or grandiose or erotic ideas. For example, a man with paranoid reactions may develop a whole system of logically related beliefs, and "evidence" for them, about how he is being persecuted by the police, how his wife is being unfaithful to him, how he has been ordained the savior of mankind, and how a famous woman he has never met is in love with him. Those with paranoid reactions are filled with extreme anxiety, are very sensitive to the hostility or simply the criticisms of others, and construct their delusions from the slightest cues that tend to support their suspicions. **Paranoia** is an extreme form of paranoid reaction in which people base very elaborate delusional systems on the misinterpretation or exaggeration of actual events. They frequently believe that they have unique, superior abilities, although often these delusions do not interfere with the rest of their thinking and social activities. Persons with paranoid psychosis lack the extreme mood changes of psychotic manics and depressives and do not become as withdrawn and disorganized as schizophrenics. Paranoid reactions are sometimes thought of as ways in which neurotic behavior disorders pass over into psychotic disorders.

Paranoid reactions tend to be concentrated among people from forty to sixty, the period when youth, attractiveness, vigor, and flexibility are inevitably diminishing. But the origins of paranoid delusions go back to infancy or early childhood, it is believed. As children, paranoids never learned to develop normal trust in others, never mastered their earliest fears, and could not achieve normal ego-superego maturation. In fact, they may often have been mistreated by their parents. Consequently they have anxious, fearful, suspicious, and solitary personalities in later life, tending to overreact to any perceived threats or mistreatment. Paranoids deny that any of their anxieties and fears come from within themselves. They become very angry at perceived mistreatment by others, deny their own anger and project it to those others, become frightened at apparent threats in the behavior

of the same or other persons, and soon see a whole conspiracy arrayed against them.

Psychotic depressive reactions are disorders of mood in which self-depreciation, guilt, and dejection are so extreme and persistent that they become delusional. Psychotically depressed people become detached from others and from their environment. They become so absorbed in their own guilt and self-hatred that they often have thoughts of suicide and sometimes attempt it. Unlike neurotic depressives, psychotic depressives do not seek reassurance and support from others; they are totally convinced of their complete hopelessness, worthlessness, failure, and guilt. Typically they can give no particular reason for their despair, or attribute it to an event that is fairly common in life situations. At one time or another we all fail to make the team or the club, lose a job, or have to deal with a serious illness, and every one of us must experience the death of someone we love. We mourn, which is a natural and necessary thing to do, but our unhappiness does not prevent us from carrying on our daily lives, and in time we cease to mourn. The depressed psychotic is disabled by a wide variety of stressful events (see Figure 15-4).

Psychotic depressives slump in hopelessness, staring, limp, motionless. They cannot sleep, their appetites wane, and they become sexually unresponsive. They find it difficult to initiate anything and impossible to accomplish anything. They cannot carry on a normal conversation, they talk slowly and repetitiously and answer questions briefly or incompletely. They may eventually become stuporous, helpless, unable to carry out any of their functions. They would starve if no one fed them. Their depressions are marked by the prevalence of self-castigation. The most trivial mistakes of the past are elaborated in their delusions into terrible sins or colossal failures. Their self-hatred becomes masochistic cruelty, and they appear to gloat over their own doom.

Interestingly, psychotic depression has been found to be associated with depletion of the biogenic amines required for the proper func-

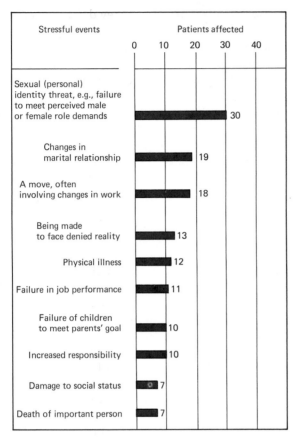

Stressful events	Patients affected

Figure 15-4 Stress factors associated with severe depression. (Leff, Roatch, & Bunney, 1970)

tioning of the central nervous system, referred to earlier as accompaniments of neurotic depressions. Fortunately, psychotic depressions can be ameliorated to some extent by the electroshock and drug treatments that have done so much for neurotic depression (see Chapter 16).

PERSONALITY OR CHARACTER DISORDERS

Over and beyond the neurotic and psychotic disorders are a group of behavior disorders that are referred to as character or personality disorders. As you saw in Chapter 14, personality is comprised of consistent and permanent traits, or those kinds of behavior that are essentially characteristic of an individual, as opposed to temporary or incidental behavior. The American Psychiatric Association's *Manual of Mental Disorders* (1968) defines **personality disorders** as "characterized by deeply ingrained maladaptive patterns of behavior that are perceptibly different in quality from psychotic and neurotic symptoms. Generally, these are life-long patterns, often recognizable by the time of adolescence or earlier." These personality disorders are distortions or warpings in people's basic patterns or styles of living that are maladaptive in that they tend to be injurious to them, particularly in their interactions with other people.

Aggressive Disorders

The **explosive personality** is prone to outbursts of excessive rage or verbal or physical aggressiveness. When not under stress or in conflict, these people may seem quite well adjusted. But with minor stresses they are likely to explode into temper tantrums or physical assaults in which their perception, judgment, and thought processes become disorganized and overwhelmed, reminiscent of the rage of little children. Explosive personalities may easily become overly critical and argumentative, trying to intimidate others in order to bolster their own self-esteem. When such approaches do not work, they may lose control, make violent "scenes," and provoke a great deal of anxiety and hostility in others. Afterward they may regret their behavior and express repentance, but guilt, if any, is short-lived, and aggressiveness continues to be their final solution to frustration or stress. Some of the sudden violent deaths that are so prevalent may be attributed to such explosive personalities.

The **passive-aggressive personality** sounds like a living contradiction. It is manifested by people who express their constant underlying hostility in passive or covert ways, as opposed to the overt attacks of the explosive personality. Passive-aggressive people are usually overly dependent, almost childishly so, on others in the family, their friends, or those in authority. But when this dependence is threatened in any way, they may become stubborn and sullen, like disobedient children, failing to cooperate, procrastinating, complaining, and acting in inefficient, obstructive ways. These covert expressions of aggression may be very disruptive of the activities and the morale of others associating with them.

The **passive-dependent personality** is a closely related type. These people depend on others to the point of childishness, although they may be hostile underneath. But they cannot express this anger, and appear to be overly anxious and fearful in any situation making the slightest demands on them.

Disorders Resembling Psychoses

Several other types of personality disorder resemble psychotic reactions but do not result in the delusions or loss of contact with reality that accompany the psychoses. For example, the **schizoid personality** is typified by shy, oversensitive, withdrawn, and often eccentric behavior patterns. Such people may be prone to daydreaming, to avoiding any intimate or competitive interactions with others, and to suppressing any direct hostility.

The **paranoid personality,** on the other hand, is characterized by predominant behavior patterns of suspicion, envy, extreme sensitivity to criticism, and a tendency to feel superior to others and blame them for purposefully creating any difficulties that the person experiences. Consequently, it is difficult for these people to make or maintain any very close relationships with others, and they may devote most of their energies to nonhuman or solitary pursuits.

The **obsessive-compulsive personality** tends to be rigid, inhibited, overly conscientious, and conforming in behavior patterns. People of this type may demand excessive order and

organization in everything they do and display an overburdening need to do their duty, whatever they conceive it to be.

The **cyclothymic** or **affective personality,** on the other hand, may frequently shift in mood from intense elation to sadness and depression, and consequently present an unpredictable personality to others. Sometimes gay and enthusiastic, at other times worried and pessimistic, these people give a basic impression of instability, with variations in mood not caused by their circumstances, or triggered by only minor happenings.

The **hysterical personality** is even more extreme in excitability and emotional instability, given to overdramatization, so this is also called the **histrionic personality.** Although people of this type do not develop conversion reactions, as do hysterical neurotics, they are usually immature and overly dependent on others, as well as self-centered, trying to attract attention with their extreme antics. They seem to want to live in the midst of earth-shaking emergencies. They cannot express their feelings freely, and often turn to physical actions in order to communicate. The relations of these individuals with others, on whom they seem childishly dependent, are often seriously impaired by their overreactions—they "cry wolf" too often.

Antisocial Personalities

One of the most serious, and perhaps widespread, of the personality disorders is manifested in those who are basically unsocialized, so it is called **antisocial** or **sociopathic personality disorder.** An obsolete name for this disorder is "psychopathic personality." The childishness and dependence observed in other personality disorders make them border on the antisocial disorder, except that sociopaths make fewer or no social demands. On the contrary, they are chronically in conflict with society, and are apparently incapable of loyalty to other individuals or groups, or to values held by others. In this they differ from **dyssocial personalities,** such as most delinquents and criminals, who do maintain loyalties to their own groups or subcultures. Antisocial personalities are extremely self-centered, impulsive, and irresponsible by any social norms. Characteristically they are callous and do not feel guilt for their antisocial behavior, nor is this behavior correctable by punishment. They lay the blame for their actions on others and can create very plausible rationalizations for their unacceptable behavior in this way. In childhood they may play truant from school, steal, run away from home, and mingle with other people who share their scorn for society. As adults they may be vagrants, criminals, confidence operators. They have poor military, marital, and job histories, and frequently turn to drugs. A large part of their behavior is aimed at deceiving others, and consequently they are frequently involved in quarrels.

Somehow those with antisocial personalities have never grown up to the point of accepting the social norms and controls, whether external or internalized, that most people follow in the main. They do not manifest any remorse for anything they do. Studies have shown that antisocial personalities often derive from broken homes or have parents who provide no consistent discipline, but these observations do not explain why some children become antisocial under these conditions and others do not. Somehow, some develop a profound reaction against authority of any kind.

ORGANIC BEHAVIOR DISORDERS

Biochemical and genetic components have been mentioned in connection with neurotic and psychotic depressions and with schizophrenia. Although these disorders have been thought to be basically functional, it appears likely that a part, if not the whole, of the conditions causing them will be discovered to be physical. Whatever the case with these disorders, there is an unfortunately large number of other behavior disorders that are known to be principally organic. **Mental retardation,** for example, a disorder of subnormal intellectual functioning that originates before birth or early in development, is known to be caused by a great variety of physical conditions: infectious conditions within the mother, like rubella (German measles) and syphilis, or other drug or toxic agents that affect the fetus; traumas that mechanically damage the central nervous system of the fetus during birth; and disorders of metabolism, nutrition, or growth after birth, some genetic and some environmental. Although great progress has been made in identifying the agents that can cause mental retardation, in preventing its occurrence, and in rehabilitating the mentally retarded, much more remains to be accomplished. Other **organic brain disorders** are caused by concussions, by brain tumors, by diseases like encephalitis, and by convulsive disorders like epilepsy, in which the rhythms of brain waves (EEG) are disturbed.

Many organic brain disorders are associated with psychotic states, in which those afflicted lose contact with reality and develop delusions and hallucinations. Among these are the alcoholic psychoses: **delirium tremens,** with frightening hallucinations, and the **Wernicke-Korsakoff syndrome,** a condition induced by the nutritional deficiency that often accompanies prolonged alcoholism, in which memory is impaired.

About a quarter of new admissions to mental hospitals are over 65 years of age and three-fourths of these have **senile dementia,** a disorder marked by childish emotions and self-centeredness. The exact cause of senile dementia is unknown but is related to aging of brain tissue.

Psychoses may also result from many other organic conditions, like cerebral arteriosclerosis and endocrine, metabolic, and nutritional disorders, and may follow intoxication from drugs or poisons of many kinds.

ADVANCES IN TREATMENT

Despite the prevalence of functional and organic behavior disorders, more progress has been made in their identification, knowledge of their causes, and methods for their treatment in recent decades than ever before. In part these advances are due to the proliferation of research in the last decade or two, and in part to the interdisciplinary nature of the attacks that have been mounted against these disorders. Professionals in mental hospitals now include medical doctors, clinical psychologists, psychiatrists, and social workers, lending their talents to individual cases as required. Furthermore, behavior disorders are now less likely to be treated with abhorrence and rejection or isolation than previously, both by professionals and by the public at large. Great progress has been made in alleviating behavior disorders by means of drugs and other organic treatments, which permit many patients in mental hospitals to be released to halfway community centers and eventually to return to their normal surroundings, rather than deteriorating in hospital wards. As we shall see in the next chapter, great advances have been made also in recent years in various kinds of individual and group therapy. The most encouraging sign with all of these developments is that behavior disorders are now being treated more directly and more objectively than they used to be, with greater knowledge and, justifiably, with greater optimism.

SUMMARY

Behavior disorders consist of maladaptive behavior that tends to be ineffective in maintaining the well-being and survival of the individual.

Behavior disorders can be organic (due to physiological diseases) or functional (without known physiological causes), or both. Medical models of functional behavior disorders, which treat them as separate diseases, have not been very productive. Interpersonal models assume that behavior disorders are caused by interpersonal conflicts.

Neuroses are functional behavior disorders in which chronic or acute anxieties predominate, sometimes accompanied by depression. Neurotics are aware that their behavior is maladaptive; psychotics are usually unable to distinguish reality from unreality and to meet the demands of everyday life. Obsessive-compulsive neurotics are prey to irrational repeated thoughts or acts. Phobic persons succumb to acute fears or panics. Hypochondriacal neurotics suffer many bodily complaints with no physical cause, while neurasthenics feel weak and exhausted. Hysterical neurotics display physical paralysis, blindness, or deafness arising from conversion reactions. Some neurotics display loss of identity, amnesia, or sleepwalking.

Addictions are behavior disorders due to the chronic or continuous use of drugs to the extent of physiological and/or psychological dependence on them. Increased tolerance of doses is often accompanied by undesirable physiological reactions to withdrawal.

Psychoses are behavior disorders in which people lose contact with reality as a result of distorted perception and cognition, often with hallucinations or delusions, disturbances of speech and memory, and extreme shifts in mood and feelings. Psychotics are usually unaware that their behavior is maladaptive.

One of the principal psychoses, schizophrenia, is characterized by hallucinations and delusions, flat or inappropriate emotions, ritualistic reactions, and withdrawal from others. Manic-depressive psychosis, on the other hand, involves delusions and marked shifts in mood and emotion. The manic type shows extreme elation, the depressed type displays anxiety and depression, and the bipolar type passes through both manic and depressive episodes. Paranoid reactions, of which paranoia is an extreme type, involve persistent delusions, often of persecution or grandeur, but also of jealousy or erotic attachments. Psychotic depressive reactions are stronger than neurotic depressions, are accompanied by extreme withdrawal or stupor, and may involve delusions.

Personality or character disorders reveal maladaptive personality traits, often apparent from childhood onward. The explosive and passive-aggressive personalities are excessively aggressive, the former prone to outbursts of rage while the latter expresses aggression in covert and obstructive ways. Passive-dependent personalities resemble passive-aggressives, but their anger is manifested in anxiety rather than in disruptive interactions with others. The schizoid and paranoid personalities have characteristics resembling those of schizophrenics, but they do not lose touch with reality. The obsessive-compulsive is preoccupied with rigid behavior patterns. The cyclothymic personality has unstable variations in mood. The hysterical personality is extremely excitable and immature. The antisocial or sociopathic personality is in chronic or continuous conflict with others, without loyalties or social values.

The conditions for the initiation and development of functional behavior disorders have been extensively investigated, but the precise genetic or environmental, organic or interpersonal, causal factors have yet to be established. Behavior disorders constitute some of the severest of all human problems. Some progress is being made in their treatment, however, as discussed in the next chapter.

WHAT DO YOU THINK ABOUT IT?

1. Look back at your original list of symptoms or characteristics that identify behavior disorder or mental illness. How would you now change this list with deletions, revisions, or additions?

2. To what extent do you think lack of self-control is represented in each of the neurotic, addictive, psychotic, and personality disorders? To what extent, in addition, should persons with each of these disorders be held morally responsible and legally responsible for their actions? To what extent do you think society ought to be responsible for dealing with and giving treatment to persons with each of these disorders?

3. What major programs would you propose for (1) the prevention and (2) the treatment of neurotic, addictive, psychotic, and personality disorders? Should such programs, if any, be privately or publicly organized, administered, and funded, or initiated and paid for by the individuals concerned? Would such programs be more, equally, or less valuable for our society than the ongoing (1) social security, (2) physical health and safety, (3) national defense, (4) public welfare, and (5) educational programs in our society?

16

Psychotherapy

WHAT IS PSYCHOTHERAPY?

■ It's nearly midnight and the pages in the book you're studying have little meaning. You feel "down," discouraged, vaguely unhappy. Your friend next door is a good listener. An hour and a half and two cups of coffee later, you're all talked out. You feel tired but somehow less troubled, more relaxed. Was that psychotherapy?

A middle-aged woman leaves the confessional in a Catholic church, spends a few minutes kneeling in a pew at the rear of the church, then goes out, feeling cleansed and comforted. Did she just undergo a bit of psychotherapy?

The business executive slams the psychiatrist's door as he leaves the office. He is angry and upset about the way the session went. He wanted some specific advice about controlling recurrent emotional outbursts in the presence of his employees, but the psychiatrist gently but firmly insisted that solutions must come from the patient himself. That sounds like psychotherapy, but what makes it so?

A group of teenagers in a community center, at first tentatively and awkwardly, then with increasing self-confidence, begins to participate in an "expressive movement" class, their bodies gradually acting out feelings of anger or tenderness, optimism or despair. Is this psychotherapy?

A little boy's attempt to join a slightly older group elicits a rude and cruel rebuff. Feeling hurt and unwanted, he runs crying into his mother's arms. She fondles and comforts him, reminding him of his coming birthday party, to which his many friends of his own age will come. His crying ceases and he runs out to play with his dog, a smile on his face. Was that psychotherapy?

A couple in marital counseling is taught how to identify and respond more effectively to each other's needs for affection and security. Is this type of training psychotherapy?

What is psychotherapy? The word itself comes from two Greek words: *psyche*, or mind, and *therapeuein*, the root meaning of which is "to attend to" or "treat." "Treating the mind," however, fails to give us much useful information. Psychotherapists of any persuasion minister to people, not to conceptual abstractions like "mind." And some therapists attempt to alleviate the most severe behavior disorders described in Chapter 15 by directly manipulating *bodily* conditions, with drugs, electroshock treatments, even brain surgery, all of which constitute a separate category of treatments called **somatic therapy. Psychotherapy** can be broadly defined, then, as a way of helping people to deal with and overcome their behavior disorders.

EARLY PSYCHOTHERAPY

Intellectual progress does not follow a straight line. There are stops and starts and even complete regressions. The Greeks and Romans, inspired by remarkable physicians like Hippocrates and Galen, were guided by the view that mental states resulted from bodily illness (see Figure 16-1). While their explanations were often incorrect, they did look for natural rather than supernatural causes of such phenomena as delusions, hallucinations, and depression. With the coming of the Dark Ages and the growth of Christianity, naturalistic interpretations were replaced by **demonological theories** of behavior disorders, views that can still be found today. Thus a person displaying what would normally be called psychotic behavior today was then normally considered to be possessed by agents of Satan. Madness became the sign of possession by demons. The therapy was simple enough: exorcism. For witches, whose possession was the result of deliberate contracts made with the devil, the

therapy prescribed could not fail to purify the individual: It was death (see Figure 16-2).

Not until the seventeenth century was madness once more ascribed, and only by a few, to illness rather than to Satan. Medical treatises, most notably *The Anatomy of Melancholy* (Burton, 1621), led to the establishment of asylums for the confinement of the insane. Confinement, however, was hardly treatment. As shown in Figure 16-3, patients were chained to the walls of their cells by iron collars, they were treated like animals, and tickets of admission were sold to "normal" citizens who came to be amused by the antics of the "lunatics." The uproar and confusion in the asylums were deafening. "Bedlam," in fact, is derived from the local pronunciation of "Bethlehem," the common designation of the Hospital of St. Mary of Bethlehem, a London asylum. Although illness had replaced the devil as the cause of bizarre behavior, little progress in treatment practices occurred until the end of the eighteenth century, when Philippe Pinel, director of an asylum in Paris, freed the patients of their heavy chains and began to treat them with compassion and respect (see Figure 16-4).

Figure 16-1 Medieval woodcut illustrating the four temperaments that Hippocrates assumed resulted from excesses of four bodily "humors." From left to right: a cheerful and hopeful man (too much blood); a melancholic man (too much dark bile); an irascible man (too much yellow bile); and a sluggish man (too much phlegm).

Figure 16-2 Sixteenth-century engraving of a woman thought to be a witch being prepared for burning.

Figure 16-3 William Hogarth's painting of the Hospital of St. Mary of Bethlehem (Bedlam) in London.

Figure 16-4 Philippe Pinel unshackling mental patients at the Salpêtrière in Paris.

The nineteenth century witnessed a growing emphasis on physical factors as the basis for mental illness. Louis Pasteur's germ theory of disease and increasing evidence that the delusions and general mental dysfunction of a disease called **paresis** were linked to syphilis strengthened the organic view. Lesions in the central nervous system were accepted as the primary cause of mental illness through the late nineteenth century, when the French neurologists Jean Martin Charcot and Pierre Janet, through hypnotism, dramatically demonstrated how hysterical symptoms could be induced and removed by suggestion. Freud's own use of hypnotism, and later of free association, left him, if not his medical colleagues, convinced that many symptoms were psychogenic, and were not the result of brain lesions. Problems of a psychological origin and nature required psychological, not somatic, therapy, and Freud's method of psychoanalysis became the earliest and most famous of the psychotherapies.

PSYCHOANALYTIC THEORY

Freud's **psychoanalytic theory,** as you saw in Chapter 14, attempted to explain both normal and abnormal personality development according to the manner in which the individual resolves certain conflicts between basic instinctive drives, on the one hand, and the constraints of reality and the pangs of conscience on the other. One of the most important conflicts concerns the attachment of the male child for his mother, the Oedipus complex, a fixation that Freud considered essentially sexual. The child's sexual impulses give rise to fear that his father may retaliate against his incestuous yearnings by depriving him of his most valued possession, the source of his deepest pleasure, his penis. This fear is traditionally called the **castration complex.** The term is a misnomer, since castration of the male involves the removal of the testes, not the amputation of the penis. In the normal course of development, the mother is abandoned as a love object and the child sublimates his sexual impulses into tender feelings for her. Furthermore, he identifies with his father, sharing his values and adopting many of his traits.

Freudian Therapy

When the child's libido is not successfully redirected away from the forbidden parent, the tabooed impulses must be excluded from consciousness by the process of repression. The mechanism of repression, like any other in the Freudian model, runs on energy. The total amount of energy available is fixed. If too much of this energy is used for the purpose of maintaining the repression of forbidden thoughts, the individual has too little energy left over to power the ego functions involved in coping with reality. These functions include thinking, problem solving, judging, and perceiving.

Psychoanalytic therapy is a method for liberating energy tied up in infantile love objects and energy consumed in keeping unacceptable thoughts repressed. With such therapy, the individual then has more internal energy available for dealing effectively with the problems of everyday life. Freud used the concept of **resistance** to refer to the patient's inability or reluctance to permit repressed impulses from emerging in consciousness. The concept of **transference** refers to the process during psychoanalysis in which the therapist comes to represent a parent substitute, allowing the patient to recapture the emotional attitudes of childhood, redirected now toward the analyst.

By re-creating the dynamics of the patient's childhood relationships with the parents, the early emotional patterns of love and hate, dependence and independence, acceptance and rejection are reawakened. This time, however, the family drama has a better chance of coming out well, with conflicts resolved and misperceptions corrected. It's as if the therapist were saying, "Your emotional relationship with your mother never got straightened out and you're still suffering the effects of it. I will now stand in for your mother while we go back to the emotional crises of childhood, and this time let's work it all out together." The process, however, is far more subtle than this statement suggests. In fact, the transference relationship actually terminates when the analyst finally interprets the patient's emotional attitudes toward him as a reinstatement of his attitudes toward his parents. The goals of psychoanalytic therapy, then, are to help the patient overcome his resistances so that repressed wishes will come to consciousness, and to establish an effective transference relationship within which the unresolved emotional relationships of childhood can be examined and more adult attitudes developed. The overall aim is to help patients to achieve insight into their emotional dynamics, and thereby relieve their symptoms.

To achieve these goals, psychoanalytic therapy employs the techniques of free association and dream analysis. In **free association,** patients are encouraged to relax and verbalize everything going through their minds, no matter how trivial or how embarrassing they may consider it to be. The analyst listens carefully for signs of repressed material appearing in disguised form, or for hesitations, blocks, and expressions of impatience or anger, which may indicate resistance. In **dream analysis,** the patient's dreams are accepted on two levels: (1) the *manifest* content, consisting of the dream material the patient remembers upon awakening, which often serves as an important point of departure for free association; (2) the *latent* content, consisting of the repressed impulses and memories that find expression in disguised form in the manifest content of the dream. Thus the latent content is inferred from the manifest content, as well as from free-association material and other verbalizations of the patient.

Psychoanalysis is a long process, often requiring several sessions a week over a period of years. Psychoanalysts are not in abundant supply. Most **psychoanalysts** have a degree in medicine, followed by a special training program in psychoanalytic therapy that includes their own psychoanalysis. Some, who have no medical degree but who have received formal training in the psychoanalytic method, are called lay analysts. Clinical psychologists and psychiatric social workers may also become psychoanalysts by completing the appropriate period of training.

Some psychoanalysts, like Erik Erikson (1963) and even Anna Freud (1946), the master's own daughter, emphasize the improvement of ego functioning. They depart from Freud's conception of the id as the source of all energy, asserting that the ego can develop into an independent, self-powered set of functions. Their form of therapy places great emphasis on teaching patients how to cope more effectively with their environments, how to plan more judiciously, and how generally to achieve a higher level of competence in dealing with life's problems. Conscious processes receive far more attention from the *ego analysts* than from orthodox Freudian analysts.

Adlerian Therapy

Alfred Adler, you may recall from Chapter 14, broke with Freud over the issue of dominant drives. Freud insisted on the primacy of the sexual drive, and Adler on the primacy of striving to overcome initial and universal *feelings of inferiority*. All people, in the course of trying to reconcile their personal strivings with social reality, develop their own individual life styles. In the neurotic personality, however, the integration of personal needs, compensatory reactions, and social skills is deficient. Neurotics spend too much time and energy preserving their own myths of personal superiority, and not enough in developing satisfactory social relations. Adler's form of psychoanalysis tries to get patients to analyze their characteristic styles in coping with feelings of inadequacy. The aim of therapy is not only to give patients insight into the various stratagems they use in order to achieve power, and

thereby escape their nagging feelings of inferiority, but also to teach them how to find security in cooperative relationships with others. Adler had a remarkable faith in people's potential for growth. By interpreting neurotic behavior as symptomatic of a faulty life style, Adler set the stage for more modern conceptions of therapy as an educative process, rather than as treatment for an illness.

Jungian Therapy

Far more emphasis is placed by **Jungian therapy** on elucidating the influence of unconscious forces than by Alderian therapy, but both approaches differ from Freudian psychoanalysis in their explicit attempt to help patients discover and develop their latent possibilities. *Wholeness* and *self-realization* are two important goals of Jungian therapy. Patients are encouraged to find meaning and dignity in their lives through a variety of means, such as artistic expression, religious experience, and the study of myths. The aim is always growth and development, as opposed to the Freudian stress on impulse and defense.

The drift in the direction of social determinants of neurotic behavior and psychotherapy as a process of education or self-actualization, begun by Adler and Jung, was extended in the United States by the neo-psychoanalytic therapists Karen Horney (1945), Erich Fromm (1941), and Harry Stack Sullivan (1953). While free association and dream analysis may be used by the followers of these analysts, these methods are employed primarily as aids in analyzing the patient's self-concept, current conflicts and anxieties, and interpersonal situations.

CLIENT-CENTERED THERAPY

Unlike psychoanalysis, **client-centered** or **nondirective therapy** begins with the here and now of the person's experience, rather than in a probing for infantile fixations and repressed impulses. Carl Rogers developed nondirective or *Rogerian therapy* on the premise that the potentiality for growth exists in every individual, and that therapists can best assist their clients' self-actualizing tendencies by helping them develop self-insight. First of all, therapists should not regard their clients as sick. Notice that they are called "clients," not "patients." Second, therapists should avoid imposing their own interpretations on what their clients' report and should not influence the direction the conversations take. Therapists may restate or rephrase clients' comments, reflecting back the emotional quality of the things that clients say, but not interpret them. Throughout, therapists strive to maintain and display complete acceptance of their clients, an approach Rogers calls **unconditional positive regard,** neither approving nor disapproving of what they say, but accepting as wholly valid and important the feelings that clients show toward themselves and others. Together, therapist and client explore the latter's idealized self-concept and the degree to which it differs from actual self-concept.

Because client-centered therapy insists upon clients' responsibility for determining their own growth, for arriving at their own insights, and for making their own choices, it has also been classified among the humanistic-existential therapies. The Rogerian approach has had an enormous impact on methods and theory of psychological counseling (Rogers, 1951; Snyder, 1947). Unlike most founders of "schools" of therapy, Rogers has consistently urged that research be conducted to assess changes occurring in the client during the course of therapy. By introducing the use of the tape recorder during therapy sessions, he made it possible to study the therapeutic process objectively and to obtain direct measures of behavior change. Seeman (1949), for example, found in his clients an orderly decrease in the time they devoted to the discussion of problems and an increase in comments denoting insight and self-understanding as therapy progressed. Positive attitudes toward the self systematically increased, while negative attitudes declined.

Since the Rogerian therapist is quite interested in seeing such attitudinal changes develop, some critics have maintained that, by selectively attending to certain statements and not to others, the therapist may be inadvertently "shaping" the client's report. Analysis of transcripts made in one of Rogers' own therapy sessions showed this to be the case (Truax, 1966).

A SAMPLE OF NONDIRECTIVE THERAPY

The following excerpt is taken from a third counseling session (Snyder, 1947). The client, a 20-year-old student, had originally come for counseling because of her feelings of inferiority. A hand deformed from birth had contributed to her negative self-image. In the second interview she had expressed self-consciousness about her hand, and resentment against her parents' attitudes toward her handicap. In this brief segment from the third interview, the significance of both the student's (S) and counselor's (C) comments is indicated in the headings. Note how the counselor tried to let the student know that he understood the content and feeling she was trying to communicate. Also note how he clarified and synthesized the meaning of her statements.

Problem—Negative Attitude Toward Others

Student. After I left here last time—that night during dinner the student dean in our house asked to speak to my roommate. My roommate told me about it afterwards—Miss Hansen asked if I would be embarrassed as hostess at the table. She said she didn't want to hurt me! These darn student deans who think that they must guard us! The other student dean I had before never raised the issue. It makes me so mad!

Clarification of Feeling

Counselor. You feel that this incident helped to accentuate the difficulty.

Problem—Negative Attitude Toward Others

Student. That was the first time with a student dean. Really though, it struck me very funny. She watches us like a hawk. We can't make a move but she knows it.

Clarification of Feeling

Counselor. You resent her activity.

Agreement; Insight

Student. I just don't like it on general principles. Oh, I suppose that she was trying to save me embarrassment.

Restatement of Content

Counselor. You can see why she did that.

Insight

Student. I think that she is really afraid of us—she's queer. I don't know, but as far as I am concerned, I'm pretty indifferent to her.

Restatement of Content

Counselor. You feel that she doesn't affect you one way or the other.

Agreement; Problem

Student. No. A few weeks ago a girl in my house that I talked with about it last year asked me why I hid my hand all the time. I said that I just always have done it and I can't break the habit.

Restatement of Content

Counselor. A habit which you can't overcome.

Problem—Ambivalent Attitude Toward Self

Student. I don't see any reason to—except that maybe it makes it more obvious when I try to hide it. But I really don't know it when I do it. There was a time when I wouldn't even buy any clothes without pockets. They all had to have pockets and I wouldn't have an evening dress because it didn't have any.

Restatement of Content

Counselor. You feel there is no reason why you should not hide your hand.

Problem—Ambivalent Attitude Toward Self; Insight

Student. I really can't decide if I'm right or wrong. If it is wrong, I think I'd try to break it. I do it so completely automatically that I really don't have any time to think about it.

Restatement of Content

Counselor. You can't quite decide which is right, or which is wrong.

Agreement; Problem—Ambivalent Attitude Toward Self

Student. That's it. Yes, it is not at all clear to me. Should I keep it out of sight or keep it out in the open? I still don't know.

Clarification of Feeling

Counselor. There are advantages in either direction.

Problem—Ambivalent Attitude Toward Self

Student. I honestly don't know what to do. I think that if I could use it, if I could bring it out in the open and feel all right about it, I'd be all right.

Clarification of Feeling

Counselor. If you could display your hand and still feel all right about it, you think that would be the thing that you would want to do.

Agreement; Insight

Student. Yes. I will meet this thing my whole lifetime. I need to get over it.

Clarification of Feeling

Counselor. You want to live more comfortably with yourself.

Since changes in the self-concept are considered to be a paramount goal of Rogerian therapy, much research has been directed toward the measurement of the discrepancy between the perceived self and the ideal self. A method frequently employed by Rogers and his colleagues is the **Q-sort technique,** which requires clients to sort cards bearing self-statements, like "I am self-reliant," "I express my emotions freely," and "I often feel guilty," into nine piles, according to the closeness with which they think a given statement applies to themselves. This sorting produces a measure of the way in which clients see themselves—the perceived self. They are then asked

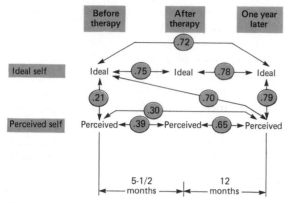

Figure 16-5 The relation between perceived self and ideal self before and after therapy, and one year later, as measured in a 40-year-old neurotic woman by the Q-sort technique. The numbers are correlation coefficients (see Appendix: Statistics). The higher the number, the greater the congruence between self measures. Note that while the biggest discrepancy (.21) between perceived and ideal selves occurred before therapy began, a year after therapy there was considerable similarity (.79) between the way she saw herself and the way she wanted to be. The results also show a high consistency in the ideal self-concept and, of course, considerable change in the perceived self. (Adapted from Rogers, 1961)

to sort the statements again, this time according to the way they would like to be—the ideal self. Q-sorts are obtained at various times, before and during therapy, and after its termination to see how the relation between the perceived and ideal self changes. In a typical study using the Q-sort technique, J. M. Butler and Gerard Haigh (1954) reported that before therapy began, student clients showed a wider discrepancy between perceived self and ideal self than a control group of students who were not going into therapy. As a result of therapy, measures of perceived self and ideal self became much more congruent. Figure 16-5 shows the correlation between ideal-self and perceived-self measures in a female client before and after therapy, and at a final follow-up a year later. A great deal of psychotherapy research of the client-centered approach has been reported by Carl Rogers and Rosalind F. Dymond (1954).

Client-centered therapy continues to be the dominant approach employed in college and university counseling services, and in many child-guidance clinics. As you have probably inferred, this method is used mainly with mildly disturbed people and may be totally inappropriate for the treatment of psychotics.

RATIONAL-EMOTIVE THERAPY (RET)

Many students feel that they would choose Rogers' nondirective counseling if they ever decided to seek professional help. Perhaps the qualities of empathic understanding, warmth, and acceptance characteristic of the Rogerian approach contribute to its popularity. Do you think you'd do well as a client in nondirective counseling? Consider then a diametrically opposed approach, one in which you would be scolded and nagged rather than "understood." Suppose you were given a therapy homework assignment to do before the next session, but for some reason you failed to complete it; how do you think a Rogerian therapist would react? Certainly not like this:

So you didn't feel like doing the assignment. Tough! Well, you darned well better do it if you want to overcome the nonsense you keep telling yourself. And you didn't like me for giving you the assignment. Well, I don't give a shit whether you like me or not. We're here not to have a lovey-dovey relationship . . . but to convince you that unless you get off your ass and do that assignment I gave you . . . you're probably going to keep stewing in your own neurotic juices forever. Now when are you going to cut out the crap and do something to help yourself?

Does this seem rather belligerent and nasty? Albert Ellis (1962), quoted above, believes that patients must usually be badgered into doing the work of psychotherapy and that warmth and tender feelings are no substitute for the hard work of confronting and repudiating the many logical fallacies that determine their self-defeating behavior.

What are some of these fallacies, according to Ellis, and how do they make people miserable?

1. I must be loved or approved by virtually everyone for everything I do. "*Why* must everyone love you?" Ellis asks. And what are the consequences if not everyone does? Is it not irrational to expect everyone to love you? And does it not doom you to feel rejected by at least some people? Ellis teaches his patients that a certain amount of social approval is useful, but that universal approval is neither realistic nor useful.

2. I am worthless unless I am perfect in everything I do. While this sounds like a silly assumption, some people consider every less-than-perfect performance as justifying their conclusion that they are incompetent and inadequate. Ellis tries to show patients that this assumption is irrational and self-defeating. He teaches them to concentrate instead on the things one *can* do in life to produce the greatest enjoyment and rewards.

3. My unhappiness is externally caused; there is nothing I can do to control my sorrow. This is another illogical assumption, since happiness or unhappiness depends on the view you take of events. There is nothing that can *force* you to be unhappy.

4. I should be upset over other people's problems and disturbances. Ellis' view is that other people's problems are not at all alleviated by your feeling upset, and that other people's deficiencies are, after all, their problem, not yours.

These are some of the irrational views Ellis thinks lead to neurotic problems like excessive self-blaming and hypercritical attitudes, overdependence on others, and reluctance to accept responsibility for creating one's own misery. There are obvious similarities in this approach to the existential-humanistic therapies, which are discussed later. The difference is Ellis' strong *cognitive* approach, his conviction that we make ourselves feel miserable because our thinking is faulty and because we live out our

lives in accordance with impossible, irrational assumptions. "She doesn't like me, therefore *nobody* likes me."

In recent years, as forms of therapy based on learning principles have been extended to include attempts to change thinking and perceptual processes (Bandura, 1969), Ellis' rational-emotive approach has begun to attract more and more attention, especially in the area of behavioral self-control (Goldfried & Merbaum, 1973).

HUMANISTIC-EXISTENTIAL THERAPIES

The existentialist movement in philosophy, represented by philosophers like Sören Kierkegaard, Martin Heidegger, and Jean-Paul Sartre, developed the position that the essence of being lies in our affirmation of our existence, in the importance of individual choices as the basis of human freedom. Derived from similar notions, several existential forms of psychotherapy have been developed by such proponents as Ludwig Binswanger (1956) and Viktor Frankl (1963) in Europe, and Rollo May (1960), Abraham Maslow (1970), and Fritz Perls (1970) in the United States. These therapeutic approaches agree in their view of human beings as thinking, knowing, and free agents, fully capable of taking responsibility for their decisions and actions, and always evolving and changing in the process of achieving their potential. People's lives are not determined by the external forces acting on them; rather, they themselves determine events, participating in and changing the world, not simply reacting to it.

Existential Therapy

Clients are seen not as objects in **existential therapy,** but as experiencing human beings whose points of view therapists must try to understand. Therapists develop real, rather than professional, relationships with their clients, and attempt to share clients' experiences rather than interpret or reflect them. Understanding of clients' dynamics is derived less from formal theory than from clients' personal life situations. The aim is to help clients understand the properties of their own existence, to discover themselves as unique, loving, and evolving individuals, to accept responsibility for their decisions, for constructing a meaningful existence for themselves, and for developing significant commitments to themselves and to others.

Gestalt Therapy

Developed by Fritz Perls (1970) within the humanistic-existential tradition, **Gestalt therapy** is based on the assumption that people are innately good and possess the ability to take command of their lives and grow. The aim of Gestalt therapy is to help people become more creative and expressive, more in contact with their feelings, more capable of accepting responsibility for what they are and wish to be. As in Rogerian and existential therapies, what is important are present perceptions, feelings, and activities, not the forbidden impulses and unresolved conflicts of the past. Clients are encouraged to experience their feelings rather than take refuge in thinking about them. "Living in the moment," opening one's awareness to all aspects of existence, functioning as a *whole* person—these are some of the goals of Gestalt therapy (Fagan & Shepherd, 1970).

Gestalt therapy is difficult to describe in detail, for systematic analyses of the therapy process are lacking. Instead, you find descriptions of the rules and games involved in therapy exercises (Levitsky & Perls, 1970; Perls, Hefferline, & Goodman, 1951). Some of the rules call for speaking in the present tense (principle of the now) and using "I" language ("I am trembling," not "It [the hand] is trembling"). In one type of game, the "game of dialogues," the patient personifies different aspects of his personality, like his aggressive and

Figure 16-6 Fritz Perls, the founder of Gestalt therapy.

passive sides, or nice-guy and tough-guy sides, and makes up a dialogue between them. In another game the patient states, "I take responsibility for it," for every statement he makes about his feelings or behavior. In "I have a secret," all the participants in a group try to imagine how the others would react to their own personal secrets involving guilt or embarrassment.

Some critics feel that much of the flavor of Gestalt therapy may stem from Perls's own personality rather than from the therapeutic procedures themselves. Perls was an earthy, warm, egotistical, ebullient, and brash showman, and enjoyed staging impressive demonstrations of therapy exercises (see Figure 16-6). Yet the popularity of Gestalt therapy has continued to grow since his death in 1970. Many people who never heard of either Fritz Perls or Gestalt therapy have nonetheless developed a fondness for one of his most quoted statements:

I do my thing and you do your thing. I am not in this world to live up to your expectations and you are not in this world to live up to mine. You are you and I am I. And if by chance we find each other, it's beautiful. If not, then not.

GROUP THERAPY

The individual forms of psychotherapy discussed so far have both practical and theoretical disadvantages. On the practical side, one-to-one therapy is terribly inefficient. If a therapist meets each client only once a week and schedules 30 clients a week, no more than 30 or so patients are treated by one therapist over a period of several years—not an uncommon term for traditional psychotherapy. In view of the increasing need for treatment as more people are educated to seek help and as the field of preventive therapy develops, the one-to-one approach can aggravate an existing therapist shortage. Obviously, ways must be found to distribute the efforts of skilled therapists over a wider range of the population. Group therapies attempt to do just that, and the average cost of therapy per person is also reduced. Reducing the expense of psychotherapy is a problem of the greatest importance if treatment is to be made available to people of all economic levels.

A Social Context

The theoretical disadvantage of individual therapy is that both therapist and patient are precluded from systematically observing the patient's characteristic modes of interacting with other people. If it is true, as many contend, that behavior disorders are essentially problems in living (Szasz, 1960) and rooted in the history of the person's interpersonal transactions (Sullivan, 1953), it follows that therapeutic change might well occur most rapidly in a social context. In **group therapy,** people have a chance to learn, quickly and decisively, how their behavior affects others, and whether their perceptions of themselves and of the world coincide with those of others or are idiosyn-

cratic and distorted. Therapists, too, have an advantage: They can directly see how their patients relate to others, what defensive stratagems they employ, and what interpersonal skills need to be improved, without having to rely on each patient's possibly distorted reports of outside relationships.

But how shall group therapy be conducted? There are as many forms of group therapy as there are of individual therapy. Each "school" seems to have evolved its own variant of group therapy. For example, a fairly orthodox psychoanalytic orientation provides the foundation for Samuel R. Slavson's (1943) group therapy, perhaps the oldest systematic approach to the treatment of people in groups. Typically, patients and one or more therapists sit in a circle and discuss their own or each other's problems (see picture at beginning of this chapter). The therapist may elicit expressions of feelings, clarify meanings, offer tentative interpretations and also encourage others to do so, and generally act in an accepting, nonthreatening manner. Often people in such a group discover they are not so peculiar or different as they feared, and that other people have the same or similar conflicts, anxieties, and misery. People who have difficulty relating to others often find comfort in belonging to a group that cares enough to listen to them and offer constructive suggestions, and to accept them with all their problems.

Group therapy is commonly combined with individual therapy, and is usually begun after some prior experience in individual therapy.

Psychodrama

A technique developed by J. L. Moreno (1971), which encourages patients to act out their feelings as if they are in a play, is called **psychodrama.** Thus people with unresolved ambivalent feelings toward their parents might be required to improvise scenes in which other patients or staff members take the roles of the parents (see Figure 16-7). By acting out

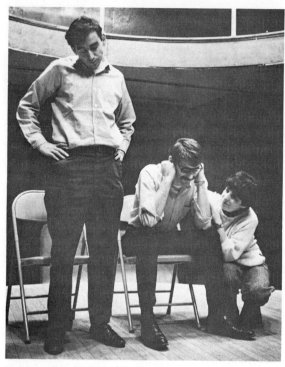

Figure 16-7 A psychodrama scene. The protagonist (center) struggles to decide whether to break off a love relationship. The auxiliary ego on his left portrays his mother, consoling him. The male auxiliary figure embodies his dejection and inability to come to a decision.

their emotional attitudes instead of merely verbalizing them, people presumably obtain clearer insight into the bases of their maladjustment. This method is often used as an adjunct to other forms of therapy, and is used with increasing frequency in therapy with adolescents and in marital counseling.

Sensitivity Training

The **sensitivity training group**, or **T-group**, originated at the National Training Laboratories in Bethel, Maine, and was developed by the followers of Kurt Lewin, whose phenomenological analysis of conflict was mentioned in Chapter 13. Originally the participants were drawn from business and industry, and the goal was to increase the efficiency of execu-

tives by increasing their sensitivity to the people with whom they worked. Thus the original aim was more educational than therapeutic. In fact, even today it is recommended that psychotics, certain types of neurotics, and hysterics be excluded (Kuehn & Crinella, 1969). The training is brief, several hours a day for one or two weeks. The procedures vary considerably, but often include reporting of dreams and daydreams, role playing, and special methods for involving timid, suspicious, or aloof group members.

Sociometric methods are used to facilitate important feedback to individuals who frequently are excluded from social groupings. For example, a group of five persons may be assigned a problem like this one:

All of you have been together on a ship that has just sunk. You (point to one member) have just found a small life raft capable of holding three other people. Ahead is an island on which you can live fairly comfortably; but, because it is out of the shipping lanes, you will have to be there at least six months. What three other people in this group will you ask to join you on the raft, row to the island, and live there together? What do you expect of them during that six-month period [Gottschalk & Davidson, 1971]?

Since all members of the group must announce and explain their choices, those who are left out have the opportunity to confront the fact of their exclusion and obtain valuable feedback about the reasons other people avoid them. You can see how such exercises might help people to learn more about their feelings and those of other people. Elliot Aronson (1972) puts it this way: ". . . in a college psychology course, I learn how people behave; in a T-group, I learn how *I* behave . . . how others see me, how my behavior affects them, and how I am affected by other people." He states that the general goals of most groups are:

1. To develop a willingness to examine one's own behavior and try out different ways of relating to others.

2. To become more sensitive to other people.
3. To become more genuine and free in interpersonal relations.
4. To learn how to be more cooperative, rather than authoritative or submissive.
5. To learn how to resolve conflicts and disputes by reasoning rather than by manipulating or coercing people.

As you may well imagine, the competence and skill of the leader is an important determinant of a T-group's functioning. A leader who tries to function more as a therapist, offering depth analyses and maintaining a superordinate position to the group members, will probably not be so effective as one who functions as a regular participating member. The leader's task is to facilitate group processes, giving and receiving feedback, providing supportive comments, easing the flow of communication, and intervening to protect participants from unfair attacks.

Encounter Groups

Encounter groups are a more recent innovation than T-groups and usually stress some sort of physical contact between participants, like touching, massage, and body movement (see Figure 16-8). Originating on the West Coast and identified particularly with the Esalen Institute, encounter groups are now functioning throughout the United States. The effectiveness of these group experiences is difficult to measure, but a number of research reports have begun to appear. A study of 18 different encounter groups at Stanford University (Lieberman, Yalom, & Miles, 1973) revealed that the outcome of such experiences is quite variable. Immediately after the sessions ended, most participants reported positive effects, including increased self-esteem, improved ability to express justified anger, and a more permissive attitude toward themselves and others.

Not everyone fared so well, however, and six to eight months later a tenth of the partici-

pants were still suffering some adverse effects of the emotional pummeling they had taken during the group sessions. These "casualties" displayed some enduring psychological harm directly traceable to the encounter experience. Some became markedly withdrawn and depressed. Others experienced a reduction in self-esteem. In some groups led by aggressive, authoritarian leaders, many participants sim-

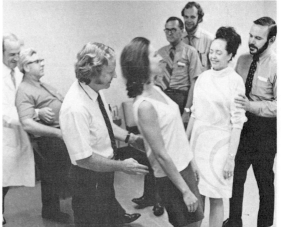

Figure 16-8 Nonverbal exercises in sensitivity training. The hand dance (top) is used to create an awareness of another person through touch. The trust–distrust exercise (bottom) teaches group members to trust others by requiring them to fall backward into their partners' arms. (Courtesy L. A. Gottschalk)

ply dropped out. Interestingly, while group members were only moderately successful in predicting which participants would become casualties, group leaders were even less successful.

It seems, then, that encounter groups are not everyone's cup of tea. First of all, it does not follow that good procedures taken to an extreme degree will necessarily produce a better outcome. Yet that assumption seems to underlie crash programs in self-awareness:

If something is good, more is better. If self-disclosure is good in groups, then total . . . disclosure in the nude must be better. . . . If expression of feeling is good, then, hitting, touching, feeling, kissing, and fornicating must be better. If human relations training is good, then it is good for everyone in all stages of the life cycle, in all life situations [Yalom, 1970].

Not everyone is able, or needs, to take the intense pressure for self-disclosure or to suffer the heavy emotional pounding of a hostile group and an "aggressive stimulator" (leader). Some participants can escape injury only by refusing to take the whole thing very seriously. The nature of the group, the leader, and the participant should all be carefully considered before anyone joins such a group. Here are some suggestions that anyone contemplating joining an encounter group would do well to follow (Shostrom, 1969):

1. *Don't respond to a newspaper ad.* Trained professionals are ethically forbidden to advertise.
2. *Don't join groups consisting of fewer than 6 members, or more than 16.* Too few may lead to scapegoating and ganging up. Too large a group makes it hard to keep track of what's going on.
3. *Don't join a group on impulse.* If you're in the middle of an emotional crisis or have trouble maintaining a firm grasp on reality, a group experience is not for you.
4. *Don't join any group that includes people who are close to you, professionally or socially.*
5. *Don't be impressed by the place or the people.* Good sessions can occur in plain settings. A diverse rather than homogeneous group helps bring out the many sides of each individual.
6. *Avoid groups that have a specific ax to grind,* that insist on a preferred cultural, social, political, or philosophic point of view.
7. *Avoid groups that have no connection with a professional whose credentials you can check.* A key question to ask is, *Is your professional consultant licensed to practice in this state?*

DOES PSYCHOTHERAPY WORK?

Psychoanalysis is a long-drawn-out, expensive, and often painful experience. Other forms of psychotherapy are usually shorter, less expensive (but still expensive), and less painful (but still painful). Is psychotherapy worth it? Just how effective is it? The answer to this question depends, of course, on the criteria of effectiveness and on the methods used to measure improvement. Freudian, client-centered, and other traditional psychotherapists share the view that insight into underlying dynamics is essential for a successful outcome. They view the therapist's role as that of a facilitator, one who makes it possible for people to perceive clearly what their real problems and conflicts are. While the achievement of insight does not automatically eliminate the problems, the process of self-discovery is considered crucial. For this reason, it is disquieting to learn that the types of insights patients report can be predicted more readily from a knowledge of their therapists' schools of psychotherapy than from a knowledge of the patients' own problems and background (Marmor, 1962). Since each school trains its therapists to look for different causes of neuroses, in practice they tend to come up with diagnoses favored by their school rather than by those of a rival system. Somehow these theories get communicated to the patients, who apparently learn rather well to develop Freudian or Adlerian or Rogerian insights, depending on their therapists' theoretical predilections (Heine, 1953). This raises the possibility that patients' insights may index the successful adoption of their therapists' ways of thinking, rather than self-discovery of the true causes of their behavior.

Criticism of Psychotherapy

While psychotherapy may convert a patient to the therapist's orientation, isn't it still possible for patients treated by one method to improve more than patients treated by other methods? Apparently not. A review of research on the effectiveness of various forms of psychotherapy revealed that no school was more effective than any others (Luborsky, Chandler, Auerbach, Cohen, & Bachrach, 1971). In fact, it has even been argued that the more psychotherapy patients receive, the lower the recovery rate. Some years ago (1952), Hans Eysenck, a foremost critic of insight forms of psychotherapy, examined 19 studies dealing with the results of psychoanalytic and other traditional types of psychotherapy. The 7000 patients covered by these studies were grouped according to the amount of improvement they displayed. Eysenck sent a shock wave through the psychotherapeutic profession by reporting that while 72 per cent of patients receiving only custodial care improved, only 44 per cent of those undergoing psychoanalysis improved, and 64 per cent of those who were treated by a variety of other methods improved. Eysenck's implication was clear: More psychotherapy means poorer chance of recovery.

Eysenck's conclusion has been severely criticized on the grounds that the studies on which it was based were so different in such procedural matters as duration of treatment, experience of therapists, types of cases, follow-up information, and assessment procedures that legitimate comparisons were not possible. More recent analyses of research reports (Bergin, 1966, 1971) have shown that Eysenck's original conclusion was too pessimistic, since modest improvement above chance expectancy does occur, especially when therapy is especially intensive and of long duration. However, the average change shown by treated patients is not very different from that shown by untreated control subjects, and some of the people who receive treatment get worse.

Patients' Evaluations

Against this background, how can the frequently encountered claims of therapeutic success by psychotherapists and former patients or clients be explained? The main questions, of course, are whether the changes claimed have really occurred, whether they are long lasting, and whether it was the therapy, and not other factors, that was responsible for the improvement. Much research has shown that **spontaneous remission** of behavior disorders does occur. Out of any group of people who intermittently suffer anxiety attacks, at some point a percentage of them will stop experiencing this type of distress, and the reasons for the "cure" are often unknown. The percentage of such spontaneous cures among untreated patients is called the base rate. When people announce that their therapy has been "successful," it is difficult to know whether it was the therapy that cured them, or whether they would have recovered in any case. On a larger scale, a therapist's claim of a 75 per cent success rate is difficult to evaluate unless we know the percentage of patients who would have improved with other treatments, or with no treatment at all.

The enthusiasm of some "cured" ex-patients may be stronger evidence for a placebo effect than for the efficacy of the therapeutic procedures themselves. Just as taking a sugar pill is often followed by the relief of bodily symptoms in a person who believes the pill to be an effective medicine, so too psychiatric patients may improve because they *believe* in the therapy, or in the therapist, rather than because of the effectiveness of the procedures themselves. The therapist's personality may be a powerful determinant of the placebo effect. Confident, authoritative, charismatic therapists will inspire more faith in their curative powers than will hesitant, doubt-ridden, vacillating ones.

It is fair to assume that patients who seek out a therapist genuinely want to improve. In some cases, the desire to improve is tied to a desire to please the therapist; that is, to gain the approval of a person whom they respect and admire, and who, after all, does seem to bestow social rewards when patients give signs of making progress. How much genuine improvement occurs in psychotherapy because of the **demand characteristics** of the situation—that is, patients' perception of the changes that are expected of them—is often difficult to determine. Yet this is an important question. Patients who somehow learn to suppress self-destructive comments because they sense this is a change expected of them by the therapist do not necessarily transfer this effect to real-life situations.

Patients may feel they have improved, more than objective evidence would justify, for another reason: Having spent much time and money on psychotherapy, they are powerfully motivated to magnify any slightest indication of improvement. A perception of the treatment as unsuccessful would be evidence of one more failure, and hence extremely aversive. Our belief systems often reflect our strong needs to reconcile discrepant perceptions (Festinger, 1957), and the perception of having spent a lot of time and money on therapy does seem easier to reconcile with the perception of therapeutic success than with that of therapeutic failure.

All these considerations add up to a cautionary statement: Assessments of psychotherapeutic effectiveness based on patient self-reports are not very reliable. Objective assessment made by someone other than the patient is preferred. But who should the objective observer be?

Therapists' Evaluations

Therapists themselves are closest to their patients' behavior, and see more of it than anyone else. Why can't one simply ask the therapist to judge the amount of improvement, or lack of it? In evaluating questions of fact, especially when the evaluation is complex and subject to error, an impartial observer is invaluable. In scientific investigation, verification of a reported finding by a different laboratory is mandatory. Therapists may see more improvement than is there to be seen, they may focus on behavioral changes that others might consider trivial, they may have selected for treatment only patients whose particular problems were relatively easy to solve. Moreover, therapists assessing their own effectiveness are always handicapped by lack of knowledge about the fate of patients who abruptly terminate therapy after it has begun. Do such patients get worse after they leave? Did the incomplete therapy they received make them worse? Did they leave because the therapy itself was making things worse? Even when patients complete a full course of therapy, few therapists make follow-up efforts to check on the longevity of any beneficial changes that may have occurred in therapy. These considerations all point to the need for impartial and objective assessment of psychotherapy. They provide good reasons for mistrusting effectiveness claims made by individual psychotherapists who base their judgments on their own impressions of patient improvement.

Recently the focus of research has shifted from attempts to measure the relative effectiveness of various schools of psychotherapy to the identification of the personal qualities of patients and of therapists that are related to therapeutic effectiveness. Studies by Lester Luborsky and his associates (1971) and Allen Bergin (1971) provide a general picture of the type of people who are most likely to profit from therapy. They are generally intelligent, likable, socially able persons, who are highly motivated to improve. Anxious and depressed types tend to be among those who improve most, but the less disturbed they are to begin with, the greater the likelihood of a successful outcome. As you might expect, patients make faster progress with therapists who rank high in experience and skill (regardless of theoretical orientation), who are warm and sensitive, and who share patients' attitudes and values (and, probably, social class). Unfortunately, this adds up to saying that the people already most favored by society and their own psychosocial adjustment are likely to benefit most from psychotherapy, while those who are most disturbed and most in need stand to benefit least, and in fact are more likely to deteriorate in therapy. Not a very optimistic conclusion.

THE BEHAVIOR THERAPIES

Beginning in the late 1950s and early 1960s, a variety of new psychotherapeutic approaches was developed. Although a diversity of labels has been employed (behavior therapy, behavior modification, reinforcement therapy, contingency management, behavioral self-control), **behavior therapy** is widely accepted as the general term for a group of techniques that share the following properties: (1) dissatisfaction with certain theoretical assumptions and the success rate of the traditional psychotherapies, (2) the conviction that neurotic behavior is learned, and that the principles of learning can be applied to help people unlearn neurotic "habits" and acquire more adaptive habits, and (3) an appreciation of the need to provide objective evidence of treatment effectiveness.

Dissatisfaction with Traditional Approaches

At the beginning of this chapter it was explained how somatic conceptions of mental illness eventually gave way to psychological or psychodynamic explanations, especially owing to the influence of Sigmund Freud. The older medical model that views neurotic and psychotic behavior as signs of organic disease was discarded, but the concept of disease—"mental" disease now—was retained. To this day we speak of diagnosing the nature of mental *illness,* and sometimes speak of people as mentally *sick.* These are signs of a disease conception, a medical model of behavior disorders. As you saw (Chapter 15), people like Dr. Thomas Szasz have challenged the usefulness of this idea, arguing for a more social conception of such disorders as "problems in living."

Behaviorists have also vigorously protested that traditional therapists, while discarding the organic basis of behavior disorders, have retained all the trappings of the medical model. The clinical psychologist is often called upon to apply a battery of tests to help *diagnose* the *underlying* problem, of which the overt behavior is only a *symptom.* The *patient* is *treated* for the *illness* in the hope of effecting a *cure.* Doesn't this sound like a disease? Yet while it is usually fairly easy to diagnose the cause of a medical disease, it is difficult to identify the source of the inner disorder of which the overt behavior is but a symptom. While an elevated sugar level in the urine is accepted as a symptom of a diabetic condition the world over, behavioral symptoms may reflect a disorder in some parts of the world but not in others. In many countries—Greece, for one—it is considered perfectly normal for men to dance together, but in the United States this behavior is often taken as symptomatic of homosexuality. In this country, oral forms of sexual behavior were regarded as "sick" at one time, but are now regarded as one among many acceptable types of sexual behavior.

B. F. Skinner (1959), whose work in the psychology of learning and behavioral technology has already been described (see Chapter 7), offered a more serious objection to the quasimedical model of mental disorders. As long as the "real causes" of the troubling behavior are ascribed to the workings of inferred inner events like needs, emotions, and conflicts, the task of scientific analysis, the identification of causal relations between behavior and its environmental determinants, is neglected. While the traditional Freudian might wish to diagnose self-punitive behavior as a symptom of a raging inner battle being won by a powerful, vindictive superego against libidinal forces while a puny ego stands by too weak to mediate, Skinner would urge a behavioral analysis of external sources of reinforcement that could be maintaining the behavior in question.

With the focus of attention shifted to observable or measurable aspects of behavior, behavior therapists have increasingly argued for objective assessment of therapeutic outcomes, preferring to measure improvement in the form of changed behavior as opposed to shifts in psychological test scores, assessment by researchers other than the therapist, and designs that include appropriate controls for placebo, base rate, and other spurious factors affecting outcome (Bandura, 1969).

Learned Basis of Behavioral Disorders

All behavior therapists assume that neurotic behavior is learned behavior. Irrational fears, lack of self-confidence, excessive suspiciousness and distrust, overly hostile or submissive tendencies, obsessions, sexual dysfunctions, enuresis, and compulsions all represent maladaptive habits that the individual acquires through some form of learning. Some therapists assume that the principles of classical conditioning and instrumental learning are sufficient to explain most forms of neurotic behavior. Others feel that while the *elimination* of neurotic behavior proceeds according to principles of learning, the acquisition of some fears is difficult to explain in terms of simple conditioning. The origin of the bizarre behavior shown by schizophrenic patients, for example, is more and more often attributed to biochemical factors (see Chapter 15), yet the

principles of operant conditioning are of considerable effectiveness in improving the general behavioral competence of these patients. The important implication of the view that abnormal behavior is subject to the laws of learning is that psychotherapy comes to be regarded as an educational process in which the individual is trained to abandon faulty habits and acquire new skills. The sharp differences between psychodynamic therapies and behavioral therapies are summarized in Table 16-1.

The Origins of Behavior Therapy

Since the behavior therapies are based on the experimental psychology of learning, their origin goes back to the beginnings of the psychology of conditioning. In Chapter 7 you saw that Pavlov was very much interested in applying the principles of conditioning to the treatment of mental patients. Vladimir Bekhterev was another Russian who, early in this century, used conditioning procedures in treating hysteria, obsessional neurosis, and paranoia.

The influence of the Russian psychopathologists on American psychologists was enormous, but was restricted mainly to the shaping of learning *theory*, not the treatment of behavior disorders. Thus, while theorists like John B. Watson, Edward L. Thorndike, Edwin R. Guthrie, and Clark L. Hull developed complex theories of learning firmly grounded in the associationist tradition of Russian reflexology, their efforts were not aimed at producing new systems of psychotherapy.

Since the aim of psychotherapy, regardless of orientation, is some form of change, it was inevitable that at some point the principles of behavior change through learning would be applied to systems of treatment. A major event occurred in 1950, with the publication of John Dollard and Neal Miller's *Personality and Psychotherapy*, in which the origins of neuroses and the dynamics of psychoanalytic treatment are interpreted in the language of learning

Table 16-1 Basic Differences Between Psychodynamic and Behavior Therapies

Psychodynamic Therapies	Behavior Therapies
1. Emphasis on inner dynamics as the locus of the problem.	1. Emphasis on maladaptive behavior as the problem.
2. Symptoms considered indirect evidence of unconscious conflicts.	2. Symptoms considered maladaptive habits.
3. Treatment directed toward resolution of inner conflicts, not elimination of symptoms.	3. Treatment involves extinguishing inappropriate habits and learning more appropriate behaviors.
4. Techniques based on analytic or psychodynamic principles.	4. Techniques based on learning principles.
5. Patient-therapist relation emphasized.	5. Patient-therapist relationship secondary to techniques used.
6. Interpretation of motives underlying symptoms deemed crucial.	6. Analysis of stimulus control and reinforcement contingencies deemed crucial.
7. Aim: to restructure personality.	7. Aim: to change behavior.
8. Therapy, especially psychoanalytic, tends to be long-term.	8. Therapy tends to be short-term (often 10 to 20 hours).

theory. This volume is a landmark because it served to demonstrate the compatibility between principles derived from rigorous experimental research in learning and the development of neurotic behavior and its treatment.

Dollard and Miller's work, important as it was, did not argue for a new therapeutic method based on learning; it provided a linguistic connection between learning principles and therapy. The new methods, collectively called **behavior therapy,** resulted from the influence of two major figures, a South African psychiatrist and an American animal behaviorist well known to you by now. And strangely, just as the basic principles of learning can be divided into those of classical and operant conditioning, so too the two dominant forms of behavior therapy represent applications of the principles of classical and operant conditioning. The psychiatrist, Joseph Wolpe, devised a system called **psychotherapy by reciprocal inhibition** (1958), which combines fear extinction and counterconditioning principles with deep-muscle relaxation, as you saw in Chapter 8. This approach is more com-

monly called **systematic desensitization therapy,** or simply **desensitization therapy.** The American behaviorist, B. F. Skinner, has inspired the application of reinforcement principles, especially in the treatment of severe psychotic disorders and mental retardation. These methods are often grouped under the term **behavior modification.**

Systematic Desensitization

Wolpe's system of therapy grew out of earlier experiments that showed how cats that had been shocked in a particular cage could be made to overcome their fear of the shock area by allowing them to feed in another room at first, and then letting them feed closer and closer to the place where they had been shocked. Wolpe wanted to break the connection between stimuli in the shock cage and the fear that had been conditioned to them. Feeding is a response antagonistic to fear. Have you ever tried eating a full meal when you're terribly frightened about something? By letting the cats feed in places that elicited weak fear, and then gradually letting them feed closer and closer to the most feared place, Wolpe was eventually able to destroy the fear-eliciting power of the shock-cage stimulus.

When applied to human fears, Wolpe's method (1973) is first to train patients to relax deeply. Relaxation is assumed to be a response incompatible with anxiety. Having already made a list of the situations or events that make the patient anxious, Wolpe then teaches the patient to relax deeply while imagining the weakest anxiety-arousing item in the hierarchy of feared stimuli. Gradually, as relaxation responses supplant anxiety responses, the patient learns to relax while imagining ever more potent fear-eliciting stimuli. Finally the individual has learned to relax in the presence of all the stimuli that had earlier aroused anxiety.

Wolpe's systematic desensitization has been applied not only to phobic behavior like fear of animals, heights, and elevators, but also to the treatment of sexual dysfunction, stuttering, speech anxiety, sexual deviations, obesity, depression, and character and obsessional neuroses, and to the development of assertive behaviors.

DESENSITIZATION OF A WASHING COMPULSION

An 18-year-old boy, Michael T., had spent most of his time in bed for two months before his treatment began because his neurotic washing compulsion had made getting up seem hardly worthwhile (Wolpe, 1973). His terrible fear of contaminating other people with his urine made him take four hours showering when he got up, and whenever he urinated it took him 45 minutes to clean his genitals and another two hours to wash his hands. During interviews he would place the New York Times on his chair before he sat down. Similar compulsive attempts to prevent urine contamination almost completely incapacitated him.

Michael's parents had forced him to sleep with his older sister until he was 15 because of her fear of being alone. This situation had quite naturally aroused erotic responses, about which Mi-

chael felt extremely guilty. His anger and hostility toward his parents was expressed in many destructive fantasies and had led to his washing compulsion.

Michael's desensitization treatment first consisted of imagining a stranger dipping his hand into a trough of water containing only one drop of urine. Although this caused anxiety, Michael gradually came to accept greater concentrations of urine in the water, and finally pure urine, without disturbance. This long process, which took about five months of sessions five times a week, did reduce his shower time to about an hour and the hand-washing ritual to 45 minutes. Then Michael imagined placing his own hand in greater and greater concentrations of urine, and came to accept this in imagination though not in actuality. So he was then gradually desensitized to accepting a closed bottle of urine across the room; it was brought closer, and finally, after a long series of tiny steps, he became able to touch his own urine. By then he was able to dress daily, his shower time had decreased to 40 minutes, and his cleaning-up routine had almost disappeared. He came to be able to "contaminate" other things with his uriniferous hands, like magazines, doorknobs, and even other people's hands. But although he was able to go back to school, he did not make further progress until treatments were resumed weekly on an outpatient basis. Shower time was reduced to 20 minutes and hand-washing to 3 minutes. Before long Michael reported he was leading a normal life, and follow-ups indicated that his recovery had been maintained. Although it had been a long process of treatment, requiring great effort, Michael was finally rid of his crippling compulsion.

Assessment of the effectiveness of systematic desensitization has taken many forms, from simple clinical observation to controlled studies in which matched groups of patients receive a variety of treatments (including no treatment), and their behavior is objectively evaluated before, immediately after, and long after treatment by "blind" researchers. (In a **blind evaluation,** the researcher does not know what treatment the patient has received.) The earliest reports were based on individual case studies in which therapists themselves judged the degree of improvement resulting from treatment. Table 16-2 compares the success rate of systematic desensitization against analytic and general hospital therapy. In the Wolpe (1958) study referred to in the table, the assessment of improvement or "cure" was based on criteria originally proposed by R. P. Knight (1941) for the purpose of improving research on the effectiveness of psychoanalytic therapy. These criteria are: (1) symptomatic improvement, (2) increased productivity at work, (3) improved adjustment and pleasure in sex, (4) improved interpersonal relationships, and (5) enhanced ability to handle ordinary psychological conflicts and reasonable reality stresses. The data in Table 16-2 show a substantially higher recovery rate for patients receiving Wolpe's form of behavior therapy.

Controlled investigations began to appear in the 1960s as research activity sharply increased. While only 13 reports appeared between 1952 and 1962, 182 were published in the following 10 years, ranging from single case studies to highly sophisticated controlled studies. Reviews (Paul, 1969a, 1969b) of evaluation research have left little doubt concerning the effectiveness of systematic desensitization, compared with traditional forms of therapy, over a wide range of behavior problems and therapy settings. Furthermore, it is now amply

clear that, contrary to the warnings of traditional therapists, **symptom substitution** — the cropping up of some other symptom after behavior therapy has eliminated the original symptom — has not been observed to occur (Paul, 1968).

In a good example of a well-controlled investigation of the effectiveness of systematic desensitization, Gordon Paul (1966) divided college students suffering from intense speech anxiety into four treatment groups. One group received desensitization-relaxation therapy, another conventional insight-oriented psychotherapy; members of a third, "attention-placebo," group received a placebo that was identified as an anxiety-reducing drug, and also met with a therapist who offered no therapy beyond giving them attention; a control group received no treatment at all. Before the experiment began, all students were put through the stressful procedure of giving an impromptu speech before a critical audience. Just before their talks, pulse rate and palm sweat were measured. In addition, the subjects rated their own anxiety and were given anxiety ratings by trained observers in the audience. Five practicing clinicians, all experienced in the use of traditional insight-oriented therapy, administered the treatments over a six-week period. To make sure "good" therapists would not be inadvertently assigned to only one of the treatment conditions, each therapist

Table 16-2 Results of Various Forms of Psychotherapy

Type of Therapy	Number of Cases	Apparently Cured or Much Improved	Percentage Recoveries
Systematic desensitization			
Wolpe (1958)	210	188	90%
Psychoanalytic therapy			
Brody (1962)	210	126	60
General hospital therapy			
Hamilton & Wall (1941)	100	53	53

Source: Wolpe, 1973.

administered each of the three treatments. Only five therapy sessions were given, since the therapists felt this was the number they would normally use to treat such cases by insight-oriented methods in daily practice. At the end of treatment, each subject had to give another stressful speech during which behavior ratings were made, and measures of pulse rate, sweating, and subjective fear were again taken.

Figure 16-9 shows the results of this study. It is apparent that the percentage of subjects evidencing a reduction in anxiety was greatest in the desensitization-relaxation group, whether physiological responses, behavior ratings, or subjective reports were used to measure anxiety. Although the insight-oriented treatment and the nonspecific treatment given the attention-placebo group also produced some anxiety reduction, as indicated by behavior ratings and subjective reports, only the desensitization-relaxation treatment resulted in a significant reduction in physiological signs of anxiety. A six-week follow-up indicated no evidence of symptom substitution. A second follow-up two years later (Paul, 1967), in which the same subjects were readministered the original battery of personality tests, revealed that 85 per cent of the desensitization-relaxation group still showed less public-speaking anxiety than originally; only 50 per cent of the subjects in the insight or the attention-placebo groups were less anxious than before treatment; in the nontreated control group, only 22 per cent reported less anxiety. Again, no evidence of symptom substitution was found.

This type of well-controlled study represents a marked improvement over the earlier case-study evidence of behavior-therapy effectiveness. Even the therapists involved, who were themselves trained in psychodynamic-

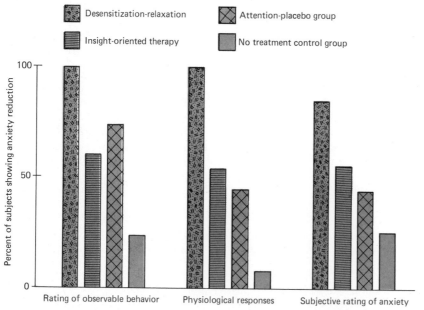

Figure 16-9 Per cent of subjects in each of four groups showing decreases in public-speaking anxiety as measured by behavior ratings, physiological responses (sweating, pulse rate), and subjective reports. (Adapted from INSIGHT Vs. DESENSITIZATION IN PSYCHO-THERAPY by Gordon L. Paul with the permission of the publishers, Stanford University Press © 1966 by the Board of Trustees of the Leland Stanford Junior University)

oriented methods and who favored insight-oriented techniques in their daily practices, rated the subjects in the behavior-therapy group as the most improved and gave them the most promising prognosis.

Implosive Therapy

If you had used Pavlovian conditioning to make a dog fear a certain room in the house, perhaps by having periodically given the animal his bath in that place, it's quite likely this fear would persist a very long time and be expressed as a "dogged" refusal to approach that place. Assuming you've long ago stopped bathing the dog there, how would you go about eliminating the continuing fear? If you were Wolpe, you might feed your dog some delectable tidbits at some distance from the hated room, then closer and closer, trying to countercondition the good feeling produced by the tidbits to the stimuli that heretofore have been eliciting fear. But let's be Pavlov, instead of Wolpe, for a moment. What would Pavlov do to extinguish a fear CR to the CS of the hated room? Forcing the dog to stay in the room (without dousing him!), in the presence of fear-producing CSs, should lead to pretty rapid extinction, shouldn't it?

This procedure of fear extinction by forced exposure to the CS, when used in animal studies, is called **flooding** (Baum, 1970). When the technique is applied to fear extinction in humans (Stampfl & Levis, 1967), it is called **implosive therapy.** The patient is asked to *imagine* threatening scenes (as in Wolpe's method), not actually to confront them. But while the desensitization-relaxation method moves up the hierarchy of imagined fear-inducing stimuli ever so slowly, implosion therapy begins with the most terrifying imagery imaginable. There is little concern with counterconditioning or relaxation training, only with the forced and continued contemplation of the worst features of the feared event or situation. It sounds like a "sink or swim" proce-dure, and you may wonder about the number of patients whose anxiety is so highly aroused by the procedure that they fail to return for further treatment. While initial reports of the relative effectiveness of implosion therapy published by practitioners were quite enthusiastic (Hogan & Kirchner, 1967), the methodological sophistication of the research studies has been severely criticized (Morganstern, 1973). This leaves us with no clear basis for concluding that implosion therapy is any more effective than desensitization-relaxation therapy.

FEAR OF SNAKES

Implosive therapy aims to achieve anxiety reduction by a straightforward Pavlovian extinction procedure, except that the CS is *imagined* rather than actually encountered. Moreover, the therapist not only encourages the patient to visualize the feared object as it really is or may be encountered; by using dramatic narrative he does his best to exaggerate the fearsome qualitites of the phobic stimulus.

Here is a sample of the technique applied to the treatment of a snake-phobic individual (Hogan, 1968):

Therapist. I want you to picture yourself getting ready to get into your bed and there in your bed are thousands of snakes. Can you see them crawling around in your bed? I want you to lie down with them. Get down with them. Feel yourself moving around with the snakes and they are crawling all over you. And you are moving and turning in bed and they are touching you. Feel them crawling on you, touching you, slimy and slithering. Feel yourself turn over in your bed, and they are under you and on you and around you, and touching your face and in your hair. And they are crawling across your face. Can you feel them touch you?

Subject. Kind of cold.

Therapist. Feel, you are now cold and clammy like a snake and they are touching you with their cold, clammy, wet, slimy, drippy, cold bodies that are wiggling and touching your skin and feel them. Uhhhh, now can you feel them touch you? They are touching you. Can you feel them touch you? Move around so you can get greater contact. Move your body like that woman in the Sealy ad and feel them touch you, uhhh, wiggly and slimy, they are crawling on you, on your face. Uhhh!

If you detect a little sexual overtone in this passage, this is not accidental, for the incorporation of psychodynamic themes is an important part of the procedure. Psychodynamic theory is used primarily to generate themes for the therapist's vivid narration, not as a basis for either interpreting the origin of an individual patient's phobia or for guiding progress toward the achievement of insight. Actually snakes are not slimy or wet (unless they're water snakes, of course), but this was a therapy session, not a lesson in herpetology.

Desensitization and Cognitive Therapy

In recent years, increasing recognition has been given by **cognitive therapy** to the role played by cognitive processes in modifying feelings and actions. There is growing acceptance of the belief that the way we feel and behave in a given situation depends on the way we perceive or think about that situation, or about ourselves in that situation. If we think most people are out to do us in and if we see ourselves as pretty inept and defenseless types, it's quite understandable that we might feel rather anxiety-ridden most of the time. Now, if our thinking, and also our perceptions of other people and of our own qualities, could be changed, the basis for our terror would dissolve. This is the type of notion underlying a number of therapy methods that have in common the aim of modifying those aspects of our thinking and/or perceptions that make us miserable.

Ellis' **rational-emotive therapy,** previously discussed, is an example of methods used to modify illogical thought patterns. Used in combination with desensitization-relaxation, rational-emotive therapy to train the patient to cognitively "restructure" or relabel the situa-

tion can help to convert the perception of threat or rejection into the perception of social acceptance (A. A. Lazarus, 1971). When office mates leave for lunch without you, you can either perceive their departure as their rejection of you (and it is this way of perceiving the scene that makes you feel miserable), or interpret their behavior as an oversight, with no rejection of you intended. The way you choose to interpret the scene determines the way you will feel. Cognitive therapy attempts to modify the way you perceive and feel by modifying what you say to yourself (Meichenbaum, 1973).

OPERANT CONDITIONING TECHNIQUES

The behavior therapy procedures discussed so far were largely directed toward the elimination of anxiety states, and were based mainly on classical conditioning principles. In the therapeutic modification of behavior, it is often desirable to achieve effects other than the weakening of anxiety. For example, there are the problems of reducing the deficit of behavioral skills displayed by retarded people, of increasing interpersonal activity among withdrawn psychotic patients, and of training any hospitalized person to become less dependent on supervising personnel.

Operant, or reinforcement, methods have been developed and are being widely used in cases in which appropriate behaviors need to be acquired or strengthened, or in which it is desirable to eliminate or weaken inappropriate behaviors. The principles of operant conditioning are simple enough. You will recall (Chapters 7 and 8) that contingencies can be arranged so that (1) desirable behavior (or some approximation of it) is followed by positive reinforcement, and (2) inappropriate behavior is followed by negative reinforcement or, more commonly, by the withdrawal of positive reinforcement. A vast system of behavior modification has been developed on the basis of these two principles and variations of them.

Reinforcement Methods

The application of reinforcement principles in the treatment of hospitalized schizophrenic patients began in the 1950s, with the experimental investigations of Ogden Lindsley (1956). The methods were closely patterned after animal Skinner-box procedures. Patients could obtain rewards in the form of candy or cigarettes by manipulating a plunger protruding from the wall of a cubicle (Figure 16-10). These early procedures amounted to the superimposition of an animal research model on the human organism, but they did show that the psychotic's behavior was not simply erratic, unpredictable, or "crazy." These patients revealed an orderly pattern of responding and displayed good sensitivity to reinforcement contingencies as the effects of schedule changes were studied.

Research efforts were soon directed toward the shaping of interpersonal behavior in psychotic patients (King, Armitage, & Tilton, 1960). Severely withdrawn, uncommunicative chronic schizophrenic patients were rewarded for operating levers in the multiple-operant problem-solving apparatus shown in Figure 16-11. At first the reinforcement (candy) even had to be placed in the mouths of the most regressed patients and their hands placed on the lever. Eventually, by means of a system of differential reinforcement, patients were shaped to respond on more complex tasks, requiring listening to and verbally replying to the therapist's instructions. Later, rewards were withheld unless the patients not only communicated with each other as they worked in pairs but also cooperatively solved problems requiring conjoint motor activity. As a result of this "treatment," patients became more verbal and more interested in occupational activities, and improved more rapidly than patients who had received traditional therapy, recreational therapy, or no therapy. Such early studies encouraged further exploration of reinforcement methods in rehabilitating psychotics, the most

severely disturbed category of mental patients.

Reinforcement techniques have been used to improve verbal, social, and self-controlling behavior in autistic children (Lovaas et al., 1973; Wolf, Risley, & Mees, 1964) and are in continuous use in classroom programs designed to improve learning preparedness skills in retarded and hyperactive children (Gardner, 1971; Thompson & Grabowski, 1972).

In a series of convincing demonstrations, Teodoro Ayllon (1963) applied reinforcement principles to the elimination of bizarre behaviors in individual chronic psychotic patients. One patient was cured of food stealing by withdrawal of positive reinforcement (a meal) whenever stealing occurred. Her tendency to wear enormous quantities of clothing was eliminated by requiring the removal of some garments as the price of admission to the dining room. A third habit, that of hoarding dozens of towels in her room, was eliminated by a "satiation" procedure: Nurses kept giving

Figure 16-10 Apparatus for studying operant conditioning in psychotic patients. Operating the plunger yields rewards like candy, cigarettes, or coins.

Figure 16-11 The operant interpersonal method for establishing interpersonal behavior in schizophrenics: A, the problem-solving apparatus; B, simple operant behavior; C, simple and complex problem solving; D, cooperative problem solving. (King, Armitage, & Tilton, 1960)

her more towels to hoard until the count reached 625, after which she began to remove them. Eventually she kept no more than one or two a week in her room.

Such control over individual segments of behavior soon encouraged attempts to apply reinforcement principles on a wardwide basis, the intent being to upgrade the self-management of large groups of patients dras-

tically, making them less dependent on ward personnel and more accomplished in the types of behaviors that bring social and monetary rewards in society.

In a series of classic studies, Teodoro Ayllon and Nathan Azrin (1965) and John Atthowe and Leonard Krasner (1968) demonstrated the feasibility of **token economy systems,** in which patients are immediately rewarded with

Figure 16-12 A patient redeeming tokens for a cup of coffee.

tokens for a variety of desirable behaviors, ranging from self-grooming to occupational activities. The tokens are, essentially, secondary reinforcements, and can later be redeemed for specific reinforcements such as especially attractive personal rooms, trips to town, extra appointments with staff members, and commissary items (see Figure 16-12). Elaborate systems have been established for arriving at and communicating to all patients the number of tokens that can be earned by displaying various behaviors. The "price structure" of the reinforcements available often needs revision, since even the mental hospital is subject to inflationary trends. Because patients participate in managing the system, they have the opportunity to learn complex interpersonal and business-management skills, as well as simpler social amenities and self-care behaviors.

When reinforcements were no longer given the patients, like employees in the "real world," simply stopped working. As Figure 16-13 shows, when wages were restored, the strike terminated.

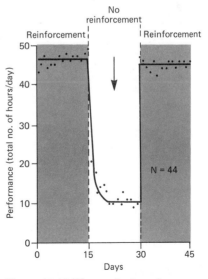

Figure 16-13 When patients no longer received "payment" for working, the number of hours worked per week plummeted. As soon as payment was restored, they resumed working. (Ayllon & Azrin, 1965)

While token economies have literally transformed the lives of many hospitalized psychotic patients, it should not be assumed that they constitute a "cure" for schizophrenia. First of all, although improvement rates are high, not every patient improves (Kazdin & Bootzin, 1972). Second, patients living in a token economy are usually being treated with antipsychotic drugs. It is questionable whether the remarkable improvement that large numbers of patients show in token economies would occur if chemotherapy were withdrawn. One interpretation is that while reinforcement methods don't cure the psychosis, they maximize the patient's ability to function effectively within the constraints imposed by the disorder.

Another question concerns the degree to which behavior that improves within the regimen of a token economy will generalize to the patients' activities in the community after they have been discharged. While discharge rates for patients assigned to a token-economy ward are sometimes double the rate of traditionally organized wards, the subsequent success of these patients in the larger society depends on the adequacy of the transitional programs that are established to facilitate their reentry. The most favorable outcomes occur when training for effective generalization is begun in the hospital and transitional houses or lodges are ready to receive the patients upon discharge. In an elaborate study, George Fairweather (1964) devised a program that progressively developed complex social and self-directive behavior in a selected group of patients. The group met often to evaluate members' progress, manage the incentive system, review policy matters, and make decisions. These patients rapidly developed self-directive behavior and impressive interpersonal skills. After discharge, the group ran its own employment counseling service, conducted informal educational programs for its members, and maintained a good record of gainful employment. Despite these advantages of preparatory programs, however, readmission rates for these patients were no lower than for control groups.

Additional research has shown the major factor in boosting the chances of a favorable outcome after discharge to be a well-organized transitional program in a community residence. In a later project (1969), Fairweather and his associates placed discharged patients in a community lodge, which was essentially run by the patients. They did all their own shopping, kept records, ran their own savings and loan bank, and even set up an income-producing business in which the members worked and held shares. A 40-month follow-up showed a dramatic improvement in the level of functioning of the members of the transitional lodge, compared with patients whose training had been confined to the hospital. Figure 16-14 shows that full-time employment among discharged patients trained in the lodge program remained much higher than among those trained in the hospital programs. The conclusion seems clear: For maximal effectiveness, positive reinforcement systems should deliberately incorporate transi-

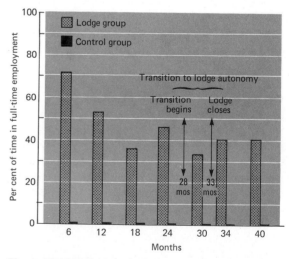

Figure 16-14 Patients in the lodge program had very favorable records of full-time employment; patients in the hospital program were unable to keep jobs. (Fairweather et al., 1969)

tional training in the very environmental setting in which the patients will live and work following discharge. In the light of such information, consider the current practice of releasing mental patients into often hostile communities, with a minimum of transitional training and postdischarge care.

CAUGHT IN BETWEEN

With the development of calming drugs and various therapies, many patients are being quickly released from mental institutions to reenter the communities from which they came. During a recent year almost 36,000 patients were turned out of New York State's mental hospitals, more than 14,000 of them going back to New York City alone. When such patients are assisted in their rehabilitation in halfway houses, sheltered workshops, and evening hospitals, very little trouble results. There are not nearly enough of such facilities, however, and most of the patients go onto welfare, into nursing homes for the aged, or into run-down hotels or private houses in which they receive no supervision, have no medical attention, and mean nothing to anyone but a quick profit for the operators. No wonder many of the patients wander the streets and frighten children and adults with their occasional odd behavior. Although they cause very little real harm, over half of the released patients are returned to mental hospitals.

The abrupt release of mental patients, though it is known to be undesirable, frequently cannot be avoided under present circumstances. Neighborhoods and communities do not want halfway houses or other rehabilitation establishments in their midst, fearing a sharp increase in the number of "odd" people in the neighborhood. Many people are still fearful of and prejudiced against those exhibiting signs of deviance. Others, like the members of the American Civil Liberties Union, contend that, once released, mental patients should have their freedom and not be forced to submit to rehabilitation procedures. Harold Wolfe, associate commissioner of the New York Department of Mental Hygiene, says, "We are caught in a squeeze. We are accused of dumping patients into neighborhoods. And we are accused of imprisoning patients in violation of their civil rights." The city of Long Beach, Long Island, even passed a law barring patients released in the future from taking up residence in the community.

Hardly anyone questions the benefits of returning patients to the community quickly. But no one wants to be inconvenienced or to pay for the extensive and costly rehabilitation procedures that seem to be required if the process is to work. Perhaps rapid rehabilitation will gradually be improved for the benefit of the patients and accepted by the general public, but it will be a long, slow process.

SOMATIC THERAPIES

Three major forms of somatic, or physical, therapy are in use today: **psychosurgery, electroconvulsive-shock therapy (ECT),** and drug therapy or **chemotherapy.**

Psychosurgery

The least employed of the three forms of somatic therapy mentioned, psychosurgery remains the most controversial. Intending to disconnect thinking (frontal lobes) and emotional (thalamus) centers in the brains of patients suffering from severe emotional disorders, Egas Moniz (1936) performed an operation called a prefrontal leucotomy. Six years later W. Freeman and J. W. Watts (1942) described a similar operation that they called **prefrontal lobotomy.** Small holes were first drilled in the skull, and a sharp instrument was then inserted to cut the fibers connecting the thalamus and frontal lobes (see Figure 16-15). The operation used to be carried out mainly on severely disturbed psychotics, and sometimes on violent or hallucinating patients. The main effect was to reduce the emotional turbulence raging within these patients. One reason for the ensuing controversy is simply that the effects of these operations is irreversible. Another is that the results have been equivocal.

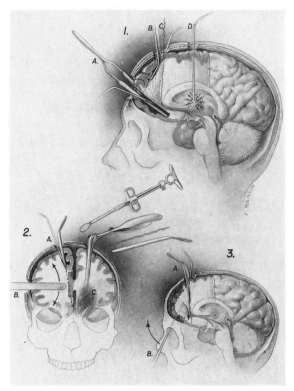

Figure 16-15 Three psychosurgical techniques for cutting connections between various portions of the brain. (Courtesy W. B. Scoville)

Still another is that the operations produced such undesirable side effects as a severe flattening of affect, reduction of interest in the environment, occasionally *increases* in impulsive behavior, seizures, and often a stuporous state. The development of drug therapy, especially the advent of the phenothiazines, has sharply limited the number of psychosurgical procedures now performed.

Electroconvulsive-shock Therapy (ECT)

John F. Fulton (1951) described how physicians of ancient Rome would use electric eels to administer electric charges to patients' heads, stunning them and perhaps also relieving their headaches. It wasn't until 1938, however, that modern ECT methods were introduced by two Italians, U. Cerletti and L. Bini. A current of 80 to 150 volts, lasting less than two seconds, is applied through electrodes placed on the patient's forehead. The effect is a convulsion, during which the patient loses consciousness. To reduce the likelihood of fractures and bruises, muscle relaxants are administered before the treatment. Although patients show some memory loss following treatment, this effect is dissipated within a few weeks. (Recall of events just prior to ECT occurs within an hour.)

Many people find the thought of ECT quite upsetting. Yet the treatment is, first of all, quite painless. In addition, ECT is very successful in treating severely depressed patients. A series of 5 to 10 treatments will produce full recovery from depression in 80 to 90 per cent of patients. Just why such convulsions are effective is still something of a mystery. Some researchers claim that the shock itself is the therapeutic factor and others hold that it is the coma following shock that is critical. Although drug therapy is supplanting ECT, it remains a valuable method of treating those patients who do not improve under medication with antidepressants.

Chemotherapy

Three major categories of drugs have been developed for the treatment of behavior disorders: **minor tranquilizers,** such as Miltown, Librium, and Valium; **major tranquilizers,** such as Thorazine and Stelazine; and **antidepressants.** Minor tranquilizers are usually prescribed for the alleviation of anxiety and tension. Although little controlled research has been completed, the habitual use of such tranquilizers has become quite widespread. Major tranquilizers have become the favored treatment for schizophrenics. For this reason, phenothiazines, the drug class to which Thorazine belongs, are classed as antipsychotic drugs. It has been estimated that over 85 per cent of all patients in state mental hospitals in 1970 were receiving Thorazine or some other phenothiazine (Davison & Neale, 1974). Controlled studies conducted by the National Institute of Mental Health, using a placebo control group and ratings made on a double-blind basis, revealed phenothiazines to be very effective in reducing the severity of psychotic behavior (Cole, 1964). Unfortunately, these drugs can also have side effects: fatigue, blurred vision, motor disturbances, and low blood pressure. Furthermore, readmission rates for patients discharged and kept on maintenance doses are high, with a "revolving door" pattern.

Antidepressants are of two types: *tricyclics* (like Elavil and Tofranil) and *monoamine oxidase* (MAO) *inhibitors* (like Nardil). Tricyclics, the more frequently used type, are primarily effective in cases of **endogenous depression,** where the disorder is usually attributed to some biochemical malfunction rather than, or in conjunction with, environmental stresses. The effectiveness of MAO inhibitors has not been so well established (Davis, Klerman, & Schildkraut, 1967) and the use of this type of drug has been declining. Unfortunately, drug effectiveness research is still plagued by the placebo effect: Even taking a placebo has been known to produce complex effects, attenuating some disorders while aggravating others.

Most recently, enthusiasm has been aroused by the possible usefulness of a drug called lithium carbonate as a treatment for manic and depressive states. Substantial agreement about the effectiveness of this drug has not yet been reached (Davis & Fann, 1971).

SUMMARY

Psychotherapy, in the broadest sense, is a way of helping people overcome their behavior disorders, decreasing their maladaptive behaviors and increasing their adaptive ones.

Psychoanalytic therapies apply the psychodynamic theories of Freud, Adler, Jung, or neo-Freudians like Erikson, Horney, and Sullivan to overcome patients' resistance and to uncover their early repressed inner conflicts by free association and dream analysis. These techniques aim at enabling patients, through transference with the analyst, to resolve their conflicts satisfactorily.

In client-centered therapy, developed by Rogers, the therapist maintains unconditional positive regard for the client, supports the client's positive insights but does not direct them, and assists the client in developing self-actualizing tendencies. Changes in the client's perceived and ideal selves can be inferred from self-statements of the Q-sort technique.

In rational-emotive therapy, patients are urged by the therapist to expose, confront, and repudiate their many fallacious ideas about themselves. The aim of this tough-minded cognitive approach is to overcome self-pity and develop self-esteem. Humanistic, existential, and Gestalt therapies use a variety of techniques to help people discover their real selves and take responsibility for making decisions that will realize their own potentialities in society.

The popularity of group therapy has increased in recent years, making therapy less expensive and available to many more people. Group therapy enables people to see the direct effects of their attitudes and behavior on other people, allowing clients to adjust their conceptions of themselves accordingly. In psychodrama, people can act out their emotional conflicts with others, playing various roles; and in sensitivity training people become more sensitive to others and learn how to interact more cooperatively with them rather than submissively or authoritatively. Encounter groups, involving close and usually physical contacts between participants, have produced marked changes in behavior but sometimes adverse effects persist.

Proponents of the effectiveness of psychotherapies often overlook the fact that many behavior disorders undergo spontaneous remission, that some patients improve because of placebo effects, and that others improve because of a deep desire to live up to the expectations of the therapist. Much research has indicated the need to improve or change psychotherapeutic methods, particularly for seriously disturbed patients.

Attributing behavior disorders to the learning of maladaptive patterns, behavior therapies aim to change these by the application of classical or operant conditioning principles. Wolpe's systematic desensitization therapy attempts to countercondition relaxation responses to cues that normally elicit anxiety. Implosive therapy requires the patient to confront and deal with imaginary situations designed to arouse the strongest emotional responses, but a thorough evaluation of the effects of these "flooding," or extinction, procedures has yet to be made. Reinforcement methods, based on the operant conditioning principles of Skinner, use positive and negative reinforcers, often in the form of tokens, to strengthen adaptive and weaken maladaptive behavior patterns. Some objective evaluations have shown behavior therapy to be more effective than traditional therapies based on psychodynamic principles, particularly with severely disturbed patients.

In contrast to psychotherapy, somatic therapies may include drugs, electric shock, and brain surgery in the treatment of behavior disorders. The use of psychosurgery and electroconvulsive-shock (ECS) therapies has waned in recent years because of serious questions about their long-run or side effects, although these techniques are still resorted to when others fail. The use of chemotherapy has greatly increased in recent years, however, because tranquilizers and antidepressants have proved effective in treating serious behavior disorders and in alleviating minor emotional disorders.

HOW WOULD YOU DO IT?

1. Imagine that you have (*a*) a serious anxiety neurosis, (*b*) an obsessive-compulsive neurosis, (*c*) a severe depression, and (*d*) an incapacitating phobia. Considering what you have read about various therapies, which type of therapy would you choose for treatment of each condition and why?

2. What features of psychoanalytic therapy, behavior therapy, or other therapies have impressed you most favorably or unfavorably and what evidence can you give to argue for one of these types of therapy and against the other types? Or are you of the opinion that there is really no choice between these types? Or that it would be best for most people to avoid therapy entirely? Whatever your conclusion, what evidence can you present for it?

3. In dealing with friends who appeal to you for assistance by discussing some of their most serious and intimate problems with them, do you tend to adopt a directive or a nondirective approach? Which type of therapy would you say these discussions most closely resemble? Do you ever indulge in a kind of "group therapy" in your discussions with friends? What insights, if any, does this chapter give you as to the way individual or group discussions with friends could be more beneficial?

Social Behavior

DIRECT VISUAL CONTACT

■ Sit fairly close to another person, within a foot or two, while the two of you look each other directly in the eyes for up to a minute without saying anything, if you can. Since you will be gazing into each other's eyes, you will have to estimate the time. Observe what happens to the other person and within yourself while you are looking into each other's eyes. What do you and your partner notice in particular? Discuss the effects you both noticed. Were the effects the same for both of you, or different? Why does direct visual contact have such noticeable effects?

PERSONAL SPACE AND SPATIAL INVASION

■ How do you usually find yourself a seat when you enter a bus or train in which only a few people are seated? Where do you usually take a seat when you go into a movie theater or other assembly of seated people where only some of the seats are occupied? Now try doing it a different way by taking the seat right next to a person you do not know in an *uncrowded* cafeteria, on a bus, in the reading room of a library, or in some other place where people are assembled, like a student union. Say nothing after you sit down. Simply go about your own activity but observe how the other person reacts. How do you think that person is feeling? How do you feel?

Social behavior is studied by investigators in many fields—social psychologists, sociologists, anthropologists, ethologists, economists, political scientists, historians. To get some sense of the character of social behavior as it is investigated by social psychologists, try the activities described in "Direct Visual Contact" and "Personal Space and Spatial Invasion" and examine the conclusions below that psychologists have reached about such activities.

THE NATURE OF SOCIAL PSYCHOLOGY

Surely one of the simpler ways in which people interact is by looking at each other, whether in silence or while speaking or listening to each other.

Visual Contact

A social psychologist, Ralph Exline, who has studied visual interactions during silence and speech, reports that partners in silent and **direct visual contact,** in which the eyes meet for sixty seconds, often begin to fidget, giggle, smile, or grimace nervously (Exline, 1972). Others gaze fixedly at each other deadpan for the full time, although the gaze shifts from one eye of the partner to the other. Many break eye contact before the minute is up. Feelings during such eye contact are often called "spooky" or "weird," ranging from strong awareness of the other to great tension, or even a sense of loss of self. In a report on an investigation of the feelings of college students in visual and verbal interactions with others, Exline reported that they feel most comfortable when the other person spends only half the time looking at them, less comfortable when they are looked at the whole time, and least comfortable when they are not looked at at all. Students of both sexes are less disconcerted by the silent stares of younger people than by those of their peers or older persons (see Figure 17-1). Both sexes also feel more comfortable being gazed at fixedly by a peer of the opposite sex than by one of their own sex. Students of both sexes find the silent stares of older people are the least comfortable. Generally, people seem to prefer a moderate amount of visual contact when they are interacting face to face with another person to no visual contact at all or to a continuous gaze.

Other investigations of the eye contact have indicated that we gaze directly more often at those praising us than at those criticizing us (Ellsworth & Carlsmith, 1968), and more often at those who are familiar and friendly than at strangers (Efran & Broughton, 1966). Direct eye contact increases with attraction (Mehrabian, 1969), and the stronger the feelings of love between two people, the more the eyes will meet (Rubin, 1970). Remember the lines from an old song: "Don't sigh and gaze at me . . . people will say we're in love." The one who feels more powerful in an interaction with another will gaze at the less powerful person *less* frequently. But a monkey will use direct visual engagements to express dominance or to challenge it in another monkey. Perhaps human beings reduce direct visual contact, particularly during silence, in order to avoid disrupting struggles for dominance (Exline, 1972). In summary, direct eye contact seems to be a very significant factor in a variety of interactions between people.

Personal Space

Everyone has a sense of **personal space,** a surrounding area with invisible boundaries into which others cannot intrude without producing some aversive effect on our feelings and actions (Sommer, 1969). This personal space is perhaps a form of human **territoriality,** an urge to maintain a given amount of space for oneself, or keep a certain **individual distance** from others (Hall, 1966). Personal space is not symmetrical, for people can tolerate strangers closer to them at either side than in front of them. The size of personal space varies from culture to culture. If the space is invaded, people react by moving, by disapproving looks, by expressing some protest, or simply by withdrawing rapidly within themselves the way many do in crowded elevators and subways. Did you observe these or similar reactions when you broke the unwritten rules and sat close to another person in the activity "Personal Space and Spatial Invasion"? In large crowds, however, when people cannot avoid being packed together, concepts of personal space are temporarily suspended. Why do you find it easy to tolerate the crushing closeness of an unfamiliar person in a crowded bus, but become uncomfortable when a stranger sits next to you in a sparsely filled theater? Do you think it may have something to do with the probability that the other person may try to interact with you? The same behavior in different contexts often receives very different interpretations.

Many experiments have probed the dimensions of personal space and individual distance and the factors affecting them. Thus it has been found that extroverts tolerate a closer conversational distance than introverts. Students in an experiment who had been led to expect praise sat closer to the experimenter's chair than those who were expecting neither praise nor criticism. Those who expected criticism sat farthest away. Subjects asked to "stand as close as comfortable to see well"

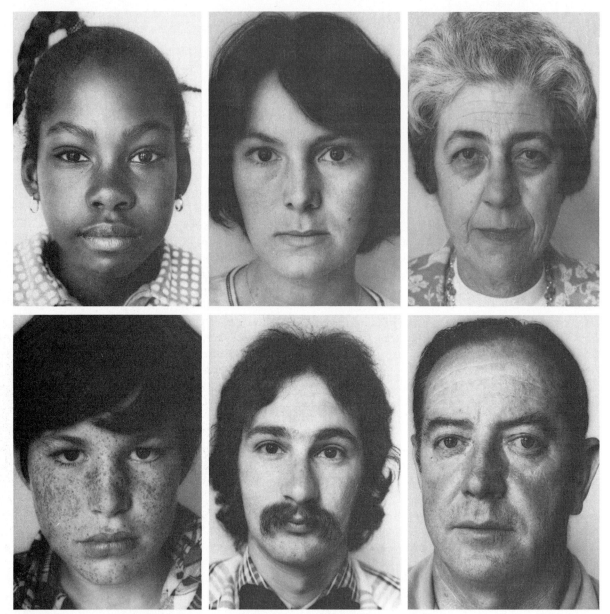

Figure 17-1 Stare for some time directly into the eyes of one of the youngsters (left), then of a person about your own age (center), and of an older person (right). Which is easiest, or least disconcerting, for you to trade stares with? How can you explain your judgments?

even approached closer to a *photograph* of a person with the eyes closed than to one with open eyes (Argyle & Dean, 1965). When an experimenter joined a student sitting on an outdoor bench, the student tended to shift po-

sition on the bench more frequently than students alone on other benches and tended to leave the bench earlier. Another experimenter sat on a chair at a table occupied by women students in a study hall (see Figure 17-2). She

Figure 17-2 What indications of individual distances do you find in this photograph of students in a library reading room?

found that the quickest departures of the students occurred when she sat down in the chair next to them and moved it closer (Sommer, 1969). Protests over invasions of space are not usually expressed verbally, for personal space is treated rather like our own sexual feelings—we acknowledge them and try to cope with them, but we usually don't talk about them.

People who are perceived as objects or "nonpersons" can break the unwritten space rules and enter our personal space with impunity. Waiters can clear off our table and janitors can sweep a room without making us feel our private space has been "invaded" or even interrupting our conversations. Personal space and individual distance have been found to affect interactions between people in many different ways.

The activities you were encouraged to carry out and the investigations reported on direct visual contact and personal space are one part of that division of psychology known as social psychology. **Social psychology** studies the interactions between individuals or groups as they influence individual or group behavior. Distinctively psychological concepts are used: perception, motivation, learning. You have already read about person perception (Chapter 5), for example, about prejudices (Chapter 11),

and about needs for achievement, affiliation, and power (Chapter 12), in which people's behavior is influenced by that of others. Conformity and nonconformity, dominance and submission, high and low morale, and attitudes are all concepts involved in the interactions of individuals and groups. The social psychologist tries to relate these constructs to the behavior of individuals rather than to the behavior of organizations, social classes, institutions, communities, customs, status, or kinship relations, as sociologists and anthropologists are interested in doing.

GROUP EFFECTS ON INDIVIDUAL BEHAVIOR

In its broadest sense, a **group,** whether of persons, coins, or anything else, is a collection of things that have some common characteristic. Thus you may see a group of books on a shelf, a flock of ducks flying overhead, or a group of people talking in a room. If the thing or persons simply chance to be together in space and time, they are known collectively as an **aggregate group.** The members of a **functional group,** on the other hand, act together to fulfill some common interest, purpose, or goal, often with organized roles or differentiated patterns of behavior. A group of students

Figure 17-3 An aggregate of people doing a variety of different things. Still, what indications do you see of people functioning together in groups?

Figure 17-4 A small class of students with an instructor in a seminar—a functional group.

waiting for the doors of a library to open, for example, is an aggregate group; although they have the same interest in getting into the library, they are not acting in concert (see Figure 17-3). Nor do the individuals have status or role relations to each other. A group of students in a class is a functional group; they have deliberately chosen to come together for a common goal, and they interact with the instructor and among themselves according to established roles and behavioral norms (see Figure 17-4). Groups may consist of two or more individuals. **Dyadic groups,** or **dyads,** consist of two people, like man and wife, mother and child, physician and patient, or lovers, and have their own characteristics (see Figure 17-5). Whatever their number, social psychologists usually study functional groups, although the behavior of aggregate groups may also be investigated, as in studies of invasion of personal space and of crowds gathered by chance.

Figure 17-5 A dyadic group.

Social Facilitation

Does it seem strange to you that social psychology was the last branch of psychology to develop experimentally? Science appears to have advanced in this manner historically from the least human, like astronomy and physics, to the most human, like psychology, sociology, and anthropology. Perhaps human cultural, moral, and religious traditions are so strong and thoroughly ingrained that we feel we already know all the answers, or hesitate to do experiments whose conclusions might run counter to such traditions. Whatever the reasons, social psychology developed relatively recently. Some of the earliest experimental studies dealt with the effects of groups on the efficiency of their members. Do you think you usually work better alone or in a group? In the first experimental social study by psychologists, for example, it was found that subjects competing with each other in pairs were able to

wind turns of line on a fishing reel more rapidly than subjects doing the winding alone (Triplett, 1897). The improvement of individual behavior in groups came to be known as **social facilitation** (Allport, 1924), although it was soon found that groups can also prove detrimental to the behavior of their individual members.

Audience Effects

Probably you have often wondered about the **audience effects** of people who are simply watching the behavior of another person; in fact, you may have had problems performing before an audience. The results of experiments on the effects of audiences on individual performances have seemed contradictory. In some experiments, subjects performing *simple activities,* like multiplying numbers or observing the flashing of lights with a passively watching audience or an occasionally visiting supervisor, performed better than subjects working alone (Dashiell, 1930). However, other experiments in which subjects had to learn *new material,* such as lists of words, showed better results and fewer errors when the subjects worked alone than when they worked in the presence of even passive spectators. In general, an audience of passive watchers seems to impair the learning of new tasks and to enhance the performance of habitual or already learned tasks (Zajonc, 1965). In your first attempts at public speaking, for example, you may stumble miserably because you are unaccustomed to the audience, even though your speech went beautifully when you rehearsed it alone. Then after more experience you may find that the audience stimulates your performance tremendously. Actors, musicians, and other public performers often say that they are "inspired" by their audiences, although singers, for example, may still falter in "putting over" a song if the audience response is poor (see Figure 17-6).

In problem solving, you have seen how a dominant but incorrect response tendency can retard a solution that requires the emergence of different, novel responses (see Chapter 11). An explanation of the effects of an audience on the efficiency of individual behavior has been proposed in terms of a similar competition between appropriate behavior (the thing you want to do well) and interfering responses (Zajonc, 1965). The presence of spectators tends to arouse individuals, increasing their alertness and nervousness to the extreme of stage fright. Even if they can only imagine their audiences, radio and TV performers get mike fright. With such general and often intense arousal, the dominant response tends to be made, whether it is an error or not. Inexperienced speakers are impelled to say something, for example, whether it is appropriate or not. Consequently, in the learning of tasks or performing of activities that are not already well learned, the efficiency of behavior decreases if an audience is present; but the performance of well-learned, highly practiced behaviors and skills improves

Figure 17-6 Audience behavior often affects the behavior of the performer. An approving, enthusiastic audience may enhance performance (top), while a bored, disapproving audience may disrupt it (bottom).

when they are performed before an audience.

What is it about an audience that accounts for its effects on an individual's behavior? In an experiment designed to answer this question, Nickolas Cottrell (1968) provided his subjects with various audience conditions: (1) blindfolded strangers sitting in the darkened experimental room while they were supposedly being dark-adapted for another experiment, (2) others who were supposedly waiting for another experiment but wanted to observe the ongoing experiment, and (3) no audience of any kind. The subjects had been thoroughly trained to pronounce certain nonsense words (dominant responses) but had received little training on others. In the experiment, they were asked to pronounce both types of words without help as each was flashed on a screen. Those subjects who had an audience of blindfolded strangers performed almost exactly as well on both types of words as those who performed alone, while the subjects with an audience of observers pronounced the less well-practiced words much more poorly than the words they had practiced well. Cottrell concluded that the mere presence of others is not as important as the presence of others who are specifically observing one's efforts and who may be judging how well one is doing. Enhancement of well-learned behavior apparently requires the presence of an audience that watches and presumably evaluates us.

Coaction Effects

Coaction effects appear when people are acting in a group on the same task, whether each is doing the task individually or all of them are doing the task together. For example, a group of people may individually be addressing, stuffing, sealing, and stamping envelopes for a mailing, or they may be working at the task collectively, with two people addressing, one stuffing, and others sealing and stamping the envelopes in a division of labor. In an early experiment on coaction effects, F. H. Allport (1920) gave many subjects a series of tests. On one trial, the subjects took the tests alone in cubicles. On another trial they took the tests around a table, but were instructed not to compare the results of their tests with each other. In one test, subjects were required simply to cancel all vowels they found in reading through newspaper articles. In another test they listed the associations that occurred to them, starting with a word, writing a second word that they associated with the first, then writing a third word associated with the second, and so on. In other tests, subjects multiplied numbers, tried to determine what was wrong with a series of false syllogism problems, or had to judge the relative weights of

several objects or the pleasantness of several odors. In all but the problem-solving and judgment tests, subjects performed better working in groups around the table than working alone. Although they did not give each other their results, in the routine, well-practiced types of tests the presence of others probably aroused them more, made them more alert, and exposed them to the example of others working diligently at the task. The problem-solving and judgmental tasks presented new situations, however, or required new solutions, for which the presence of others might too quickly trigger dominant but wrong responses. These tasks could be done more efficiently when the subjects were alone. Other experiments have shown similar kinds of coaction effects. When the individuals in a group can see or hear each other at work on an easy, familiar, or well-learned task, they tend to perform more efficiently.

Conformity Affects Perception

Suppose you are with three or four of your friends deciding what to do of an evening. One friend suggests going to see a popular movie that is showing for the first time in the vicinity. You suggest spending the evening at a nearby lake with some refreshments. Another friend seconds the movie motion, and after you argue a bit a third goes for the movie too. You decide to go along with them, but a fourth friend pulls out—she can think of better things to do. Leaving her, the rest of you go off to the movie. This situation illustrates a process of **group evaluation and decision** that you frequently experience. The members of the group influence each other's behavior, as your own is often influenced, even against your wishes or perhaps even your better judgment. What is the nature of the pressure to conform to the group, as you did, or to stand out independently, as the fourth friend did? And how strong are conformity pressures as opposed to individual desires or judgments?

A LIGHT THAT SEEMS TO MOVE

■ In this activity you take advantage of an illusion to test group conformity pressure on perception. The illusion is known as the **autokinetic effect,** in which a stationary pinpoint of light shown to a person in a darkened room appears to move over a period of a minute or so. Although the exact cause of this illusion is not entirely understood, it is probably due to minor eye movements of the subject (Matin and MacKinnon, 1964). Since this is an activity in social psychology, you need two or three subjects who are not familiar with this illusion. You can make a pinpoint of light by cutting a piece of cardboard to fit the head of a flashlight, making a small pinhole in the center of the cardboard, and taping it over the flashlight head. Make a room as dark as possible, preferably at night, unless you can completely cover window and door with blankets. Light leaking under a single door can destroy the effect. Then you are ready for your subjects.

Have one subject sit at one end of the room while the others wait outside. You stand at the other end yourself, telling the subject to watch a small light that will come on for a minute. Switch on the flashlight, which you have already placed on a desk or chest so it will be stationary. Keep it on for about a minute, switch it off, and ask your subject how far the light moved. Repeat this procedure several times. You will find that the subject's first judgments of distance moved may vary a good deal. They will then settle down close to a self-established norm, like five inches.

Then bring in two or more other subjects and have all of them, including your first subject, judge the distance the light moves, announcing their judgments out loud. Note the judgments on a pad each time, as you repeat the process a number of times. Again the group judgments may vary widely at first, then settle down to a group norm. Now have your first subject stay and let the others leave. Repeat the procedure a number of times again. What are your first subject's judgments like this time, compared with this subject's original individual judgments? How do they compare with the group's judgments?

When the autokinetic experiment described in "A Light That Seems to Move" was done with many subjects (Sherif, 1936), all of them quickly established their own individual characteristic response norms about the number of inches the object appeared to move, whatever the direction. This standard was each subject's **individual norm.** Members of a group soon established a **group norm** in the same manner, their judgments beginning to cluster around a given distance of perceived movement. When members from the group were tested individually later, they did not return to their old individual standard nor establish new ones, but held close to the group norm. Group norms thus proved stronger than their own. They tended to perceive an event in accordance with the perceptions of people no longer present, although most of them were not conscious of the group pressures. Our perceptions of things can thus be affected by groups in many ways.

The effects of majority perceptual judgments on judgments made by an individual were explored further in a series of experiments in which college students were asked to select the one line of three on a card that was equal in length to a line on another card (Asch, 1955). Of the seven subjects, six were confederates of the experimenter. The seventh was a "naive" or real subject and made his own judgments. After a couple of trials in which all the participants picked the correct equivalent line, the confederates began to select incorrect lines, as the experimenter had preinstructed them to do. This created a majority opinion opposed to that of the lone uninformed subject. The naive subject quickly became nervous and hesitant, and ended up making judgments that agreed with the obviously incorrect responses of the majority 37 per cent of the time.

About a quarter of the naive subjects remained independent in their judgments, never accepting the majority's incorrect judgments. On the other hand, many of those naive subjects who conformed to the majority did so nearly all the time, even when the difference between the lines judged equivalent was as much as seven inches. Having one other subject who at least agreed with their correct judgments a part of the time helped some naive subjects maintain their correct though minority judgments. Although many intelligent, capable naive subjects were strongly influenced by the incorrect majority judgments, nearly all subjects, confederates and naive subjects alike, later agreed that in general, independence of judgment was a trait to be preferred to conformity.

Undoubtedly most persons have a strong tendency to conform to the ideas, judgments, and standards of the groups to which they belong. Often they trust group judgments or norms more than their own, even when these conflict with their own perceptions. People also are accustomed to learning by imitating others. Conformity to the behavior of others usually earns the approval of others, while nonconformity often exposes us to expressions of disapproval. These tendencies to think, act, and feel like the group to which one belongs have thus been positively reinforced many times, and strongly affect the perceptual and cognitive behavior of individual members of the group. The principles of instrumental conditioning described in Chapter 7 help to explain the development and maintenance of conformity behavior. Now, can you see how they might be applied to train individuals to *resist* group pressures?

Conformity Produces Obedience

Many social groups depend on the obedience of subordinates to superiors for their effective functioning. You have only to think of an army, a business, a school, a church, or a family to see how much obedience to authority is required in the groups that account for nearly all of our social institutions. Even political mavericks and other opponents of the establishment quickly form establishments of their own. Soldiers, employees, pupils, church members, and children are all expected to conform, in the main, to the norms of those in authority, abide by their decisions, and follow their orders. This thoroughly ingrained **obedience** can serve many useful functions in

groups, but it can also lead to devastating results in many spheres of group activity.

In a series of experiments early in the 1960s, Stanley Milgram investigated the extent to which obedience to authority would lead subjects to conform to orders, even though they thought that their actions were causing another person extreme pain (Milgram, 1963, 1965). Milgram's subjects were told that they were to teach word associations to "learners" (who were confederates of the experimenter). The learners sat in an adjoining room with electrodes on their arms. The wall between the rooms was provided with windows through which the teacher-subjects could observe them. The teacher was instructed to give the learners shocks of increasing strengths when the learners made errors, by pushing buttons marked for increasing voltages. Although the confederate-learners actually received no shocks, they pretended to react with greater protests as the shocks increased. But the experimenter encouraged the teachers to continue, insisting that they administer shocks at the highest voltage settings as the learners continued to make errors. Despite signs that the learners were in great pain and might even have collapsed, two-thirds of the teachers administered shock at the highest voltages marked on the panel. Undoubtedly many of them would have stopped on their own, but the authoritative experimenter overrode their objections and they obeyed him. Milgram varied the physical, auditory, and visual distances between teacher-subjects and learners in some experiments and found that obedience increased with greater distances (with learners secluded in another room), but decreased when teachers and learners were actually close to each other. Still, one-third of the teachers faithfully followed orders to the limit, some even to the point of holding the learner's hand against a metal plate through which the electricity was presumably being conducted.

Treatment of subjects in such a deceptive and stressful manner has been sharply restricted under ethical standards developed by the American Psychological Association (1973). These standards require openness and honesty in the relationship between investigators and subjects, who should be protected from all forms of mental stress and free to discontinue participation in an experiment whenever they wish.

Eliciting such obedient reactions from normal, average subjects helps us to understand how some authorities have successfully directed people to behave brutally toward each other. Torture, massacre, and genocide take place because people are "only following orders." Milgram's results have been confirmed in experiments by others; in fact, one experiment with subjects instructed to assume the roles of guards and prisoners had to be stopped, as the "guards" showed signs of getting out of control in their treatment of the "prisoners" (Zimbardo, 1972). Carried to such extremes, even though unwillingly, human beings' obedience to authority offers a sad commentary on our usual idealistic views of human nature and presents many problems to be solved: How can obedience to authority be made more selective and judicious? How can we train people to refuse to obey when the effects of obedience become obviously destructive and immoral? Are certain personality types, like authoritarian or conforming personalities, distinguishable from others, so that dangerous extremes can be identified and treated before they create catastrophes? Would groups organized on a democratic basis, rather than under authoritarian leadership, be more likely to avoid the dangers of excessive conformity? Or must situations productive of authoritarianism be avoided, if most people cannot resist the commands of their leaders, whatever the consequences?

THE EFFECTS OF ATTITUDES

Some of the ways in which other persons affect the individual have been discussed. But this doesn't even begin to describe the complexity of interactions between people, for each of us has hundreds of attitudes that develop from our interactions with single individuals and with groups of people. The identification, measurement, and study of these attitudes are the core activities of social psychologists. They are also the most difficult. You may have seen the old movie in which Fred Astaire sings, "Did you ever see a dream walking?" He goes on, "Well, I did!" But no one has yet seen an attitude walking or talking, or been able to put a finger on one or examine it through a microscope. Since attitudes are complex constructs arising in our experiences, they are difficult to pin down. Perhaps the best way to see what attitudes are like is to look into a couple of your own.

TWO EXTREME ATTITUDES

■ Select a person whom you like very much, or love, and another person whom you dislike very much, or even hate. We have attitudes toward those we love and hate, like and dislike, approve and disapprove. In your behavioral interactions with these persons you will tend to express the intense attitudes that you have toward them. Consider your attitudes toward these persons and write out your answers to the following questions about each of them:

- What *feelings* or *emotions* do you have about the person you love and the person you hate, particularly when you are with them?
- What *motivations*—that is, desires, needs, drives, or expectations—do you have in regard to these persons?
- What *thoughts*, opinions, or beliefs do you have about these persons?
- What *values* do you find are created or fulfilled in your interactions and relationships with these persons?
- How do you usually *behave* when you are with these persons, including your facial expressions and your verbal behavior?

Compare what you have written about the person you like and the person you dislike. All of these things you have observed about your relations with them express your attitudes toward them. Is it any wonder that attitudes are difficult to define and study? Our attitudes apply not simply to individuals, but also to groups, toward all of whose members we react in much the same way.

The Nature of Attitudes

Attitudes are fairly permanent dispositions or tendencies involving emotions, motives, thoughts or beliefs, judgments, and behavior in our reactions toward ourselves, other individuals and groups, things, and events. Thus you undoubtedly have specific attitudes toward your father and mother, other relatives, friends and strangers, many kinds of groups in which you function, your home, your possessions, your various activities at work and play, and your ideas and feelings. One may also have attitudes toward nonliving and even fictional people—a deceased grandparent, Adolf Hitler, Santa Claus.

Like the construct of personality that summarizes a number of traits (see Chapter 14), the attitude construct is made up of several components: certain feelings, beliefs, and tendencies to act with respect to the object of our attitudes. Attitudes always involve some feelings, some emotional reaching toward or against a person, group, activity, or situation, the target of our attitudes. The feelings may be positive or negative, happy or sad, pleasant or angry, but some emotional component is usually involved and it is directed toward some target. If you sometimes merely feel sad without directing the sadness toward a target, you are feeling an emotion but not an attitude.

Attitudes also involve some **beliefs,** or ideas that are accepted, about the target. Our attitudes about legalizing marijuana include some beliefs concerning the effects of pot smoking on health, or on the likelihood that it will stimulate increased consumption of marijuana or narcotic drugs. Needless to say, the factual validity of such beliefs need not be firmly es-

tablished for the belief to be strong and an important component of an attitude.

When not one but several beliefs provide the basis for a given attitude, we speak of a **belief system.** Belief systems may vary from an unorganized group of isolated beliefs to a coherent, well-integrated collection of beliefs, each of which has been verified by reference to factual information. A fruitful analysis of one's own attitudes should include an attempt to identify each component of the belief system on which the attitude is based, to see whether the individual beliefs are consistent with each other or are contradictory, and to determine what evidence exists in favor of or against each belief. Obviously, such an analysis can be a chore and hardly worthwhile in the case of trivial attitudes (for example, attitudes toward holding a dinner fork with the right or left hand). But careful analysis of our belief structures may indeed become mandatory when we deal with more serious attitudes (for example, attitudes toward the busing of children to remote schools for the purpose of desegregation).

The third component of an attitude, an **action tendency,** merely indicates that feelings and beliefs usually express themselves in some form of behavior toward the target. Thus a person with powerful negative emotions against busing, as well as strongly held beliefs that busing is bad for children, would be more likely to join an antibusing demonstration than would a person with contrary beliefs and emotions. Young men who believed that American participation in the Vietnam war was not justifiable and who believed they would be forced into combat fled the United States by the thousands in the 1960s and early 1970s. Feelings and beliefs, together with behavior toward the target, are the components of every attitude.

The Measurement of Attitudes

Since attitudes are such complex affairs, you may wonder how they could possibly be measured. Yet surely attitudes do range widely in direction, favorable or unfavorable, positive or negative, and in intensity or strength, as you can see if you review the kinds of food that you like and dislike, for example. Some foods you like very much, some are only slightly appetizing to you, others you feel neutral about, still others you avoid if you can, and certain foods you would not touch unless you were starving to death. You know your own opinions about many kinds of food, and these opinions express your attitudes toward them. It should then be possible to measure the direction and intensity of your attitudes toward foods, the women's liberation movement, communism, or anything else by asking you to express your feelings or beliefs about them, as well as to indicate your actual or potential behavior toward them.

Rating scales have been used, then, to measure the direction and intensity of people's attitudes. These rating scales are similar to those used to measure personality traits (see Chapter 14). **Attitude scales** are developed by first gathering a large number of statements about the subject of the attitude to be rated. The *Thurstone attitude scale,* one of the earliest, was made up by having 100 or more judges sort statements about a subject into piles, ranging from most positive (scored 1) to most negative (scored 11) attitudes on the subject (Thurstone & Chave, 1929). Those statements rated in the same way by most of the judges were then selected to make up the rating scale and assigned the scores given them by the judges. Thus, in a scale rating attitudes toward capital punishment, the statement ''Capital punishment should be abolished at once'' might be scored 11 and the statement ''Capital punishment should be extended to all kidnappers'' might be scored 1. After such a scale has been constructed, an individual whose attitude is being measured simply checks agreement or disagreement with each statement, and the attitude rating is the average score (1 to 11) of the statements with which the subject agrees. When attitude rating scales are administered to a representative sample of a group of peo-

ple, like police officers, doctors, or college students, the general or prevalent attitudes of the group can be determined.

The *Likert scale* is another type of scale widely used to rate attitudes. The Likert scale is constructed by having many judges rate various statements on a subject according to the intensity of their approval or disapproval of the statements, ranging from strong to moderate approval, to undecided, to moderate, to strong disapproval (Likert, 1932). A statement that usually evokes strong approval might then be scored 1 while a statement that evokes strong disapproval might be scored 5. A whole series of statements rated by the judges over a wide range of approval to disapproval are then selected for the rating scale in order to cover the range of individual differences in attitudes. Individuals whose attitudes are being rated then indicate the intensity of their agreement or disagreement with each of the various statements, and their average scores on all the statements become the measures of their attitudes on the subject.

Still another way of measuring attitudes is the *Osgood semantic-differential technique* (Osgood, Suci, & Tannenbaum, 1957), described in Chapter 11. The scale consists of a series of bipolar adjective pairs, each pair arranged on a 7-point scale. People whose attitudes are being measured rate the target concept (for example, love, Catholicism) for each of the adjective pairs, thereby expressing their attitudes toward the subject. A scale for rating attitudes on corporal punishment, for example, might include such bipolar adjectives as ''kind–cruel,'' ''passive–active,'' ''soft–hard,'' ''bad–good,'' and so on. Rating corporal punishment on many such dimensions in this way should tend to reveal what it means emotionally to individuals, or how they evaluate it.

Attitudes Toward the Sexes

The semantic-differential technique was used in a recent study to explore the attitudes that 140 black and white students of both sexes in an eastern university held toward their own and the other sex (Turner & Turner, 1974). The subjects were asked to rate on the semantic-differential scale the statements "Most men are . . ." and "Most women are . . ." in terms of the bipolar adjectives quick–slow, happy–sad, useful–useless, healthy–sick, changing–unchanging, calm–excited, good–bad, giving–taking, strong–weak, warm–cold, smart–dumb, and active–passive. The first adjective of each pair is at the positive end of the dimension, the second adjective at the negative end. The students also rated their concepts of men and women in terms of the adjective pairs responsible–irresponsible, trustworthy–untrustworthy, and reliable–unreliable.

Although the group of subjects in this study was drawn more from the lower than middle or upper socioeconomic levels, making it difficult to apply the results to all social levels, some challenging results emerged from the study. The subjects could be divided into four sex-race groups: black females, black males, white females, and white males. All four of these groups evaluated men at least slightly more positively than women. Perhaps this is not surprising in a culture that seems to exalt masculinity so much over femininity. White females evaluated men considerably more positively than any other group. The investigators noted that white women are socialized for the "feminine" functions of "stroking" men, or offering them emotional favor and support. This helps to explain why advances toward sexual equality are so slow and difficult in our society.

On the specific trait of reliability, the black women evaluated men as considerably less reliable than did the other groups, and were the only group to find men less reliable than women. Strangely enough, white women evaluated men as more reliable than did the men themselves. The investigators suggested that black women have a lack of trust in men, which may have a negative effect on the relationships between the sexes. However, the belief that men can't be counted on could also make black

women more self-reliant, which in turn might result in the more equalitarian position that black women hold in the black family than white women hold in theirs. Perhaps, the researchers suggested, the attitudes of blacks may stimulate more equal relations between the sexes, so interactions between black liberation and women's liberation movements might be productive. They pointed out, however, that this was just a pilot study and that more research must be done before their findings on a small group of college students of lower socioeconomic levels can be generalized reliably.

YOUR OWN SEX ATTITUDES

■ If you are interested in your own attitudes toward the sexes, you can rate men on the seven-point scale shown in Figure 17-7 using Turner & Turner's pairs of adjectives. Then rate women in terms of the same adjectives. Finally, average your numerical scores on the ratings for men and for women. Also average your reliable–unreliable ratings for the two sexes. A low average score is on the positive side, a high score on the negative side.

Attitudes and Behavior

Another way to measure attitudes, other than verbally expressed opinions and beliefs, is in terms of *actual behavior*. You know all too well how you may think and say one thing and then do another. You may resolve, "I'll get an hour of physical exercise every day," and find after the first few days that many other

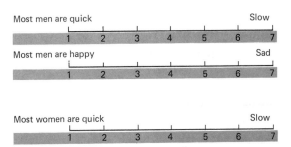

Figure 17-7 Semantic-differential polar pairs of adjectives for rating attitudes toward men and women.

demands take precedence. This difference between verbal and other behavior was well brought out in a study of prejudice displayed toward a Chinese couple that stopped at many motels, hotels, and restaurants while traveling with a white couple on the Pacific Coast, where prejudice against Orientals has been strong in the past (La Piere, 1934). In staying overnight in 66 accommodations and eating in 184 restaurants, the Chinese couple was refused service only once. Yet when those same places were later sent questionnaires asking, "Will you accept members of the Chinese race as guests in your establishment?" 92 per cent of those who responded indicated that they would not, and the remainder checked "Uncertain, depends upon circumstances." Their attitudinal beliefs, expressed in their verbal responses, varied widely from their actual practices, which may have been influenced by the character of the Chinese couple, the white couple accompanying them, and other factors.

As indicated previously, prejudices are emotionalized, irrational, or unfounded attitudes of a persistent nature. Yet prejudices can be distinguished from **discrimination,** which is differential behavior for or against a group, or any members of that group, on grounds reasonably irrelevant to the situation. You may remember the concept of stimulus discrimination, discussed in Chapter 7, which showed how the organism can be trained to overlook similarities and to respond differently to closely related stimuli. And a prejudice does not lead inevitably to discriminatory behavior. Unbigoted people, for example, may be described as unprejudiced nondiscriminators — they feel no inner tensions or hostility about a minority and are likely to protest to others when they see them discriminating against members of a minority group. Hard-core bigots, on the other hand, are prejudiced discriminators — injurious behavior toward the members of a minority group accompanies their prejudiced attitudes, although they may pay lip service to freedom and the

equality of all people. Between these two extremes we find unprejudiced discriminators, who feel they must conform with their peers or their neighbors in rejecting minority members although they actually have no prejudicial attitudes toward them. And then there are the timid bigots, who are prejudiced nondiscriminators, expressing strong attitudinal prejudices yet not carrying these into action, since others often look askance at discriminatory behavior these days or step in to argue against it. There is, then, no necessary link between prejudice and discrimination, although they often accompany each other. The more intense the attitudes, the more likely they are to find expression in overt behavior.

This relationship between attitudes and actual behavior, as opposed to the verbal expression of attitudes, has been used to measure attitude intensity. Subjects are first given an attitude rating scale to fill out and then, to see how strong their attitudes may actually be, they are asked whether they would act in various ways in manifesting their attitudes (De Fleur & Westie, 1958). Thus, if their attitudes toward blacks (or whites) are being investigated, they may be asked to sign a release form indicating willingness to be photographed with a black (or white) person of the opposite sex. Then they are asked if they will permit such a photograph to be used in a national publicity campaign against this prejudice, whether they will appear on a radio or TV show to argue against it, and whether they will march in protest of discrimination. Or their behavior may be directly observed as they are placed in various situations that encourage behavioral expression of prejudice or lack of prejudice. Still, actions cannot be the sole measure of attitudes, for as the various types of discriminators show, factors other than attitudes may affect the actions that are taken. Furthermore, you have already seen how attitudes are a composite of feelings and beliefs as well as actions. A more complete understanding of a person's attitudes, then, requires getting some measure of emotional and belief systems, usually by using some sort of objective or projective test, as well as some sample of behavior in everyday life.

The Formation of Attitudes

Think of a few of your own attitudes for a moment. You undoubtedly have strong attitudes toward a great many individuals and groups, such as your mother and father, brother or sister, the mentally retarded and the aged, and teachers, dentists, and policemen, to name just a few. When you examine them, how do you find that these attitudes originated and were shaped?

The formation and development of attitudes have been investigated in many studies, and these have indicated that most of them are products of social learning. Do biological factors play any role at all in the formation of attitudes? In Chapter 2 you saw how acceptance or rejection of certain odors may well be innate, manifested in the first postnatal hours. These reactions may be a part of our survival equipment, to help us accept foods likely to be nourishing and reject substances that could be injurious. Whether other genetic factors may play roles in the formation of human attitudes remains to be established, but certainly our physiological drives and other physiological conditions do affect our attitudes. Hormones and a variety of psychopharmacological agents, like alcohol and marijuana, also affect attitudes, at least temporarily. Beyond these, very enjoyable or exciting as well as disastrous or traumatic personal experiences can also initiate or change attitudes suddenly and sharply. Undoubtedly you can muster plenty of evidence of such effects on your own attitudes.

Far more significant than individual factors in the formation of attitudes, however, are the groups and institutions within which individuals become socialized as they grow. The process of socialization begins in infancy in the mother-child relationship. It soon includes the father and other members of the infant's family. When parents are affectionate toward their children and attentive to their needs, children are more likely to use parental attitudes as models (Mussen & Parker, 1965). Soon infants begin to display the same or similar attitudes toward everything in their environments.

To select a very general and key attitude that everyone develops early in childhood, consider the studies of self-esteem in boys 10 to 12 years of age made by a number of social psychologists (Coopersmith, 1968). **Self-esteem** and its contrary, **self-derogation,** are the attitudes of favor and scorn that people take toward themselves. These may be expressed in the beliefs they hold about themselves and the extent to which they have or lack trust in themselves. Self-attitudes can be manifested in almost everything people do and in their interactions with others. Teachers' descriptions of the boys' reactions to failures and criticism and their self-assurance or timidity, as well as Rorschach and TAT tests and the boys' own judgments of their self-esteem, were used to separate the boys into high, medium, and low self-esteem groups. Then they were placed in a variety of typical situations, such as playing together, having discussions, throwing beanbags into boxes, and making drawings of people, to see how their levels of self-esteem might affect their behavior.

The studies showed that the boys with high self-esteem were much less destructive than those with medium or low self-esteem, and less frequently had feelings of anxiety or distress. They also had fewer psychosomatic symptoms than the other groups. High self-esteem boys participated the most in social groups, and argued for their own opinions; the other groups of boys tended to withdraw from arguments. Furthermore, those with high self-esteem were concerned with public affairs; those with low self-esteem wished to avoid involvement with other people. Those with high self-esteem also displayed higher goals and were more successful in fulfilling their aspirations. They reacted less extremely to the criticisms of others than did lower self-esteem groups. Studies of the parents of the high-esteem boys revealed that they set clear standards of high performance for their boys, gave them definite challenges rather than being fully permissive, and encouraged independence and self-reliance as the boys began to explore the world around them. Doesn't this remind you of the research that showed that mothers of boys with a high need to achieve tend to give their sons independence training at an early age (see Chapter 12)?

Coopersmith concluded, "From our studies of a sample of preadolescent boys in a typical American environment we have become convinced that learning at an early age to respond constructively to challenges and troublesome conditions is essential to becoming a self-respecting individual." Once attitudes of self-esteem or self-derogation have been formed, they tend to influence many other attitudes, as well as behavior within groups.

As children venture beyond their families, they play with other children and associate with them in school and other institutions. Although their families have set their basic attitudes, peer conformity is very strong in childhood and adolescence, as well as striving to be like one's heroes or heroines, real or imagined, whose every act and attitude serve as models to be copied. Youngsters follow social norms or standards of behavior in the groups of which they are members. These norms serve as patterns of excellence or of appropriate attitudes for them. Certain styles of clothing and adornment and ways of talking become the objects of enthusiastic or derogatory attitudes for children, just as they do later for adults. People are open to, and tend to adopt, the attitudes of those social groups with which they are closely associated, whatever the functions of the groups may be. We are likely to associate, in the first place, with groups that have attitudes similar to our own. Then, as we become integrated into the group, we accept more of its attitudes, and become more susceptible to the group pressure to conform. If group pressure does not succeed in shaping our behavior, we are likely to find ourselves on the outside looking in. Favored **in-groups,** composed of similar members, often of the same socioeconomic status, are opposed to scorned **out-groups,** those with differing socioeconomic status, attitudes, customs, and activities. Group members who often act together have very similar experiences, and these also serve to strengthen the similarity of their attitudes. They tend to pat each other on the back, and form mutual admiration societies.

THE GROUPNESS ATTITUDE

What appears to be a very basic social "groupness" attitude was explored in a series of experiments with 64 British schoolboys, 14 and 15 years of age (Tajfel, 1970). The boys were brought into a lecture room and told they would be tested for visual judgment. They were separated into groups of eight, ostensibly matched on the basis of their scores on the visual judgment test, but in fact assigned quite randomly. Then they were individually given a series of sheets to mark in separate cubicles indicating how they would determine the distribution of rewards and penalties in the form of small amounts of money, giving it to or taking it away from others. None of the money could be assigned to themselves. The other boys' names were coded on the sheets, so friendliness or hostility toward specific individuals could not play a part in their decisions. On different sheets, the boys were asked to distribute money (1) to members identified as belonging to their own group (the in-group), (2) to members belonging to another group (the out-group), and (3) to members of both groups.

When asked to distribute the money solely to (1) other members of their in-group or to (2) members of an out-group, the boys tended to be extremely fair in the judgments. But when asked to distribute the money (3) between members of both in- and out-groups, they always gave more money (as much as they could) to members of their own group than to members of the out-group. Although they could have distributed the money fairly on a maximum joint-profit basis for the whole group of 64 boys, they chose instead to be unfair, or to discriminate against the out-groups, even though they did not know who the members of these groups were.

Tajfel pointed out that these experiments isolated a **groupness attitude,** or a tendency to favor the in-group, even though the boys had no basis for any hostility toward or conflict of interest with the out-group, nor for friendliness toward the in-group. He suggested that, as children become socialized, they must learn powerful social motives to behave fairly toward members of their in-groups and to discriminate against members of out-groups, simply because they see these attitudes expressed time and again in all kinds of group situations and activities. Groupness and fairness attitudes lead people to "play favorites" in such a way as to reward their in-groups and penalize out-groups, irrespective of other motives, just as the boys did. Tajfel concluded, "Socialization into 'groupness' is powerful and unavoidable; it has innumerable valuable functions. It also has some odd side effects that may—and do—reinforce acute intergroup tensions whose roots lie elsewhere." Could constant reinforcement of behavior that expresses such a groupness attitude be a strong factor in the development of prejudices and discrimination?

Prejudices and Stereotypes

Prejudices have been defined previously as emotionally charged, persistent, and irrational attitudes. They may be either positive or negative, expressing favor or scorn, and are not founded on actual facts or evidence, often persisting despite evidence to the contrary. Thus they may be said to consist, at least in part, of a cognitive component of irrational ideas or beliefs. Prejudices may favor an in-group or derogate an out-group. In one of their most destructive forms in societies—and prejudices are prevalent in all cultures—they are directed against minority groups, whether racial or national in character, by the dominant in-groups.

Used this way, prejudices function to maintain and enforce the privileges of the dominant groups and the low status of the submissive groups by means of unjust, discriminatory treatment. Many Americans have prejudices against such minority groups in our society as blacks, the Spanish-speaking, and Jews, for example, and prejudices favoring "real" Americans, or white Anglo-Saxon Protestants (WASPs). On the other hand, WASPs, being in a real numerical minority, are frequently discriminated against in situations where other groups are dominant.

Stereotypes, first described as such by the political writer Walter Lippman (1922), are oversimplified caricatures of people or things, "pictures in our heads" that often form parts of the cognitive component of prejudices. Stereotypes of blacks may picture them as lazy, lawless, pleasure-loving, gregarious, and musical, for example. The Irish may be pictured as quick-tempered, religious, very nationalistic, and argumentative. Stereotypes are expressed in this manner as a set of adjectives referring to the character traits of those to whom they are applied, thus building supposedly typical mental pictures of them. Stereotypes often consist of both positive and negative qualities. Thus blacks are often considered to be gregarious and musical (positive traits) as well as lazy. You may recall Razran's experiment (Chapter 11) indicating that girls with Jewish surnames were perceived as intelligent and ambitious, but also less attractive than others.

Prejudices and the stereotyped pictures accompanying them are largely formed and developed in the family, then in peer groups, and in other in-groups as socialization proceeds. Prejudices are passed on to the young from one generation to the next. Rooted in the traditions of a society, they are very persistent and difficult to change. Often youngsters absorb prejudices about minorities without ever having had any personal contact with them. One American reared in a small village in a largely rural state reported that he was indoctrinated with prejudices against blacks, Jews, Chinese, and Communists, even though he knew none of them. To these were added prejudices against Poles, Catholics, Germans, union members, and people who lived over the mountains in the western part of his state, of whom he was hardly aware.

Studies have shown that persons of lower intelligence, less problem-solving ability, and less flexible cognitive functioning are more prone to develop and maintain ethnic prejudices. One investigator compared the cognitive abilities of seven-year-old children living in an upper-middle-class suburb of Boston who were divided into those high and low in prejudice (Kutner, 1958). The highly prejudiced children proved to be rigid and dogmatic, tending to overgeneralize, overclassify, and oversimplify, while the unprejudiced children were more flexible and open, thinking less in concrete than in abstract terms and tending to generalize realistically, to individualize, and to be tolerant of ambiguities. Cognitive abilities have a bearing on the number and intensity of prejudices that are absorbed, although such abilities can be overridden, of course, by the emotional force of prejudices and pressures to conform.

Prejudices are transmitted not only through direct modeling by others, but also through the communication and entertainment media of a society, like newspapers, mass magazines, popular fiction, the theater, movies, and TV. The stereotypes are simply presented with the accompanying approving or disapproving attitudes and are often absorbed no matter how distant from reality they may be. Studies of the first-grade reading textbooks published in the United States between 1965 and 1966, for example, compared the new texts that attempted to present many racial and national minorities fairly with the traditional prejudiced texts (Blum, Waite, & Zimet, 1967; Waite, 1968). Even though some of the stories in the new texts deliberately brought in minority characters, these were often stereotyped, and very few of them were major characters in the stories. In the typical story, one black family is described living in the midst of a happy and prosperous white suburban neighborhood. When traditional stereotypes are transmitted in this manner through most members of in-groups, dominate communication media, and are passed on as traditions, it is no wonder that prejudices are slow to change.

Although they cannot be equated with prejudices, stereotypes make up much of the cognitive component of prejudices, which have strong emotional aspects as well. Stereotypes have often been studied in connection with prejudices, particularly those against racial and national minorities. A distinction must be made between **personal stereotypes,** the collection of traits assigned to individuals or to the members of a group by an individual, and **social stereotypes,** the traits typically assigned to members of a group by another whole group. Social stereotypes constitute the social norms of most members of any social group in relation to any other group. The character of personal stereotypes is to some extent influenced by the personality and the experience of the individuals who hold them, though they tend to conform more or less to the social stereotypes of their in-groups.

YOUR PERSONAL SELF-STEREOTYPE

■ The list of terms for traits given in Table 17-1 is made up from studies of the terms used by many people in describing their own stereotypes of various minority groups. Glancing through the list, you can see that some of the terms are favorable, some unfavorable, and some may be almost neutral and difficult to evaluate as favorable or unfavorable. Go through the list, term by term, and carefully consider which of these terms you judge to apply to yourself; that is, which are fairly characteristic of your actions, in the main. Make a list of these terms on a separate sheet of paper. This will give you a picture of your personal self-stereotype.

Many college students have rated the favor-

Table 17-1 Checklist of Terms Used in Studies of Stereotypes

Aggressive	Imaginative	Quick-tempered
Alert	Imitative	Quiet
Ambitious	Impulsive	Radical
Argumentative	Individualistic	Reserved
Arrogant	Industrious	Revengeful
Artistic	Intelligent	Rude
Boastful	Jovial	Scientifically minded
Brilliant	Kind	Sensitive
Conceited	Lazy	Sensual
Conservative	Loud	Shrewd
Conventional	Loyal to family ties	Slovenly
Courteous	Materialistic	Sly
Cowardly	Meditative	Sophisticated
Cruel	Mercenary	Sportsmanlike
Deceitful	Methodical	Stolid
Efficient	Musical	Straightforward
Evasive	Naive	Stubborn
Extremely nationalistic	Neat	Stupid
Faithful	Ostentatious	Suave
Frivolous	Passionate	Suggestible
Generous	Persistent	Superstitious
Gluttonous	Physically dirty	Suspicious
Grasping	Pleasure-loving	Talkative
Gregarious	Ponderous	Tradition-loving
Happy-go-lucky	Practical	Treacherous
Honest	Progressive	Unreliable
Humorless	Pugnacious	Very religious
Ignorant	Quarrelsome	Witty

Source: Karlins, Coffman, & Walters, 1969.

ableness of these terms. To do this, they used a rating scale of +2 for very favorable, +1 for favorable, 0 for neutral, −1 for unfavorable, and −2 for very unfavorable. The average values from all their ratings are given for each of these terms in Table 17-3, at the end of this chapter. Transfer to your list the ratings for the traits you judged applied to yourself. In this way you can distinguish the favorableness, unfavorableness, or neutrality of the traits in your self-stereotype. Add all the plus ratings and all the minus ratings and average them. An average of about +1.00 would be favorable, an average of −1.00 unfavorable, and anything over these values extremely so. How favorable and unfavorable are you about yourself in your personal self-stereotype? This will give

you some notion, if you evaluated your traits objectively and honestly, about how much or how little self-esteem you have and perhaps some insight into your idealized and derogatory images of yourself.

Considering what you know about and have experienced of prejudices and stereotypes in America, past and present, would you judge that social stereotypes are now tending to fade and disappear, particularly among college students like yourself and your friends, who these days often wholly disapprove of prejudices? Investigations of the social stereotypes of groups of Princeton students (100 or more), made in 1933, 1951, and 1967, furnish some evidence for the answer to this question (Karlins, Coffman, & Walters, 1969). In all the studies, the list of stereotypical traits shown in Table 17-1 were given the students and they were asked to select those key traits that best described 10 different minority groups, adding other traits if they felt they needed to. In 1933, the first generation of students perceived the various ethnic groups so uniformly that 75 per cent of the students used the same five key traits in characterizing them. The smaller the number of traits consistently applied, the greater the uniformity in the way these groups were perceived.

In 1951, however, many of the second generation of students reacted negatively to being asked to make such stereotyped judgments of minorities, many of which they hardly knew. Data analysis revealed that they made use of 12 key traits, rather than the 5 that had been sufficient in 1933. It was concluded that perhaps social stereotypes were disappearing, or were at least being diluted and losing influence with students. In 1967, however, the third generation of students displayed more uniformity in their stereotypes of minority groups than had those in 1951. Again many objected to making such generalizations and nearly 20 per cent refused to judge groups about which they had no evidence. In general, it did not appear that students had become less stereotypical in judging the traits of minority groups. The apparent fading of social stereotypes envisioned in 1951 was not confirmed in 1967. Even though the stereotypes remained, however, there were some changes in the key traits selected to characterize each of the minority groups.

Table 17-2 shows the principal traits students applied to Americans as a whole, blacks, Germans, Jews, Japanese, and Chinese in 1933, 1951, and 1967. The traits the students used to characterize Americans in 1967 were decidedly less favorable than those used in 1933 and 1951. The stereotyped picture of the Chinese became considerably more favorable. The ratings of the Germans and Japanese showed the effects of World War II in 1951 and then became more favorable as the war receded into the past. How would you describe what happened to the images of Jews and blacks? And what changes do you think would be found if the study were done today? Considering the amount of money this country spends to increase goodwill toward Americans in other countries, can you see how the measurement of stereotypes could be used to get an objective assessment of the way people all over the world see us at different times in history?

In general, over the generations, social stereotypes are so uniform and persistent, even though changes occur in details as shown in this study, that even the very tolerant are not entirely free of them, although their stereotypes may rarely be so strong that they affect their emotions or their judgments. But how can such strong attitudes be changed?

Changes in Attitudes

Both positive and negative attitudes serve natural and very valuable functions in directing and integrating the activities of individuals and groups of people. Without attitudes, which impel us to prize some things and scorn others, we would have no general guidance for our individual and group behavior, which would either be aimless or require decisions moment by moment. We would have no personal values or social standards to control behavior that reduces our drives, satisfies our genuine needs, and enables us to live together fruitfully. However, certain attitudes, with their associated personal and social stereotypes, are not based on reality, and are emotionally extreme and irrational. Such attitudes, called prejudices, are bound to function destructively for both the individuals and the groups that hold them, either obediently or compulsively, for they present false pictures of reality and distort human relations. They yield

Table 17-2 Comparison of Stereotype Trait Frequencies for Americans as a Whole, Blacks, Germans, Jews, Japanese, and Chinese

Americans as a Whole:

Trait	1933	1951	1967
Industrious	48	30	23
Intelligent	47	32	20
Materialistic	33	37	67
Ambitious	33	21	42
Progressive	27	5	17
Pleasure-loving	26	27	28
Alert	23	7	7
Efficient	21	9	15
Aggressive	20	8	15
Straightforward	19	—	9
Practical	19	—	12
Sportsmanlike	19	—	9
Individualistic	—	26	15
Conventional	—	—	17
Scientifically minded	—	—	15
Ostentatious	—	—	15

Blacks:

Trait	1933	1951	1967
Superstitious	84	41	13
Lazy	75	31	26
Happy-go-lucky	38	17	27
Ignorant	38	24	11
Musical	26	33	47
Ostentatious	26	11	25
Very religious	24	17	8
Stupid	22	10	4
Physically dirty	17	—	3
Naive	14	—	4
Slovenly	13	—	5
Unreliable	12	—	6
Pleasure-loving	—	19	26
Sensitive	—	—	17
Gregarious	—	—	17
Talkative	—	—	14
Imitative	—	—	13

Germans:

Trait	1933	1951	1967
Scientifically minded	78	62	47
Industrious	65	50	59
Stolid	44	10	9
Intelligent	32	32	19
Methodical	31	20	21
Extremely nationalistic	24	50	43
Progressive	16	3	13
Efficient	16	—	46
Jovial	15	—	5
Musical	13	—	4
Persistent	11	—	4
Practical	11	—	9
Aggressive	—	27	30
Arrogant	—	23	18
Ambitious	—	—	15

Jews:

Trait	1933	1951	1967
Shrewd	79	47	30
Mercenary	49	28	15
Industrious	48	29	33
Grasping	34	17	17
Intelligent	29	37	37
Ambitious	21	28	48
Sly	20	14	7
Loyal to family ties	15	19	19
Persistent	13	—	9
Talkative	13	—	3
Aggressive	12	—	23
Very religious	12	—	7
Materialistic	—	—	46
Practical	—	—	19

Japanese:

Trait	1933	1951	1967
Intelligent	45	11	20
Industrious	43	12	57
Progressive	24	2	17
Shrewd	22	13	7
Sly	20	21	3
Quiet	19	—	14
Imitative	17	24	22
Alert	16	—	11
Suave	16	—	—
Neat	16	—	7
Treacherous	13	17	1
Aggressive	13	—	19
Extremely nationalistic	—	18	21
Ambitious	—	—	33
Efficient	—	—	27
Loyal to family ties	—	—	23
Courteous	—	—	22

Chinese:

Trait	1933	1951	1967
Superstitious	34	18	8
Sly	29	4	6
Conservative	29	14	15
Tradition-loving	26	26	32
Loyal to family ties	22	35	50
Industrious	18	18	23
Meditative	19	—	21
Reserved	17	18	15
Very religious	15	—	6
Ignorant	15	—	7
Deceitful	14	—	5
Quiet	13	19	23
Courteous	—	—	20
Extremely nationalistic	—	—	19
Humorless	—	—	17
Artistic	—	—	15

Source: Karlins, Coffman, & Walters, 1969.

no end of grief, hostility, and tragedy, both for those against whom they are directed and for those who hold them. The aspirations of many members of society to change these attitudes are understandable.

UNREALISTIC BELIEFS

In a recent investigation, a sample of 375 men and women in the greater Boston area were interviewed on their beliefs about the welfare poor (Williamson, 1974). Here are some of the questions the respondents were asked and their answers, contrasted with the actual facts as investigated and reported by the U.S. Department of Health, Education, and Welfare:

What per cent of welfare recipients are able-bodied unemployed males?

    Respondents: 37 per cent
            In reality: 0.9 per cent

What per cent of children in families receiving aid for dependent children are born out of wedlock?

    Respondents: 33 per cent [on target!]
            In reality: 31 per cent

What per cent of welfare recipients lie about their financial situations?

    Respondents: 41 per cent
            In reality: 0.4 per cent or less

How many children under age 18 are there in the average family receiving aid to dependent children?

    Respondents: 4.8 children
            In reality: 2.6 children

In recent years has the birth rate for families receiving aid to dependent children been increasing, decreasing, or remaining about the same?

    Respondents: 44 per cent said increasing
        20 per cent said decreasing
            In reality: decreasing since 1967

In addition to such marked misconceptions about the welfare poor (with the exception of birth out of wedlock), Williamson found that strong conservative beliefs about welfare issues and about the work ethic were involved in antagonistic attitudes toward additional relief for the poor. He acknowledged that such strong ideological attitudes are resistant to change, and that misconceptions are not easily corrected by information and education. Williamson therefore suggested that the greatest force for change in such attitudes will be found in the increasing efforts of the welfare poor themselves to organize. He concluded, "As the poor begin to take collective action on their own behalf with increasing frequency, it is likely that there will be a reduction in the prevalence of the belief that they are lazy and unmotivated."

Many studies have been made of the ways in which prejudices, as well as other attitudes, can be influenced. Undoubtedly you have seen discrimination in operation in all kinds of derogatory and destructive behavior that expressed prejudiced attitudes toward racial, national, or sex groups. And undoubtedly you have experienced discrimination yourself when, for instance, a supervisor at work, an instructor in school, or another student puts you down, expressing great disapproval, rejecting whatever you do, putting obstacles in your way, and even beginning to make of you a scapegoat for others. Rejected groups and individuals seem to have four courses of action open to them in dealing with prejudice. They may (1) accept it, submitting to the inequities as best they can, feeling there is nothing to be done about it; (2) avoid the situation, if this is feasible, trying to stay away from it and to develop other resources compensating for it on their own; (3) work peacefully but determinedly to expose the faulty beliefs underlying prejudices, demonstrating by their own behavior that the prejudice directed toward the groups of which they are members is unjustified; (4) react with counterrejection, protest, and hostility. Today you can see all of these ways of responding to prejudice in the behavior of various groups and their members. None of them, except (3), seems very effective in itself.

Still other courses of action can be taken, however, to combat discrimination both by those discriminated against and by others who wish to ease the tensions and overcome the inequities of our society. In a democratic culture like ours, (5) there are some laws against various prevalent forms of discrimination, like discrimination based on sex, creed, race, nationality, and age (whether young or old), in such spheres of life as employment, housing, recreation, and public accommodations. These laws prescribe sanctions against those who so discriminate, preventing or at least punishing some of this behavior and providing stronger bulwarks against it than individuals can muster by themselves. Even so, laws are often disregarded by groups convinced of the righteousness of their convictions or not willing to relinquish the presumed benefits from their discriminatory practices, despite the devastating effects on society as a whole. And do laws touch the prejudices themselves, can they reach the strongly emotionalized and irrational attitudes held by such people?

Beyond such legal limitations on discriminatory behavior, and beyond direct protests against it, lie (6) methods of persuasion and education directed toward changing the prejudiced attitudes themselves. In **persuasion,** a person or group attempts to change destructive attitudes by communications of various kinds, oral or written. Investigations have shown that the attractiveness and the credibility of the communicators play a large role in effecting changes in attitudes. The influence, authority, or power of communicators, and their capacity to determine rewards or punishments, have significant influence. People's opinions can be swayed by an authority much more than by some relatively powerless person like themselves. Thus in one investigation people tended to accept extreme and even unbelievable opinions about the amount of sleep per night that is necessary when such views were attributed to "Sir John Eccles, a Nobel Prize–winning physiologist," but not when they were attributed to "Mr. Harry Olsen, director of the Fort Worth YMCA" (Bochner & Insko, 1966). Other variables influencing attitude change include the nature and content of the communications themselves.

How do communications bring about changes in attitudes? Do they simply furnish information that provides evidence to counter irrational prejudices, like those against the welfare poor, or do they arouse positive or negative emotions about the subject that will stir the receivers to change their attitudes? Weak or strong arousal of emotions has been found to be less effective in changing attitudes than moderate emotional arousal. Still other variables arise in the character and circumstances of the receivers of the communications. How suggestible are they? Are they intelligent enough to grasp the arguments presented? To what extent do they tend to conform or not to conform, what is their level of anxiety, and what values do they hold? If they tend to be conformists and are exposed to strong group disapproval of their prejudice, they will be more likely to reconsider and relinquish it. If their prejudice is shown to be inconsistent with their basic beliefs or values, then they are much more likely to modify their prejudiced attitude accordingly, and on their own. A great many factors play a role, then, in the success of any systematic attempt to change attitudes, particularly if one is striving for a permanent change rather than a temporary digression or a superficial modification.

SOCIAL INTERACTIONS

In addition to group effects on individuals and the effects of attitudes on social behavior, social psychologists study social interactions, reciprocal relationships between two or more persons whose behavior is mutually dependent on each other. Many of our daily activities involve such social interactions, from the way we drive in traffic, following certain traffic regulations and expecting other drivers to do the same, to the ways we act in formal or informal groups with other people in the course of our work or leisure.

Studies have shown that self-concepts are based, to a great extent, on **reference groups,** those social groups with which people identify and whose norms they tend to accept as their own (Gordon, 1968). Children's reference groups include their families and friends. Their self-concepts derive from the roles they are expected to play with them, based upon the norms they follow or impose. So even our concept of ourselves depends in large measure on the social groups with which we interact and of which we feel we are members.

Interpersonal Attraction

When you first meet other people, men or women, what determines whether you will like them or dislike them? Do your first impressions of others usually appear to be sound, or do you often have to change them? The bases for attraction and repulsion between two people have proved to be very complex. What factors, for example, do you think should be most significant in selecting a marital partner?

Physical attractiveness (or unattractiveness) has been found to be one factor that affects liking (or disliking) of other persons. It at least plays a part in the formation of immediate impressions, for a person does not have too much more to go on at first acquaintance. Cultural and subcultural norms greatly affect personal characteristics found to be attractive and unattractive. In the same category is *physical closeness* or *proximity* of one person to another, so that the two often meet and are readily available to each other. One intensive study of college students living in the same building through a semester showed that, initially, proximity was influential in determining their attraction to each other (Newcomb, 1961). As the semester wore on, however, the degree of similarity in the students' attitudes and values became dominant and displaced proximity in significance. "Birds of a feather flock together," as the maxim goes. The importance of *similarity of attitudes* for attraction has been proved time after time, regardless of other factors like physical attractiveness, race, sex, or status (Byrne, 1971). However, it has been found that happily married couples tend to overestimate their similarity, while unhappy couples underestimate it (Levinger & Breedlove, 1966), so perceived similarity rather than actual similarity is related to happiness in marriage. But don't "opposites attract" also? you may well ask. There seems to be a proverb supporting every possibility.

We are all acquainted with the aggressive wife and the dependent husband, or the dominant husband and submissive wife. Have you noticed obsessive talkers who have patient listeners for friends? Perhaps people make friends of those who seem to satisfy their own needs, which in some instances require *complementary qualities.* Some research has indicated that this is the case, particularly in long-lasting relationships (Winch, 1958). But another investigation found that such relationships may be more determined in their early stages by *social-status factors,* like socioeconomic class and religion, than by a similarity of attitudes and values, and finally by complementarity of needs as the relationship ripens (Kerckhoff & Davis, 1962). Still, the satisfaction of each other's needs, even though they may be quite opposite in character, undoubtedly plays some role in personal attractions.

A **reward** or **reinforcement theory** of interpersonal attraction explains the degree of intensity of attraction or repulsion, of liking or disliking, as due to the positive or negative reinforcements the persons derive from their interactions. Pleasure and satisfaction of needs, or displeasure and frustration of needs, would be derived from the physical attractiveness or ugliness, the similarity or dissimilarity of attitudes, and the compatibility or lack of compatibility in needs and interests, resulting in greater or lesser attraction or repulsion. A **social-exchange theory** of interpersonal attraction holds, however, that many interpersonal situations involve not only rewards but also costs for the persons involved. The costs may be values given in return or forgone for those values received from the relationship, and costs must be subtracted from rewards in evaluating what each member gets out of any interpersonal relationship (Murstein, 1971). Social-exchange theory stresses that the persons interacting with each other and considering long-run relationships do evaluate the relationship on such a social-exchange basis, in comparison with other alternatives that are or might be available. Such evaluations are not necessarily verbalized by the parties involved, however, and some might take offense at the description of a "sacred trust" in exchange terms.

With such a host of variables to contend with, how can one ever hope to understand, let alone predict, the intricacies of courtship and marriage? What is needed, it would seem, is a tightly constructed theory broad enough to cover the vast domain of variables operating from the time two potential lovers lock their gaze "across a crowded room," past the rocky shoals of courtship, and into the various stages of marriage. Such a theory, the most comprehensive of its kind, has been developed (Murstein, 1971), and it suggests that very different factors play critical roles at different times in the relationship.

In the initial stages, *stimulus factors,* such as physical attraction, play an important part in getting a relationship started. But the individuals' estimates of what they have to offer and how desirable a partner they have a right to expect will also influence who approaches whom. In a later stage, as people get to know each other better, there is the opportunity to compare each other's *values.* At this stage of courtship many couples discover that they want quite different things out of life and that their needs are hardly complementary. If the relationship survives this stage, the couple moves on to the third, or *role,* stage, in which the partners can assess the degree of compatibility between the roles each wants to—or feels compelled to—play, as parent, provider, com-

panion, or critic. **Stimulus-value-role (SVR) theory** thus attempts to relate the dynamic changes occurring in successive stages of courtship and marriage to a complex constellation of both psychological and sociological variables.

FINGERTIP AURAS AND ATTRACTION?

In 1939 Semyon Kirlian, a Russian electrician, discovered that when a person's fingertips are placed on a photographic film over an electrically charged steel plate, circular auras were produced around them which could be seen when the film was developed. Just why an electrostatic field makes these auras—called the **Kirlian effect**—which vary in size, brightness, and "spikiness," is not known, although it has been claimed that they are not related to heat, galvanic skin response (GSR), vasoconstriction, skin temperature, or sweat (see Figure 17-8). Then, strangely enough, a recent experiment proved these auras to be reliably related to the degree of interpersonal attraction between one person (the subject) and another (the photographer-experimenter) who placed the subject's fingers on the photographic film (Murstein & Hadjolian, 1975).

In this experiment, analysis of the fingertip auras of many college students demonstrated that the auras were significantly greater for (1) students whose auras were obtained by a "photographer" of the opposite sex than for those who dealt with a "photographer" of the same sex; (2) students whose fingers were placed on the film close to the fingers of another student of the opposite sex, rather than a student of the same sex; and (3) students who were tested together with a student of the same sex whom they liked, rather than one they disliked. The researchers concluded that the size and brightness of these fingertip auras, which can be measured and scored very accurately by "blind" judges, provide a fairly reliable measure of interpersonal attraction. Since the effect is not easily influenced by conscious intentions, the method may therefore prove to be a useful tool.

The investigators also tried to measure the Kirlian effects of seductive behavior by having the "photographer" hold the hands of opposite-sex subjects for a few seconds before placing their fingers on the film, tell the subjects they were very attractive, and, in the case of a female "seducer," offer the subjects her first name, phone number, and address, or in the case of a male "seducer," ask for this information. Under such seductive conditions, however, the subjects exhibited smaller auras than under "normal" conditions, rather than the larger ones that had been taken to indicate attraction. The investigators concluded that the photographers may have been too directly forward in their advances and may have actually "turned off" the subjects by their behavior. They suggested that more subtle seductive behavior might show the expected increase in attraction, and concluded:

Future research also might concern itself with the relation of auras and physical attractiveness, similarity, self-esteem, and other variables studied earlier in interpersonal attraction experiments. It would likewise be of value to study different kinds of relationships: dating, engagement, marriage, divorce as well as different degrees of marriage adjustment to determine their relationship to aural patterns.

Love

Perhaps the strongest form of interpersonal attraction, more profound than simply liking or even intimate friendship, is **love,** sometimes called "true love" or "romantic love." Normally this intense attraction develops between persons of opposite sexes, although homosexuals of both sexes may also have intense and long-lasting love affairs. As love begins between a pair, direct eye contact may be one of the first signs. Eye contacts between mother and nursing child have been cited by child psychologists as a factor in the establishment of bonds of mutual attachment and affection. The pupils of the eye widen, permitting more light to enter the eye and facilitating vision, with the fixed attention, the stirring of interest, and the arousal of emotions. The open pupils and wide-open, attentive eyes are considered to be a most sensitive measure of the beginning of attraction and arousal.

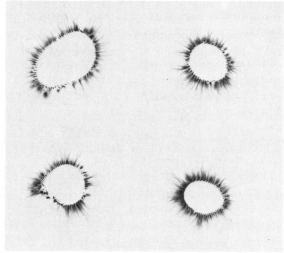

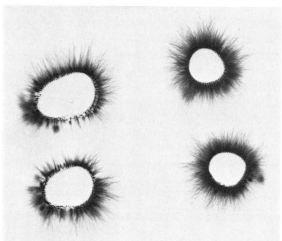

Figure 17-8 Examples of fingertip auras illustrating the Kirlian effect. The auras at the top appeared around the fingertips of college students who felt unattracted to each other. Those on the bottom were recorded for two students who felt attracted to each other. (Courtesy of B. I. Murstein and R. Milardo)

Popular songs, as well as casual observation, indicate that people in love gaze more than usual at each other. "Millions of people go by, but they all disappear from view, 'cause I only have eyes for you," runs one lyric. Now an experiment has confirmed this gazing of couples in love (Rubin, 1970). Couples that had indicated by their own judgments that they were either weakly or intensely in love were seated across from each other at a table and left alone, while two observers watched their eye contacts through mirrors that permitted observation from an adjoining room. The couples were then individually seated with strangers and observed. The study gave conclusive proof that couples intensely in love gaze simultaneously at each other much more than do strangers or those weakly in love.

In 1958 Harry Harlow, then president of the American Psychological Association, observed, "So far as love or affection is concerned, psychologists have failed in their mission. The little we know about love does not transcend simple observation, and the little we write about it has been written better by poets and novelists" (Harlow, 1958). In the last decade, however, the study of love has blossomed. A paper-and-pencil scale has even been developed for the measurement of romantic love (Rubin, 1969). The scale contains some statements for the purpose of identifying romantic love, others for identifying intimate or platonic friendship. Use of the scale has indicated that romantic love is definitely distinguishable from strong liking or intimate friendship. The three major components of **romantic love** suggested by the scale are (1) affiliative and dependent need for the other, indicated by such items as "If I could never be with ____, I would feel miserable," and "It would be hard for me to get along without ____"; (2) a predisposition to help the other, shown in items like "I would do almost anything for ____," and "If ____ were feeling badly, my first duty would be to cheer him (her) up"; and (3) a sense of exclusiveness of the other and absorption in the other, signified by "I feel very possessive toward ____," and "I feel that I can confide in ____ about virtually everything." When this scale was administered to 158 dating (but nonengaged) couples at the University of Michigan, it proved capable of distinguishing love from liking and showed that the love scores of the men and the women were almost identical. On the other hand, women *liked* their boy friends somewhat more than men *liked* their girl friends. This finding reflected the higher ratings women gave their boy friends on such traits as intelligence, good judgment, and potential for leadership (Rubin, 1970).

True or romantic love has sometimes been disparaged by self-appointed experts on the relations between the sexes. Parents will often tell a son or daughter who has fallen in love that this is just a passing fancy, with the implication that he or she will get over this disease with emotional maturity. Parents who try to disrupt a relationship often come up against the "Romeo and Juliet complex," an intensification of the emotional attachment when obstacles are encountered.

Both experts and parents have tended to promulgate many myths about romantic love. An investigation of more than 1000 college students of both sexes (Kephart, 1970) has revealed that these myths are without much substance. The students were given the Bell Adjustment Inventory to indicate the level of their emotional adjustment. On the average the subjects had experienced their first infatuations at the age of 13, and had their first serious love affairs at 17. No relationship was found between their emotional adjustment and the ages at which infatuations and love affairs first occurred. Falling in love was not a sign of emotional immaturity, as has often been charged.

According to another myth, the emotionally immature find it easier to become attracted to the other sex. In actual fact, the reports of the students showed that the emotionally immature found it most difficult to become so attracted. The notion that early infatuations imply promiscuity had to be discarded as well, for both mature and immature students had experienced about five infatuations and had fallen in love once or twice. However, those who had managed to have 12 or more loves by the time they were in college had poor emotional scores on the Bell Inventory.

Romantic "bigamy" was relatively rare among the students sampled. Only about 5 per cent had experienced falling in love with two persons at the same time, although about half of them reported brief simultaneous infatuations. Emotionally immature men reported romantic bigamy more frequently than did the emotionally secure. These students had dated an average of more than 30 persons each, and the greater their emotional immaturity, the greater the number of persons dated. Two-thirds of the men had been infatuated or fallen in love with at least one older woman, and one-third of the women with a younger man, but these women showed signs of greater immaturity than those who had not.

Overall, the investigation tended to reveal a selection process that might be explained by the social-exchange theory of attraction, as the students passed through several infatuations and a love affair or two. After extensive attractive encounters, dating, infatuations, and loves for a decade or so, usually this screening process eventually resulted in the selection of a more permanent mate, often a marriage partner. The investigator suggested that when students fall in and out of love they are manifesting a pattern of normal emotional maturation. The conclusions of this study tended to be confirmed in an investigation of married couples (Spanier, 1972). Spanier found that romanticism plays an important role in attitudes toward dating, mate selection, and marriage, after which it may begin to decrease in intensity and significance. He concluded that "romanticism does not appear to be harmful to marriage relationships in particular or the family system in general, and is therefore not generally dysfunctional in our society."

SUMMARY

Social psychology deals with the influence on individuals or groups of their interactions with other individuals or groups, using concepts drawn from psychological areas like perception, learning, and motivation rather than sociological concepts like social classes, institutions, and status. Direct visual contact and invasion of personal space illustrate the all-pervasive effects of social interactions on individuals.

Functional groups made up of people acting together for some common goal provide social facilitation of well-learned performances but not of new tasks or tasks requiring problem-solving behavior. When individuals feel that audiences are observing and evaluating their performance, they are likely to be affected by them.

Conformity strongly affects perception and behavior, bringing individual standards into accord with group norms, particularly when groups are authoritative. The need to conform often has advantages in terms of group efficiency, but disadvantages when it overrides constructive efforts.

Attitudes are persistent tendencies involving a complex of motives, emotions, thoughts, and behavior, directed toward behavior, a belief system supporting the behavior, and action tendencies expressing the feelings and beliefs. Attitudes are measured with various kinds of rating scales and by observation of actual behavior or action tendencies.

The formation of attitudes is indirectly influenced by genetic and physiological factors, by individual experiences, and by the copying of models of behavior as socialization proceeds. Among key early attitudes are self-esteem and self-derogation, and a "groupness" attitude favoring in-groups and rejecting out-groups.

Prejudices, favorable or unfavorable, are persistent, emotionally charged, and irrational attitudes, not based on adequate or correctly interpreted evidence. Oversimplified caricatures of target people or things, called stereotypes, accompany prejudices. Personal stereotypes are held by particular individuals, while social stereotypes involve conceptions generally held by groups about other groups.

Attitudes, including prejudices, may be changed gradually by individual efforts, by legal sanctions, or by methods of persuasion and education applied by credible authorities who attempt to substitute rational beliefs for the irrational attitudes.

Interpersonal attraction is influenced by many factors, such as physical attractiveness and proximity, similarity or complementarity

of attitudes and needs, and reinforcement and costs of interactions in terms of social exchange. According to stimulus-value-role (SVR) theory, long-term interpersonal relations, like courtship and marriage, seem to be affected especially by stimulus conditions, values, and roles in successive stages as the relationship deepens.

The strongest interpersonal attraction, love, seems to involve an affiliative and dependent need between the partners, a predisposition to

Table 17-3 Mean Favorableness (+) and Unfavorableness (−) of Terms Used in Studies of Stereotypes, Based on Ratings on a 5-Point Scale from +2 to −2

Term	Mean Rating	Term	Mean Rating	Term	Mean Rating
Aggressive	+0.18	Imaginative	+1.39	Quick-tempered	−0.90
Alert	+1.44	Imitative	−0.63	Quiet	+0.20
Ambitious	+1.06	Impulsive	−0.22	Radical	−0.45
Argumentative	−0.50	Individualistic	+1.01	Reserved	+0.12
Arrogant	−1.30	Industrious	+1.32	Revengeful	−1.28
Artistic	+1.34	Intelligent	+1.61	Rude	−1.67
Boastful	−1.11	Jovial	+0.92	Scientifically	
Brilliant	+1.70	Kind	+1.29	minded	+0.81
Conceited	−1.50	Lazy	−1.12	Sensitive	+0.99
Conservative	−0.06	Loud	−0.83	Sensual	+0.39
Conventional	−0.30	Loyal to family		Shrewd	+0.18
Courteous	+1.18	ties	+0.57	Slovenly	−1.25
Cowardly	−1.63	Materialistic	−0.45	Sly	−0.58
Cruel	−1.77	Meditative	+0.59	Sophisticated	+0.74
Deceitful	−1.73	Mercenary	−0.88	Sportsmanlike	+1.19
Efficient	+1.18	Methodical	+0.24	Stolid	+0.32
Evasive	−0.83	Musical	+0.90	Straightforward	+0.96
Extremely		Naive	−0.66	Stubborn	−0.58
nationalistic	+0.10	Neat	+0.86	Stupid	−1.59
Faithful	+1.23	Ostentatious	−0.89	Suave	+0.45
Frivolous	−0.53	Passionate	+0.41	Suggestible	−0.55
Generous	+1.17	Persistent	+0.85	Superstitious	−0.84
Gluttonous	−1.13	Physically dirty	−1.45	Suspicious	−0.75
Grasping	−0.97	Pleasure-loving	+0.46	Talkative	−0.13
Gregarious	+0.30	Ponderous	−0.23	Tradition-loving	+0.25
Happy-go-lucky	+0.45	Practical	+0.82	Treacherous	−1.65
Honest	+1.56	Progressive	+0.99	Unreliable	−1.64
Humorless	−0.92	Pugnacious	−0.73	Very religious	+0.23
Ignorant	−1.37	Quarrelsome	−1.11	Witty	+1.01

Source: Karlins, Coffman, & Walters, 1969.

help each other, and a feeling of being exclusively absorbed in each other, as opposed to less intense degrees of liking or friendship.

Romantic love does not simply express emotional immaturity, but rather a constructive maturing process through which people pass as they gradually select permanent partners.

APPLY IT YOURSELF

Select individuals of the same or opposite sex who are (1) an acquaintance, (2) a person in one of your in-groups, (3) a person in an out-group, (4) a person you are prejudiced for, (5) a person you are prejudiced against, (6) a person you feel neutral about, (7) a person you hate, (8) an intimate friend, and (9) a person you love. Consider your behavior in the company of each of these people, the attitudes you and they manifest, and your influences on each other. Then try the same analysis for a group with which you are acquainted, an in-group, an out-group, a group you are prejudiced for, and so on. Then explore all these individual and group relationships in terms of the social exchanges that occur within the relationships. Do you begin to sense a picture of what your general social behavior and relationships are like?

Appendix Statistics

The methods of psychologists are essentially improvements on ordinary, common-sense ways of observing behavior. Psychological observations are controlled, precise, and refined, as you saw in Chapter 1. Psychologists have developed more reliable procedures for investigating behavior than are available to untrained persons. Their observations are called **data,** the plural form of the Latin word for *fact*. Psychologists work with data in the form of **symbols,** like numbers, words, or other signs, representing the observations. They then employ these symbols in the analysis and interpretation of their observations and draw their conclusions with them. The symbols also provide an efficient way to communicate psychological observations and conclusions to others. As you may well imagine, the huge number of observations made in a psychological investigation is much too great to communicate one at a time, using either words or numbers. Imagine having to describe to someone the reaction times of 20 subjects to each of 20 words in a word-association test. You'd have your listener confused by a myriad of numbers, and the overall forest would be lost among the individual trees. Somehow all of these results must be pulled together and abbreviated—and that brings us to **statistics,** the analysis, interpretation, and presentation of masses of numerical data in an effective manner.

BRANCHES OF STATISTICS

The problem of providing a clear and concise summary of a large group of data is met by one of the two main branches of statistics, called descriptive statistics. **Descriptive statistics** is composed of procedures for describing and summarizing observations that have been **quantified**—that is, numbers have been assigned to the data. The aim is to reduce a large number of data to a simply described, easily understood form. At some time, for example, the semester grades you receive in your various courses may have shown considerable variation: 81, 72, 90, 83, and 76. You are heartened by the fact that the majority of your grades range from 81 to 90. That seems pretty good, but did you make the Dean's list with an 80 overall score? It may look as if you've done so easily, until you take the average, a descriptive statistic that is obtained by totaling the scores and dividing the total by the number of scores. You find that you just squeaked through with an 80 average. You really use statistics all the time in ways like this, and you can see their value even in such a small example.

The second major branch, **inferential statistics,** deals with procedures for making predictions about other data, not yet collected, on the basis of a relatively small sample of data on hand from observations already made. For example, inferential statistics are used to estimate the probability that the results of one experiment with a group of people would be obtained again if the experiment were repeated many times, with other people serving as subjects. A **sample** of data is a small group of data selected as more or less representative of a much larger **population** of data, the whole set of data of a particular kind from which the sample is selected. We also speak of a population of data when all the possible observations that make up the set have not been made but might potentially be made. A simple example of the application of inferential statistics is the Gallup poll, which is used, on the basis of the responses of a very small sample of voters, to predict the voting behavior of an entire nation.

Inferential statistics are also an integral part of the experimental method, in which the behaviors of experimental and control groups are compared (see Chapter 1). How much do the average scores of the two groups have to differ before you can be confident in concluding that the independent variable produced a real difference in the behaviors of the two groups, a difference that would appear time after time if the experiment were repeated? To have scientific value, the research done with a modest sample of subjects must yield conclusions that hold for much larger groups of subjects. If psychologists can't generalize beyond their given data, their major aim, the prediction of behavior, becomes unattainable. Inferential statistics extends their vision beyond a small sample of subjects, allowing them to make general statements, or **generalizations,** about the whole population from which the subjects were drawn.

The combination of descriptive and inferential statistics provides many valuable tools for the investigation of behavior. Some of the basic and most useful descriptive and inferential methods are presented here.

DESCRIPTIVE STATISTICS

Suppose you are a psychology instructor with a class of 100 students. One day you return their midterm exams, which you have graded, to them. After looking at their own scores, with manifest approval or disapproval as the case may be, several of them ask how well the class performed on the exam. They want some sort of standard against which to measure their own scores. If descriptive statistics did not exist, you either would have to mumble a vague and really meaningless "Not so bad," or, wishing to be precise, might feel compelled to recite the whole set of 100 exam scores. Wouldn't your students shake their heads? Neither way would help. Let's see how you could use descriptive statistics to give a good quantitative summary of the midterm-exam data.

Frequency Distributions

One statistical method you could use would be to set up the exam scores in a **frequency distribution,** so called because it shows the frequency with which individual scores fall into a number of classes or groups of scores. In making a frequency distribution, you divide the full range of the scores into a suitable number of classes and then count, or tabulate, the number of scores that fall into each class. Table A-1 shows a frequency distribution that you might get for the midterm scores of your 100 students. In this distribution, the **class intervals,** or range of scores making up each class of data, are kept at 5 points, as from 96 to 100 and 91 to 95. About 10 or 12 class intervals are often suitable with this and larger number of scores, although a smaller number of class intervals may be right for fewer scores. The frequency distribution is made up by tabulating each score, placing it in its proper class

Table A-1 Frequency Distribution with Class Intervals of 5 and Tabulation of 100 Midterm Exam Scores

Score Intervals	Tabulation	Frequency
96–100	I	1
91–95	++++	5
86–90	++++ IIII	9
81–85	++++ ++++ I	11
76–80	++++ ++++ ++++	15
71–75	++++ ++++ ++++ III	18
66–70	++++ ++++ ++++ I	16
61–65	++++ ++++ III	13
56–60	++++ III	8
51–55	IIII	4
Total		100

interval, then totaling the number of scores in each interval. The frequency distribution shown in Table A-2, with class intervals of 10 corresponding to letter grades, might be a better way of reporting the scores of the class on the exam to your students. Reporting either frequency distribution to the class would certainly provide a pretty good description of the class performance against which students could evaluate their own scores. Since there just happen to be 100 students in your class, the frequencies given are also the percentages of scores in each class interval. For any other size class, calculating and adding the percentages of the scores in each class interval would

also provide valuable information for the students.

Histograms

Often, descriptive data like the midterm-exam scores are presented in the form of a **bar graph**, or **histogram**, as shown in Figure A-1, in which the frequency of scores in each class interval is represented as a bar. The class intervals are arranged in increasing value from left to right in the graph. Comparing this with Table A-1, you see that the histogram is only an adaptation of a frequency distribution, the height of the bars representing the number of cases falling within each class interval. As shown in Figure A-2, you can sometimes produce a rough histogram at the same time you are tabulating your data in a frequency distribution by placing an X or filling in a box of a graph for each score as you place it in its appropriate class interval. Then the height of the bars made by your Xs when you have finished tabulating them represents the number of cases falling within each class interval, and you have saved time and effort.

Frequency Polygons

"Polygon" means many-sided, and the term aptly describes the line shown in Figure A-3. This is the kind of line, usually called a curve, most often used to represent research data.

Table A-2 Frequency Distribution with Class Intervals of 10 Corresponding to Letter Grades and Tabulation of 100 Midterm Exam Scores

Letter Grade	Score Intervals	Tabulation	Frequency
A	91–100	++++ I	6
B	81–90	++++ ++++ ++++ ++++	20
C	71–80	++++ ++++ ++++ ++++ ++++ ++++ III	33
D	61–70	++++ ++++ ++++ ++++ ++++ IIII	29
E	51–60	++++ ++++ II	12
Total			100

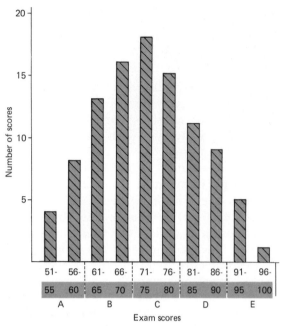

Figure A-1 A bar graph, or histogram, displays in graphic form the frequency distribution of exam scores for a class.

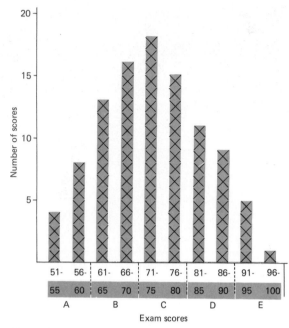

Figure A-2 Tabulation of scores by placing Xs within their class intervals makes a histogram.

Note that each data point is equal to the height of its corresponding bar in the histogram (Figure A-1). As the number of scores, or cases, increases and the class intervals become smaller, the curve tends to become smoother. A really smooth curve, like those shown in Figure A-4, can be thought of as consisting of an infinite number of points, each representing the midpoint of a tiny class interval. In a frequency polygon, however, the lines between the points do not actually represent a number of scores per interval under them, but only serve to show more clearly in what way the points for actual scores vary from one class interval to the next. Thus the line between the first two points on the left-hand side of the curve in Figure A-3 shows that the number of scores goes up sharply between the class interval 51–55 and the class interval 56–60. But the line between the third and fourth points, going up at a lesser angle, shows that the number of scores between the class intervals 61–65 and 66–70 goes up less sharply.

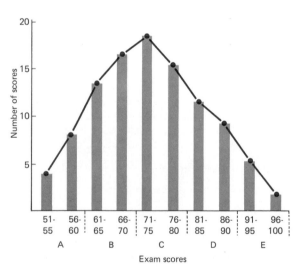

Figure A-3 Frequency polygon of exam scores with lines connecting the top of the bars representing the number of scores in each class interval.

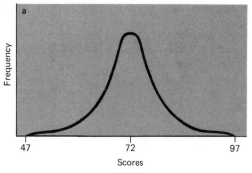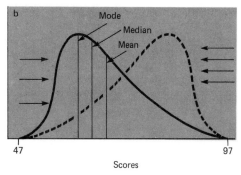

Figure A-4 (a) A normal distribution of scores with the mean, median, and mode all equal to 72. (b) The solid curve describes a distribution of scores skewed to the right; note that the median falls between the mode and the mean. The dashed curve traces a distribution skewed to the left.

The Normal Curve

As an instructor describing the way the students performed on an exam, you might be able to say simply, "The scores were distributed according to a normal curve," or "The scores had a normal distribution." The students could then visualize a curve like that in the left panel (*a*) of Figure A-4. Such a **normal curve**, or **normal distribution**, with identical slopes on both sides of the midpoint, is commonly obtained for measures of certain psychological traits like intelligence (IQ), although seldom obtained for measures of other traits like anxiety (see Figure 13-2). Note some of the properties of the normal curve: A perpendicular line dropped from the peak of the curve to the baseline bisects the curve into two parts, each the mirror image of the other.

Skewed Distributions

As shown in panel *b* of Figure A-4, **skewed distributions** are those whose slopes are not equally steep on both sides of the peak. The scores tend to pile up on one side or the other. A distribution skewed to the right has many scores bunched at the low end of the scale and fewer at the higher end, while the contrary is true for a distribution skewed to the left. If you

received a very low score on an exam, for example, would it look worse for you if the class distribution was skewed left or right?

Measures of Central Tendency

A **measure of central tendency** is a number representative of a distribution of scores. One kind of representative number, the **mean (M)**, is obtained by adding up all the scores and then dividing by the number of scores. The general formula for the mean is:

$$\text{Mean} = \frac{\Sigma X}{N}$$

in which ΣX equals the sum (Σ) of the scores (X), and N equals the number of scores. Since the mean is a value around which many scores tend to cluster, it is called a measure of central tendency.

Another measure of central tendency, the **median**, is the midpoint in a distribution. For example, suppose you have the following 11 scores arranged in order of magnitude:

49, 56, 57, 62, 67, |68,| 74, 74, 81, 85, 97

The median, 68, is the middle score, with an equal number of scores above and below it. But suppose you have an *even* number of 12 scores arranged in order of magnitude:

49, 56, 57, 62, 67, 68, | 74, 74, 81, 85, 97, 100
                        71

Then the median becomes a new number, 71, halfway between the two scores (68 and 74) that divide the number of scores into two equal parts. Half of the range of 6 from 68 to 74 is 3, and 68 + 3 (or 74 − 3) equals 71. In a perfectly normal curve, as in panel *a* of Figure A-4, the mean and the median are identical. Can you see why they must be? Compute the mean for the set of 11 scores given above (49–97). Are the mean and the median identical? Why, or why not?

The mode is still another measure of central tendency. The **mode** is simply the most frequently appearing score in a distribution of scores. In the set of 11 scores given (49–97), the mode is 74, which is the only score that appears twice. And you see that 74 is also the mode for the set of 12 scores given (49–100).

Why are so many different measures of central tendency needed? If the distributions to be described were all perfectly normal, like that shown in panel *a* of Figure A-4, different measures would not be needed, for the mean, median, and mode are identical in such distributions. However, many distributions are not normal, like those shown in panel *b* of Figure A-4. For an extreme case, consider the following set of annual incomes earned by five individuals:

$6,000, $7,000, $8,000, $8,500, $970,500

The mean annual income is $200,000. This value is typical of no individual in the sample. Now find the median. Isn't $8,000 the more typical value, far more representative of 80 per cent of the incomes? You can see, then, that the mean is a poor measure of central tendency if the sample includes one or more really extreme scores; that's where the median comes in handy, since it is relatively unaffected by extreme values.

Measures of Variability

Remembering that the goal of descriptive statistics is to convey an accurate and concise appreciation of a lot of data, consider this question: Would you be able to visualize a distribution of grades on the basis of the information that (1) the distribution was perfectly symmetrical, (2) the mean, and necessarily also the median and mode, was 70, and (3) the range, the difference between highest and lowest scores, was 40, the grades ranging from 50 to 90? If you think such a distribution can look only one way, refer to Figure A-5. The three distributions fit the description given, but differ in the degree to which the scores tend to cluster around the mean of 70. You can see that the mean of 70 is most representative of the scores in the tallest, skinniest distribution.

Adding some information about the variability of the distribution—that is, about the dispersion of the grades around the mean—improves the description of the distribution immensely. What is needed is a way

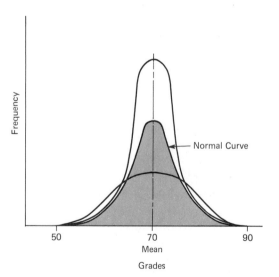

Figure A-5 Three symmetrical distributions of grades differing in degree of variability of grades about the mean.

to describe this dispersion of scores around the mean with a single number, similar to the way we can express the central tendency of a distribution by one number like the mean, mode, or median. Such a number for expressing dispersion is called the **standard deviation**, abbreviated **SD.** The standard deviation tells how far on either side of the mean you have to go to include about two-thirds of the scores in the distribution. Figure A-6 shows two distributions, *a* and *b*, with the same mean, 70, and both symmetrical, but varying widely in dispersion. The SD of distribution *a* is 10, since it is necessary to cover a range of 10 points on either side of the mean (mean ± 10) in order to take in two-thirds of the scores. The SD of distribution *b* is only 4, since the range of 66 to 74 points (mean ± 4) takes in two-thirds of the space under the curve.

Now that you see the value of the SD as a measure of dispersion or variability, let's see how it is computed. As you can surmise, the method must include some measure of the degree to which each score deviates from the mean: Many big deviations give a large SD; small deviations, a small SD. Consider two sets of scores:

Set A	Set B
50	68
60	69
70	70
80	71
90	72
Mean A = 70	Mean B = 70

Satisfy yourself that the means are identical. Yet the mean is certainly more representative of the scores in Set B than of those in Set A. That is, the amount of dispersion around the mean is greater in Set A than in Set B. Here's how to calculate the SD, the measure of dispersion, for Set A:

Set A Scores (X)	Deviation from Mean (D)	Deviation Squared (D²)
50	−20	400
60	−10	100
70	0	0
80	+10	100
90	+20	400
Mean A = 70		$\Sigma D^2 = 1000$

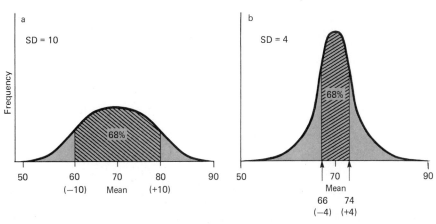

Figure A-6 The more widely dispersed the grades about the mean, the greater the value of the SD. The range covered by one SD above and below the mean always includes 68 per cent of the distribution, regardless of the amount of dispersion.

The sum of the 5 deviations squared (ΣD^2) is 1000. Let's take the average of these squared deviations by dividing 1000 by 5, to get 200. The final step requires you to take the *square root* of the average squared deviations, that is $\sqrt{200}$ or 14.14. This is the SD of the distribution of scores in Set A. The generalized formula for standard deviation is, then:

$$SD = \sqrt{\frac{\Sigma D^2}{N}}$$

Now you can compute the SD for the distribution of scores in Set B. Compare the two SDs against these general conclusions about standard deviations: (1) The larger the SD, the greater the dispersion of scores around the mean of the distribution; and (2) the smaller the SD, the more representative is the mean of the scores in the distribution. As you can see, the instructor who supplies both the mean and the SD for the distribution of midterm-exam scores can communicate a great deal about a large quantity of data with just two values.

The SD has other uses. It allows you to compare a person's performance with that of others on a number of different measures. For example, suppose Bill gets a score of 52 on an anxiety scale that has a mean of 40 and an SD of 7. Suppose he also has an IQ of 130, tested with a scale that has a mean of 100 and an SD of 15. How can you evaluate Bill's relative standing on the two tests, even though the means and ranges and even the very meaning of the two tests are very different? This can be done by expressing his scores in terms of distance from the mean in SD units. His score converted to SD units is called a **standard score,** or **Z score.** To compute a Z score, all you need is the score you wish to convert and the mean and SD of the distribution of scores from which it came, then use the formula

$$Z = \frac{X - M}{SD}$$

That is, the Z score equals the score you wish to convert (X) minus the mean of the distribu-

tion (M) divided by the standard deviation of the distribution (SD). For Bill's anxiety test score,

$$Z = \frac{52 - 40}{7} = \frac{12}{7} = 1.7$$

Converting his intelligence test score,

$$Z = \frac{130 - 100}{15} = \frac{30}{15} = 2.0$$

Bill's Z score of 1.7 on the anxiety test means that he is 1.7 SD units above the mean for that distribution, while he is 2.0 SD units above the mean of the intelligence-test distribution. Thus Bill is relatively brighter than anxious, compared with the groups on which the distributions of these tests have been based.

Figure A-7 shows a normal distribution of IQ scores and reveals important interrelations between scores, SD values, and percentiles. A **percentile** is one one-hundredth, or 1 per cent, of the whole range of scores in a distribution. Observe that almost the entire distribution of scores (99.6 per cent) is included within 3 SDs of the mean (± 3 SD), but a good bulk of scores (68 per cent) falls between one SD above and below the mean (± 1 SD). Since the curve is symmetrical, you can see that there should be as many people scoring above 130 as below 70, and as many between 55 and 70 as between 130 and 145. Look at the percentiles row. The **percentile value** of a given IQ score is obtained by arranging the scores in numerical order and then computing the percentage of scores that are smaller than the given score. If your score was 130 in the distribution shown in Figure A-7, this would mean that 97.5 per cent of the people in the population would be expected to have IQ scores lower than yours. You can see that less than 1 per cent of the population is estimated to have IQs above 145. According to the figure, what per cent of the population has an IQ between 70 and 85? Suppose you make a new acquaintance in a queue the next time you go to a movie. Assuming that moviegoers represent a random sampling of the population, what are the chances that your new acquaintance will have an IQ above 115? Another question: Assuming the distribution shown in Figure A-7, if a person's Z score is 0.66, what is his IQ score? When you have a normal distribution, you can see how much information can be gleaned from it.

INFERENTIAL STATISTICS

While statistical methods are useful for describing data in hand, psychologists are usually interested in generalizing these descriptive statements to the wider population of individuals from which the sample of their subjects is drawn. Inferential statistics are the most powerful instruments used by psychologists in their attempts to discover wide-ranging principles of behavior. In experimental research, two group means are usually compared, the mean for the experimental group and the mean for the control group (see

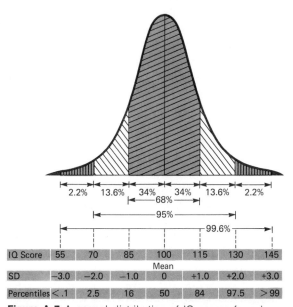

Figure A-7 A normal distribution of IQ scores for a large sample. Note the relationships among scores, SD, and percentiles, and observe the per cent of cases falling within various SD ranges around the mean.

Chapter 1). But how can you decide whether the observed difference between these two means reflects the real effect of the experimental, or independent, variable or whether the difference could be attributed to chance factors? You will see that evaluating the significance of the difference between two means requires a careful weighing of two factors: the reliability of the means—that is, the degree to which they are representative of the group scores—and the actual difference between them.

Reliability of Means

Suppose you want to know whether the knowledge that a woman is a member of a feminist movement influences her perceived attractiveness to men. You could expose a set of 10 photographs of women to two random samples of male college-student subjects: For one group (experimental), the photographed women would be described as members of a feminist organization; for the other group (control), no identification of the women would be provided. Each male subject would rate the attractiveness of each photograph on a 10-point scale, and the 10 ratings would be summed to provide a total score.

First, let's examine hypothetical results obtained from two *control* groups consisting of randomly selected male subjects, a large group of 100 and a small group of 20. Figure A-8 shows two possible—and extreme—distributions of scores for the two control groups. Both groups have a mean of 60. Since each is a sample taken from the population to which you wish to generalize the results of the experiment, wouldn't you have more confidence in the reliability, or representativeness, of the mean if it came from a large sample with a small SD, like the one in Figure A-8*a*, than if it came from a small sample with a large SD, like the one in Figure A-8*b*? Eventually, from the mean of a sample, you'd like to get a reliable estimate of the mean of the population. You

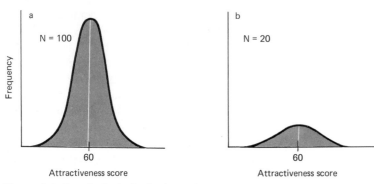

Figure A-8 Hypothetical distributions of attractiveness scores obtained from two groups.

would have less confidence that the mean would be a reliable estimate of the population mean if it came from a small sample with wide dispersion than you would have if the mean came from a larger sample. Two factors, then, need to be weighed in assessing the reliability of the mean: the SD and the size (N) of the sample.

The **standard error of the mean (SE)** combines the two factors that influence the reliability of the mean in a single expression, according to the formula

$$SE = \frac{SD}{\sqrt{N}}$$

Note carefully: The lower the variability (SD), the smaller the SE; the larger the sample (N), the smaller the SE; and, of course, the smaller the SE, the more reliable the mean.

Differences Between Group Means

Let's see how you can use what you've learned about the reliability of means to determine the significance of the difference between two group means. This time, only one control group (Group C), receiving no information about the women in the photos, will be used. Subjects in a second group, being told the women are members of the feminist movement on campus, constitute the experimental group (Group E). Suppose the mean attractiveness rating given by Group E is 40, while

that of the control group (Group C) is 60. Is there a significant difference between the two means? That is, does the difference between the two mean attractiveness ratings result from the fact that one group was given information about the women in the photographs and the other was not? Or could a difference this large between means have occurred by chance? If both groups had received the same information, a small difference between means would have been expected due to individual differences among the people in the two groups. A **significant difference** between group means occurs when statistical tests indicate the difference is probably too large to have occurred by chance. Consider: How reliable are these means? Observe the hypothetical distributions shown in Figure A-9. Although the difference between the means of the distributions of Groups E and C is the same in both the upper and lower panels, note the difference in the amount of dispersion of scores around the mean in each distribution. In the upper panel, note that the highest attractiveness ratings given by males who thought they were evaluating "feminists" are barely more flattering than the *lowest* attractiveness ratings given by control-group males. The small amount of overlap between these distributions adds to your confidence in concluding that the experimental variable (labeling versus no labeling of photos) had a real

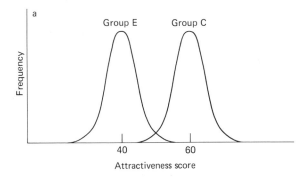

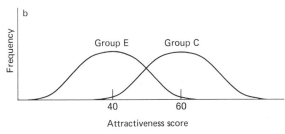

Figure A-9 Hypothetical distributions of attractiveness scores obtained by Groups E and C. Although the difference in the means for the groups is the same, the distributions in the upper panel (a) show less dispersion, hence the standard error of the mean (SE) is lower than in the lower panel (b). Accordingly, the likelihood the difference between the means of the distributions shown in (a) represents a true difference in the population is much greater than in the case of the distributions shown in panel (b).

and discriminative effect on perceived attractiveness. If these figures reflected the true intensity of antifeminist prejudice among college men—which they do not, as you will see—this problem would clearly be of gigantic proportions.

Compare the upper panel (a) with the lower panel (b). Although the mean difference is the same, note the much greater dispersion within each distribution and the overlap between distributions in panel b. You can readily see that the reliability of the means is much lower in panel b. What you now need is a single expression that takes into account the SE of both means. The **standard error of the difference**

between means, (SE_{diff}), does exactly that, as you can see from its formula:

$$SE_{diff} = \sqrt{SE^2_{M_1} + SE^2_{M_2}}$$

in which SE_{M_1} and SE_{M_2} represent the SEs of the two group means. The only new twist is that each SE value is squared and the square root is taken of the sum of the two squared values. The SE_{diff} is a very important value, because it reflects the factors of sample size and dispersion in the distribution of the scores of *both* groups. If the SE_{diff} is small (as it would be for the distributions shown in panel *a* of Figure A-9), even a small difference between the sample means may be taken to reflect a real difference in the population. If the SE_{diff} is very large, the difference between the means would have to be very large indeed to override the disadvantages of high dispersion and/or a small number of cases that a large value for the SE_{diff} implies. Accordingly, the final step is a comparison of the size of the difference between the two sample means and the SE_{diff}. The ratio obtained, the **critical ratio (CR)** (also called the *t* value), is expressed in the following formula:

$$CR = \frac{M_1 - M_2}{SE_{diff}}$$

Tables are available that show how large the CR must be to support the conclusion, at various levels of confidence, that a "true difference" exists between the means. For example, a CR of 1.96 would indicate, according to such tables, that if the experiment were repeated 100 times, you could expect to find a difference between the experimental and control groups in the direction indicated 95 times. Only 5 times in 100 would such a result be expected purely on the basis of chance. The higher the CR, the more confident you can be that the difference obtained between the means of the two groups in your experiment reflect a real difference in the population. This is what inferential statistics is all about: It helps you predict something about the future.

A recent study did investigate the perceived attractiveness of feminist women, using a somewhat different design (Goldberg, Gottesdiener, & Abramson, 1975). These investigators found that there *was* a difference in perceived attractiveness, but it was much smaller than the difference indicated by our hypothetical example. The investigators first had a large number of students rate the attractiveness of 30 photographed women, using a 5-point Likert scale like that described in Chapter 17. Once a mean attractiveness rating was established for each photo, 82 new subjects were asked to sort out the photos of women they guessed were supporters and nonsupporters of women's liberation. It was found that women perceived to be supporters of the feminist movement had a mean attractiveness rating of 2.75, a bit lower than the mean rating of 2.86 computed for nonsupporters. The difference between these means is quite tiny, but the authors reported a less than one-in-a-thousand chance that it could be due to chance on the basis of statistical analysis. What does this tell you about the reliability of the means? Can you visualize the distributions of attractiveness ratings of perceived supporters and nonsupporters?

Correlations

You encountered the correlational method in Chapter 1 as one of the several approaches used by psychologists to investigate behavior. Covariation is another term for correlation. Correlation expresses the observation that when systematic variations occur in the measures assigned to one variable, systematic variations also occur in the measures of another variable. Thus **correlation** measures the interrelationship between variations occurring in two sets of scores. But how can the degree of correlation be computed and expressed in a single numerical value?

In Chapter 1 you saw hypothetical scores for 10 students on both math and logic tests.

These scores appear in Table A-3, in the columns headed X and Y. The table shows the steps involved in computing the **correlation coefficient (r)**, a number reflecting the degree of correlation between variables. In the example in Table A-3, $r = +0.99$, indicating a strong *positive correlation* between math and logic scores: Students who make high scores in math tend to make high scores in logic, and those who make low scores in math tend to make low scores in logic. A correlation is *negative*, on the other hand, when a high score on one test indicates a low score on the other test. For a perfect positive correlation, r would be $+1.00$, and for a perfect negative correlation, r would be -1.00. And if two variables are totally uncorrelated, the value of r is 0.00. Figure 1-19 in Chapter 1 shows how a **scatter diagram**, or **scattergram**, a graph that displays the extent of correlation between variables, can be plotted. Figure A-10 shows a series of such scatter diagrams that illustrate different degrees of positive and negative correlation. You know that the correlation coefficient (r) for the X and Y scores in Table A-3 is 0.99. Try plotting these scores on a scatter diagram that you set up for yourself, to see what such a high degree of correlation looks like.

It is very easy to misinterpret the meaning of a correlation coefficient. Here are some points to keep in mind:

1. The correlation, no matter how strong, does not guarantee a *causal* relationship between the two variables. There is, for example, a high positive correlation between midterm and final exam grades, but it would be absurd to assert that midterm exam grades *cause* the final exam grades. There is a negative correlation between the number of mules in a state and the number of Ph.D.'s in that state; a relationship, yes, but hardly a causal one. There is also correlation (positive or negative, would you say?) between the length of boys' pants and their mental age as measured by an IQ test. Correlation *may* reflect a causal relationship, but not necessarily. Experimental

Table A-3 Computing the Pearson Product-Moment Correlation (r)

Student	Math Score X	Logic Score Y	$(X - M_x)$ x	$(Y - M_y)$ y	x^2	y^2	xy
1	75	74	−3	−3	9	9	9
2	89	90	11	13	121	169	143
3	100	98	22	21	484	441	462
4	92	94	14	17	196	289	238
5	57	53	−21	−24	441	576	504
6	87	85	9	8	81	64	72
7	60	63	−18	−14	324	196	252
8	71	67	−7	−10	49	100	70
9	82	80	4	3	16	9	12
10	67	66	−11	−11	121	121	121

$M_x = 78 \quad M_y = 77 \qquad \Sigma x^2 = 1842 \quad \Sigma y^2 = 1974 \quad \Sigma xy = 1883$

$$r = \frac{\Sigma xy}{\sqrt{(\Sigma x^2)(\Sigma y^2)}} = \frac{1883}{\sqrt{(1842)(1974)}} = \frac{1883}{\sqrt{3636108}} = 0.99$$

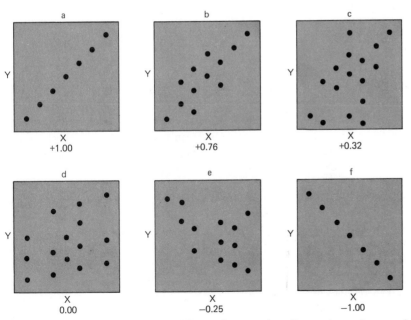

Figure A-10 Scattergrams showing different degrees of positive and negative correlation. The correlation coefficient r is shown immediately below each scattergram.

methods must be used to determine whether the relationship is a causal one.

2. A correlation coefficient does not indicate the *percentage* of relationship between two variables. For example, suppose the correlation between the IQ scores of parents and children is 0.50. This doesn't imply a 50 per cent relationship. Rather, it is necessary to square the value of r to get an estimate of the percentage of relationship between two variables. Thus with $r = 0.50$ between IQ of parents and their children, you can say that 0.50^2, or about 25 per cent, of the variation in the IQ scores of a number of children is accounted for by variations in parental IQ scores. This is another way of saying that an r of 0.50 implies a 25 per cent relationship between the variables.

3. Correlation coefficients are not directly proportional. If the correlation between two variables is 0.60, the relationship between them is not twice as strong as if the correlation were only 0.30. A better comparison is obtained by squaring the two correlations and then dividing the larger product by the smaller. Thus $0.60^2 = 0.36$; $0.30^2 = 0.09$; 0.36 divided by $0.09 = 4$. An r of 0.60 therefore implies a relationship four times stronger than an r of 0.30.

While it is clear that a correlation coefficient can be used as a descriptive statistic to measure the relationship between two sets of data already collected, correlational methods are also used for inferential purposes. For example, just suppose that, on a number of occasions, an instructor has always found a correlation of $+1.00$ between midterm and final exam grades (not very likely, but just *suppose*). This would mean that given knowledge of the midterm grades, the instructor could predict with perfect accuracy the final exam grades (and thus no final exam would need to be given). Take another example: If the amount of TV violence observed by children were perfectly correlated with measures of subsequent display of aggressiveness, you'd be able to predict beforehand *which* children would be likely to show future aggressive behavior. Or, if you like, by watching current aggressiveness, you could tell how much TV violence a child had viewed. Correlations high enough to permit such inferences about aggressiveness have, of course, not been found. In other areas, however, a fair amount of inference is possible. IQ scores of identical twins have shown correlation coefficients as high as 0.90. What predictive uses can you think of for a coefficient this high? The correlation between scores obtained on the same personality test on two separate occasions by the same persons (*test–*

Table A-4 Midterm and Final Exam Grades for Students in Two Discussion Sections, *A* and *B*, in an Introductory Psychology Course

Student	Discussion Section	Exam Scores for Midterm	Final
1	A	93	92
2	A	84	83
3	B	76	81
4	A	91	85
5	B	58	86
6	A	76	80
7	B	82	69
8	B	93	90
9	A	62	73
10	B	88	90
11	A	89	86
12	A	90	79
13	A	86	88
14	B	92	87
15	B	89	84
16	B	81	79
17	A	83	71
18	B	91	96
19	A	72	75
20	A	83	75
21	B	92	93
22	B	78	77
23	A	88	77
24	B	70	55
25	B	88	73
26	A	92	93

retest reliability) is also usually very high. How can such high correlations be used to help design better measuring instruments?

APPLICATIONS OF STATISTICS

Now that you have seen some of the basic concepts and procedures of statistics, you undoubtedly realize that you often use or need to understand at least the basic concepts of statistics, like percentages and means, and its fundamental procedures, like frequency distributions and scatter diagrams. You will find knowledge of these statistical principles and procedures valuable in working with this book, to say nothing of reading psychological reports in journals and other books, as well as in other scientific disciplines, ranging from physics and chemistry to sociology and economics. Finally, you will find statistics both necessary and valuable as you collect data for your own psychological or other investigations.

Review the statistical procedures shown here by applying them to the following problem: The data in Table A-4 give the actual midterm and final exam grades for a class of 26 students taking a course in introductory psychology. The students were divided into two discussion sections, A and B. Analyze and interpret these data for the two sections as follows:

1. Make up frequency distributions, histograms, and frequency polygons for each section for the midterm and final grades.
2. Are the distributions normal or skewed?
3. What are the means, modes, and medians for the distributions?
4. What are the standard deviations and standard errors of the means for midterm and final scores?
5. What are the Z scores for several students?
6. What is the correlation coefficient (r) between the midterm and the final scores? (If a calculator is not available, limit your computation to the scores of the first ten students.)
7. What is the critical ratio of the difference between final grades for students in sections A and B? Would you say that students in section A are more or less consistent than students in B, and how can you tell?

Glossary

absolute rating scale A rating scale according to which the rater assigns a score to each subject on each characteristic being rated on the basis of comparison with a standard for each characteristic. See also *relative rating scale*.

absolute threshold The minimum level of stimulus intensity of which an organism is aware or to which it responds. See also *difference threshold*.

abstract theory A theory that employs mathematical or purely imaginary concepts or principles to summarize and explain events or relationships. See also *reductionistic theory; theory*.

achievement motivation See *need for achievement*.

accommodation The focusing of the image of an object on the retina of an observer by means of a change in the shape of the lens of the eye, serving as a cue, by kinesthetic feedback from muscles controlling the lens, for the distance of objects in monocular vision. See also *monocular depth perception*.

accommodation, cognitive The process by means of which individuals adjust their existing cognitive structures when they encounter new observations that do not fit into the framework; according to Piaget, one of the major methods of cognitive development. See also *assimilation*.

acetylcholine One of the chemical transmitters at synapses throughout the nervous system, which stimulates drinking when applied to the lateral nucleus of the hypothalamus.

Achievement Anxiety Test (AAT) A specific anxiety measure of both debilitating and facilitating effects of test anxiety.

acoustic confusion Confusion that results in errors in reading words visually when the spelling of words as seen does not correspond with the sounds of words as heard.

acquired motives See *secondary motives*.

action tendency The regular way in which a person with an attitude toward another person or thing acts toward that target of the attitude, expressing favorable or unfavorable feelings and beliefs.

actualization An archetype in the collective unconscious, predisposing an individual to strive for realization and giving rise to the self, seeking the highest values, according to Jung; also, the principal human motive, according to Maslow and other humanistic psychologists. See also *archetype; collective unconscious*.

acupuncture anesthesia A Chinese medical procedure consisting of the insertion of needles in various precisely determined locations in the patient's body, which is purported to alleviate symptoms, including pain, and cure disease.

adaptation, receptor or **sensory** The process by which a sensory receptor tends to respond less and less to constant stimulation until partial or complete failure of response occurs. See also *dark adaptation; light adaptation*.

adaptation-level theory A theory that analyzes and explains perception on the basis of the organism's adaptation or adjustment to the specific conditions of stimulation, including the immediate focal stimuli, background stimuli, and residual stimuli representing past experience.

adaptive behavior Behavior of an organism that tends to restore it to equilibrium or homeostasis, satisfy its needs, or adjust it to environmental and social conditions, and is conducive in the long run to its survival. See also *homeostasis; maladaptive behavior*.

addiction, drug A condition manifested in a strong craving for a drug that results in an overwhelming preoccupation with obtaining and using it, based on extreme psychological or physical dependence. See also *dependence, drug; drugs, psychoactive.*

addictive disorder The behavior disorder resulting from physiological and/or psychological dependence on drugs. See also *addiction, drug; dependence, drug.*

Adlerian therapy A type of psychoanalytic therapy based on Alfred Adler's emphasis on the universal striving to overcome feelings of inferiority, the reconciliation of personal drives with social realities, and the development of one's own life style.

adrenal glands Endocrine glands located above the kidneys that secrete several hormones, including epinephrine (adrenaline), which produce the peripheral activation, or excitement, accompanying many emotions.

adrenaline See *epinephrine.*

adrenocortical hormones Hormones from the adrenal glands that prepare the body for psychological or physical stress.

affect The psychological component of an emotion; the feeling quality of an experience, such as the quality of pleasantness of unpleasantness accompanying certain behavior or situations. See also *emotion; feeling; hedonic quality.*

affective personality See *cyclothymic personality.*

affective psychosis See *manic-depressive psychosis.*

afterglow A tingling sensation arising from stimulation of the skin around the lips, in creases between nose and cheeks, other facial areas, and the back of the hand, lasting from several seconds to several minutes after the stimulation has ceased. The receptor for these sensations has not been identified.

afterimage An image or sensation that remains in the visual field for some time after the cessation of the stimulation that produced it. Staring at a colored shape and closing the eyes will produce a negative afterimage of the complementary color. Blue and yellow, red and green are complementary colors.

age regression The psychoanalytic method of assisting a patient to recall the first occurrence of a conflict, often having taken place in childhood, by means of such techniques as free association and hypnosis.

aggregate group A group of persons who simply chance to gather in space and time without a common goal. See also *functional group; group.*

aggression Behavior of an organism intended to threaten or to inflict injury on another organism, often accompanying anger or rage and sometimes turned against the organism itself. See also *masochistic behavior.*

aggressive reaction A frequent reaction to frustration, consisting of an attack on the barrier that blocks access to the desired goal; often accompanied by anger or rage. See also *barrier; displacement; frustration; scapegoat.*

"Aha" experience The surprising and agreeable experience of sudden insight when the solution of a problem suddenly dawns, expressed in exclamations like "Aha!" See also *insight; problem solving; sudden solution.*

alcohol A natural drug, ethyl alcohol, that acts as a depressant, in low doses inducing behavior that is normally inhibited, in high doses inducing mental confusion and motor impairment. See also *depressant.*

alcoholism Addiction to the use of ethyl alcohol, involving dependence on the drug to the extent of heavy use for three months or more or inability to go one day without use. See also *addiction, drug.*

alpha waves or **rhythms** Slow, high-voltage patterns of brain waves, recorded on electroencephalograms, usually accompanying states of wakeful mental alertness and relaxation, particularly when the eyes are closed. See also *electroencephalogram.*

altered state of consciousness A state of awareness or experience differing markedly from the normal waking state, characterized by changes in attention, memory, thought, and judgment; changes in sense of time; loss of self-control; increased suggestibility; strong emotional reactions; hallucinations. See also *consciousness.*

Alternate Uses Test (AUT) A test for creativity in which subjects are asked to think of unusual uses to which common things, like eyeglasses or automobile tires, could be put, thereby demonstrating one component of creative behavior.

amnesia Partial or total loss of memory resulting from extreme repression due to severe aversive emotion or conflict, or from organic brain damage. See also *fugue; hysterical neurosis; repression.*

amniocentesis Collection of a sample of the amniotic fluid around an embryo by inserting a needle through the mother's abdominal wall into the uterus; analysis of the amniotic fluid yields information on the genetic character of the embryo.

amphetamine A drug that stimulates the central nervous system. Methamphetamine, or "speed," is a popular form of this drug. See also *stimulant*.

amplitude Half the distance between the trough and the height of the crest of a wave. The sensation of intensity of light and sound varies with the amplitude of light and sound waves. See also *brightness; light wave; loudness; sound wave*.

analgesia A state of insensibility to pain without loss of consciousness.

anal stage According to Freudian theory, the stage during the second and third years of life in which children concentrate on the excretory functions for libidinal gratification and aggression.

androgens Sex hormones found in both sexes, but in higher concentrations in the male.

anima, animus The female archetype possessed by men and the male archetype possessed by women, respectively, as a part of their collective unconscious, according to Jung.

animism The view that all events, including human behavior, are governed by spiritual forces.

antidepressant One of a group of drugs used for the alleviation of depression, primarily for endogenous depression in which the disorder is attributed to some biochemical malfunction rather than, or in addition to, environmental stresses.

antisocial or **sociopathic personality** A deviant personality, also known as psychopathic personality, characterized by self-centered, impulsive, and irresponsible behavior patterns, in chronic conflict with society, without loyalty to other individuals or groups, and uninterested in the values of others. See also *dyssocial personality*.

anvil See *ossicles*.

anxiety A complex emotional and motivational state, subjectively involving feelings of fear, dread, or worry, and accompanied by such physical manifestations as a pounding heart, perspiration, and dizziness. See also *fear*.

anxiety inventory A set of statements, selected as descriptive of reliable symptoms of anxiety, to which subjects respond by indicating whether or to what degree the statements apply to them. See also *specific anxiety measure; Taylor Manifest Anxiety Scale; Test Anxiety Questionnaire*.

anxiety neurosis A neurotic behavior disorder characterized by sensitivity to tension-producing conflicts and a tendency to react with anxiety, dread, or fright, and with bodily disturbances.

apathy A frequent withdrawal reaction to persistent or severe frustration in which the individual becomes helpless to initiate activity. See also *learned helplessness; withdrawal reaction*.

approach–approach conflict A type of conflict in which equally strong approach tendencies are pitted against each other. See also *behavioral model of conflict*.

approach–avoidance conflict A type of conflict in which approach and avoidance tendencies are pitted against each other, often yielding persistent conflicts. See also *behavioral model of conflict*.

archetype An inborn, emotionalized predisposition, like a fear of snakes, passed on through human evolution, according to Jung. See also *collective unconscious*.

arrhythmia An irregularity in the rhythmic action of the heart, either in time or force, due to organic or emotional conditions. See also *premature ventricular contraction*.

assessment The measurement or evaluation of any behavioral process, like personality or emotionality, by means of a test, an inventory, or a scale. See also *personality assessment*.

assimilation The process by means of which individuals fit new observations into their already existing cognitive structures; according to Piaget, one of the principal methods of cognitive development. See also *accommodation, cognitive*.

association cortex See *cortex*.

associationism The doctrine that simple elements, like sensations, combine through various types of association to form all of the compounds of the mind, like images and ideas.

astrology The unverified theory that the positions of celestial bodies—sun, moon, stars, planets—determine personality types and influence human behavior.

attachment A bond characterized by mutual affection between an infant and a caretaker, normally the mother.

attention The focusing of an organism on stimulation in such a way that awareness of the stimulus is heightened. Factors influencing attention include stimulus intensity, novelty, significance, and motivation. See also *selective attention*.

attitude A persistent response tendency of an individual toward a target, either favorable or unfavorable, involving a complex of motives, emotions, thoughts, and behavior. See also *action tendency; belief; direction; prejudice.*

attitude scale A rating scale used to measure the strength of favorable and unfavorable attitudes toward target persons or things. See also *Likert attitude scale; rating scale; semantic differential technique; Thurstone attitude scale.*

attraction The motive directed toward behavior that brings individuals together; possibly a non-learned motive. See also *primary motive; secondary motive.*

attraction, interpersonal A liking, favoring, or approving relationship between two or more people, based on such factors as physical attractiveness, physical proximity, similar or complementary attitudes, and like social status. See also *reward theory of attraction; social-exchange theory of attraction.*

audience effects The effects on the performance of an individual produced by observers, particularly those who evaluate the observed activities. See also *coaction effects.*

auditory canal The canal leading from the outer ear to the tympanic membrane.

auditory cortex The area in the top of the temporal lobe in both left and right hemispheres of the brain to which the primary auditory nerve pathways lead.

auditory nerve or **pathway** The nerve, consisting of a bundle of axons of spiral ganglion cells, carrying neural messages from the ear to the auditory cortex.

autism A behavior disorder of early childhood, generally considered a form of psychosis, characterized by mutism, repetitive meaningless acts, and failure to manifest normal awareness of or responsiveness to others.

autogenic training Training in self-control of various physical functions, like the temperature of one's hands, by the verbalization of a series of statements to oneself while imagining the results. See also *biofeedback.*

autokinetic effect The apparent movement of a stationary pinpoint of light in a darkened room, probably caused by minor movements of the observer's eyes.

autonomic nervous system The major division of the peripheral nervous system, composed of a system of ganglia, or groups of nerve cell bodies, and associated nerves lying outside the central nervous system that regulate the glands and other internal organs. See also *central nervous system; somatic nervous system.*

average See *mean; median; mode.*

avoidance–avoidance conflict A type of conflict in which two negative and incompatible avoidance tendencies are pitted against each other, often causing the individual to react with withdrawal —by leaving the field, for example—or by fantasy, regression, hysterical disorders, or amnesia. See also *behavioral model of conflict.*

avoidance conditioning See *negative reinforcement.*

awareness Attention to, fixation on, consciousness, realization, perception, or knowledge of anything or event.

axon That part of the neuron that transmits nerve impulses away from the neuron cell body to other neurons or to muscles or glands.

babbling The repeated sounds all infants make, unrelated to the language of their cultures but including the sounds of most languages, and selectively reinforced by caretakers when the sounds appear to be meaningful in their language.

barbiturates A class of depressant drugs that produce drowsiness. See also *depressant.*

bar graph See *histogram.*

barrier An event or condition, either external or internal, that thwarts progress toward a desired goal or target toward which behavior is directed, thereby instigating frustration. See also *aggressive reaction; frustration; withdrawal reaction.*

basal age On the Stanford-Binet Intelligence Scale, the subtest age level at which the examinee passes all of the test items.

baseline (of target behavior) The frequency and/or strength of the target behavior to be modified by behavioral-technology procedures, which is used to determine whether the behavior is increasing or decreasing as desired under the modification program. See also *target behavior.*

basilar membrane The membrane within the cochlea of the inner ear on which the organ of Corti is located.

behavioral control Manipulation of relevant environmental conditions for the purpose of modifying one's own behavior or that of others. See also *stimulus control.*

behavioral model of conflict A theory of conflict,

developed by Neal Miller and his associates, based on the tension created by incompatible tendencies to approach and to avoid objects, events, or situations. See also *approach–approach conflict; approach–avoidance conflict; avoidance–avoidance conflict; double approach–avoidance conflict.*

behavioral rehearsal A therapeutic technique in which a person is trained to overcome behavioral inhibitions in real life by rehearsing components of the inhibited behavior during therapy.

behavioral technology The application of classical and instrumental conditioning principles in medicine, education, psychotherapy, and self-control to help eliminate behavior disorders or control behavior undesirable to the individual involved.

behavior disorder Behavior that tends, chronically or acutely, to be maladaptive for the organism, such as neurotic or psychotic behavior; also called "mental illness," "insanity," "abnormal behavior." See also *functional behavior disorder; interpersonal model; maladaptive behavior; medical model; neurosis; organic behavior disorder; psychosis.*

behavior modification See *behavior therapy.*

behavior therapy Treatment of behavior disorders on the basis of learning principles, based on the assumption that the disorders are basically learned maladaptive patterns of behavior; related terms are behavior modification, reinforcement therapy, contingency management, and behavioral self-control. See also *desensitization therapy; implosive therapy.*

belief An idea or thought on which a person is ready to act, accepting it as true; sets of interrelated ideas, or belief systems, are involved in attitudes.

belief system See *belief.*

binaural discrepancy The difference in the time of arrival and loudness of a sound at the two ears of an observer, serving as a cue to the direction of the sound source. See also *sound localization.*

binocular depth perception Perception of the depth or distance of an object derived from cues provided by both eyes, such as binocular disparity. See also *binocular disparity; monocular depth perception.*

binocular disparity The difference between the views from two eyes of an object fairly close to an observer, which occurs because the separation of the eyes gives each a slightly different visual field; one of the principal cues for binocular depth perception. See also *binocular depth perception.*

binocular vision Vision with both eyes. See also *monocular vision.*

biofeedback The communication, or feedback, to an individual of changes in the physical system, such as heartbeat, brain waves, and muscular tension, to indicate the success or failure of attempts to control these and other processes.

biological drive A drive directed toward maintaining the optimal physiological condition of an organism. See also *homeostatic drive; nonhomeostatic drive.*

biophilous type The life-loving type of personality according to Fromm. See also *life instinct.*

bipolar cell A cell in the middle layer of the retina that interconnects various rod and cone receptor cells, carrying the nerve message to ganglion cells.

blind evaluation Evaluation of a technique, like one of the psychotherapeutic methods, by a judge who does not know what technique has been used on the patients, and consequently can be objective in evaluating their degree of improvement.

blind spot The small spot in the retina where nerve fibers pass out of the eye and receptors for vision are lacking.

body language Gestures, postures, and other body or facial expressions that convey information about a person's state of mind or characteristics and supplement verbal expressions.

brainstem The part of the brain that connects the spinal cord with higher brain regions. It consists of the medulla, pons, and midbrain, and regulates such automatic functions as respiration, blood pressure, and heart rate.

brightness The sensation of intensity of light, produced by the amplitude of the light waves stimulating the retina of the eye.

caffeine A stimulant drug that is a natural constituent of coffee and tea, and is found as well in many cola-flavored drinks.

caffeinism Nervousness, headache, agitation, irritability, heart palpitations, nausea, and diarrhea arising from consumption of excessive amounts of caffeine-containing beverages. The symptoms mimic those of anxiety neurosis.

Cannabis sativa See *marijuana.*

cardiovascular processes The processes by which the heart, blood vessels, and capillaries function in an organism, which in a variety of investigations have been shown to be conditionable.

case-history technique The reconstruction of a subject's past based on self-reports, reports of family members and others, and records about the subject from other sources. See also *retrospective method*.

castration complex According to Freudian theory, a condition attributed to children in the throes of the Oedipus conflict, involving fear of losing the penis for males and anxiety at having "lost" the penis for females, in punishment for desiring sexual relations with the parent of the opposite sex.

catatonic schizophrenia A type of schizophrenia marked by either excited, sometimes violent behavior or negative, withdrawn behavior in which limb positions or body posture remain unchanged (waxy flexibility) for long periods of time. See also *schizophrenia*.

causal relationship An invariant relationship between independently defined events such that the occurrence of one, the cause or independent variable, is uniformly followed by the occurrence of the other, the effect or dependent variable. See also *correlation; dependent variable; experimental method; functional relationship; independent variable; intervening variable; stimulus-response relationship*.

cause See *causal relationship; independent variable*.

cell-assembly theory A theory that analyzes and explains perception in terms of a cell assembly, or group of cells in the brain that function together, firing impulses simultaneously, because they have been bonded by prior experiences with the stimulating object.

central nervous system The most highly developed part of the nervous system, composed of the brain and spinal cord and lying within the bony skull and spine. See also *peripheral nervous system*.

cerebellum The part of the brain close to the brainstem, serving as a control center for movement, muscle coordination, and balance.

cerebral hemispheres The largest and most recently evolved part of the brain, whose surface layer is called the cortex, or neocortex, arranged in two nearly symmetrical halves. See also *cortex*.

chaining The linking together of a number of separate responses of an organism to form the desired complete pattern of behavior in the instrumental conditioning of the organism. See also *shaping*.

character disorder See *personality disorder*.

character trait See *personality trait*.

chemotherapy The use of drugs in the treatment of behavior disorders. See also *antidepressant; tranquilizer*.

chiasma See *optic chiasma*.

chromosome Threadlike materials composed of many genes, found in the nucleus of all living cells, through which inheritance is transmitted.

chronic anxiety An anxious condition persisting for long periods of time and tending to recur. See also *anxiety*.

chronological age Age in years. See also *mental age*.

chunking The reducing or grouping together of elements of information into a small number of chunks, in a coding strategy that aids transfer from short-term memory to storage in long-term memory. See also *coding strategies; long-term memory*.

clairvoyance Alleged extrasensory perception of objects or events; that is, perception by means other than the known sensory modalities. See also *extrasensory perception*.

classical conditioning A kind of learning, usually involving a glandular or visceral response, in which a neutral stimulus (like the sound of a bell) is paired with a potent stimulus or reinforcer (like food) enough times so that the neutral stimulus comes to elicit a response (salivation) similar to that produced by the potent stimulus. The originally neutral stimulus is called a conditioned stimulus (CS); the potent stimulus is called an unconditioned stimulus (US); and the original response (unconditioned response or UR) becomes a conditioned response (CR). See also *instrumental conditioning; learning; operant learning*.

class interval The range of scores used in grouping individual scores into a number of classes of equal size, having the same range of scores. See also *frequency distribution*.

client-centered therapy A type of psychotherapy in which the client's self-actualizing tendencies are emphasized by the therapist's encouragement of self-insight and self-acceptance; developed by Carl Rogers. See also *Q-sort technique; unconditional positive regard*.

clinical psychology The division of psychology that deals with people suffering from emotional or adjustment problems or behavior disorders. See also *counseling psychology*.

cloning The process of replicating the entire genetic makeup of an individual in a new organism, producing an identical genetic copy.

clustering   A procedure—for example, grouping items of information into classes—serving as a coding strategy to aid transfer of information from short-term memory to storage in long-term memory. See also *coding strategies; hierarchical tree.*

coaction effects   The effects on the performance of members of a group of working on the same task, whether individually or in a division of labor. See also *audience effects; social facilitation.*

cocaine   A stimulant made from the extract of coca leaves; also used as a local anesthetic. Produces excitability and talkativeness, but long-term effects may include depression and convulsions. While no physical dependence results from extended use, psychological dependence may develop.

cochlea   The coiled tube of the inner ear, transmitting vibrations from the ossicles to the basilar membrane containing the sound receptors, the hair cells in the organ of Corti.

coding strategies   Procedures that assist the transfer of information from short-term memory to storage in long-term memory. See also *chunking; clustering; mnemonic device; retrieval strategies.*

cognition   The process by which individuals gain understanding and acquire knowledge, including imagining, remembering, conceiving, inferring, thinking, and reasoning, and which is manifested in such varied activities as simple problem solving and complex scientific investigation.

cognitive development   The ways in which the capacity to use cognitive processes develop during childhood, passing through several distinct stages, according to the theory of Jean Piaget. See also *accommodation, cognitive; assimilation; cognition; concrete operational stage; formal operational stage; preoperational stage; sensorimotor stage.*

cognitive therapy   A type of therapy, like Albert Ellis' rational-emotive therapy, emphasizing the strong influence of perceptions and cognitions on emotions; also used in some forms of desensitization therapy to help the patient convert the perception or thought of threat or rejection into one of social acceptance. See also *desensitization therapy; rational-emotive therapy.*

collective unconscious   An unconscious entity composed of latent memories inborn in human beings as residues of evolution and consisting of archetypes, or emotionalized predispositions (such as fear of the dark), developed under the primitive conditions of prehistoric eras; a construct of Carl Jung. See also *archetype.*

color   The quality of visual sensations, also called "hue," varying through the spectrum from red (produced by physical light stimuli of long wavelength) to violet (produced by stimuli of short wavelength).

color blindness   The inability to distinguish all or some colors, resulting from failure of the red, green, or blue discriminatory cones to function properly.

comparative psychology   The study of the behavioral similarities and differences of various species of animals.

complex   An organized nucleus of extreme feelings, thoughts, and perceptions, such as the mother complex, in part derived from experience and in part, according to Jung, from the collective unconscious.

compulsion   See *obsessive-compulsive neurosis.*

concept   A general idea combining the essential features common to a group or class of similar things, such as the idea of dogs, or "doggishness," as opposed to the image of a particular dog.

concrete operational stage   The stage in Piaget's theory of cognitive development, from about 7 to 12 years of age, during which children begin to grasp logical relationships, classify things according to their common properties, and understand how such properties of things as their number, volume, and weight remain constant despite changes in their shape or arrangement. See also *cognitive development.*

concurrent validity   The ability of a test to discriminate between groups of subjects known to differ in the characteristic it is intended to measure. See also *construct validity; validity.*

conditioned emotional response (CER)   An emotional response, like fear or anger, that has been classically or instrumentally conditioned. In operant appetitive learning, a CER is measured by the amount of disruption produced in hunger-motivated responding by a fear stimulus.

conditioned response (CR)   A response (like salivation) elicited by a previously neutral stimulus (like a sound) after it has been paired a number of times with an unconditioned stimulus (like food). See also *reflex, acquired.*

conditioned stimulus (CS)   A previously neutral stimulus that comes to elicit a response like a biological reflex as a result of repeated pairing with an unconditioned stimulus (US). See also *reflex, acquired; unconditioned stimulus.*

conditioning See *classical conditioning; instrumental conditioning.*

cone The receptor cell in the retina of the eye differentially sensitive to various wavelengths of light and thereby distinguishing colors, concentrated particularly in the central, or foveal, portion of the retina.

conflict A process in which opposing reaction tendencies are pitted against each other, thus blocking action by the organism. See also *behavioral model of conflict; Freudian model of conflict; Oedipus conflict; phenomenological model of conflict.*

connotative meaning The meaning that a word or other symbol may acquire through mediated generalization, as opposed to the external stimulus object or event to which the word refers. See also *mediated generalization.*

consciousness Awareness or perception of internal or external facts or events, ranging in degree from sleep to alert awake, arousal, and altered states. See also *altered state of consciousness.*

conservation of number The principle that regardless of placement or arrangement, the number of objects in a group remains the same; a principle not grasped before the concrete operational stage of cognitive development, according to Piaget.

conservation of volume The principle that regardless of shape of container, a given amount of liquid retains the same volume; a principle not grasped before the concrete operational stage of cognitive development, according to Piaget.

consolidation Certain changes occurring in the nervous system over the critical period of time involved in the reliable storage of experiences in long-term memory.

constancy See *perceptual constancy.*

construct validity The degree to which predictions based on the theoretical properties of the characteristic being measured by a test are actually confirmed. See also *concurrent validity.*

contingency The degree of probability that an event, like a CS, will be followed by another event, like a US. Contingency relationships range from −1.0 (CS never followed by US) through 0.0 (no relationship between CS and US occurrence) to +1.0 (CS always followed by US).

control group The group of subjects not exposed to or affected by the independent variable in an experiment. See also *dependent variable; experi-*

mental group; independent variable; method of difference.

convergence The inward motion of the eyes of an observer toward each other, providing kinesthetic feedback cues from the eye muscles for the perception of distance of objects in binocular vision. See also *binocular depth perception.*

convergent hierarchy A number of associated external stimuli that elicit the same response, like the standardized traits of people associated in stereotypes. See also *divergent hierarchy.*

conversion reaction A neurotic syndrome, motivated by extreme levels of anxiety, expressed as a loss or impairment of sensory or motor functions. See also *dissociation reaction; hysteric conversion.*

cornea A tough transparent membrane protecting the eye, through which light enters.

corpus callosum A large tract of fibers interconnecting the right and left hemispheres of the cerebral cortex and integrating their functions. The severance of this tract, performed in order to control epileptic seizures, has revealed a difference in the functions of the left and right hemispheres.

correlation The degree of covariation between measurable properties of things or events. See also *correlational method; correlation coefficient; negative correlation; positive correlation; variable.*

correlational method A method of determining whether measures of variables, things, or events tend to covary consistently with each other, either positively or negatively. See also *correlation; negative correlation; positive correlation; variable.*

correlation coefficient (*r*) A number reflecting the degree of correlation between two sets of scores or variables, ranging from +1.00 for a perfect positive correlation to −1.00 for a perfect negative correlation. A value of 0.00 indicates that the two sets of scores are not correlated.

cortex or **neocortex** The thin surface area of the cerebral hemispheres of the brain. It is divided in each hemisphere into four lobes: the frontal lobe contains an area controlling motor movement; the parietal lobe contains an area that processes sensory information from the body; the temporal lobe contains an area that processes auditory information; the occipital lobe contains an area that processes visual information. The remainder of the cortex, primarily neither sensory nor motor in function, is called the association cortex.

counseling psychology A branch of clinical psychology in which personal advising and guidance are emphasized, usually practiced in educational or business settings and dealing with less severe problems than those encountered in mental hospitals. See also *clinical psychology; industrial psychology; management psychology; personnel psychology; school psychology.*

counterconditioning The substitution of a more adaptive response for an anxiety response by conditioning the stimuli that previously elicited the anxiety to the adaptive behavior. See also *desensitization-relaxation therapy.*

covert process A process, such as thinking and imagining, that takes place privately within the individual and is not directly observable by others. See also *overt process.*

covert sensitization A behavior-modification technique in which the individual is taught to associate the urge to eat (drink, smoke, etc.) with very aversive, nauseating imagery.

creative process A process by means of which something novel or original is produced. According to one analysis, the process consists of the stages of preparation, incubation, illumination or insight, and verification. See also *creativity; insight; problem solving.*

creativity The widely varying ability to produce some new and original thing, event, or idea. See also *Alternate Uses Test; creative process; Remote Associates Test.*

critical period A period in the life of an organism during which a response or behavior is readily established, and before and after which such acquisition occurs slowly or not at all; in imprinting, a brief period early in development during which social attachment is established. See also *imprinting.*

critical ratio (CR) The number expressing the comparison of the size of the difference between two sample means against the standard error of the difference between the means:

$$CR = \frac{M_1 - M_2}{SE_{diff}}$$

CR is the critical ratio, M_1 and M_2 are the two means, and SE_{diff} is the standard error of the difference between the means.

cross-modal perception The perceptual ability to recognize identity of an object across sensory modalities; for instance, recognizing that an object seen is the same as one previously only touched.

cyclothymic personality A mildly deviant personality, also known as affective personality, characterized by the shifting of moods from extreme elation to profound depression.

dark adaptation A kind of visual adaptation in which the eye adjusts to low light intensity with enlargement of the pupil and a shift from cone to rod vision. See also *adaptation; light adaptation.*

data Facts; observations that may be transformed into symbols (numbers, words, or other signs) for the purpose of drawing inferences or constructing an intellectual system; "data" is plural, "datum" singular. See also *statistics; symbol.*

death instinct A drive, deriving from the id, destructive of the self, according to Freudian theory. See also *life instinct.*

decibel The unit of measurement of the loudness of sounds, consisting of one-tenth of a bel; a bel is the logarithm of the ratio between two sound intensities, the sound in question and the threshold sound.

defaced image The image of the self produced by childhood insecurities, significant in the development of personality; a construct of Karen Horney. See also *idealized image.*

defense mechanism A process used by the ego, like repression or displacement, to avoid or diminish conflicts and the anxiety they produce; a construct of Freud. See also *displacement; regression; repression; sublimation.*

delayed-reaction experiment An experiment in which the period of time between stimulus and response is extended, providing the opportunity to investigate the mediational processes that enable organisms to respond correctly to the stimulus. See also *mediational process; proprioceptive stimulus.*

delirium tremens A violent delirium characterized by terrifying hallucinations, tremor, sweating, and mental confusion, resulting from withdrawal from prolonged excessive use of alcohol.

delusion A fixed but erroneous belief strongly held even though it does not correspond to physical or social realities; characteristic of psychosis. See also *hallucination; paranoid reaction.*

demand characteristics The influence of perception of the changes expected during psychotherapeutic treatment on the patient's actual improvement or on the patient's judgment of improvement.

demonological theory An early theory of behavior disorders, attributing them to seizure by demons, bewitchment, or possession by other evil spirits; still prevalent in some preliterate cultures.

dendrite That part of the neuron that, with the neuron cell body, receives stimulation either from the environment or from other neurons.

deoxyribonucleic acid (DNA) Genetic material, found in the chromosomes, whose complex structure carries the genetic code through ribonucleic acid.

dependence, drug Inability to function without a drug, *physical* when continued use is necessary to prevent undesirable physiological reactions and *psychological* when a user feels that continued use is necessary to maintain a minimal state of well-being. See also *addiction, drug.*

dependent variable An event that, under the controlled conditions of an experiment, is caused by a prior event, the independent variable. See also *independent variable.*

depressant A drug that depresses the central nervous system and tends to decrease alertness and induce drowsiness, and may produce depression. See also *alcohol; barbiturates.*

depression See *neurotic depression; psychotic depressive reaction.*

depression, endogenous A depression attributed to a biochemical malfunction in the patient rather than or in conjunction with environmental stresses or internal conflicts.

depth perception Visual perception of the depth or distance of an object. See also *binocular depth perception; monocular depth perception.*

descriptive hypothesis A statement expressing the kind of results to be determined or observed when conditions expressed in the statement hold, such as "to determine differences in aggressive behavior in groups of subjects who watch violent and nonviolent TV shows." See also *predictive hypothesis.*

descriptive statistics The branch of statistics involving procedures for describing and summarizing observations that have been quantified as data. See also *frequency distribution; inferential statistics.*

desensitization-relaxation therapy (DRT) A procedure for overcoming anxiety or phobias by training clients in deep muscular relaxation, then having them imagine anxiety-inducing situations of gradually increasing intensity and gradually substitute relaxation for the incompatible tensions of anxiety. See also *counterconditioning.*

desensitization technique A method of counteracting anxiety by learning to relax the muscles of the body when anxiety-arousing scenes are imagined. See also *behavioral control; relaxation technique.*

desensitization therapy A type of behavior therapy in which patients first learn to relax deeply and then imagine a successively more intense series of anxiety-producing situations, letting the relaxation responses substitute for the anxiety responses until the situations no longer produce aversive feelings or discomfort. See also *behavior therapy; cognitive therapy; relaxation technique.*

detection theory A psychophysical theory that analyzes and explains the detection of stimuli in terms of the discriminability of signal against background "noise," emphasizing the importance of factors that affect that discrimination. See also *false alarm; hit; noise; psychophysics; signal.*

developmental psychology The division of psychology concerned with the study of integrated physical and psychological changes occurring during the growth of the individual from conception through maturity to old age.

deviation IQ An intelligence quotient based on a comparison of an individual's score on an intelligence test with that of a standardization group of the same age.

difference threshold The minimum level of change in stimulus intensity that results in an experienced or reported difference in sensation. See also *absolute threshold.*

differential inhibition, law of See *law of differential inhibition.*

dimensions See *emotional dimensions.*

direction The positive or negative characteristic of an attitude, either accepting or rejecting the target of the attitude.

direct relationship A relationship between independent and dependent variables such that both increase or decrease together. See also *inverse relationship.*

direct visual contact See *visual contact, direct.*

disciplinary technique The approach taken to control the behavior of others, particularly children, and to instill in them the norms of behavior acceptable in their culture or subculture. Discipline may be enforced with either reward or punishment. Love-oriented techniques are based on maintaining a positive relationship between the parent and child. Power-assertive techniques are based on the authority of the parent over the child.

discrepant stimulus   A stimulus that differs from, or disagrees with, an infant's cognitive structure, so that the child cannot at once assimilate it, according to Piaget, but must accommodate the structure to it. See also *accommodation, cognitive; assimilation; stimulus.*

discrete-trial learning   A kind of instrumental conditioning in which the organism's learned behavior terminates once it produces its desired effect. For example, after inserting a coin in a vending machine and receiving candy, an individual ends the behavior until more candy is desired. See also *operant learning.*

discrimination (conditioning)   A conditioning process in which an excitatory conditioned stimulus (CS+) is strengthened by reinforcement and a similar CS+ is weakened by extinction to become an inhibitory conditioned stimulus (CS−), so that the organism differentiates its responses to the two stimuli and can be said to discriminate between them. See also *operant discrimination.*

discrimination (social)   Differential behavior, either favoring or rejecting a person or group. See also *action tendency; attitude; prejudice.*

discriminative stimulus (S^D)   A stimulus that serves as a signal that reinforcement will follow a given response. Thus the sight of a vending machine is a discriminative stimulus (S^D) for the response of putting a coin into it to receive candy. See also *discrimination (conditioning).*

displacement   The substitution of other targets for an aggressive reaction in place of the original instigator of the frustration; according to Freudian theory, a defense mechanism by which the ego, when it is blocked from satisfying libidinal drives, finds other means of satisfaction and thereby decreases or prevents anxiety. See also *aggressive reaction; defense mechanism; frustration; scapegoat; sublimation.*

displacement activity   A fixed-action pattern of behavior that is inappropriate to the situation, often displayed by animals in conflict situations.

dissociation   A separation of consciousness into two or more seemingly independent or partially independent states.

dissociation reaction   A pattern of hysterical neurotic behavior in which the identity or state of consciousness is altered, as in amnesia, somnambulism, and multiple-personality neurosis.

distributed practice   Practice periods that are separated by rest periods of relatively long duration. See also *massed practice.*

disuse theory   The oldest theory of forgetting, which holds that memory fades or diminishes with the passage of time; largely discredited by evidence that many memories are retained indefinitely.

divergent hierarchy   A number of associated responses elicited by a single verbal or other symbolic stimulus, whether the responses are made separately on different occasions or in a series on one occasion, like the series of responses to the words "The End" at the completion of a movie. See also *convergent hierarchy.*

DNA   See *deoxyribonucleic acid.*

doctrine of formal discipline   The now-discarded belief that exposure to such formal subjects as Latin, Greek, logic, and mathematics tends to strengthen such abilities as reasoning, remembering, and judging. See also *nonspecific transfer; transfer of training.*

dominant gene   A gene with the capacity to express itself wholly, to the exclusion of the other member of the pair of genes. See also *recessive gene.*

double-alternation maze   An apparatus in which the maze pattern is so arranged that it gives subjects no cues for their next responses, which must therefore be derived from mediational processes. See also *delayed-reaction experiment; mediational process.*

double approach–avoidance conflict   A type of conflict in which two possibilities for action yield approach–avoidance tendencies, since both positive and negative consequences attend each possible choice. This conflict tends to be persistent.

double bind   A situation involving two contradictory injunctions, one verbal and the other usually conveyed by tone of voice or posture, and a third implied injunction forbidding the victim to leave the field, so that the victim is forced to choose between two responses, either of which will constitute disobedience to one of the contradictory injunctions; postulated as a factor in the development of schizophrenia but not consistently confirmed.

dowser   A person who claims to possess the ability to locate underground water or other objects, usually by means of Y-shaped sticks.

dream analysis   A psychoanalytic technique

whereby the patient describes the dream (called manifest content) and the analyst uses the patient's free association to interpret the meaning (latent content) of the dream.

drive A basic or physiological motive. See also *biological drive; homeostatic drive.*

drive reduction Diminution of the state of tension and discomfort of an organism by the achievement of a reinforcing goal, as the hunger drive of a fasting animal is diminished by eating.

drive-reduction theory A theory of motivation that holds that organisms are motivated to direct their behavior toward reinforcing goals that tend to reduce drives or diminish tensions. See also *law of effect; reinforcement.*

drive state A state of tension and discomfort produced by deprivation or by exposure to intense stimulation, like the thirst drive of an animal deprived of water or the state produced by electric shock.

drug addiction See *addiction, drug.*

drug dependence See *dependence, drug.*

drugs, psychoactive Chemical substances that alter the state of consciousness, including stimulants, depressants, and hallucinogens, affecting central nervous system functioning. In general, stimulants increase nervous system activity and depressants decrease it. See also *depressant; hallucinogens; stimulant.*

drug therapy See *chemotherapy.*

dualistic conception, dualism An interpretation of human nature in terms of the body, part of the material or physical world, and the spirit, part of the immaterial or mental world.

dyadic group, dyad A group of two persons, such as husband and wife or mother and child, with characteristics often different from those of larger groups.

dynamism A behavioral tendency of individuals in interaction, like the infant's crying and the adult's talking, directed toward the satisfaction of needs, on the basis of which personality is developed and the frustration of which creates basic anxieties; a construct of Harry Stack Sullivan.

dyssocial personality A personality disorder exhibited by delinquents and criminals, characterized by aggressive and destructive behavior toward other individuals and groups but loyalty to one's own group or subculture, in contrast to antisocial personality.

eardrum See *tympanic membrane.*

echolocation The location of objects in the vicinity of an observer, such as a blind person, by the use of sound cues reflected from the objects that are approached. Bats and porpoises are some of the animals that depend on echolocation for navigation.

educational psychology The division of psychology that studies the educational process in schools, including interactions among students, teachers, and administrators.

effect See *causal relationship; dependent variable.*

egg A female reproductive cell, or gamete, produced in the ovary, with one-half of the number of chromosomes of the parental cell.

ego That portion of the personality which attempts to satisfy the drives of the id by mediating between it and conditions in the environment in accordance with the reality principle, according to Freudian theory. See also *id; superego.*

egocentrism The inability to understand that the outlook or attitudes of others may differ from one's own, particularly characteristic of younger children.

Electra conflict or **complex** Freud's Oedipus conflict applied to girls.

electrical stimulation of the brain (ESB) Electrical stimulation given to precisely selected locations in the brain by means of tiny implanted electrodes, in order to investigate the functions of the brain in those locations.

electrocardiogram (EKG) The permanent record of the functioning of a heart, traced on a tape by an electrocardiograph.

electrocardiograph (EKG) apparatus An instrument that electrically records the bioelectric activity of the heart so that normal and abnormal heart conditions can be monitored and diagnosed by analysis of the taped tracing, known as an electrocardiogram (EKG).

electroconvulsive shock (ECS) A brief electrical shock to the brain of sufficient intensity to produce convulsions, occasionally used for the treatment of severe depression.

electroconvulsive-shock therapy (ECT) A type of somatic therapy, diminishing in use with the advent of drug therapy, in which convulsions are produced by electric shock, particularly effective for depressed patients.

electrode A thin wire, insulated except at the tip, which is passed into the brain to electrically stimulate or record neural activity from precisely selected areas; used to study the relationship between brain activity and behavior.

electroencephalogram (EEG)   A recording of electrical brain waves made by electrodes placed in various positions on a person's head.

electromagnetic spectrum   All of the varieties of electromagnetic radiation ranging from gamma and X rays through light waves to radio and microwaves.

electromyograph (EMG)   An instrument for recording and reporting the electrical waves accompanying the activity of skeletal muscles, used in the diagnosis of neuromuscular disorders and to provide feedback of the progress of muscular relaxation and tension. See also *biofeedback*.

embryo   An unborn organism in the early stages of development; the unborn human organism during the first eight weeks after conception, after which it is called a fetus.

emission rate   The rate at which operantly conditioned responses are emitted, often used as a measure of the strength of the conditioning. See also *latency; resistance to extinction*.

emotion   An aroused state of an organism, consisting of a strong affective or feeling component, like love, hate, anger, or fear, and visceral reactions.

emotional dimensions   The polar dimensions that are held to characterize emotions: pleasantness and unpleasantness, attention and rejection, activation and inactivation.

encounter group   A group formed for an intensive type of group therapy, often involving nudity and physical contact between participants, such as touching, massage, and body movement, and an emphasis on self-disclosure and emotional interaction.

endocrine system   The coordinating glands that secrete hormones into the bloodstream, specialized for the control of ongoing, principally metabolic functions. The adrenal and pituitary glands are examples.

endogenous depression   See *depression, endogenous*.

engram   A hypothetical physical trace by which a memory is stored in the neurons of the association cortex or other areas of the cortex.

environmental psychology   The division of psychology, related to social psychology, concentrated on the influences of environmental conditions on individual and social behavior.

epinephrine   A hormone from the adrenal gland that produces arousal of the body. Also called adrenaline.

escape conditioning   See *negative reinforcement*.

estrogens   Sex hormones present in both sexes but found in higher concentrations in the female.

ethnic group   A large group of people with shared language, cultural traditions, and institutions, so that they manifest many similar traits. Often equivalent to a national or regional group, such as the French, Germans, and Basques.

excitation   A process by which a synaptic transmitter from the axon of one neuron causes an increase in the tendency of an adjacent neuron to create nervous activity.

excitation, law of   See *law of excitation*.

excitatory conditioned stimulus (CS+)   A conditioned stimulus (CS) that is paired repeatedly with an unconditioned stimulus (US) and increases the strength of a conditioned response (CR). See also *inhibitory conditioned stimulus*.

existential psychologist   A psychologist, such as Rollo May and Adrian Van Kaam, who tends to follow the thought of existential philosophers, emphasizing the freedom and responsibility of the self and the significant role it plays in the development of personality.

existential therapy   See *humanistic-existential therapies*.

expectancy-value theory   The theory that the probability that a person will behave in a certain manner depends on that person's level of expectation that the action will yield certain rewards available in the situation.

experimental design   The manner in which an experiment is set up and arranged, in order to test the hypotheses the investigator has in mind and either confirm or refute them decisively.

experimental group   The group of subjects in an experiment that is exposed to levels of the independent variable (cause) assumed to affect measures of a dependent variable (effect). See also *control group; method of difference*.

experimental method   A method of investigation in which conditions are thoroughly controlled, so that the causes of events are reliably determined. See also *method of concomitant variations; method of difference*.

experimental psychology   The division of psychology concentrated on basic or theoretical research, aimed more toward the discovery of laws of behavior than toward practical application of known laws.

explosive personality A personality disorder characterized by chronic outbursts of verbal or physical aggressiveness.

expressive language Verbal expressions used to communicate ideas and feelings to others; the capacity for expressive language develops later than the ability to recognize and comprehend language. See also *receptive language*.

extinction The weakening and eventual disappearance of a conditioned response (CR) after the conditioned stimulus (CS) is presented repeatedly without an unconditioned reinforcing stimulus (US). Instrumentally conditioned responses can be similarly extinguished by withholding the reinforcer whenever the response occurs.

extinctive inhibition, law of See *law of extinctive inhibition*.

extrasensory perception (ESP) Presumed human psychic capacities that extend beyond the usual sensory and perceptual limits. See also *clairvoyance; dowser; parapsychology; precognition; psychokinesis; telepathy*.

extroversion The attitude adopted by the ego oriented toward the external world and other people, the contrary of introversion, and of great significance in the development of personality; a construct of Jung.

eye arrest The brief complete stoppage of eye movements between saccades, noted in connection with schizophrenia.

face validity The immediate and apparent indication that a test measures the characteristic it is intended to measure.

false alarm A term used in detection theory of perception for the report of a signal when none is present. See also *detection theory*.

fantasy A set of images or daydreams that serve as substitutes for satisfactions unattained in real life; often a consequence of persistent frustration. See also *withdrawal reaction*.

fear A complex motivational and emotional state aroused by threatening situations. Although sometimes distinguished from "anxiety," the term "fear" is often used interchangeably with it. See also *anxiety*.

feeling An effect, or qualitative aspect of sensations, awareness, or consciousness, such as the quality of pleasantness or unpleasantness. See also *affect; emotion; hedonic quality*.

fetus The unborn human organism from the eighth week after conception until birth or abortion. See also *embryo*.

figure and ground The apparently innate organizing process, stressed by Gestalt psychologists, in accordance with which a perceptual field tends to be perceived as a distinct figure, or shape, against a less distinct ground, or background. See also *Gestalt theory*.

fixation A process resulting from extreme anxiety or conflicts in which a person does not develop beyond a certain early stage, according to Freudian theory. See also *regression*.

fixed-action pattern A relatively complex, repetitious set of responses of an unchanging form, which, once elicited by a single sign stimulus, is independent of further environmental control.

fixed-interval schedule (FI) A schedule of partial reinforcement in operant learning in which responses are reinforced only after certain set intervals of time. See also *reinforcement schedule*.

fixed-ratio schedule (FR) A schedule of partial reinforcement in operant learning in which a fixed number of responses is required for each reinforcement given. See also *reinforcement schedule*.

flooding The attempt to extinguish conditioned fear or other undesirable emotional responses to conditioned stimuli by frequent presentation of such stimuli of an intense degree without accompanying aversive effects, a principle on which implosive therapy is based. See also *implosive therapy*.

forgetting The inability to reproduce previously learned verbal or motor behavior, or to reexperience earlier images or ideas. See also *memory*.

forgetting, theories of See *disuse theory; interference theories; motivational theories; organizational theories*.

formal operational stage The stage in Piaget's theory of cognitive development from about 12 to 15 years of age, during which adolescents begin to grasp the skills of complex logical reasoning, becoming capable of formulating hypotheses, deducing their implications, and testing them against observation.

fovea The small central area of the retina in which the cones are concentrated, providing vision of greatest acuity.

fraternal twins Siblings who develop from the simultaneous fertilization and development of two eggs, and thus are genetically no more alike than any other two children of the same parents; also known as dizygotic twins. See also *identical twins.*

free association A technique used in psychoanalytic therapy in which patients express whatever comes into their minds, thereby revealing to the analyst repressed conflicts, complexes, sources of resistance, and defense mechanisms.

free-recall method The method of measuring memory by means of the reproduction of previously learned materials, in the absence of any cues. See also *recognition method; relearning method.*

frequency The number of waves passing a given point in one second, expressed in terms of cycles, or Hertz, per second.

frequency distribution The frequency with which individual scores fall into a number of classes of scores, each class having the same class interval, or range, of scores.

frequency polygon A many-sided curve composed of lines connecting the points that represent the frequencies of scores in the class intervals of a frequency distribution.

Freudian model of conflict A theory of conflict based on the Freudian concept that the superego and ego tend to block immediate expression of the drives of the id. See also *behavioral model of conflict; defense mechanism; Oedipus conflict; phenomenological model of conflict; repression.*

frontal lobes See *cortex.*

frustration A complex state aroused in a motivated organism when it is blocked or impeded in its progress toward a desired goal. See also *aggressive reaction; barrier; withdrawal reaction.*

frustration-aggression hypothesis The hypothesis that frustration always increases the tendency of an organism to react aggressively, proposed by John Dollard, L. W. Doob, Neal Miller, and colleagues.

fugue A psychological and physical flight from one's life situation and environment, during which the individual assumes a new identity. Following recovery from the fugue state the individual experiences amnesia in regard to all activities during the fugue state.

functional behavior disorder A behavior disorder for which no causal physiological conditions have been found or are known. See also *behavior disorder; interpersonal model; medical model; organic behavior disorder.*

functional fixedness The tendency to think of objects as useful only for their usual function and to ignore other possible ways of using them. See also *response set.*

functional group A group of persons who act together to fulfill some common interest, purpose, or goal, often with organized roles for different group members. See also *aggregate group.*

functional relationship A relationship between variables in which a dependent variable changes as some property of an independent variable changes, identifying the independent variable as cause and the dependent variable as effect. See also *causal relationship; stimulus-response relationship.*

galvanic skin response (GSR) A change in electrical resistance of the skin that may occur during many emotions.

gamete A reproductive cell capable of fusing with a gamete of the other parent to produce a new individual. Each male sperm and female egg is a gamete. See also *egg; sperm.*

ganglion (plural, *ganglia*) A group or cluster of many nerve cells, usually in the peripheral nervous system.

ganglion cell A cell in the retina, its axon forming the optic nerve, which carries nerve impulses to the brain. See also *bipolar cell.*

gender or **sex-role identification** The process by which a child learns the sex to which he or she belongs and acquires the behavior typical of that sex in the child's culture; gender forms an important part of the child's self-concept. See also *identification; self-concept.*

gene A tiny segment of DNA found in chromosomes, which governs transmission of a hereditary trait.

general anxiety measure A test that measures many manifestations of anxiety in various situations. See also *anxiety inventory; Taylor Manifest Anxiety Scale.*

generalization A statement descriptive of relationships holding for all members of a population from which the sample studied was drawn. See also *law.*

generalized reinforcement Reinforcement in instrumental conditioning by means of reinforcers, such as money or social approval or disapproval, that acquire their effects by association with many primary reinforcers, so that they reinforce many different kinds of behavior. See also *primary reinforcement; secondary reinforcement.*

genetic counseling Counseling individuals by tracing the incidence of genetic traits in their families in order to predict undesirable traits in an individual or in future offspring.

genetic technology Techniques for altering and directing the gene action of cells in order to replace defective genes and overcome hereditary disorders.

genital stage The stage during and after adolescence in which people gradually find and accept socially approved mates, according to Freudian theory.

genotype The complex genetic constitution of an individual. See also *phenotype.*

gestalt A perceptual whole, in which the total effect is greater than that produced by the sum of the parts, as three dots (the parts) in sequence may be perceived as a line (the whole), or two dots with a third one centered above them may be perceived as a triangle. See also *Gestalt theory.*

Gestalt theory A theory that explains perception in terms of certain innate organizing processes, or gestalts, such as figure and ground, and the grouping of stimuli in orderly patterns. See also *grouping processes.*

Gestalt therapy A type of psychotherapy related to existential and Gestalt psychology, which aims to expand one's awareness to all aspects of existence, using a variety of therapy exercises for leading patients toward understanding themselves and acting as whole persons.

glial cell One type of cell in the nervous system that does not conduct nervous impulses, but provides nourishment and structural support.

gonads Endocrine glands, consisting of the testes in males and the ovaries in females, that secrete the male and female sex hormones, androgens and estrogens, respectively.

grade-point average (GPA) The mean grade for a number of courses, summarizing the quality of academic behavior over a period of one or more semesters.

gradient A regular change in a property of an object that occurs with changes in distance from the observer, such as the regular decrease in the detail and apparent size of a pebble in a gravel road the farther it is from the observer; one of the principal cues for monocular depth perception. See also *monocular depth perception.*

grammar The set of rules that are followed in a language in expressing meaningful combinations of words in sentences.

ground See *figure and ground.*

group A collection of persons or things that have some characteristic in common, similar to a set or class of things. See also *aggregate group; dyadic group; functional group.*

group evaluation and decision The joint evaluation and judgment of problems, issues, or tasks by the members of a functional group.

grouping processes The apparently innate organizing processes, stressed by Gestalt psychologists, by which patterns of stimuli are perceived on the basis of regularity, symmetry, simplicity, proximity, continuity, and closure. See also *Gestalt theory.*

groupness attitude A basic attitude, probably established during childhood, leading to a tendency to favor the in-group and treat it fairly and to disfavor any out-groups and treat them unfairly.

group norm A standard arising from a series of interactions of a group of people, affecting the judgments of individual group members. See also *individual norm; reference group.*

group therapy A type of psychotherapy in which people in a small group interact with a therapist and with each other, learning how their self-perceptions and attitudes match those of others and how their behavior affects others. See also *encounter group; psychodrama; sensitivity training group.*

GSR See *galvanic skin response.*

habit A theoretical construct used to explain why repeated pairings of conditioned and unconditioned stimuli lead to progressive increases in the strength of the conditioned response. See also *classical conditioning; inhibition.*

hallucination A sensory perception experienced in the waking state in the absence of any external causal stimulus, as a result of a drug or mental disorder.

hallucinogens Drugs that produce distortions in cognition and perception, often resulting in hallucinations. See also *drugs, psychoactive; hallucination; LSD; marijuana.*

halo effect The positive or negative influence on later judgments produced by first judgments on the initial responses of a person being tested or interviewed. See also *stereotyped judgment.*

hammer See *ossicles.*

hebephrenic schizophrenia A type of schizophrenia, characterized by shallow and inappropriate emotions, regressive behavior, and hypochondriacal complaints.

hedonic quality The feeling tone or quality of pleasure or displeasure accompanying an emotion. See also *affect; feeling.*

heredity The transmission of potentialities for characteristics from parent to offspring through a mechanism lying primarily in the chromosomes of the gametes.

heritability The degree to which a trait is controlled by genetic, as opposed to environmental, factors.

Hertz (Hz) The unit of measurement of wave frequency, consisting of one cycle per second.

heterozygous The condition of an organism in which two genes of a pair are different, carrying different instructions for an inherited trait. See also *homozygous.*

hierarchical tree A clustering procedure—for example, the organization of items of information into a classification system—serving as a coding strategy to aid transfer of information from short-term memory to storage in long-term memory. See also *clustering.*

hippocampus A region of the brain located below the temporal cortex that may be involved in the normal functioning of memory, especially in the storage by transfer from short- to long-term memory.

histogram or **bar graph** A graphing procedure in which the frequency of scores in each class interval in a frequency distribution is represented as a bar. See also *frequency distribution.*

histrionic personality See *hysterical personality.*

hit A term used in detection theory of perception for a correct report of the detection of a signal.

homeostasis The tendency of the body to maintain a constant, optimal internal environment.

homeostatic drive A biological drive that serves to restore the physiological equilibrium of an organism, like the drives of hunger, thirst, respiration, excretion, and temperature regulation. See also *biological drive; nonhomeostatic drive.*

homozygous The condition of an organism in which two genes of a pair are identical, carrying the same instructions for an inherited trait. See also *heterozygous.*

hormones The secretions of the endocrine glands that alter the rate of certain chemical reactions in the body. Epinephrine and androgens are examples. See also *endocrine system.*

humanistic-existential therapies Type of psychotherapy based on humanistic (Maslow) and existential (Frankl and May) principles that emphasize the freedom of individuals to make their own decisions and take responsibility for them.

hunger The biological motive or drive produced in an organism by food deprivation. See also *homeostatic drive; motive; need.*

hunger center The region of the hypothalamus that seems to control hunger. See also *lateral nucleus (hypothalamus).*

hyperkinesis A condition of overactivity in children. The cause is unknown, but it may result from a central nervous system abnormality.

hypertension, essential (primary) A condition of abnormally high blood pressure, the exact cause of which is unknown.

hypnosis A subjective state in which a person is highly suggestible, tolerates incongruity, and presents a trancelike appearance, although its distinction from the waking state is questioned.

hypochondriacal neurosis A behavioral disorder marked by a chronic preoccupation with imagined physical illness and exaggerated concern with bodily functions.

hypothalamus A structure at the base of the brain that, with the limbic system, controls sleep, emotions, and such basic motivations as hunger, sex, and temperature regulation.

hypothermia Reduced body temperature, which can impair storage in long-term memory during consolidation periods.

hypoxia Reduced supply of oxygen to the brain, which can impair storage in long-term memory during consolidation periods.

hysterical neurosis A neurotic syndrome that often appears as one of two types: conversion reaction, with impairment of sensory or motor functions, and dissociative reaction, with alterations of conscious states, as in amnesia, fugue, and somnambulism.

hysterical personality A personality disorder characterized by overdependence on others, emotional instability, and excitability. The hysterical personality attracts attention by treating many situations as emergencies, but lacks the conversion reactions of hysterical neurosis. Also known as histrionic personality.

hysteric conversion A neurotic reaction in which an emotional problem is converted into a physical symptom that has no physical basis.

id The unconscious, infantile reservoir of psychic energy, which follows the pleasure principle; a construct of Freud. See also *ego; superego.*

idealized image The image of the self developed in childhood to combat the basic anxiety created by threats to security, significant in the development of personality; a construct of Karen Horney. See also *defaced image.*

identical twins Siblings that develop from the splitting of a single fertilized egg, having exactly the same genetic material; also known as monozygotic twins. See also *fraternal twins.*

identification One of the defense mechanisms, according to Freudian theory, by which the individual deals with anxiety by adopting the traits and values of another person, as a boy associates himself with his father and a girl with her mother. See also *defense mechanism; transference.*

identity The strong sense of a stable and competent self (ego identity) and of organized and persistent groups (group identity), which are attained by the adequately developing personality, according to Erikson.

illusion See *perceptual illusion.*

imagery The mental pictures of things, events, or relationships, based on and derived from memory, used in cognitive activities of acquiring knowledge, in addition to thoughts or verbal processes.

implosive therapy A type of behavior therapy in which the patient is directed to imagine many intense anxiety-producing situations in the attempt to extinguish the anxiety response by a process similar to flooding.

impossible object A drawing of an object containing inconsistent cues for shape and distance so that it is impossible to interpret just what object is represented.

imprinting The tendency of an organism during a critical period of its early development to follow a moving object and to form a lasting attachment to that object.

incentive The goal toward which motivated behavior is directed, as the behavior of a hungry orga-

nism is directed toward finding and eating food (the incentive). See also *motive; need.*

independent variable An event that, under controlled conditions, causes another event (its effect), known as the dependent variable.

individual distance The distance within which other persons may not approach an individual without eliciting protests or withdrawal, depending on circumstances, roles of the persons involved, and culture. See also *personal space; territoriality.*

individual norm A standard developed by an individual on the basis of his or her own series of judgments. See also *group norm.*

individual psychology Adler's theory of personality, crediting people with striving for goals, particularly the goal of superiority or self-assertion, rather than being moved primarily by unconscious sexual drives.

industrial psychology The division of psychology dealing with the efficiency of human performance in an organizational setting. See also *management psychology; personnel psychology.*

infantile autism See *autism.*

inferential statistics Statistical procedures for making predictions about the characteristics of a large group of people on the basis of a relatively small sample of data. See also *descriptive statistics.*

inferiority The feelings aroused by failures or imperfections in achieving superiority, which must be overcome if the personality is to develop adequately, according to Adler. See also *individual psychology; superiority.*

in-group A group to which a person belongs, often of the same socioeconomic status and customs, and which the individual tends to favor. See also *attitude; discrimination; out-group.*

inherited, inborn, or **innate behavior** Behavior that is present or potentially present from birth, passed on from generation to generation through the genes.

inhibition A process by which a synaptic transmitter from an axon of one neuron causes a decrease in the tendency of an adjacent neuron to create nervous activity.

inhibition A theoretical construct to explain the reduction of the strength of conditioned responses by extinction, by assuming the growth of an inhibitory factor that competes against the tendency of the conditioned stimulus to elicit the conditioned response. See also *habit; laws of inhibition.*

inhibitory conditioned stimulus (CS−) A conditioned stimulus (CS) that is presented repeatedly alone, without the reinforcing unconditioned stimulus (US). See also *law of extinctive inhibition.*

Initial Training Alphabet (ITA) A 44-character phonetic alphabet comprising all the sounds of the English language, as opposed to the 26-character conventional alphabet. It is being used experimentally in initially teaching children to read and write.

insight The sudden solution of a problem accompanied by a grasping of the elements in the situation as a whole, according to Gestalt principles, and the sudden reorganization of the elements to produce the perceived solution. See also *"Aha" experience; problem solving.*

instant learning See *sudden solution.*

instigating condition A condition, such as deprivation of water, that initiates the motivational sequence, culminating in a goal response that reduces or terminates the motivational condition.

instinct or **instinctive behavior** Specific, complex, and adaptive behavior of an organism in reaction to environmental or internal stimuli, largely stable and inherited, although modifiable by learning. Nest-building behaviors of birds and rats are examples. Also called species-characteristic behavior.

instrumental conditioning A kind of learning, usually modifying a muscular response or response of the whole body, which either produces some reward (positive reinforcement) or avoids or terminates some unpleasant result (negative reinforcement). See also *classical conditioning; discrete-trial learning; learning; operant learning.*

instrumental response Usually a muscular response, or an act of the entire organism, which either produces reward or avoids or escapes aversive stimulation.

intelligence The general capacity to engage in insightful, goal-directed behavior requiring complex cognitive skills. See also *cognition.*

intelligence quotient (IQ) A number obtained by dividing mental age, determined by an intelligence test, by chronological age, then multiplying the result by 100.

interference theories Theories that explain forgetting by reference to disruption of memories by events intervening since the time of original learning. See also *forgetting, theories of; proactive interference; retroactive interference.*

interpersonal attraction See *attraction, interpersonal.*

interpersonal model A theory that attributes functional behavior disorders to conflicts arising from interactions between people, rather than to organic conditions. See also *functional behavior disorder; medical model.*

interposition The occlusion, or cutting off from view, of one object by a nearer object in the same line of vision, providing a cue for monocular depth perception.

intervening variable A variable that summarizes relationships between one or more independent variables (cause) and various measures of the dependent variable (effect), often treated as a hypothetical construct with explanatory value. See also *dependent variable; independent variable.*

introspection Self-observation of the contents of consciousness or awareness; also, the analysis of one's own conscious experiences in an attempt to analyze their component elements. See also *consciousness.*

introversion The orientation of the ego toward the inner, subjective world, the contrary of extroversion, and of great significance in the development of personality, according to Jung. See also *extroversion.*

inverse relationship A relationship between independent and dependent variables such that when either one increases the other decreases. See also *direct relationship.*

IQ See *intelligence quotient.*

iris The circular muscular tissue between the cornea and lens of the eye whose expansion and contraction governs the amount of light entering the eye.

irradiation See *stimulus generalization.*

James-Lange theory The theory that emotional experiences result from awareness of, rather than cause, visceral reactions to external emotional situations. See also *emotion; visceral reactions.*

Jungian therapy A type of psychoanalytic therapy based on Jung's principles, emphasizing the attainment of wholeness and self-realization through the clarification of the influence of unconscious forces, including the archetypes.

just noticeable difference (jnd) A barely detectable change in the intensity of a physical stimulus. See also *difference threshold; Weber's law.*

kinesthesis See *kinesthetic sense.*

kinesthetic receptors Receptors in the body joints

responsible for the kinesthetic sense of orientation of parts of the body.

kinesthetic sense The human sensory system responding to internal, bodily stimulation from the muscles and joints, resulting in the sensations of motion, weight, and position or posture of the body. See also *sensory system.*

Kirlian effect The rings around the fingertips made when a person's fingertips are placed on photographic film over an electrostatic field on an electrically charged plate, apparently indicative of the degree of emotional arousal; potentially a measure of interpersonal attraction. See also *attraction, interpersonal.*

Korsakov psychosis See *Wernecke-Korsakov syndrome.*

language The complex processes of communicating by means of the conventional oral, written, or gestural symbols of a human culture. See also *expressive language; language structure; psycholinguistics; receptive language.*

language structure The two structural levels on which language functions, according to Noam Chomsky: (1) deep structure, which represents thoughts or meanings, and (2) surface structure, by which these meanings are expressed verbally in phrases or sentences, with the aid of grammar. See also *grammar; language.*

latency The period of time elapsing between the onset of a stimulus and the start of the response to it, used as one measure of the strength of classical conditioning. The shorter the latency, the stronger the conditioning. See also *emission rate; resistance to extinction.*

latent stage The stage from the fifth to tenth or eleventh years of life, in which children obtain gratification from and displace their drives in learning skills at school and in play with other children, according to Freudian theory.

lateral eye movement The shifting of the eyes toward the left or right when attention is turned inward, possibly related to dominance of one or the other hemisphere of the cerebral cortex.

lateral geniculate body A region in the thalamus to which the optic nerves lead from the optic chiasma. Neurons in the lateral geniculate body send axons to the visual cortex in the occipital lobe.

lateral nucleus (hypothalamus) A region of the hypothalamus that largely controls the motivated behavior resulting from the biological drives of hunger and thirst, serving as a center for these drives. See also *biological drive; hypothalamus.*

law A general statement of uniform invariant relationships between objectively defined events. See also *generalization; theory.*

lawful relationship A uniform relationship repeatedly found between independent and dependent variables under controlled experimental conditions.

law of differential inhibition A uniform relationship such that responding to generalized stimuli resembling the excitatory conditioned stimulus (CS+) will diminish and cease when these stimuli are never followed by the unconditioned stimulus (US), even though the CS+, when presented on interspersed trials, is always followed by the US. Under these conditions, the responding to the generalized stimulus is inhibited, while the excitatory stimulus retains its strength.

law of effect A law of learning, formulated by Edward Thorndike, that states that responses producing satisfaction will be repeated and responses producing dissatisfaction will not be repeated. See also *drive-reduction theory.*

law of excitation The uniform and repeated relationship found in classical conditioning between pairings of a conditioned stimulus (CS) and an unconditioned stimulus (US) with an increase in the strength of the conditioned response (CR). This CS is sometimes labeled CS+ and is called an excitatory conditioned stimulus.

law of extinctive inhibition A uniform relationship such that after a conditioned response (CR) has been conditioned to a conditioned stimulus (CS) by pairing of the CS to an unconditioned stimulus (US), repeated presentation of the CS alone will lead to a reduction in the CR strength. This CS is often labeled CS— and is called an inhibitory conditioned stimulus. See also *law of differential inhibition.*

laws of inhibition Uniform conditioning relationships that involve a reduction in the strength of the conditioned response (CR) as stated in the laws of extinctive and differential inhibition.

learned helplessness A depressed and apathetic condition produced by repeated exposure to inescapable aversive stimulation, suggested as a condition analogous to severe human depressions. See also *depression; withdrawal reaction.*

learning A relatively permanent change in the behavior of an organism resulting from reinforced practice and to be distinguished from the temporary effects of drugs and sensory adaptation, as well as from the effects of maturation.

learning set See *response set.*

lens The transparent body in the eye so shaped that it focuses light passing through it on the retina.

libido The basic sexual drive or instinct that predominates in the id, according to Freudian theory.

life-events inventory A list of common psychosocial stressors—serious and stressful situations in which people may find themselves—scored as to relative severity and used to gauge the stress to which a person is or has been subjected.

life instinct The libidinal drive, deriving from the id, predominantly sexual and directed toward the maintenance of the individual and the reproduction of the species, according to Freudian theory.

life style The typical attitudes and behavior constituting the essential ways a person lives, as opposed to superficial, momentary, or atypical ways of behaving. See also *personality.*

light The visual sensations resulting from the reception of light waves in the eye; also, the physical stimulus for vision. See also *light waves.*

light adaptation The adjustment of the eye to high light intensity, with reduction of pupil size and a depletion of visual pigments built up by lower light intensities. See also *dark adaptation.*

light receptors Rod and cone cells in the retina of the eye, containing light-sensitive pigments that transduce light energy into nerve messages, producing vision.

light waves Waves occurring in a narrow band of the electromagnetic spectrum, serving as the physical stimuli for vision, ranging from 380 to 780 nanometers in wavelength. See also *amplitude; frequency; wavelength.*

Likert attitude scale A scale that measures the direction and intensity of attitudes, consisting of a series of statements about the targets of attitudes; subjects indicate the degree of their agreement or disagreement with these statements. See also *attitude scale; direction.*

limbic system A group of closely interconnected structures at the core of the brain that works with the hypothalamus to control the emotions and such basic motivations as hunger, sex, and temperature.

locus-of-control scale A scale that measures the extent to which subjects perceive the locus of control of their behavior to be either internal, within themselves, or external, outside themselves in other people and events. See also *rating scale.*

long-term memory (LTM) The memory process in which information is transformed by coding, stored, and retained for long periods of time, if not indefinitely, available for retrieval. See also *coding strategies; organizational theories; short-term memory.*

loudness The sensed quality of intensity or magnitude of sound (usually expressed in decibels), resulting from the amplitude of sound waves stimulating the ear.

love or **romantic love** An intense form of interpersonal attraction characterized by an affiliative need for the other, a predisposition to help the other, and a sense of the exclusiveness of and absorption in the other. See also *attraction, interpersonal.*

LSD (lysergic acid diethylamide) A potent hallucinogen that induces sensory distortions and illusions and sometimes induces psychotic reactions.

maladaptive behavior Behavior that tends to result in disequilibrium or diminish homeostasis, frustrate the organism's needs, or bring it into conflict with environmental and social conditions; behavior that is not conducive in the long run to survival. See also *adaptive behavior; homeostasis.*

malingering The conscious pretense of some form of illness in order to gain attention or avoid responsibility, as opposed to actual organic, neurotic, or psychotic disorders.

management psychology The branch of industrial psychology concentrated on management effectiveness and problems.

manic-depressive psychosis A psychosis characterized by delusions and marked shifts in mood and emotion. The manic type is characterized by extreme elation and talkativeness, with flight of ideas; the depressed type is characterized by extreme depression, with strong anxiety and stupor; the rare bipolar type is characterized by both manic and depressive episodes. See also *psychotic depressive reaction.*

mantra See *Transcendental Meditation.*

marijuana (Cannabis sativa) A minor hallucinogen, obtained from the Indian hemp plant, which tends to induce a mild euphoria, but also results in disturbances in perception and cognition.

masochistic behavior Behavior that is injurious to oneself, explained in Freudian terms as displaced aggression. See also *displacement*.

massed practice Practice periods that are separated by very brief rest periods. See also *distributed practice*.

maturation The changes in behavior of an organism resulting from physiological growth, whose timing and character are largely determined by heredity.

maturational readiness Physiological readiness to acquire a new type of behavior, such as the readiness of an infant to sit up, stand, and walk.

mean A measure of the central tendency of a distribution of scores, obtained by adding all the scores and dividing the sum by the number of scores. See also *measure of central tendency; median; mode*.

meaning The property of cues, signs, words, or symbols standing for, expressing, or representing something else, as the word "table" stands for a whole class of similar objects. See also *connotative meaning; mediated generalization*.

measure of central tendency A measure—mean, median, or mode—that identifies the central location in a distribution of scores. See also *mean; median; mode*.

measure of variability A measure, like the standard deviation, that represents the dispersion of scores around the mean in a distribution of scores. See also *standard deviation*.

median A measure of the central tendency of a distribution, obtained by finding the number halfway between the highest and lowest scores in the distribution. See also *mean; measure of central tendency; mode*.

mediated generalization Generalization from conditioned stimuli to other stimuli having the same or similar meanings, as opposed to the same or similar physical properties.

mediational process A process, such as thinking, planning, and problem solving, that intervenes between environmental stimuli and observable responses, serving in the selection or guidance of the appropriate response to given stimuli. See also *delayed-reaction experiment; double-alternation maze; mediated generalization*.

medical model A theory that explains functional behavior disorders according to the model of organic diseases; thus behavioral events are considered as "symptoms," from which a specific

"mental illness" may be "diagnosed." See also *interpersonal model*.

meditation Inner withdrawal and concentration by means of a variety of procedures, resulting in an altered state of consciousness that gives a sense of unity of self and universe. See also *altered state of consciousness; samadhi; satori; Transcendental Meditation*.

medulla See *brainstem*.

meiosis The sequence of changes in the nucleus of a cell resulting in the production of two reproductive cells, or gametes, each with half the number of chromosomes present in the original cell.

memory The ability to reproduce previously learned verbal or motor behavior, or to reexperience earlier images or ideas. See also *forgetting; long-term memory; sensory storage; short-term memory*.

memory, measurement of See *free-recall method; recognition method; relearning method*.

mental age Mental development expressed in years as determined by an intelligence test. See also *chronological age*.

mental retardation A behavior disorder of subnormal intellectual functioning caused by any of a number of prenatal or infant physical conditions, some genetic and some environmental.

metaneed A motive over and beyond the basic needs, such as a desire for beauty, goodness, truth, order, or wisdom; a construct of Abraham Maslow. See also *metapathology*.

metapathology Lack of fulfillment of the metaneeds, resulting in lowered self-actualization, alienation, and loss of self-esteem; a construct of Abraham Maslow. See also *metaneed*.

methamphetamine See *amphetamine*.

method of concomitant variations An experimental method for determining the cause of events by observing whether the systematic manipulation of one event, the cause, will produce systematic changes in a second event, the effect. See also *dependent variable; experimental method; independent variable; method of difference*.

method of difference An experimental method for determining the causes of events by observing whether the event (effect or dependent variable) occurs in the presence of another event (cause or independent variable) but does not occur in its absence, other conditions remaining the same. See also *control group; dependent variable; experi-*

mental group; experimental method; independent variable; method of concomitant variations.

method of limits The method of measuring absolute or difference thresholds by alternate increases and decreases in the intensity of the stimulus until the organism detects the stimulus or its change on 50 per cent of its occurrences. See also *absolute threshold; difference threshold.*

method of loci A mnemonic device for storing and retrieving information in long-term memory by associating items to be remembered with a series of locations (loci), such as along a street or in rooms of a house. See also *coding strategies; mnemonic device; retrieval strategies.*

midbrain See brainstem.

Minnesota Multiphasic Personality Inventory (MMPI) A personality inventory consisting of many statements designed basically to diagnose personality disorders, but also used to measure a variety of personality characteristics. See also *personality inventory.*

mirror tracing A task requiring the tracing of the outlines of a figure, such as a star, while the subject observes only the reversed mirror image of the figure; used in investigating the acquisition of simple sensorimotor skills.

mnemonic device A memory device, such as rhyme or acronym, whose use serves as a coding strategy that aids transfer of information from short-term memory to storage in long-term memory. See also *coding strategies; method of loci.*

modality Any one of the sensory systems by means of which an organism receives a kind of stimulus energy, such as vision or audition. Each modality produces a unique type of sensation. See also *sensation; sensory system.*

mode The most frequently appearing score in a distribution of scores; a measure of central tendency representative of the distribution. See also *mean; measure of central tendency; median.*

monocular depth perception Perception of depth or distance of an object derived from cues provided by vision with one eye, such as size of the image of the object on the retina. See also *binocular depth perception.*

monocular vision Vision with one eye. See also *binocular vision.*

monogenetic trait A trait, such as eye or hair color, that is determined by a single gene pair. See also *polygenetic trait.*

mood Susceptibility to a certain feeling over a period of time, lasting from several hours to a day or so. Moods are not as permanent as temperament or as brief as the usual emotional reactions. See also *temperament.*

Moro reflex A species-characteristic behavior of human infants in response to loud noises or loss of support, consisting of a clasping movement of the arms.

motion parallax The apparent motion of objects as an observer's head turns from side to side, serving as a monocular cue for the distance of objects. See also *monocular depth perception.*

motivated behavior Behavior that is aroused, persists, and is directed toward a goal. See also *motive.*

motivational theories (forgetting) Theories of forgetting that depend on the general notion that people are motivated to forget things that make them anxious and emotionally upset. See also *amnesia; repression.*

motive A goal-directed, aroused, and persistent state of an organism, often arising from a need. Motives are numerous and have been classified in various ways, such as biological, safety, personal, and interpersonal. See also *biological drive; homeostatic drive; motivated behavior; primary motive; secondary motive.*

motive to avoid success or **achievement (M−s)** The need to avoid doing well, or excelling, with reference to some standard of excellence, sometimes opposing the need for achievement. $M-_s$ is measured by means of a form of the Thematic Apperception Test.

motor cortex See *cortex.*

multiple-personality neurosis A neurotic behavior disorder in which the patient exhibits a dissociation reaction involving behaviors suggestive of distinct personalities on various occasions.

multivariate factor analysis A statistical technique to determine intercorrelations among the scores of many variables, such as personality traits.

mutation A spontaneous sudden change in the genetic material of any cell, inheritable when it occurs in gametes.

narcolepsy A disorder in which a person uncontrollably falls asleep during the day.

naturalistic observation The process of observing the behavior of organisms as it occurs under real-life conditions. See also *observation.*

necrophilous type The death-loving type of personality, according to Erich Fromm. See also *death instinct.*

need An internal state of an organism involving a deficit, such as lack of food or water, resulting in a motive or drive.

need for achievement (n-Ach) The need to do well, to excel, with reference to some standard of excellence, usually measured by means of a form of the Thematic Apperception Test.

need for affiliation (n-Aff) The need to initiate or maintain friendly, affectionate interactions with others, measured by a form of the Thematic Apperception Test.

need for power (n-Pow) The need to control other people or to influence their decisions, measured by a form of the Thematic Apperception Test.

negative afterimage See *afterimage.*

negative correlation The relationship between measures of variables, things, or events such that as one increases the other decreases consistently. See also *correlation; positive correlation.*

negative reinforcement The strengthening of responses that reduce or terminate an aversive event. Negative reinforcement is used in escape and avoidance conditioning. See also *positive reinforcement.*

negative transfer A decrease in the ease or efficiency in a new learning task or situation due to interference by learning transferred from prior tasks or situations. See also *nonspecific transfer; positive transfer; transfer of training.*

neoanalytic theory A theory, sometimes called neo-Freudian, that reshapes Freudian theory but still retains many of its basic concepts and principles, such as the theories of Erik Erikson and Karen Horney.

neocortex See *cortex.*

nerve A bundle of nerve fibers from many neurons, covered with a protective sheath and connecting parts of the nervous system with other parts of the body or with other nerves.

nerve fiber An axon or dendrite of a neuron, many of which together form a nerve, transmitting nerve impulses to and from the central nervous system. See also *axon; dendrite; nerve; neuron.*

nerve impulse A brief bioelectrical change in a neuron that travels from the initial segment of the dendrite near the cell body to the terminal ends of the axon carrying neural messages.

nervous system The brain, spinal cord, and neurons interconnecting the sense organs and muscles, functioning by the transmission of nerve impulses, and controlling processes like consciousness, sensory experience, and memory. See also *central nervous system; peripheral nervous system.*

neurasthenic neurosis A behavioral disorder marked by extreme fatigue and weakness in the absence of any physical causes.

neuron A nerve cell that has the specialized capacity to transmit nerve impulses. Sensory neurons are activated by environmental stimuli, motor neurons control the body's muscles and glands, and interneurons link the sensory and motor neurons.

neurosis Any of a group of behavior disorders characterized primarily by anxiety and manifested in behavioral or physical symptoms, unaccompanied by misperception or gross distortion of external reality or by gross personality disorganization. See also *behavior disorder; hypochondriacal neurosis; neurotic depression; hysterical neurosis; neurasthenic neurosis; obsessive-compulsive neurosis; phobia.*

neurotic depression A neurotic behavior disorder characterized by extreme dejection, self-depreciation, hopelessness, and bodily complaints. See also *psychotic depressive reaction.*

neurotic disorder See *neurosis.*

noise A sound produced by sound waves of many different frequencies randomly mixed together; also, in detection theory, background stimuli accompanying a signal stimulus.

nondirective therapy A kind of direct humanistic therapy, developed by Carl Rogers, emphasizing encouragement of self-acceptance and self-realization. See also *client-centered therapy.*

nonhomeostatic drive A biological drive that is not essential for the maintenance of the physiological equilibrium of an organism, such as sex and parental drives. See also *biological drive; homeostatic drive; motive.*

nonspecific transfer The transfer of learning strategies from the learning of one kind of task to the learning of a different kind of task; sometimes called "learning how to learn," because it is general principles or approaches, rather than specific behaviors, that are transferred. See also *transfer of training.*

norepinephrine   One of the chemical transmitters at synapses throughout the nervous system, which stimulates eating when applied to the lateral nucleus of the hypothalamus. See also *lateral nucleus (hypothalamus)*.

norm   See *group norm; individual norm*.

normal curve   See *normal distribution*.

normal distribution   A bell-shaped frequency distribution in which the slopes on both sides of the midpoint or peak are identical, commonly obtained with large numbers of scores of certain psychological traits, such as intelligence (IQ). See also *frequency distribution; skewed distribution*.

NREM sleep   The physiologically quiet stage of sleep. See also *REM sleep*.

nucleus   A cluster of cell bodies in the central nervous system having a similar function, such as the lateral nucleus of the hypothalamus.

obedience   Submission by a member of a group to an authority, a leader, or other members of the group.

observation   The act of attending to, recognizing, and recording facts or events and often of measuring them in some way. See also *naturalistic observation; retrospective method; self-observation; unobtrusive measures*.

obsessive-compulsive neurosis   A neurotic behavior disorder characterized by frequent repetition of apparently useless words or actions (compulsions) or thoughts (obsessions), reinforced by temporary reduction of chronic anxiety.

obsession   See *obsessive-compulsive neurosis*.

obsessive-compulsive personality   A personality disorder characterized by rigid, inhibited, and overly conscientious and conforming behavior, with an overburdening need for order and organization.

occipital lobes   See *cortex*.

Oedipus conflict or **complex**   The conflict of the young boy between the striving for sexual expression with his mother and the fear of punishment by the father; a construct of Freud.

olfactory cell   The receptor cell in the olfactory membrane of the nasal cavity responsible, when stimulated by particles in the air, for the sense of smell, or olfaction.

operant conditioning   See *operant learning*.

operant discrimination   An instrumental conditioning process in which the response rate in the presence of one stimulus (S^D) is increased by positive reinforcement and reduced in the presence of a second stimulus (S^Δ) by nonreinforcement. Thus the organism learns to discriminate between the two stimuli, responding in the presence of one but not in the presence of the other. See also *discrimination (conditioning)*.

operant (free-responding) learning   A kind of instrumental conditioning in which the organism, free to respond whenever it wishes, increases its rate of responding in ways that lead to reinforcers. See also *discrete-trial learning*.

operational definition   The definition of a thing, event, or relationship in terms of the way(s) in which it is observed to act or the procedures used in its measurement.

opiate addiction   Addiction to opium or one of its derivatives—heroin, morphine, codeine—involving physiological and/or psychological dependence, as well as increasing tolerance of the drug. See also *addiction, drug; tolerance*.

opponent-process theory   A theory of motivation that states that extremely pleasant or unpleasant emotions are followed by the opposite type of affective response when the original stimulus is terminated.

optic chiasma   The crossing of nerve fibers where the optic nerves from each eye meet, with fibers from the left half of each eye's retina going to the left lateral geniculate body and fibers from the right half going to the right lateral geniculate body. See also *lateral geniculate body; nerve fiber; optic nerve*.

optic nerve or **pathway**   The nerve, consisting of a bundle of axons of ganglion cells, carrying neural messages from the eye to the visual cortex.

oral stage   The stage during the first year of life in which libidinal gratification and aggression are centered on the mouth, according to Freudian theory.

organic behavior disorder   A behavior disorder resulting from known physiological conditions, such as brain concussions and hardening of the arteries in the brain. See also *functional behavior disorder*.

organic brain disorder   An abnormal brain condition, originating from any of numerous physiological conditions, such as concussion, tumor, encephalitis, and convulsive disorders like epilepsy, which result in behavior disorders.

organism   Any discrete or individual form of animal or plant life; in psychology, an individual animal, human or other.

organizational theories Theories that attribute forgetting to the breakdown of memory systems by means of which input information is transformed and stored. See also *forgetting, theories of; long-term memory; sensory storage; short-term memory.*

organ of Corti The structure of the inner ear carrying the hair-cell sound receptors that are stimulated by vibrations of the basilar membrane in the cochlea.

ossicles Tiny bones, called the hammer, anvil, and stirrup, in the middle ear, which transmit and increase force of vibrations from the tympanic membrane to the cochlea.

out-group A group of individuals, often of different socioeconomic status and customs, which is disfavored by individuals belonging to other groups in the society. See also *attitude; discrimination (social); in-group.*

oval window The membrane of the cochlea of the inner ear through which sound vibrations are transmitted from the ossicles to the fluid therein.

overlearning Learning beyond the point of mastery to the criterion of at least one perfect recitation. See also *learning.*

overt process A process, like speaking or smiling, carried on publicly by the individual and directly observable by others. See also *covert process.*

pain perception The perception of pain stimuli, which can be modified by motivation, expectation, prior experience, and the cultural background of the perceiver.

paired-associate learning The learning of lists of pairs of items—words, nonsense syllables, or pictures—in order to master the task of responding with the second item of a pair when the first item is presented.

panic An attack of acute anxiety with extreme tension, with which the person is unable to deal. See also *anxiety; chronic anxiety; neurosis.*

paradoxical cold The sensing of very high temperatures on the skin as very cold at the moment of stimulation. The paradox occurs because the cold receptors react to very high temperatures as well as to low temperatures.

paradoxical sleep See *sleep, rapid-eye-movement.*

parallax angle The angle made by a line from either eye of an observer to an object in relation to the baseline between the two eyes.

paranoia A rare psychosis characterized by the development of an elaborate system of delusions of persecution and/or grandeur, based on misinterpretation or exaggeration of a real event or series of events; other cognitive behavior may be relatively unaffected, and extreme mood changes are lacking. See also *delusion; paranoid reaction.*

paranoid personality A personality disorder characterized by suspicion, envy, sensitivity to criticism, a sense of superiority, and a tendency to blame others for any difficulties.

paranoid reaction A psychotic disorder characterized by delusions of persecution and/or grandeur. When delusions are bizarre, fragmented, and accompanied by hallucinations, the disorder is considered a variety of schizophrenia; when delusions are well systematized, it is considered a form of paranoia.

paranoid schizophrenia A subtype of schizophrenia, characterized by bizarre, fragmented delusions of persecution or of grandeur, often accompanied by hallucinations, aggressive behavior, and delusions.

parapsychology The scientific study of processes beyond ordinary human sensations and perceptions. See also *extrasensory perception.*

parasympathetic division The part of the autonomic division of the peripheral nervous system that acts primarily to promote the body's maintenance processes. See also *autonomic nervous system.*

paresis An organic brain disease characterized by brain lesions resulting from syphilis and manifested in delusions and general mental dysfunctions.

parietal lobes See *cortex.*

passive-aggressive personality A personality disorder characterized by apparent passivity and dependence that covertly express aggressions with stubborn, procrastinating, uncooperative, and obstructive behavior patterns.

passive-dependent personality A personality disorder characterized by childish dependence and extreme anxiety in situations in which demands are made.

peak experience An intense and spontaneous experience associated with the process of self-actualization, according to psychologist Abraham

Maslow, characterized by feelings of self-sufficiency, beauty, wholeness, and harmony with others. See also *self-actualization.*

pedigree analysis   The study of the incidence of certain traits in blood relatives of an individual (parents, siblings, aunts and uncles, grandparents) in comparison with their incidence in the population at large.

peer   A person belonging to the same group in society as the person in question, such as those of the same age, same grade in school, or same status.

percentile   One-hundredth, or 1 per cent, of the whole range of scores in a distribution.

percentile value or **rank**   The value of an individual score obtained by arranging all the scores in a distribution in numerical order and computing the percentage of scores smaller than the given individual score.

perception   An experience of objects, events, or relationships obtained by extracting information from and interpreting sensations. See also *sensation.*

perceptual constancy   The ability to perceive objects as relatively unchanged in size, shape, color, brightness, and so on, under varying viewing conditions. See also *shape constancy; size constancy.*

perceptual illusion   A perception that is an incorrect interpretation of the actual object or event perceived, or fluctuating and conflicting interpretations of the same object.

performance   Overt measurable behavior, often used as an indirect measure of changes in inferred processes such as learning and motivation.

peripheral nervous system   The part of the nervous system that lies outside the skull and spine, consisting of nerves and ganglia. See also *autonomic nervous system; central nervous system; somatic nervous system.*

personal interview   A method for measuring and evaluating personality, in which the interviewer asks a series of questions and the interviewee answers them. Clinical and psychiatric interviews tend to be more uniformly structured and penetrating than informal job or counseling interviews. See also *personality assessment.*

personality   The complex of stable behavioral characteristics, patterns, and traits that uniquely distinguish the whole person and one person from another.

personality assessment   The observation, measurement, and evaluation of personality characteristics. See also *personal interview; personality inventory; projective test; rating scale.*

personality disorder   An enduring maladaptive pattern of behavior characterized by distortions or intensification of common personality traits. See also *antisocial personality; behavior disorder; cyclothymic personality; dyssocial personality; explosive personality; hysterical personality; obsessive-compulsive personality; paranoid personality; passive-aggressive personality; passive-dependent personality; schizoid personality.*

personality inventory   A structured test composed of a series of questions or statements to which subjects respond, revealing interests, attitudes, values, or traits characteristic of their personalities. See also *personality assessment; Strong-Campbell Interest Inventory; structured test.*

personality or **character trait**   An established pattern of behavior not changing over periods of time, manifested by many people, and expressed in a variety of situations. Character traits, like courage and honesty, are sometimes distinguished from personality traits, like sociability and assertiveness.

personality theory   A theory that attempts to identify and integrate the principles that explain human personality and the ways it develops and changes. Personality theories include type, trait, psychoanalytic, social learning, humanistic, and existential theories.

personal space   The asymmetrical area with invisible boundaries surrounding a person into which others cannot intrude without affecting the person aversively. See also *individual distance.*

personal stereotype   The image of a person or group held by an individual, made up of a simplified collection of assigned traits. See also *social stereotype; stereotype.*

personification   A good or bad image of oneself and others, which combines with other images to form conceptions of the self and others, enabling one to gain security and ward off anxiety, according to Harry Stack Sullivan.

personnel psychology   The branch of industrial psychology that deals with employee efficiency and problems.

person perception   The interpretation of a person's intentions, emotions, and personality characteristics based on nonverbal cues derived from observations of behavior, such as body language.

persuasion The attempt of a person or group to change prejudiced attitudes of others by means of communications of various kinds, oral and written.

phallic stage The stage from the third to fifth years of life in which children concentrate for sexual and aggressive gratification on the genitals, and experience the Oedipus complex, according to Freudian theory.

phenomenological model of conflict A theory developed by Kurt Lewin and his followers, which explains conflict in terms of psychological vectors, or forces, pushing the individual toward or away from valenced activities or objects. See also *behavioral model of conflict; Freudian model of conflict.*

phenotype The traits actually manifested or expressed by an individual organism as a result of the interaction between genotype and environment.

phenylketonuria A monogenetic disorder of metabolic deficiency that produces mental retardation and other symptoms.

phi phenomenon The perceptual illusion of movement of a light when a series of stationary lights flash one after another in succession. This is the fundamental principle upon which motion pictures are based.

phobia An intense, irrational fear aroused by specific objects, people, or places, providing the basis for reinforcement of any behavior, usually avoidance, that produces relief. See also *relief-seeking behavior.*

phrenology The refuted theory that personality types can be identified by means of the size and shape of the skull.

phylogenetic Based on natural evolutionary relationships; acquired in the course of evolutionary development.

phylum (plural, **phyla**) One of the primary divisions of the animal kingdom, composed of organisms sharing a fundamental organizational pattern and presumably common ancestors.

physiological psychology The division of psychology that concentrates on the biological or organic, rather than the environmental or cognitive, determinants of behavior.

pigmented layer The black membrane layer at the back of the retina that prevents light from being reflected and scattered throughout the eye before it reaches the receptor cells in the retina.

pitch The sensed quality of sound resulting from the frequency of the sound waves stimulating the ear.

placebo A substance or procedure described to a patient as therapeutic, although it is not itself effective, prescribed for psychological effects or used as a control in experiments.

placebo effect The influence of faith or belief in a psychotherapeutic or other method of treatment on the success of the treatment and the patient's judgment of its success.

pleasure center One of the areas in the brain, principally located in the limbic system, the stimulation of which is extremely pleasureable. See also *punishment center.*

pleasure principle The basic infantile drive for pleasure through the gratification of needs and avoidance of pain, expressing the energies of the libido, according to Freudian theory.

polygenetic trait A trait of an organism, like height, that is determined by more than one gene pair. See also *monogenetic trait.*

pons See *brainstem.*

population The whole set of data of a particular kind, from which a representative sample can be selected. See also *inferential statistics.*

positive correlation The relationship between measures of variables, things, or events such that as one increases the other consistently increases, or as one decreases the other consistently decreases. See also *negative correlation.*

positive reinforcement The strengthening of responses that immediately precede a rewarding event. Positive reinforcement is used in reward conditioning. See also *negative reinforcement.*

positive transfer The increase in ease or efficiency in a new learning task or situation due to the transfer of learning from prior tasks or situations. See also *negative transfer; nonspecific transfer; transfer of training.*

precognition A presumed extrasensory awareness of future events. See also *extrasensory perception.*

predictability The capacity to tell beforehand that an event will occur given a certain condition or set of conditions, based, for example, on a high correlation or a causal relationship between the event and another event. See also *causal relationship; correlation.*

predictive hypothesis   A hypothetical statement expressing the results expected, given a specific set of conditions, such as "If some subjects watch more violent TV shows than other subjects, then the former subjects will display more aggressive behavior." See also *descriptive hypothesis.*

prefrontal lobotomy   The cutting of the fibers connecting the frontal lobes and thalamus, in order to relieve severe emotional disorders, but sometimes having severe side effects and now largely abandoned.

prejudice   A strongly emotional, irrational or unfounded, and persistent attitude for or against a person, group of people, things, or events. See also *attitude; discrimination, stereotype.*

premature   In the human infant, birth before the usual gestation period in the uterus of about 38 weeks or 270 days after conception.

premature ventricular contraction (PVC)   A contraction of the left ventricle, one of the chambers of the heart, a little sooner than should normally occur, causing the heart to function less efficiently. See also *arrhythmia.*

preoperational stage   The stage in Piaget's theory of cognitive development, from about two to six years of age, during which children begin to acquire knowledge through the use of concepts and symbols standing for objects.

primary or **basic anxiety**   The anxiety aroused in the helpless infant by strong hunger, pain, discomfort, loud noises, and rough handling, the first source of conflicts and maladaptive behavior, according to Freudian psychodynamic theory. See also *anxiety.*

primary motive   One of the physiological drives designed to maintain homeostasis, like hunger and thirst. See also *biological drive; homeostatic drive; secondary motive.*

primary reinforcement   Reinforcement in instrumental conditioning by means of reinforcers, such as food, water, sex, and shock, that yield unconditioned or innate effects on the organism, not requiring training for reinforcement. See also *generalized reinforcement; secondary reinforcement.*

proactive interference (PI)   The tendency of earlier learning to disrupt the recall of later learning. See also *interference theories; retroactive interference.*

problem box   A box from which animals can escape only by solving a problem, such as releasing a catch on the door, used in the study of problem-solving behavior by E. L. Thorndike and others. See also *problem situation; problem solving.*

problem situation   A situation in which an individual has no immediately available behavior for attaining a desired goal. See also *problem solving.*

problem solving   Behavior in which normal responses are blocked, immediate solutions do not work, and a variety of strategies, like trial-and-error behavior, are implemented, often with the assistance of symbolic mediational behavior. See also *"Aha" experience; creative process; insight; mediational process; sudden solution.*

projective test   An unstructured personality test, such as the Rorschach test, in which responses to vague or ambiguous stimuli require use of imagination and reveal something about the subject's underlying personality characteristics. See also *personality assessment; Rorschach test; Thematic Apperception Test.*

proprioceptive stimulus   Stimulus feedback from the muscles and joints to indicate the position and movement of limbs and body; probably involved as a mediator in the ability of animals to make delayed reactions to stimuli. See also *delayed-reaction experiment.*

psychiatry   A medical practice that specializes in the treatment of behavior disorders, using psychotherapy and in some cases drugs.

psychoactive drugs   See *drugs, psychoactive.*

psychoanalysis   The theory, developed by Freud and his followers, that personality development results from the manner in which the individual progresses through a series of psychological stages; also, a therapeutic method designed to help individuals by uncovering unconscious motives. See also *psychoanalytic therapy.*

psychoanalyst   A practitioner of psychoanalytic therapy, who has a degree in medicine, has received formal psychoanalytic training, and has been psychoanalyzed by another analyst. Lay analysts lack the medical degree but undergo the same special training. See *psychoanalytic therapy.*

psychoanalytic theory   A theory of normal behavior and its disorders developed by Sigmund Freud and his followers, based on the dynamic interactions of the id, ego, and superego.

psychoanalytic therapy   The method of psychotherapy developed by Freud and his followers, aimed at liberating the energies tied up in infantile love objects and consumed in repression of impulses unacceptable to the superego. The method aims to overcome resistances and achieve transference with the use of such techniques as free association and dream analysis. See also *dream analysis; free association; psychotherapy; repression; resistance; transference.*

psychodrama A technique developed by J. L. Moreno in which psychiatric patients are encouraged to play various roles in acting out scenes involving their conflicts.

psychokinesis A presumed capacity of the mind to influence physical events, such as the movement of an object simply by mental effort. See also *extrasensory perception.*

psycholinguistics The division of psychology in which the acquisition and use of language is investigated in terms of the psychological processes involved. See also *language.*

psychology The investigation of human and animal behavior and associated mental and physical processes.

psychopathic personality See *antisocial personality.*

psychopharmacology The scientific study of the behavioral and psychological effects of drugs, including effects on perceptual, emotional, and cognitive functions. See also *drugs, psychoactive.*

psychophysics The investigation under controlled laboratory conditions of the relationships between changes in the values of physical stimuli and changes in the qualities of sensations. See also *sensation; stimulus.*

psychosis Any of a group of serious behavior disorders characterized by distorted perception and cognition, hallucinations or delusions, extreme effects on speech and memory, and marked shifts in mood and feeling, often resulting in inability to distinguish reality from unreality. See also *delusion; hallucination; manic-depressive psychosis; paranoia; paranoid reaction; psychotic depressive reaction; schizophrenia.*

psychosomatic disorder An organic disorder, such as asthma, headache, cramp, ulcers, and colitis, in which symptoms are originated and maintained by emotional factors.

psychosurgery A controversial type of somatic therapy, such as prefrontal lobotomy, in which connections between various parts of the brain are cut in order to relieve certain kinds of severe emotional disorders.

psychotherapy Methods utilizing direct communication and interaction to help alleviate or overcome behavior disorders that hamper the well-being of patients and others. See also *behavior therapy; client-centered therapy; group therapy; psychoanalytic therapy; somatic therapy.*

psychotherapy by reciprocal inhibition See *desensitization therapy.*

psychotic depressive reaction One kind of psychosis in which self-depreciation, guilt, and hopelessness are so extreme and persistent that they become delusional and withdrawal is severe. See also *neurotic depression.*

psychotic disorders See *psychosis.*

punishment An aversive stimulus produced by a certain response. Punishment lowers the probability that the response will occur in the future. See also *negative reinforcement.*

punishment center One of the areas in the brain of an organism, principally in the limbic system, the stimulation of which is strongly aversive. See also *pleasure center.*

pupil The round opening between the cornea and lens of the eye whose diameter varies in size with the expansion and contraction of the iris, thereby varying the amount of light passing into the eye.

pursuit-rotor tracking A task requiring that a stylus be kept in contact with a small disk moving around on the surface of a platter rotating at a constant speed, used in investigating the acquisition of simple sensorimotor skills.

Q-sort technique A technique used in client-centered therapy in which the client sorts cards bearing a variety of self-statements into piles that represent degrees of approximation first to the perceived self and second to the ideal self.

qualitative See *quantitative.*

quantify To assign symbols, such as numbers, to observations; for example, to count the subjects in an experiment and arrive at the number 10, standing for the number of subjects. See also *descriptive statistics.*

quantitative Pertaining to the expression of observations or characteristics in numerical terms, on which mathematical operations can be performed; opposed to qualitative, nonnumerical observations or characteristics. Thus a sound can be judged quantitatively as two or three times louder than another sound, but beauty is judged qualitatively as "much more" or "much less," but not two or three times more or less beautiful.

questionnaire   A set of systematically arranged and often pretested questions about respondents' past or usual behavior, opinions, or feelings. See also *retrospective method; self-report inventory.*

rating scale   A scale representing a series of degrees or qualities, used to indicate the judged degree or quality of any specific characteristic, such as a personality trait, possessed or manifested by a person or thing. See also *absolute rating scale; relative rating scale.*

rating test   A test composed of a series of rating scales.

rational-emotive therapy (RET)   A type of psychotherapy, developed by Albert Ellis, emphasizing a cognitive approach to emotional conflicts, in which neurotic behavior is attributed to irrational and erroneous assumptions and ideas. See also *cognitive therapy.*

reality principle   The basic tendency of the conscious ego to guide behavior toward real situations that will satisfy the libidinal drives of the id, according to Freudian theory.

receptive language   The reception and understanding of language. In children, receptive language is usually more advanced than expressive language. See also *expressive language.*

receptor   The part of each sensory system that is sensitive to a particular kind of physical stimulation, such as the rods and cones in the retina of the eye, the sensory system for vision. Receptors transform physical energy into neural activity. See also *sensory system.*

recessive gene   A gene that expresses itself only when paired with a similar gene. When paired with a dominant gene, the recessive gene is masked. See also *dominant gene.*

recognition method   The method of measuring memory by means of the correct identification of previously learned materials. See also *free-recall method; relearning method.*

reductionistic theory   A theory that employs concepts or principles from a lower or simpler level of explanation than that normally used for the explanation of the events. Thus, such a theory might attempt to explain human sexual behavior in terms of hormones or brain mechanisms. See also *abstract theory; theory.*

reference group   A social group with which a person tends to identify; a group whose attitudes, values, and interests an individual shares. See also *group norm; individual norm; in-group.*

reflex, acquired   An innate biological reflex triggered by a previously neutral stimulus through experience. See also *conditioned response.*

reflex, biological   A simple, innate, and automatic response to stimulation, like the withdrawal of a limb from a painful stimulus. See also *unconditioned response.*

regression   The adoption of behavior patterns more appropriate to earlier, often childish or infantile stages of life, sometimes resulting from extreme frustration; according to Freudian theory, a defense mechanism in which behavior reverts to an earlier stage of development, as to the anal stage, in order to overcome anxiety.

regression, age   See *age regression.*

rehearsal   See *behavioral rehearsal.*

rehearsal buffer   The set of items of information that is actively rehearsed in short-term memory long enough to facilitate its transfer to long-term memory.

reinforcement   The process by which positive or negative reinforcers classically or instrumentally strengthen the responses of an organism. See also *generalized reinforcement; negative reinforcement; positive reinforcement; reinforcer.*

reinforcement methods   In behavior therapy, the use of principles of reinforcement based on operant conditioning to reduce behavior deficits and extinguish undesirable behavior patterns. See also *behavior therapy; operant learning; reinforcement.*

reinforcement of alternate behavior (RAB)   Conditioning principles applied to change an individual's undesirable behavior. Alternate behavior is positively reinforced while the undesirable behavior is punished.

reinforcement schedule   A pattern of reinforcement in operant learning. Patterns fall into two major categories: regular or continuous reinforcement, in which every correct response is reinforced; and partial or intermittent reinforcement, in which only some of the correct responses are reinforced. See also *fixed-interval schedule; fixed-ratio schedule; variable-interval schedule; variable-ratio schedule.*

reinforcement theory of attraction   See *reward theory of attraction.*

reinforcer   In classical conditioning, the originally potent or unconditioned stimulus (US); in instrumental conditioning, the stimulus that increases the probability of the response that produces it (positive reinforcer) or of the response that avoids or escapes from it (negative reinforcer). See also *negative reinforcement; positive reinforcement.*

reinforcing goal See *incentive.*

reinforcing stimulus An unconditioned stimulus that, through conditioning, makes a previously neutral stimulus become effective in eliciting a similar response. See also *reinforcement; reinforcer.*

relative rating scale A rating scale according to which the rater ranks each subject in relation to the other subjects on each of the characteristics being rated. See also *absolute rating scale.*

relaxation technique A method of learning to relax the muscles of the body progressively, used in conjunction with desensitization techniques in behavior therapy. See also *desensitization technique.*

relearning method The method of measuring memory by noting the reduction, or "savings," in the number of trials required to relearn the material to the original criterion of mastery. See also *free-recall method; recognition method; savings score.*

reliability The degree to which a method of measurement yields consistent results. See also *validity.*

relief-seeking behavior Behavior directed toward avoiding or changing situations conducive to the arousal of anxiety or other aversive emotions. Such avoidance or escape responses are often symptoms of phobias or anxiety neuroses.

REM sleep The physiologically more active stage of sleep during which rapid-eye-movements and dreaming occur. See also *NREM sleep.*

reminiscence Improved performance or recall of a learned task some time after the learning trials have ceased, presumably due to the dissipation of work inhibition during the intervening period. See also *warm-up effect.*

Remote-Associates Test (RAT) A test in which subjects are required to produce a word association common to three different words. The test measures the ability to identify the common or mediating element among different words, even though the words belong to remote associative clusters, and thus presumably measures creativity. *Alternate Uses Test.*

repression A type of motivated forgetting of information stored in long-term memory in which memories that arouse anxiety or other disagreeable emotions are prevented from being retrieved. See also *amnesia; conflict; defense mechanism.*

resistance The reluctance or inability of individuals undergoing psychoanalytic therapy to permit repressed impulses to emerge into consciousness.

resistance to extinction The number of trials or period of time required for extinction of a classically or instrumentally conditioned response, used as one measure of the strength of conditioning. The greater the resistance to extinction, the stronger the conditioning. See also *emission rate; latency.*

response A name often given the dependent variable in psychological experiments. See also *dependent variable; stimulus-response relationship.*

response-contingent event An event whose occurrence depends on, or is contingent on, a prior response. Punishment, an aversive consequence following undesirable behavior, is such an event, as praise or some other reward is a positive consequence for strengthening desirable behavior.

response set A relatively permanent, usually learned tendency to respond in a certain way to given stimulus situations or to problems requiring creative approaches. See *functional fixedness; learning; problem solving.*

retina The tissue lining the back of the eye, containing the rod and cone receptor cells, whose stimulation by light results in vision.

retrieval strategies Procedures for recovering information that has been coded and stored in long-term memory, often the reverse of the coding strategies used in storing it there. See also *coding strategies; method of loci.*

retroactive interference (RI) The tendency of later learning to disrupt the recall of earlier learning. See also *interference theories; proactive interference.*

retrospective method The reconstruction of prior behavior from the accounts given by participants in the events. See also *case-history technique; observation; questionnaire; self-report inventory.*

reward conditioning See *positive reinforcement.*

reward theory of attraction The theory that interpersonal attraction is based on positive reinforcements derived from the interactions of the persons involved. See also *attraction, interpersonal; reinforcement; social-exchange theory of attraction; stimulus–value–role theory.*

ribonucleic acid (RNA) A large protein molecule that translates genetic instructions from DNA into specific cellular processes, such as the synthesis of needed proteins, and may be involved in or the site of the physical storage of memories in neurons of the brain.

rod   The receptor cell in the retina of the eye sensitive to light energy of all wavelengths and concentrated particularly in the periphery of the retina. See also *cone.*

role playing   See *psychodrama.*

romantic love   See *love.*

rooting response   A species-characteristic behavior of the human newborn in which the head turns back and forth sideways in apparent search for the breast.

Rorschach test   A projective technique consisting of ten symmetrical inkblots that subjects are asked to interpret. See also *projective test; unstructured test.*

rote learning   Learning by constant repetition, as in learning a poem "by heart."

round window   The membrane of the cochlea of the inner ear that relieves the pressure changes of cochlear fluid caused by sound vibrations.

saccades   The brief and intermittent movements of the eyes apparent when a person reads long lines of printed material, for example. See also *eye arrest.*

saccule   See *vestibular apparatus.*

samadhi   A state induced by meditation, as taught by Hindu yogis, leading to deep mental and physical relaxation, unawareness of external and internal stimuli, and an eventual ecstatic condition. See also *satori.*

sample   A small group of data selected as representative of a much larger population of data. See also *inferential statistics.*

satiety center   The region of the hypothalamus that indicates when enough has been eaten. See also *ventromedial nucleus (hypothalamus).*

satori   The ultimate state induced by meditation, according to Zen Buddhists, resulting in final awareness that life is totally good and everything wholly agreeable. See also *meditation; samadhi.*

savings score   The score expressing the degree of retention of material learned, obtained by dividing the number of trials required for relearning by the number of trials required to learn the material originally. See also *relearning method.*

scale   See *rating scale.*

scapegoat   A person or group of people who become the target of displaced aggressive reactions of another individual or group. See also *aggressive reaction; displacement.*

scapegoat theory   A theory of schizophrenia that assumes that the family unconsciously selects and exploits one of its members as the victim for latent pathological components within the family.

scatter diagram or **scattergram**   A type of graph that displays the degree of correlation between variables or scores, with one variable represented on the vertical dimension of the graph and the other variable on the horizontal dimension. See also *correlation.*

schizoid personality   A personality disorder characterized by withdrawn, introvertive, and eccentric behavior patterns.

schizophrenia   A group of psychotic behavior disorders characterized by common disturbances in perceiving (hallucinations and delusions), thinking (bizarre ideas), mood (flat or inappropriate emotions), behavior (ritualistic reactions and withdrawal), and speech ("word salad"). See also *catatonic schizophrenia; hebephrenic schizophrenia; paranoid schizophrenia; simple schizophrenia.*

school psychology   A branch of clinical psychology concerned with the emotional and developmental problems of children in elementary and secondary schools, and emphasizing diagnostic testing and counseling as well as methods and theories of learning and instruction.

secondary generalization   See *mediated generalization.*

secondary (acquired) motives   Motives that may be derived from primary motives and normally are acquired through learning. Many complex human motives, though learned, do not seem to be based on primary biological motives; for example, gregariousness and motives for prestige or achievement. See also *motive; primary motive.*

secondary reinforcement   In instrumental conditioning, reinforcement by means of reinforcers, such as praise or blame, that acquire their effects through conditioning or training. See also *generalized reinforcement; primary reinforcement.*

selective attention   The process of directing attention to certain features of the environment while disregarding other features. See also *attention.*

selective breeding   The process of mating animals for a specific trait for the purpose of studying the heritability of the trait. If the trait is governed primarily by heredity, continued mating of individuals with the trait for a number of generations will produce a strain with a high incidence of the trait. See also *heritability.*

self-actualization The creative realization of one's capacities, a need recognized by the psychologist Abraham Maslow. See also *motive; secondary motive.*

self-concept The general ideas and feelings that all people acquire about themselves as unique individuals of special significance, developed early in childhood.

self-control procedures The behavioral-technology procedures that any individual can use to modify everyday habits in more desirable directions, by such methods as changing the external stimuli controlling such habits, reinforcing behavior incompatible with them, and monitoring one's own progress toward such change.

self-derogation A negative attitude toward oneself, varying in degree of disfavor or disapproval and affecting many other attitudes and much of the individual's behavior. See also *defaced image; self-concept; self-esteem.*

self-esteem A positive attitude toward oneself, varying in degree of favor or approval and affecting many other attitudes and much of the individual's behavior. See also *idealized image; self-concept; self-derogation.*

self-observation The process of observing one's own internal and external reactions, or covert and overt behavior, in a given situation. See also *observation.*

self-report inventory A set of systematically arranged and often pretested questions or statements for subjects to answer, sometimes used as personality tests. See also *questionnaire; retrospective method.*

semantic differential A technique for measuring the qualitative meanings or feeling tones of words or other symbols by means of a series of rating scales of contrary adjectives like "good–bad," "active–passive." See also *connotative meaning; meaning.*

semicircular canals See *vestibular apparatus.*

senile dementia An organic brain disease marked by childish emotions, self-centeredness, and failure of memory for recent events, resulting from aging of brain tissues.

sensation The kind of conscious awareness or experience produced by the action of a given sensory system, such as sound sensed by the ear, light sensed by the eye, and pressure sensed by touch receptors in the skin. See also *sensory quality; sensory system.*

sense See *sensory system.*

sensitivity training group or **T-group** A group formed for a type of group therapy in which dreams or daydreams are analyzed, role playing is encouraged, and special methods are used to involve timid, suspicious, or aloof group members. See also *group therapy; psychodrama.*

sensorimotor skill Learned behavior that involves both sensory processes and muscular reactions, like typing or playing tennis, in which verbal behavior plays a relatively small part.

sensorimotor stage The stage in Piaget's theory of cognitive development, from birth to about two years, during which infants acquire knowledge simply by sensing and physically reacting to the objects in their environment.

sensory cortex See *cortex.*

sensory deprivation The lack of adequate sensory stimulation for the normal maintenance or development of an organism.

sensory quality The quality or property of sensations produced within a sensory system, such as the brightness and color of light and the loudness, pitch, and timbre of sound.

sensory storage The brief perceptual memory process of storage of sensory input for less than a second. The process is sometimes called iconic memory for visual storage and echoic memory for auditory storage. See also *organizational theories.*

sensory system Any one of the sensory pathways of an organism that receives stimulation and transforms it into nerve impulses transmitted to the central nervous system. These systems include the visual, auditory, smell, and taste senses, as well as the somesthetic senses (touch, pain, temperature), kinesthetic senses (motion, weight, position), and vestibular sense (balance and motion). See also *kinesthetic sense; somesthetic sense; vestibular sense; receptor.*

sex-role identification See *gender identification.*

sex-typed behavior Behavior that members of a society consider appropriate for one sex but not the other.

shadow The archetype in the collective unconscious predisposing individuals to sin or break taboos of the society; an inborn vestige of human beings' animal instincts, according to Jung.

shape constancy The visual perception of an object as constant in shape when perceived from various points of view, even though the shape of the retinal image of the object changes from different points of view. See also *perceptual constancy*.

shaping   The instrumental conditioning of behavior into highly refined skills by means of the reinforcement of a series of successive approximations, each response approaching closer and closer to the responses desired. See also *chaining*.

short-term memory (STM)   The memory process by means of which information is stored for 10 to 20 seconds, and can be retrieved provided the information is constantly rehearsed. See also *long-term memory; organizational theories; rehearsal buffer*.

sickle-cell anemia   A physical disorder caused by a trait resulting from a mutation that is prevalent in the populations of various areas, principally Africa. Severe anemia results when an individual is homozygous for the recessive gene involved.

signal   A term used for the stimulus in the detection theory of perception. See also *detection theory*.

significant difference   A difference between two means that would be likely to recur if the observations or experiment were repeated. See also *standard error of the difference between means*.

sign stimulus   A highly specific cue from the environment of an organism, or from within it, that serves to elicit species-characteristic behavior.

simple schizophrenia   A type of schizophrenia characterized by lack of attachment to others, apathy and withdrawal, deterioration of mental capacities, lack of interest in practically everything, and regression to a childish level. Delusions and hallucinations are absent. See also *schizophrenia*.

situational measure   The measurement of personality or other characteristics by placing individuals to be assessed in typical situations that will reveal their reactions of the type under study. See also *personality assessment*.

size constancy   The visual perception of an object as constant in size when viewed at varying distances, even though the size of the retinal image of the object diminishes with greater distance from the observer. See also *perceptual constancy*.

skewed distribution   A graphed curve in which the slopes at the sides of the peak are not equally steep, with the scores piling up on one side of the peak or the other. See also *normal distribution*.

sleep   A normal state of existence of higher animal organisms consisting of a loss of consciousness and occurring in a number of stages identifiable by electroencephalograms of brain waves. See also *NREM sleep; REM sleep*.

smell receptor   See *olfactory cell*.

social-exchange theory of attraction   The theory that interpersonal attraction is based on both the rewards and the costs accruing to the persons involved, such as values given in return for values received, or values forgone discounted from the rewards. See also *attraction, interpersonal; reward theory of attraction; stimulus–value–role theory*.

social facilitation   The improvement of individual behavior in the presence of others.

social psychology   The objective study of the influences on individuals or groups of their interactions with other individuals or groups, emphasizing psychological concepts drawn from areas like perception, learning, and motivation more than sociological concepts like social class, institutions, and status.

social reinforcement   The reinforcement, either positive or negative, of a person's behavior by means of the reward or punishment, praise or criticism, approval or disapproval given by other people. See also *reinforcement*.

social stereotype   The image held by many members of a society of out-groups within the society, like minority groups, made up of a simplified collection of assigned traits. See also *personal stereotype; stereotype*.

sociopathic personality   See *antisocial personality*.

somatic nervous system   The major division of the peripheral nervous system composed of all sensory neurons and their associated nerves connecting the sense organs with the central nervous system, and all nerves from the central nervous system to the body's muscles. See also *autonomic nervous system*.

somatic therapy   The use of drugs, electroshock, and psychosurgery in the treatment of behavior disorders. See also *chemotherapy; electroconvulsive therapy*.

somesthetic or **skin sense**   The human sensory system responding to bodily stimulation, resulting in the sensations of temperature, touch, and pain. See also *sensory system*.

somnambulism   Sleepwalking, one of the dissociation reactions.

sound   The auditory sensations resulting from the reception of sound waves in the ear, varying in sensory qualities of pitch, loudness, and timbre.

sound localization   Perception of the distance and direction of a sound source by means of cues provided by the sound alone. See also *binaural discrepancy.*

sound receptor   The hair cells in the organ of Corti, sensitive to vibrations transmitted from the basilar membrane.

sound wave   A vibration in the air consisting of successive condensations and rarefactions of molecules produced by a moving body, perceived as sound.

source traits   Certain key personality traits, like tough- and tender-mindedness, based on clusters of surface traits and manifesting basic aspects of personality, according to R. B. Cattell's trait theory of personality. See also *surface traits.*

species-characteristic or **species-specific behavior**   Inherited, complex, and coordinated behavior common to nearly all members of a species. See also *instinct.*

specific anxiety measure   A test, such as the Test Anxiety Questionnaire, that measures the individual's anxiety in a particular kind of situation, such as taking examinations or tests. See also *Achievement Anxiety Test; anxiety inventory; Test Anxiety Questionnaire.*

speech centers   Those regions in the human cortex, usually in the left frontal and temporal lobes, in which speech processes are carried on.

sperm   A male reproductive cell, or gamete, produced in the testis, possessing one-half of the number of chromosomes of the parental cell.

spinal cord   That part of the central nervous system encased in the backbone, which transmits nerve impulses to and from the brain by means of interneurons that travel up and down it.

spiral ganglion cell   A cell in the inner ear that is activated by hair-cell receptors on the organ of Corti and whose axon forms the auditory nerve.

spontaneous recovery   The recovery of part of the strength of a classically or instrumentally conditioned response some time after it has been extinguished.

spontaneous remission   The diminishing of or recovery from a behavior disorder without psychotherapeutic treatment. The percentage of such spontaneous cures, the base rate, must be kept in mind in judging the success of various types of psychotherapeutic treatment.

stages of development   The periods of life through which people pass from infancy to maturity, each stage marked by its own characteristic conflicts, according to Freudian theory. See also *anal stage; genital stage; latent stage; oral stage; phallic stage.*

standard deviation (SD)   A number representing the dispersion of scores in a distribution around the mean of that distribution, obtained by summing the squares of the deviations of each score from the mean, taking the mean of this sum, and finding the square root of the mean:

$$SD = \sqrt{\frac{\Sigma D^2}{N}}$$

SD = the standard deviation, Σ = the sum, D = the deviation of each score from the mean, and N = the number of scores. See also *measure of variability.*

standard error of the difference between means (SE$_{diff}$)   The square root of the summed squares of the standard errors of two sample means:

$$SE_{diff} = \sqrt{SE_{M_1}{}^2 + SE_{M_2}{}^2}$$

SE$_{diff}$ = the standard error of the difference between the means, SE$_{M_1}$ = the standard error of mean 1, and SE$_{M_2}$ = the standard error of mean 2.

standard error of the mean (SE)   The number expressing the reliability of the mean of a given distribution of scores, obtained by dividing the standard deviation of the distribution by the square root of the number of scores in the distribution:

$$SE = \frac{SD}{\sqrt{N}}$$

SE = the standard error of the mean, SD = the standard deviation of the distribution, and N equals the total number of scores in the distribution.

standardization group   The group of people whose performance on a given test is used as a standard, against which the performance of other individuals is compared.

standard score or **Z score**   An individual score in comparison with the mean of a distribution of scores in terms of distance from the mean in standard-deviation units.

$$Z = \frac{X - M}{SD}$$

Z = the standard score, X = the individual's score,

M = the mean score for the distribution, and SD = the standard deviation of the distribution.

Stanford-Binet Intelligence Scale A standardized intelligence test used most frequently for children.

startle pattern An unlearned pattern of bodily reactions following a sudden and intense stimulus, such as "jumping" at a loud noise.

statistics The analysis, interpretation, and presentation of masses of numerical data in an effective manner. See also *descriptive statistics; inferential statistics.*

stereoscope An instrument that presents two slightly different pictures of the same scene to the eyes, giving the illusion of the perception of depth and distance in the scene.

stereotype A group of standardized ascribed characteristics forming an oversimplified image of something or someone, often associated with outgroups. See also *attitude; belief; personal stereotype; prejudice; social stereotype.*

stereotyped judgment A judgment influenced by the preconceived notions of the evaluator. See also *halo effect.*

stimulant A drug that stimulates the central nervous system and tends to increase alertness, reduce fatigue, and induce euphoria; in high doses it may induce irritability and anxiety. See also *amphetamine; caffeine; cocaine.*

stimulus (plural, *stimuli*) Physical energy of the types to which the sense receptors of an organism are adapted, impinging on a receptor and causing it to react. Thus electromagnetic waves and sound waves of the proper frequencies affect the eyes and the ears, respectively, and initiate nerve impulses in these receptors.

stimulus condition A name often given the independent variable in psychological experiments. See also *independent variable; stimulus-response relationship.*

stimulus control The high probability of occurrence of certain behaviors in the presence of specific classes of stimuli, achieved through classical and instrumental conditioning.

stimulus generalization A process in which a response (CR) conditioned to one specific conditioned stimulus (CS+) may also be elicited by other stimuli that resemble the CS+. Stimulus generalization occurs both in classical and instrumental conditioning.

stimulus–response (S–R) relationship A relationship between the stimulus condition and the response as the independent and dependent variables in psychological experiments. See also *causal relationship; functional relationship; dependent variable; independent variable.*

stimulus–value–role theory (SVR) The theory that stimulus factors, values, and roles are, successively, the major determinants of interpersonal attraction. See also *attraction, interpersonal; reward theory of attraction; social-exchange theory of attraction.*

stirrup See *ossicles.*

Strong-Campbell Interest Inventory A personality inventory of statements to which a subject's responses, compared with those of many people in various occupations, indicate the relative degree of the subject's own interests. See also *personality inventory.*

structured test A test, such as a personality inventory, made up of a selected series of questions or statements to which subjects respond, "Yes," "No," or "Don't know." See also *personality inventory; unstructured test.*

sublimation One of the defense mechanisms, according to Freudian theory, in which achievements in various areas of endeavor, like art or science, are used as substitutes for direct sexual satisfaction of libidinal drives. See also *defense mechanism; displacement.*

subliminal Related to external stimulation of an organism below the threshold of its conscious awareness.

successive approximations The conditioning procedures that select and reward behavior that approaches more and more closely to the final specific behavior desired. See also *chaining; shaping.*

sudden solution (instant learning) The solution of a problem that occurs in a flash, attributed either to some kind of creative insight or to the transfer of previous learning experiences.

suicide Self-destruction, sometimes interpreted as aggression displaced inward against the self, sometimes as an extreme form of withdrawal.

superego The conscience, which internalizes the prohibitions of society and serves to inhibit the instinctive, pleasure-seeking drives of the id, according to Freudian theory.

superiority The innate, dynamic goal of self-assertion and achievement, of greatest significance in the development of personality, according to Alfred Adler, and the contrary of inferiority.

surface traits Certain personality traits, such as assertiveness and aggressiveness, which are highly correlated with each other, according to R. B. Cattell's trait theory of personality. See also *source traits.*

symbol A number, word, or other sign, representing or standing for something, as the number 10 can stand for 10 subjects or 10 trials in an experiment.

symbolic control The control of an individual's behavior by antecedent symbol processes, such as images or ideas, so that the probability that the behavior will occur is changed by the presence or absence of such processes. See also *stimulus control; symbolic processes.*

symbolic processes Activities involving symbols, or cues standing for other things, such as thinking, imagining, or verbalizing.

sympathetic division The part of the autonomic division of the peripheral nervous system that acts primarily to prepare the body for fight or flight.

symptom substitution The appearance of new disorders in a patient after the original maladaptive behavior has been eliminated by some form of therapy; often assumed but rarely observed to be a consequence of behavior therapy.

synapse The short gap across which a nerve message passes from the axon of one neuron to the dendrites of another by means of chemicals that serve as synaptic transmitters.

synaptic transmitter One of a number of chemicals, such as acetylcholine, released by an axon that diffuses across the synapse to excite or inhibit the adjacent neuron.

systematic desensitization technique See *desensitization technique.*

systematic desensitization therapy See *desensitization therapy.*

target behavior The behavior that an individual wishes to change, eliminate, or strengthen by a behavioral-technology procedure, using principles of classical or instrumental conditioning. This behavior is recorded and analyzed in detail before the attempt is made to modify it.

taste The sensation produced by taste-cell receptors in the mouth, resulting in at least four primary taste sensory qualities: bitter, sweet, salty, and sour.

taste bud A structure consisting of many taste cells arranged around a pore, located in the mouth and throat, but concentrated on the tongue.

taste cell A specialized receptor occurring in clusters called taste buds on the tongue, larynx, and pharynx, and stimulated by chemical solutions to yield taste experiences.

taste receptor The taste cell, with its taste hairs, contained in taste buds and reacting to chemicals in the saliva to produce the sensation of taste.

Taylor Manifest Anxiety Scale (TMAS) A measure of general anxiety, consisting of statements to which subjects respond by indicating whether the statements are true or false as they apply to them.

telepathy A presumed capacity for the direct transfer of thoughts from one mind to another without the employment of verbal communication. See also *extrasensory perception.*

temperament An individual's typical, basic inclination, emotional response, or disposition. See also *mood.*

temporal lobe See *cortex.*

territoriality Maintenance of a certain area by an animal or group of animals for its exclusive use, observed in many species and attributed by some to human beings as well. See also *personal space.*

Test Anxiety Questionnaire (TAQ) A measure of anxiety specifically related to taking examinations or tests.

testosterone A male hormone produced by the testes, or made synthetically, which is responsible for inducing and maintaining male secondary sex characteristics.

thalamus The major relay station in the brain for the transmission and initial processing of sensory messages to the cortex.

Thematic Apperception Test (TAT) A projective technique in which the subject is required to tell a story based on each of a set of pictures depicting individuals in ambiguous situations; presumably individuals project their own motives onto the characters in the pictures.

theory A logically coherent system of principles or laws for the prediction and explanation of a number of related events. See also *abstract theory; law; reductionistic theory.*

thirst The biological homeostatic motive or drive aroused in an organism by lack of sufficient fluids.

thought The cognitive process in which ideas, usually expressed in verbal terms, are used to arrive at an understanding of things, events, or relationships. See also *cognition; imagery.*

threshold The minimum level of stimulus intensity, or the minimum level of change in stimulus intensity, of which an organism is aware or to which it responds. See also *absolute threshold; difference threshold.*

Thurstone attitude scale An attitude scale for which judges sort statements about the targets of attitudes into groups representing degrees of favor or disfavor, on the basis of which scores are assigned to the statements, then summed to determine the direction and intensity of their attitudes.

timbre The sensory quality of sounds that characterizes a given source, as the quality of the sound of a clarinet is discriminable from the sounds of other wind instruments, such as flutes and saxophones.

time out (TO) The withholding of positive reinforcement for a period of time, as by seclusion in a "quiet" room, used as a form of punishment in reducing the strength of undesirable behavior.

tip-of-the-tongue phenomenon (TOT) The state of not quite being able to recall a word but still recalling some of its features, such as the first letter or number of syllables in the word.

token-economy system A system of tokens, essentially secondary reinforcers, varying in value, used in accordance with operant conditioning techniques for the establishment and maintenance of adaptive behavior patterns.

tolerance The diminishing effect of a drug with its repeated use.

trait A fairly enduring behavioral characteristic that can be rated or measured along a dimension, such as aggressiveness. See *personality or character trait.*

tranquilizer One of a group of drugs used for the relief of minor anxiety and tension and for the treatment of psychoses.

Transcendental Meditation (TM) A kind of meditation developed by Maharishi Mahesh Yogi, based on concentration on one source of stimulation, a particular sound called a mantra, to the exclusion of all others. See also *meditation; samadhi; satori.*

transducer See *transduction.*

transduction The process by means of which sensory receptors transform the physical energy of stimuli into neural energy. See also *receptor.*

transference The process whereby a patient identifies with a psychoanalyst, who becomes a parent substitute, allowing for reestablishment of the emotions of childhood and a resolution of conflict with the help of the analyst. See also *identification.*

transfer of training The carry-over effects of training or learning in one kind of situation, or of learning one specific skill, to other situations or other skills. Such effects sometimes assist and sometimes hamper new learning. See also *negative transfer; nonspecific transfer; positive transfer.*

transitive inference The process of inferring a relationship between two or more objects or events on the basis of knowledge of the relationship between other objects or events.

trial and error A variety of random behavior that organisms tend to emit in attempting to solve a problem, until the correct behavior is finally learned and emitted immediately when the problem is presented. See also *learning; problem solving.*

tympanic membrane or **eardrum** The circular membrane between the auditory canal and the middle ear, which vibrates in response to the sound waves that act on it, transmitting the vibrations to the middle ear.

Umweg problem A kind of problem used in studying problem-solving behavior that cannot be solved with the direct and obvious behavior likely to be emitted first by the problem solver. See also *problem situation.*

unconditional positive regard The attitude of the therapist toward the client in client-centered therapy, accepting the client's statements and feelings as important and valid.

unconditioned response (UR) An innate reflex elicited by an unconditioned stimulus, as the salivary reflex is elicited by the stimulus of food presented to a hungry animal. See also *reflex, biological.*

unconditioned stimulus (US) A biologically potent stimulus that automatically elicits a reflex response, as food presented to a hungry animal elicits a reflex salivary response. See also *conditioned stimulus; reflex, biological.*

unobtrusive measures Covert methods of observing behavior such that subjects are totally unaware that they are being observed.

unstructured test A test, such as the Thematic Apperception Test, composed of ambiguous pictures, to which the subject responds imaginatively, thereby revealing the characteristics being tested. See also *personality inventory; structured test*.

utricle   See *vestibular apparatus*.

vacuum behavior   A fixed-action pattern that occurs in the absence of the appropriate sign stimulus.

validity   The degree to which a test or other method of assessment actually measures what it was designed to measure. See also *concurrent validity; construct validity; reliability*.

variable   Any event occurring under experimental conditions that causes or is caused by another event. See also *dependent variable; independent variable; intervening variable*.

variable-interval schedule (VI)   A schedule of partial reinforcement in operant learning in which responses are reinforced only after varying intervals of time.

variable-ratio schedule (VR)   A schedule of partial reinforcement in operant learning in which a variable and unpredictable number of responses is required before reinforcement is given.

ventromedial nucleus (hypothalamus)   A region of the hypothalamus that operates as a satiety center for the hunger drive, indicating when enough food has been eaten. See also *lateral nucleus (hypothalamus)*.

verbal behavior   The use of spoken or written language in communicating with others. One form, called "verbal reports," made by a subject to an experimenter, often involves references to conscious, subjective experiences. See also *language*.

vertebrate   The major division of animals that have a spinal column, including birds, reptiles, fish, and mammals.

vestibular apparatus   The combination of semicircular canals, saccule, and utricle in the inner ear responsible for the sense of balance and movement of the head, called the vestibular sense.

vestibular sense   The human sensory system consisting of the semicircular canals and utricle of the inner ear, resulting in the sensation of position and movement of the head.

virtue   According to the Greek philosopher Aristotle, the golden mean of a trait between two extremes, which are the vices of deficiency and excess of the trait.

visceral organs   Organs of the body, such as the heart, blood vessels, stomach, bladder, and glands, regulated by the hypothalamus and the autonomic nervous system. See also *autonomic nervous system; hypothalamus; visceral reactions*.

visceral reactions   Reactions of the visceral organs involved in emotional responses and governed by the autonomic division of the nervous system. See also *autonomic nervous system; emotion; visceral organs*.

visual acuity   The varying capacity to distinguish fine details in the visual field of the eye.

visual contact, direct   The simultaneous meeting of eyes of two people, often significant of their relationship with each other.

visual cortex   The area at the rear of the occipital lobe in both left and right hemispheres of the brain to which the primary visual nerve pathways lead.

WAIS   See *Wechsler Adult Intelligence Scale*.

warm-up effect   The improved performance or recall of a learned task shortly after going back to practicing it again after a period of rest. See also *reminiscence*.

wavelength   The distance between successive troughs or crests of waves. The sensation of color varies with the length of light waves. See also *color; light wave; sound wave*.

Weber's law   The psychophysical law that states that just noticeable differences in sensations are constant percentages of the intensities of the physical stimuli that produce the sensations. See also *difference threshold; just noticeable difference; psychophysics*.

Wernecke-Korsakov syndrome   An organic brain condition marked by impairment of memory resulting from nutritional deficiencies, frequently associated with prolonged alcoholism. See also *organic brain disorder*.

withdrawal reaction   A frequent reaction to persistent or severe frustration, marked by fantasy, apathy, and depression, with diminished aggressive behavior and often the renunciation of the originally desired goals. See also

withdrawal syndrome   Physiological effects resulting from the abrupt withdrawal of a drug after physical dependence has been established. See also *dependence, drug*.

work inhibition   The tendency toward inhibition of response occurrence that increases with the number of responses that occur without a rest and with the effort involved in responding. Work inhibition is assumed to dissipate during rest, accounting for improved performance in distributed-practice learning.

Wechsler Adult Intelligence Scale (WAIS)   A standardized intelligence test for adults combining both performance and verbal items.

Zeigarnik effect   The observation that uninterrupted and completed learning tasks are more easily forgotten than uncompleted tasks.

Z score   See *standard score*.

zygote   A cell formed by the union of two gametes, or a fertilized egg, constituting a new individual.

References

Aaronson, S. A., & Todaro, G. J. Human diploid cell transformation by DNA extracted from the tumor virus SV40. *Science*, 1969, *166*, 390–391.

Adams, J. A. The second facet of forgetting: A review of warm-up decrement. *Psychological Bulletin*, 1961, *58*, 257–273.

Adamson, R. B. Functional fixedness as related to problem solving: A repetition of three experiments. *Journal of Experimental Psychology*, 1952, *44*, 288–291.

Agarival, K. L., Buchi, H., Caruthers, M. H., Guipta, N., Khorana, H. G., Kleppe, K., Kumar, A., Ohtsuka, E., Rajbhandary, U. L., van de Sande, J. H., Sgaramella, V., Weber, H., & Yamada, I. Total synthesis of the gene for an alanine transfer ribonucleic acid from yeast. *Nature*, 1970, *227*, 27–34.

Agranoff, B. W. Memory and protein synthesis. *Scientific American*, 1967, *216* (June), 115–122.

Agras, W., Sylvester, D., & Oliveau, D. The epidemiology of common fears and phobias. *Comprehensive Psychiatry*, 1969, *10*, 151–156.

Akiskal, H. S., & McKinney, W. T., Jr. Depressive disorders: Toward a unified hypothesis. *Science*, 1973, *182*, 20–29.

Allport, F. H. The influence of the group upon association and thought. *Journal of Experimental Psychology*, 1920, *3*, 159–182.

Allport, F. H. *Social psychology.* Boston: Houghton Mifflin, 1924.

Allport, G. W., & Kramer, B. M. Some roots of prejudice. *Journal of Psychology*, 1946, *22*, 9–29.

Allport, G. W., Vernon, P. E., & Lindzey, G. A. *Manual: Study of values* (3rd ed.). Boston: Houghton Mifflin, 1970.

Alpert, R., & Haber, R. N. Anxiety in academic achievement situations. *Journal of Abnormal and Social Psychology*, 1960, *61*, 207–215.

American Psychiatric Association. *Diagnostic and statistical manual of mental disorders* (2nd ed.). Washington, D.C.: American Psychiatric Association, 1968.

American Psychological Association. *Ethical principles in the conduct of research with human participants.* Washington, D.C.: American Psychological Association, 1973.

Ames, J. B. The sense of self of nursery school children as manifested by their verbal behavior. *Journal of Genetic Psychology*, 1952, *81*, 193–232.

Amsel, A. Frustrative nonreward in partial reinforcement and discrimination learning: Some recent history and a theoretical extension. *Psychological Review*, 1962, *69*, 306–328.

Amsel, A., & Roussel, J. Motivational properties of frustration: I. Effect on a running response of the addition of frustration to the motivational complex. *Journal of Experimental Psychology*, 1952, *43*, 363–368.

Anand, B. K., Chkina, G. S., & Singh, B. Some aspects of electroencephalographic studies in yogis. *EEG and Clinical Neurophysiology*, 1961, *13*, 452–456.

Anderson, B. Thirst and brain control of water balance. *American Scientist*, 1971, *59*, 408–415.

Andrew, R. J. Some remarks on behaviour in conflict situations, with special reference to *Emberiza* spp. *British Journal of Animal Behaviour*, 1956, *4*, 85–91.

Argyle, M., & Dean, J. Eye contact, distance, and affiliation. *Sociometry*, 1965, *28*, 289–304.

Aronson, E. *The social animal.* San Francisco: W. H. Freeman, 1972.

Asch, S. E. Opinions and social pressure. *Scientific American*, 1955, *193* (November), 31–35.

Ashman, R. The inheritance of simple musical memory. *The Journal of Heredity*, 1952, *43*, 51–52.

Atkinson, J. W., Heyns, R. W., & Veroff, J. The effect of experimental arousal of the affiliation motive on thematic apperception. *Journal of Abnormal and Social Psychology*, 1954, *49*, 405–410.

Atthowe, J. M., Jr., & Krasner, L. Preliminary report on the application of contingent reinforcement procedures (token economy) on a "chronic" psychiatric ward. *Journal of Abnormal Psychology*, 1968, *73*, 37–43.

Ayllon, T. Intensive treatment of psychotic behaviour by stimulus satiation and food reinforcement. *Behaviour Research and Therapy*, 1963, *1*, 53–61.

Ayllon, T., & Azrin, N. H. The measurement and reinforcement of behavior of psychotics. *Journal of Experimental Analysis of Behavior*, 1965, *8*, 357–383.

Azrin, N. H. Pain and aggression. *Psychology Today*, 1967, *1* (January), 26–33.

Azrin, N. H., & Foxx, R. M. *Toilet training in less than a day.* New York: Simon & Schuster, 1974.

Ball, W., & Tronick, E. Infant response to impending collision: Optical and real. *Science*, 1971, *171*, 818–820.

Bandura, A. *Principles of behavior modification.* New York: Holt, Rinehart and Winston, 1969.

Bandura, A. Social learning theory of aggression. In J. F. Knutson (Ed.), *Control of aggression: Implications from basic research.* Chicago: Aldine, 1971.

Bandura, A., Ross, D., & Ross, S. A. Imitation of film-mediated aggressive models. *Journal of Abnormal and Social Psychology*, 1963, *66*, 3–11.

Barber, T. X. *Hypnosis: A scientific approach.* New York: Van Nostrand Reinhold, 1969.

Barber, T. X. *LSD, meditation, yoga, and hypnosis.* Chicago: Aldine, 1970.

Barber, T. X., Walker, P. C., & Hahn, K. W., Jr. Effects of hypnotic induction and suggestions on nocturnal dreaming and thinking. *Journal of Abnormal Psychology*, 1973, *82*, 414–427.

Bard, P., & Mountcastle, V. B. Some forebrain mechanisms involved in the expression of rage, with special reference to suppression of angry behavior. In J. F. Fulton (Ed.), *The frontal lobes*, pp. 362–404. Baltimore: Williams & Wilkins, 1948.

Barker, R., Dembo, T., & Lewin, K. Frustration and regression: An experiment with young children. University of Iowa Studies: *Studies in Child Welfare*, 1941, *18*, No. 1.

Barron, F. The psychology of creativity. In *New directions in psychology* (Vol. 2), pp. 3–134. New York: Holt, Rinehart and Winston, 1965.

Barry, H., Bacon, M. K., & Child, I. L. A cross-cultural survey of some sex differences in socialization. *Journal of Abnormal and Social Psychology*, 1957, *55*, 327–332.

Bateson, G., Jackson, D. D., Haley, J., & Weakland, J. Toward a theory of schizophrenia. *Behavioral Science*, 1956, *1*, 251–264.

Baum, M. Extinction of avoidance responding through response prevention (flooding). *Psychological Bulletin*, 1970, *74*, 276–284.

Beary, J. F., Benson, H., & Klemchuk, H. P. A simple psychophysiologic technique which elicits the hypometabolic changes of the relaxation response. *Psychosomatic Medicine*, 1974, *36*, 115–120.

Beck, A. T. *Depression: Causes and treatment.* Philadelphia: University of Pennsylvania Press, 1972.

Becker, W. C. Consequences of different kinds of parental disciplines. In M. L. Hoffman & L. W. Hoffman (Eds.), *Review of child development research* (Vol. 1), pp. 169–208. New York: Russell Sage Foundation, 1964.

Beecher, H. K. Increased stress and effectiveness of placebos and "active" drugs. *Science*, 1960, *132*, 91–92.

Bell, S. M., & Ainsworth, M. D. S. Infant crying and maternal responsiveness. *Child Development*, 1972, *43*, 1171–1190.

Bennett, E. L., Diamond, M. C., Krech, D., & Rosenzweig, M. R. Chemical and anatomical plasticity of brain. *Science*, 1964, *146*, 610–619.

Benson, H., Beary, J. F., & Carol, M. P. The relaxation response. *Psychiatry*, 1974, *37*, 37–46.

Benson, H., Shapiro, D., Tursky, B., & Schwartz, G. E. Decreased systolic blood pressure through operant conditioning techniques in patients with essential hypertension. *Science*, 1971, *173*, 740–742.

Bergin, A. E. Some implications of psychotherapy research for therapeutic practice. *Journal of Abnormal Psychology*, 1966, *71*, 235–246.

Bergin, A. E. The evaluation of therapeutic outcomes. In A. E. Bergin & S. L. Garfield (Eds.), *Handbook of psychotherapy and behavior change: An empirical analysis*, pp. 217–270. New York: Wiley, 1971.

Bexton, W. H., Heron, W., & Scott, T. H. Effects of decreased variation in the sensory environment. *Canadian Journal of Psychology*, 1954, *8*, 70–76.

Binswanger, L. Existential analysis and psychotherapy. In F. Fromm-Reichmann & J. L. Moreno (Eds.), *Progress in psychotherapy*, pp. 144–148. New York: Grune & Stratton, 1956.

Birch, H. G. The relation of previous experience to insightful problem-solving. *Journal of Comparative Psychology*, 1945, *38*, 367–383. (a)

Birch, H. G. The role of motivational factors in insightful problem-solving. *Journal of Comparative Psychology*, 1945, *38*, 295–317. (b)

Blakemore, C., & Cooper, G. F. Development of the brain depends on the visual environment. *Nature*, 1970, *228*, 477–478.

Blank, M., Altman, L. D., & Bridger, W. H. Cross-model transfer of form discrimination in pre-school children. *Psychonomic Science*, 1968, *10*, 51–52.

Bloom, L. *Language development: Form and function in emerging grammars*. Cambridge: M.I.T. Press, 1970.

Blum, G. E., Waite, R. R., & Zimet, S. F. Ethnic integration and urbanization of a first grade reading text book: A research study. *Psychology in the Schools*, 1967, *4*, 176–181.

Bochner, S., & Insko, C. A. Communication discrepancy, source credibility and opinion change. *Journal of Personality and Social Psychology*, 1966, *4*, 614–621.

Bolles, R., & Petrinovich, L. A technique for obtaining rapid drive discrimination in the rat. *Journal of Comparative and Physiological Psychology*, 1954, *47*, 378–380.

Boneau, C. A., & Cuca, J. M. An overview of psychology's human resources. *American Psychologist*, 1974, *29*, 821–840.

Boring, E. G. Apparatus notes: A new ambiguous figure. *American Journal of Psychology*, 1930, *42*, 444–445.

Bower, G. H. Organizational factors in memory. *Cognitive Psychology*, 1970, *1*, 18–46.

Bower, T. G. R. The object in the world of the infant. *Scientific American*, 1971, *225* (December), 30–38.

Bowlby, J. The nature of the child's tie to his mother. *International Journal of Psychoanalysis*, 1958, *39*, 350–373.

Brady, J. V. Ulcers in "executive" monkeys. *Scientific American*, 1958, *199* (October), 95–100.

Braine, M. D. S. The ontogeny of English phrase structure: The first phase. *Language*, 1963, *39*, 1–13.

Breggin, P. R. The psychophysiology of anxiety. *Journal of Nervous and Mental Disease*, 1964, *139*, 558–568.

Breuer, J., & Freud, S. [*Studies in hysteria*](A. A. Brill, trans.) New York: Nervous and Mental Disease Publishing Co., 1936.

Bridges, K. M. B. Emotional development in early infancy. *Child Development*, 1932, *3*, 324–341.

Briggs, R., & King, T. J. Nucleocytoplasmic interactions in eggs and embryos. In J. Brachet & A. E. Muskey (Eds.), *The cell* (Vol. 1), pp. 538–618. New York: Academic Press, 1959.

Brody, M. W. Prognosis and results of psychoanalysis. In J. H. Nodine & J. H. Moyer (Eds.), *Psychosomatic Medicine*. Philadelphia: Lea & Febiger, 1962.

Brown, J., & Wald, G. Visual pigments in single rods and cones of the human retina. *Science*, 1964, *144*, 45–52.

Brown, J. S. Gradients of approach and avoidance responses and their relation to motivation. *Journal of Comparative and Physiological Psychology*, 1948, *41*, 450–465.

Brown, J. S., *The motivation of behavior*. New York: McGraw-Hill, 1961.

Brown, R., & McNeill, D. The "tip of the tongue" phenomenon. *Journal of Verbal Learning and Verbal Behavior*, 1966, *5*, 325–337.

Bruner, J. S., Olver, R. R., & Greenfield, P. M. (Eds.), *Studies in cognitive growth*. New York: Wiley, 1966.

Brunswik, E. *Perception and the representative design of psychological experiments*. Berkeley: University of California Press, 1956.

Brunswik, E., & Reiter, L. Eindrucks-Charaktere schematisierter Gesichter. *Zeitschrift für Psychologie*, 1938, *142*, 67–134.

Bryant, P. E., Jones, P., Claxton, V., & Perkins, G. M. Recognition of shapes across modalities by infants. *Nature*, 1972, *240*, 303–304.

Bryant, P. E., & Trabasso, T. Transitive inferences and memory in young children. *Nature*, 1971, *232*, 456–458.

Budinger, T. F., Bichsel, H., & Tobias, C. A. Visual phenomena noted by human subjects on exposure to neutrons of energies less than twenty-five million electron volts. *Science*, 1971, *172*, 868–870.

Budzynski, T., Stoyva, J., & Adler, C. Feedback-induced muscle relaxation: Application to tension headache. *Journal of Behavior Therapy and Experimental Psychiatry*, 1970, *1*, 205–211.

Burton, R. *The anatomy of melancholy* (13th ed.).

London: Thomas Dawson, White Friars, 1827. (Originally published, 1621.)

Butcher, J. N., & Ryan, M. Personality stability and adjustment to an extreme environment. *Journal of Applied Psychology*, 1974, *59*, 107–109.

Butler, J. M., & Haigh, G. V. Changes in the relation between self-concepts and ideal concepts consequent upon client-centered counseling. In C. R. Rogers & R. F. Dymond (Eds.), *Psychotherapy and personality change*, pp. 55–75. Chicago: University of Chicago Press, 1954.

Butler, R. A. Discrimination learning in rhesus monkeys to visual-exploration motivation. *Journal of Comparative and Physiological Psychology*, 1953, *46*, 95–98.

Byrne, D. The effect of a subliminal food stimulus on verbal responses. *Journal of Applied Psychology*, 1959, *43*, 249–252.

Byrne, D. *The attraction paradigm.* New York: Holt, Rinehart and Winston, 1971.

Cabanac, M. Physiological role of pleasure. *Science*, 1971, *173*, 1103–1107.

Cameron, N. *Personality development and psychopathology: A dynamic approach.* Boston: Houghton Mifflin, 1963.

Campbell, D. P. *Manual for the Strong-Campbell interest inventory.* Stanford, Calif.: Stanford University Press, 1974.

Campbell, H. J. Peripheral self-stimulation as a reward. *Nature*, 1968, *218*, 104–105.

Casey, A. The effect of stress on the consumption of alcohol and reserpine. *Quarterly Journal of Studies on Alcohol*, 1960, *21*, 208–216.

Casswell, S., & Marks, D. Cannabis-induced impairment of performance of a divided attention task. *Nature*, 1973, *241*, 60–61.

Cattell, R. B. *Personality: A systematic, theoretical, and factual study.* New York: McGraw-Hill, 1950.

Cattell, R. B. *Personality and motivation structure and measurement.* Yonkers, N.Y.: World, 1957.

Cautela, J. R. Covert sensitization. *Psychological Reports*, 1967, *20*, 459–468.

Ceraso, J. The interference theory of forgetting. *Scientific American*, 1967, *217* (October), 117–124.

Chafetz, M. E. Addiction. II. Alcoholism. In A. M. Freedman & H. I. Kaplan (Eds.), *Comprehensive textbook of psychiatry*, pp. 1011–1026. Baltimore: Williams & Wilkins, 1967.

Chambers, J. A. College teachers: Their effect on creativity of students. *Journal of Educational Psychology*, 1973, *65*, 326–334.

Chomsky, N. Review of Skinner's *Verbal Behavior. Language*, 1959, *1*, 26–58.

Chomsky, N. *Language and mind.* New York: Harcourt Brace Jovanovich, 1968.

Christensen, P. R., Guilford, J. P., Merrifield, P. R., & Wilson, R. C. *The alternate uses test.* Beverly Hills, Calif.: Sheridan Supply Company, 1960.

Claridge, G. S., Carter, S., & Hume, W. I. *Personality differences and biological variations: A study of twins.* Elmsford, N.Y.: Pergamon, 1973.

Cochrane, R., & Robertson, A. The life-events inventory: A measure of the relative severity of psycho-social stresses. *Journal of Psychosomatic Research*, 1973, *17*, 135–139.

Cohen, B. D., Kalish, H. I., Thurston, J. R., & Cohen, E. Experimental manipulation of verbal behavior. *Journal of Experimental Psychology*, 1954, *47*, 106–110.

Cohen, J. *Personality assessment.* Chicago: Rand McNally, 1969.

Cohen, N. E. (Ed.). *The Los Angeles riots: A socio-psychological study.* New York: Praeger, 1970.

Cole, J. O. Phenothiazine treatment in acute schizophrenia: Effectiveness. *Archives of General Psychiatry*, 1964, *10*, 246–261.

Condon, W. S., & Smith, L. W. Neonate movement is synchronized with adult speech: Interactional participation and language acquisition. *Science*, 1974, *183*, 99.

Cooper, R. M., & Zubek, J. P. Effects of enriched and restricted early environments on the learning ability of bright and dull rats. *Canadian Journal of Psychology*, 1958, *12*, 159–164.

Coopersmith, S. Studies in self-esteem. *Scientific American*, 1968, *218* (February), 96–106.

Corcoran, D. W. J. An acoustic factor in letter cancellation. *Nature*, 1966, *210*, 658.

Corcoran, D. W. J. Acoustic factor in proof reading. *Nature*, 1967, *214*, 815–852.

Coren, S. Subjective contours and apparent depth. *Psychological Review*, 1972, *79*, 359–367.

Cormack, R. M. Haptic illusion: Apparent elongation of a disk rotated between the fingers. *Science*, 1973, *179*, 590–592.

Cornish, R. D., & Dilley, J. S. Comparison of three methods of reducing test anxiety: Systematic desensitization, implosive therapy, and study counseling. *Journal of Counseling Psychology*, 1973, *20*, 499–503.

Cottrell, N. B.: Performance in the presence of other

human beings: More presence, audience, and affiliation effects. In E. C. Simmel, R. A. Hoppe, & G. A. Milton (Eds.), *Social facilitation and imitative behavior.* Boston: Allyn & Bacon, 1968.

Crick, F. H. C. The genetic code. *Scientific American,* 1962, *207* (October), 66–74.

Daly, H. B. Learning of a hurdle-jump response to escape cues paired with reduced reward or frustration nonreward. *Journal of Experimental Psychology,* 1969, *79,* 146–157.

Dashiell, J. F. An experimental analysis of some group effects. *Journal of Abnormal and Social Psychology,* 1930, *25,* 190–199.

Davenport, R. K., & Rogers, C. M. Intermodal equivalence of stimuli in apes. *Science,* 1970, *168,* 279–280.

Davenport, R. K., & Rogers, C. M. Perception of photographs by apes. *Behaviour,* 1971, *39,* 318–320.

Davies, J. D. *Phrenology: Fad and science.* New Haven: Yale University Press, 1955.

Davis, B. Prospects for genetic intervention in man. *Science,* 1970, *170,* 1279–1283.

Davis, C. M. Self-selection of diet by newly weaned infants. *American Journal of Disturbed Children,* 1928, *36,* 651–679.

Davis, J. M., & Fann, W. E. Lithium. In *Annual review of pharmacology,* pp. 285–302. Palo Alto, Calif.: Annual Reviews, 1971.

Davis, J. M., Klerman, G., & Schildkraut, J. Drugs used in the treatment of depression. In L. Efron, J. O. Cole, D. Levine, & J. R. Wittenborn, *Psychopharmacology: A review of progress.* Washington, D.C.: U.S. Clearinghouse of Mental Health Information, 1967.

Davison, G. C. Systematic desensitization as a counterconditioning process. *Journal of Abnormal Psychology,* 1968, *73,* 91–99.

Davison, G. C., & Neale, J. M. *Abnormal psychology: An experimental clinical approach.* New York: Wiley, 1974.

De Fleur, M. L., & Westie, F. R. Verbal attitudes and overt acts: An experiment on the salience of attitudes. *American Sociological Review,* 1958, *23,* 667–673.

Delgado, J. M. R., Roberts, W. W., & Miller, N. E. Learning motivated by electrical stimulation of the brain. *American Journal of Physiology,* 1954, *179,* 587–593.

de Lint, J., & Schmidt, W. The epidemiology of alcoholism. In Y. Israel and J. Mardones (Eds.), *Bio-*

logical basis of alcoholism, pp. 423–442. New York: Wiley, 1971.

Dember, W. H. Birth order and need affiliation. *Journal of Abnormal and Social Psychology,* 1964, *68,* 555–557.

Dement, W. The effect of dream deprivation. *Science,* 1960, *131,* 1705–1707.

Denenberg, V. H. Effects of exposures to stresses in early life upon later behavioral and biological processes. In L. Levi (Ed.), *Society, stress, and disease: Childhood and adolescence,* pp. 269–281. London: Oxford University Press, 1975.

Denenberg, V. H., & Zarrow, M. X. Effects of handling in infancy upon adult behavior and adrenocortical activity: Suggestions for a neuroendocrine mechanism. In D. N. Walcher & D. L. Peters (Eds.), *Early childhood: The development of self-regulation mechanisms,* pp. 39–64. New York: Academic Press, 1971.

De Nike, L. D. The temporal relationship between awareness and performance in verbal conditioning. *Journal of Experimental Psychology,* 1964, *68,* 521–529.

Dennis, W. The effect of cradling practices upon the onset of walking in Hopi children. *Journal of Genetic Psychology,* 1940, *56,* 79–86.

Descartes, R. *De homine.* Leyden, 1662. Translated as *Treatise on man.* Cambridge: Harvard University Press, 1972.

Descartes, R. *Meditationes de prima philosophia.* Amsterdam, 1642. Translated as *Meditations on the first philosophy: A discourse on method.* London: J. M. Dent & Sons, 1934.

Desiderato, O., & Koskinen, P. Anxiety, study habits, and academic achievement. *Journal of Counseling Psychology,* 1969, *16,* 162–165.

Desiderato, O., & Sigal, S. Associative productivity as a function of creativity level and type of verbal stimulus. *Psychonomic Science,* 1970, *18,* 357–358.

Dethier, V. G., & Stellar, E. *Animal behavior* (3rd ed.). Englewood Cliffs, N.J.: Prentice-Hall, 1970.

Deutsch, J. A., & Deutsch, D. *Physiological psychology.* Homewood, Ill.: Dorsey Press, 1973.

Diven, K. E. Certain determinants in the conditioning of anxiety reactions. *Journal of Psychology,* 1937, *3,* 291–308.

Dobzhansky, T. Differences are not deficits. *Psychology Today,* 1973, *7* (December), 96–101.

Dollard, J., Doob, L. W., Miller, N. E., Mowrer, O. H., Sears, R. R., Ford, C. S., Hovland, C. I., &

Sollenberger, R. I. *Frustration and aggression.* New Haven: Yale University Press, 1939.

Dollard, J., & Miller, N. E. *Personality and psychotherapy: An analysis in terms of learning, thinking, and culture.* New York: McGraw-Hill, 1950.

Duncan, C. P. The retroactive effect of electroshock on learning. *Journal of Comparative and Physiological Psychology,* 1949, *42,* 32–44.

Efran, J. S., & Broughton, A. Effect of expectancies for social approval on visual behavior. *Journal of Personality and Social Psychology,* 1966, *4,* 103–107.

Eibl-Eibesfeldt, I. *Ethology: The biology of behavior.* New York: Holt, Rinehart and Winston, 1970.

Ekman, P. Conditioning opinions about capital punishment as a function of verbal and nonverbal reinforcement. *American Psychologist,* 1959, *14,* 347. (Abstract)

Ekman, P., Sorenson, E. R., & Friesen, W. V. Pancultural elements in facial displays of emotion. *Science,* 1969, *164,* 86–88.

Ellis, A. *Reason and emotion in psychotherapy.* New York: Lyle Stuart, 1962.

Ellsworth, P. C., & Carlsmith, J. Effects of eye contact and verbal content on affective response to dyadic interaction. *Journal of Personality and Social Psychology,* 1968, *10,* 15–20.

Engel, B. T. Operant conditioning of cardiac function: A status report. *Psychophysiology,* 1972, *9,* 161–177.

Engen, T., Levy, N., & Schlosberg, H. The dimensional analysis of a new series of facial expressions. *Journal of Experimental Psychology,* 1958, *55,* 454–458.

Epstein, S., & Fenz, W. O. Steepness of approach and avoidance gradients in humans as a function of experience: Theory and experiment. *Journal of Experimental Psychology,* 1965, *70,* 1–12.

Erikson, E. H. *Childhood and society* (Rev. ed.). New York: Norton, 1963.

Eron, L. D., Huesmann, L. R., Lefkowitz, M. M., & Walder, L. O. Does television violence cause aggression? *American Psychologist,* 1972, *27,* 253–263.

Esch, H. The evolution of bee language. *Scientific American,* 1967, *216* (April), 97–104.

Evarts, E. V. Unit activity in sleep and wakefulness. In G. C. Quarton, T. Melnechuk, & F. D. Schmitt (Eds.), *The neurosciences: A study program,* pp. 545–556. New York: Rockefeller University Press, 1967.

Exline, R. V. Visual interaction: The glances of power and preference. In J. K. Cole (Ed.), *Nebraska symposium on motivation, 1971,* pp. 163–206. Lincoln: University of Nebraska Press, 1972.

Eysenck, H. The effects of psychotherapy: An evaluation. *Journal of Consulting Psychology,* 1952, *16,* 319–324.

Fagan, J., & Shepherd, I. L. (Eds.). *Gestalt therapy now: Therapy, techniques, applications.* Palo Alto, Calif.: Science & Behavior Books, 1970.

Fairweather, G. W. *Social psychology in treating mental illness: An experimental approach.* New York: Wiley, 1964.

Fairweather, G. W., Saunders, D. H., Maynard, H., & Cressler, D. L. *Community life for the mentally ill: An alternative to institutional care.* Chicago: Aldine, 1969.

Fangel, C., & Kaada, B. R. Behavioral "attention" and fear induced by cortical stimulation in the cat. *Electroencephalography and Clinical Neurophysiology,* 1960, *12,* 575–588.

Fantz, R. L. Visual perception from birth as shown by pattern selectivity. *Annals of the New York Academy of Sciences,* 1965, *118,* 793–814.

Fantz, R. L., & Fagan, J. F., III. Visual attention to size and number of pattern details by term and preterm infants during the first six months. *Child Development,* 1975, *46,* 3–18.

Fantz, R. L., & Miranda, S. B. Newborn infant attention to form of contour. *Child Development,* 1975, *46,* 224–228.

Farina, A. *Schizophrenia.* New York: General Learning Press, 1972.

Feshbach, S., & Singer, R. D. *Television and aggression: An experimental field study.* San Francisco: Jossey-Bass, 1971.

Festinger, L. *A theory of cognitive dissonance.* Stanford, Calif.: Stanford University Press, 1957.

Festinger, L., Riecken, H. W., & Schachter, S. *When prophecy fails.* Minneapolis: University of Minnesota Press, 1956.

Fisher, A. E. Maternal and sexual behavior induced by intracranial chemical stimulation. *Science,* 1956, *124,* 228–229.

Flynn, J. P. The neural basis of aggression in cats. In D. C. Glass (Ed.), *Neurophysiology and emotion,* pp. 40–60. New York: Rockefeller University Press, 1967.

Foulkes, R. A. Dowsing experiments. *Nature,* 1971, *229,* 163–168.

Frankenburg, W. K., & Dobbs, J. B. The Denver Development Screening Test. *Journal of Pediatrics,* 1967, *71,* 181–191.

Frankl, V. E. *Man's search for meaning* (Rev. ed.). New York: Washington Square Press, 1963.

Fredenburg, N. C. *Response strength as a function of alley length and time of deprivation.* Unpublished master's thesis, State University of Iowa, 1956.

Freedman, D. G. Smiling in blind infants and the issue of innate vs. acquired. *Journal of Child Psychology and Psychiatry,* 1964, *5,* 171–184.

Freedman, D. G., & Freedman, N. C. Behavioral differences between Chinese-American and European-American newborns. *Nature,* 1969, *224,* 1227.

Freeman, W., & Watts, J. *Psychosurgery.* Springfield, Ill.: Charles C Thomas, 1942.

Freud, A. *The ego and mechanisms of defense.* New York: International Universities Press, 1946.

Frijda, N. H. Emotion and recognition of emotion. In M. B. Arnold (Ed.), *Feelings and emotions,* pp. 241–250. New York: Academic Press, 1970.

Fromm, E. *Escape from freedom.* New York: Holt, Rinehart and Winston, 1941.

Fromm, E. Psychoanalysis and Zen Buddhism. In D. T. Suzuki, E. Fromm, & R. De Martino (Eds.), *Zen Buddhism and psychoanalysis,* pp. 77–141. New York: Harper & Row, 1960.

Fulton, J. F. *Frontal lobotomy and affective behavior.* New York: Norton, 1951.

Garcia, J., & Koelling, R. A. Relation of cue to consequence in avoidance learning. *Psychonomic Science,* 1966, *4,* 123–124.

Gardner, B. T., & Gardner, R. A. Two-way communication with an infant chimpanzee. In A. Schrier & F. Stollnitz (Eds.), *Behavior of non-human primates* (Vol. 4), pp. 117–184. New York: Academic Press, 1971.

Gardner, E. J. *Principles of genetics* (4th ed.). New York: Wiley, 1972.

Gardner, R. A., & Gardner, B. T. Early signs of language in child and chimpanzee. *Science,* 1975, *187,* 752–753.

Gardner, W. I. *Behavior modification in mental retardation.* Chicago: Aldine, 1971.

Gates, A. I. Recitation as a factor in memorizing. *Archives of Psychology,* 1917, *6* (40).

Gazzaniga, M. The split brain in man. *Scientific American,* 1967, *217* (August), 24–29.

Geen, R. G. Effects of evaluation apprehension on memory over instances of varying length. *Journal of Experimental Psychology,* 1974, *102,* 908–910.

Glucksberg, S. The influence of strength of drive on functional fixedness and perceptual recognition. *Journal of Experimental Psychology,* 1962, *63,* 36–41.

Glucksberg, S., & King, L. J. Motivated forgetting mediated by implicit verbal chaining: A laboratory analog of repression. *Science,* 1967, *158,* 517–518.

Glueck, B. C., & Stroebel, C. F. Biofeedback meditation in the treatment of psychiatric illnesses. *Comprehensive Psychiatry,* 1975, *16,* 303–321.

Goldberg, P. A., Gottesdiener, M., & Abramson, P. R. Another put-down of women?: Perceived attractiveness as a function of support for the feminist movement. *Journal of Personality and Social Psychology,* 1975, *32,* 113–115.

Goldfried, M. R. Systematic desensitization as training in self-control. *Journal of Consulting and Clinical Psychology,* 1971, *37,* 228–235.

Goldfried, M. R. Reduction of generalized anxiety through a variant of systematic desensitization. In M. R. Goldfried & M. Merbaum (Eds.), *Behavior change through self-control,* pp. 297–304. New York: Holt, Rinehart and Winston, 1973.

Goldfried, M. R., & Merbaum, M. *Behavior change through self-control.* New York: Holt, Rinehart and Winston, 1973.

Goldiamond, I. Self-control procedures in personal behavior problems. *Psychological Reports,* 1965, *17,* 851–868.

Gordon, C. Self-conceptions: Configurations of content. In C. Gordon & K. Gergen (Eds.), *The self in social interaction.* New York: Wiley, 1968.

Gottesman, I. I., & Shields, J. Contributions of twin studies to perspectives on schizophrenia. In B. A. Maher (Ed.), *Progress in experimental personality research* (Vol. 3), pp. 1–84. New York: Academic Press, 1966.

Gottschalk, L. A., & Davidson, R. S. Sensitivity groups, encounter groups, training groups, marathon groups, and the laboratory movement. In H. I. Kaplan & B. J. Sadock (Eds.), *Comprehensive group psychiatry,* pp. 422–459. Baltimore: Williams & Wilkins, 1971.

Goy, R. W. Early hormonal influences on the development of sexual and sex-related behavior. In F. O. Schmitt (Ed.), *The neurosciences: Second study program,* pp. 196–207. New York: Rockefeller University Press, 1970.

Gray, F., Graubard, P. S., & Rosenberg, H. Little brother is changing you. *Psychology Today,* 1974, *7* (March), 42–46.

Greden, J. E. Anxiety or caffeinism: A diagnostic

dilemma. *American Journal of Psychiatry*, 1974, *131*, 1089–1092.

Greenspoon, J. The reinforcing effect of two spoken sounds on the frequency of two responses. *American Journal of Psychology*, 1955, *68*, 409–416.

Gregory, R. L. *The intelligent eye.* New York: McGraw-Hill, 1970.

Griffin, D. R., & Galambos, R. The sensory basis of obstacle avoidance by flying bats. *Journal of Experimental Zoology*, 1941, *86*, 481–506.

Griffin, D. R., & Galambos, R. Obstacle avoidance by flying bats: The cries of bats. *Journal of Experimental Zoology*, 1942, *89*, 475–490.

Grinker, R. R., & Spiegel, J. P. *War neurosis.* New York: Blakiston, 1945.

Grinspoon, L. Marihuana. *Scientific American*, 1969, *221* (December), 17–25.

Grossman, S. P. Eating or drinking elicited by direct adrenergic or cholinergic stimulation of the hypothalamus. *Science*, 1960, *132*, 301–302.

Guilford, J. P. *Personality.* New York: McGraw-Hill, 1959.

Guiton, P. The development of sexual responses in the domestic fowl, in relation to the concept of imprinting. *Symposium of the Zoological Society of London*, 1962, *8*, 227–234.

Haber, R. N., & Hershenson, M. *The psychology of visual perception.* New York: Holt, Rinehart and Winston, 1973.

Hailman, J. P. The pecking response in chicks of the laughing gull (*larus articilla L.*) and related species. *Behaviour Supplement*, XV, 1967.

Hall, C. S. What people dream about. *Scientific American*, 1951, *184* (May), 60–64.

Hall, E. *The hidden dimension.* New York: Doubleday, 1966.

Hall, K. R. L., & Stride, E. The varying responses to pain in psychiatric disorders: A study in abnormal psychology. *British Journal of Medical Psychology*, 1954, *27*, 48–60.

Hamilton, D. M., & Wall, J. H. Hospital treatment of patients with psychosomatic disorders. *American Journal of Psychiatry*, 1941, *98*, 551–557.

Harlow, H. F. The formation of learning sets. *Psychological Review*, 1949, *56*, 51–65.

Harlow, H. F. The nature of love. *American Psychologist*, 1958, *13*, 673–685.

Harlow, H. F., Harlow, M. K., & Suomi, S. J. From thought to therapy: Lessons from a primate laboratory. *American Scientist*, 1971, *59*, 538–549.

Harlow, H. F., & McKinney, W. T. Nonhuman primates and psychoses. *Journal of Autism and Childhood Schizophrenia*, 1971, *1*, 368–375.

Harris, F. R., Wolf, M. R., & Baer, D. M. Effects of adult social reinforcement on child behavior. *Journal of Nursery Education*, 1964, *20*, 8–17.

Harris, M. B. Self-directed program for weight-control: A pilot study. *Journal of Abnormal Psychology*, 1969, *74*, 263–270.

Harvey, O. J., & Campbell, D. T. Judgments of weight as affected by adaptation range, adaptation duration, magnitude of unlabeled anchor, and judgmental language. *Journal of Experimental Psychology*, 1963, *65*, 12–21.

Hathaway, S. R., & McKinley, J. C. *Minnesota multiphasic personality inventory* (Rev. ed.). New York: Psychological Corporation, 1951.

Hebb, D. O. *The organization of behavior.* New York: Wiley, 1949.

Heine, R. W. A comparison of patients' reports on psychotherapeutic experience with psychoanalytic, nondirective, and Adlerian therapists. *American Journal of Psychotherapy*, 1953, *1*, 16–23.

Helson, H. Adaptation-level as frame of reference for prediction of psychophysical data. *American Journal of Psychology*, 1947, *60*, 1–29.

Hendrickson, G., & Schroeder, W. Transfer of training in learning to hit a submerged target. *Journal of Educational Psychology*, 1941, *32*, 206–213.

Heron, W. The pathology of boredom. *Scientific American*, 1957, *196* (January), 52–56.

Hess, E. H. Imprinting in birds. *Science*, 1964, *146*, 1128–1139.

Hess, W. R. The diencephalic sleep centre. In J. F. Delafresnaye (Ed.), *Brain mechanisms and consciousness*, pp. 117–136. Springfield, Ill.: Charles C. Thomas, 1954.

Hildum, D. C., & Brown, R. W. Verbal reinforcement and interviewer bias. *Journal of Abnormal and Social Psychology*, 1956, *53*, 108–111.

Hilgard, E. R. Individual differences in hypnotizability. In J. E. Gordon (Ed.), *Handbook of clinical and experimental hypnosis*, pp. 391–443. New York: Macmillan, 1967.

Hoebel, B. G., & Teitelbaum, P. Effects of force-feeding and starvation on food intake and body weight of a rat with ventromedial hypothalamic lesion. *Journal of Comparative and Physiological Psychology*, 1966, *61*, 189–193.

Hoffman, H. S., Fleshler, M., & Jensen, P. Stimulus aspects of aversive controls: The retention of conditioned suppression. *Journal of the Experimental Analysis of Behavior,* 1963, *6,* 575–583.

Hogan, R. A. The implosive technique. *Behaviour Research and Therapy,* 1968, *6,* 423–432.

Hogan, R. A., & Kirchner, J. H. A preliminary report of the extinction of learned fears via short term implosive therapy. *Journal of Abnormal Psychology,* 1967, *72,* 106–111.

Holzman, P. S., Proctor, L. R., & Hughes, D. W. Eye-tracking patterns in schizophrenia. *Science,* 1973, *181,* 179–181.

Horner, M. S. Toward an understanding of achievement-related conflicts in women. *Journal of Social Issues,* 1972, *28,* 157–175.

Horney, K. *Our inner conflicts.* New York: Norton, 1945.

Houston, J. P., & Mednick, S. A. Creativity and the need for novelty. *Journal of Abnormal and Social Psychology,* 1963, *66,* 137–141.

Hubel, D. H., & Wiesel, T. N. Receptive fields and functional architecture of monkey striate cortex. *Journal of Physiology,* 1968, *195,* 215–243.

Hunter, W. S. The delayed reaction in animals and children. *Behavior Monographs,* 1913, *2,* 21–30.

Hunter, W. S. The white rat and the double alternation temporal maze. *Pedagogical Seminary and Journal of Genetic Psychology,* 1931, *39,* 303–319.

Hydén, H. Biochemical changes accompanying learning. In G. C. Quarton, T. Melnechuk, & F. O. Schmitt (Eds.), *The neurosciences: A study program,* pp. 765–771. New York: Rockefeller University Press, 1967.

Hydén, H., & Egyházi, E. Change in RNA content and base composition in cortical neurons of rats in a learning experiment involving transfer of handedness. *Proceedings of the National Academy of Science,* 1964, *52,* 1030–1035.

Jackson, D. N. *Manual for the personality research form.* Goshen, N.Y.: Research Psychologists Press, 1967.

Jacobson, E. *Progressive relaxation.* Chicago: University of Chicago Press, 1938.

James, W. What is emotion? *Mind,* 1884, *9,* 188–205.

Jenkins, H. M., & Harrison, R. H. Effect of discrimination training on auditory generalization. *Journal of Experimental Psychology,* 1960, *59,* 246–252.

Jensen, A. R. How much can we boost IQ and scholastic achievement? *Harvard Educational Review,* 1969, *39,* 1–123.

Jensen, A. R. The differences are real. *Psychology Today,* 1973, *7* (December), 79–86.

Kagan, J. The determinants of attention in the infant. *American Scientist,* 1970, *58,* 298–305.

Kagan, J. *Understanding children: Behavior, motives and thought.* New York: Harcourt Brace Jovanovich, 1971.

Kagan, J. Do infants think? *Scientific American,* 1972, *226* (March), 74–82.

Kallman, F. J. The genetics of mental illness. In S. Arieti (Ed.), *American handbook of psychiatry* (Vol. 1), pp. 175–196. New York: Basic Books, 1959.

Kamin, L. J. *The science and politics of I.Q.* New York: Halsted Press, 1974.

Kamiya, J. Conditional discrimination of the EEG alpha rhythm in humans. Paper presented at the meeting of the Western Psychological Association, San Francisco, April 1962.

Kanizsa, G. Marzini quasi-percettivi in campi con stimolazione omogenea. *Rivista di Psicologia,* 1955, *49,* 7–30.

Karlins, M., Coffman, T. L., & Walters, G. On the fading of social stereotypes: Studies in three generations of college students. *Journal of Personality and Social Psychology,* 1969, *13,* 1–16.

Kasamatsu, A., & Hirai, T. An electroencephalographic study of Zen meditation (Zazen). In J. Kamiya, T. X. Barber, L. V. Di Cara, N. E. Miller, D. Shapiro, & J. Stoyva (Eds.), *Biofeedback and self-control,* pp. 613–625. Chicago: Aldine, 1971.

Kaufman, L., & Rock, I. The moon illusion. *Scientific American,* 1962, *207* (July), 120–130.

Kazdin, A. E., & Bootzin, R. R. The token economy: An evaluative review. *Journal of Applied Behavior Analysis,* 1972, *5,* 343–372.

Kephart, W. H. The "dysfunctional" theory of romantic love: A research report. *Journal of Comparative Family Studies,* Autumn, 1970.

Kerckhoff, A. C., & Davis, K. E. Value concensus and need complementarity in mate selection. *American Sociological Review,* 1962, *27,* 295–303.

Kety, S. S., Rosenthal, D., Wender, P. H., & Schulsinger, F. The types and prevalence of mental illness in the biological and adoptive families of adopted schizophrenics. In D. Rosenthal & S. S. Kety (Eds.), *The transmission of schizophrenia,* pp. 345–362. London: Pergamon, 1968.

King, G. F., Armitage, S. G., & Tilton, J. R. A therapeutic approach to schizophrenics of extreme pathology. *Journal of Abnormal and Social Psychology,* 1960, *61,* 276–286.

Kleitman, N. Patterns of dreaming. *Scientific American,* 1960, *203* (November), 82–88.

Klonoff, H. Marijuana and driving in real-life situations. *Science,* 1974, *186,* 317–324.

Knight, R. P. Evaluation of the results of psychoanalytic therapy. *American Journal of Psychiatry,* 1941, *98,* 434–446.

Köhler, W. *The mentality of apes.* New York: Harcourt, Brace, 1925.

Krieg, W. J. S. *Functional neuroanatomy.* New York: McGraw-Hill, 1953.

Krueger, W. C. F. The effect of overlearning on retention. *Journal of Experimental Psychology,* 1929, *12,* 71–78.

Kuehn, J. L., & Crinella, F. M. Sensitivity training: Interpersonal "overkill" and other problems. *American Journal of Psychiatry,* 1969, *126,* 840–845.

Kutner, B. Patterns of mental functioning associated with prejudice in children. *Psychological Monographs,* 1958, *72* (Whole No. 460).

Landis, C., & Mettler, F. A. *Varieties of psychopathological experience.* New York: Holt, Rinehart and Winston, 1964.

Lange, C. G. *Om sindsbevægelser: Et psykofysiologisk studie.* Copenhagen: J. Lunde, 1885.

La Piere, R. T. Attitude versus actions. *Social Forces,* 1934, *13,* 203–237.

Lashley, K. S. *Brain mechanisms and intelligence.* Chicago: University of Chicago Press, 1929.

Layzer, D. Heritability analyses of IQ scores: Science or numerology? *Science,* 1974, *183,* 1259–1266.

Lazarus, A. A. *Behavior therapy and beyond.* New York: McGraw-Hill, 1971.

Lazarus, R. S., Speisman, J. C., Mordkoff, A. M., & Davison, L. A. A laboratory study of psychological stress produced by a motion picture film. *Psychological Monographs,* 1962, *76* (Whole No. 556).

Leavitt, H. J., & Schlosberg, H. The retention of verbal and motor skills. *Journal of Experimental Psychology,* 1944, *34,* 404–417.

Leff, M., Roatch, J. F., & Bunney, W. E., Jr. Environmental factors preceding the onset of severe depressions. *Psychiatry,* 1970, *33,* 293–311.

Leiderman, P. H., Babu, B., Kagla, J., Kraemer, H. C., & Leiderman, G. F. African infant precocity and some social influences during the first year. *Nature,* 1973, *242,* 247–249.

Lenneberg, E. H. *Biological foundations of language.* New York: Wiley, 1967.

Levin, S. M. The effects of awareness on verbal conditioning. *Journal of Experimental Psychology,* 1961, *61,* 67–75.

Levine, S. Sex differences in the brain. *Scientific American,* 1966, *214* (April), 84–90.

Levine, S., Chevalier, J. A., & Korchin, S. J. The effects of early shock and handling on later avoidance learning. *Journal of Personality,* 1956, *24,* 475–493.

Levinger, G., & Breedlove, J. Interpersonal attraction and agreement: A study of marriage partners. *Journal of Personality and Social Psychology,* 1966, *3,* 367–372.

Levitsky, A., & Perls, F. S. The rules and games of Gestalt therapy. In J. Fagan & I. L. Shepherd (Eds.), *Gestalt therapy now: Therapy, techniques, applications,* pp. 140–149. Palo Alto, Calif.: Science & Behavior Books, 1970.

Lewin, K. *A dynamic theory of personality.* New York: McGraw-Hill, 1935.

Lieberman, M. A., Yalom, I. D., & Miles, M. B. *Encounter groups: First facts.* New York: Basic Books, 1973.

Liebert, R. M., Sobol, M. D., & Davidson, E. S. Catharsis of aggression among institutionalized boys: Fact or artifact? In G. A. Comstock, E. A. Rubenstein, & J. P. Murray (Eds.), *Television and social behavior* (Vol. 5), Washington, D.C.: Government Printing Office, 1972.

Likert, R. A. Technique for the measurement of attitudes. *Archives of Psychology,* 1932, *22* (Whole No. 140).

Lindsley, O. R. Operant conditioning methods applied to research in chronic schizophrenia. *Psychiatric Research Reports,* 1956, *5,* 118–139.

Lippmann, W. *Public opinion.* New York: Harcourt, Brace, 1922.

Lorenz, K. Der Kumpan in der Umwelt des Vögels. *Journal für Ornithologie,* 1935, *83,* 137–213, 289–413.

Lorenz, K. *On aggression.* New York: Harcourt, Brace & World, 1966.

Lovaas, O. I., Berberich, J. P., Perloff, B. F., & Schaeffer, B. Acquisition of imitative speech by schizophrenic children. *Science,* 1966, *151,* 705–707.

Lovaas, O. I., Koegel, R., Simmons, J. Q., & Long, J. S. Some generalization and follow-up measurement on autistic children in behavior therapy.

Journal of Applied Behavior Analysis, 1973, *6,* 1–36.

Lowell, E. L. The effect of need for achievement on learning and speed of performance. *Journal of Psychology,* 1952, *33,* 31–40.

Luborsky, L., Chandler, M., Auerbach, A. H., Cohen, J., & Bachrach, H. M. Factors influencing the outcome of psychotherapy: A review of quantitative research. *Psychological Bulletin,* 1971, *75,* 145–185.

Luchins, A. S. Mechanization in problem solving: The effect of Einstellung. *Psychological Monographs,* 1942, *54* (Whole No. 6).

Ludwig, A. M. Altered states of consciousness. *Archives of General Psychiatry,* 1966, *15,* 225–234.

McClelland, D. C. *n* achievement and entrepreneurship: A longitudinal study. *Journal of Personality and Social Psychology,* 1965, *1,* 389–392.

McClelland, D. C. *Assessing human motivation.* New York: General Learning Press, 1971. (a)

McClelland, D. C. *Motivational trends in society.* New York: General Learning Press, 1971. (b)

McClelland, D. C., Atkinson, J. W., Clark, R. A., & Lowell, E. L. *The achievement motive.* New York: Appleton-Century-Crofts, 1953.

McClelland, D. C., Rindlisbacher, A., & De Charms, R. Religious and other sources of parental attitudes toward independence training. In D. C. McClelland (Ed.), *Studies in motivation,* pp. 389–397. New York: Appleton-Century-Crofts, 1955.

McConnell, J. V., Cutler, R. L., & McNeil, E. B. Subliminal stimulation: An overview. *American Psychologist,* 1958, *13,* 229–242.

McKeachie, W. J., Pollie, D., & Speisman, J. Relieving anxiety in classroom examinations. *Journal of Abnormal and Social Psychology,* 1955, *50,* 93–98.

McLaren, D. S., & Yaktin, U. S. Infant precocity. *Nature,* 1973, *244,* 587.

Mahoney, M. J., & Thoresen, C. E. *Self-control: Power to the person.* Monterey, Calif.: Brooks/Cole, 1974.

Marmor, J. Psychoanalytic therapy as an educational process: Common denominators in the therapeutic approaches of different psychoanalytic schools. In J. H. Masserman (Ed.), *Science and psychoanalysis,* pp. 286–299. New York: Grune & Stratton, 1962.

Marshack, A. *The roots of civilization: The cognitive beginnings of man's first art, symbol and notation.* New York: McGraw-Hill, 1972.

Martin, B. The assessment of anxiety by physiological behavioral measures. *Psychological Bulletin,* 1961, *58,* 234–255.

Maslow, A. H. *Motivation and personality.* New York: Harper & Row, 1954.

Maslow, A. H. *Toward a psychology of being.* Princeton, N.J.: Van Nostrand, 1962.

Maslow, A. H. *Motivation and personality* (2nd ed.). New York: Harper & Row, 1970.

Masserman, J. H. *Principles of dynamic psychiatry.* Philadelphia: Saunders, 1946.

Masserman, J. H. Experimental neuroses. *Scientific American,* 1950, *182* (March), 38–43.

Masserman, J. H., & Yum, K. S. An analysis of the influence of alcohol on experimental neurosis in cats. *Psychosomatic Medicine,* 1946, *8,* 36–52.

Matin, L., & MacKinnon, G. E. Autokinetic movement: Selective manipulation of directioned components by image stabilization. *Science,* 1964, *143,* 147–148.

Maugh, T. H., II. Marijuana: The grass may no longer be greener. *Science,* 1974, *185,* 683–685.

May, R. *Existential psychology.* New York: Random House, 1960.

May, R. *Existential psychology* (2nd ed.). New York: Random House, 1969.

Mayfield, E. C. The selection interview: A re-evaluation of published research. *Personnel Psychology,* 1964, *17,* 239–260.

Mead, M. *Sex and temperament in three primitive societies.* New York: Morrow, 1937.

Mednick, M. T. Mediated generalization and the incubation effect as a function of manifest anxiety. *Journal of Abnormal and Social Psychology,* 1957, *55,* 315–321.

Mednick, S. A. The associative basis of the creative process. *Psychological Review,* 1962, *69,* 220–232.

Meehl, P. E. *Clinical versus statistical prediction: A theoretical analysis and a review of the evidence.* Minneapolis: University of Minnesota Press, 1954.

Mehler, J., & Bever, T. G. Cognitive capacity of very young children. *Science,* 1967, *158,* 141–142.

Mehrabian, A. Significance of posture and position in the communication of attitude and status relationships. *Psychological Bulletin,* 1969, *71,* 359–372.

Meichenbaum, D. H. Cognitive factors in behavior modification: Modifying what clients say to themselves. In C. Franks & T. Wilson (Eds.), *Annual review of behavior therapy, theory, and practice,* pp. 416–431. New York: Brunner-Mazel, 1973.

Melzack, R. The perception of pain. *Scientific American,* 1961, *204* (February), 41–49.

Melzack, R., & Eisenberg, H. Skin sensory afterglows. *Science,* 1968, *159,* 445–447.

Merrylees, K. W. Dowsing experiments criticized. *Nature,* 1971, *233,* 502.

Michael, R. T. Estrogen-sensitive neurons and sexual behavior in female cats. *Science,* 1962, *136,* 322–323.

Milgram, S. Behavioral study of obedience. *Journal of Abnormal and Social Psychology,* 1963, *67,* 371–378.

Milgram, S. Some conditions of obedience and disobedience to authority. *Human Relations,* 1965, *18,* 57–76.

Miller, G. A. The magical number seven plus or minus two: Some limits on our capacity for processing information. *Psychological Review,* 1956, *63,* 81–97.

Miller, N. E. Studies of fear as an acquirable drive: I. Fear as motivation and fear-reduction as reinforcement in the learning of new responses. *Journal of Experimental Psychology,* 1948, *38,* 89–101. (a)

Miller, N. E. Theory and experiment relating psychoanalytic displacement to stimulus–response generalization. *Journal of Abnormal and Social Psychology,* 1948, *43,* 155–178. (b)

Miller, N. E. Learnable drives and rewards. In S. S. Stevens (Ed.), *Handbook of experimental psychology,* pp. 435–472. New York: Wiley, 1951.

Miller, N. E. Liberalization of basic S–R concepts: Extensions to conflict behavior, motivation, and social learning. In S. Koch (Ed.), *Psychology: A study of a science* (Vol. 2). New York: McGraw-Hill, 1959.

Miller, N. E., & Bugelski, B. R. Minor studies of aggression: II. The influence of frustrations imposed by the in-group on attitudes expressed toward out-groups. *Journal of Psychology,* 1948, *25,* 437–442.

Miller, N. E., & Dworkin, B. R. Visceral learning: Recent difficulties with curarized rats and significant programs for human research. In P. A. Obrist, A. H. Black, J. Brener, & L. V. Di Cara (Eds.), *Contemporary trends in cardiovascular psychophysiology,* pp. 312–331. Chicago: Aldine, 1973.

Mischel, W. *Personality and assessment.* New York: Wiley, 1968.

Mishler, E., & Waxler, N. E. *Interaction in families: An experimental study of family processes and schizophrenia.* New York: Wiley, 1968.

Mitchell, K. R., & Ng, K. T. Effects of group counseling and behavior therapy on the academic achievement of test-anxious subjects. *Journal of Counseling Psychology,* 1972, *19,* 491–497.

Mittelman, B., Wolff, H. G., & Scharf, M. P. Emotions and gastroduodenal function: Experimental studies on patients with gastritis, duodenitis, and peptic ulcer. *Psychosomatic Medicine,* 1942, *4,* 5–61.

Moniz, E. *Tentatives opératoires dans le traitement de certain psychoses.* Paris: Masson, 1936.

Montague, E. K. The role of anxiety in serial rote learning. *Journal of Experimental Psychology,* 1953, *45,* 91–96.

Montgomery, K. C. The role of the exploratory drive in learning. *Journal of Comparative and Physiological Psychology,* 1954, *47,* 60–64.

Moore, J. W. Stimulus control: Studies of auditory generalization in rabbits. In A. H. Black & W. F. Prokasy (Eds.), *Classical conditioning: II. Current theory and research,* pp. 206–230. New York: Appleton-Century-Crofts, 1972.

Moreno, J. L. Psychodrama. In H. I. Kaplan & B. J. Sadock (Eds.), *Comprehensive group psychiatry,* pp. 460–500. Baltimore: Williams & Wilkins, 1971.

Morganstern, K. P. Implosive therapy and flooding procedures: A critical review. *Psychological Bulletin,* 1973, *79,* 318–334.

Moruzzi, G. Functional significance of sleep for brain mechanisms. In J. C. Eccles (Ed.), *Brain and conscious experience,* pp. 345–388. New York: Springer, 1966.

Mowrer, O. H. On the dual nature of learning: A reinterpretation of "conditioning" and "problem solving." *Harvard Educational Review,* 1947, *17,* 102–148.

Mowrer, O. H. "Sin," the lesser of two evils. *American Psychologist,* 1960, *15,* 301–304.

Munn, N. L. *Handbook of psychological research on the rat.* Boston: Houghton Mifflin, 1950.

Munn, N. L. The evolution of mind. *Scientific American,* 1957, *196* (June), 140–150.

Murstein, B. I. *Theory and research in projective techniques (Emphasizing the TAT).* New York: Wiley, 1963.

Murstein, B. I. A theory of marital choice and its applicability to marriage adjustment. In B. I. Murstein (Ed.), *Theories of attraction and love,* pp. 100–151. New York: Springer, 1971.

Murstein, B. I., & Hadjolian, S. E. Baby, light my aura. *Human Behavior,* 1975, *4* (September), 40–41.

Mussen, P. H., & Parker, A. L. Mother nurturance and girls' incidental imitative learning. *Journal of Personality and Social Psychology,* 1965, *2,* 94–97.

Newcomb, T. M. *The acquaintance process.* New York: Holt, Rinehart and Winston, 1961.

Nideffer, R. M. Alpha and the development of human potential. In D. Shapiro, T. X. Barber, L. V. Di Cara, J. Kamiya, N. E. Miller, & J. Stoyva (Eds.), *Biofeedback and self-control, 1972,* pp. 167–188. Chicago: Aldine, 1973.

Nisbett, R. E. Taste, deprivation, and weight determinants of eating behavior. *Journal of Personality and Social Psychology,* 1968, *10,* 107–116. (a)

Nisbett, R. E. Determinants of food intake in obesity. *Science,* 1968, *159,* 1254–1255. (b)

Nolan, J. D. Self-control procedures in the modification of smoking behavior. *Journal of Consulting and Clinical Psychology,* 1968, *32,* 92–93.

Norman, D. A. *Memory and attention.* New York: Wiley, 1969.

Nowlis, D. P., & Kamiya, J. The control of electroencephalographic alpha rhythms through auditory feedback and the associated mental activity. *Psychophysiology,* 1970, *6,* 476–484.

Office of Strategic Services Assessment Staff. *Assessment of men.* New York: Rinehart, 1948.

Olds, J. Differential effects of drive and drugs on self-stimulation at different brain sites. In D. E. Sheer (Ed.), *Electrical stimulation of the brain,* pp. 350–366. Austin: University of Texas Press, 1961.

Olds, J., & Milner, P. Positive reinforcement produced by electrical stimulation of septal areas and other regions of rat brain. *Journal of Comparative and Physiological Psychology,* 1954, *47,* 419–427.

Orme-Johnson, D. W. Autonomic stability and transcendental meditation. *Psychosomatic Medicine,* 1973, *35,* 341–349.

Orne, M. T. On the simulating subject as a quasi-control group in hypnosis research: What, why, and how. In E. Fromm & R. E. Shor (Eds.), *Hypnosis: Research, development, and perspectives,* pp. 399–443. Chicago: Aldine, 1972.

Osgood, C. E. The nature and measurement of meaning. *Psychological Bulletin,* 1952, *49,* 197–237.

Osgood, C. E., Suci, G. J., & Tannenbaum, P. H. *The measurement of meaning.* Urbana: University of Illinois Press, 1957.

Ostfeld, A. M. *The common headache syndrome: Biochemistry, pathophysiology, therapy.* Springfield, Ill.: Charles C Thomas, 1962.

Ostwald, P. The sounds of infancy. *Developmental Medicine and Child Neurology,* 1972, *14,* 350–361.

Otis, L. S. Changes in drug usage patterns of practitioners of transcendental meditation (TM). Unpublished report, Stanford Research Institute, Menlo Park, California, 1972.

Pagano, R. R., Ross, R. M., Stivers, R. M., & Warrenburg, S. Sleep during transcendental meditation. *Science,* 1976, *191,* 308–310.

Paivio, A. *Imagery and verbal processes.* New York: Holt, Rinehart and Winston, 1971.

Paskewitz, D. A., & Orne, M. T. Visual effects or alpha feedback training. *Science,* 1973, *181,* 360–363.

Patten, W. *Evolution.* Hanover, N.H.: Dartmouth College Press, 1922.

Pattie, F. A. A brief history of hypnotism. In J. E. Gordon (Ed.), *Handbook of clinical and experimental hypnosis,* pp. 10–43. New York: Macmillan, 1967.

Paul, G. L. *Insight versus desensitization in psychotherapy.* Stanford, Calif.: Stanford University Press, 1966.

Paul, G. L. Insight versus desensitization in psychotherapy two years after termination. *Journal of Consulting Psychology,* 1967, *31,* 333–348.

Paul, G. L. Two-year follow-up of systematic desensitization in therapy groups. *Journal of Abnormal Psychology,* 1968, *73,* 119–130.

Paul, G. L. Outcome of systematic desensitization: I. Background, procedures, and uncontrolled report of individual treatment. In C. M. Franks (Ed.), *Behavior therapy: Appraisal and status,* pp. 63–104. New York: McGraw-Hill, 1969. (a)

Paul, G. L. Outcome of systematic desensitization: II. Controlled investigations of individual treatment, technique variations, and current status. In C. M. Franks (Ed.), *Behavior therapy: Appraisal and status,* pp. 105–159. New York: McGraw-Hill, 1969. (b)

Paul, G. L., & Shannon, D. T. Treatment of anxiety through systematic desensitization in therapy groups. *Journal of Abnormal Psychology,* 1969, *74,* 425–437.

Pavlov, I. P. *Conditioned reflexes: An investigation of the physiological activity of the cerebral cortex.* (G. V. Anrep, trans.). London: Oxford University Press, 1927.

Pavlov, I. P. *Lectures on conditioned reflexes.* (Vol. 1). (W. H. Gantt, trans.). New York: International Publishers, 1928.

Pellegrini, R. J. The astrological "theory" of personality: An unbiased test by a biased observer. *The Journal of Psychology*, 1973, *85*, 21–28.

Penfield, W. *The excitable cortex in conscious man.* Liverpool: Liverpool University Press, 1958.

Perls, F. S. Four lectures. In J. Fagan & I. L. Shepherd (Eds.), *Gestalt therapy now: Therapy, techniques, applications*, pp. 14–38. Palo Alto, Calif.: Science & Behavior Books, 1970.

Perls, F. S., Hefferline, R. E., & Goodman, P. *Gestalt therapy: Excitement and growth in the human personality.* New York: Julian Press, 1951.

Peterson, L. R., & Peterson, M. J. Short-term retention of individual verbal items. *Journal of Experimental Psychology*, 1959, *58*, 193–198.

Petry, H. The subjective Necker cube. Paper presented at the meeting of the Eastern Psychological Association, New York, April 1975.

Piaget, J. *The origins of intelligence in children.* New York: International Universities Press, 1952.

Pinneau, S. R. *Changes in intelligence quotient from infancy to maturity.* Boston: Houghton Mifflin, 1961.

Pinsky, L. S., Osborne, W. Z., Hoffman, R. A., & Bailey, J. V. Light flashes observed on Skylab 4. *Science*, 1975, *188*, 928–930.

Poppel, E., Held, R., & Frost, H. Residual visual function after brain wounds involving the central visual pathways in man. *Nature*, 1973, *243*, 295–296.

Postman, L., & Rau, L. Retention as a function of the method of measurement. *University of California Publications in Psychology*, 1957, *8*, 217–270.

Postman, L., Stark, K., & Fraser, J. Temporal changes in interference. *Journal of Verbal Learning and Verbal Behavior*, 1968, *7*, 672–694.

Premack, A. J., & Premack, D. Teaching language to an ape. *Scientific American*, 1972, *227* (October), 92–99.

Premack, D. Reinforcement theory. In D. Levine (Ed.), *Nebraska symposium on motivation, 1965*, pp. 123–180. Lincoln: University of Nebraska Press, 1965.

Pritchard, R. M. Stabilized images on the retina. *Scientific American*, 1961, *204* (June), 72–78.

Quay, H. The effect of verbal reinforcement on the recall of early memories. *Journal of Abnormal and Social Psychology*, 1959, *59*, 254–257.

Rachlin, H. *Introduction to modern behaviorism.* San Francisco: W. H. Freeman, 1970.

Ray, O. A. *Drugs, society, and human behavior.* St. Louis: C. V. Mosby, 1972.

Razran, G. A quantitative study of meaning by a conditioned salivary technique (semantic conditioning). *Science*, 1939, *90*, 89–91.

Razran, G. Ethnic dislikes and stereotypes: A laboratory study. *Journal of Abnormal and Social Psychology*, 1950, *45*, 7–27.

Razran, G. The observable unconscious and the inferable conscious in current Soviet psychophysiology: Interoceptive conditioning, semantic conditioning, and the orienting reflex. *Psychological Review*, 1961, *68*, 81–147.

Read, P. P. *Alive: The story of the Andes survivors.* Philadelphia: Lippincott, 1974.

Reedy, J. J., Szczes, T., & Downs, T. D. Tongue rolling among twins. *The Journal of Heredity*, 1971, *62*, 125–127.

Richter, C. P. Total self-regulatory functions in animals and human beings. *The Harvey Lecture Series*, 1942, *38*, 63–103.

Ringuette, E. L., & Kennedy, T. An experimental study of the double-bind hypothesis. *Journal of Abnormal Psychology*, 1966, *71*, 136–142.

Rizley, R. C., & Rescorla, R. A. Associations in second-order conditioning and sensory preconditioning. *Journal of Comparative and Physiological Psychology*, 1972, *81*, 1–11.

Robinson, B. W. Forebrain alimentary responses: Some organizational principles. In M. J. Wayner (Ed.), *Thirst: First international symposium on thirst in the regulation of body water*, pp. 411–427. New York: Pergamon, 1964.

Robinson, J. O., & Wilson, J. A. The impossible colonnade and other variations of a well-known figure. *British Journal of Psychology*, 1973, *64*, 363–365.

Roffwarg, H. P., Muzio, J. N., & Dement, W. C. Ontogenetic development of the human sleep-dream cycle. *Science*, 1966, *152*, 604–619.

Rogers, C. R. *Client-centered therapy.* Boston: Houghton Mifflin, 1951.

Rogers, C. R. *On becoming a person.* Boston: Houghton Mifflin, 1961.

Rogers, C. R., & Dymond, R. F. (Eds.), *Psychotherapy and personality change.* Chicago: University of Chicago Press, 1954.

Rosenhan, D. L. On being sane in insane places. *Science*, 1973, *179*, 1–9.

Rosenthal, R., & Jacobson, L. *Pygmalion in the*

classroom. New York: Holt, Rinehart and Winston, 1968.

Rosenzweig, M. R., Bennett, E. L., & Diamond, M. C. Brain changes in response to experience. *Scientific American,* 1972, *226* (February), 22–29.

Rosenzweig, S., III. Need-persistive and ego-defensive reactions to frustration as demonstrated by an experiment on repression. *Psychological Review,* 1941, *48,* 347–349.

Ross, J., & Lawrence, K. A. Some observations on memory artifice. *Psychonomic Science,* 1968, *13,* 107–108.

Rotter, J. B. Generalized expectancies for internal vs. external control of reinforcement. *Psychological Monographs,* 1966, *80* (Whole No. 609).

Roubíček, J. Anxiety and higher nervous functions. In *Studies in anxiety. British Journal of Psychiatry,* special publication, No. 3, 21–25. Ashford, Kent: Headley Brothers, 1969.

Rovee, C. K. Psychophysical scaling of olfactory responses to the aliphatic alcohols in human neonates. *Journal of Experimental Child Psychology,* 1969, *7,* 245–254.

Rubin, Z. *The social psychology of romantic love.* Ann Arbor, Mich.: University Microfilms, 1969. No. 70-4179.

Rubin, Z. Measurement of romantic love. *Journal of Personality and Social Psychology,* 1970, *16,* 265–273.

Rumbaugh, D. M., Gill, T. V., & von Glasersfeld, E. C. Reading and sentence completion by a chimpanzee. *Science,* 1973, *182,* 731–733.

Russell, J. A., & Mehrabian, A. Distinguishing anger and anxiety in terms of emotional response factors. *Journal of Consulting and Clinical Psychology,* 1974, *42,* 79–83.

Sano, T. Motor and other responses elicited by electrical stimulation of the cat's temporal lobe. *Folia Psychiatrica et Neurologica Japonica,* 1958, *12,* 152–176.

Sarason, I. G. Interrelationships among individual difference variables, behavior in psychotherapy, and verbal conditioning. *Journal of Abnormal and Social Psychology,* 1958, *56,* 339–344.

Sarason, S. B., Davidson, K. S., Lighthall, F. F., Waite, R. R., & Ruebush, B. K. *Anxiety in elementary school children.* New York: Wiley, 1960.

Sarason, S. B., & Mandler, G. Some correlates of test anxiety. *Journal of Abnormal and Social Psychology,* 1952, *47,* 810–817.

Sargent, J. D., Walters, E. D., & Green, E. E. Psychosomatic regulation of migraine headaches. *Seminars in Psychiatry,* 1973, *5,* 415–428.

Scarr-Salapatek, S., & Williams, M. L. The effects of early stimulation on low-birth-weight infants. *Child Development,* 1973, *44,* 94–101.

Schachter, S., & Singer, J. E. Cognitive social and physiological determinants of emotional state. *Psychological Review,* 1962, *69,* 379–399.

Schachter, S., & Wheeler, L. Epinephrine, chlorpromazine, and amusement. *Journal of Abnormal and Social Psychology,* 1962, *65,* 121–128.

Schaffer, H., & Emerson, P. Patterns of response to physical contact in early human development. *Journal of Child Psychology and Psychiatry,* 1964, *5,* 1–13.

Scheerer, M. Problem solving. *Scientific American,* 1963, *208* (April), 118–128.

Schlosberg, H. The description of facial expressions in terms of two dimensions. *Journal of Experimental Psychology,* 1952, *44,* 229–237.

Schneidman, E. S., Farberow, N. L., & Litman, R. L. *The psychology of suicide.* New York: Science House, 1970.

Schultz, J. H., & Luthe, W. *Autogenic therapy.* New York: Grune & Stratton, 1959.

Schwartz, G. E. Biofeedback as therapy: Some theoretical and practical issues. *American Psychologist,* 1973, *28,* 666–673.

Sechenov, I. M. *Refleksy golovnogo mozga.* St. Petersburg, 1863. Translated as *Reflexes of the brain.* Cambridge: M.I.T. Press, 1965.

Seeman, J. A study of the process of nondirective therapy. *Journal of Consulting Psychology,* 1949, *13,* 157–168.

Seeman, W., Nidich, S., & Banta, T. Influence of transcendental meditation on a measure of self-actualization. *Journal of Counseling Psychology,* 1972, *19,* 184–187.

Seligman, M. E. P. Learned helplessness. In A. C. De Graff (Ed.), *Annual review of medicine* (Vol. 23), pp. 407–412. Palo Alto, Calif.: Annual Reviews, 1972.

Seligman, M. E. P. *Helplessness: On depression, development, and death.* San Francisco: W. H. Freeman, 1975.

Seligman, M. E. P., & Hager, J. L. *Biological boundaries of learning.* New York: Appleton-Century-Crofts, 1972.

Seligman, M. E. P., & Maier, S. F. Failure to escape

traumatic shock. *Journal of Experimental Psychology*, 1967, *74*, 1–9.

Sem-Jacobsen, C. W., & Torkildsen, A. Depth recording and electrical stimulation in the human brain. In E. R. Ramsey & D. S. O'Doherty (Eds.), *Electrical studies on the unanesthetized brain*, pp. 275–287. New York: P. Hoeber, 1960.

Shapiro, D., Schwartz, G. E., & Tursky, B. Control of diastolic blood pressure in man by feedback and reinforcement. *Psychophysiology*, 1972, *9*, 296–304.

Sharpless, S. K. Hypnotics and sedatives. In L. Goodman & A. Gilman (Eds.), *The pharmacological basis of therapeutics*, pp. 98–134. New York: Macmillan, 1970.

Sheffield, F. D., & Roby, T. B. Reward value of nonnutritive sweet taste. *Journal of Comparative and Physiological Psychology*, 1950, *43*, 471–481.

Sheffield, F. C., Wulff, J. J., & Backer, R. Reward value of copulation without sex drive reduction. *Journal of Comparative and Physiological Psychology*, 1951, *44*, 3–8.

Sherif, M. An experimental approach to the study of attitudes. *Sociometry*, 1936, *1*, 90–98.

Sherman, S. J. Internal-external control and its relationship to attitude change under different social influence techniques. *Journal of Personality and Social Psychology*, 1973, *26*, 23–29.

Sherrod, D. R. Lateral eye movements and reaction to persuasion. *Perceptual and Motor Skills*, 1972, *35*, 355–358.

Shostrom, E. L. Group therapy: Let the buyer beware. *Psychology Today*, 1969, *2* (May), 37–40.

Sidman, M. Avoidance conditioning with brief shock and no exteroceptive warning signal. *Science*, 1953, *118*, 157–158.

Singer, J. L. *Imagery and daydream methods in psychotherapy and behavior modification*. New York: Academic Press, 1974.

Singer, R. D. Verbal conditioning and generalization of prodemocratic responses. *Journal of Abnormal and Social Psychology*, 1961, *63*, 43–46.

Skinner, B. F. *The behavior of organisms: An experimental analysis*. New York: Appleton-Century-Crofts, 1938.

Skinner, B. F. *Walden II*. New York: Macmillan, 1948.

Skinner, B. F. Are theories of learning necessary? *Psychological Review*, 1950, *57*, 193–216.

Skinner, B. F. *Science and human behavior*. New York: Macmillan, 1953.

Skinner, B. F. *Verbal behavior*. New York: Appleton-Century-Crofts, 1957.

Skinner, B. F. What is psychotic behavior? In B. F. Skinner, *Cumulative record*, pp. 202–219. New York: Appleton-Century-Crofts, 1959.

Skinner, B. F. *About behaviorism*. New York: Knopf, 1974.

Slavson, S. R. *An introduction to group therapy*. New York: Commonwealth Fund, 1943.

Slotnick, B. M., & Katz, H. M. Olfactory learning-set formation in rats. *Science*, 1974, *185*, 796–798.

Smith, D. G. More about dowsing. *Nature*, 1971, *233*, 501.

Smith, W. F., & Rockett, F. C. Test performance as a function of anxiety, instructor, and instructions. *Journal of Educational Research*, 1958, *52*, 138–141.

Snyder, S. H., Banerjee, S. P., Yamamura, H. I., & Greenberg, D. Drugs, neurotransmitters, and schizophrenia. *Science*, 1974, *184*, 1243–1253.

Snyder, W. U. *Casebook of non-directive counseling*. Boston: Houghton Mifflin, 1947.

Solomon, R. L. Punishment. *American Psychologist*, 1964, *19*, 237–253.

Solomon, R. L., & Corbit, J. D. An opponent-process theory of motivation: I. Temporal dynamics of affect. *Psychological Review*, 1974, *81*, 119–145.

Sommer, R. *Personal space: The behavioral basis of design*. New York: Prentice-Hall, 1969.

Spanier, G. B. Romanticism and marital adjustment. *Journal of Marriage and the Family*, 1972, *34*, 481–487.

Spence, K. W. A theory of emotionally based drive (D) and its relation to performance in simple situations. *American Psychologist*, 1958, *13*, 131–141.

Spielberger, C. D. The role of awareness in verbal conditioning. In C. W. Eriksen (Ed.), *Behavior and awareness: A symposium of research and interpretation*, pp. 73–101. Durham, N.C.: Duke University Press, 1962. (a)

Spielberger, C. D. The effects of manifest anxiety on the academic achievement of college students. *Mental Hygiene*, 1962, *46*, 420–426. (b)

Spielberger, C. D., Levin, S. M., & Shepard, M. The effects of awareness and attitude toward the reinforcement on the operant conditioning of verbal behavior. *Journal of Personality*, 1962, *30*, 106–121.

Spielberger, C. D., & Smith, L. H. Anxiety (drive), stress, and serial-position effects in serial-verbal learning. *Journal of Experimental Psychology*, 1966, *72*, 589–595.

Spielberger, C. D., Weitz, H., & Denny, J. P. Group counseling and the academic performance of anxious college freshmen. *Journal of Counseling Psychology*, 1962, *9*, 195–204.

Spranger, E. *Types of men.* New York: Stechert, 1928.

Staats, C. K., & Staats, A. W. Meaning established by classical conditioning. *Journal of Experimental Psychology*, 1957, *54*, 74–80.

Stampfl, T. G., & Levis, D. J. Essentials of implosive therapy: A learning-theory–based psychodynamic behavioral therapy. *Journal of Abnormal Psychology*, 1967, *72*, 496–503.

Steinbach, R. A. *Pain: A psychophysiological analysis.* New York: Academic Press, 1968.

Steiner, J. E. Innate, discriminative human facial expressions to taste and smell stimulation. *Annals of the New York Academy of Sciences*, 1974, *237*, 229–233.

Steuer, F. B., Applefield, J. M., & Smith, R. Televised aggression and the interpersonal aggression of preschool children. *Journal of Experimental Child Psychology*, 1971, *11*, 442–447.

Stricker, L. J., Jacobs, P. I., & Kogan, N. Trait interrelations in implicit personality theories and questionnaire data. *Journal of Personality and Social Psychology*, 1974, *30*, 198–207.

Stuart, R. B., & Davis, B. *Slim chance in a fat world: Behavioral control of obesity.* Champaign, Ill.: Research Press, 1972.

Sue, D. The role of relaxation in systematic desensitization. *Behavior Research and Therapy*, 1972, *10*, 153–158.

Suga, N., & Schlegel, P. Neural attenuation of responses to emitted sounds in echolocating bats. *Science*, 1972, *177*, 82–84.

Suga, N., & Shimozawa, T. Site of neural attenuation of responses to self-vocalized sounds in echolocating bats. *Science*, 1974, *183*, 1211–1213.

Sullivan, H. S. *The interpersonal theory of psychiatry.* New York: Norton, 1953.

Sumner, W. G. *Folkways: A study of the sociological importance of usages, manners, customs, mores, and morals.* Boston: Ginn, 1906.

Supa, P., Cotzin, M., & Dallenbach, K. M. "Facial vision": The perception of obstacles by the blind. *American Journal of Psychology*, 1944, *57*, 133–183.

Surgeon General's Scientific Advisory Committee on Television and Social Behavior. *Television and social behavior* (5 vols. and summary). Washington, D.C.: Government Printing Office, 1971.

Szasz, T. S. The myth of mental illness. *American Psychologist*, 1960, *15*, 113–118.

Tajfel, H. Experiments in intergroup discrimination. *Scientific American*, 1970, *223* (November), 96–102.

Tanner, W. P., Jr., & Swets, J. A. A decision-making theory of visual detection. *Psychological Review*, 1954, *61*, 401–409.

Targ, R., & Puthoff, H. Information transmission under conditions of sensory shielding. *Nature*, 1974, *251*, 602–607.

Taub, A. Acupuncture anesthesia in the People's Republic of China. *Yale Medicine*, 1974 (Fall), 4–6.

Taylor, J. A. The relationship of anxiety to the conditioned eyelid response. *Journal of Experimental Psychology*, 1951, *41*, 81–92.

Taylor, J. A. A personality scale of manifest anxiety. *Journal of Abnormal and Social Psychology*, 1953, *48*, 285–290.

Teichman, Y. Emotional arousal and affiliation. *Journal of Experimental Social Psychology*, 1973, *9*, 591–605.

Templer, D. I., Goldstein, R., & Penick, S. B. Stability and interrater reliability of lateral eye movement. *Perceptual and Motor Skills*, 1972, *34*, 469–470.

Thomas, A., Chess, S., & Birch, H. G. The origin of personality. *Scientific American*, 1970, *223* (August), 102–109.

Thomas, A., Chess, S., Birch, H. G., Hertzig, M. E., & Korn, S. *Behavioral individuality in early childhood.* New York: New York University Press, 1964.

Thompson, T., & Grabowski, J. (Eds.). *Behavior modification of the mentally retarded.* New York: Oxford University Press, 1972.

Thorndike, E. L. Animal intelligence. *Psychological Monographs*, 1898, *2* (Whole No. 8).

Thorpe, W. H. *Bird-song.* Cambridge: The University Press, 1961.

Thurstone, L. L., & Chave, E. J. *The measurement of attitudes.* Chicago: University of Chicago Press, 1929.

Tinbergen, N. *The study of instinct* (2nd ed.). Oxford: Clarendon Press, 1969.

Torrance, E. P. *Guiding creative talent.* Englewood Cliffs, N.J.: Prentice-Hall, 1962.

Triplett, N. The dynamogenic factors in pacemaking and competition. *American Journal of Psychology*, 1897, *9*, 507–533.

Truax, C. B. Reinforcement and non-reinforcement

in Rogerian therapy. *Journal of Abnormal Psychology*, 1966, *71*, 1–9.

Tryon, R. C. Genetic differences in maze-learning ability in rats. *39th Yearbook, National Society for the Study of Education*, 1940, Part 1, 111–119.

Tulving, E. When is recall higher than recognition? *Psychonomic Science*, 1968, *10*, 53–54.

Turner, B. F., & Turner, C. B. The political implications of social stereotyping of women and men among black and white college students. *Sociology and Social Research*, 1974, *58*, 155–162.

Underwood, B. J. Interference and forgetting. *Psychological Review*, 1957, *64*, 49–60.

U.S. Children's Bureau. *Infant care*. Care of Children Series No. 2. Bureau of Publications No. 8 (rev.), 1924.

U.S. Department of Health, Education, and Welfare. *The Health Consequences of Smoking*. Supplement to the 1967 *Public Health Service Review*. Washington, D.C.: Government Printing Office, 1969.

Valins, S., & Ray, A. A. Effects of cognitive desensitization on avoidance behavior. *Journal of Personality and Social Psychology*, 1967, *7*, 345–350.

Van Kaam, A. *Existential foundations of psychology*. Pittsburgh: Duquesne University Press, 1966.

Vaughan, E., & Fisher, A. E. Male sexual behavior induced by intracranial electrical stimulation. *Science*, 1962, *137*, 758–760.

Veroff, J. Development and validation of a projective measure of power motivation. *Journal of Abnormal and Social Psychology*, 1957, *54*, 1–8.

Veroff, J., Atkinson, J. W., Feld, S., & Gurin, G. The use of thematic apperception to assess motivation in a nationwide interview study. *Psychological Monographs*, 1960, *74* (Whole No. 12).

Victor, M., Angevine, J. B., Mancall, E. L., & Fisher, C. M. Memory loss with lesions of hippocampal formation. *Archives of Neurology*, 1961, *5*, 26–45.

Violence on TV: Does it affect our society? *TV Guide*, June 14, 1975, pp. 4–31.

von Bekésy, G. The variation of phase along the basilar membrane with sinusoidal vibrations. *Journal of the Acoustical Society of America*, 1947, *19*, 452–460.

von Frisch, K. *Bees: Their vision, chemical senses, and language*. Ithaca, N.Y.: Cornell University Press, 1950.

Wade, N. Psychical research: The incredible in search of credibility. *Science*, 1973, *181*, 138–143.

Waite, R. R. Further attempts to integrate and urbanize first grade reading textbooks: A research

study. *Journal of Negro Education*, 1968, *37*, 62–70.

Walk, R. D., & Gibson, E. J. A comparative and analytical study of visual depth perception. *Psychological Monographs*, 1961, *75* (Whole No. 519).

Walker, E. L., & Heyns, R. W. *An anatomy for conformity*. Englewood Cliffs, N.J.: Prentice-Hall, 1962.

Wallace, R. K., & Benson, H. The physiology of meditation. *Scientific American*, 1972, *226* (February), 85–90.

Watson, J. B. *Psychological care of infant and child*. New York: Norton, 1928.

Watson, J. D. *The double helix*. New York: Signet, 1968.

Webb, E. J., Campbell, D. T., Schwartz, R. D., & Sechrest, L. *Unobtrusive measures: Nonreactive research in the social sciences*. Chicago: Rand McNally, 1966.

Wechsler, D. Intelligence defined and undefined: A relativistic appraisal. *American Psychologist*, 1975, *30*, 135–139.

Weil, A. Parapsychology: Andrew Weil's search for the true Geller, Part I. *Psychology Today*, 1974, *8* (June), 45–50. Part II: The letdown, *Psychology Today*, 1974, *8* (July), 74–82.

Weiss, T., & Engel, B. T. Operant conditioning of heart rate in patients with premature ventricular contractions. *Psychosomatic Medicine*, 1971, *33*, 301–321.

Weitzenhoffer, A. M., & Hilgard, E. R. *Stanford hypnotic susceptibility scale, forms A and B*. Palo Alto, Calif.: Stanford University Press, 1959.

Welker, W. I. Variability of play and exploratory behavior in chimpanzees. *Journal of Comparative and Physiological Psychology*, 1956, *49*, 181–185.

Wenger, M. A., Bagchi, B. K., & Anand, B. K. Experiments in India on "voluntary" control of the heart and pulse. *Circulation*, 1961, *24*, 1319–1325.

Wertheimer, M. Experimentelle Untersuchungen uber das Sehen von Bewegung. *Zeitschrift für Psychologie*, 1912, *61*, 161–265.

Wertheimer, M. Psychomotor coordination of auditory and visual space at birth. *Science*, 1961, *134*, 1692–1693.

White, R. W. Motivation reconsidered: The concept of competence. *Psychological Review*, 1959, *66*, 297–333.

Wiener, M., Devoe, S., Rubinow, S., & Geller, J. Nonverbal behavior and nonverbal communication. *Psychological Review*, 1972, *79*, 185–214.

Williamson, J. B. Beliefs about the welfare poor.

Sociology and Social Research, 1974, *58*, 163–175.

Winch, R. F. *Mate selection: A study of complementary needs.* New York: Harper & Row, 1958.

Winchester, A. M. *Genetics: A survey of the principles of heredity* (4th ed.). Boston: Houghton Mifflin, 1972.

Winterbottom, M. R. The relation of need for achievement to learning experience in independence and mastery. In J. W. Atkinson (Ed.), *Motives in fantasy, action, and society*, pp. 453–478. New York: Van Nostrand, 1958.

Wolf, M. M., Risley, T., & Mees, H. Application of operant conditioning procedures to the behavior problems of an autistic child. *Behavior Research and Therapy*, 1964, *1*, 305–312.

Wolf, S., & Wolff, H. G. *Human gastric function: An experimental study of a man and his stomach* (2nd ed.). New York: Oxford University Press, 1947.

Wolfe, J. B. Effectiveness of token-rewards for chimpanzees. *Comparative Psychology Monographs*, 1936, *12* (Whole No. 60).

Wolff, H. G. *Headache and other head pain.* New York: Oxford University Press, 1963.

Wolff, P. The causes, controls, and organization of behavior in the neonate. *Psychological Issues*, 1966, *5*, Monograph 17.

Wolpe, J. *Psychotherapy by reciprocal inhibition.* Stanford, Calif.: Stanford University Press, 1958.

Wolpe, J. *The practice of behavior therapy* (2nd ed.). New York: Pergamon, 1973.

Woodworth, R. S., & Schlosberg, H. *Experimental psychology* (Rev. ed.). New York: Holt, 1954.

Wynne, L. C., & Solomon, R. L. Traumatic avoidance learning: Acquisition and extinction in dogs deprived of normal peripheral autonomic function. *Genetic Psychology Monographs*, 1955, *52*, 241–284.

Yalom, I. D. *The theory and practice of group psychotherapy.* New York: Basic Books, 1970.

Yerkes, R. M., & Dodson, J. D. The relation of strength of stimulus to rapidity of habit-formation. *Journal of Comparative Neurology and Psychology*, 1908, *18*, 459–482.

Zajonc, R. B. Social facilitation. *Science*, 1965, *149*, 269–274.

Zax, M., & Stricker, G. *Patterns of psychopathology.* New York: Macmillan, 1963.

Zeigarnik, B. Über das Beholten von erledigten und unerledigten Handlungen. *Psychologische Forschung*, 1927, *9*, 1–85.

Zelazo, P. R., Zelazo, N. A., & Kalb, S. "Walking" in the newborn. *Science*, 1972, *176*, 314–315.

Zimbardo, P. Pathology of imprisonment. *Society*, 1972, *9* (6), 4–8.

Zotterman, Y. Special senses: Thermal receptors. In V. H. Hall (Ed.) *Annual Review of Physiology*, pp. 357–372. Stanford, Calif.: Annual Reviews, 1953.

Zubek, J. P., Welch, G., & Saunders, M. G. Electroencephalographic changes during and after 14 days of perceptual deprivation. *Science*, 1963, *139*, 490–492.

Zwerling, I., & Rosenbaum, A. Alcoholic addiction and personality. In S. Arieti (Ed.), *American handbook of psychiatry*, pp. 623–644. New York: Basic Books, 1959.

Author Index

Subject Index